RESEARCH **METHODS**
for the
Behavioral Sciences

SECOND EDITION

Charles Stangor
University of Maryland

Houghton Mifflin Company Boston New York

To Leslie, for her boundless compassion, generosity, and love

Vice President and Publisher: Charles Hartford
Senior Sponsoring Editor: Kerry Baruth
Editorial Assistant: Caryn Yilmaz
Project Editor: Jane Lee
Editorial Assistant: Talia Kingsbury
Production/Design Assistant: Bethany Schlegel
Senior Manufacturing Coordinator: Marie Barnes
Senior Marketing Manager: Katherine Greig
Marketing Associate: Anne Tousey

Cover Image: © Jake Rajs/Photonica

Printed in the U.S.A.

Library of Congress Control Number: 2002109678

ISBN: 0-618-31287-0

23456789-MP-07 06 05 04

Brief Contents

Contents

Preface

Research Methods for the Behavioral Sciences grew out of my perceived need for a textbook that covers a complete body of research approaches, is accessible for a first-year undergraduate methods or laboratory class, and yet is still detailed enough to serve as a reference book for students as they progress to higher-level courses. I think you will find this book to be easily understood by sophomores, and yet comprehensive enough to serve as a useful handbook for students working as research assistants or writing theses. Indeed, I use the textbook as a test for my graduate students—if they know everything in it, I can trust that they will be able to fully and adequately analyze their data or be able to realize what other information they might need to do so.

Furthermore, I wanted a book that is balanced in emphasis between conducting and consuming research. For the consumer of research, I have incorporated many sections and much pedagogy on how to draw inferences from existing research (see the Hands-on Experiences in Chapters 11, 12, and 14). I have devoted two full chapters to the essential topics of internal and external validity and have endeavored to use these chapters to help develop students' critical thinking and interpretive skills. But I have also filled the book with practical advice for students who are conducting their own research, including:

- "Goals of an ethical research project" in Chapter 3
- "Guide to improving the reliability and validity of questionnaires" in Chapter 5
- Sections in Chapter 12 concerned with designing valid and powerful experiments
- Appendix A on writing research reports
- The section on data preparation and analysis in Appendix B
- Appendix F on using computers to collect data

A number of examples of SPSS printouts have been placed in the chapters in this edition, allowing students to see how the statistics look when they are initially computed.

I have placed as much emphasis on nonexperimental research methods as I have on experimental ones, arguing that all three research approaches—descriptive, correlational, and experimental—have unique strengths and weaknesses (see Table 1.3). Although the focus is primarily on quantitative research,

I have also pointed out the appropriate use of qualitative research, such as focus groups and case studies. I have devoted two full chapters (4 and 5) to the important concerns of creating measures and evaluating their effectiveness. My guess is that many of the students in this course will some day have to design a survey, and in order to do so they will have to know how to write effective, reliable, and valid items. Issues of measurement are frequently underdeveloped in research methods texts, and I have tried to correct this omission.

I believe that this book simultaneously serves the needs of even the most demanding instructor and yet can be enjoyed by students. I have tried to make it thorough, interesting, integrative, accessible, and to provide an effective pedagogy. From an instructor's perspective, I think this book will help students enjoy learning about research methods, understand them well, and think critically and creatively about research. From a student's perspective, the book is brief and succinct, concepts are easy to grasp, and there are several helpful examples. As one reviewer put it, "The book basically represents the most important concepts—what a student might highlight in a longer book."

Organization and Coverage

The book is divided into four sections. Part One covers the background of research. Chapter 1 emphasizes the importance of research to citizens in contemporary society and the potential implications of using (or failing to use) research to make decisions. Chapter 2 explains how science is conducted—the scientific method and the use of the literature review to develop and refine the research hypothesis. Chapter 3 represents a broad overview of research ethics, including practical guides for conducting ethical research.

Part Two deals with measures and measurement. Chapter 4 teaches students how to develop both self-report and behavioral measures and reviews the strengths and weaknesses of each. Practical hints for constructing useful measures are given. Chapter 5 covers the important aspects of reliability and construct validity, and in more detail than any competing text. Chapter 6 presents the elements of surveys and sampling, and Chapter 7 introduces observational and archival methods. I have attempted to point out to students (and instructors might note this as well) that the methods covered in these chapters are both research designs (descriptive research), but also methods that can be used as measured variables in correlational and experimental research.

The chapters in Part Three present the basics of testing research hypotheses. Chapter 8 covers the principles of hypothesis testing and inferential statistics, while Chapters 9 and 10 cover the logic of correlational and experimental research, respectively. Chapter 9 includes sections on multiple regression, longitudinal designs, path analysis, and structural equation modeling.

Part Four considers the design and interpretation of complex experiments, including factorial experimental designs and means comparison tests (Chapter 11). Internal and external validity are covered in Chapters 12 and 13, respectively, and the Hands-on Experiences in these chapters provide a wealth of examples. Chapter 12 also gives practical advice for designing effective experiments. Chapter 14 reviews the strengths and difficulties of quasi-experimental research designs, with a focus on the many threats to internal validity that they contain and how these threats can be overcome.

The Appendices are designed to supplement the text. They can be assigned at any time during the course or used for reference afterward. Appendix A presents an overview of how scientists share their data with others, including a detailed description of how to write a research report following APA style. This appendix also includes an annotated example of a research report written in APA format.

Appendices B and C provide the formulas for most of the univariate statistical tests contained in an introductory statistics text. Appendix B also includes practical advice for analyzing data using computer software programs, along with many examples of SPSS outputs. Students who are collecting and analyzing their own data should therefore find Appendix B extremely helpful in helping them understand how to interpret their results. Appendix D summarizes the most commonly used multivariate research techniques, along with sample computer output. Although it is not likely that a first-year methods student will need to conduct a factor or structural equation analysis, these techniques are so common in contemporary research reports that students should have a place to go to learn the basics of such techniques, and accomplished students (for instance, those writing theses) should be able to learn how to conduct them if necessary.

Statistical Issues

I assume that most students who are taking a research methods or laboratory course are familiar with univariate statistical procedures, but I have designed this book to function effectively even for courses in which the students are not familiar with statistics. Although I cover many statistical issues in the book itself (Chapter 6, "Surveys and Sampling"; Chapter 8, "Hypothesis Testing and Inferential Statistics"; Chapter 9, "Correlational Research Designs"; and Chapters 10 and 11 on ANOVA), students who need a refresher can be directed to Appendices B and C at any point in the semester. The text always references the Appendices that cover the calculations of the statistics under discussion. The placement of all calculations in the Appendices allows instructors to choose whether and when to assign this material.

Because of the increasing importance of students' learning to use computers to conduct statistical analyses, Appendix B introduces this process, and the newly added Appendix F, "Using Computers to Collect Data," expands upon this topic. Many examples of computer output are presented in the text and in the Appendices. The discussion is framed around the Statistical Package for the Social Sciences—in my opinion the package with the most user-friendly platform. I also recommend the accompanying manual, *Using SPSS for Windows*, described below, for students who are going to be calculating statistics.

Pedagogical Features

To promote mastery of the broad array of concepts, terms, and applications central to the research methods course, each chapter of the book includes both standard pedagogical elements and several unique features:

- A *chapter outline* provides a basic orientation to the chapter.
- Unique chapter-opening *Study Questions* help you learn to formulate appropriate questions about the topics that are to come before reading the chapter. You can review these questions again when preparing for exams.
- *Boldface key terms* and an *end-of-text glossary* are useful tools for learning and reviewing the vocabulary of the course.
- A chapter *Summary* highlights the key points of the chapter.
- *Review and Discussion Questions* help you assess your mastery of chapter concepts and provide productive points of departure for classroom discussion.
- Particularly useful *Hands-on Experiences* supply a wealth of practical problems and exercises that complement and expand upon the examples given in the text.

New to this Edition

The second edition of *Research Methods for the Behavioral Sciences* has been updated to include more in-depth discussion of key topics throughout and an updated art program to make the text more informative for students. Particularly, the second edition focuses to an even greater extent on providing information for students who are conducting their own research. New outputs from SPSS analyses have been added in Chapters 6, 9, and 10, and a new table of tips for writing the research report is included in Appendix A. The addition of Appendix F, "Using Computers to Collect Data," covers the pertinent issue of gathering data from electronic sources. More examples of operational definitions have been presented in Chapter 4. Expanded discussion of popular statistical and methodological techniques, including psychophysiological measures (Chapter 4), structural equation modeling (Chapter 9), and meta-analysis (Chapter 13) has been included.

Supplements to the Text

The following supplementary materials are available with *Research Methods for the Behavioral Sciences*. Contact your local Houghton Mifflin representative for more information.

For Instructors:

Instructor's Manual and Test Bank.   Full answers to the Review and Discussion Questions and the Hands-on Experiences, along with a complete set of multiple-choice and essay test questions, can be found in the instructor's manual, which is author-written.

Computerized Test Bank.   Test Bank questions are available in the HMTesting 6.0 package, a new version of our testing software that offers a new, easy-to-use interface; complete cross-platform flexibility; as well as other new features to make the product flexible and easy to use.

Instructor Web Site.   An array of useful and innovative teaching resources can be found at the instructor's Web site, including author-written sample answers to essay questions from the Instructor's Resource Manual.

For Students:

Using SPSS for Windows.   I have also written a manual called *Using SPSS for Windows* that introduces students to the basics of SPSS. This handbook, with step-by-step instructions, sample output, and student exercises based on data sets provided on CD-ROM, can be shrinkwrapped with the text.

Student Web Site.   To enhance the classroom experience, students can visit the text's Web site where they will find resources on how to read a textbook, time management issues, and more useful learning aids.

Acknowledgments

It is not possible for me to acknowledge all of the people who helped me write this book. The list would include my students, whose questions, comments, and complaints taught me how to better teach research methods; convinced me of the need for this book; and helped me make the book more useful. My wife, Leslie, supported me as only she can during and after the long hours in front of the word processor. I am grateful to those who gave me feedback and materials, including Lisa Aspinwall, Jude Cassidy, Jack Fyock, Paul Hanges, Madeline Heilman, Bill Hodos, John Jost, Dave Kenny, James Lange, and Gretchen Sechrist. I am particularly indebted to Jud Mills, who read just about every word at least once and who was my own best instructor in research methods. Thanks also to the Department of Psychology at the University of Maryland, to the members of the Society for Personality and Social Psychology, and to the editorial and production group at Houghton Mifflin, including Senior Sponsoring Editor Kerry Baruth, Editorial Assistant Caryn Yilmaz, and Project Editor Jane Lee.

I would also like to acknowledge the helpful comments of the manuscript reviewers. They helped shape the book and make it even more user-friendly, and caught some of the most glaring errors.

Kimberly J. O'Farrell, Tulane University

Dr. James Hoeffner, Department of Psychology, University of Michigan

Jennifer Devenport, California State University, Fullerton

Lisa M. Dinella, Arizona State University

Barry E. Collins, Department of Psychology, UCLA

Kay Coleman, Boston University

I am always interested in receiving comments from instructors and students. You can write me at the Department of Psychology, University of Maryland, College Park, MD 20742 or contact me via e-mail: Stangor@psyc.umd.edu. I hope you find this book useful and enjoyable.

Orrtanna, Pennsylvania
July 2003

PART **ONE**
Getting Started

CHAPTER ONE
Introduction to Research

STUDY QUESTIONS

- What is behavioral research, and why is it conducted?

- What are the limitations of "everyday science" and intuition for understanding behavior?

- What is the scientific method, and why do scientists use it?

- What is the difference between a fact and a value, and how do a scientist's values influence his or her research?

- What are the goals of basic research and of applied research, and how do the two types of goals relate to each other?

- What benefits are there to be gained from learning how to evaluate research, conduct it, and think critically about it?

- What are the goals of descriptive, correlational, and experimental research? What are the advantages and disadvantages of each research approach?

Part of the excitement of contemporary life is observing the speed at which the world around us changes. It was only one hundred years ago that people first flew in an airplane. Today astronauts spend months at a time in space. It was only a little over five hundred years ago that Johannes Gutenberg printed the first page of a book. Today more printed text is sent via e-mail in a few seconds than could be published in a lifetime only a few years ago. A doctor who studied medicine one hundred years ago learned that most diseases were incurable—medicine could hope only to make the remaining life of a patient more comfortable. Today doctors routinely give people new life by replacing the coronary arteries of the heart and preventing the growth of tumors through the use of chemical and radiation treatments.

Yet despite the benefits that technological change has brought, many of the problems facing humanity appear to be as great as ever. There are still many children, in all parts of the world, who are hungry and who do not have adequate housing or health care. Physical violence is prevalent, including child and spousal abuse, gang violence in cities, ethnic conflicts within nations, and warfare between nations. Divorce continues to have an impact on the lives of thousands of children, and people continue to expose themselves to deadly viruses such as acquired immune deficiency syndrome (AIDS), even when there are ways to avoid contracting these diseases. Although people are living longer and enjoy many of the comforts of technological achievement, the dramatic technological advances that have occurred over the past few decades have not generally been paralleled by advances in the quality of our interpersonal and social behavior.

And it is this behavior, among both humans and animals, and the scientific research designed to study it that are the focus of this book. Indeed, the purpose of behavioral research is to increase our understanding of behavior and, where possible, to provide methods for improving the quality of our lives. The results of such research are becoming increasingly relevant to our perception of such human problems as homelessness, illiteracy, psychological disorders, family instability, and violence. Thus it is not surprising that research is being used more and more frequently to help guide public policy. For instance, behavioral research has been used to guide court rulings on racism, such as in the landmark *Brown* v. *Board of Education* (1954), and sexism (Fiske, Bersoff, Borgida, Deaux, & Heilman, 1991), as well as on the use of lie detectors in criminal trials (Saxe, Dougherty, & Cross, 1985). Behavioral research is also being used to help us understand which methods of educating children are most effective, and teachers are being trained to make use of the most effective techniques.

Behavioral research also provides important information that complements other scientific approaches. For instance, in the field of medicine infectious diseases such as measles and polio were once major causes of death. Today people's own behavior is implicated in most of the leading killers, including homicide, lung cancer, heart disease, and AIDS. Furthermore, much of the productive capability of modern societies is now dependent not only on further technological advances but also on the availability of an educated and skilled work force.

In sum, behavioral research is used to study important human problems and provide solutions to them. Because research has such a significant impact on scientific decisions and public policy, informed citizens, like you, are wise to understand it.

Behavioral Research

Behavioral research is conducted by scientists in such fields as behavioral medicine, communications, criminology, human development, education, psychology, and sociology. The goal of **behavioral research** is to discover, among other things, how people perceive their world, how they think and feel, how they change over time, how they learn and make decisions, and how they interact with others. Behavioral scientists study behavior both because they want to understand it and also because they want to contribute to creating solutions to the everyday problems that face human beings.

Of course, behavioral scientists aren't the only people who are concerned with human behavior or the only ones who propose solutions to social problems. Philosophers, religious leaders, and politicians, for instance, also attempt to provide explanations for social behavior. But what sets behavioral scientists apart from many other people who are concerned with human behavior is their belief that, just as dramatic technological advances have occurred through scientific research, personal and social behavior can be understood, and potentially improved, through the application of scientific research methods. In contrast to many statements made by philosophers, politicians, and religious leaders, which are based only on their own personal beliefs, faith, or intuition, the statements made by social scientists are **empirical,** which means that they are based on systematic collection and analysis of data, where **data** are information collected through formal observation or measurement.[1] Behavioral scientists draw their conclusions about human behavior from systematic collection and analysis of data.

Behavioral scientists believe that research is the best tool for understanding human beings and their relationships with others. For instance, rather than accepting the claim of a religious leader that the adoption of traditional religious beliefs will change behavior, a behavioral scientist would collect data to empirically test whether highly religious people are more helpful and less aggressive toward others than are less religious people. Rather than accepting a politician's contention that creating (or abandoning) a welfare program will improve the condition of poor people, a behavioral scientist would attempt to empirically assess the effects of receiving welfare on the quality of life of welfare recipients. And, rather than relying on a school principal's beliefs about which teaching methods are most effective, behavioral scientists would

---

[1]Although the word *data* is technically a plural noun, scientists frequently treat it as a singular noun, and this practice is now accepted by linguists. Although it is thus correct to say either "the data were collected" or "the data was collected," this book uses the more traditional plural form.

Q
why such a focus on human behavior?

A
because it is observable! what about emotion and motivation (studied by proxy)

e.g.) self-report measures as a proxy for everything

∴ you can do an empirical study on something if you can find a behavioral proxy for it!

systematically test and compare the effectiveness of different methods. In short, behavioral scientists believe in the value of scientific research to answer questions about human behavior.

The claim that human behavior is best known through the use of a scientific approach is not something that everyone believes or that is without controversy. Indeed, although I hope that you will become convinced of the utility of behavioral research for understanding people, I also hope that you will think critically about its value as you study this book. I hope that you will continually ask yourself what behavioral research methods offer in the way of understanding and improving our lives that other approaches do not. And, most important, I hope that you will learn how to evaluate behavioral research.

Finally, although behavioral research is conducted in large part to provide information about important social problems and to further scientific understanding about the principles of human behavior, I also hope that you will find it interesting in its own right—you might even discover that conducting research is fun! If you have ever wondered about how we learn and why we forget, what dreams are for and whether they influence us when we are awake, whether we can tell if others are lying to us, or even whether some people have extrasensory perception (ESP), you will find that behavioral research is the best way to provide answers to these interesting questions. Studying behavioral research and conducting it yourself is exciting, because it allows you to discover and understand new things. In sum, I hope you will enjoy this book, both because you like behavioral research, and also because you realize that it has a significant impact on human behavior, scientific decisions, and public policy.

Everyday Science Versus Empirical Research

Just like scientists, most of us have an avid interest in asking and answering questions about our world. We want to know why things happen, when and if they are likely to happen again, and how to reproduce or change them. Such knowledge enables us to predict our own behavior and that of others. We even collect data to aid us in this undertaking. Indeed, it has been argued that people are "everyday scientists" who conduct research projects to answer questions about behavior (Nisbett & Ross, 1980). When we perform poorly on an important test, we try to understand what caused our failure to remember or understand the material and what might help us do better the next time. When our good friends Eva and Joshua break up, despite what appeared to have been a relationship made in heaven, we try to determine what happened. When we contemplate the growing ranks of the homeless in our cities, we try to investigate the causes of this problem by looking at the people themselves, the situation around them, and the responses of others to them.

The results of these "everyday" research projects can teach us many principles of human behavior. We learn through experience that if we give someone bad news, she or he may blame us even though the news was not our fault. We learn that people may become depressed after they fail at a task. We see that aggressive behavior occurs frequently in our society, and we develop theories to explain why this is so. These insights are part and parcel of everyday social life. In fact, much behavioral research involves the scientific study of everyday behavior (Heider, 1958; Kelly, 1967).

Relying on Our Intuition

Many people believe that they can find answers to questions about human behavior by using their own intuition. They think that since they spend their whole lives with others, they should certainly have learned what makes people do what they do and why. As a result, many may believe that behavioral research is basically "common sense" and that therefore formal study of it is not necessary. Although there is no question that we do learn about other people by observing them, because our observations are conducted informally, they may lead us to draw unwarranted or incorrect conclusions. In fact, we are often incorrect in our intuition about why others do what they do and even (as Sigmund Freud so insightfully noted) why we ourselves do what we do!

The problem with the way people collect and interpret data in their everyday lives is that they are not always particularly thorough. Often, when one explanation for an event seems to make sense, they adopt that explanation as the truth even when other explanations are possible and potentially more accurate. To take a couple of examples, eyewitnesses to violent crimes are often extremely confident in their identifications of the perpetrators of these crimes. But evidence shows that eyewitnesses are no less confident of their identifications when they are incorrect than when they are correct (Wells, Leippe, & Ostrom, 1979). People also become convinced of the existence of extrasensory perception, or the predictive value of astrology, when there is no evidence for either. Accepting explanations without testing them thoroughly may lead people to think that they know things that they do not really know.

but what defines thoroughly? is there an ultimate test?

Discovering the Limitations of Using Intuition

In one empirical demonstration of how difficult it can be to understand even our own behavior, Nisbett and Wilson (1977) had college students read a passage describing a woman who was applying for a job as a counselor in a crisis intervention center. Unknown to the students, the descriptions of the interview were varied so that different students read different information about what occurred during the interview. Some students read that the woman had superb academic credentials, whereas others did not learn this information. And for some students the woman was described as having spilled a cup of coffee over the interviewer's desk during the interview, whereas for others no such event was mentioned. After reading the information, the students first judged the woman they had read about in terms of her suitability for the job on rating scales such as how much they liked her and how intelligent they thought she was. They also indicated how they thought each of the behaviors they had read about (for instance, being highly intelligent or spilling coffee over everything) influenced their judgments.

On the basis of these data, the researchers were able to determine how the woman's behaviors actually influenced the students' judgments of her. They found, for instance, that being described as having excellent academic credentials increased ratings of intelligence and that spilling coffee on the interviewer's desk actually *increased* how much the students liked her.[2] But when the actual effects of the behaviors on the judgments were compared to the students' reports about how the behaviors influenced their judgments, the researchers found that the students were not always correct. Although the students were aware that information about strong academic credentials increased their judgments of intelligence, they had no idea that the applicant's having spilled coffee made them like her more.

Still another way that intuition may lead us astray is that, once we learn about the outcome of a given event (for instance, when we read about the results of a research project), we frequently believe that we would have been able to predict the outcome ahead of time. For instance, if half of a class of students is told that research concerning interpersonal attraction has demonstrated that "opposites attract" and the other half is told that research has demonstrated that "birds of a feather flock together," both sets of students will frequently report believing that they would have predicted this outcome before they read about it. The problem is that reading a description of the research finding leads us to think of the many cases that we know that support it, and thus makes it seem believable. The tendency to think that we could have predicted something that we probably could not have predicted is called the **hindsight bias.**

In sum, although intuition is useful for getting ideas, and although our intuitions are sometimes correct, they are not infallible. Peoples' theories about how they make judgments do not always correspond well to how they actually make decisions. And people believe that they would have predicted events that they would not have, making research findings seem like they are just common sense. This does not mean that intuition is not important—scientists frequently rely on their intuition to help them solve problems. But, because they realize that this intuition is frequently unreliable, they always back up their intuition empirically. Behavioral scientists believe that, just as research into the nature of electrons and protons guided the development of the transistor, so behavioral research can help us understand the behavior of people in their everyday lives. And these scientists believe that collecting data will allow them to discover the determinants of behavior and use this knowledge productively.

---

[2]A person who seems "too good to be true" on the surface can sometimes endear him- or herself to observers by accidentally making a small, humanizing mistake (such as spilling coffee). Such a blunder is known as a *pratfall*.

The Scientific Method

All scientists (whether they are physicists, chemists, biologists, sociologists, or psychologists) are engaged in the basic processes of collecting and organizing data and drawing conclusions about those data. The methods used by scientists to do so have developed over many years and provide a basis for collecting, analyzing, and interpreting data within a common framework in which information can be shared. We can label the set of assumptions, rules, and procedures that scientists use to conduct research the **scientific method.** Indeed, the focus of this book is the use of the scientific method to study behavior.

In addition to requiring that science be empirical—based on observation or measurement of relevant information—the scientific method demands that the procedures used be **objective,** or free from the personal bias or emotions of the scientist. The scientific method prescribes how scientists collect and analyze data, how they draw conclusions from data, and how they share data with others. These rules increase objectivity by placing data under scrutiny by other scientists and even by the public at large. Because data are reported objectively, other scientists know exactly how the scientist collected and analyzed the data. This means that they do not have to rely only on the scientist's own interpretation of the data; they may also draw their own, potentially different, conclusions. Of course, we frequently trust scientists to draw their own conclusions about their data (after all, they are the experts), and we rely on their interpretations. However, when conclusions are made on the basis of empirical data, a knowledgeable person can check up on these interpretations should she or he desire to do so. This book will demonstrate how.

The scientific method also demands that science be based on what has come before it. As we will discuss in Chapter 13, most new research is designed to *replicate*—that is, to repeat, add to, or modify—previous research findings. The scientific method results in an *accumulation* of scientific knowledge, through the reporting of research and the addition to and modifications of these reported findings through further research by other scientists.

Values Versus Facts in Scientific Research

Although scientific research is an important method of studying human behavior, not all questions can be answered using scientific approaches. Statements that cannot be objectively measured or objectively determined to be true or false are not within the domain of scientific inquiry. Scientists therefore draw a distinction between values and facts. **Values** are personal statements such as "Abortion should not be permitted in this country," "I will go to heaven when I die," or "It is important to study behavioral research." **Facts** are objective statements determined to be accurate through empirical study. Examples are "There were over 20,000 homicides in the United States in 1993," or

"Behavioral research demonstrates that individuals who are exposed to highly stressful situations over long periods of time are particularly likely to develop health problems such as heart disease and cancer."

Facts and the Formation of Values.   Because values cannot be considered to be either true or false, science cannot prove or disprove them. Nevertheless, as shown in Table 1.1, behavioral research can sometimes provide facts that can help people develop their values. For instance, science may be able to objectively measure the impact of unwanted children on a society or the psychological trauma suffered by women who have abortions. The effect of capital punishment on the crime rate in the United States may also be determinable. This factual information can and should be made available to help people formulate their values about abortion and capital punishment, as well as to enable governments to articulate appropriate policies. Values also frequently come into play in determining what research is appropriate or important to conduct. For instance, the U.S. government has recently supported and provided funding for research on HIV and AIDS while at the same time limiting the possibility of conducting research using human stem cells.

Distinguishing Between Facts and Values.   Although scientists use research to help distinguish facts from values, the distinction between the two is not always as clear-cut as they might like. Sometimes statements that scientists consider to be factual later turn out to be partially or even entirely incorrect. This happens because there is usually more than one way to interpret data. As a result, scientists frequently disagree with each other about the meaning of observed data. One well-known example concerns the interpretation of race-related differences in IQ. Data show that, on average, African-American students score more poorly on standardized exams than do white students (Herrnstein & Murray, 1994). Some scientists argue that these data indicate inherent genetic differences in intelligence among racial groups, whereas others contend that these differences are caused by social effects, such as differences

TABLE 1.1   Examples of Values and Facts in Scientific Research

Personal Value	Scientific Fact
Welfare payments should be reduced for unmarried parents.	The U.S. government paid over $21 billion in unemployment insurance in 1994.
Handguns should be outlawed.	There were over 35,000 deaths caused by handguns in the United States in 1992.
Blue is my favorite color.	Over 35 percent of college students indicate that blue is their favorite color.
It is important to quit smoking.	Smoking increases the incidence of cancer and heart disease.

Mary Hesse -? the underdetermination of data.

in nutrition, interests, and schooling. Still others maintain that the data demonstrate not that intelligence is unequal between races but that the tests themselves are culturally biased to favor some groups over others. In most cases such as this, the initial disagreement over the interpretation of data leads to further data collection designed to resolve the disagreements.

Although data must also be interpreted in the natural sciences, such as chemistry and physics, interpreting data is even more difficult in the behavioral sciences. And because people have their own hypotheses and beliefs about human behavior, they can easily make their own interpretations of the results of behavioral research, such as the meaning of differences on IQ tests between white and African-American students. Furthermore, the measures used by behavioral scientists, such as asking people questions and observing their behaviors, often appear less sophisticated than those used in other sciences. As a result, to many people behavioral science research does not appear to be as "scientific" as research in the natural sciences.

Something unique about humans that is not like atoms or particles! (Howard)

Even though behavioral research has not advanced as far as research in the natural sciences, behavioral scientists follow the same procedures as do scientists in other fields. These procedures involve creating a systematic set of knowledge about the characteristics of individuals and groups and the relationships among them. In this sense behavioral science research is just as scientific as that in any other field. Furthermore, just because data must be interpreted does not mean that behavioral research is not useful. Although scientific procedures do not necessarily guarantee that the answers to questions will be objective and unbiased, science is still the best method currently known for drawing objective conclusions about the world around us. When old facts are discarded, they are replaced with new facts, based on newer and more correct data. Although science is not perfect, the requirements of empiricism, objectivity, and accumulation still result in a much greater chance of producing an accurate understanding of human behavior than is available through other approaches.

Values and Facts in the Research Report.   Although the goal of the scientific method is to be objective, this does not mean that values do not come into play in science. Scientists must make decisions about what to study, how to study it, whom to use as research participants, and how to interpret their data. Thus the goal of science is not to make everything objective, but rather to make clear which parts of the research process are objective and which parts are not.

Scientific findings are made publicly available through the publication of *research reports*. The **research report** is a document that presents scientific findings using a standardized written format. Different research report formats are used in different fields of science, but behavioral science frequently uses the format prepared by the *American Psychological Association (APA)*. An overview of this approach is presented on the inside cover of this book, and a complete description of APA format can be found in Appendix A. If you are not familiar with it, you may wish to read Appendix A now.

One of the most important requirements of the research report is that the appropriate information goes in the appropriate section. In this regard, two of the sections—Introduction and Discussion—are relatively subjective, because they involve such questions as what topics are of importance to study and how the data should be interpreted. However, two other sections—Results and Discussion—are completely objective, describing the actual procedures of the experiments and the statistical analyses. Again, the point is that science has both objective and subjective components, and it attempts to clearly differentiate the two. One of the major things you will learn in this book is how to draw the important distinction between the values and facts (that is, between the subjective and the objective aspects) in behavioral research.

[handwritten margin note: errata / Method + Results / are "objective"]

Basic and Applied Research

One way that the scientist's values influence research is in the types of research that he or she finds important to study. Some scientists conduct research primarily for the intellectual satisfaction of knowing something, whereas others conduct research for the purpose of gaining practical knowledge about a particular social issue or problem.

Basic research answers fundamental questions about behavior. For instance, cognitive psychologists study how different types of practice influence memory for pictures and words, and biological psychologists study how nerves conduct impulses from the receptors in the skin to the brain. There is no particular reason to study such things except to acquire a better knowledge of how these processes occur.

Applied research investigates issues that have implications for everyday life and provide solutions to everyday problems. Applied research has been conducted to study such issues as what types of psychotherapy are most effective in reducing depression, what types of advertising campaigns will reduce drug and alcohol abuse, how to predict who will perform well at managerial positions, and what factors are associated with successful college performance. One type of applied research is called **program evaluation research,** which is conducted to study the effectiveness of methods designed to make positive social changes, such as training programs, antiprejudice programs, and after-school learning programs. We will more fully discuss how to conduct program evaluation research in Chapter 14.

Although research usually has either a basic or an applied orientation, in most cases the distinction between the two types is not clear-cut. Scientists who conduct basic research are frequently influenced by practical issues in determining which topics to study. For instance, although research concerning the role of practice on memory for lists of words is basic in orientation, the results could someday be used to help children learn to read. Correspondingly, scientists who are interested in solving practical problems are well aware that the results of basic research can help them do so. Programs designed to reduce the spread of AIDS or to promote volunteering are frequently founded on the results of basic research concerning the factors that lead people to change their behaviors.

In short, applied research and basic research inform each other (Lewin, 1944). Basic research provides underlying principles that can be used to solve specific problems, and applied research gives ideas for the kinds of topics that basic research can study. Advances in the behavioral sciences occur more rapidly when each type of research is represented in the enterprise. Accordingly, we will discuss both approaches in this book.

 ## The Importance of Studying Research Methods

I hope that you are now beginning to understand why instructors find it so important for students to take research methods or research laboratory courses as part of their behavioral science degree. To fully understand the material in a behavioral science course, you must first understand how and why the research you are reading about was conducted and what the collected data mean. A fundamental understanding of research methodology will help you read about and correctly interpret the results of research in any field of behavioral science.

Evaluating Research Reports

One goal of this book is to help you learn how to evaluate scientific research reports. We will examine how behavioral scientists develop ideas and test them, how they measure behavior, and how they analyze and interpret the data they collect. Understanding the principles and practices of behavioral research will be useful to you because it will help you determine the quality of the research that you read about. If you read that ibuprofen relieves headaches faster than aspirin, or that children learn more in private than in public schools, you should not believe it just because the findings are based on "research." As we will discuss in more detail in later chapters, research can mislead you if it is not valid. Thus the most important skill you can gain from the study of research methods is the ability to distinguish good research from bad research.

Conducting Research

The second goal of this book is to help you learn how to conduct research. Such skills will obviously be useful to you if you plan a career as a behavioral scientist, where conducting research will be your most important activity. But the ability to design and execute research projects is also in demand in many other careers. For instance, advertising and marketing researchers study how to make advertising more effective, health and medical researchers study the impact of behaviors (such as drug use and smoking) on illness, and computer scientists study how people interact with computers. Furthermore, even if you are not planning a career as a researcher, jobs in almost any area of social, medical, or mental health science require that a worker be informed about behavioral research. There are many opportunities for college graduates who have developed the ability to conduct research (American Psychological Association, 1995), and this book is designed to help you learn these skills.

There is no question that conducting behavioral research is difficult. Unlike beakers full of sulfuric acid, the objects of study in the behavioral sciences—human beings and animals—differ tremendously from each other. No two people are alike, nor do they respond to attempts to study them in the same way. People are free to make their own decisions and to choose their own behaviors. They choose whether to participate in research, whether to take it seriously, and perhaps even whether to sabotage it. Furthermore, whereas the determinants of the pressure of a gas or the movement of a particle can be fairly well defined, the causes of human behavior are not at this time well understood. Although these difficulties represent real challenges, they also represent the thrill of conducting behavioral research. The path is difficult, but the potential rewards of understanding behavior are great.

for Stanger, this is just a hurdle - for others, this is the reason why "empiricism" or "science" is imp-ossible with humans

Thinking Critically About Research

Progress in the behavioral sciences depends on people, like you, who have the skills to critically create, read, evaluate, and criticize research. As you read this book, you will acquire skills that allow you to think critically about research. And once you have learned these skills, you will be able to conduct sound research and to determine the value of research that you read about. In short, you will be able to ask the important questions, such as "How was the research conducted?" "How were the data analyzed?" and, more generally, "Are the conclusions drawn warranted by the facts?" In the remainder of this chapter, we will turn to these questions by considering the three major research approaches to studying human behavior.

Research Designs: Three Approaches to Studying Behavior

Behavioral scientists agree that their ideas and their theories about human behavior must be backed up by data to be taken seriously. However, although all scientists follow the basic underlying procedures of scientific investigation, the research of different scientists is designed with different goals in mind, and the different goals require different approaches to answering the researcher's questions. These different approaches are known as research designs. A **research design** is the specific method a researcher uses to collect, analyze, and interpret data. Although there are many variants of each, there are only three basic research designs used in behavioral research. These are descriptive research designs, correlational research designs, and experimental research designs.

Because these three research designs will form the basis of this entire book, we will consider them in some detail at this point. As we will see, each

research design
↓
data
↓
statistical analysis
↓
interpretation & communicate

of the approaches has both strengths and limitations, and therefore all three can contribute to the accumulation of scientific knowledge. To fully understand how the research designs work, you need to be aware of the statistical tests that are used to analyze the data. If you are not familiar with statistical procedures (or if you feel that you need a bit of a brushup), you should read Appendix B and Appendix C before you continue.

Descriptive Research: Assessing the Current State of Affairs

The first goal of behavioral research is to describe the thoughts, feelings, and behavior of individuals. Research designed to answer questions about the current state of affairs is known as **descriptive research.** This type of research provides a "snapshot" of thoughts, feelings, or behaviors at a given place and a given time.

Surveys and Interviews.   One type of descriptive research, which we will discuss in Chapter 6, is based on *surveys*. Millions of dollars are spent yearly by the U.S. Bureau of the Census to describe the characteristics of the U.S. population, including where people work, how much they earn, and with whom they live. Descriptive data in the form of surveys and interviews are regularly found in articles published in newspapers and magazines and are used by politicians to determine what policies are popular or unpopular with their constituents.

Sometimes the data from descriptive research projects are rather mundane, such as "Nine out of ten doctors prefer Tymenocin," or "The average income in Montgomery County is $36,712." Yet other times (particularly in discussions of social behavior), descriptive statistics can be shocking: "Over 40,000 people are killed by gunfire in the United States every year," or "Over 45 percent of sixth graders at Madison High School report that they have used marijuana."

One common type of descriptive research, frequently reported in newspaper and magazine articles, involves surveys of the "current concerns" of the people within a city, state, or nation. The results of such a survey are shown in Figure 1.1. These surveys allow us to get a picture of what people are thinking, feeling, or doing at a given point in time.

Naturalistic Observation.   As we will discuss more fully in Chapter 7, another type of descriptive research—known as *naturalistic observation*—is based on the observation of everyday events. For instance, a developmental psychologist who watches children on a playground and describes what they say to each other while they play is conducting descriptive research, as is a biological psychologist who observes animals in their natural habitats or a sociologist who studies the way in which people use public transportation in a large urban city.

Qualitative Versus Quantitative Research.   One distinction that is made in descriptive research concerns whether it is *qualitative* or *quantitative* in orientation. **Qualitative research** is descriptive research that is focused on observing and describing events as they occur, with the goal of capturing all of

FIGURE 1.1   Survey Research: Current Concerns of U.S. Citizens

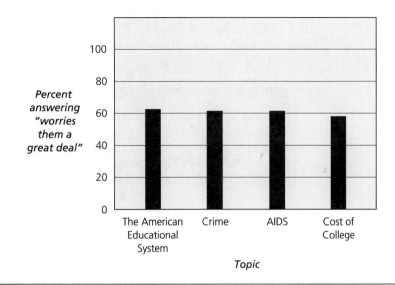

This graph represents the top worries of 1,000 randomly selected adults interviewed in June through July, 1996. Sampling error is plus or minus 3 percentage points.

Source: Adapted from *The Washington Post,* September 15, 1996.

the richness of everyday behavior and with the hope of discovering and understanding phenomena that might have been missed if only more cursory examinations had been used (Denzin & Lincoln, 2000). The data that form the basis of qualitative research are in their original rich form—for instance, descriptive narratives such as field notes and audio or video recordings. **Quantitative research** is descriptive research that uses more formal measures of behavior, including questionnaires and systematic observation of behavior, which are designed to be subjected to statistical analysis. The strength of qualitative research is that it vividly describes ongoing behavior in its original form. However, because it does not use statistical analysis, it is generally more subjective and may not fully separate the values of the researcher from the objectivity of the research process. In many cases, however, qualitative data are reported along with quantitative data to provide a fuller description of the observed behavior; this combination of approaches can be very informative.

Strengths and Limitations of Descriptive Research.   One advantage of descriptive research is that it attempts to capture the complexity of everyday behavior. For instance, surveys capture the thoughts of a large population of people, and naturalistic observation is designed to study the behavior of people or animals as it occurs naturally. Thus descriptive research is used to provide a relatively complete understanding of what is currently happening. Nevertheless, descriptive research has a distinct disadvantage in that although it allows us to get an idea of what is currently happening, it is limited to providing static pictures. A study of the current concerns of individuals, for instance, cannot tell us how those concerns developed or what impact they have on people's voting behavior.

Correlational Research: Seeking Relationships Among Variables

In contrast to descriptive research, which is designed to provide static pictures, **correlational research** involves the measurement of two or more relevant variables and an assessment of the relationship between or among those variables. A **variable** is any attribute that can assume different values among different people or across different times or places. Sometimes variables are rather simple—for instance, measures of age, shoe size, or weight. In other cases (and as we will discuss fully in Chapters 4 and 5), variables represent more complex ideas, such as egomania, burnout, sexism, or cognitive development.

As we will see in Chapter 9, the goal of correlational research is to uncover variables that show systematic relationships with each other. For instance, the variables of height and weight are systematically related, because taller people generally weigh more than shorter people. In the same way, study time and memory errors are also related, because the more time a person is given to study a list of words, the fewer errors she or he will make. Of course, a person's score on one variable is not usually perfectly related to his or her score on the other. Although tall people are likely to weigh more, we cannot perfectly predict how tall someone is merely by knowing that person's weight.

The Pearson Product-Moment Correlation Coefficient. Because the size of the relationships of interest to behavioral scientists is usually very small, statistical procedures are used to detect them. The most common measure of relationships among variables is the **Pearson product-moment correlation coefficient,** which is symbolized by the letter r.

The correlation coefficient ranges from $r = -1.00$ to $r = +1.00$. Positive values indicate positive correlations, in which people who are farther above average on one variable (for instance, height) generally are also farther above average on the other variable (for instance, weight). Negative values of r indicate negative correlations, in which people who are farther above average on one variable (for instance, study time) generally are also farther below average on the other variable (memory errors). Values of the correlation coefficient that are farther from zero (either positive or negative) indicate stronger relationships, whereas values closer to zero indicate weaker relationships.

The Use of Correlations to Make Predictions. One type of correlational research involves predicting future events from currently available knowledge. In this case one or more variables of interest are measured at one time, and other variables are measured at a later time. To the extent that there is a correlation between what we know now and what will occur later, we can use

TABLE 1.2   Predictors of College Performance

Predictor Variable	r
SAT score	.31
High school GPA	.30
Socioeconomic status	.12
Study habits	.30
Interfering social problems	−.39
Feelings of faculty involvement	.19

The column labeled r indicates the observed Pearson correlation coefficient between the predictor variable and college GPA. Note that most of the variables are *positively* correlated with college GPA, whereas the presence of interfering social problems is *negatively* correlated with GPA.

knowledge about the things that we already know to predict what will happen later. For instance, Nettles, Thoeny, and Gosman (1986) used a correlational research design to predict whether college students would stay in school or drop out. They measured characteristics of 4,094 college students at thirty different colleges and universities and assessed the ability of these characteristics to predict the students' current college grade-point average (GPA). In addition to intellectual variables such as high school GPA and Scholastic Aptitude Test (SAT) scores, they also assessed social variables including socioeconomic status, the students' reports of interfering social problems such as emotional stress and financial difficulties, and the students' perceptions of the quality of faculty-student relations at their university. The last measure was based on responses to questions such as "It is easy to develop close relationships with faculty members," and "I am satisfied with the student-faculty relations at this university." As shown in Table 1.2, the researchers found that students' ratings of the social problems they experienced on campus were as highly predictive of their grade-point average as were the standardized test scores they had taken before entering college. This information allows educators to predict which students will be most likely to finish their college education and suggests that campus experiences are important in this regard.

Strengths and Limitations of Correlational Research.   One particular advantage of correlational research is that it can be used to assess behavior as it occurs in people's everyday lives. Imagine, for instance, a researcher who finds a negative correlation between the row in which his students normally sit in his class and their grade on the final exam. This researcher's data demonstrate a very interesting relationship that occurs naturally for students attending college—those who sit nearer the front of the class get better grades.

Despite the ability of correlational studies to investigate naturally occurring behavior, they also have some inherent limitations. Most important, correlational studies cannot be used to identify causal relationships among the variables. It is just as possible that getting good grades causes students to sit in the front of the class as it is that sitting in the front of the class causes good grades. Furthermore, because only some of all the possible relevant variables are measured in correlational research, it is always possible that neither of the variables caused the other and that some other variable caused the observed variables to be correlated. For instance, students who are excited by the subject matter or who are highly motivated to succeed in school might both choose to sit in the front of the class and also end up getting good grades. In this case seating row and grades will be correlated, even though neither one caused the other.

In short, correlational research is limited to demonstrating relationships between or among variables or to making predictions of future events, but it cannot tell us why those variables are related. For instance, we could use a correlational design to predict the success of a group of trainees on a job from their scores on a battery of tests that they take during a training session. But we cannot use such correlational information to determine whether the training caused better job performance. For that, researchers rely on experiments.

Experimental Research: Understanding the Causes of Behavior

Behavioral scientists are particularly interested in answering questions about the causal relationships among variables. They believe that it is possible, indeed necessary, to determine which variables cause other variables to occur. Consider these questions: "Does watching violent television cause aggressive behavior?" "Does sleep deprivation cause an increase in memory errors?" and "Does being in a stressful situation cause heart disease?" Because it is difficult to answer such questions about causality using correlational designs, scientists frequently use experimental research. As we will discuss more fully in Chapters 10 and 11, **experimental research** involves the active creation or *manipulation* of a given situation or experience for two or more groups of individuals, followed by a measurement of the effect of those experiences on thoughts, feelings, or behavior. Furthermore, experimental research is designed to create *equivalence* between the individuals in the different groups before the experiment begins, so that any differences found can confidently be attributed to the effects of the experimental manipulation.

Elements of Experiments.   Let us look, for instance, at an experimental research design used by social psychologists Macrae, Bodenhausen, Milne, and Jetten (1994). The goal of this experiment was to test the hypothesis that suppressing the use of stereotypes may cause an unexpected "rebound" in which those stereotypes are actually used to a greater extent at a later time. In the experiment college students were shown a picture of a "skinhead" and asked to write a short paragraph describing what they thought he was like. While doing so, half of the students were explicitly told not to let their stereotypes about skinheads influence them when writing their descriptions. The other half of the students were just asked to write a description.

After the students had finished writing their descriptions, they were told that they were going to be meeting with the person they had written about and were taken into a separate room. In the room was a row of nine chairs, with a jean jacket and a book bag sitting on the center one. The experimenter explained that the partner (the skinhead) had evidently left to go to the bathroom but that he would be right back and the students should take a seat and wait. As soon as the students sat down, the experiment was over. The prediction that students who had previously suppressed their stereotypes would sit, on average, farther away from the skinhead's chair than the students who had not suppressed their stereotypes was confirmed.

Strengths and Limitations of Experimental Research.   This clever experiment nicely demonstrates one advantage of experimental research. The experiment can be interpreted as demonstrating that suppressing stereotypes caused the students to sit farther away from the skinhead because there was only one difference between the two groups of students in this experiment, and that was whether they had suppressed their stereotypical thoughts when writing. It is this ability to draw conclusions about causal relationships that makes experiments so popular.

Although they have the distinct advantage of being able to provide information about causal relationships among variables, experiments, like descriptive and correlational research, also have limitations. In fact, experiments cannot be used to study the most important social questions facing today's society, including violence, racism, poverty, and homelessness, because the conditions of interest cannot be manipulated by the experimenter. Since it is not possible (for both practical and ethical reasons) to manipulate whether a person is homeless, poor, or abused by her or his parents, these topics cannot be studied experimentally. Thus descriptive and correlational designs must be used to study these issues. Because experiments have their own limitations, they are no more "scientific" than are other approaches to research.

The Selection of an Appropriate Method

The previous sections have described the characteristics of descriptive, correlational, and experimental research designs. Because these three approaches represent fundamentally different ways of studying behavior, they each provide different types of information. And, as summarized in Table 1.3, each research design has a unique set of advantages and disadvantages. In short, each of the three research designs contributes to the accumulation of scientific knowledge, and thus each is necessary for a complete study of behavior.

To determine which research approach is best for a given research project, the researcher must look at several matters. For one, practical issues such as the availability of research participants, researchers, equipment, and space will determine the research approach. And as we will see in Chapter 3, ethical principles of research will shape the researcher's choice. But the decision will also derive from the researcher's own ideas about research—what she or he

TABLE 1.3 Characteristics of the Three Research Designs

Research Design	Goal	Advantages	Disadvantages
Descriptive	To create a snapshot of the current state of affairs	Provides a relatively complete picture of what is occurring at a given time	Does not assess relationships among variables
Correlational	To assess the relationships between and among two or more variables	Allows testing of expected relationships between and among variables and making of predictions	Cannot be used to draw inferences about the causal relationships between and among the variables
Experimental	To assess the impact of one or more experimental manipulations on a dependent variable	Allows drawing of conclusions about the causal relationships among variables.	Cannot experimentally manipulate many important variables

thinks is important to study. And it is to the development of research ideas that we will turn in the next chapter.

Furthermore, because each of the three research designs has different strengths and weaknesses, it is often effective to use them together. For instance, the impact of population density on mental health has been tested using naturalistic observation, correlational studies, and experimental research designs. Using more than one technique (such as more than one research design) to study the same thing, with the hope that all of the approaches will produce similar findings, is known as **converging operations.** As we will see, the converging-operation approach is common in the behavioral sciences.

SUMMARY

Behavioral research is conducted by scientists who are interested in understanding the behavior of human beings and animals. These scientists believe that knowledge gained through personal intuition or the claims of others is not a sufficient basis for drawing conclusions about behavior. They demand that knowledge be gained through the accumulation of empirical data, as prescribed by the scientific method. Behavioral scientists understand that the scientific approach is not perfect, but it is better than any other known way of drawing conclusions about behavior.

Although science is designed to create a collection of facts, it is not entirely free of values. The values of scientists influence how they interpret their data, what and whom they study, and how they report their research. For instance, some scientists conduct basic research, whereas others conduct applied research. One of the important goals of the scientific method is to make clear to others which aspects of the research process are based on facts and which are based on values.

There are three major research designs in behavioral research. There are advantages and disadvantages to each of the approaches, and each provides an essential avenue of scientific investigation. Descriptive research, such as surveys and naturalistic observation, is designed to provide a snapshot of the current state of affairs. Descriptive research may be either qualitative or quantitative in orientation. Correlational research is designed to discover relationships among variables and to allow the prediction of future events from present knowledge. The relationships among variables are frequently described using the Pearson correlation coefficient. Because correlational research cannot provide evidence about causal relationships between variables, experimental research is often employed to do so. Experiments involve the creation of equivalence among research participants in more than one group, followed by an active manipulation of a given experience for these groups and a measurement of the influence of the manipulation. The goal is to assess the causal impact of the manipulation. Because each of the three types of research designs has both strengths and limitations, it is very important to learn to think critically about research. Such critical evaluation will allow you to select the appropriate research design and to determine what conclusions can and cannot be drawn from research.

KEY TERMS

applied research 11
basic research 11
behavioral research 4
converging operations 20
correlational research 16
data 4
descriptive research 14
empirical 4
experimental research 18
facts 8
hindsight bias 7

objective 8
Pearson product-moment
    correlation coefficient (r) 16
program evaluation research 11
quantitative research 15
qualitative research 14
research design 13
research report 10
scientific method 8
values 8
variable 16

REVIEW AND DISCUSSION QUESTIONS

1. What is behavioral research? What are its fundamental goals and limitations? Why is learning about behavioral research important?

2. In what ways is behavioral research similar to and different from research in the natural sciences, such as chemistry, biology, and physics?

3. Why are behavioral scientists wary of using their intuition to understand behavior?

4. What is the scientific method, and how does it guide research?

5. Discuss the basic characteristics of scientific inquiry (empiricism, objectivity, and accumulation) and their value to science.

6. In what ways is science objective, and in what ways is it subjective? What prevents the subjectivity of science from compromising it as a discipline?

7. Consider the similarities and differences between basic research and applied research. What does each contribute to our knowledge about behavior?

8. Describe the characteristics of descriptive, correlational, and experimental research designs, and discuss the advantages and disadvantages of each.

HANDS-ON EXPERIENCE

1. Locate a newspaper or magazine article that reports a behavioral science research project.
   a. Determine whether the project is a descriptive, a correlational, or an experimental research design.
   b. What variables are measured in the research?
   c. Is the research applied or basic in orientation?
   d. What are the most important findings of the research?
   e. What do you perceive as potential limitations of the research?

2. Consider whether each of the following research reports seems to describe an applied or a basic research project, and explain why:

   An experimental analysis of the impact of contingent reinforcement on salespersons' performance behavior
   The theory of crystallized and fluid intelligence
   The effect of prison crowding on inmate behavior
   The role of schemata in memory for places
   Neonatal imitation

3. Create predictions about the relationships between behavioral variables that interest you. For each relationship that you develop, indicate how the prediction could be tested using a descriptive, a correlational, and/or an experimental research design. What would be the advantages and disadvantages of studying the relationship using each of the different designs?

4. Generate three beliefs about human behavior using the following as models. Indicate whether each is based on fact or opinion and how you could tell the difference.

a. Women are more socially skilled than men.

b. It is more difficult for a person to learn how to play the piano when she or he is older than when she or he is younger.

c. Dogs are smarter than cats.

d. It is difficult for a person to study while loud music is playing nearby.

5. Consider the data reported in Table 1.2. Interpret the observed correlations between the predictor variables and college GPA. What do these correlations indicate about the causes of college grade-point averages? What are the limitations of the research findings?

6. Consider the meaning of data showing that, on average, African-American students score more poorly on standardized exams in comparison to white students (Herrnstein & Murray, 1994). What type of data might be collected to help determine the meaning of such differences?

7. Find and read the following articles about whether scientists should look for and report differences between men and women in their research. Consider how the values of the scientist might influence his or her decisions in this regard and how these decisions might affect the scientific rigor of the research report.

Eagly, A. H. (1990). On the advantages of reporting sex comparisons. *American Psychologist, 45,* 560–562.

Baumeister, R. F. (1988). Should we stop studying sex differences altogether? *American Psychologist, 43,* 1092–1095.

8. Read a qualitative research report such as one of the following, and report on how the research is used to get a detailed picture of the ongoing behavior of the research participants.

Festinger, L., Riechen, H. W., & Schachter, S. (1956). *When prophecy fails.* Minneapolis: University of Minnesota Press.

Humphreys, L. (1970). *Tearoom trade: Impersonal sex in public places.* Chicago: Aldine.

CHAPTER TWO
Developing the Research Hypothesis

STUDY QUESTIONS

- How do behavioral scientists get ideas for their research projects?

- What is a literature search? Why is a literature search necessary, and how is it conducted?

- What computer databases contain listings of behavioral research reports?

- How are previous research findings used to develop ideas for further research?

- What role do laws and theories play in scientific research?

- What are research hypotheses, and what is their purpose?

As we have seen in Chapter 1, this book concerns the scientific study of behavior. In this chapter we will begin our investigation of the research process by considering the initial stages in conducting scientific research, including how scientists get their ideas for research and how they conduct a background literature review to see what research has already been conducted on their topic. We will also consider the principles that are used to organize research—laws, theories, and research hypotheses. Because research hypotheses are the most basic tool of the scientist, we will be spending a major part of this book discussing their development and testing, and this chapter will provide an important background for the chapters to come.

Getting Ideas

As you can well imagine, there are plenty of topics to study and plenty of approaches to studying those topics. For instance, my colleagues within the Psychology Department at the University of Maryland study such diverse topics as:

present list
of research
from CH45

Anxiety in children
The interpretation of dreams
The effects of caffeine on thinking
How birds recognize each other
How praying mantises hear
What makes people enjoy their experiences in banks
How to reduce stereotyping and prejudice

The point is, there are a lot of things to study!

You may already be developing such ideas for your research projects. As with most things based on creative and original thinking, these ideas will not come to you overnight. For the best scientists, research is always in the back of their minds. Whether they are reading journal articles, teaching classes, driving in the car, or exercising, scientists are continually thinking about ways to use research to study the questions that interest them. Good behavioral scientists are always alert to their experiences and ready to apply those experiences to their research.

elicit ideas for
research project
in a brainstorm.
or discussion
(phrased as a
question?)

Because there are so many things to study, you may think it would be easy to come up with research ideas. On the contrary, informative research ideas are hard to come by. For instance, although you may be interested in studying depression, nurturance, memory, or helping, having an idea of a research interest is only a very preliminary first step in developing a testable research idea. Before you can begin your research project, you must determine what aspects of your topic you wish to focus on and then refine these interests into a specific research design. And for your ideas to result in an accumulation of knowledge, they must be informed by past research. This is going to take time and require a lot of thought on your part.

Bas

Apl.

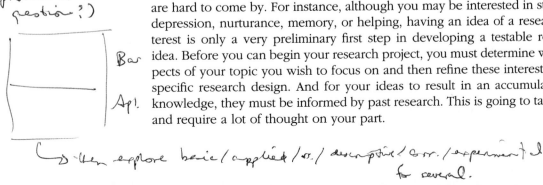

↳ then explore basic/applied/vs./descriptive/corr./experimental
for several.

Scientists develop their ideas about what to study in a number of different ways, and in the next sections we will consider some methods for getting ideas.[1] As you read this section, keep in mind the types of research that we discussed in Chapter 1. You may want to begin your search for ideas by determining whether you are more interested in a basic research project or in a specific applied question. And you will want to think about whether your research question is best tested using a descriptive, a correlational, or an experimental research design.

Solving Important Real-World Problems

Many behavioral scientists develop their research programs around their concerns with human problems. For instance, behavioral scientists have studied how to improve children's reading skills, how to alleviate stress in corporate managers, how to promote volunteering, and how to reduce aggression among gang members. Other scientists have studied methods for reducing risky behavior such as unprotected sex and cigarette smoking. Still others have studied the effectiveness of psychotherapy or how juries make decisions. Thus one way to get ideas for research is to develop an applied research project that has the goal of producing a better understanding of the causes of, or potential solutions to, everyday problems.

Using Observation and Intuition

Because much behavioral research involves the study of people in their everyday lives, it is often possible to develop research ideas on the basis of intuition or hunches, which are themselves based on observation of everyday behavior. Getting ideas about the relationships among variables by observing specific facts is known as the **inductive method.** In this approach your own curiosity becomes the source of your ideas. For instance, you may have noticed that several friends of yours have had trouble developing satisfactory romantic relationships. You may have developed a theory about why these particular people have this particular behavioral problem, and you may want to test this idea in a research project. As we have seen in Chapter 1, it is useful to test hunches about behavior because those hunches often "feel" more right to us than they actually turn out to be. Only by subjecting our hunches to systematic investigation can we be sure of their validity.

Some important scientific ideas have been developed through observation. For instance, Sigmund Freud developed his theory of personality by carefully observing the patients in his clinical practice. In a similar way Jean Piaget developed his theory of cognitive development in children by watching the development of his own children.

---

[1]The social psychologist William McGuire recently argued that there were forty-nine different ways of getting research ideas (!), and you may want to look at some of these in his chapter in the *Annual Review of Psychology:* McGuire, W. J. (1997). Creative hypothesis generating in psychology: Some useful heuristics. *Annual Review of Psychology, 48,* 1–30.

Although using observation and intuition has the potential of producing new ideas and approaches, there is also a possible danger to this approach. Studies that are based on intuition alone but do not relate to existing scientific knowledge may not advance the field very far. Consider a research project designed to test the idea that people learn more in a class taught by left-handed teachers than in a class taught by right-handed teachers. In the long run such research could make a contribution to science by linking brain symmetry and creativity to teaching effectiveness. But the results of a single study testing this prediction will probably not make much of a contribution to the larger body of scientific knowledge because there is no existing explanation for why a left-handed instructor should be better than a right-handed instructor other than the hunch of the person who developed the idea.

Although you may use your observations of everyday behavior to generate research ideas, or develop your research around solutions to a practical social problem, you should try to link your research to the findings from other studies investigating the same concepts. A study concerning creative thinking will be more useful if it is related to existing research about creativity, even if the goal of the study is to demonstrate that the existing research has drawn incorrect conclusions or is incomplete. The more links you can draw between your research and existing research, the greater is the likelihood that your research will make an important contribution to the field.

Using Existing Research

The previous discussion has perhaps already suggested to you that I think that the best way to generate research ideas is by reading about and studying existing scientific research and then using this existing knowledge to generate new research ideas and topics. Although basing your research ideas on already existing research may seem to limit the contribution that your project can make, this is not the case. In fact, research that is based on or related to previous research findings tends to advance science more rapidly because it contributes to the accumulation of a unified and integrated body of knowledge. Our substantial knowledge about topics such as the causes of prejudice or the development of reading skills in children exists precisely because of the cumulative work of hundreds of investigators who have conducted research that built on previously conducted research.

Finding Limiting Conditions. Because every research project is limited in some way or another, goal of most research is to expand on or improve existing research. One useful strategy for developing research ideas is to consider the potential *limiting conditions* of previous research. For instance, for many years people believed that women were more likely to conform to the opinions of others than men were. Only when scientists began to consider the types of tasks that had been used in conformity research was a basic limiting condition found. Previous research had relied to a large extent on topics (such as football and baseball) in which men were more knowledgeable than women. However, subsequent research demonstrated that the original conclusion was too broad. This research showed that women do conform more than men, but only when the topic is one about which women believe that men have more knowledge than they do (Eagly & Chravala, 1986). If the topic is one in which women believe they are more knowledgeable (for instance, fashion design), then men are found to conform more than women. In this case research assessing the limiting conditions of existing findings made a significant contribution by developing a new explanation for a phenomenon. A finding that had previously been explained in terms of differences between men and women was now explained in terms of differences in knowledge about the topic.

Explaining Conflicting Findings. Another strategy for developing research ideas is to attempt to explain conflicting findings in a research area. In many cases some studies testing a given idea show one pattern of data, whereas other studies do not show that pattern. And some studies may even show the opposite pattern. Research that can account for these discrepancies can be extremely useful. One classic example of this approach occurred in the 1960s when Robert Zajonc (1965) noted that some studies had demonstrated that tasks such as bicycle riding or jogging were performed better in the presence of others, whereas other studies showed that tasks such as solving mathematical problems were usually solved more efficiently when people were alone. There was no known explanation for these differences.

Zajonc proposed that being with others increased psychological arousal and that arousal amplified the "dominant" or most likely response in a given setting. Because the dominant response was usually the correct response on easy or well-learned tasks (such as jogging) but the incorrect response on difficult or poorly learned tasks (such as math problems), the presence of others might either increase or decrease performance depending on task difficulty. This became a very important principle in social psychology, and the findings have been confirmed in many different experiments. Zajonc's research was particularly valuable because it was able to account in a consistent way for what had previously appeared to be inconsistent research findings.

In short, because existing research provides so many ideas for future research, it is very important to be aware of what other research has been done in an area. Indeed, one of the most important qualities of a good scientist is an open mind. Careful and creative analysis of existing research can produce many important ideas for future research projects.

Doing a Literature Search

Because all good research is designed to build on and expand existing knowledge, it would be wasteful for a scientist to begin working on a project without knowing what others working in the area have already done. This is why scientists receive years of training in which they learn both methods of conducting research and the current content of knowledge in their field. It is also why scientists spend a lot of time reading about research in scientific journals and participating at conferences where research is presented. In short, scientists are keenly aware that their research will make a contribution to the field only if it is based on and adds significantly to what is already known.

Once you have begun to develop an idea for your research, you should perform a *literature search* to locate the journals and books that contain reports of previous research (Reed & Baxter, 1983). Conducting a literature search before beginning a research project is essential because it helps prevent duplication of effort and may help you avoid problems that others have had. The literature search is also a great time-saver because it can provide you with invaluable information about how to measure the variables you are interested in and what research designs will be most useful to you. There is so much literature in behavioral science journals and books that no matter what your research idea is, others will probably have done something relevant to it. This does not mean that your idea is not important—in fact, it suggests that others have also found it to be so.

Locating Sources of Information

There are many sources of research literature relevant to your interest. Probably the most important sources of information are research reports that contain complete descriptions of the collected data and the data analyses. These research reports are known as *primary sources* and usually appear in professional journals. *Secondary sources* are documents that contain only summaries or interpretations of the research reports rather than a complete description of them. Secondary sources include textbooks, books written by a single author, and edited books that contain a collection of chapters on a single topic, each contributed by a different author. Some journals, such as *Psychological Bulletin* and the *Annual Review of Psychology,* also publish primarily secondary-source articles.

In many cases, the sources that you locate can be found online through the databases maintained by university libraries. If the source is not online, you will have to find it on the shelves of your library using the call number of the book or journal. If your library does not subscribe to the journal or have the book on its shelves, you may be able to get it through the interlibrary loan system.

You may also wish to use the Web to get ideas. It is likely that no matter what your topic is, you will find one or more Internet sites that contain data and other relevant information about it. In many cases, however, Web sites provide only secondary-source information. Since this information may be based primarily on intuition rather than on data, it is difficult to determine its accuracy and credibility. Therefore, although Web sites are useful for getting initial ideas, they should always be backed up with primary-source information.

Other valuable sources of information are experts in the field in which you are interested. An instructor may be a good source in this regard or may be able to direct you to an even more knowledgeable expert. Experts can also be useful in directing you to specific journals that are known to contain the best published research in your topic area. Do not be shy about contacting experts. Although they may be busy, scientists are usually happy to put their knowledge to use.

Conducting the Search

Generally, a literature search will be most efficient if it (1) starts at a broad, general level (secondary sources) and then progresses to more specific levels (primary sources) and (2) starts with the newest available information and uses this information to progress backward toward previous research.

One approach to beginning a literature search in an area that you do not know much about is to use one or more introductory textbooks in that field as the most general secondary sources. Choose a chapter in which your topic is discussed, and read the chapter carefully. Although using secondary sources can be a time-saver because they generally provide more information in fewer pages, it is absolutely essential that you also consult primary sources in your literature search. Secondary sources may not adequately summarize the primary-source research. Journal articles are also more complete and objective than secondary sources because (as we will discuss in Appendix A), they have passed a rigorous review process.

After you have begun to focus on a topic area, you will want to move from general information toward more specific treatments of the topic area by reading book chapters and journal articles. As you begin to move deeper into your topic, do not be too inflexible about what you are interested in. It is best to keep an open mind at this point because you may find that your research idea has already been well tested or that another research idea interests you more than the one you began with. Remember that your goal is not only to read about the research but also to use the research to develop and refine ideas for your own research. Being open-minded is important in all stages of the research process, especially because research that originally seemed irrelevant may later turn out to be valuable to you when you have a broader idea of the scope of the topic you are studying. The literature search should be used to help you modify and refine your original ideas.

Investigating Computer Databases.   The most efficient way to find primary sources relevant to your topic is through the use of a computer-aided literature search. Behavioral science databases are provided by most libraries and are available online. The databases contain summaries (called **abstracts**) of thousands of journal articles and book chapters. Reading these abstracts will give you a basic idea of whether the material will provide information you are interested in, and where to locate a journal article or book chapter if you decide to read it.

The two most relevant databases in psychology are PsycINFO® and PsycARTICLES®. PsycINFO indexes almost 2 million references to psychological literature published from 1887 to the present. Some of these articles may be online in your library. PsycARTICLES provides the full text of articles from over forty journals published by the American Psychological Association. These represent some of the most important journals in psychology. The American Psychological Association Web site (*www.apa.org*) has more information about both of these databases. Similar databases are found in other fields. For instance, SocialSciIndex® is a sociological database containing abstracts from over 1,600 journals. Medline® indexes journals in the areas of health care, environmental health, and behavioral medicine, and ERIC® is a collection of databases including those related to education and training.

Another useful database is the Social Science Citation Index (SSCI). Although the normal search procedure is to use the reference lists of newer journal articles to locate older articles, SSCI allows you to work the other way around. If you have an older article that you have found to be very important to your topic, you can use SSCI to find other, more recent articles that have cited that article in their references.

One potential problem is that it takes some time for the databases to be updated. As a result, if you believe that there are some very new articles that have been published on your topic, and if you know which journals they might have been published in, then you can use Current Contents to locate them. Current Contents is essentially a table of contents for all journals within certain disciplines that have been published in the previous two weeks.

Using Keywords Effectively.   Before beginning your search in a database, you will need to have a few keywords to use in locating your materials. Most of your keywords will be of subjects, such as *learning, memory, stress,* or *paranoia.* However, you can also use author names or journal titles as keywords. You can develop your own keywords on the basis of your interests, but if you are not sure about what keywords to use, consult the *Thesaurus*—an index of all of the keywords used in the database. Ask your reference librarian for help if you are unsure how to proceed.

Once you have entered a keyword, the computer checks the titles and abstracts of all of the books or articles in the database for the occurrence of that word. One problem is that some keywords are so broad that there are way too many articles using them. For instance, I recently searched PsycINFO using the keyword *learning* and found over 182,000 journal articles listed! The database thus allows you to combine keywords to make your target more specific. For instance, when I combined the keywords *learning* and *children,* the list was reduced to about 31,735 articles, and a search for *learning* and *children* and *television* produced only 278 articles. Finally, I indicated that I wanted only articles from the years 2000–2002, and this reduced the output to a manageable list of 28 articles. You can also limit your search to include only journal articles, to include only certain authors, and (in case your foreign language skills aren't that good) to include only articles in English.

Figure 2.1 shows the input that I gave to my search. You can see that the database is PsycINFO, that there are three keywords—*children, learning,* and *television*—and that I have indicated to search only in the years 2000–2002.

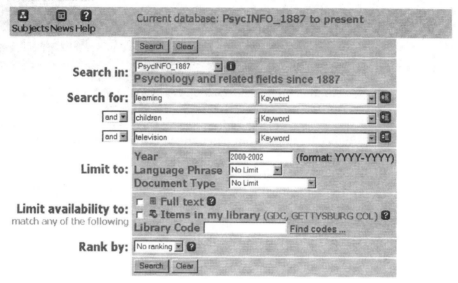

Figure 2.1   Input to PsycINFO Search

Author(s): Oates, Caroline ; Blades, Mark ; Gunter, Barrie
Affiliation: 1. U Sheffield, Management School, Sheffield, England; 2. U Sheffield, Dept of Psychology, Sheffield, England; 3. U Sheffield, Dept of Journalism Studies, Sheffield, England

Title: **Children and television advertising: When do they understand persuasive intent?**

Source: *Journal of Consumer Behaviour* Vol 1(3), Feb 2002, 238-245.
Additional Info: United Kingdom : Henry Stewart Publications

Standard No: ISSN: 1472-0817 (Print)

Language: English

Abstract: Children's response to television advertising is investigated in this paper. Children (aged 4-10 yrs) were tested for their recall, recognition and understanding of novel television advertisements and compared to a group of 12 adults. Children were able to recognize scenes from the advertisements after one exposure but recall of the brand names was poor for the younger children, even after three exposures. Recall for the advertising content increased by age and number of exposures. None of the 6-yr-olds and only a quarter of the 8-yr-olds and a third of the 10-yr-olds discussed advertising in terms of persuasion. Therefore, although children remember television advertisements, their purpose is not fully understood, even by any 10-yr-olds. (PsycINFO Database Record (c) 2002 APA, all rights reserved):

Figure 2.2   Output of PsycINFO Search

Figure 2.2 presents the first listing that came out of my search, and you can see the type of information it contains. It includes the title and authors of the article, as well as their university affiliations. Also included is information about the journal in which the article is published and the abstract. The listing also allows me to see whether the article is available in my library and whether it is available online. In this case, the full text of the article turned out to be available, and I could go right to reading it.

Using the keyword system will get you started, but it is only the beginning of your literature search. As you read journal articles, you will find that those articles contain other relevant articles in their reference sections. Working backward through the reference lists of the articles you read will allow you to find many new articles that did not appear in the initial keyword search. To adequately prepare a research topic for investigation, you must do an extensive search of the literature, which will take quite a bit of time. Keep in mind that you can often do a large part of the preparation for your research project at this point by taking good notes or making copies of the articles and by thinking about how these references will relate to your final report.

Using Abstracts to Select Important Documents. Once you have developed a smaller list of articles relevant to your area of interest, you will begin to read their abstracts to determine if the articles may be of interest to you. As you read through journal abstracts, you will probably find that there are certain authors who have published frequently in your topic area. These are the scientists who have made major contributions to the literature, and you may wish to locate their contributions by entering their names as keywords.

Remember that it is important to read at least some of the articles that you have located. It is not sufficient to just read the abstracts, because they are too brief to give you a complete understanding of the research.

Formalizing Ideas into Research Hypotheses

As you conduct your literature search, you will want to pay close attention to the organizing principles that form the basis of behavioral research. These principles include laws, theories, and research hypotheses. As we will see in the next sections, once you have read a great deal about your topic area, you will begin to develop more specific ideas about what you want to study, and you will be ready to begin formalizing your interests into a specific research hypothesis that you will test.

Laws

Principles that are so general as to apply to all situations are known as **laws.** There are well-known laws in the physical sciences, such as the law of gravity and the laws of thermodynamics, but there currently are very few universally accepted laws within the behavioral sciences. This is partly because behavioral science research has not progressed as far as that in the natural sciences and partly because it is more difficult to specify laws of social behavior. In any case, because laws are such general principles and are considered so only because their validity has already been well established, they are themselves rarely directly subjected to scientific test.

Theories

The next step down from laws in the hierarchy of organizing principles is the theory. A **theory** is an integrated set of principles that explains and predicts many, but not all, observed relationships within a given domain of inquiry. Because theories integrate many observations into a relatively simple whole and yet are not too general to be tested, they form the basic building blocks of science. Existing theories (or ones that you develop) may help provide you with ideas for developing your own research. The process of using a theory to generate specific ideas that can be tested through research is known as the **deductive method.**

The Components of a Good Theory.   Consider, for instance, the stage theory of cognitive development, which states that children pass through a series of cognitive stages and that children cannot perform certain activities until the appropriate cognitive stage has been reached (Piaget, 1952). This is an extremely useful theory in human development because it can be applied to many different content areas and can be tested in many different ways.

The utility of a theory can be judged on the basis of how well it meets some fundamental requirements. First, good theories are **general,** meaning that they summarize many different outcomes. Second, they are **parsimonious,** meaning that they provide the simplest possible account of those outcomes. The stage theory of cognitive development meets both of these requirements. It can account for developmental changes in behavior across a wide variety of domains, and yet it does so parsimoniously—by hypothesizing a simple set of cognitive stages.

Third, good theories provide ideas for future research. For instance, the stage theory suggested many different types of experiments in many different areas that have since been used to study cognitive development. Research has demonstrated, for instance, that children cannot conserve volume or mass until they have reached an appropriate stage of development (Piaget, 1952), that they learn about what it means to be a boy or a girl in stages (Stangor & Ruble, 1987), and that moral reasoning follows a stage sequence (Kohlberg, 1969). Taken together, these different research findings, all predicted by the stage theory, provide overall support for the theory.

Fourth, good theories are **falsifiable** (Popper, 1959), which means that the variables of interest can be adequately measured and the relationships between the variables that are predicted by the theory can be shown through research to be incorrect. The stage theory of cognitive development is falsifiable because the stages of cognitive reasoning can be measured and because if research discovers that children learn new tasks gradually, rather than quickly, as they pass into a new stage, then the theory will be shown to be incorrect. In general, when a theory is falsified, it will be replaced by a new, more accurate theory.

Judgment of a Theory's Utility.   Some theories meet some of the requirements for a good theory but not others. The theory of social reinforcement, for instance, proposes that people will be more likely to subsequently perform a behavior after they have been rewarded for performing it. This is an extremely important theory because it summarizes much of everyday social behavior in a parsimonious manner and also provides ideas for testing it. For instance, the theory would predict that children would more likely share their toys if their mother praises them for doing so.

However, the definitions of "reward" in social behavior involve both external factors, such as money and praise, and internal factors, such as mood improvement and guilt reduction. Because internal factors are difficult to define and measure, a supporter of social learning theory could easily argue that when a behavior occurs, it has been rewarded, and that when a behavior does not occur, it has not been rewarded. For instance, when a person helps a complete stranger escape from a burning building, there is obvious cost to the helper, but the potential reward is not clear. But a supporter of social reinforcement theory would say that the reward was something such as "feeling good about helping" or "avoiding guilt if one didn't help." In this case the problem is that the theory is not falsifiable because the variable "reward" is defined as "that which increases the occurrence of behavior." Theories in which the variables cannot be measured or in which the variables are vague enough that they cannot provide information to falsify the theory are called **tautological.**

No single theory is able to account for all behavior in all cases. Rather, a theory is inevitably found to be limited in that it makes accurate predictions in some situations or for some people but not in other situations or for other people. As a result, there is a constant interplay between theory and data: existing theories are modified on the basis of collected data, and the new modified theories then make new predictions which are tested by new data, and so forth. In time a theory will either change so much that it becomes a new and different theory or be entirely replaced by another, more accurate theory. A theory survives only to the extent that it is "good enough" and no currently known alternative theory is better. When a better theory is found, it will replace the old one. This is part of the accumulation of scientific knowledge.

The Research Hypothesis

Although good theories are designed to be falsifiable, they are usually framed too broadly to be tested in a single experiment. Therefore, scientists use a more precise statement of the presumed relationship among specific parts of the theory—a research hypothesis—as a basis for correlational and experimental research (remember that relationships among variables are never tested in descriptive research). Because research hypotheses are the most basic tool of the scientist, we will be spending a major part of this book discussing their development and testing.

A **research hypothesis** can be defined as a specific and falsifiable prediction regarding the relationship between or among two or more variables. The research hypothesis states the existence of a relationship between the variables of interest and the specific direction of that relationship. For instance:

> Observing violent television shows will cause increased aggressive behavior.
>
> Participating in psychotherapy will reduce anxiety.
>
> Smoking marijuana will reduce the ability to learn new information.

As we will discuss more fully in Chapters 10 and 11, in experimental research designs the research hypothesis involves the relationship between an **independent variable** (the experimental manipulation) and a **dependent variable** (the variable that is caused by the independent variable). The independent variable is created by the experimenter through the experimental manipulation, and the research hypothesis is that the manipulated independent variable causes changes in the measured dependent variable. Causal relationships can be depicted graphically using straight arrows that point in one direction:

INDEPENDENT   DEPENDENT
VARIABLE   VARIABLE

In correlational research designs, both the independent variable and the dependent variable are measured. Furthermore, because it is not possible to state the causal relationships between variables in correlational designs, the terms *independent variable* and *dependent variable* are sometimes replaced with the terms *predictor variable* and *outcome variable,* respectively. The research hypothesis is that there is a correlation between the variables, and this correlation is shown using a curved line with arrows that point in both directions:

PREDICTOR   OUTCOME
VARIABLE   VARIABLE

Because the research hypothesis is only a guess and is designed to be falsifiable, its validity must be tested. Moreover, there are many ways to measure the variables of interest and many ways to test the relationship between them. The major focus of this book is on how to develop research designs and test research hypotheses.

SUMMARY

The first stage in a research project is developing an idea. These ideas can come through an interest in solving important social problems, through the use of the inductive method to organize existing facts, and through the exercise of the deductive method to derive predictions from existing theories. The last approach is perhaps the most useful because it ensures that the new research is related to existing research and thus contributes to the accumulation of scientific knowledge.

Before beginning a research project the scientist conducts a literature search, usually by using computer databases to locate abstracts of relevant articles. The literature search involves locating both secondary- and primary-source material. Being knowledgeable about previous research from other research laboratories is essential to the development of effective research. The literature search frequently leads the scientist to modify and refine his/her original research ideas.

One of the goals of science is to organize relationships into explanatory principles such as laws and theories. Laws are general principles that apply to all situations. Theories are integrated set of principles that explain and predict many observed events within a given domain. Good theories are both general and parsimonious, they form the basis of future scientific research, and they make predictions that can be tested and falsified.

Theories are tested in the form of research hypotheses—specific and testable predictions regarding the relationship between or among two or more variables. Once a scientist develops a research hypothesis, she or he tests it using either a correlational or an experimental research design.

KEY TERMS

abstracts 30
deductive method 34
dependent variable 36
falsifiable 34
general 34
independent variable 36

inductive method 26
laws 33
parsimonious 34
research hypothesis 36
tautological 35
theory 34

REVIEW AND DISCUSSION QUESTIONS

1. How do scientists get ideas for research? What are the advantages and potential disadvantages of each method for doing so?

2. What guidelines do scientists use to conduct an effective literature search? What specific literature databases are most useful to behavioral scientists?

3. What makes a good theory? Why are theories so important in behavioral research?

4. What makes a theory falsifiable? What makes a theory tautological?

5. What is a research hypothesis? Why are research hypotheses, rather than theories or laws, tested in behavioral research?

HANDS-ON EXPERIENCE

1. Turn each of the following statements into a research hypothesis and indicate whether the hypothesis is falsifiable:

    God answers our prayers.
    Birds of a feather flock together.
    You can't teach an old dog new tricks.
    Elderly individuals don't remember things well.
    Practice makes perfect.
    Single-parent families produce delinquent children.
    Aggression is increasing in our society.
    People work harder when they are in a good mood.
    Cats can understand English.

2. Consider the following variables. For each one (a) create a research hypothesis in which the variable serves as an independent (or predictor) variable and (b) create a research hypothesis in which the variable serves as a dependent (or outcome) variable.

    Helping
    Paranoia
    Memory
    Performance on a mathematics test
    Color preference
    Life satisfaction

3. Consider how each of the research hypotheses you generated in problems 1 and 2 could (or could not) be tested using a correlational and an experimental research design.

4. Conduct a literature search on one of the research hypotheses that you developed in problem 2. Generate a list of five of the references that you locate. Be sure to include both primary and secondary sources.

5. On the basis of your literature review, consider whether your original research hypothesis is still reasonable or whether it needs to be modified. Develop at least one research hypothesis different from the one you originally developed.

6. Find a newspaper article that reports the results of a scientific study. Identify the variables, and specify the research hypothesis. What research design was used to test the hypothesis?

7. Find a newspaper article that states a potential research hypothesis but does not test the hypothesis using a scientific study. State the research hypothesis, and identify the variables. Indicate whether the hypothesis could be best tested using a correlational or an experimental approach.

8. Consider the limitations of a research hypothesis that states that "hyperactivity in children is caused by either increases or decreases in the amount of attention that parents pay to the child."

CHAPTER THREE
Ethics in Research

STUDY QUESTIONS

- What are some of the concerns guiding ethical research?

- What are the potential psychological threats to participants in behavioral science research projects?

- What factors may interfere with participants' freedom to choose whether or not to participate in research?

- What is the function of informed consent?

- How might a researcher abuse his or her power in the research relationship?

- When and why is deception used in research?

- What is debriefing, and how is it used?

- What procedures do researchers use to ensure that behavioral research is ethical?

- What procedures do researchers follow to ensure the ethical treatment of animals in behavioral research?

One of the major difficulties involved in studying human beings, and even animals, is that they often behave quite differently when they are being studied than they would otherwise. As a result, behavioral scientists are faced with a basic challenge: to learn what people do when they are not being studied, behavioral scientists must create research designs that measure important everyday phenomena and that allow research participants the freedom and motivation to openly and honestly express their thoughts, feelings, and behavior. And scientists must do this in a way that prevents participants from guessing what is being studied and altering their responses as a result.

To create situations in which behavior can be validly assessed, scientists sometimes engage in practices that may be questioned on ethical grounds. For instance, researchers may lead people to participate in research without telling them that they are participating. Researchers may require introductory psychology students to participate in research projects and then deceive these students, at least temporarily, about the nature of the research. In some cases researchers may induce stress, anxiety, or negative moods in the participants, expose them to weak electrical shocks, or convince them to behave in ways that violate their moral standards. And researchers may sometimes use animals in their research, potentially harming them in the process.

Of course, behavioral scientists have a basic reason for engaging in these practices. For one, as we will discuss in more detail in the chapters to come, creating such situations is frequently the only way that important behavioral phenomena can be objectively studied. Second, they feel that although there may well be some costs to research participants when they participate in research, there is also a great benefit to humanity to be gained from the research. This benefit is, of course, the knowledge about human behavior that accrues through the conduct of behavioral research. Furthermore, scientists also believe that there are potential benefits to the research participants in the form of learning about how research is conducted and experiencing the satisfaction of having contributed to the scientific literature. In each case, before beginning to conduct the research, scientists have come to the conclusion that the potential benefits of conducting the research outweigh the potential costs to the research participants.

What Is Ethical Research?

Although the focus of this chapter is the ethical treatment of human and animal participants in behavioral science research, concern about the welfare of research participants is only one aspect of ethics in behavioral research. The ethical concerns of scientists also involve maintaining honesty in conducting and reporting scientific research, giving appropriate credit for ideas and effort, and considering how knowledge gained through research should be used. Determining whether a research project is ethical is a difficult enterprise because there are no clearly "right" or clearly "wrong" answers to ethical questions. By definition, ethics involves values, not facts. Nevertheless, as we will see, there is an agreed-on set of basic ethical principles that must be adhered to by those conducting research.

Ethical concerns are not unique to the behavioral sciences. Rather, they are part of the process of conducting research in any scientific field. Physicists have long debated the ethics of having helped develop the nuclear bomb. Biologists worry about the potential outcomes of creating genetically engineered human babies, and chemists are concerned about the environmental effects of the chemicals they devise. Medical researchers agonize over the ethics of withholding potentially beneficial drugs from control groups in clinical trials in which only some of the participants are given the drugs and of using animals to test potentially dangerous medical treatments. In each of these cases, however, scientists have justified their decision to conduct the research with the belief that in the long run the potential gains of the resulting knowledge will outweigh any potential costs that may be incurred by participants or by society at large.

Some research, such as the forced participation in medical experiments conducted on prisoners by the Nazis during World War II (which gave rise to the Nuremberg code), is perceived as immoral by almost everyone. Other procedures, such as the use of animals in research testing the effectiveness of drugs, or even the practice of asking an individual to complete a questionnaire without first informing him or her what the questionnaire is designed to assess, are more controversial. However, because scientific research is designed to and has provided information that has improved the lives of many people, it is not reasonable to argue that because scientific research has costs, no research should be conducted. This argument fails to consider the fact that there are significant costs to *not* doing research and that these costs may be greater than the potential costs involved in going ahead with the research project (Rosenthal, 1994).

Treating research participants ethically matters not only for the welfare of the individuals themselves but also for the continued effectiveness of behavioral science as a scientific discipline. For one thing, if society begins to question the ethics of behavioral research, this may create a general suspicion about and mistrust of the results of scientific research. Unethical behavior may also lead to government sanctions against the conduct of behavioral research. For instance, the concealed recording of jury sessions by psychologists led to the passing of legislation that entirely banned such studies (Vaughan, 1967). These issues demand that scientists assess the ethical principles of each and every research project and realize that they may have to change or potentially even abandon certain research procedures.

This chapter discusses how scientists make judgments about ethical

TABLE 3.1   APA Guidelines on Research with Humans

The following are some of the most important ethical principles from the American Psychological Association's guidelines on research with human participants.

General Principles

Psychologists respect and protect civil and human rights and the central importance of freedom of inquiry and expression in research, teaching, and publication.

Psychologists obtain appropriate approval prior to conducting research. They conduct the research in accordance with the approved research protocol.

Informed Consent

Psychologists inform participants about

the purpose of the research, expected duration, and procedures,
their right to decline to participate and to withdraw from the research once participation has begun;
reasonably foreseeable factors that may be expected to influence their willingness to participate
any prospective research benefits and
whom to contact for questions about the research and research participants' rights.

Psychologists obtain informed consent from research participants prior to recording their voices or images for data collection unless (1) the research consists solely of naturalistic observations in public places, and it is not anticipated that the recording will be used in a manner that could cause personal identification or harm, or (2) the research design includes deception, and consent for the use of the recording is obtained during debriefing.

Psychologists make reasonable efforts to avoid offering excessive or inappropriate financial or other inducements for research participation when such inducements are likely to coerce participation.

Deception

Psychologists do not conduct a study involving deception unless they have determined that the use of deceptive techniques is justified by the study's significant prospective scientific, educational, or applied value and that effective nondeceptive alternative procedures are not feasible.

Psychologists do not deceive prospective participants about research that is reasonably expected to cause physical pain or severe emotional distress.

Psychologists explain any deception that is an integral feature of the design and conduct of an experiment to participants as early as is feasible, preferably at the conclusion of their participation, but no later than at the conclusion of the data collection, and permit participants to withdraw their data.

Debriefing

Psychologists provide a prompt opportunity for participants to obtain appropriate information about the nature, results, and conclusions of the research, and they take reasonable steps to correct any misconceptions that participants may have of which the psychologists are aware.

If scientific or humane values justify delaying or withholding this information, psychologists take reasonable measures to reduce the risk of harm.

When psychologists become aware that research procedures have harmed a participant, they take reasonable steps to minimize the harm.

Source: American Psychological Association (2002). Ethical principles of psychologists. *American Psychologist, 57,* 1060–1073.

principles regarding the use of humans and animals as research participants. These decisions rely on the individual values of the scientist, as well as established ethical codes developed by scientific organizations and federal governments. In the United States, the Department of Health and Human Services provides the guidelines for ethical standards in research, and these are available at **http://ohrp.osophs.dhhs.gov/humansubjects/guidance/45cfr46.htm.** Perhaps the most relevant organization for behavioral scientists is the American Psychological Association (APA); a summary of this organization's guidelines for ethical research with human participants is presented in Table 3.1. The basic goal of the chapter is to inform you about these guidelines and to thoroughly discuss the relevant issues, so that you will be able to use this knowledge to develop your own conclusions and guide your own decisions. We will focus on four basic goals of ethical research (Diener & Crandall, 1978):

- Protecting participants from physical and psychological harm
- Providing freedom of choice about participating in the research
- Maintaining awareness of the power differentials between researcher and participant
- Honestly describing the nature and use of the research to participants

Protecting Research Participants from Physical and Psychological Harm

The most direct ethical concern of the behavioral scientist is the possibility that his or her research will cause harm to the research participants. Fortunately, the danger of physical harm from participation in behavioral science research is very low. Nevertheless, given scientists' interest in studying people's emotions, participation in behavioral research may in some cases produce rather extreme emotional reactions, and these may have long-term negative outcomes.

Types of Threats

Some past research has posed severe threats to the psychological welfare of the participants. One example is the well-known research of Stanley Milgram (1974) investigating obedience to authority. In these studies, participants were induced by an experimenter to administer electric shock to another person so that Milgram could study the extent to which they would obey the demands of a scientist. Most participants evidenced high levels of stress resulting from the psychological conflict they experienced between engaging in aggressive and dangerous behavior and following the instructions of the experimenter. In another experiment (Bramel, 1962), male college students were told, on the basis of false data, that they had "homosexual tendencies." Although it was later revealed to them that this feedback was not true, the participants may have experienced psychological stress during the course of the experiment and after it was over.

Although studies such as those of Milgram and Bramel would no longer be conducted because the scientific community is now much more sensitized to the potential of such procedures to create emotional discomfort or harm, other studies that present less severe, but potentially real, threats are still conducted. For instance, to study the effects of failure on self-esteem or alcohol consumption, experimenters may convince research participants that they have failed on an important self-relevant task such as a test of social skills or intelligence (Hull & Young, 1983). Or to better understand the effects of depression on learning, researchers may place individuals in negative moods (Bower, 1981).

In other cases, although the research does not directly create stressful situations, it does have the unfortunate outcome of leading the participants to discover something unpleasant about themselves, such as their tendency to stereotype others or to make unwise decisions. Although it might be argued that the participants could make good use of this information and improve their lives from it, having found out the information might nevertheless be stressful to them, and they certainly did not ask to be told about these aspects of their personality. In still other cases participants are led to perform behaviors that they may later be embarrassed about or ashamed of. For instance, in one experiment investigating the factors that lead college students to cheat (Kahle, 1980), a test was administered to students and the test papers collected. Then the papers were returned to the students for grading, and it was made rather easy for them to change their answers on the exam so as to improve their score. Many students did so. Unknown to the students, however, their original responses had been recorded, so that the experimenters could discover how many students cheated by changing their answers.

The Potential for Lasting Impact

Obviously, procedures that have the potential to create negative moods, stress, self-doubts, and anxiety in research participants involve some potential costs to these individuals. Although the psychological states created in these situations are assumed to be only temporary, there is no guarantee that they will not have longer-lasting consequences. Individuals who have been induced to shock another person or to cheat on an examination may be permanently changed as a result of their participation in the research. Furthermore, these harmful psychological outcomes may not even be immediately apparent to the participant or the experimenter, but occur only later.

Although researchers should always treat the possibility that their research will produce psychological harm seriously, and choose alternative methods of testing their research hypotheses whenever possible, fortunately most evidence suggests that participation in psychological research does not produce long-term psychological damage. For instance, even though the men in Milgram's experiment obviously felt stress during the experiment itself, they did not report any long-term negative outcomes, nor did a team of psychiatrists find any evidence of harmful effects (Milgram, 1974). In fact, the participants in social research usually report that they experienced only minor disturbances and that they learned much about themselves and about the conduct of social science from their participation. Nevertheless, there is always the possibility that at least some research participants may be psychologically hurt by participating in behavioral research.

Providing Freedom of Choice

The second goal of ethical research is to guarantee that participants have free choice regarding whether they wish to participate in research. In an ideal situation each individual has the opportunity to learn about the research and to choose to participate or not participate without considering any other factors. In reality, freedom of choice is more difficult to attain. An individual who is in financial need of the money being offered for participation by a researcher is less able to decline to participate than one who is not in such need, and a college student who has trekked across campus to a laboratory is likely to choose to participate rather than having to return later for another study.

Conducting Research Outside the Laboratory

Although threats to freedom of choice may occur in experiments conducted in scientific laboratories, they are even more common in research conducted in real-world settings, particularly in naturalistic observational studies where the behavior of individuals is observed without their knowledge. In lab studies the individual volunteers to participate and knows that an experiment is occurring. But in observational research the participant may not even know that research is being conducted. We can ask whether it is ethical to create situations that infringe on passersby, such as research designed to see who helps in a situation created by the researchers (Piliavin, Rodin, & Piliavin, 1969), particularly because the individuals who were the "participants" in the experiment were never informed that the helping situation was staged.

Concerns with free choice also occur in institutional settings, such as schools, psychiatric hospitals, corporations, and prisons, when individuals are required by the institutions to take certain tests, or when employees are assigned to or asked by their supervisors to participate in research. Such issues are often debated in colleges and universities in which all students enrolled in introductory psychology are required either to participate in research or to perform other potentially less interesting tasks, such as writing papers about research reports.

University scientists and instructors argue that participation in psychological research teaches students about the conduct of research and that if there were no research participants, there would be no psychology to study. They also argue that it is more scientifically valid to require students to participate, rather than to have a volunteer system, because volunteer participants react differently from nonvolunteers (Rosenthal & Rosnow, 1975). The students, however, may argue that the time they spend going to these research sessions might be better used studying, that the specific experiments are sometimes not related to the subject matter of their course or are not well explained to them, and thus that the requirement seems more motivated to serve the convenience of researchers.

There are, again, no easy answers to these questions. However, keep in mind that there are potential gains for the participants in the form of knowledge about behavior and the practice of behavioral research. Furthermore, this research can be expected to benefit society at large. However, benefit to the participants occurs only when the researchers fully explain the purposes and expected results of research to participants when the research has ended. It is the duty of the experimenter to do so. Students should make a point to use their participation in research projects to learn something about how and why research is conducted. They should ask questions and attempt to find out what the research is designed to test and how their data will be used.

Securing Informed Consent

The most important tool for providing freedom of choice and reducing psychological stress from participation in behavioral science research is the use of **informed consent.** According to guidelines provided by the U.S. Department of Health and Human Services (2001), informed consent must include

(1) a statement that the study involves research and the expected duration of the participation; a description of the procedures to be followed, and identification of any procedures which are experimental;

(2) a description of any reasonably foreseeable risks or discomforts to the participant;

(3) a description of any benefits to the participant or to others which may reasonably be expected from the research;

(4) a disclosure of appropriate alternative procedures or courses of treatment, if any, that might be advantageous to the participant;

(5) a statement describing the extent, if any, to which confidentiality of records identifying the participant will be maintained;

(6) for research involving more than minimal risk, an explanation as to whether any compensation is to be made and an explanation as to whether any medical treatments are available if injury occurs and, if so, what they consist of, or where further information may be obtained;

(7) an explanation of whom to contact for answers to pertinent questions about the research and research participants' rights, and whom to contact in the event of a research-related injury to the participant; and

(8) a statement that participation is voluntary, refusal to participate will involve no penalty or loss of benefits to which the participant is otherwise entitled, and the participant may discontinue participation at any time without penalty or loss of benefits to which the participant is otherwise entitled.

A sample informed consent form is shown in Table 3.2. Informed consent involves several aspects, each of which is designed to reduce the possibility of

TABLE 3.2 Sample Informed Consent Form

Consent Form: Interactions

I state that I am 18 years of age or older and wish to participate in a program of research being conducted by Dr. Charles Stangor at the University of Maryland, College Park, Department of Psychology.

The purpose of the research is to study how individuals get to know each other. In the remainder of the study I will be having a short conversation with another person. This interaction will be videotaped. At the end of the interaction, I will be asked to complete some questionnaires about how I felt during and what I remember about the interaction.

I furthermore consent to allow the videotape that has been made of me and my partner to be used in the research. I understand that the videotape will be used for research purposes only, and no one else except the present experimenter and one other person who will help code the tape will ever view it.

I understand that code numbers will be used to identify the videotapes, and that all written material that I contribute will be kept separate from the videos. As a result, it will not be possible to connect my name to my videotape.

I understand that both myself and my partner have the right to withdraw the tape from the study at any point.

I understand that the experiment is not designed to help me personally, but that the researchers hope to learn more about interpersonal interactions.

I understand that I am free to ask questions or to withdraw from participation at any time without penalty.

Dr. Charles Stangor
Department of Psychology
Room 3123
555-5921

Signature of participant _____
Date _____

ethical problems. First, the potential participant is presented with a sheet of paper on which to record demographic information, including age. This information assures the experimenter that the research participant is old enough to make her or his own decision about whether to participate. When children are used in research, the corresponding ethical safeguards are even more rigorous. In this case a parent or guardian must give approval for the individual to participate in research. The American Psychological Association (APA) and the Society for Research in Child Development (SRCD) have developed guidelines for research with children as well as adults.

Second, the potential participant is given an informed consent form explaining the procedure of the research, who is conducting it, how the results of the research will be used, and what is going to happen during the research session. Third, the potential participant is informed of her or his rights during the research. These rights include the freedom to leave the research project at any point without penalty and the knowledge that the data will be kept confidential. After carefully reading this information, the individual is given the opportunity to ask any questions. At this point the participant signs the form to indicate that she or he has read and (the researcher hopes) understood the information.

It is rare that an individual declines to participate in or continue a behavioral research project. This is perhaps because of the use of informed consent and the determination by the researcher that the research project is not ethically problematic, but it may also be due to social factors that reduce the likelihood of quitting. Once a participant has arrived at the research session (and even more so when the project has begun), it becomes difficult for him or her to express a desire to leave. As a result, the researcher must continually keep in mind that he or she has great control over the behaviors of the research participant, must continually be on the lookout for signs that the participant is uncomfortable, and must be prepared to stop the research if any problems surface.

Because many students participate in research projects to earn credit in behavioral science courses, one issue that sometimes arises concerns how to treat a student who decides not to participate. When this decision is made before the research begins, it seems reasonable not to give credit because the student can usually find another experiment to participate in with which he or she is more comfortable. However, for a person who has already begun the procedure under the good faith of finishing but later decides to quit, it is usually better to award full credit.

Weighing Informed Consent Versus the Research Goals

Although informed consent has obvious advantages from the point of view of the participant, it has disadvantages from the point of view of the researcher. Consider what might have happened if Milgram had told his research participants that his experiment was about obedience to authority, rather than telling them that he was studying learning. In this case the participants would probably have carefully monitored their behavior to avoid being seen as "obedient" types, and he would have obtained very different results. However, the participants' behavior in this case would seem to reflect more a reaction to the informed consent form than what might be expected if the participants had not been alerted. In such cases the preferred strategy is to tell participants as much as possible about the true nature of the study, particularly everything that might be expected to influence their willingness to participate, while still withholding the pieces of information that allow the study to work. Often creative uses of informed consent may allow researchers to provide accurate information to participants and still enable the research to continue. For instance, participants may be told that they may or may not be given alcohol or that their behavior may or may not be videotaped at some point. In these cases the individuals are informed of the procedures and potential risks and give their consent to participate in any or all of the procedures they might encounter, but the research is not jeopardized.

Maintaining Awareness of Power Differentials

One of the basic ethical concerns in research with humans involves the inherent power differential between the researcher and the research participant. This differential occurs because the researcher has higher status than the participant and thus is able (and indeed expected) to control the participant's behavior and also how the data contributed are used. The experimenter tells the participant what to do and when to do it and also determines whether the participant receives course credit or payment for participation. Although, as we will discuss in the next section, ethical procedures require that the participant always have the option to choose not to participate in the research and to withdraw his or her data, the high-status researcher may be influential in preventing him or her from doing so.[1]

Avoiding Abuses of Power

The fact that the researcher has power over the participant places him or her in a position in which there is the possibility for abuse of this power. Such abuse might range from showing up late to the research session without apology, to promising the participant money for participation that is not actually available, or even to hypnotizing the participant and attempting to learn intimate details about his or her life without the participant's knowledge. Any time the research participant is coerced into performing a behavior that he or she later regrets, the power relationship between the researcher and the participant has been misused. The inherent power differential between researcher and participant demands that the former continually and carefully ensure that all research participants have been treated fairly and respectfully.

Respecting Participants' Privacy

One potential source of ethical concern in behavioral research, which stems from the control the researcher has over the use of the participant's data, involves the invasion of the privacy of the research participants or violations of the confidentiality of the data that they contribute. The private lives of research participants may be invaded in field research when, for instance, the researcher searches through the garbage in a neighborhood or observes behavior in a public setting such as in a small town. These issues become particularly problematic when the research results are later published in a manner in which the

---

[1]This power relationship is explicit in the use of the term *subject* to refer to the research participant. Although it is now more acceptable to use less impersonal terms, such as *participant* or *respondent* (American Psychological Association, 1994), the true power relationship between the experimenter and the research participant has not changed.

identities of the individuals might be discovered. As a result, scientists often use fictitious names of persons and places in their research reports.

The privacy of research participants may also be violated in questionnaire and laboratory studies. In many cases, respecting the privacy of participants is not a major problem because the data are not that personally revealing. Exceptions may occur when the questionnaires involve intimate personal information such as sexual behavior or alcohol and drug use. In such cases the data should be kept *anonymous*. The respondent does not put any identifying information onto the questionnaire, and therefore the researcher cannot tell which participant contributed the data. To help ensure that the data are anonymous, individuals can seal their questionnaires in an envelope and place them with other sealed envelopes in a box. (As we will see in later chapters, making the data anonymous may also lead the respondents to answer questions more honestly.)

In other cases the data cannot be anonymous because the researcher needs to keep track of which respondent contributed the data. This holds true when questionnaires are given to the same people at more than one time point or when participants are selected on the basis of their questionnaires for follow-up research. Here the solution that respects the privacy of the individual is to keep the data *confidential*. One technique is to have each participant use a unique code number to identify her or his data, such as the last four digits of the social security number. In this way the researcher can keep track of which person completed which questionnaire, but others will not be able to connect the data with the individual who contributed it. In all cases collected data that have any identifying information must be kept in locked rooms or storage cabinets to ensure confidentiality, and the researcher must be aware of the potential for abuse of such information. Since many data are now stored on computer disks, the researcher must be especially careful that no copies of these data are in the public domain, such as stored on public access computer networks.

Honestly Describing the Nature and Use of the Research

Perhaps the most widespread ethical concern to the participants in behavioral research is the extent to which researchers employ deception. **Deception** occurs whenever research participants are not completely and fully informed about the nature of the research project before participating in it. Deception may occur in an active way, such as when the researcher tells the participants that he or she is studying learning when in fact the experiment really concerns obedience to authority. In other cases the deception is more passive, such as when participants are not told about the hypothesis being studied or the potential use of the data being collected. For instance, a researcher studying eyewitness testimony might create a fake crime scene and then later test the participants on their memory of it.

Both active and passive deception can be problematic. For instance, an experiment in which individuals participated in a study about interviewing without first being told that the results of the research were going to be used to develop interrogation procedures for prisoners of war would be highly unethical, even though the deception was passive in nature, because participants might have decided not to participate in the research had they been fully informed.

When Deception Is Necessary

The argument against the use of deception in behavioral research is straightforward. The relationship between the researcher and the participant is based on mutual trust and cooperation. If deception is involved, this trust may be broken. Although some have argued that deception of any sort should never be used in any research (Baumrind, 1985), there are also persuasive arguments supporting its use. Social psychologists defend the use of deception on the grounds that it is needed to get participants to act naturally and to enable the study of social phenomena. They argue that it would be impossible to study such phenomena as altruism, aggression, and stereotyping *without* using deception because if participants were informed ahead of time what the study involved, this knowledge would certainly change their behavior. Furthermore, social psychologists argue that to study some phenomena, such as stress, it is more ethical to deceive the participants into thinking that they are going to participate in a stressful situation than to actually expose them to the stress itself.

One review found that 58 percent of social psychological experiments used some form of deception (Adair, Dushenko, & Lindsay, 1985). The need to employ deception in order to conduct certain types of research has been recognized by scientists, and the code of ethics of the APA allows deception (including concealed observation) when necessary. However, given the potential dangers of deception, the APA code also requires researchers to explicitly consider how their research might be conducted without the use of deception. (Other scientific organizations also have codes of ethics regarding the treatment of research participants.)

Simulation Studies: An Alternative to Deception

One technique for avoiding deception in some cases is the use of simulation studies (Rubin, 1973). In a **simulation study** participants are fully informed about the nature of the research and asked to behave "as if" they were in a social setting of interest. A situation is set up that is similar to that in the real world in terms of important elements. For instance, people might be asked to imagine that they are a manager of a large corporation and to make decisions the way they think a manager would, or they might be asked to imagine a situation in which they might or might not help another person. Unfortunately, as we have seen in Chapter 1, asking people what they think they would do often does not reflect what they actually do. In fact, the power of much behavioral research is the demonstration that people cannot predict what they, or others, would do in a given setting.

Despite these problems, some simulation studies have been very effective in providing insights into human behavior. One well-known example is the "Stanford Prison Study" (Haney, Banks, & Zimbardo, 1973). In this study college students were randomly assigned to play the role of either prisoners or prison guards in a mock prison. Those assigned to be prisoners were "arrested," issued prison numbers, and put in cells. The participants who became "guards" were given uniforms and nightsticks. This simulation was so successful in the sense of participants taking it seriously that on the first day the "guards" began to create demeaning experiences for "prisoners" who banded together in a hunger strike. The study had to be canceled after only a few days because of the potential for psychological stress to the "inmates."

The Consequences of Deception

As with any ethical decision, there are differences of opinion about the appropriateness of using deception. Some scientists believe that deception should never be used in any research (Ortmann & Hertwig, 1997), whereas others believe that deception is a normal and useful part of psychological research (Kimmel, 1998). Although it is always preferable, when possible, to avoid the use of deception (and in fact many experiments are entirely "honest"), research investigating the effects of deception on participants in behavioral research suggests that its use does not normally produce any long-lasting psychological harm. In fact, students who have participated in experiments in which they have been deceived report enjoying them more and receiving more educational benefits from them than have those who participated in nondeceptive research (Smith & Richardson, 1983). It is ironic, in fact, that the use of deception may be more harmful to the ability of the researchers to continue their research than it is to the research participants. Because the use of deception is so widespread, participants may arrive at studies expecting to be deceived. As a result, the deception used in the research is not likely to be effective in accomplishing the goals for which it was designed. Thus the most powerful argument against the use of deception is that its continued use may defeat the goals of behavioral science research itself!

Debriefing

Because behavioral science research has the potential for producing long-term changes in the research participants, these participants should be fully debriefed after their participation. The **debriefing** occurs immediately after the research has ended and is designed to explain the purposes and procedures of the research and remove any harmful aftereffects of participation. Although debriefing is an essential part of all behavioral research, it is particularly important in research that involves deception because it can be used both to assess the effectiveness of the deception and to alleviate its potential impact on research participants. Since this portion of the experiment is so important, sufficient time to do it properly should always be allotted.

Conducting a Postexperimental Interview.

In many cases the debriefing procedure is rather elaborate and is combined with a **postexperimental interview** in which the participants' reactions to the research are assessed. The participants may first be asked to verbally express or (if they are run in groups) to write down their thoughts about the research. These reactions may often indicate whether the respondents experienced the research as expected, if they were suspicious, and if they have taken the research seriously.

When deception has been used, the researcher may want to determine if it has been effective through the use of a **suspicion check**—questioning the participants to determine whether they believed the experimental manipulation or guessed the research hypothesis. One approach, proposed by Mills (1976), is to tell the participants that "there is more to this experiment than I have told you. I'm curious—do you know what it might be?" The idea is that if the participant is suspicious about the deception, he or she will say so ("I knew that there really wasn't anyone in the other room"), whereas participants who are not suspicious will not know how to answer the question or will answer with something irrelevant.

After this initial part of the debriefing is completed, the researcher next fully explains in detail the purposes of the experiment, including the research hypothesis and how it is being tested. The scientist should explain the goals of the research in an accurate and fair manner, and the importance of the research should not be overstated. Thus the debriefing also serves an educational function in which the participants learn something about behavioral science research and how it is conducted. Because the educational value of participation in a research project is one of the benefits of behavioral research, the researcher should be sure to design the debriefing to maximize this function.

The last goal of the debriefing is to try to eliminate long-term consequences of having participated in the research. Any deception that has been used is fully explained to the participants, and its necessity is justified. A thorough debriefing procedure has been shown to be an effective method of reducing the harmful effects of deception (Smith & Richardson, 1983).

Finally, the participants are given ample time to ask questions about the research and may be requested not to discuss the research with others until the end of the semester, or whenever the data collection will have finished. The experimenter should be certain to supply his or her name and telephone number to the participants and encourage them to call with any questions or concerns.

Ensuring the Effectiveness of the Debriefing.

Debriefing does not solve all the problems of treating participants with respect, nor does it guarantee that the outcomes of unethical procedures can be "taken back" through follow-up procedures. Ill effects may persist even after debriefing (Ross, Lepper, & Hubbard, 1975), particularly when the participant has been led to engage in embarrassing or stressful behaviors. When this might be the case, the experimenter may conduct a **process debriefing**—an active attempt to undo any changes that might have occurred. For instance, if the experiment has involved the creation of a negative mood state, a positive mood induction procedure might be given to all participants before they leave. However, despite the use of careful debriefing procedures, it is often almost impossible to entirely undo the effects of experimental manipulations, and a participant who has engaged in behaviors that he or she later regrets may be affected by these behaviors despite a careful debriefing.

In the end, what is most important is that the participants feel that they have been treated fairly in the experiment. Some of the most important characteristics of an ethical research project using human participants are outlined in Table 3.3. The manner in which the debriefing is conducted may have a large impact on the participants' feelings about being deceived and their perceptions of the research. Other experimenter behaviors that can lead to more positive experiences for the participants include showing up on time, acting in a friendly manner, allowing enough time for questions to arise, and offering to send the written results of research projects to participants if they want them (and then actually doing so). Of course, when participants receive course credit for participation, the experimenter is also expected to report their participation in the research to the appropriate people in a timely manner. Because experimenters have higher status than participants, this relationship can easily be abused, and researchers must continually strive to avoid such problems.

TABLE 3.3   Characteristics of an Ethical Research Project Using Human Participants

Trust and positive rapport are created between the researcher and the participant.

The rights of both the experimenter and participant are considered, and the relationship between them is mutually beneficial.

The experimenter treats the participant with concern and respect and attempts to make the research experience a pleasant and informative one.

Before the research begins, the participant is given all information relevant to his or her decision to participate, including any possibilities of physical danger or psychological stress.

The participant is given a chance to have questions about the procedure answered, thus guaranteeing his or her free choice about participating.

After the experiment is over, any deception that has been used is made public, and the necessity for it is explained.

The experimenter carefully debriefs the participant, explaining the underlying research hypothesis and the purpose of the experimental procedure in detail and answering any questions.

The experimenter provides information about how he or she can be contacted and offers to provide information about the results of the research if the participant is interested in receiving it.

Using Animals as Research Participants

To this point in this chapter we have been considering the ethical decisions involved in conducting research with human beings. But because animals make up an important part of the natural world, and because some research cannot be conducted using humans, animals are also participants in behavioral research. Probably to a large extent because of ethical concerns, most research is now conducted with rats, mice, and birds, and the use of other animals in research is declining (Thomas & Blackman, 1992). As with ethical decisions regarding human participants, a set of basic principles has been developed that helps researchers make informed decisions about such research.

Because the use of animals in research involves a personal value, people naturally disagree about this practice. Although many people accept the value of such research (Plous, 1996), a minority of people, including animal-rights activists, believe that it is ethically wrong to conduct research on animals. They base this argument on the assumption that because animals are also living creatures, they have the same status as humans and no harm should ever be done to any living thing.

Most scientists, however, reject this view. They argue that such beliefs ignore the potential benefits that have and continue to come from such research.

TABLE 3.4   APA Guidelines on Humane Care and Use of Animals in Research

The following are some of the most important ethical principles from the American Psychological Association's guidelines on research with animals.

Psychologists acquire, care for, use, and dispose of animals in compliance with current federal, state, and local laws and regulations, and with professional standards.

Psychologists trained in research methods and experienced in the care of laboratory animals supervise all procedures involving animals and are responsible for ensuring appropriate consideration of their comfort, health, and humane treatment.

Psychologists ensure that all individuals under their supervision who are using animals have received instruction in research methods and in the care, maintenance, and handling of the species being used, to the extent appropriate to their role. (See also Standard 2.05, Delegation of Work to Others.)

Psychologists make reasonable efforts to minimize the discomfort, infection, illness, and pain of animal subjects.

Psychologists use a procedure subjecting animals to pain, stress, or privation only when an alternative procedure is unavailable and the goal is justified by its prospective scientific, educational, or applied value.

Psychologists perform surgical procedures under appropriate anesthesia and follow techniques to avoid infection and minimize pain during and after surgery.

When it is appropriate that an animal's life be terminated, psychologists proceed rapidly, with an effort to minimize pain and in accordance with accepted procedures.

Source: American Psychological Association (2002). Ethical principles of psychologists. *American Psychologist, 57,* 1060–1073.

For instance, drugs that can reduce the incidence of cancer or acquired immune deficiency syndrome may first be tested on animals, and surgery that can save human lives may first be practiced on animals. Research on animals has also led to a better understanding of the physiological causes of depression, phobias, and stress, among other illnesses (Miller, 1985).

In contrast to animal-rights activists, then, scientists believe that because there are many benefits that accrue from animal research, such research can and should continue as long as the humane treatment of the animals used in the research is guaranteed. And the animals that are used in scientific research are treated humanely. The scientists who use them in their research are extremely careful to maintain the animals in good health—after all, a healthy animal is the best research participant. Furthermore, they use the fewest animals necessary for the research, and they subject them to the least possible amount of stress. A summary of the American Psychological Association's guidelines regarding the care and use of animals in research is presented in Table 3.4.

Ensuring That Research Is Ethical

Making decisions about the ethics of research involves weighing the costs and benefits of conducting versus not conducting a given research project. We have seen that these costs involve potential harm to the research participants, and to the field, whereas the benefits include knowledge about human behavior and educational gains to the individual participants. Most generally, the ethics of a given research project is determined through a cost-benefit analysis, in which the costs are compared to the benefits. If the potential costs of the research appear to outweigh any potential benefits that might come from it, then the research should not proceed.

Of course, arriving at a cost-benefit ratio is not simple. For one thing, there is no way to know ahead of time what the effects of a given procedure will be on every person or animal who participates or what benefit to society the research is likely to produce. In addition, what is ethical is defined by the current state of thinking within society, and thus costs and benefits change over time. Consider, for instance, a classic experiment by Aronson and Mills (1959) investigating the hypothesis that individuals who underwent a severe initiation in order to be admitted to a group would later have greater attraction to the group than to individuals who had not been so initiated.

Female undergraduates were told that they would subsequently be joining a discussion group on the "psychology of sex." In some of the conditions, participants were asked if they would be embarrassed to talk about sex. If they answered no, they were admitted to the group. But in the "severe initiation" condition, participants were told that they had to prove that they could discuss sex frankly, and they were asked to read aloud (to the male experimenter) a list of twelve obscene words and two vivid descriptions of sexual activity from contemporary novels before joining the group.

Because today's standards are different than they were in 1959, such an experiment would probably be perceived by most as a violation of ethical principles. Society no longer considers it appropriate for a powerful male experimenter to require a less powerful female undergraduate to talk about sexual behavior in his presence. Although the women were given the choice of not participating, it was most certainly difficult for them to do so, as they would have lost their experimental credit as well as the time they had spent signing up for and reporting to the experiment.

One interesting tack on determining the cost-benefit ratio is to assess it empirically. One approach (Berscheid, Baron, Dermer, & Libman, 1973) is to describe the research project in its entirety to a separate group of individuals who are similar to potential participants and inquire whether they would participate. Alternatively, the research could be described and people asked to rate the potential costs to participants (Schlenker & Forsyth, 1977). Again, potential participants do not seem to perceive most research as unethical. In fact, students generally rate the potential benefits as greater than the costs and estimate a lower cost-benefit ratio than do the scientists conducting the research!

The Institutional Review Board

The U.S. Department of Health and Human Services regulations require that all universities receiving funds from the department set up an **institutional review board (IRB)** to determine whether proposed research meets department regulations. The IRB consists of at least five members, including, in addition to scientists, at least one individual whose primary interest is in nonscientific domains (for instance, a community member, a religious leader, or a legal specialist) and at least one member who is not affiliated with the institution at which the research is to be conducted. This composition ensures that the group represents a variety of areas of expertise, not just other scientists, who may tend to overrate the importance of scientific research.

All federally funded research, and almost all university research that is not federally funded, must be approved by the IRB. To gain approval, the scientist submits a written application to the IRB requesting permission to conduct research. This proposal must include a description of the experimental procedure and, if the research uses human participants, an explanation of how informed consent will be obtained and how the participants will be debriefed.

In addition, the application must detail any potential risks to the participants, as well as the potential benefits to be gained from the research. The basic goal of the IRB is to determine, on the basis of the research description, the cost-benefit ratio of a study. The IRB may suggest modifications to the procedure or (in rare cases) may inform the scientist that the research violates Department of Health and Human Services guidelines and thus cannot be conducted at the university. A similar committee, the animal care and use committee, makes decisions about animal research and ensures that animals used in research are treated in a humane manner. Board members conduct regular inspections of all of the animal labs at the institution to be certain that the animals are healthy and free from stress and that the research is conducted in accordance with appropriate guidelines.

The Researcher's Own Ethics

Despite the possibility of empirical assessment of ethical questions and the availability of institutional guidelines, because questions of scientific ethics are at heart issues of personal value, each person must draw her or his own conclusions about what is right and what is wrong in scientific research. Thus the ultimate responsibility lies with the investigator. Unfortunately, there is no single method for anticipating and alleviating all the possible ethical problems that can arise in the conduct of behavioral research. Rather, what is involved is an attempt to find an appropriate balance between the rights and dignity of the research participants and the importance of continuing scientific inquiry.

Overall, when the proper safeguards are followed, the rights and dignity of human participants are generally upheld. Yet each research project has to be evaluated in terms of potential ethical problems. Sometimes alternative procedures can be used; at other times the study must be canceled. When in doubt, consult with instructors or colleagues and others outside of the field. In many cases the IRB at your university will be the final judge of the ethics of your research.

Correctly and Honestly Reporting Research Results

Although to this point we have focused on the safety, rights, and dignity of the research participant, ethical behavior in science includes honesty not only in conducting research, but also in reporting it and giving proper credit for ideas. Science is based on truth, and scientists are expected to be truthful in all aspects of their research. In this sense the rules are simple—report exactly what you did and what you discovered in your research. Do not lie or mislead the reader in any way. The methods of the research should be completely and fully described, and the statistical analyses reported accurately. According to American Psychology Association guidelines, scientists are also obligated to publish corrections to existing publications if they later discover significant errors in them. Furthermore, scientists are obligated to interpret their data as fairly as they can. Remember that it is completely appropriate to use the work of others as a basis for your research—but do not plagiarize. When you have taken ideas from others, be certain to appropriately cite the sources of the work.

Although we can assume that most scientists are honest, they are nevertheless only human, and therefore some errors will occasionally be made. In some cases mistakes are made because the scientist is not careful about how he or she collects and analyzes data. For instance, errors may be made in keypunching the data or in the process of conducting the statistical analyses. It is therefore extremely important that researchers check their data carefully to be sure that their statistical analyses are correct. Some suggestions for ensuring that data are analyzed correctly can be found in Appendix B of this book.

In rare cases a scientist may intentionally alter or fabricate data, and in such cases we say that he or she has committed **scientific fraud.** Although scientific fraud does not happen very often, it is a very serious event when it does occur, because it can lead people to adopt unwise social policies on the basis of the fraudulent data, or can lead scientists to spend time conducting follow-up research that is based on invalid knowledge.

Because scientific fraud is so costly, scientists are naturally concerned to prevent its occurrence. The most effective route is for each scientist to take full responsibility for his or her research and to carefully monitor the behavior of his or her co-workers. Fortunately, most scientists do not want to commit fraud, because if they do so they know that their research results will not be able to be replicated by others, and, as we will see in Chapter 12, it is this replication that leads to scientific progress.

SUMMARY

Because research using humans and animals has the potential to both benefit and harm those participants, the ethics of conducting versus not conducting a research project must be carefully evaluated before it is begun. There are no clear-cut right or wrong answers to questions about research ethics, but there are a set of ethical principles, developed by scientific organizations and regulatory agencies, that must be adhered to by those conducting behavioral research.

Conducting ethical research with human participants involves avoiding psychological and physical harm to research participants, providing freedom of choice, treating participants with respect, and honestly describing the nature and use of the research. Behavioral research with animals must be conducted such that the animals are treated humanely at all times.

Decisions about what research is appropriate and ethical are based on careful consideration of the potential costs and benefits to both the participants in the research and the advancement of science. The procedures that are followed to ensure that no harm is done to the participants include the use of informed consent before the experiment begins and a thorough debriefing in which the purposes and procedures of the research are explained in detail to the participants.

In most cases the institutional review board (IRB) at the institution where the research is being conducted will help the scientist determine whether his or her research is ethical.

KEY TERMS

debriefing 53
deception 51
informed consent 47
institutional review board (IRB) 58
postexperimental interview 54

process debriefing 55
scientific fraud 60
simulation study 52
suspicion check 54

REVIEW AND DISCUSSION QUESTIONS

1. Compare the ethical dilemmas faced by behavioral scientists with those faced by scientists in other scientific fields. What are the particular ethical problems that arise in behavioral science research?

2. Explain why deception is used in behavioral research, and then express your personal feelings about the use of deception. Should deception ever be used? If not, why not? If so, what are the allowable limits of deception?

3. Consider the four principles of ethical research with human participants outlined in the chapter. What procedures are used by behavioral scientists to help ensure that their research conforms to these principles?

4. What are informed consent and debriefing, and what is their purpose in behavioral research? Is it ever ethical to conduct research that does not use informed consent? Is it ever ethical to conduct behavioral research that does not use debriefing?

5. What are the arguments for and against the use of animals in research? What steps are taken to ensure the health and welfare of research animals?

HANDS-ON EXPERIENCE

1. For each of the following studies, consider whether or not you think the research is ethical, how the research may have violated principles of ethical behavior, and what, if any, alternative research methods for testing the research hypothesis might have been used:

   a. College students were asked to volunteer for an experiment involving betting behavior. Then they were told that they could choose either to receive $3.00 for their participation or they could gamble for the possibility of earning more money. After the experiment was conducted, participants were told that the experimenters did not actually have any money to pay them, but that the deception had been necessary in order to obtain their participation in the research.

   b. A study was done in a small company in which most of the employees knew each other. Detailed reports of the interactions of the workers were published in a book. Although some attempt was made to disguise the names of the individuals, any employee who read the book could identify who was being referred to.

c. A researcher was studying initial interactions between people. While two students were supposedly waiting for an experiment to begin, the researcher covertly videotaped their actions and conversation. The researcher then told them about the research and gave them the opportunity to have the tape erased.

d. A researcher worked for a time on the production line of a large manufacturing plant. His status as a researcher was unknown to his co-workers. It was not until he was about to leave that he revealed his purpose and identity to the workers.

e. Students who were interested in attending medical school participated in a study where the researcher gave them false negative feedback about their scores on the Medical College Admission Tests (MCAT). The students were presented with "sample" MCAT questions that did not have any correct answers. Consequently, the students performed very poorly on the exam, and the researchers studied their anxiety and how they coped with failure.

f. To study what types of people are most likely to give money to a stranger, people on city streets were asked for money by an individual who said he had just lost his wallet. No one was ever told that he or she was part of a research project.

g. To study the effects of alcohol on decision making, a graduate student interviewed college students after they had left a campus bar. With a portable breathalyzer, he registered their blood alcohol content. Although some of them were found to be intoxicated beyond the legal state limits, and although many of them were going to be driving home, he did not inform them of their blood alcohol levels.

h. A psychologist teaching a large lecture class conducted an experiment in which the letter grades assigned the students in different sections of the course were deliberately raised or lowered so that the same score on an examination might be an "A" in one section and a "C" in another section. The purpose of the experiment was to determine the effect of this feedback on achievement on the final examination.

2. Contact the chairperson of the institutional review board at your university. Find out who are the current members of the committee and what types of research they have recently considered for approval.

3. Consider any potential ethical problems for each of the research designs you developed in Hands-on Experience 1 in Chapter 2.

4. Animal-rights activists argue that all living things have the same status. Imagine that you are caught in a burning building with your family dog and a child who is a complete stranger to you. If you could save only one of the two, which one would you choose, and why?

5. View the film of Stanley Milgram's experiment on obedience. Discuss the ethical implications of the research.

6. Read and report to your class about one of the following reports about scientific fraud. Why did the fraud occur, and what damage was done by it?

Kamin, L. (1974). *The science and politics of IQ.* New York: Wiley.

Green, B. F. (1992). Exposé or smear? The Burt affair. *Psychological Science, 3,* 328–331.

Debliev, J. (1983). The Darsee affair. *Emory Magazine,* 7–15.

Higgins, A. C., & Meadows, P. (2001). *The bibliography on scientific fraud* (3rd ed.). Albany, NY: Exams Unlimited.

You may also wish to look at other related articles on the Web at **www. onlineethics.org.**

PART **TWO**
Measuring and Describing

CHAPTER FOUR
Measures

STUDY QUESTIONS

- What is the difference between conceptual and measured variables?

- What is an operational definition?

- What are the differences among nominal, ordinal, interval, and ratio scale variables?

- What are projective tests, associative lists, and think-aloud protocols? What is each designed to measure?

- What are Likert, semantic differential, and Guttman scales? What is each used to measure?

- What is reactivity, and how can measured variables be designed to avoid it?

- How are behavioral measures used in research?

- What are the advantages and disadvantages of using self-report versus behavioral measures?

We have seen in Chapters 1 and 2 that the basis of science is empirical measurement of relevant variables. Formally, **measurement** refers to the assignment of numbers to objects or events according to specific rules (Coombs, 1964). We assign numbers to events in everyday life, for instance, when we rate a movie as a "nine out of ten" or when a hotel is rated "three star." As in everyday life, measurement is possible in science because we can use numbers to represent the variables we are interested in studying. In this chapter and the next, we will discuss how behavioral scientists decide what to measure, the techniques they use to measure, and how they determine whether these measures are effective.

Fundamentals of Measurement

You will recall from Chapter 2 that the research hypothesis involves a prediction about the relationship between or among two or more variables—for instance, the relationship between self-esteem and college performance or between study time and memory. When stated in an abstract manner, the ideas that form the basis of a research hypothesis are known as **conceptual variables.** Behavioral scientists have been interested in such conceptual variables as self-esteem, parenting style, depression, and cognitive development.

Measurement involves turning conceptual variables into **measured variables,** which consist of numbers that represent the conceptual variables.[1] The measured variables are frequently referred to as **measures** of the conceptual variables. In some cases the transformation from conceptual to measured variable is direct. For instance, the conceptual variable "study time" is straightforwardly represented as the measured variable "seconds of study." But other conceptual variables can be assessed by many different measures. For instance, the conceptual variable "liking" could be assessed by a person rating, from one to ten, how much he or she likes another person. Alternatively, liking could be measured in terms of how often a person looks at or touches another person or the number of love letters that he or she writes. And liking could also be measured using physiological indicators such as an increase in heart rate when two people are in the vicinity of each other.

Operational Definition

The term **operational definition** refers to a precise statement of how a conceptual variable is turned into a measured variable. Research can only proceed once an adequate operational definition has been defined. In some cases the conceptual variable may be too vague to be operationalized, and in other cases the variable cannot be operationalized because the appropriate technology has not been developed. For instance, recent advances in brain imaging

---

[1]You will recall that in correlational research all of the variables are measured, whereas in experiments only the dependent variable is measured.

have allowed new operationalizations of some variables that could not have been measured even a few years ago. Table 4.1 lists some potential operational definitions of conceptual variables that have been used in behavioral research. As you read through this list, note that in contrast to the abstract conceptual variables (employee satisfaction, frustration, depression), the measured variables are very specific. This specificity is important for two reasons. First, more specific definitions mean that there is less danger that the collected data will be misunderstood by others. Second, specific definitions will enable future researchers to replicate the research.

Converging Operations

That there are many possible measures for a single conceptual variable might seem a scientific problem. But it is not. In fact, multiple possible measures represent a great advantage to researchers. For one thing, no single operational definition of a given conceptual variable can be considered the best. Different types of measures may be more appropriate in different research contexts. For instance, how close a person sits to another person might serve as a measure of liking in an observational research design, whereas heart rate might be more appropriate in a laboratory study. Furthermore, the ability to use different operationalizations of the same conceptual variable allows the researcher to hone in, or to "triangulate," on the conceptual variable of interest. When the same conceptual variable is measured using different measures, we can get a fuller and better measure of it. Because this principle is so important, we will discuss it more fully in subsequent chapters. This is an example of the use of *converging operations,* as discussed in Chapter 1.

TABLE 4.1 Operational Definitions

Conceptual Variable	Operational Definitions
Employee satisfaction	Number of days per month that the employee shows up to work on time
	Rating of job satisfaction from 1 (not at all satisfied) to 9 (extremely satisfied)
Aggression	Number of presses of a button that administers shock to another student
	Time taken to honk the horn at the car ahead after a stoplight turns green
Attraction	Number of inches that an individual places his or her chair away from another person
	Number of millimeters of pupil dilation when one person looks at another
Depression	Number of negative words used in a creative story
	Number of appointments with a psychotherapist
Decision-making skills	Number of people correctly solving a group performance task
	Speed at which a task is solved

The researcher must choose which operational definition to use in trying to assess the conceptual variables of interest. In general, there is no guarantee that the chosen measured variable will prove to be an adequate measure of the conceptual variable. As we will see in Chapter 5, however, there are ways to assess the effectiveness of the measures once they have been collected.

Conceptual and Measured Variables

The relationship between conceptual and measured variables in a correlational research design is diagrammed in Figure 4.1. The conceptual variables are represented within circles at the top of the figure, and the measured variables are represented within squares at the bottom. The two vertical arrows, which lead from the conceptual variables to the measured variables, represent the operational definitions of the two variables. The arrows indicate the expectation that changes in the conceptual variables (job satisfaction and job performance in this example) will cause changes in the corresponding measured variables. The measured variables are then used to draw inferences about the conceptual variables.

FIGURE 4.1   Conceptual and Measured Variables in a Correlational
Research Design

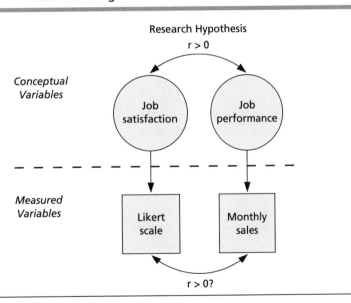

The research depicted here tests the correlational relationship between the conceptual variables of job satisfaction and job performance, using a specific operational definition of each. If the research hypothesis (that job performance is correlated with job satisfaction) is correct, and if the measured variables actually measure the conceptual variables, then a relationship between the two measured variables (the bottom curved arrow) should be observed.

You can see that there are also two curved arrows in Figure 4.1. The top arrow diagrams the research hypothesis—namely, that changes in job satisfaction are related to changes in job performance. The basic assumption involved in testing the research hypothesis is as follows:

- if the research hypothesis (that the two conceptual variables are correlated) is correct, and
- if the measured variables are adequate—that is, if there is a relationship between both of the conceptual and measured variables (the two vertical arrows in the figure)—then
- a relationship between the two measured variables (the bottom arrow in the figure) will be observed (cf. Nunnally, 1978).

The ultimate goal of the research is to learn about the relationship between the conceptual variables. But the ability to learn about this relationship is dependent on the operational definitions. If the measures do not really measure the conceptual variables, then they cannot be used to draw inferences about the relationship between the conceptual variables. Thus the adequacy of a test of any research hypothesis is limited by the adequacy of the measurement of the conceptual variables.

Nominal and Quantitative Variables

Measured variables can be divided into two major types: nominal variables and quantitative variables. A **nominal variable** is used to name or identify a particular characteristic. For instance, sex is a nominal variable that identifies whether a person is male or female, and religion is a nominal variable that identifies whether a person is Catholic, Buddhist, Jewish, or some other religion. Nominal variables are also frequently used in behavioral research to indicate the condition that a person has been assigned to in an experimental research design (for instance, whether she or he is in the "experimental condition" or the "control condition").

Nominal variables indicate the fact that people who share a value on the variable (for instance, all men or all the people in the control condition of an experiment) are equivalent in some way, whereas those that do not share the value are different from each other. Numbers are generally used to indicate the values of a nominal variable, such as when we represent the experimental condition of an experiment with the number 1 and the control condition of the experiment with the number 2. However, the numbers used to represent the categories of a nominal variable are arbitrary, and thus we could change which numbers represent which categories, or even label the categories with letters or names instead of numbers, without losing any information.

In contrast to a nominal variable, which names or identifies, a **quantitative variable** uses numbers to indicate the extent to which a person possesses a characteristic of interest. Quantitative variables indicate such things as how attractive a person is, how quickly she or he can complete a task, or how many siblings she or he has. For instance, on a rating of perceived attractiveness, the number 10 might indicate greater attractiveness than the number 5.

Measurement Scales

Specifying the relationship between the numbers on a quantitative measured variable and the values of the conceptual variable is known as **scaling.** In some cases in the natural sciences the mapping between the measure and the conceptual variable is quite precise. As an example, we are all familiar with the use of the Fahrenheit scale to measure temperature. In the Fahrenheit scale, the relationship between the measured variable (degrees Fahrenheit) and the conceptual variable (temperature) is so precise that we can be certain that changes in the measured variable correspond exactly to changes in the conceptual variable.

In this case we can be certain that the difference between any two points on the scale (the degrees) refers to equal changes in the conceptual variable across the entire scale. For instance, we can state that the difference in temperature between 10 and 20 degrees Fahrenheit is exactly the same as the difference in temperature between 70 and 80 degrees Fahrenheit. When equal distances between scores on a measure are known to correspond to equal changes in the conceptual variable (such as on the Fahrenheit scale), we call the measure an **interval scale.**

Now consider measures of length, such as feet and inches or the metric scale, which uses millimeters, centimeters, and meters. Such scales have all of the properties of an interval scale because equal changes between the points on the scale (centimeters for instance) correspond to equal changes in the conceptual variable (length). But measures of length also have a true zero point that represents the complete absence of the conceptual variable—zero length. Interval scales that also have a true zero point are known as **ratio scales** (the Kelvin temperature scale, where zero degrees represents absolute zero, is another example of a ratio scale). In addition to being able to compare intervals, the presence of a zero point on a ratio scale also allows us to multiply and divide scale values. When measuring length, for instance, we can say that a person who is 6 feet tall is twice as tall as a child who is 3 feet tall.

In most behavioral science research the scaling of the measured variable is not as straightforward as it is in the measurement of temperature or length. Measures in the behavioral sciences normally constitute only ordinal scales. In an **ordinal scale,** the numbers indicate whether there is more or less of the conceptual variable, but they do not indicate the exact interval between the individuals on the conceptual variable. For instance, if you rated the friendliness of five of your friends from 1 (least friendly) to 9 (most friendly), the scores would constitute an ordinal scale. The scores tell us the ordering of the people (that you believe Malik, whom you rated as a 7, is friendlier than Guillermo, whom you rated as a 2), but the measure does not tell us how big the difference between Malik and Guillermo is. Similarly, a hotel that receives a four-star rating is probably not exactly twice as comfortable as a hotel that receives a two-star rating.

Selltiz, Jahoda, Deutsch, and Cook (1966) have suggested that using ordinal scales is a bit like using an elastic tape measure to measure length. Because the tape measure can be stretched, the difference between 1 centimeter and

2 centimeters may be greater or less than the difference between 7 centimeters and 8 centimeters. As a result, a change of 1 centimeter on the measured variable will not exactly correspond to a change of 1 unit of the conceptual variable (length), and the measure is not interval. However, although the stretching may change the length of the intervals, it does not change their order. Because 2 is always greater than 1 and 8 is always greater than 7, the relationship between actual length and measured length on the elastic tape measure is ordinal.

There is some disagreement of opinion about whether measured variables in the behavioral sciences can be considered ratio or interval scales or whether they should be considered only ordinal scales. In most cases it is safest to assume that the scales are ordinal. For instance, we do not normally know whether the difference between people who score 8 versus 10 on a measure of self-esteem is exactly the same as that between two people who score 4 versus 6 on the same measure. And because there is no true zero point, we cannot say that a person with a self-esteem score of 10 has twice the esteem of a person with a score of 5. Although some measures can in some cases be considered interval or even ratio scales, most measured variables in the behavioral sciences are ordinal.

Self-Report Measures

In the next sections we will consider some of the many types of measured variables used in behavioral research. We begin by considering how we might gain information by directly asking someone about his or her thoughts, feelings, or behavior. To do so involves using **self-report measures,** in which individuals are asked to respond to questions posed by an interviewer or a questionnaire. Then in the following sections we will consider the use of **behavioral measures,** designed to directly measure what people do.

Free-Format Self-Report Measures

Perhaps the most straightforward use of self-report measures involves asking people to freely list their thoughts or feelings as these come to mind. One of the major advantages of such **free-format self-report measures** is that they allow respondents to indicate whatever thoughts or feelings they have about the topic, without any constraints imposed on respondents except the effort it takes to write these thoughts or feelings down or speak them into a tape recorder.

Projective Measures.   A **projective measure** is a measure of personalities in which an unstructured image, such as an inkblot, is shown to participants, who are asked to freely list what comes to mind as they view the image. One common use of free-format self-report measures is the assessment of personality variables through the use of projective tests such as the Thematic Apperception Test, or TAT (Morgan & Murray, 1935) or the Rorschach inkblots. The TAT, for instance, consists of a number of sketches of people, either alone or with others, who are engaging in various behaviors, such as gazing out a window or pointing at each other. The sketches are shown to individuals, who are asked to tell a story about what is happening in the picture. The TAT assumes that people may be unwilling or unable to admit their true feelings when asked directly but that these feelings will show up in the stories about the pictures. Trained coders read the stories and use them to develop a personality profile of the respondent.

Associative Lists.   Free-format response formats in the form of associative lists have also been used to study such variables as stereotyping. In one of these studies (Stangor, Sullivan, & Ford, 1991), college students were presented with the names of different social groups (African Americans, Hispanics, Russians) and asked to list whatever thoughts came to mind about the groups. The study was based on the assumption that the thoughts listed in this procedure would be those that the individual viewed as strongest or most central to the group as a whole and would thus provide a good idea of what the person really thought about the groups. One student listed the following thoughts to describe different social groups:

> Whites: "Materialistic and prejudiced."
> Hispanics: "Poor, uneducated, and traditional. Willing to work hard."
> Russians: "Unable to leave their country, even though they want to."

Think-aloud Protocols.   Another common type of free-format response formats is a **think-aloud protocol** (Ericsson & Simon, 1980). In this procedure individuals are asked to verbalize into a tape recorder the thoughts that they are having as they complete a task. For instance, the following protocol was generated by a college student in a social psychology experiment who was trying to form an impression of another person who was characterized by conflicting information (Fiske, Neuberg, Beattie, & Milberg, 1987): "Professor. Strong, close-minded, rowdy, red-necked, loud. Hmmmm. I've never met a professor like this. I tend to make a stereotype of a beer-guzzling bigot. . . . I can sort of picture him sitting in a smoky, white bar, somewhere in, off in the suburbs of Maryland." The researchers used the think-aloud protocols, along with other data, to understand how people formed impressions about others.

The Difficulties of Coding Free-Format Data.   Despite the fact that free-format self-report measures produce a rich set of data regarding the thoughts and feelings of the people being studied, they also have some disadvantages. Most important, it is very difficult and time-consuming to turn the generated thoughts into a set of measured variables that can be used in data analysis. Because each individual is likely to have used a unique set of thoughts, it is hard to compare individuals. One solution is to simply describe the responses verbally (such as the description of the college professor on this page) and to treat the measures as qualitative data. However, because correlational and experimental research designs require the use of quantitative data (measured variables that can be subjected to statistical analysis), it is frequently useful to convert the free responses into one or more measured variables. For instance, the coders can read the answers given on projective tests and tabulate the extent to which different themes are expressed, or the responses given on associative lists can be tallied into different categories. However, the process of fitting the free responses into a structured coding system tends to reduce the basic advantage of the approach—the freedom of the individual to give unique responses. The process of coding free-response data is known as *content analysis,* and we will discuss it in some detail in Chapter 7.

Fixed-Format Self-Report Measures

Partly because of the difficulty of coding free-format responses, most research using self-report measures relies on **fixed-format self-report measures.** On these measures, the individual is presented with a set of questions (the questions are called **items**), and the responses that can be given are more structured than in free-format measures.

In some cases the information that we wish to obtain is unambiguous, and only one item is necessary to get it. For instance:

Enter your ethnic identification (please check one):

———— White
———— African American
———— Asian
———— Hispanic
———— Other (please specify) ————————

In other cases—for instance, the measurement of personality variables such as self-esteem, anxiety, intelligence, or mood—the conceptual variable is more difficult to assess. In these cases fixed-format self-report measures containing a number of items may be used. Fixed-format self-report measures that contain more than one item (such as an intelligence test or a measure of self-esteem) are known as **scales.** The many items, each designed to measure the same conceptual variable, are combined together by summing or averaging, and the result becomes the person's score on the measured variable.

One advantage of fixed-format scales is that there is a well-developed set of response formats already available for use, as well as a set of statistical procedures designed to evaluate the effectiveness of the scales as measures of underlying conceptual variables. As we will see in the next chapter, using more than one item is very advantageous because it provides a better measure of the conceptual variable than would any single item.

The Likert Scale. The most popular type of fixed-format scale is the Likert scale (Likert, 1932). A **Likert scale** consists of a series of items that indicate agreement or disagreement with the issue that is to be measured, each with a set of responses on which the respondents indicate their opinions. One example of a Likert scale, the Rosenberg self-esteem scale, is shown in Table 4.2. This scale contains ten items, each of which is responded to on a four-point response format ranging from "strongly disagree" to "strongly agree." Each of the possible responses is assigned a number, and the measured variable is the sum or average of the responses across all of the items.

You will notice that five of the ten items on the Rosenberg scale are written such that marking "strongly agree" means that the person has high self-esteem, whereas for the other half of the items marking "strongly agree" indicates that the individual does *not* have high self-esteem. This variation avoids a potential problem on fixed-format scales known as **acquiescent responding** (frequently called a yeah-saying bias). If all the items on a Likert scale are phrased in the same direction, it is not possible to tell if the respondent is simply a "yeah-sayer" (that is, a person who tends to agree with everything) or if he or she really agrees with the content of the item.

To reduce the impact of acquiescent responding on the measured variable, the wording of about one-half of the items is reversed such that agreement with these items means that the person does *not* have the characteristic being measured. Of course, the responses to the reversed items must themselves be *reverse-scored,* so that the direction is the same for every item, before the sum or average is taken. On the Rosenberg scale, the reversed items are changed so that 1 becomes 4, 2 becomes 3, 3 becomes 2, and 4 becomes 1.

TABLE 4.2 The Rosenberg Self-Esteem Scale

Please rate yourself on the following items by writing a number in the blank before each statement, where

4 = Strongly agree

3 = Agree

2 = Disagree

1 = Strongly disagree

3	(1) I feel that I'm a person of worth, at least on an equal base with others.
4	(2) I feel that I have a number of good qualities.
2	(3) All in all, I am inclined to think that I am a failure. (R)
3	(4) I am able to do things as well as other people.
2	(5) I feel I do not have much to be proud of. (R)
4	(6) I take a positive attitude toward myself.
3	(7) On the whole, I am satisfied with myself.
2	(8) I wish I could have more respect for myself. (R)
1	(9) I certainly feel useless at times. (R)
1	(10) At times I think I am no good at all. (R)

(R) denotes an item that should be reverse-scored before the total is calculated. The measured variable is the sum or average score across the ten items. For this person, the sum score is 34, and the mean is 3.40.

Source: Rosenberg (1965).

Although the Likert scale shown in Table 4.2 is a typical one, the format can vary to some degree. Although "strongly agree" and "strongly disagree" are probably the most common endpoints, others are also possible:

I am late for appointments:

Never   1   2   3   4   5   6   7   Always

It is also possible to label the midpoint of the scale (for instance, "neither agree nor disagree") as well as the endpoints, or to provide a label for each of the choices:

I enjoy parties:

1   Strongly disagree
2   Moderately disagree
3   Slightly disagree
4   Slightly agree
5   Moderately agree
6   Strongly agree

In still other cases, for instance, in the study of children, the response scale has to be simplified:

When an even number of response choices is used, the respondent cannot choose a neutral point, whereas the provision of an odd number of choices allows a neutral response. Depending on the purposes of the research and the type of question, this may or may not be appropriate or desirable. One response format that can be useful when a researcher does not want to restrict the range of input to a number of response options is to simply present a line of known length (for instance 100 mm) and ask the respondents to mark their opinion on the line. For instance:

I enjoy making decisions on my own:

Agre _____ Disagree

The distance of the mark from the end of the line is then measured with a ruler, and this becomes the measured variable. This approach is particularly effective when data are collected on computers because individuals can use the mouse to indicate on the computer screen the exact point on the line that represents their opinion and the computer can precisely measure and record the response.

The Semantic Differential.   Although Likert scales are particularly useful for measuring opinions and beliefs, people's feelings about topics under study can often be better assessed using a type of scale known as a semantic differential (Osgood, Suci, & Tannenbaum, 1957). Table 4.3 presents a semantic differential designed to assess feelings about a university. In a **semantic differential,** the topic being evaluated is presented once at the top of the page, and the items consist of pairs of adjectives located at the two endpoints of a standard response format. The respondent expresses his or her feelings toward the topic by marking one point on the dimension. To quantify the scale, a number is assigned to each possible response, for instance, from –3 (most negative) to +3 (most positive). Each respondent's score is computed by averaging across his or her responses to each of the items after the items in which the negative response has the higher number have been reverse-scored. Although semantic differentials can sometimes be used to assess other dimensions, they are most often restricted to measuring people's evaluations about a topic—that is, whether they feel positively or negatively about it.

The Guttman Scale.   There is one more type of fixed-format self-report scale, known as a Guttman scale (Guttman, 1944), that is sometimes used in behavioral research, although it is not as common as the Likert or semantic differential scale. The goal of a Guttman scale is to indicate the extent to which an individual possesses the conceptual variable of interest. But in contrast to Likert and semantic differential scales, which measure differences in the extent to which the participants agree with the items, the Guttman scale involves the creation of differences in the items themselves. The items are created ahead of time to be cumulative in the sense that they represent the degree of the conceptual variable of interest. The expectation is that an individual who endorses any given item will also endorse every item that is less extreme. Thus the **Guttman scale** can be defined as a fixed-format self-report scale in which the

TABLE 4.3   A Semantic Differential Scale Assessing Attitudes Toward a University

My university is:

Beautiful	____	____	____	____	____	____	____	Ugly
Bad	____	____	____	____	____	____	____	Good
Pleasant	____	____	____	____	____	____	____	Unpleasant
Dirty	____	____	____	____	____	____	____	Clean
Smart	____	____	____	____	____	____	____	Stupid

Respondents are told to check the middle category if neither adjective describes the object better than the other and to check along the scale in either direction if they feel the object is described better by either of the two adjectives. These ratings are usually scored from –3 to +3 (with appropriate reversals). Scores are averaged or summed to provide a single score for each individual.

items are arranged in a cumulative order such that it is assumed that if a respondent endorses or answers correctly any one item, he or she will also endorse or correctly answer all of the previous scale items.

Consider, for instance, the gender constancy scale shown in Table 4.4 (Slaby & Frey, 1975). This Guttman scale is designed to indicate the extent to which a young child has confidently learned that his or her sex will not change over time. A series of questions, which are ordered in terms of increasing difficulty, are posed to the child, who answers each one. The assumption is that if the child is able to answer a given question correctly, then he or she should also be able to answer all of the questions that come earlier on the scale correctly because those items are selected to be easier. Slaby and Frey (1975) found that although the pattern of responses was not perfect (some children did answer a later item correctly and an earlier item incorrectly), the gender

TABLE 4.4   The Gender Constancy Scale

1. Are you a boy or a girl?
2. (Show picture of a girl) Is this a boy or a girl?
3. (Show picture of a boy) Is this a boy or a girl?
4. (Show picture of a man) Is this a man or a woman?
5. (Show picture of a woman) Is this a man or a woman?
6. When you were a baby, were you a girl or a boy?
7. When you grow up, will you be a man or a woman?
8. This grownup is a woman (show picture of woman). When this grownup was little, was this grownup a boy like this child (show picture of boy) or a girl like this child (show picture of girl)?
9. This child is a boy (show picture of boy). When this child grows up, will this child be a woman like this grownup (show picture of woman) or a man like this grownup (show picture of man)?
10. If you wore clothes like this (show picture of a boy who is wearing girls' clothing), would you still be a boy, or would you be a girl?
11. If this child wore clothes like these (show picture of a girl who is wearing boys' clothing), would this child still be a girl, or would she be a boy?
12. If you played games that girls play, would you then be a girl, or would you be a boy?
13. (Show picture of man) If this grownup did the work that women usually do, would this grownup then be a woman, or would this grownup then be a man?
14. (Show picture of woman) If this grownup did the work that men usually do, would this grownup then be a man, or would the grownup then be a woman?

The gender constancy scale (Slaby & Frey, 1975) is a Guttman scale designed to measure the extent to which children have internalized the idea that sex cannot change. The questions are designed to reflect increasing difficulty. Children up to six years old frequently get some of the questions wrong. The version here is one that would be given to a boy. The sex of the actors in questions 8 through 12 would be reversed if the child being tested was a girl.

constancy scale did by and large conform to the expected cumulative pattern. They also found that older children answered more items correctly than did younger children.

Reactivity as a Limitation in Self-Report Measures

Taken together, self-report measures are the most commonly used type of measured variable within the behavioral sciences. They are relatively easy to construct and administer and allow the researcher to ask many questions in a short period of time. There is great flexibility, particularly with Likert scales, in the types of questions that can be posed to respondents. And, as we will see in Chapter 5, because a fixed-format scale has many items, each relating to the same thought or feeling, they can be combined together to produce a very useful measured variable.

However, there are also some potential disadvantages to the use of self-report. For one thing, with the exception of some indirect free-format measures such as the TAT, self-report measures assume that people are able and willing to accurately answer direct questions about their own thoughts, feelings, or behaviors. Yet as we have seen in Chapter 1, people may not always be able to accurately self-report on the causes of their behaviors. And even if they are accurately aware, respondents may not answer questions on self-report measures as they would have if they thought their responses were not being recorded. Changes in responding that occur when individuals know they are being measured are known as **reactivity.** Reactivity can change responses in many different ways and must always be taken into consideration in the development of measured variables (Weber & Cook, 1972).

The most common type of reactivity is **social desirability**—the natural tendency for research participants to present themselves in a positive or socially acceptable way to the researcher. One common type of reactivity, known as **self-promotion,** occurs when research participants respond in ways that they think will make them look good. For instance, most people will overestimate their positive qualities and underestimate their negative qualities and are usually unwilling to express negative thoughts or feelings about others. These responses occur because people naturally prefer to answer questions in a way that makes them look intelligent, knowledgeable, caring, healthy, and nonprejudiced.

Research participants may respond not only to make themselves look good but also to make the experimenter happy, even though they would probably not respond this way if they were not being studied. For instance, in one well-known study, Orne (1962) found that participants would perform tedious math problems for hours on end to please the experimenter, even though they had also been told to tear up all of their work as soon as they completed it, which made it impossible for the experimenter to check what they had done in any way.

The desire to please the experimenter can cause problems on self-report measures; for instance, respondents may indicate a choice on a response scale even though they may not understand the question or feel strongly about their answer but want to appear knowledgeable or please the experimenter. In such cases the researcher may interpret the response as meaning more than it really does. Cooperative responding is particularly problematic if the participants are able to guess the researcher's hypothesis—for instance, if they can figure out what the self-report measure is designed to assess. Of course, not all participants have cooperative attitudes. Those who are required to participate in the research may not pay much attention or may even develop an uncooperative attitude and attempt to sabotage the study.

There are several methods of countering reactivity on self-report measures. One is to administer other self-report scales that measure the tendency to lie or to self-promote, which are then used to correct for reactivity (see, for instance, Crowne and Marlow's [1964] social-desirability scale). To lessen the possibility of respondents guessing the hypothesis, the researcher may disguise the items on the self-report scale or include unrelated filler or distracter items to throw the participants off the track. Another strategy is to use a cover story—telling the respondents that one thing is being measured when the scale is really designed to measure something else. And the researcher may also be able to elicit more honest responses from the participant by explaining that the research is not designed to evaluate him or her personally and that its success depends upon honest answers to the questions (all of which is usually true). However, given people's potential to distort their responses on self-report measures, and given that there is usually no check on whether any corrections have been successful, it is useful to consider other ways to measure the conceptual variables of interest that are less likely to be influenced by reactivity.

Behavioral Measures

One alternative to self-report is to measure behavior. Although the measures shown in Table 4.1 are rather straightforward, social scientists have used a surprising variety of behavioral measures to help them assess the conceptual variables of interest. Table 4.5 represents some that you might find interesting that were sent to me by my social psychology colleagues. Indeed, the types of behaviors that can be measured are limited only by the creativity of the researchers. Some of the types of behavioral variables that form the basis of measured variables in behavioral science include those based on:

Frequency (for instance, frequency of stuttering as a measure of anxiety in interpersonal relations)

Duration (for instance, the number of minutes working at a task as a measure of task interest)

Intensity (for instance, how hard a person claps his or her hands as a measure of effort)

Latency (for instance, the number of days before a person begins to work on a project as a measure of procrastination)

TABLE 4.5   Some Conceptual Variables and the Behavioral Measures That Have Been Used to Operationalize Them

Conceptual Variable	Behavioral Measure
Personality style	Observation of the objects in and the state of people's bedrooms (with their permission, of course!) (Gosling, Ko, Mannarelli, & Morris, 2002)
Aggression	Amount of hot sauce that a research participant puts on other participants' food in a taste test (Lieberman, Solomon, Greenberg, & McGregor, 1999)
Desire for uniqueness	Extent to which people choose an unusual, rather than a common, color for a gift pen (Kim and Markus, 1999)
Honesty	Whether children, observed through a one-way mirror, followed the rule to "take only one candy" when they were trick or treating (Diener, Fraser, Beaman, & Kelem, 1976)
Dieting	Number of snacks taken from a snack bowl during a conversation between a man and a woman (Mori, Chaiken, & Pliner, 1987)
Cold severity	Change in the weight of a tissue before and after a research participant blew his or her nose with it (Cohen, Tyrrell, & Smith, 1993)
Interest in a task	Number of extra balls played on a pinball machine in free time (Harackiewicz, Manderlink, & Sansone, 1984)
Environmental behavior	How long participants let the water run during a shower in the locker room after swimming (Dickerson, Thibodeau, Aronson, & Miller, 1992)
Friendliness	How close together a person puts two chairs in preparation for an upcoming conversation (Fazio, Effrein, and Falender, 1981)
Racial prejudice	How far away a person sits from a member of another social category (Macrae, Bodenhausen, Milne, & Jetten, 1994)

Speed (for instance, how long it takes a mouse to complete a maze as a measure of learning)

Although some behaviors, such as how close a person sits to another person, are relatively easy to measure, many behavioral measures are difficult to operationally define and effectively code. For instance, you can imagine that it would be no easy task to develop a behavioral measure of "aggressive play" in children. In terms of the operational definition, decisions would have to be made about whether to include verbal aggression, whether some types of physical aggression (throwing stones) should be weighted more heavily than other types of physical aggression (pushing), and so forth. Then the behaviors would have to be coded. In most cases complete coding systems are worked out in advance, and more than one experimenter makes ratings of the behaviors, thereby allowing agreement between the raters to be assessed. In some cases videotapes may be made so that the behaviors can be coded at a later time. We will discuss techniques of coding behavioral measures more fully in Chapter 7.

Nonreactive Measures

Behavioral measures have a potential advantage over self-report measures—because they do not involve direct questioning of people, they are frequently less reactive. This is particularly true when the research participant (1) is not aware that the measurement is occurring, (2) does not realize what the measure is designed to assess, or (3) cannot change his or her responses, even if he or she desires to.

Nonreactive behavioral measures are frequently used to assess attitudes that are unlikely to be directly expressed on self-report measures, such as racial prejudice. For instance, Word, Zanna, and Cooper (1974) coded the nonverbal behavior of white male participants as they conducted an interview with another person, who was either black or white. The researchers found that the interviewers sat farther away from the black interviewees than from the white interviewees, made more speech errors when talking to the blacks, and terminated the interviews with the blacks sooner than with the whites. This experiment provided insights into the operation of prejudice that could not have been obtained directly because, until the participants were debriefed, they did not know that their behavior was being measured or what the experiment was about.

Some behavioral measures reduce reactivity because they are so indirect that the participants do not know what the measure is designed to assess. For instance, some researchers studying the development of impressions of others will provide participants with a list of behaviors describing another person and then later ask them to remember this information or to make decisions about it. Although the participants think that they are engaging in a memory test, what they remember about the behaviors and the speed with which they make decisions about the person can be used to draw inferences about whether the participants like or dislike the other person and whether they use stereotypes in processing the information. The use of nonreactive behavioral measures is discussed in more detail in a book by Webb, Campbell, Schwartz, Sechrest, and Grove (1981).

Psychophysiological Measures

In still other cases behavioral measures reduce reactivity because the individual cannot directly control his or her response. One example is the use of **psychophysiological measures,** which are designed to assess the physiological functioning of the body's nervous and endocrine systems (Cacioppo, Tassinary, & Berntson, 2000).

Some psychophysiological measures are designed to assess brain activity, with the goal of determining which parts of the brain are involved in which types of information processing and motor activities. These brain measures include the electroencephalogram (EEG), magnetic resonance imaging (MRI), positron-emission tomography (PET), and computerized axial tomography

(CAT). In one study using these techniques, Harmon-Jones and Sigelman (2001) used an EEG measure to assess brain activity after research participants had been insulted by another person. Supporting their hypotheses, they found that electrical brain responses to the insult were stronger on the left side of the brain than on the right side of the brain, indicating that anger involves not only negative feelings about the other person but also a motivational desire to address the insult.

Other psychophysiological measures, including heart rate, blood pressure, respiration speed, skin temperature, and skin conductance, assess the activity of the sympathetic and parasympathetic nervous systems. The electromyograph (EMG) assesses muscle responses in the face. For instance, Bartholow and his colleagues (2001) found that EMG responses were stronger when people read information that was unexpected or unusual than when they read more expected material, and that the responses were particularly strong in response to negative events. Still other physiological measures, such as amount of *cortisol,* involve determining what chemicals are in the bloodstream—for instance, to evaluate biochemical reactions to stress.

Although collecting psychophysiological measures can be difficult because doing so often requires sophisticated equipment and expertise and the interpretation of these measures may yield ambiguous results (for instance, does an increase in heart rate mean that the person is angry or afraid?), these measures do reduce reactivity to a large extent and are increasingly being used in behavioral research.

Choosing a Measure

As we have seen in this chapter, most conceptual variables of interest to behavioral scientists can be operationalized in any number of ways. For instance, the conceptual variable of aggression has been operationalized using such diverse measures as shocking others, fighting on a playground, verbal abuse, violent crimes, horn-honking in traffic, and putting hot sauce on people's food. The possibility of multiple operationalizations represents a great advantage to researchers because there are specific advantages and disadvantages to each type of measure. For instance, as we have seen, self-report measures have the advantage of allowing researchers to get a broad array of information in a short period of time, but the disadvantage of reactivity. On the other hand, behavioral measures may often reduce reactivity, but they may be difficult to operationalize and code, and the meaning of some behaviors may be difficult to interpret.

When designing a research project, think carefully about which measures to use. Your decision will be based on traditional approaches in the area you are studying and on the availability of resources, such as equipment and expertise. In many cases you will want to use more than one operationalization of a measure, such as self-report and behavioral measures, in the same research project. In every case, however, you must be absolutely certain that you do a complete literature review before you begin your project, to be sure that you have uncovered measures that have been used in prior research. There is so much research that has measured so many constructs, that it is almost certain that someone else has already measured the conceptual variable in which you are interested. Do not be afraid to make use of measures that have already been developed by others. It is entirely appropriate to do so, as long as you properly cite the source of the measure. As we will see in the next chapter, it takes a great amount of effort to develop a good measured variable. As a result, except when you are assessing a new variable or when existing measures are not appropriate for your research design, it is generally advisable to make use of the work that others have already done rather than try to develop your own measure.

SUMMARY

Before any research hypothesis can be tested, the conceptual variables must be turned into measured variables through the use of operational definitions. This process is known as measurement.

The relationship between the conceptual variables and their measures forms the basis of the testing of research hypotheses because the conceptual variables can be understood only through their operationalizations. Measured variables can be nominal or quantitative. The mapping, or scaling, of quantitative measured variables onto conceptual variables in the behavioral sciences is generally achieved through the use of ordinal, rather than interval or ratio, scales.

Self-report measures are those in which the person indicates his or her thoughts or feelings verbally in answer to posed questions. In free-format measures the participant can express whatever thoughts or feelings come to mind, whereas in fixed-format measures the participant responds to specific preselected questions. Fixed-format measures such as Likert, semantic differential, and Guttman scales contain a number of items, each using the same response format, designed to assess the conceptual variable of interest.

In contrast to self-report measures, behavioral measures can be more unobtrusive and thus are often less influenced by reactivity, such as acquiescent responding and self-promotion. One example of such nonreactive behavioral measures are those designed to assess physiological responding. However, behavioral measures may be difficult to operationalize and code, and the meaning of some behaviors may be difficult to interpret.

KEY TERMS

acquiescent responding 75
behavioral measures 72
conceptual variables 67
fixed-format self-report measures
    74
free-format self-report measures
    72
Guttman scale 77
interval scale 71
items 74
Likert scale 74
measured variables 67
measurement 67
measures 67
nominal variable 70

nonreactive behavioral measures 82
operational definition 67
ordinal scale 71
projective measure 72
psychophysiological measures 82
quantitative variable 70
ratio scales 71
reactivity 79
scales 74
scaling 71
self-promotion 79
self-report measures 72
semantic differential 77
social desirability 79
think-aloud protocol 73

REVIEW AND DISCUSSION QUESTIONS

1. Describe in your own words the meaning of Figure 4.1. Why is measurement so important in the testing of research hypotheses?

2. Indicate the relationships between nominal, ordinal, interval, and ratio scales and the conceptual variables they are designed to assess.

3. Generate three examples of nominal variables and three examples of quantitative variables that were not mentioned in the chapter.

4. On a piece of paper make two columns. In one column list all of the advantages of free-format (versus fixed-format) self-report measures. In the other column list all of the advantages of fixed-format (versus free-format) self-report measures. Given these comparisons, what factors might lead a researcher to choose one approach over the other?

5. Behavioral measures frequently have the advantage of reducing participant reactivity. Since they can capture the behavior of individuals more honestly, why are they so infrequently used in behavioral research?

6. Consider some examples of psychophysiological measures that are used in behavioral research.

HANDS-ON EXPERIENCE

1. Develop at least three behavioral measures of each of the following conceptual variables. Consider measures that are based on frequency, speed, duration, latency, and intensity. Consider the extent to which each of the measures you develop is nonreactive.
   a. Conformity
   b. Enjoyment of reading
   c. Leadership
   d. Paranoia
   e. Independence

2. Develop a ten-item Likert scale to measure one of the conceptual variables in problem 1.

3. Develop a free-format self-report measure for each of the conceptual variables listed in problem 1.

4. Find an example of a Likert, a semantic differential, and a Guttman scale used in a published research report other than those discussed in this chapter.

CHAPTER FIVE
Reliability and Validity

STUDY QUESTIONS

• What are random error and systematic error, and how do they influence measurement?

• What is reliability? Why must a measure be reliable?

• How are test-retest and equivalent-forms reliability measured?

• How are split-half reliability and coefficient alpha used to assess the internal consistency of a measured variable?

• What is interrater reliability?

• What are face validity and content validity?

• How are convergent and discriminant validity used to assess the construct validity of a measured variable?

• What is criterion validity?

• What methods can be used to increase the reliability and validity of a self-report measure?

• How are reliability and construct validity similar? How are they different?

We have seen in Chapter 4 that there are a wide variety of self-report and be-havioral measured variables that scientists can use to assess conceptual vari-ables. And we have seen that because changes in conceptual variables are assumed to cause changes in measured variables, the measured variables are used to make inferences about the conceptual variables. But how do we know whether the measures that we have chosen actually assess the conceptual vari-ables they are designed to measure? This chapter discusses techniques for evaluating the relationship between measured and conceptual variables.

In some cases, demonstrating the adequacy of a measure is rather straight-forward because there is a clear way to check whether it is measuring what it is supposed to. For instance, when a physiological psychologist investigates perceptions of the brightness or color of a light source, she or he can compare the participants' judgments with objective measurements of light intensity and wavelength. Similarly, when we ask people to indicate their sex or their cur-rent college grade-point average, we can check up on whether their reports are correct.

In many cases within behavioral science, however, assessing the effective-ness of a measured variable is more difficult. For instance, a researcher who has created a new Likert scale designed to measure "anxiety" assumes that an individual's score on this scale will reflect, at least to some extent, his or her actual level of anxiety. But because the researcher does not know how to meas-ure anxiety in any better way, there is no obvious way to "check" the re-sponses of the individual against any type of factual standard.

Random and Systematic Error

The basic difficulty in determining the effectiveness of a measured variable is that the measure will in all likelihood be influenced by other factors besides the conceptual variable of interest. For one thing, the measured variable will certainly contain some chance fluctuations in measurement, known as **ran-dom error.** Sources of random error include misreading or misunderstanding of the questions, and measurement of the individuals on different days or in different places. Random error can also occur if the experimenter misprints the questions or misrecords the answers or if the individual marks the answers incorrectly.

Although random error influences scores on the measured variable, it does so in a way that is self-canceling. That is, although the experimenter may make some recording errors or the individuals may mark their answers incorrectly, these errors will increase the scores of some people and decrease the scores of other people. The increases and decreases will balance each other and thus cancel each other out.

In contrast to random error, which is self-canceling, the measured variable may also be influenced by other conceptual variables that are not part of the conceptual variable of interest. These other potential influences constitute **sys-tematic error** because, whereas random errors tend to cancel out over time,

FIGURE 5.1   Random and Systematic Error

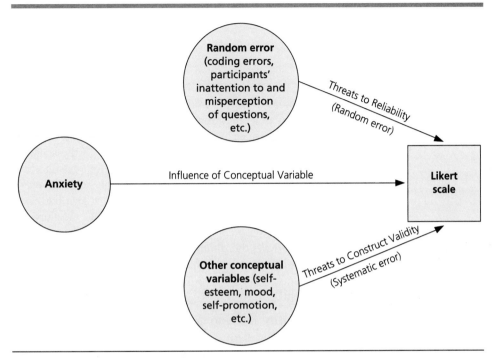

Scores on a measured variable, such as a Likert scale measure of anxiety, will be caused not only by the conceptual variable of interest (anxiety), but also by random measurement error as well as other conceptual variables that are unrelated to anxiety. Reliability is increased to the extent that random error has been eliminated as a cause of the measured variable. Construct validity is increased to the extent that the influence of systematic error has been eliminated.

these variables systematically increase or decrease the scores on the measured variable. For instance, individuals with higher self-esteem may score systematically lower on the anxiety measure than those with low self-esteem, and more optimistic individuals may score consistently higher. Also, as we have discussed in Chapter 4, the tendency to self-promote may lead some respondents to answer the items in ways that make them appear less anxious than they really are in order to please the experimenter or to feel better about themselves. In these cases, the measured variable will assess self-esteem, optimism, or the tendency to self-promote in addition to the conceptual variable of interest (anxiety).

Figure 5.1 summarizes the impact of random and systematic error on a measured variable. Although there is no foolproof way to determine whether measured variables are free from random and systematic error, there are techniques that allow us to get an idea about how well our measured variables "capture" the conceptual variables they are designed to assess rather than being influenced by random and systematic error. As we will see, this is accomplished through examination of the correlations among a set of measured variables.[1]

Reliability

The **reliability** of a measure refers to the extent to which it is free from random error. One direct way to determine the reliability of a measured variable is to measure it more than once. For instance, you can test the reliability of a bathroom scale by weighing yourself on it twice in a row. If the scale gives the same weight both times (we'll assume your actual weight hasn't changed in between), you would say that it is reliable. But if the scale gives different weights each time, you would say that it is unreliable. Just as a bathroom scale is not useful if it is not consistent over time, an unreliable measured variable will not be useful in research.

The next section reviews the different approaches to assessing a measure's reliability; these are summarized in Table 5.1.

Test-Retest Reliability

Test-retest reliability refers to the extent to which scores on the same measured variable correlate with each other on two different measurements given at two different times. If the test is perfectly reliable, and if the scores on the conceptual variable do not change over the time period, the individuals

TABLE 5.1   Summary of Approaches to Assessing Reliability

Approach	Description
Test-retest reliability	The extent to which scores on the same measure, administered at two different times, correlate with each other
Equivalent-forms reliability	The extent to which scores on similar, but not identical, measures, administered at two different times, correlate with each other
Internal consistency	The extent to which the scores on the items of a scale correlate with each other. Usually assessed using coefficient alpha
Interrater reliability	The extent to which the ratings of one or more judges correlate with each other

Reliability refers to the extent to which a measured variable is free from random error. As shown in this table, reliability is assessed by computing the extent to which measured variables correlate with each other.

[1]Be sure to review Appendix B in this book if you are uncertain about the Pearson correlation coefficient.

should receive the exact same score each time, and the correlation between the scores will be $r = 1.00$. However, if the measured variable contains random error, the two scores will not be as highly correlated. Higher positive correlations between the scores at the two times indicate higher test-retest reliability.

Although the test-retest procedure is a direct way to measure reliability, it does have some limits. For one thing, when the procedure is used to assess the reliability of a self-report measure, it can produce reactivity. As you will recall from Chapter 4, reactivity refers to the influence of measurement on the variables being measured. In this case reactivity is a potential problem because when the same or similar measures are given twice, responses on the second administration may be influenced by the measure having been taken the first time. These problems are known as **retesting effects.**

Retesting problems may occur, for instance, if people remember how they answered the questions the first time. Some people may believe that the experimenter wants them to express *different* opinions on the second occasion (or else why are the questions being given twice?). This would obviously reduce the test-retest correlation and thus give an overly low reliability assessment. Or respondents may try to duplicate their previous answers exactly to avoid appearing inconsistent, which would unnaturally increase the reliability estimate. Participants may also get bored answering the same questions twice. Although some of these problems can be avoided through the use of a long testing interval (say, over one month) and through the use of appropriate instructions (for instance, instructions to be honest and to answer exactly how one is feeling right now), retesting poses a general problem for the computation of test-retest reliability.

To help avoid some of these problems, researchers sometimes employ a more sophisticated type of test-retest reliability known as **equivalent-forms reliability.** In this approach two different but equivalent versions of the same measure are given at different times, and the correlation between the scores on the two versions is assessed. Such an approach is particularly useful when there are correct answers to the test that individuals might learn by taking the first test or be able to find out during the time period between the tests. Because students might remember the questions and learn the answers to aptitude tests such as the Graduate Record Exam (GRE) or the Scholastic Aptitude Test (SAT), these tests employ equivalent forms.

Reliability as Internal Consistency

In addition to the problems that can occur when people complete the same measure more than once, another problem with test-retest reliability is that some conceptual variables are not expected to be stable over time within an individual. Clearly, if optimism has a meaning as a conceptual variable, then people who are optimists on Tuesday should also be optimists on Friday of next week. Conceptual variables such as intelligence, friendliness, assertiveness, and optimism are known as **traits,** which are personality variables that are not expected to vary (or at most to vary only slowly) within people over time.

Other conceptual variables, such as level of stress, moods, or even preference for classical over rock music, are known as **states.** States are personality variables that are expected to change within the same person over short periods of time. Because a person's score on a mood measure administered on Tuesday is not necessarily expected to be related to the same measure administered next Friday, the test-retest approach will not provide an adequate assessment of the reliability of a state variable such as mood. Because of the problems associated with test-retest and equivalent-forms reliability, another measure of reliability, known as internal consistency, has become the most popular and most accurate way of assessing reliability for both trait and state measures. Internal consistency is assessed using the scores on a single administration of the measure.

You will recall from our discussion in Chapter 4 that most self-report measures contain a number of items. If you think about measurement in terms of reliability, the reason for this practice will become clear. You can imagine that a measure that had only one item might be unreliable because that specific item might have a lot of random error. For instance, respondents might not understand the question the way you expected them to, or they might read it incorrectly. In short, any single item is not likely to be very reliable.

True Score and Random Error.   One of the basic principles of reliability is that the more measured variables are combined together, the more reliable the test will be. This is so because, although each measured variable will be influenced in part by random error, some part of each item will also measure the **true score,** or the part of the scale score that is not random error, of the individual on the measure. Furthermore, because random error is self-canceling, the random error components of each measured variable will not be correlated with each other, whereas the parts of the measured variables that represent the true score will be correlated. As a result, when they are combined together by summing or averaging, the use of many measured variables will produce a more reliable estimate of the conceptual variable than will any of the individual measured variables themselves.

The role of true score and random error can be expressed in the form of two equations that are the basis of reliability. First, an individual's score on a measure will consist of both true score and random error:

$$\text{Actual score} = \text{True score} + \text{Random error}$$

and reliability is the proportion of the actual score that reflects true score (and not random error).

$$\text{Reliability} = \frac{\text{True score}}{\text{Actual score}}$$

To take a more specific example, consider for a moment the Rosenberg self-esteem scale that we examined in Table 4.2. This scale has ten items, each designed to assess the conceptual variable of self-esteem in a slightly different way. Although each of the items will have random error, each should also measure the true score of the individual. Thus if we average all ten of the items together to form a single measure, this overall scale score will be a more reliable measure than will any one of the individual questions.

Internal consistency refers to the extent to which the scores on the items correlate with each other and thus are all measuring the true score rather than random error. In terms of the Rosenberg scale, a person who answers above average on question 1, indicating she or he has high self-esteem, should also respond above the average on all of the other questions. Of course, this pattern will not be perfect because each item has some error. However, to the extent that all of the items are measuring true score, rather than random error, the average correlation among the items will approach $r = 1.00$. To the extent that the correlation among the items is less than $r = 1.00$, it tells us either that there is random error or that the items are not measuring the same thing.

Coefficient Alpha. One way to calculate the internal consistency of a scale is to correlate a person's score on one half of the items (for instance, the even-numbered items) with her or his score on the other half of the items (the odd-numbered items). This procedure is known as **split-half reliability.** If the scale is reliable, then the correlation between the two halves will approach $r = 1.00$, indicating that both halves measure the same thing. However, because split-half reliability uses only some of the available correlations among the items, it is preferable to have a measure that indexes the average correlation among all of the items on the scale. The most common, and the best, index of internal consistency is known as **Cronbach's coefficient alpha,** symbolized as α. This measure is an estimate of the average correlation among all of the items on the scale and is numerically equivalent to the average of all possible split-half reliabilities.

Coefficient alpha, because it reflects the underlying correlational structure of the scale, ranges from $\alpha = 0.00$ (indicating that the measure is entirely error) to $\alpha = +1.00$ (indicating that the measure has no error). In most cases statistical computer programs are used to calculate coefficient alpha, but alpha can also be computed by hand according to the formula presented in Appendix D.

Item-to-Total Correlations. When a new scale is being developed, its initial reliability may be low. This is because, although the researcher has selected those items that he or she believes will be reliable, some items will turn out to contain random error for reasons that could not be predicted in advance. Thus one strategy commonly used in the initial development of a scale is to calculate the correlations between the score on each of the individual items and the total scale score excluding the item itself (these correlations are known as the *item-to-total correlations*). The items that do not correlate highly with the total score can then be deleted from the scale. Because this procedure deletes the items that do not measure the same thing that the scale as a whole does, the result is a shorter scale, but one with higher reliability. However, the approach of throwing out the items that do not correlate highly with the total is used only in the scale development process. Once the final version of the scale is in place, this version should be given again to another sample of participants, and the reliability computed without dropping any items.

Interrater Reliability

To this point we have discussed reliability primarily in terms of self-report scales. However, reliability is just as important for behavioral measures. It is common practice for a number of judges to rate the same observed behaviors and then to combine their ratings to create a single measured variable. This computation requires the internal consistency approach—just as any single item on a scale is expected to have error, so the ratings of any one judge are more likely to contain error than is the averaged rating across a group of judges. The errors of judges can be caused by many things, including inattention to some of the behaviors, misunderstanding of instructions, or even personal preferences. When the internal consistency of a group of judges is calculated, the resulting reliability is known as **interrater reliability.**

If the ratings of the judges that are being combined are quantitative variables (for instance, if the coders have each determined the aggressiveness of a group of children on a scale from 1 to 10), then coefficient alpha can be used to evaluate reliability. However, in some cases the variables of interest may be nominal. This would occur, for instance, if the judges have indicated for each child whether he or she was playing "alone," "cooperatively," "competitively," or "aggressively." In such cases a statistic known as **kappa (κ)** is used as the measure of agreement among the judges. Like coefficient alpha, kappa ranges from $\kappa = 0$ (indicating that the judges' ratings are entirely random error) to $\kappa = +1.00$ (indicating that the ratings have no error). The formula for computing kappa is presented in Appendix C.

Construct Validity

Although reliability indicates the extent to which a measure is free from random error, it does not indicate what the measure actually measures. For instance, if we were to measure the speed with which a group of research participants could tie their shoes, we might find that this is a very reliable measure in the sense that it shows a substantial test-retest correlation. However, if the researcher then claimed that this reliable measure was assessing the conceptual variable of intelligence, you would probably not agree.

Therefore, in addition to being reliable, useful measured variables must also be construct valid. **Construct validity** refers to the extent to which a measured variable actually measures the conceptual variable (that is, the construct) that it is designed to assess. A measure only has construct validity if it measures what we want it to. There are a number of ways to assess construct validity; these are summarized in Table 5.2.

TABLE 5.2 Construct and Criterion Validity

Type of Validity	Description
Construct validity	The extent to which a measured variable actually measures the conceptual variable that it is designed to measure
Face validity	The extent to which the measured variable appears to be an adequate measure of the conceptual variable
Content validity	The extent to which the measured variable appears to have adequately covered the full domain of the conceptual variable
Convergent validity	The extent to which a measured variable is found to be related to other measured variables designed to measure the same conceptual variable
Discriminant validity	The extent to which a measured variable is found to be unrelated to other measured variables designed to measure other conceptual variables
Criterion validity	The extent to which a self-report measure correlates with a behavioral measured variable
Predictive validity	The extent to which a self-report measure correlates with (predicts) a future behavior
Concurrent validity	The extent to which a self-report measure correlates with a behavior measured at the same time

Face Validity

In some cases we can obtain an initial indication of the likely construct validity of a measured variable by examining it subjectively. **Face validity** refers to the extent to which the measured variable appears to be an adequate measure of the conceptual variable. For example, the Rosenberg self-esteem scale in Table 4.2 has face validity because the items ("I feel that I have a number of good qualities"; "I am able to do things as well as other people") appear to assess what we intuitively mean when we speak of self-esteem. However, if I carefully timed how long it took you and ten other people to tie your shoelaces, and then told you that you had above-average self-esteem because you tied your laces faster than the average of the others did, it would be clear that, although my test might be highly reliable, it did not really measure self-esteem. In this case the measure is said to lack face validity.

Even though in some cases face validity can be a useful measure of whether a test actually assesses what it is supposed to, face validity is not always necessary or even desirable in a test. For instance, consider how white college students might answer the following measures of racial prejudice:

I do not like African Americans:

Strongly disagree 1 2 3 4 5 6 7 Strongly agree

African Americans are inferior to whites:

Strongly agree 1 2 3 4 5 6 7 Strongly disagree

These items have high face validity (they appear to measure racial prejudice), but they are unlikely to be valid measures because people are unlikely to answer them honestly. Even those who are actually racists might not indicate agreement with these items (particularly if they thought the experimenter could check up on them) because they realize that it is not socially appropriate to do so.

In cases where the test is likely to produce reactivity, it can sometimes be the case that tests with *low* face validity may actually be more valid because the respondents will not know what is being measured and thus will be more likely to answer honestly. In short, not all measures that appear face valid are actually found to have construct validity.

Content Validity

One type of validity that is particularly appropriate to ability tests is known as **content validity.** Content validity concerns the degree to which the measured variable appears to have adequately sampled from the potential domain of questions that might relate to the conceptual variable of interest. For instance, an intelligence test that contained only geometry questions would lack content validity because there are other types of questions that measure intelligence (those concerning verbal skills and knowledge about current affairs, for instance) that were not included. However, this test might nevertheless have content validity as a geometry test because it sampled from many different types of geometry problems.

Convergent and Discriminant Validity

Although face and content validity can and should be used in the initial stages of test development, they are relatively subjective, and thus limited, methods for evaluating the construct validity of measured variables. Ultimately, the determination of the validity of a measure must be made not on the basis of subjective judgments, but on the basis of relevant data. The basic logic of empirically testing the construct validity of a measure is based on the idea that there are multiple operationalizations of the variable:

> If a given measured variable "*x*" is really measuring conceptual variable "*X*," then it should correlate with other measured variables designed to assess "*X*," and it should not correlate with other measured variables designed to assess other conceptually unrelated variables.

According to this logic, construct validity has two separate components. **Convergent validity** refers to the extent to which a measured variable is found to be related to other measured variables designed to measure the same conceptual variable. **Discriminant validity** refers to the extent to which a measured variable is found to be unrelated to other measured variables designed to assess different conceptual variables.

Assessment of Construct Validity. Let's take an example of the use of how convergent and discriminant validity were used to demonstrate the construct validity of a new personality variable known as self-monitoring. *Self-monitoring* refers to the tendency to pay attention to the events that are occurring around you and to adjust your behavior to "fit in" with the specific situation you are in. High self-monitors are those who habitually make these adjustments, whereas low self-monitors tend to behave the same way in all situations, essentially ignoring the demands of the social setting.

Social psychologist Mark Snyder (1974) began his development of a self-monitoring scale by constructing forty-one items that he thought would tap into the conceptual variable self-monitoring. These included items designed to directly assess self-monitoring:

"I guess I put on a show to impress or entertain people."
"I would probably make a good actor."

and items that were to be reverse-scored:

"I rarely need the advice of my friends to choose movies, books, or music."
"I have trouble changing my behavior to suit different people and different situations."

On the basis of the responses of an initial group of college students, Snyder deleted the sixteen items that had the lowest item-to-total correlations. He was left with a twenty-five-item self-monitoring scale that had a test-retest reliability of .83.

Once he had demonstrated that his scale was reliable, Snyder began to assess its construct validity. First, he demonstrated discriminant validity by showing that the scale did *not* correlate highly with other existing personality scales that might have been measuring similar conceptual variables. For instance, the self-monitoring scale did not correlate highly with a measure of extraversion ($r = +.19$), with a measure of responding in a socially acceptable manner ($r = -.19$), or with an existing measure of achievement anxiety ($r = +.14$).

Satisfied that the self-monitoring scale was not the same as existing scales, and thus showed discriminant validity, Snyder then began to assess the test's convergent validity. Snyder found, for instance, that high self-monitors were more able to accurately communicate an emotional expression when asked to do so ($r = .60$). And he found that professional actors (who should be very sensitive to social cues) scored higher on the scale and that hospitalized psychiatric patients (who are likely to be unaware of social cues) scored lower on the scale, both in comparison to college students. Taken together, Snyder concluded that the self-monitoring scale was reliable and also possessed both convergent and discriminant validity.

One of the important aspects of Snyder's findings is that the convergent validity correlations were not all $r = +1.00$ and the discriminant validity correlations were not all $r = 0.00$. Convergent validity and discriminant validity are never all-or-nothing constructs, and thus it is never possible to definitively "prove" the construct validity of a measured variable. In reality, even measured variables that are designed to measure different conceptual variables will often be at least moderately correlated with each other. For instance, self-monitoring relates, at least to some extent, to extraversion because they are related constructs. Yet the fact that the correlation coefficient is relatively low ($r = .19$) indicates that self-monitoring and extraversion are not identical. Similarly, even measures that assess the same conceptual variable will not, because of random error, be perfectly correlated with each other.

The Nomological Net.   Although convergent reality and discriminant validity are frequently assessed through correlation of the scores on one self-report measure (for instance, one Likert scale of anxiety) with scores on another self-report measure (a different anxiety scale), construct validity can also be evaluated using other types of measured variables. For example, when testing a self-report measure of anxiety, a researcher might compare the scores to ratings of anxiety made by trained psychotherapists or to physiological variables such as blood pressure or skin conductance.

The relationships among the many different measured variables, both self-report and otherwise, form a complicated pattern, called a **nomological net.** Only when we look across many studies, using many different measures of the various conceptual variables and relating those measures to other variables, does a complete picture of the construct validity of the measure begin to emerge—the greater the number of predicted relationships tested and confirmed, the greater the support for the construct validity of the measure.

Criterion Validity

You will have noticed that when Snyder investigated the construct validity of his self-monitoring scale, he assessed its relationship not only to other self-report measures, but also to behavioral measures such as the individual's current occupation (for instance, whether he or she was an actor). There are some particular advantages to testing validity through correlation of a scale with behavioral measures rather than with other self-report measures. For one thing, as we have discussed in Chapter 4, behavioral measures may be less subject to reactivity than are self-report measures. When validity is assessed through correlation of a self-report measure with a behavioral measured variable, the behavioral variable is called a **criterion variable,** and the correlation is an assessment of the self-report measure's **criterion validity.**

Criterion validity is known as **predictive validity** when it involves attempts to foretell the future. This would occur, for instance, when an industrial psychologist uses a measure of job aptitude to predict how well a prospective employee will perform on a job or when an educational psychologist predicts school performance from SAT or GRE scores. Criterion validity is known as **concurrent validity** when it involves assessment of the relationship between a self-report and a behavioral measure that are assessed at the same time. In some cases criterion validity may even involve use of the self-report measure to predict behaviors that have occurred prior to completion of the scale.

Although the practice of correlating a self-report measure with a behavioral criterion variable can be used to learn about the construct validity of the measured variables, in some applied research settings it is only the ability of the test to predict a specific behavior that is of interest. For instance, an employer who wants to predict whether a person will be an effective manager will be happy to use any self-report measure that is effective in doing so and may not care about what conceptual variable the test measures (for instance, does it measure intelligence, social skills, diligence, all three, or something else entirely?). In this case criterion validity involves only the correlation between the variables rather than the use of the variables to make inferences about construct validity.

Improving the Reliability and Validity of Measured Variables

Now that we have considered some of the threats to the validity of measured variables, we can ask how our awareness of these potential threats can help us improve our measures. Most basically, the goal is to be aware of the potential difficulties and to keep them in mind as we design our measures. Because the research process is a social interaction between researcher and participant, we must carefully consider how the participant perceives the research and consider how she or he may react to it. The following are some useful tips for creating valid measures:

1. Conduct a pilot test. **Pilot testing** involves trying out a questionnaire or other research on a small group of individuals to get an idea of how they react to it before the final version of the project is created. After collecting the data from the pilot test, you can modify the measures before actually using the scale in research. Pilot testing can help ensure that participants understand the questions as you expect them to and that they cannot guess the purpose of the questionnaire. You can also use pilot testing to create self-report measures. You ask participants in the pilot study to generate thoughts about the conceptual variables of interest. Then you use these thoughts to generate ideas about the types of items that should be asked on a fixed-format scale.

2. Use multiple measures. As we have seen, the more types of measures are used to assess a conceptual variable, the more information about the variable is gained. For instance, the more items a test has, the more reliable it will be. However, be careful not to make your scale so long that your participants lose interest in taking it! As a general guideline, twenty items are usually sufficient to produce a highly reliable measure.

3. Ensure variability within your measures. If 95 percent of your participants answer an item with the response 7 (strongly agree) or the response 1 (strongly disagree), the item won't be worth including because it won't differentiate the respondents. One way to guarantee variability is to be sure that the *average* response of your respondents is near the middle of the scale. This means that although most people fall in the middle, some people will fall above and some below the average. Pilot testing enables you to create measures that have variability.

4. Write good items. Make sure that your questions are understandable and not ambiguous. This means the questions shouldn't be too long or too short. Try to avoid ambiguous words. For instance, "Do you regularly feel stress?" is not as good as "How many times per week do you feel stress?" because the term *regular* is ambiguous. Also watch for "double-barreled" questions such as "Are you happy most of the time, or do you find there to be no reason to be happy?" A person who is happy but does not find any real reason for it would not know how to answer this question. Keep your questions as simple as possible, and be specific. For instance, the question "Do you like your parents?" is vaguer than "Do you like your mother?" and "Do you like your father?"

5. Attempt to get your respondents to take your questions seriously. In the instructions you give to them, stress that the accuracy of their responses is important and that their responses are critical to the success of the research project. Otherwise carelessness may result.

6. Attempt to make your items nonreactive. For instance, asking people to indicate whether they agree with the item "I dislike all Japanese people" is unlikely to produce honest answers, whereas a statement such as "The Japanese are using their economic power to hurt the United States" may elicit a more honest answer because the item is more indirect. Of course, the latter item may not assess exactly what you are hoping to measure, but in some cases tradeoffs may be required. In some cases you may wish to embed items that measure something entirely irrelevant (they are called *distracter items*) in your scale to disguise what you are really assessing.

7. Be certain to consider face and content validity by choosing items that seem "reasonable" and that represent a broad range of questions concerning the topic of interest. If the scale is not content valid, you may be evaluating only a small piece of the total picture you are interested in.

8. When possible, use existing measures, rather than creating your own, since the reliability and validity of these measures will already be established.

Comparing Reliability and Validity

We have seen that reliability and construct validity are similar in that they are both assessed through examination of the correlations among measured variables. However, they are different in the sense that reliability refers to correlations among different variables that the researcher is planning to combine into the *same* measure of a single conceptual variable, whereas construct validity refers to correlations of a measure with *different* measures of other conceptual variables. In this sense it is appropriate to say that reliability comes before validity because reliability is concerned with creating a measure that is then tested in relationship to other measures. If a measure is not reliable, then its construct validity cannot be determined. Tables 5.1 and 5.2 summarize the various types of reliability and validity that researchers must consider.

One important question that we have not yet considered is "How reliable and valid must a scale be in order to be useful?" Researchers do not always agree about the answer, except for the obvious fact that the higher the reliability and the construct validity, the better. One criterion that seems reasonable is that the reliability of a commonly used scale should be at least $\alpha = .70$. However, many tests have reliabilities well above $\alpha = .80$.

In general, it is easier to demonstrate the reliability of a measured variable than it is to demonstrate a variable's construct validity. This is so in part because demonstrating reliability involves only showing that the measured variables correlate with each other, whereas validity involves showing both convergent and discriminant validity. Also, because the items on a scale are all answered using the same response format and are presented sequentially, and because items that do not correlate highly with the total scale score can be deleted, high reliabilities are usually not difficult to achieve.

However, the relationships among different measures of the same conceptual variable that serve as the basis for demonstrating convergent validity are generally very low. For instance, the correlations observed by Snyder were only in the range of .40, and such correlations are not unusual. Although correlations of such size may seem low, they are still taken as evidence for convergent validity.

One of the greatest difficulties in developing a new scale is to demonstrate its discriminant validity. Although almost any new scale that you can imagine will be at least moderately correlated with at least some other existing scales, to be useful the new scale must be demonstrably different from existing scales in at least some critical respects. Demonstrating this uniqueness is difficult and will generally require that a number of different studies be conducted.

Because there are many existing scales in common use within the behavioral sciences, carefully consider whether you really need to develop a new scale for your research project. Before you begin scale development, be sure to determine if a scale assessing the conceptual variable you are interested in, or at least a similar conceptual variable, might already exist. A good source for information about existing scales, in addition to PsycINFO, is Robinson, Shaver, and Wrightsman (1991). Remember that it is always advantageous to use an existing measure rather than to develop your own—the reliability and validity of such measures are already established, saving you a lot of work.

SUMMARY

Assessing the effectiveness of a measured variable involves determining the extent to which the measure is free of both random error and systematic error. These determinations are made through examination of correlations among measures of the same and different conceptual variables.

Reliability refers to the extent to which a measure is free from random error. In some cases reliability can be assessed through administration of the same or similar tests more than one time (test-retest and equivalent-forms reliability). However, because such procedures can assess only the reliability of traits, and not states, and because they involve two different testing sessions, reliability is more often assessed in terms of the internal consistency of the items on a single scale using split-half reliability or Cronbach's coefficient alpha (α). *Interrater reliability* refers to the reliability of a set of judges or coders.

Construct validity is the extent to which a measure is free from systematic error and thus measures what it is intended to measure. *Face validity* and *content validity* refer to the extent to which a measured variable appears to measure the conceptual variable of interest and to which it samples from a broad domain of items, respectively. *Convergent validity* refers to the extent to which a measured variable correlates with other measured variables designed to measure the same conceptual variable, whereas *discriminant validity* refers to the extent to which a measured variable does not correlate with other measured variables designed to assess other conceptual variables. In some cases the goal of a research project is to test whether a measure given at one time can predict behavioral measures assessed either at the same time (concurrent validity) or in the future (predictive validity).

KEY TERMS

concurrent validity 99
construct validity 94
content validity 96
convergent validity 96
criterion validity 98
criterion variable 98
Cronbach's coefficient alpha (α)
    93
discriminant validity 96
equivalent-forms reliability 91
face validity 95
internal consistency 93
interrater reliability 94

kappa (κ) 94
nomological net 98
pilot testing 99
predictive validity 98
random error 88
reliability 90
retesting effects 91
split-half reliability 93
states 92
systematic error 88
test-retest reliability 90
traits 91
true score 92

REVIEW AND DISCUSSION QUESTIONS

1. Why do self-report scales use many different items that assess the same conceptual variable?

2. Consider a measure that shows high internal consistency but low test-retest reliability. What can be concluded about the measure?

3. What is the relationship between reliability and validity? Why is it possible to have a reliable measure that is not valid but impossible to have a valid measure that is not reliable?

4. Compare the assessment of face, content, and construct validity. Which of the three approaches is most objective, and why? Is it possible to have a measure that is construct valid but not face valid?

5. What is the importance of predictive validity? In what ways does predictive validity differ from construct validity?

6. Discuss the methods that researchers use to improve the reliability and validity of their measures.

HANDS-ON EXPERIENCE

1. Choose a conceptual variable that can be considered to be a trait of interest to you, and (after conducting a literature review) create a fifteen-item Likert scale to assess it. Administer the scale to at least twenty people. Compute the scale's reliability, and then, using a statistical software program, delete items until the scale's reliability reaches at least .75 or stops increasing. Consider what sources of random and systematic error might be found in the scale.

2. Develop a behavioral or a free-format self-report measure of the conceptual variable you assessed in problem 1, and collect the relevant data from the same people. Find a partner to help you code the responses, and compute the interrater reliability of the coding. Compute the Pearson correlation coefficient between the new measure and the score on the Likert scale. Does the correlation demonstrate construct validity?

3. Videotape two of your classmates engaging in a discussion. Develop a method for systematically coding their nonverbal behaviors, such as eye contact, body posture, and hand movements. Calculate the interrater reliability of the coding scheme you developed.

CHAPTER SIX
Surveys and Sampling

STUDY QUESTIONS

- When and why are surveys used in behavioral research?

- What are the advantages and disadvantages of using interviews versus questionnaires in survey research?

- How is probability sampling used to ensure that a sample is representative of the population?

- What is sampling bias, and how does it undermine a researcher's ability to draw conclusions about surveys?

- What statistical procedures are used to report and display data from surveys?

- What is the margin of error of a sample?

Now that we have reviewed the basic types of measured variables and considered how to evaluate their effectiveness at assessing the conceptual variables of interest, it is time to more fully discuss the use of these measures in descriptive research. In this chapter we will discuss the use of self-report measures, and in Chapter 7 we will discuss the use of behavioral measures. Although these measures are frequently used in a qualitative sense—to draw a complete and complex picture in the form of a narrative—they can also be used quantitatively, as measured variables. As you read these chapters, keep in mind that the goal of descriptive research is to describe the current state of affairs but that it does not by itself provide direct methods for testing research hypotheses. However, both surveys (discussed in this chapter) and naturalistic methods (discussed in Chapter 7) are frequently used not only as descriptive data but also as the measured variables in correlational and experimental tests of research hypotheses. We will discuss these uses in later chapters.

Surveys

A **survey** is a series of self-report measures administered either through an interview or a written questionnaire. Surveys are the most widely used method of collecting descriptive information about a group of people. You may have received a phone call (it usually arrives in the middle of the dinner hour when most people are home) from a survey research group asking you about your taste in music, your shopping habits, or your political preferences.

The goal of a survey, as with all descriptive research, is to produce a "snapshot" of the opinions, attitudes, or behaviors of a group of people at a given time. Because surveys can be used to gather information about a wide variety of information in a relatively short time, they are used extensively by businesspeople, advertisers, and politicians to help them learn what people think, feel, or do.

Interviews

Surveys are usually administered in the form of an **interview,** in which questions are read to the respondent in person or over the telephone. One advantage of in-person interviews is that they may allow the researcher to develop a close rapport and sense of trust with the respondent. This may motivate the respondent to continue with the interview and may lead to more honest and open responding. However, face-to-face interviews are extremely expensive to conduct, and consequently telephone surveys are now more common. In a telephone interview all of the interviewers are located in one place, the telephone numbers are generated automatically, and the questions are read from computer terminals in front of the researchers. This procedure provides such efficiency and coordination among the interviewers that many surveys can be conducted in one day.

Unstructured Interviews. Interviews may use either free-format or fixed-format self-report measures. In an **unstructured interview** the interviewer talks freely with the person being interviewed about many topics. Although a general list of the topics of interest is prepared beforehand, the actual interview focuses in on those topics that the respondent is most interested in or most knowledgeable about. Because the questions asked in an unstructured interview differ from respondent to respondent, the interviewer must be trained to ask questions in a way that gets the most information from the respondent and allows the respondent to express his or her true feelings. One type of a face-to-face unstructured interview in which a number of people are interviewed at the same time and share ideas both with the interviewer and with each other is called a **focus group.**

Unstructured interviews may provide in-depth information about the particular concerns of an individual or a group of people and thus may produce ideas for future research projects or for policy decisions. It is, however, very difficult to adequately train interviewers to ask questions in an unbiased manner and to be sure that they have actually done so. And, as we have seen in Chapter 4, because the topics of conversation and the types of answers given in free-response formats vary across participants, the data are difficult to objectively quantify and analyze, and are therefore frequently treated qualitatively.

Structured Interviews. Because researchers usually want more objective data, the **structured interview,** which uses quantitative fixed-format items, is most common. The questions are prepared ahead of time, and the interviewer reads the questions to the respondent. The structured interview has the advantage over an unstructured interview of allowing better comparisons of the responses across different individuals because the questions, time frame, and response format are controlled to be the same for each respondent.

Questionnaires

A **questionnaire** is a set of fixed-format, self-report items that is completed by respondents at their own pace, often without supervision. Questionnaires are generally cheaper than interviews because a researcher can mail the questionnaires to many people or have them complete the questionnaires in large groups. Questionnaires may also produce more honest responses than interviews, particularly when the questions involve sensitive issues such as sexual activity or annual income, because respondents are more likely to perceive their responses as being anonymous than they are in interviews and thus may be more likely to respond truthfully. In comparison to interviews, questionnaires are also likely to be less influenced by the characteristics of the experimenter. For instance, if the topic concerns race-related attitudes, how the respondent answers might depend on the race of the interviewer and how the respondent thinks the interviewer wants him or her to respond. Because the experimenter is not present when a questionnaire is completed, or at least is not directly asking the questions, such problems are less likely.

The Response Rate. Questionnaires are free of some problems that may occur in interviews, but they do have their own set of difficulties. Although people may be likely to return surveys that have direct relevance to them (for instance, a survey of college students conducted by their own university), when mailings are sent to the general population, the **response rate** (that is, the percentage of people who actually complete the questionnaire and return it to the investigator) may not be very high. This may lead to incorrect conclusions because the people who return the questionnaire may respond differently than those who don't return it would have. Investigators can sometimes increase response rates by providing gifts or monetary payments for completing the survey, by making the questionnaire appear brief and interesting, by ensuring the confidentiality of all of the data, and by emphasizing the importance of the individual in the research (Dillman, 1978). Follow-up mailings can also be used to remind people that they have not completed the questionnaire, with the hope that they will then do so.

Question Order. Another potential problem with questionnaires that does not occur with interviews is that people may not answer the questions in the order they are written, and the researcher does not know whether or not they have. To take one example, consider these two questions:

1. "How satisfied are you with your relationships with your family?"
2. "How satisfied are you with your relationship with your spouse?"

If the questions are answered in the order that they are presented here, then most respondents interpret the word *family* in question 1 to include their spouse. If question 2 is answered before question 1, however, the term *family* in question 1 is interpreted to mean the rest of the family except the spouse. Such variability can create measurement error (Schuman & Presser, 1981; Schwarz & Strack, 1991).

Use of Existing Survey Data

Because it is very expensive to conduct surveys, scientists often work together on them. For instance, a researcher may have a small number of questions relevant to his or her research included within a larger survey. Or researchers can access public-domain data sets that contain data from previous surveys. The U.S. Census is probably the largest such data set, containing information on family size, fertility, occupation, and income for the entire U.S. population, as well as a more extensive interview data set of a smaller group of citizens. The General Social Survey is a collection of over 1,000 items given to a sample of U.S. citizens (Davis, Smith, and Marsden, 2000). Because the same questions are asked each year the survey is given, comparisons can be made over time. Sometimes these data sets are given in comparable forms to citizens of different countries, allowing cross-cultural comparisons. One such data set is the Human Area Relations Files. Indexes of some of the most important social science databases can be found in Clubb, Austin, Geda, and Traugott (1985).

Sampling and Generalization

We have seen that surveys are conducted with the goal of creating an accurate picture of the current attitudes, beliefs, or behaviors of a large group of people. In some rare cases it is possible to conduct a **census**—that is, to measure each person about whom we wish to know. In most cases, however, the group of people that we want to learn about is so large that measuring each person is not practical. Thus the researcher must test some subset of the entire group of people who could have participated in the research. **Sampling** refers to the selection of people to participate in a research project, usually with the goal of being able to use these people to make inferences about a larger group of individuals. The entire group of people that the researcher desires to learn about is known as the **population,** and the smaller group of people who actually participate in the research is known as the **sample.**

Definition of the Population

The population of interest to the researcher must be defined precisely. For instance, some populations of interest to a survey researcher might be "all citizens of voting age in the United States who plan to vote in the next election," "all students currently enrolled full time at the University of Chicago," or "all Hispanic Americans over forty years of age who live within the Baltimore city limits." In most cases the scientist does not particularly care about the characteristics of the specific people chosen to be in the sample. Rather, the scientist uses the sample to draw inferences about the population as a whole (just as a medical researcher analyzes a sample to make inferences about blood that was not sampled).

Whenever samples are used to make inferences about populations, the researcher faces a basic dilemma—he or she will never be able to know *exactly* what the true characteristics of the population are because all of the members of the population cannot be contacted. However, this is not really as big a problem as it might seem if the sample can be assumed to be representative of the population. A **representative sample** is one that is approximately the same as the population in every important respect. For instance, a representative sample of the population of students at a college or university would contain about the same proportion of men, sophomores, and engineering majors as are in the college itself, as well as being roughly equivalent to the population on every other conceivable characteristic.

Probability Sampling

To make the sample representative of the population, any of several probability sampling techniques may be employed. In **probability sampling,** procedures are used to ensure that each person in the population has a known chance of being selected to be part of the sample. As a result, the likelihood that the sample is representative of the population is increased, as is the ability to use the sample to draw inferences about the population.

Simple Random Sampling. The most basic probability sample is drawn using **simple random sampling.** In this case the goal is to ensure that each person in the population has an *equal* chance of being selected to be in the sample. To draw a simple random sample, an investigator must first have a complete list (known as a **sampling frame**) of all of the people in the population. For instance, voting registration lists may be used as a sampling frame, or telephone numbers of all of the households in a given geographic location may be used. The latter list will basically represent the population that lives in that area because almost all U.S. households now have a telephone. (However, more and more people are using cell phones rather than land lines, and cell phone numbers are not normally listed in local phone directories; this has become a major headache for survey researchers.)

Then the investigator randomly selects from the frame a sample of a given number of people. Let's say you are interested in studying volunteering behavior of the students at your college or university, and you want to collect a random sample of 100 students. You would begin by finding a list of all of the students currently enrolled at the college. Assume that there are 7,000 names on this list, numbered sequentially from 1 to 7,000. Then, as shown in the instructions for using Statistical Table A (in Appendix E), you could use a random number table (or a random number generator on a computer) to produce 100 numbers that fall between 1 and 7,000 and select those 100 students to be in your sample.

Systematic Random Sampling. If the list of names on the sampling frame is itself known to be in a random sequence, then a probability sampling procedure known as **systematic random sampling** can be used. In your case, because you wish to draw a sample of 100 students from a population of 7,000 students, you will want to sample 1 out of every 70 students (100/7,000 = 1/70). To create the systematic sample, you first draw a random number between 1 and 70 and then sample the person on the list with that number. You create the rest of the sample by taking every seventieth person on the list after the initial person. For instance, if the first person sampled was number 32, you would then sample number 102, 172, and so on. You can see that it is easier to use systematic sampling than simple random sampling because only one initial number has to be chosen at random.

Stratified Sampling. Because in most cases sampling frames include such information about the population as sex, age, ethnicity, and region of residence, and because the variables being measured are frequently expected to differ across these subgroups, it is often useful to draw separate samples from each of these subgroups rather than to sample from the population as a whole. The subgroups are called **strata,** and the sampling procedure is known as **stratified sampling.**

To collect a *proportionate stratified sample,* frames of all of the people within each strata are first located, and random samples are drawn from within each of the strata. For example, if you expected that volunteering rates would be different for students from different majors, you could first make separate lists of the students in each of the majors at your school and then randomly sample from each list. One outcome of this procedure is that the different majors are guaranteed to be represented in the sample in the same proportion that they are represented in the population, a result that might not occur if you had used random sampling. Furthermore, it can be shown mathematically that if volunteering behavior does indeed differ among the strata, a stratified sample will provide a more precise estimate of the population characteristics than will a simple random sample (Kish, 1965).

Disproportionate stratified sampling is frequently used when the strata differ in size and the researcher is interested in comparing the characteristics of the strata. For instance, in a class of 7,000 students, only 10 or so might be French majors. If a random sample of 100 students was drawn, there might not be any French majors in the sample, or at least there would be too few to allow a researcher to draw meaningful conclusions about them. In this case the researcher draws a sample that includes a larger proportion of some strata than they are actually represented in the population. This procedure is called **oversampling** and is used to provide large enough samples of the strata of interest to allow analysis. Mathematical formulas are used to determine the optimum size for each of the strata.

Cluster Sampling.   Although simple and stratified sampling can be used to create representative samples when there is a complete sampling frame for the population, in some cases there is no such list. For instance, there is no single list of all of the currently matriculated college students in the United States. In these cases an alternative approach known as **cluster sampling** can be used. The technique is to break the population into a set of smaller groups (called *clusters*) for which there are sampling frames and then to randomly choose some of the clusters for inclusion in the sample. At this point every person in the cluster may be sampled, or a random sample of the cluster may be drawn.

Often the clustering is done in stages. For instance, we might first divide the United States into regions (for instance, East, Midwest, South, Southwest, and West). Then we would randomly select states from each region, counties from each state, and colleges or universities from each county. Because there is a sampling frame of the matriculated students at each of the selected colleges, we could draw a random sample from these lists. In addition to allowing a representative sample to be drawn when there is no sampling frame, cluster sampling is convenient. Once we have selected the clusters, we need only contact the students at the selected colleges rather than having to sample from all of the colleges and universities in the United States. In cluster sampling the selected clusters are used to draw inferences about the nonselected ones. Although this practice loses some precision, cluster sampling is frequently used because of convenience.

Sampling Bias and Nonprobability Sampling

The advantage of probability sampling methods is that their samples will be representative and thus can be used to draw inferences about the characteristics of the population. Although these procedures sound good in theory, in practice it is difficult to be certain that the sample is truly representative. Representativeness requires that two conditions be met. First, there must be one or more sampling frames that list the entire population of interest, and second, all of the selected individuals must actually be sampled. When either of these conditions is not met, there is the potential for **sampling bias.** This occurs when the sample is not actually representative of the population because the probability with which members of the population have been selected for participation is not known.

Sampling bias can arise when an accurate sampling frame for the population of interest cannot be obtained. In some cases there is an available sampling frame, but there is no guarantee that it is accurate. The sampling frame may be inaccurate because some members of the population are missing or because it includes some names that are not actually in the population. College student directories, for instance, frequently do not include new students or those who requested that their name not be listed, and these directories may also include students who have transferred or dropped out.

In other cases there simply is no sampling frame. Imagine attempting to obtain a frame that included all of the homeless people in New York City or all of the women in the United States who are currently pregnant with their first child. In cases where probability sampling is impossible because there is no available sampling frame, *nonprobability samples* must be used. To obtain a sample of homeless individuals, for instance, the researcher will interview individuals on the street or at a homeless shelter. One type of nonprobability sample that can be used when the population of interest is rare or difficult to reach is called **snowball sampling.** In this procedure one or more individuals from the population are contacted, and these individuals are used to lead the researcher to other population members. Such a technique might be used to locate homeless individuals. Of course, in such cases the potential for sampling bias is high because the people in the sample may be different from the people in the population. Snowball sampling at homeless shelters, for instance, may include a greater proportion of people who stay in shelters and a smaller proportion of people who do not stay in shelters than are in the population. This is a limitation of nonprobability sampling, but one that the researcher must live with because there is no possible probability sampling method that can be used.

Even if a complete sampling frame is available, sampling bias can occur if all members of the random sample cannot be contacted or cannot be convinced to participate in the survey. For instance, people may be on vacation, they may have moved to a different address, or they may not be willing to complete the questionnaire or interview. When a questionnaire is mailed, the response rate may be low. In each of these cases the potential for sampling bias exists because the people who completed the survey may have responded differently than would those who could not be contacted.

Nonprobability samples are also frequently found when college students are used in experimental research. Such samples are called **convenience samples** because the researcher has sampled whatever individuals were readily available without any attempt to make the sample representative of a population. Although such samples can be used to test research hypotheses, they may not be used to draw inferences about populations. We will discuss the use of convenience samples in experimental research designs more fully in Chapter 13.

Whenever you read a research report, make sure to determine what sampling procedures have been used to select the research participants. In some cases researchers make statements about populations on the basis of nonprobability samples, which are not likely to be representative of the population they are interested in. For instance, polls in which people are asked to call a 900 number or log on to a Web site to express their opinions on a given topic may contain sampling bias because people who are in favor of (or opposed to) the issue may have more time or more motivation to do so. Whenever the respondents, rather than the researchers, choose whether to be part of the sample, sampling bias is possible. The important thing is to remain aware of what sampling techniques have been used and to draw your own conclusions accordingly.

Summarizing the Sample Data

You can well imagine that once a survey has been completed, the collected data (known as the **raw data**) must be transformed in a way that will allow them to be meaningfully interpreted. The raw data are by themselves not very useful for gaining the desired snapshot because they contain too many numbers. For example, if we interview 500 people and ask each of them forty questions, there will be 20,000 responses to examine. In this section we will consider some of the statistical methods used to summarize sample data. Procedures for using computer software programs to conduct statistical analyses are reviewed in Appendix B, and you may want to read this material at this point.

Frequency Distributions

Table 6.1 presents some hypothetical raw data from twenty-five participants on five variables collected in a sort of "minisurvey." You can see that the table is arranged such that the variables (sex, ethnic background, age, life satisfaction, family income) are in the columns and the participants form the rows. For nominal variables such as sex or ethnicity, the data can be summarized through the use of a frequency distribution. A **frequency distribution** is a table that indicates how many, and in most cases what percentage, of in-

TABLE 6.1   Raw Data from a Sample of Twenty-five Individuals

ID	Sex	Ethnic Background	Age	Life Satisfaction	Family Income
1	Male	White	31	70	$ 28,000
2	Female	White	19	68	37,000
3	Male	Asian	34	78	43,000
4	Female	White	45	90	87,000
5	Female	African American	57	80	90,000
6	Male	Asian	26	75	43,000
7	Female	Hispanic	19	95	26,000
8	Female	White	33	91	64,000
9	Male	Hispanic	18	74	18,000
10	Female	Asian	20	10	29,000
11	Male	African American	47	90	53,000
12	Female	White	45	82	2,800,000
13	Female	Asian	63	98	87,000
14	Female	Hispanic	37	95	44,000
15	Female	Asian	38	85	47,000
16	Male	White	24	80	31,000
17	Male	White	18	60	28,000
18	Male	Asian	40	33	43,000
19	Female	White	29	96	87,000
20	Female	African American	31	80	90,000
21	Female	Hispanic	25	95	26,000
22	Female	White	32	99	64,000
23	Male	Hispanic	33	34	53,000
24	Male	Asian	22	55	43,000
25	Female	White	52	41	37,000

This table represents the raw data from twenty-five individuals who have completed a hypothetical survey. The individuals are given an identification number, indicated in column 1. The data represent the sex, ethnicity, age, and rated life satisfaction of the respondents, as well as their family income. The life satisfaction measure is a Likert scale that ranges from 0 = "not at all satisifed" to 100 = "extremely satisfied."

dividuals in the sample fall into each of a set of categories. A frequency distribution of the ethnicity variable from Table 6.1 is shown in Figure 6.1(a). The frequency distribution can be displayed visually in a **bar chart,** as shown for the ethnic background variable in Figure 6.1(b). The characteristics of the

FIGURE 6.1   Frequency Distribution and Bar Chart

(a) *Frequency Distribution*

Ethnic Background	Frequency Distribution	Percent
African American	3	12
Asian	7	28*
Hispanic	5*	20
White	10	40
Total	25	100

*Twenty-eight percent of the sample are Asians, and there are five Hispanics in the sample.

(b) *Bar Chart*

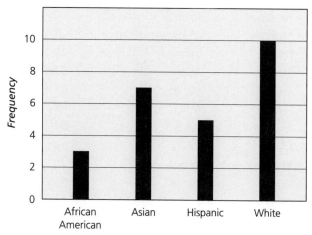

Ethnicity of respondent

The above figure presents a frequency distribution and a bar chart of the ethnicity variable from Table 6.1.

sample are easily seen when summarized through a frequency distribution or a bar chart.

One approach to summarizing a quantitative variable is to combine adjacent values into a set of categories and then to examine the frequencies of each of the categories. The resulting distribution is known as a **grouped frequency distribution.** A grouped frequency distribution of the age variable from Table 6.1 is shown in Figure 6.2(a). In this case the ages have been grouped into five categories (less than 21, 21–30, 31–40, 41–50, and greater than 50).

The grouped frequency distribution may be displayed visually in the form of a histogram, as shown in Figure 6.2(b). A **histogram** is slightly different

FIGURE 6.2   Grouped Frequency Distribution, Histogram, and Frequency Curve

(a) *Grouped Frequency Distribution*

Age	Frequency Distribution	Percent
Less than 21	5	20*
21–30	5	20
31–40	9	36
41–50	3*	12
Greater than 50	3	12
Total	25	100

*Twenty percent of the sample have not reached their twenty-first birthday, and three people in the sample are 41, 42, 43, 44, 45, 46, 47, 48, 49, or 50 years old.

(b) *Histogram*

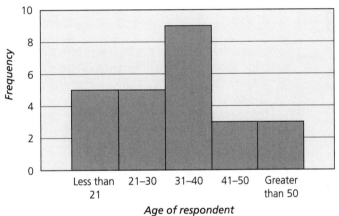

(c) *Frequency Curve*

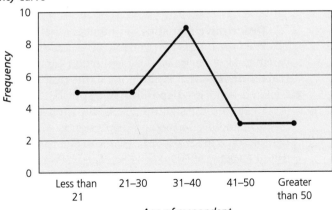

The above presents a grouped frequency distribution, a histogram, and a frequency curve of the age variable from Table 6.1.

FIGURE 6.3 Stem and Leaf Plot

Age	
Stem	Leaves
10	8899
20	024569
30	11233478
40	0557
50	27
60	3

This is a stem and leaf plot of the age variable from Table 6.1. The stems on the left represent the 10s place, and the leaves on the right represent the units place. You can see from the plot that there are twenty-five individuals in the sampling, ranging from two who are eighteen years old to one who is sixty-three years old.

from a bar chart because the bars are drawn so that they touch each other. This indicates that the original variable is quantitative. If the frequencies of the groups are indicated with a line, rather than bars, as shown in Figure 6.2(c), the display is called a **frequency curve.**

One limitation of grouped frequency distributions is that grouping the values together into categories results in the loss of some information. For instance, it is not possible to tell from the grouped frequency distribution in Figure 6.2(a) exactly how many people in the sample are twenty-three years old. A **stem and leaf plot** is a method of graphically summarizing the raw data such that the original data values can still be seen. A stem and leaf plot of the age variable from Table 6.1 is shown in Figure 6.3.

Descriptive Statistics

Descriptive statistics are numbers that summarize the pattern of scores observed on a measured variable. This pattern is called the *distribution* of the variable. Most basically, the distribution can be described in terms of its **central tendency**—that is, the point in the distribution around which the data are centered—and its **dispersion,** or spread. As we will see, central tendency is summarized through the use of descriptive statistics such as the *mean,* the *median,* and the *mode,* and dispersion is summarized through the use of the *variance* and the *standard deviation.* Figure 6.4 shows a printout from the Statistical Package for the Social Sciences (SPSS) software of the descriptive statistics for the quantitative variables in Table 6.1.

Measures of Central Tendency. The arithmetic average, or **arithmetic mean,** is the most commonly used measure of central tendency. It is computed by summing all of the scores on the variable and dividing this sum by

FIGURE 6.4   SPSS Printout of Descriptive Statistics

Descriptive Statistics

	N	Minimum	Maximum	Mean	Std. Deviation
NUMBER	25	1.00	25.00	13.0000	7.35980
AGE	25	18.00	63.00	33.5200	12.51040
SATIS	25	10.00	99.00	74.1600	23.44618
INCOME	25	18000.00	2800000	159920.0	550480.16313
Valid N (listwise)	25				

the number of participants in the distribution (denoted by the letter N). The sample mean is sometimes denoted with the symbol $\bar{x}$, read as "X-Bar," and may also be indicated by the letter M. As you can see in Figure 6.4, in our sample the mean age of the twenty-five students is 33.52. In this case the mean provides an accurate index of the central tendency of the age variable because if you look at the stem and leaf plot in Figure 6.3, you can see that most of the ages are centered at about thirty-three.

The pattern of scores observed on a measured variable is known as the variable's **distribution.** It turns out that most quantitative variables have distributions similar to that shown in Figure 6.5(a). Most of the data are located near the center of the distribution, and the distribution is symmetrical and bell-shaped. Data distributions that are shaped like a bell are known as **normal distributions.**

In some cases, however, the data distribution is not symmetrical. This occurs when there are one or more extreme scores (they are known as **outliers**) at one end of the distribution. For instance, because there is an outlier in the-family income variable in Table 6.1 (a value of $2,800,000), a frequency curve of this variable would look more like that shown in Figure 6.5(b) than that shown in Figure 6.5(a). Distributions that are not symmetrical are said to be **skewed.** As shown in Figure 6.5(b) and (c), distributions are said to be either *positively* skewed or *negatively* skewed, depending on where the outliers fall.

Because the mean is highly influenced by the presence of outliers, it is not a good measure of central tendency when the distribution is highly skewed. For instance, although it appears from Table 6.1 that the central tendency of the family income variable should be around $40,000, the mean family income is actually $159,920. The single very extreme income has a disproportionate impact on the mean, resulting in a value that does not well represent the central tendency.

The median is used as an alternative measure of central tendency when distributions are skewed. The **median** is the score in the center of the distribution, meaning that 50 percent of the scores are greater than the median and 50 percent of the scores are lower than the median. Methods for calculating the median are presented in Appendix B. In our case the median household

FIGURE 6.5 Shapes of Distributions

(a) *Normal Distribution*

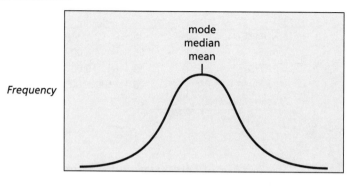

(b) *Positive Skew*

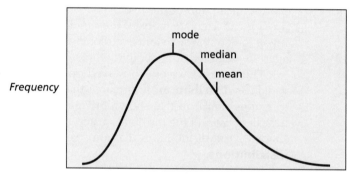

(c) *Negative Skew*

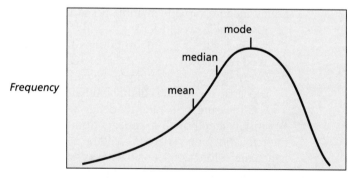

The mean, the median, and the mode are three measures of central tendency. In a normal distribution (a), all three measures fall at the same point on the distribution. When outliers are present, however, the distribution is no longer symmetrical, but becomes skewed. If the outliers are on the right side of the distribution (b), the distribution is considered positively skewed. If the outliers are on the left side of the distribution (c), the distribution is considered negatively skewed. Because the mean is more influenced by the presence of outliers, it falls nearer the outliers in a skewed distribution than does the median. The mode always falls at the most frequently occurring value (the top of the frequency curve.)

income ($43,000) is a much better indication of central tendency than is the mean household income ($159,920).

A final measure of central tendency, known as the **mode,** represents the value that occurs most frequently in the distribution. You can see from Table 6.1 that the modal value for the income variable is $43,000 (it occurs four times). In some cases there can be more than one mode. For instance, the age variable has modes at 18, 19, 31, 33, and 45. Although the mode does represent central tendency, it is not frequently used in scientific research. The relationships among the mean, the median, and the mode are described in Figure 6.5.

Measures of Dispersion.   In addition to summarizing the central tendency of a distribution, descriptive statistics convey information about how the scores on the variable are spread around the central tendency. *Dispersion* refers to the extent to which the scores are all tightly clustered around the central tendency, like this:

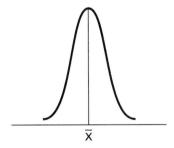

or are more spread out away from it, like this:

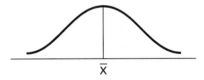

One simple measure of dispersion is to find the largest (the maximum) and the smallest (the minimum) observed values of the variable and to compute the **range** of the variable as the maximum observed score minus the minimum observed score. You can check that the range of the age variable is $63 - 18 = 45$.

The standard deviation, symbolized as s, is the most commonly used measure of dispersion. As discussed in more detail in Appendix B, computation of the standard deviation begins with the calculation of a mean deviation score for each individual. The **mean deviation** is the score on the variable minus the mean of the variable. Individuals who score above the mean have positive deviation scores, whereas those who score below the mean have negative deviation scores. The mean deviations are squared and summed to produce a statistic called the sum of squared deviations, or **sum of squares.** The sum of squares is divided by the sample size (N) to produce a statistic known as the **variance,** symbolized as s^2. The square root of the variance is the **standard deviation, s.** Distributions with a larger standard deviation have more spread. As you can see from Figure 6.4, the standard deviation of the age variable in Table 6.1 is 12.51.

Sample Size and the Margin of Error

To this point we have discussed the use of descriptive statistics to summarize the raw data in the sample. But recall that the goal of descriptive research is normally to use the sample to provide estimates about characteristics of the population from which it has been selected. We have seen that the ability to use the sample to accurately estimate the population requires that the sample be representative of the population and that this is ensured through the use of probability sampling techniques. But the extent to which the sample provides an accurate estimate of the population of interest is also determined by the size of the sample (N). Increasing the size of a sample makes it more likely that the sample will be representative of the population and thus provides more precise estimates of population characteristics.

Because of random error, the sample characteristics will most likely not be exactly the same as the population characteristics that we wish to estimate. It is, however, possible to use statistical theory to create a **confidence interval** within which we can say with some certainty that a population value is likely to fall. The procedures for creating and interpreting confidence intervals are discussed in detail in Appendix B. The confidence interval is frequently known as the **margin of error** of the sample. For instance, in Table 1.1 you can see that the margin of error of the survey is listed as "plus or minus three percentage points." In this case the margin of error is interpreted as indicating that the true value of the population will fall between the listed value minus three points and the listed value plus three points 95 percent of the time.

One very surprising fact about sampling is that, although larger samples provide more precise estimates of the population, the size of the population being estimated does not matter very much. In fact, a probability sample of 1,000 people can provide just as good an estimate for the population of the United States as can a sample of 1,000 from a small town of 20,000 people. If you are not familiar with sampling methods, you may believe that small samples cannot tell us anything about larger populations. For instance, you might think that a sample of 1,000 people cannot possibly provide a good estimate of the attitudes of the 250 million people in the United States because it represents only a very small proportion (about four one-thousandths of one percent) of the population. In fact, a carefully collected probability sample of 1,000 people can provide an extremely precise estimate of the attitudes of the U.S. population, and such small samples are routinely used to predict the outcome of national elections. Of course, probability samples are subject to many of the same problems that affect measurement more generally, including random error, reactivity, and construct invalidity. Furthermore, the results of a survey show only what people think today—they may change their mind tomorrow. Thus, although probability sampling methods are highly accurate overall, they do not guarantee accurate results.

SUMMARY

Surveys are self-report descriptive research designs that attempt to capture the current opinions, attitudes, or behaviors of a group of people. Surveys can use either unstructured or structured formats and can be administered in the form of in-person or telephone interviews or as written questionnaires.

Surveys are designed to draw conclusions about a population of individuals, but because it is not possible to measure each person in the population, data are collected from a smaller sample of people drawn from the population. This procedure is known as sampling.

Probability sampling techniques, including simple random sampling, systematic random sampling, stratified sampling, and cluster sampling, are used to ensure that the sample is representative of the population, thus allowing the researcher to use the sample to draw conclusions about the population.

When nonprobability sampling techniques are used, either because they are convenient or because probability methods are not feasible, they are subject to sampling bias, and they cannot be used to generalize from the sample to the population.

The raw data from a survey are summarized through frequency distributions and descriptive statistics. The distribution of a variable is summarized in terms of its central tendency using the mean, the mode, or the median, as well as its dispersion, summarized in terms of the variance and standard deviation.

The extent to which the sample provides an accurate picture of the population depends to a great extent on the sample size (N). In general, larger samples will produce a more accurate picture and thus have a lower margin of error.

KEY TERMS

arithmetic mean 116
bar chart 113
census 108
central tendency 116
cluster sampling 110
confidence interval 120
convenience samples 112
descriptive statistics 116
dispersion 116

distribution 117
focus group 106
frequency curve 116
frequency distribution 112
grouped frequency distribution 114
histogram 114
interview 105
margin of error 120
mean deviation 119

REVIEW AND DISCUSSION QUESTIONS

1. Compare the advantages and disadvantages of using interviews versus questionnaires in survey research.

2. Compare a sample and a population. Under what circumstances can a sample be used to draw conclusions about a population?

3. Compare and contrast the different types of probability sampling techniques.

4. When and why would nonprobability sampling methods be used?

5. Under what conditions is sampling bias likely to occur, what are its effects on generalization, and how can it be avoided?

6. Indicate the similarities and differences among the mean, the median, and the mode.

7. What is the standard deviation, and what does it represent?

HANDS-ON EXPERIENCE

1. Develop a topic of interest to you, and prepare both a structured and an unstructured interview. Collect data from your classmates, and develop a method for coding the findings.

2. Create a sampling frame, and collect a random or stratified random sample of the male and female students in your class.

3. A poll conducted by the *New York Times* shows candidate A leading candidate B by 33 to 31 percent. A poll conducted by the *Washington Post* shows candidate B leading candidate A by 34 to 32 percent. If the margin of error

of each poll is plus or minus 3 percent, what should be concluded about the polls and about the public's preferences for the two candidates?

4. Gain access to a public-domain survey data set such as the Human Area Relations Files or the General Social Survey. Ask your instructor for information about doing so, or look at the Web site *www.Icpsr.umich.edu,* which has a collection of public-domain surveys. Make some predictions about the types of data distributions that you would expect to find, and then test whether they are actually found.

5. Answer questions 1 to 7 in Appendix B.

CHAPTER SEVEN
Naturalistic Methods

STUDY QUESTIONS

- What is naturalistic research, and why is it important?

- What is ecological validity, and why do naturalistic research designs have it?

- What are the advantages and disadvantages of being an acknowledged or unacknowledged participant or observer in observational research?

- What are case studies? What are their benefits and drawbacks?

- How are behaviors systematically coded to assess their reliability and validity?

- What is archival research, and what types of questions can it be used to answer?

As we have seen in Chapter 6, self-report measures have the advantage of allowing the researcher to collect a large amount of information from the respondents quickly and easily. On the other hand, they also have the potential of being inaccurate if the respondent does not have access to, or is unwilling to express, his or her true beliefs. And we have seen in Chapter 4 that behavioral measures have the advantage of being more natural and thus less influenced by reactivity. In this chapter we discuss descriptive research that uses behavioral measures. Keep in mind as you read the chapter that, as with most descriptive research, the goal is usually not to test research hypotheses, but rather to develop ideas for topics that can be studied later using other types of research designs. However, as with survey research, naturalistic methods can also be used to create measured variables for use in correlational and experimental tests of research hypotheses.

Naturalistic Research

Naturalistic research is designed to describe and measure the behavior of people or animals as it occurs in their everyday lives. The behavior may be measured as it occurs, or it could already have been recorded by others, or it may be recorded on videotape to be coded at a later time. In any case, however, because it involves the observation of everyday behavior, a basic difficulty results—the rich and complex data that are observed must be organized into meaningful measured variables that can be analyzed. One of the goals of this chapter is to review methods for turning observed everyday behavior into measured variables.

Naturalistic research approaches are used by researchers in a variety of disciplines, and the data that form the basis of naturalistic research methods can be gathered from many different sources in many different ways. These range from a clinical psychologist's informal observations of his or her clients, to another scientist's more formal observations of the behaviors of animals in the wild, to an analysis of politicians' speeches, to a videotaping of children playing with their parents in a laboratory setting. Although these approaches frequently involve qualitative data, there are also techniques for turning observations into quantitative data, and we will discuss both types in this chapter.

In many cases naturalistic research is the only possible approach to collecting data. For instance, while researchers may not be able to study the impact of earthquakes, floods, or cult membership using experimental research designs, they may be able to use naturalistic research designs to collect a wide variety of data that can be useful in understanding such phenomena.

One particular advantage of naturalistic research is that it has **ecological validity.** *Ecological validity* refers to the extent to which the research is conducted in situations that are similar to the everyday life experiences of the participants (Aronson & Carlsmith, 1968). In naturalistic research the people whose behavior is being measured are doing the things they do every day, and in some cases they may not even know that their behavior is being recorded.

In these cases reactivity is minimized and the construct validity of the measures should therefore be increased.

Observational Research

Observational research involves making observations of behavior and recording those observations in an objective manner. The observational approach is the oldest method of conducting research and is used routinely in psychology, anthropology, sociology, and many other fields.

Let's consider an observational study. To observe the behavior of individuals at work, industrial psychologist Roy (1959–1960) took a job in a factory where raincoats were made. The job entailed boring, repetitive movements (punching holes in plastic sheets using large stamping machines) and went on eight hours a day, five days a week. There was nothing at all interesting about the job, and Roy was uncertain how the employees, some of whom had been there for many years, could stand the monotony.

In his first few days on the job Roy did not notice anything particularly unusual. However, as he carefully observed the activities of the other employees over time, he began to discover that they had a series of "pranks" that they played on and with each other. For instance, every time "Sammy" went to the drinking fountain, "Ike" turned off the power on "Sammy's" machine. And whenever "Sammy" returned, he tried to stamp a piece before "discovering" that the power had been turned off. He then acted angrily toward "Ike," who in turn responded with a shrug and a smirk.

In addition to this event, which occurred several times a day, Roy also noted many other games that the workers effectively used to break up the day. At 11:00 "Sammy" would yell, "Banana time!" and steal the banana out of "Ike's" lunch pail, which was sitting on a shelf. Later in the morning "Ike" would open the window in front of "Sammy's" machine, letting in freezing cold air. "Sammy" would protest and close the window. At the end of the day, "Sammy" would quit two minutes early, drawing fire from the employees' boss, who nevertheless let the activity occur day after day.

Although Roy entered the factory expecting to find only a limited set of mundane observations, he actually discovered a whole world of regular, complicated, and, to the employees, satisfying activities that broke up the monotony of their everyday work existence. This represents one of the major advantages of naturalistic research methods. Because the data are rich, they can be an important source of ideas.

In this example, because the researcher was working at a stamping machine and interacting with the other employees, he was himself a *participant* in the setting being observed. When a scientist takes a job in a factory, joins a religious cult (Festinger, Riecken, & Schachter, 1956), or checks into a mental institution (Rosenhan, 1973), he or she becomes part of the setting itself. Other times, the scientist may choose to remain strictly an *observer* of the setting, such as when he or she views children in a classroom from a corner without

TABLE 7.1 Participation and Acknowledgment in Observational Research

Approach	Example	Advantages and Disadvantages
Acknowledged participant	Whythe's (1993) study of "street corner society"	Ethically appropriate, but might have been biased by friendships; potential for reactivity
Acknowledged observer	Pomerantz et al.'s (1995) study of children's social comparison	Researchers able to spend entire session coding behaviors, but potential for reactivity since children knew they were being watched
Unacknowledged participant	Roy's (1959–1960) observations in the raincoat factory	Chance to get intimate information from workers, but researcher may change the situation; poses ethical questions
Unacknowledged observer	Recording the behaviors of people in a small town	Limits reactivity problems, but poses ethical questions

When conducting naturalistic observation, scientists may be either acknowledged or unacknowledged and may either participate in the ongoing activity or remain passive observers of the activity. The result is four possible approaches to naturalistic research. Which approach is best for a given project must be determined by the costs and benefits of each decision.

playing with them, watches employees in a factory from behind a one-way mirror, or observes behavior in a public restroom (Humphreys, 1975).

In addition to deciding whether to be a participant, the researcher must also decide whether to let the people being observed know that the observation is occurring—that is, to be *acknowledged* or *unacknowledged* to the population being studied. Because the decision about whether to be participant or nonparticipant can be independent of the decision to be acknowledged or unacknowledged, there are, as shown in Table 7.1, altogether four possible types of observational research designs. There are advantages and disadvantages to each approach, and the choice of which to use will be based on the goals of the research, the ability to obtain access to the population, and ethical principles.

The Unacknowledged Participant

Perhaps the most commonly used approach is that of the unacknowledged participant. When an observer takes a job in a factory, as Roy did, or infiltrates the life of the homeless in a city, without letting the people being observed know about it, the observer has the advantage of concealment. As a result, she or he may be able to get close to the people being observed and may get them to reveal personal or intimate information about themselves and their social situation, such as their true feelings about their employers or their reactions to being on the street. The unacknowledged participant, then, has the best chance of really "getting to know" the people being observed.

Of course, becoming too close to the people being studied may have negative effects as well. For one thing, the researcher may have difficulty remaining objective. The observer who learns people's names, hears intimate accounts of their lives, and becomes a friend may find his or her perception shaped more by their point of view than by a more objective, scientific one. Alternatively, the observer may dislike the people whom he or she is observing, which may create a negative bias in subsequent analysis and reporting of the data.

The use of an unacknowledged participant strategy also poses ethical dilemmas for the researcher. For one thing, the people being observed may never be told that they were part of a research project or may find it out only later. This may not be a great problem when the observation is conducted in a public arena, such as a bar or a city park, but the problem may be greater when the observation is in a setting where people might later be identified, with potential negative consequences to them. For instance, if a researcher takes a job in a factory and then writes a research report concerning the true feelings of the employees about their employers, management may be able to identify the individual workers from these descriptions.

Another disadvantage of the unacknowledged participant approach is that the activities of the observer may influence the process being observed. This may happen, for instance, when an unacknowledged participant is asked by the group to contribute to a group decision. Saying nothing would "blow one's cover," but making substantive comments would change the nature of the group itself. Often the participant researcher will want to query the people being observed in order to gain more information about why certain behaviors are occurring. Although these questions can reveal the underlying nature of the social setting, they may also alter the situation itself.

The Acknowledged Participant

In cases where the researcher feels that it is unethical or impossible to hide his or her identity as a scientist, the acknowledged participant approach can be used. Sociologist W. F. Whyte (1993) used this approach in his classic sociological study of "street corner society." Over a period of a year, Whyte got to know the people in, and made extensive observations of, a neighborhood in a New England town. He did not attempt to hide his identity. Rather, he announced freely that he was a scientist and that he would be recording the behavior of the individuals he observed. Sometimes this approach is necessary, for instance, when the behavior the researcher wants to observe is difficult to gain access to. To observe behavior in a corporate boardroom or school classroom, the researcher may have to gain official permission, which may require acknowledging the research to those being observed.

The largest problem of being acknowledged is reactivity. Knowing that the observer is recording information may cause people to change their speech and behavior, limit what they are willing to discuss, or avoid the researcher altogether. Often, however, once the observer has spent some time with the population of interest, people tend to treat him or her as a real member of the group. This happened to Whyte. In such situations the scientist may let this habituation occur over a period of time before beginning to record observations.

Acknowledged and Unacknowledged Observers

The researcher may use a nonparticipant approach when he or she does not want to or cannot be a participant of the group being studied. In these cases the researcher observes the behavior of interest without actively participating in the ongoing action. This occurs, for instance, when children are observed in a classroom from behind a one-way mirror or when clinical psychologists videotape group therapy sessions for later analysis. One advantage of not being part of the group is that the researcher may be more objective because he or she does not develop close relationships with the people being observed. Being out of the action also leaves the observer more time to do the job he or she came for—watching other people and recording relevant data. The nonparticipant observer is relieved of the burdensome role of acting like a participant and maintaining a "cover," activities that may take substantial effort.

The nonparticipant observer may be either acknowledged or unacknowledged. Again, there are pros and cons to each, and these generally parallel the issues involved with the participant observer. Being acknowledged can create reactivity, whereas being unacknowledged may be unethical if it violates the confidentiality of the data. These issues must be considered carefully, with the researcher reviewing the pros and cons of each approach before beginning the project.

Case Studies

Whereas observational research generally assesses the behavior of a relatively large group of people, sometimes the data are based on only a small set of individuals, perhaps only one or two. These qualitative research designs are known as **case studies**—descriptive records of one or more individual's experiences and behavior. Sometimes case studies involve normal individuals, as when developmental psychologist Jean Piaget (1952) used observation of his own children to develop a stage theory of cognitive development. More frequently, case studies are conducted on individuals who have unusual or abnormal experiences or characteristics or who are going through particularly difficult or stressful situations. The assumption is that by carefully studying individuals who are socially marginal, who are experiencing a unique situation, or who are going through a difficult phase in their life, we can learn something about human nature.

Sigmund Freud was a master of using the psychological difficulties of individuals to draw conclusions about basic psychological processes. One classic example is Freud's case study and treatment of "Little Hans," a child whose fear of horses the psychoanalyst interpreted in terms of repressed sexual impulses

(1959). Freud wrote case studies of some of his most interesting patients and used these careful examinations to develop his important theories of personality.

Scientists also use case studies to investigate the neurological bases of behavior. In animals scientists can study the functions of a certain section of the brain by removing that part. If removing part of the brain prevents the animal from performing a certain behavior (such as learning to locate a food tray in a maze), then the inference can be drawn that the memory was stored in the removed part of the brain. It is obviously not possible to treat humans in the same manner, but brain damage sometimes occurs in people for other reasons. "Split-brain" patients (Sperry, 1982) are individuals who have had the two hemispheres of their brains surgically separated in an attempt to prevent severe epileptic seizures. Study of the behavior of these unique individuals has provided important information about the functions of the two brain hemispheres in humans. In other individuals certain brain parts may be destroyed through disease or accident. One well-known case study is Phineas Gage, a man who was extensively studied by cognitive psychologists after he had a railroad spike blasted through his skull in an accident. An interesting example of a case study in clinical psychology is described by Rokeach (1964), who investigated in detail the beliefs and interactions among three schizophrenics, all of whom were convinced they were Jesus Christ.

One problem with case studies is that they are based on the experiences of only a very limited number of normally quite unusual individuals. Although descriptions of individual experiences may be extremely interesting, they cannot usually tell us much about whether the same things would happen to other individuals in similar situations or exactly why these specific reactions to these events occurred. For instance, descriptions of individuals who have been in a stressful situation such as a war or an earthquake can be used to understand how they reacted during such a situation but cannot tell us what particular long-term effects the situation had on them. Because there is no comparison group that did not experience the stressful situation, we cannot know what these individuals would be like if they hadn't had the experience. As a result, case studies provide only weak support for the drawing of scientific conclusions. They may, however, be useful for providing ideas for future, more controlled research.

Systematic Coding Methods

You have probably noticed by now that although observational research and case studies can provide a detailed look at ongoing behavior, since they represent qualitative data they may often not be as objective as one might like, especially when they are based on recordings by a single scientist. Because the observer has chosen which people to study, which behaviors to record or ignore, and how to interpret those behaviors, she or he may be more likely to see (or at least to report) those observations that confirm, rather than disconfirm, her or his expectations. Furthermore, the collected data may be relatively sketchy, in the form of "field notes" or brief reports, and thus not amenable to assessment of their reliability or validity. However, in many cases these problems can be overcome by using systematic observation to create quantitative measured variables (Bakeman & Gottman, 1986; Weick, 1985).

Deciding What to Observe

Systematic observation involves specifying ahead of time exactly which observations are to be made on which people and in which times and places. These decisions are made on the basis of theoretical expectation about the types of events that are going to be of interest. Specificity about the behaviors of interest has the advantage of both focusing the observers' attention on these specific behaviors and reducing the masses of data that might be collected if the observers attempted to record everything they saw. Furthermore, in many cases more than one observer can make the observations, and, as we have discussed in Chapter 5, this will increase the reliability of the measures.

Consider, for instance, a research team interested in assessing how and when young children compare their own performance with that of their classmates (Pomerantz et al., 1995). In this study one or two adult observers sat in chairs adjacent to work areas in the classrooms of elementary school children and recorded in laptop computers the behaviors of the children. Before beginning the project, the researchers had defined a specific set of **behavioral categories** for use by the observers. These categories were based on theoretical predictions of what would occur for these children and defined exactly what behaviors were to be coded, how to determine when those behaviors were occurring, and how to code them into the computer.

Deciding How to Record Observations

Before beginning to code the behaviors, the observers spent three or four days in the classroom learning, practicing, and revising the coding methods and letting the children get used to their presence. Because the coding categories were so well defined, there was good interrater reliability. And to be certain that the judges remained reliable, the experimenters frequently computed a reliability analysis on the codings over the time that the observations were being made. This is particularly important since there are some behaviors that occur infrequently, and it is important to be sure that they are being coded reliably.

Over the course of each observation period, several types of data were collected. For one, the observers coded *event frequencies*—for instance, the number of verbal statements that indicated social comparison. These included both statements about one's own performance ("My picture is the best") and questions about the performance of others ("How many did you get wrong?"). In addition, the observers also coded *event duration*—for instance, the amount of time that the child was attending to the work of others. Finally, all the children were interviewed after the observation had ended.

Choosing Sampling Strategies

One of the difficulties in coding ongoing behavior is that there is so much of it. Pomerantz et al. used three basic sampling strategies to reduce the amount of data they needed to record. First, as we have already seen, they used **event sampling**—focusing in on specific behaviors that were theoretically related to social comparison. Second, they employed **individual sampling.** Rather than trying to record the behaviors of all of the children at the same time, the observers randomly selected one child to be the focus child for an observational period. The observers zeroed in on this child, while ignoring the behavior of others during the time period. Over the entire period of the study, however, each child was observed. Finally, Pomerantz and colleagues employed **time sampling.** Each observer focused on a single child for only four minutes before moving on to another child. In this case the data were coded as they were observed, but in some cases the observer might use the time periods between observations to record the responses. Although sampling only some of the events of interest may lose some information, the events that are attended to can be more precisely recorded.

FIGURE 7.1 Strange Situation Coding Sheet

Coder name _____ Olive _____

Episode	Coding Categories			
	Proximity	Contact	Resistance	Avoidance
Mother and baby play alone	1	1	1	1
Mother puts baby down	4	1	1	1
Stranger enters room	1	2	3	1
Mother leaves room, stranger plays with baby	1	3	1	1
Mother reenters, greets and may comfort baby, then leaves again	4	2	1	2
Stranger tries to play with baby	1	3	1	1
Mother reenters and picks up baby	6	6	1	2

The coding categories are:

Proximity. The baby moves toward, grasps, or climbs on the adult.
Maintaining Contact. The baby resists being put down by the adult by crying or trying to climb back up.
Resistance. The baby pushes, hits, or squirms to be put down from the adult's arms.
Avoidance. The baby turns away or moves away from the adult.

This figure represents a sample coding sheet from an episode of the "strange situation," in which an infant (usually about 1 year old) is observed playing in a room with two adults—the child's mother and a stranger. Each of the four coding categories is scored by the coder from 1 = The baby makes no effort to engage in the behavior to 7 = The baby makes an extreme effort to engage in the behavior. The coding is usually made from videotapes and more than one coder rates the behaviors to allow calculating interrater reliability. More information about the meaning of the coding can be found in Ainsworth, Blehar, Waters, and Wall (1978).

The data of the observers were then uploaded from the laptop computers for analysis. Using these measures, Pomerantz et al. found, among other things, that older children used subtler social comparison strategies and increasingly saw such behavior as boastful or unfair. These data have high ecological validity, and yet their reliability and validity are well established. Another example of a coding scheme for naturalistic research, also using children, is shown in Figure 7.1.

Archival Research

As you will recall, one of the great advantages of naturalistic methods is that there are so many data available to be studied. One approach that takes full advantage of this situation is **archival research,** which is based on an analysis of any type of existing records of public behavior. These records might include newspaper articles, speeches and letters of public figures, television and radio broadcasts, or existing surveys. Because there are so many records that can be examined, the use of archival records is limited only by the researcher's imagination.

Records that have been used in past behavioral research include the trash in a landfill, patterns of graffiti, wear and tear on floors in museums, litter, and dirt on the pages of library books (see Webb et al., 1981, for examples). Archival researchers have found that crimes increase during hotter weather (Anderson, 1989); that earlier-born children live somewhat longer than later-borns (Modin 2002); and that gender and racial stereotypes are prevalent in current television shows (Greenberg, 1980) and in magazines (Sullivan & O'Connor, 1988).

One of the classic archival research projects is the sociological study of the causes of suicide by sociologist Emile Durkheim (1951). Durkheim used records of people who had committed suicide in seven European countries between 1841 and 1872 for his data. These records indicated, for instance, that suicide was more prevalent on weekdays than on weekends, among those who were not married, and in the summer months. From these data, Durkheim drew the conclusion that alienation from others was the primary cause of suicide. Durkheim's resourcefulness in collecting data and his ability to use the data to draw conclusions about the causes of suicide are remarkable.

Because archival records contain a huge amount of information, they must also be systematically coded. This is done through a technique known as **content analysis.** Content analysis is essentially the same as systematic coding of observational data and includes the specification of coding categories and the use of more than one rater. In one interesting example of an archival research project, Simonton (1988) located and analyzed biographies of U.S. presidents. He had seven undergraduate students rate each of the biographies on a number of predefined coding categories, including "was cautious and conservative in action," "was charismatic," and "valued personal loyalty." The interrater reliability of the coders was assessed and found to be adequate.

Simonton then averaged the ratings of the seven coders and used the data to draw conclusions about the personalities and behaviors of the presidents. For instance, he found that "charismatic" presidents were motivated by achievement and power and were more active and accomplished more while in office. Although Simonton used biographies as his source of information, he could, of course, have employed presidential speeches, information on how and where the speeches were delivered, or material on the types of appointments the presidents made, among other records.

SUMMARY

Naturalistic research designs involve the study of everyday behavior through the use of both observational and archival data. In many cases a large amount of information can be collected very quickly using naturalistic approaches, and this information can provide basic knowledge about the phenomena of interest as well as provide ideas for future research.

Naturalistic data have high ecological validity because they involve people in their everyday lives. However, although the data can be rich and colorful, naturalistic research often does not provide much information about why behavior occurs or what would have happened to the same people in different situations.

Observational research can involve either participant or nonparticipant observers, who are either acknowledged or unacknowledged to the individuals being observed. Which approach an observer uses depends on considerations of ethics and practicality. A case study is an investigation of a single individual in which unusual, unexpected, or unexplained behaviors become the focus of the research. Archival research uses existing records of public behavior as data.

Conclusions can be drawn from naturalistic data when they have been systematically collected and coded. In observational research various sampling techniques are used to focus in on the data of interest. In archival research the data are coded through content analysis. In systematic observation and content coding the reliability and validity of the measures are enhanced by having more than one trained researcher make the ratings.

KEY TERMS

archival research 133
behavioral categories 131
case studies 129
content analysis 133
ecological validity 125
event sampling 132

individual sampling 132
naturalistic research 125
observational research 126
systematic observation 131
time sampling 132

REVIEW AND DISCUSSION QUESTIONS

1. Discuss the situations in which a researcher may choose to use a naturalistic research approach and the questions such an approach can and cannot answer.

2. Consider the consequences of a researcher's decisions about observing versus participating and about being acknowledged versus unacknowledged in naturalistic observation.

3. Explain what a case study is. Discuss the limitations of case studies for the study of human behavior.

4. What is systematic observation, and what techniques are used to make observations systematic?

5. What kinds of questions can be answered through archival research, and what kinds of data might be relevant?

HANDS-ON EXPERIENCE

1. Design an observational study of your own, including the creation of a set of behavioral categories that would be used to code for one or more variables of interest to you. Indicate the decisions you have made regarding the sampling of behaviors.

2. Make a tape recording of a student meeting. Discuss methods that could be used to meaningfully organize and code the statements made by the students.

3. Design, and conduct if possible, an archival research study. Consider what type of information you will look for, how you will find it, and how it should be content coded.

4. Read about an observational study—for instance, the Festinger et al. (1956) study of a "doomsday cult."

5. Read and comment on a case study, such as one of the following:

Curtiss, S. R. (1977). *Genie: A psycholinguistic study of a modern-day "wild child."* New York: Academic Press.

Luria, A. R. (1968). *The mind of a mnemonist.* New York: Basic Books.

Rokeach, M. (1964). *The three Christs of Ypsilanti: A psychological study.* New York: Knopf.

Runyan, W. K. (1981). Why did van Gogh cut off his ear? The problem of alternative explanations in psychobiography. *Journal of Personality and Social Psychology, 40,* 1070–1077.

Schreiber, F. R. (1973). *Sybil.* Chicago: Regnery.

PART **THREE**

Testing Research Hypotheses

CHAPTER EIGHT
Hypothesis Testing and Inferential Statistics

STUDY QUESTIONS

- What are inferential statistics, and how are they used to test a research hypothesis?

- What is the null hypothesis?

- What is alpha?

- What is the p-value, and how is it used to determine statistical significance?

- Why are two-sided p-values used in most hypothesis tests?

- What are Type 1 and Type 2 errors, and what is the relationship between them?

- What is beta, and how does beta relate to the power of a statistical test?

- What is the effect size statistic, and how is it used?

We have now completed our discussion of naturalistic and survey research designs, and in the chapters to come we will turn to correlational research and experimental research, which are designed to investigate relationships among one or more variables. Before doing so, however, we must discuss the standardized method scientists use to test whether the data they collect can be interpreted as providing support for their research hypotheses. These procedures are part and parcel of the scientific method and help keep the scientific process objective.

Probability and Inferential Statistics

Imagine for a moment a hypothetical situation in which a friend of yours claims that she has ESP and can read your mind. You find yourself skeptical of the claim, but you realize that if it were true, the two of you could develop a magic show and make a lot of money. You decide to conduct an empirical test. You flip a coin ten times, hiding the results from her each time, and ask her to guess each time whether the coin has come up heads or tails. Your logic is that if she can read your mind, she should be able to guess correctly. Maybe she won't be perfect, but she should be better than chance.

You can imagine that your friend might not get exactly five out of ten guesses right, even though this is what would be expected by chance. She might be right six times and wrong only four, or she might even guess correctly eight times out of ten. But how many would she have to get right to convince you that she really has ESP and can guess correctly more than 50 percent of the time? Would six out of ten correct be enough? How about eight out of ten? And even if she got all ten correct, how would you rule out the possibility that because guessing has some random error, she might have just happened to get lucky?

Consider now a researcher who is testing the effectiveness of a new behavioral therapy by comparing a group of patients who received therapy to another group that did not, or a researcher who is investigating the relationship between children viewing violent television shows and displaying aggressive behavior. The researchers want to know whether the observed data support their research hypotheses—namely, that the new therapy reduces anxiety and that viewing violent behavior increases aggression. However, you can well imagine that because measurement contains random error, it is unlikely that the two groups of patients will show exactly the same levels of anxiety at the end of the therapy or that the correlation between the amount of violent television viewed and the amount of aggressive behavior displayed will be exactly zero. As a result of random error, one group might show somewhat less anxiety than the other, or the correlation coefficient might be somewhat greater than zero, even if the treatment was not effective or there was no relationship between viewing violence and acting aggressively.

Thus these scientists are in exactly the same position as you would be if you tried to test your friend's claim of having ESP. The basic dilemma is that it is impossible to ever know for sure whether the observed data were caused by random error. Because all data contain random error, *any pattern of data that might have been caused by a true relationship between variables might instead have been caused by chance.* This is part of the reason that research never "proves" a hypothesis or a theory.

The scientific method specifies a set of procedures that scientists use to make educated guesses about whether the data support the research hypothesis. These steps are outlined in Figure 8.1 and are discussed in the following

FIGURE 8.1 Hypothesis-Testing Flow Chart

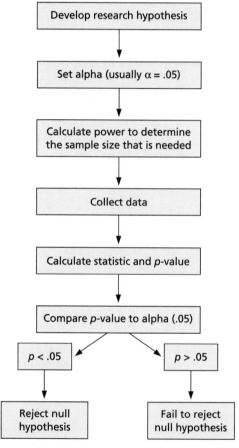

Hypothesis testing begins with the development of the research hypothesis. Once alpha (in most cases it is .05) has been chosen and the needed sample size has been calculated, the data are collected. Significance tests on the observed data may be either statistically significant ($p < .05$) or statistically nonsignificant ($p > .05$). The results of the significance test determine whether the null hypothesis should be accepted or rejected. If results are significant, then an examination of the direction of the observed relationship will indicate whether the research hypothesis has been supported.

sections. These procedures involve the use of probability and statistical analysis to draw inferences on the basis of observed data. Because they use the sample data to draw inferences about the true state of affairs, these statistical procedures are called **inferential statistics.**

Sampling Distributions and Hypothesis Testing

Although directly testing whether a research hypothesis is correct or incorrect seems an achievable goal, it actually is not because it is not possible to specify ahead of time what the observed data would look like if the research hypothesis was true. It is, however, possible to specify in a statistical sense what the observed data would look like if the research hypothesis was *not* true.

Consider, for instance, what we would expect the observed data to look like in our ESP test if your friend did *not* have ESP. Figure 8.2 shows a bar chart of all of the possible outcomes of ten guesses on coin flips calculated under the assumption that the probability of a correct guess (.5) is the same as the

FIGURE 8.2 The Binomial Distribution

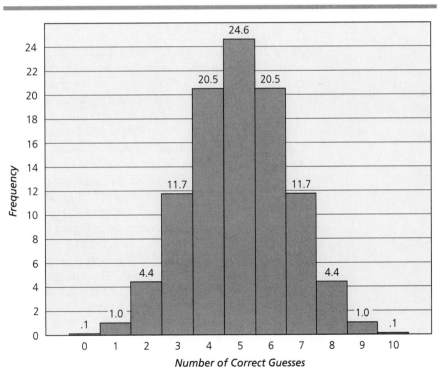

This figure represents all possible outcomes of correct guesses on ten coin flips. More generally, it represents the expected outcomes of any event where $p(a) = p(b)$. This is known as the *binomial distribution.*

FIGURE 8.3   Two Sampling Distributions

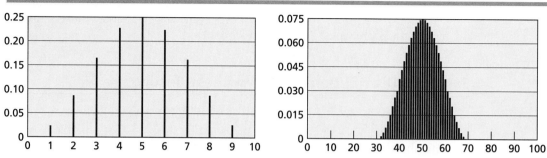

This figure shows the likely outcomes of correct guesses on ten coin flips (left side) and 100 coin flips (right side). You can see that as the sample size gets larger, the sampling distribution (in this case the binomial distribution) gets narrower.

probability of an incorrect guess (also .5). You can see that some outcomes are more common than others. For instance, the outcome of five correct guesses is expected by chance to occur 24.6 percent of the time, whereas the outcome of ten correct guesses is so unlikely that it will occur by chance only 1/10 of one percent of the time.

The distribution of all of the possible values of a statistic is known as a **sampling distribution.** Each statistic has an associated sampling distribution. For instance, the sampling distribution for events that have two equally likely possibilities, such as the distribution of correct and incorrect guesses shown in Figure 8.2, is known as the **binomial distribution.** There is also a sampling distribution for the mean, a sampling distribution for the standard deviation, a sampling distribution for the correlation coefficient, and so forth.

Although we have to this point made it sound as if each statistic has only one sampling distribution, things are actually more complex than this. For most statistics, there are a series of different sampling distributions, each of which is associated with a different sample size (N). For instance, Figure 8.3 compares the binomial sampling distribution for ten coin flips ($N = 10$) on the left side (this is the same distribution as in Figure 8.2) with the binomial sampling distribution for one hundred coin flips ($N = 100$) on the right side. You can see that the sampling distributions becomes more narrow—squeezed together—as the sample size gets bigger. This change represents the fact that, as sample size increases, extreme values of the statistic are less likely to be observed. The sampling distributions of other statistics, such as for the Pearson correlation coefficient or the F test, look very similar to these distributions, including the change toward becoming more narrow as sample size increases.

The Null Hypothesis

When testing hypotheses, we begin by assuming that the observed data do *not* differ from what would be expected on the basis of chance, and the sampling distribution of the statistic is used to indicate what is expected to happen by chance. The assumption that the observed data reflect only what would be expected under the sampling distribution is called the **null hypothesis,** symbolized as H_0. As we will see, each test of a research hypothesis begins with a null hypothesis:

> For the coin guessing experiment, H_0 is that the probability of a correct guess is = .5.
>
> For a correlational design, H_0 is that there is no correlation between the two measured variables ($r = 0$).
>
> For an experimental research design, H_0 is that the mean score on the dependent variable is the same in all of the experimental groups (for instance, that the mean of the therapy group equals the mean of the control group).

Because the null hypothesis specifies the least interesting possible outcome, the researcher hopes to be able to *reject the null hypothesis*—that is, to be able to conclude that the observed data were caused by something other than chance alone.

Testing for Statistical Significance

Setting Alpha.   You may not be surprised to hear that given the conservative nature of science, the observed data must deviate rather substantially from what would be expected under the sampling distribution before we are allowed to reject the null hypothesis. The standard that the observed data must meet is known as the **significance level** or **alpha (α).** By convention, alpha is normally set to $\alpha = .05$.[1] What this means is that we may reject the null hypothesis only if the observed data are so unusual that they would have occurred by chance at most 5 percent of the time. Although this standard may seem stringent, even more stringent significance levels, such as $\alpha = .01$ and $\alpha = .001$, may sometimes be used. The smaller the alpha is, the more stringent the standard is.

Comparing the *p*-value to Alpha.   As shown in Figure 8.1, once the alpha level has been set (we'll discuss how to determine the sample size in a moment), a statistic (such as a correlation coefficient) is computed. Each statistic has an associated **probability value** (usually called a ***p*-value** and indicated with the letter p) that shows the likelihood of an observed statistic occurring on the basis of the sampling distribution. Because alpha sets the standard for how extreme the data must be before we can reject the null hypothesis, and

---

[1]Although there is some debate within the scientific community about whether it is advisable to test research hypotheses using a preset significant level—see, for instance, Shrout (1997) and the following articles in the journal—this approach is still the most common method of hypothesis testing within the behavioral sciences.

the p-value indicates how extreme the data are, we simply compare the p-value to alpha:

If the p-value is less than alpha ($p < .05$), then we reject the null hypothesis, and we say the result is **statistically significant.**

If the p-value is greater than alpha ($p > .05$), then we fail to reject the null hypothesis, and we say the result is **statistically nonsignificant.**

The p-value for a given outcome is found through examination of the sampling distribution of the statistic, and in our case the p-value comes from Figure 8.1. For instance, we can calculate that the probability of your friend guessing the coin flips correctly all ten times (given the null hypothesis that she does not have ESP) is 1 in 1,024, or $p = .001$. A p-value of .001 indicates that such an outcome is extremely unlikely to have occurred as a result of chance (in fact, only about once in 1,000 times).

We can also add probabilities together to produce the following probabilities of correct guesses, based on the binomial distribution in Figure 8.2:

p-value for 9 or 10 correct guesses = .01 + .001 = .011

p-value for 8 or 9 or 10 correct guesses = .044 + .01 + .001 = .055

p-value for 7 or 8 or 9 or 10 correct guesses = .117 + .044 + .01 + .001 = .172

In short, the probability of guessing correctly *at least* eight times given no ESP is $p = .055$, and the probability of guessing correctly *at least* seven times given no ESP is $p = .172$.

Using One- and Two-Sided p-values.

You can see that these calculations consider the likelihood of your friend guessing better than what would be expected by chance. But for most statistical tests, unusual events can occur in more than one way. For instance, you can imagine that it would of interest to find that psychotherapy *increased* anxiety, or to find that viewing violent television *decreased* aggression even if the research hypotheses did not predict these relationships. Because the scientific method is designed to keep things objective, the scientist must be prepared to interpret any relationships that he or she finds, even if these relationships were not predicted.

Because data need to be interpreted even if they are in an unexpected direction, scientists generally use **two-sided p-values** to test their research hypotheses.[2] Two-sided p-values take into consideration that unusual outcomes may occur in more than one way. Returning to Figure 8.2, we can see that there are indeed two "sides" to the binomial distribution. There is another outcome that is just as extreme as guessing correctly ten times—guessing correctly zero times. And there is another outcome just as extreme as guessing correctly

[2]Although **one-sided p-values** can be used in some special cases, in this book we will use only two-sided p-values.

nine times—guessing correctly only once. Because the binomial distribution is symmetrical, the two-sided p-value is always twice as big as the one-sided p-value. Although two-sided p-values provide a more conservative statistical test, they allow us to interpret statistically significant relationships even if those differences are not in the direction predicted by the research hypothesis.

Using two-sided p-values, we can construct the following:

p-value for number of guesses as extreme as 10 = .001 × 2 = .002
p-value for number of guesses as extreme as 9 = .011 × 2 = .022
p-value for number of guesses as extreme as 8 = .055 × 2 = .11
p-value for number of guesses as extreme as 7 = .172 × 2 = .344

Let us return one last time to our example to finally specify how many correct guesses your friend would have to get before we could reject the null hypothesis that she does not have ESP. If we set $\alpha = .05$, then we could not reject the null hypothesis of no ESP on the basis of eight correct guesses because the two-sided p-value (.11) of an outcome as extreme as eight correct guesses is greater than alpha ($p > .05$). However, the probability of an outcome as extreme as nine correct guesses out of ten given no ESP ($p = .022$) is less than alpha ($p < .05$). Therefore, your friend would have to guess correctly nine times or more before we could reject the null hypothesis of no ESP on the basis of ten coin flips.

We will discuss the specifics of many different statistical tests in the chapters to come, but for now it is sufficient to know that each statistical test produces a p-value and that in each case the p-value is compared to alpha. The research report can notate either the exact p-value (for instance, $p = .022$ or $p = .17$) or the relationship between the p-value and alpha (for instance, $p < .05$ or $p > .05$).

Reduction of Inferential Errors

Because hypothesis testing and inferential statistics are based entirely on probability, we are bound to make errors in drawing conclusions about our data. The hypothesis-testing procedure is designed to keep such errors to a minimum, but it cannot eliminate them entirely. Figure 8.4 provides one way to think about this problem. It indicates that statistical inference can lead to both correct decisions but also, at least in some cases, to errors. Because these errors lead the researcher to draw invalid conclusions, it is important to understand what they are and how we can reduce them. On the left side of Figure 8.4 are the two possible states that we are trying to choose between—the null hypothesis may be true, or the null hypothesis may be false. And across the top of the figure are the two possible decisions that we can make on the basis of the observed data: We may reject the null hypothesis, or we may fail to reject the null hypothesis.

FIGURE 8.4   Type 1 and Type 2 Errors

		SCIENTIST'S DECISION	
		Reject null hypothesis	**Fail to reject null hypothesis**
TRUE STATE OF AFFAIRS	*Null hypothesis is true*	Type 1 Error Probability = α	Correct decision Probability = $1 - \alpha$
	Null hypothesis is false	Correct decision Probability = $1 - \beta$	Type 2 Error Probability = β

This figure represents the possible outcomes of statistical inference. In two cases the scientist's decision is correct because it accurately represents the true state of affairs. In two other cases the scientist's decision is incorrect.

Type 1 Errors

One type of error occurs when we reject the null hypothesis when it is in fact true. This would occur, for instance, when the psychologist draws the conclusion that his or her therapy reduced anxiety when it did not or if you concluded that your friend has ESP even though she doesn't. As shown in the upper left quadrant of Figure 8.4, rejecting the null hypothesis when it is really true is called a **Type 1 error.**

The probability of the researcher making a Type 1 error is equal to alpha. When $\alpha = .05$, we know we will make a Type 1 error not more than five times out of one hundred, and when $\alpha = .01$, we know we will make a Type 1 error not more than one time out of one hundred. However, because of the inherent ambiguity in the hypothesis-testing procedure, the researcher never knows for sure whether she or he has made a Type 1 error. It is always possible that data that are interpreted as rejecting the null hypothesis are caused by random error and that the null hypothesis is really true. But setting $\alpha = .05$ allows us to rest assured that a Type 1 error has most likely not been made.[3]

---

[3]Alpha indicates the likelihood of making a Type 1 error in a single statistical test. However, when more than one statistical test is made in a research project, the likelihood of a Type 1 error will increase. To help correct for this problem, when many statistical tests are being made, a smaller alpha (for instance, $\alpha = .01$) can be used.

Type 2 Errors

If you've looked carefully at Figure 8.4, you will have noticed a second type of error that can be made when interpreting research results. Whereas a Type 1 error refers to the mistake of rejecting the null hypothesis when it is actually true, a **Type 2 error** refers to the mistake of failing to reject the null hypothesis when the null hypothesis is really false. This would occur when the scientist concludes that the psychotherapy program is not working even though it really is or when you conclude that your friend does not have ESP even though she really can do significantly better than chance.

We have seen that the scientist controls the probability of making a Type 1 error by setting alpha at a small value, such as .05. But what determines **beta,** or β, the probability of the scientist making a Type 2 error? Answering this question requires a discussion of statistical power.

Statistical Power

Type 2 errors occur when the scientist misses a true relationship by failing to reject the null hypothesis even though it should have been rejected. Such errors are not at all uncommon in science. They occur both because of random error in measurement and because the things we are looking for are often pretty small. You can imagine that a biologist might make a Type 2 error when, using a microscope that is not very powerful, he fails to detect a small organism. And the same might occur for an astronomer who misses the discovery of a new planet because the earth's atmosphere creates random error that distorts the telescope's image.

The **power** of a statistical test is the probability that the researcher will, on the basis of the observed data, be able to reject the null hypothesis given that the null hypothesis is actually false and thus should be rejected. Power and beta are redundant concepts because power can be written in terms of beta:

$$\text{Power} = 1 - \beta$$

In short, Type 2 errors are more common when the power of a statistical test is low.

The Effect Size. Although alpha can be precisely set by the scientist, beta (and thus the power) of a statistical test can only be estimated. This is because power depends in part on how big the relationship being searched for actually is—the bigger the relationship is, the easier it is to detect. The size of a relationship is indicated by a statistic known as the **effect size.** The effect size indicates the magnitude of a relationship: zero indicates that there is no relationship between the variables and larger (positive) effect sizes indicate stronger relationships.

The problem is that because the researcher can never know ahead of time the exact effect size of the relationship being searched for, he or she cannot exactly calculate the power of the statistical test. In some cases the researcher may be able to make an educated guess about the likely power of a statistical test by estimating the effect size of the expected relationship on the basis of previous research in the field. When this is not possible, general knowledge about the effect sizes of relationships in behavioral science can be used. The accepted practice is to consider the approximate size of the expected relationship to be "small," "medium," or "large" (Cohen, 1977) and to calculate power on the basis of these estimates. In most cases a "small" effect size is considered to be .10, a "medium" effect size is .30, and a "large" effect size is .50.

The Influence of Sample Size.   In addition to the actual size of the relationship being assessed, the power of a statistical test is also influenced by the sample size (N) used in the research. As N increases, the likelihood of the researcher finding a statistically significant relationship between the independent and dependent variables, and thus the power of the test, also increases. We will consider this issue in more detail in a later section of this chapter.

The Tradeoff Between Type 1 and Type 2 Errors

Beginning researchers often ask, and professional scientists often still consider, what alpha is most appropriate. Clearly, if the major goal is to prevent Type 1 errors, then alpha should be set as small as possible. However, in any given research design there is a tradeoff between the likelihood of making a Type 1 and a Type 2 error. For any given sample size, when alpha is set lower, beta will always be higher. This is because alpha represents the standard of evidence required to reject the null hypothesis, and the probability of the observed data meeting this standard is less when alpha is smaller. As a result, setting a small alpha makes it more difficult to find data that are strong enough to allow rejecting the null hypothesis, and makes it more likely that weak relationships will be missed.

You might better understand the basic problem if we return for a moment to our example of testing for the presence of ESP. A person who has some degree of ESP might be able over a long period of time to guess the outcome of coin tosses correctly somewhat more than 50 percent of the time. Anyone who could do so would, according to our definition, have ESP, even if he or she was only slightly better than chance. In our test using ten guesses of ten coin flips, we have seen that if $\alpha = .05$, then the individual must guess correctly 90 percent of the time (nine out of ten) for us to reject the null hypothesis. If eight or fewer guesses were correct, we would be forced to accept the null hypothesis that the person does not have ESP. However, this conclusion would represent a Type 2 error if the person was actually able to guess correctly more than 50 percent of the time but less than 90 percent of the time.

Thus the basic difficulty is that although setting a lower alpha protects us from Type 1 errors, doing so may lead us to miss the presence of weak relationships. This difficulty can be alleviated to some extent, however, by an increase in the power of the research design. As N increases, the likelihood of the scientist detecting relationships with small effect sizes increases, even when alpha remains the same. To return once more to the ESP example, you can see by comparing the two sampling distributions in Figure 8.3 that a relatively lower percentage of correct guesses is needed to reject the null hypothesis as the sample size gets bigger. Remember that when the sample size was 10 (10 flips), your friend had to make nine correct guesses (90 percent correct) before we could reject the null hypothesis. However, if you tested your friend using 100 coin flips ($N = 100$) instead of only 10, you would have a greater chance of detecting "weak" ESP. Keeping alpha equal to .05, you would be able to reject the null hypothesis of no ESP if your friend was able to guess correctly on 61 out of 100 (that is, only 61 percent) of the coin flips. And, if you had your friend guess the outcome of 1,000 coin flips, you would be able to reject the null hypothesis on the basis of only 532 out of 1,000 (that is, only 53 percent) correct guesses.

A decision must be made for each research project about the tradeoff between the likelihood of making Type 1 and Type 2 errors. This tradeoff is particularly acute when sample sizes are small, and this is frequently the case because the collecting of data is often very expensive. In most cases scientists believe that Type 1 errors are more dangerous than Type 2 errors and set alpha at a lower value than beta. However, the choice of an appropriate alpha depends to some extent on the type of research being conducted. There are some situations in applied research where it may be particularly desirable for the scientist to avoid making a Type 2 error. For instance, if the scientist is testing a new type of reading instruction, she or he might want to discover if the program is having even a very small effect on learning, and so the scientist might take a higher than normal chance of making a Type 1 error. In such a case the scientist might use a larger alpha.

Because Type 1 and Type 2 errors are always a possibility in research, rejection of the null hypothesis does not necessarily mean that the null hypothesis is actually false. Rather, rejecting the null hypothesis simply means that the null hypothesis does not seem to be able to account for the collected data. Similarly, a failure to reject the null hypothesis does not mean that the null hypothesis is necessarily true, only that on the basis of the collected data the scientist cannot reject it.

Statistical Significance and the Effect Size

In this chapter we have discussed both statistical significance (measured by the relationship between the p-value and alpha) and the effect size as measures of relationships between variables. It is important to remember that the effect size and the p-value are two different statistics and to understand the distinction between them. Each statistical test (for instance, a Pearson correlation coefficient) has both an associated p-value and an effect size statistic.

The relationship among statistical significance, sample size (N), and effect size is summarized in the following conceptual equation (Rosenthal & Rosnow, 1991):

$$\text{Statistical significance} = \text{Effect size} \times \text{Sample size}$$

This equation makes clear three important principles that guide interpretation of research results:

- First, increasing the sample size (N) will increase the statistical significance of a relationship whenever the effect size is greater than zero. Because observed relationships in small samples are more likely to have been caused by random error, and because the p-value represents the likelihood that the observed relationship was caused by random error, larger samples are more likely to produce statistically significant results.

- Second, because the p-value is influenced by sample size, as a measure of statistical significance the p-value is not itself a good indicator of the size of a relationship. If a large sample size is used, even a very small relationship can be statistically significant. In this sense the term *significance* is somewhat misleading because although a small p-value does imply that the results are unlikely to be due to random error, it does not imply anything about the magnitude or practical importance of the observed relationship. When we determine that a test is statistically significant, we can be confident that there *is* a relationship between the variables, but that relationship may still be quite small.

- Third, we can see that the effect size is an index of the strength of a relationship that is not influenced by sample size. As we will see in the next section, this property of the effect size makes it very useful in research. When interpreting research reports, we must keep in mind the distinction between effect size and statistical significance and the effect of sample size on the latter.

Practical Uses of the Effect Size Statistic

As we have seen, the advantage of the effect size statistic is that it indicates the strength of the relationship between the independent and the dependent variables and does so independently of the sample size. Although the relationship between two or more variables is almost always tested for statistical significance, the effect size statistic provides important practical information that cannot be obtained from the p-value. In some cases, particularly in applied research, the effect size of a relationship may be more important than the statistical significance of the relationship because it provides a better index of a relationship's strength.

The Effect Size in Applied Research.   Consider, for instance, two researchers who are both studying the effectiveness of programs to reduce drug use in teenagers. The first researcher studies a classroom intervention program in which 100 high school students are shown a videotape about the dangers of drug use. The second researcher studies the effects of a television advertising campaign by sampling over 20,000 high school students who have seen the ad on TV. Both researchers find that the programs produce statistically significant increases ($p < .05$) in the perceptions of the dangers of drug use in the research participants.

In such a case the statistical significance of the relationship between the intervention and the outcome variable may not be as important as the effect size. Because the sample size of one researcher is very large, even though the relationship was found to be statistically significant, the effect size might nevertheless be very small. In this case, comparing the effect size of a relationship with the cost of the intervention may help determine whether a program is worth continuing or whether other programs should be used instead (Rossi & Freeman, 1993).

The Proportion of Variance Statistic. It is sometimes convenient to consider the strength of a relationship in terms of the proportion of the dependent variable that is "explained by" the independent variable or variables, as opposed to being "explained by" random error. The **proportion of explained variability** in the dependent variable is indicated by the square of the effect size statistic.

In many cases the proportion of explained variability is quite small. For instance, it is not uncommon in behavioral research to find a "small" effect size—that is, one of about .10. In a correlational design, for instance, this would mean that only 1 percent of the variability in the outcome variable is explained by the predictor variable (.10 × .10 = .01), whereas the other 99 percent of the variability is explained by other, unknown sources. Even a "large" effect size of .50 means that the predictor variable explains only 25 percent of the total variability in the outcome variable and that the other 75 percent is explained by other sources. Considering that they are usually quite small, it comes as no surprise that the relationships studied in behavioral research are often missed.

Determination of the Necessary Sample Size. Another use of the effect size statistic is to compute, during the planning of a research design, the power of a statistical test to determine the sample size that should be used. As shown in Figure 8.1, this is usually done in the early stages of the research process. Although increasing the sample size increases power, it is also expensive because recruiting and running research participants can require both time and money. In most cases it is not practical to reduce the probability of making a Type 2 error to the same probability as that of making a Type 1 error because too many individuals would have to participate in the research. For instance, to have power = .95 (that is β = .05) to detect a "small" effect size relationship using a Pearson correlation coefficient, one would need to collect data from over one thousand individuals!

Because of the large number of participants needed to create powerful research designs, a compromise is normally made. Although many research projects are conducted with even less power, it is usually sufficient for the estimated likelihood of a Type 2 error to be about β = .20. This represents power = .80 and thus an 80 percent chance of rejecting the null hypothesis, given that the null hypothesis is false (see Cohen, 1977).

Statistical Table G in Appendix E presents the number of research participants needed with various statistical tests to obtain power = .80 with α = .05, assuming small, medium, or large estimated effect sizes. The specifics of these statistical tests will be discussed in detail in subsequent chapters, and you can refer to the table as necessary. Although the table can be used to calculate the power of a statistical test with some precision, in most cases a more basic rule of thumb applies—run as many people in a given research project as is conveniently possible because when there are more participants, there is also a greater likelihood of detecting the relationship of interest and thus of detecting relationships between variables.

SUMMARY

Hypothesis testing is accomplished through a set of procedures designed to determine whether observed data can be interpreted as providing support for the research hypothesis. These procedures, based on inferential statistics, are specified by the scientific method and are set in place before the scientist begins to collect data. Because it is not possible to directly test the research hypothesis, observed data are compared to what is expected under the null hypothesis, as specified by the sampling distribution of the statistic.

Because all data have random error, scientists can never be certain that the data they have observed actually support their hypotheses. Statistical significance is used to test whether data can be interpreted as supporting the research hypothesis. The probability of incorrectly rejecting the null hypothesis (known as a Type 1 error) is constrained by setting alpha to a known value such as .05 and only rejecting the null hypothesis if the likelihood that the observed data occurred by chance (the p-value) is less than alpha. The probability of incorrectly failing to reject a false null hypothesis (a Type 2 error) can only be estimated. The power of a statistical test refers to the likelihood of correctly rejecting a false null hypothesis.

The effect size statistic is often used as a measure of the magnitude of a relationship between variables because it is not influenced by the sample size in the research design. The strength of a relationship may also be considered in terms of the proportion of variance in the dependent measure that is explained by the independent variable. The effect size of many relationships in scientific research is small, which makes them difficult to discover.

KEY TERMS

alpha (α) 143
beta (β) 147
binomial distribution 142
effect size 147

inferential statistics 141
null hypothesis (H_0) 143
one-sided p-values 144
power 147

REVIEW AND DISCUSSION QUESTIONS

1. With reference to the flow chart in Figure 8.1, use your own words to describe the procedures of hypothesis testing. Be sure to use the following terms in your explanation: alpha, beta, null hypothesis, probability value, statistical significance, and Type 1 and Type 2 errors.

2. Explain why scientists can never be certain whether their data really support their research hypothesis.

3. Describe in your own words the techniques that scientists use to help them avoid drawing statistically invalid conclusions.

4. What is a statistically significant result? What is the relationship among statistical significance, *N*, and effect size?

5. What are the implications of using a smaller, rather than a larger, alpha in a research design?

6. What is the likelihood of a Type 1 error if the null hypothesis is actually true? What is the likelihood of a Type 1 error if the null hypothesis is actually false?

7. What is meant by the power of a statistical test, and how can it be increased?

8. What are the practical uses of the effect size statistic?

9. What is the meaning of the proportion of explained variability?

HANDS-ON EXPERIENCE

1. Flip a set of ten coins one hundred times, and record the number of heads and tails each time. Construct a frequency distribution of the observed data. Check whether the observed frequency distribution appears to match the expected frequency distribution shown in the binomial distribution in Figure 8.2.

2. For each of the following patterns of data,

   • What is the probability of the researcher having made a Type 1 error?
   • What is the probability of the researcher having made a Type 2 error?
   • Should the null hypothesis be rejected?

- What conclusions can be drawn about the possibility of the researcher having drawn a statistically invalid conclusion?

	p-value	N	alpha	beta
a.	.03	100	.05	.05
b.	.13	100	.05	.30
c.	.03	50	.01	.20
d.	.03	25	.01	.20
e.	.06	1,000	.05	.70

3. A friend of yours reports a study that obtains a *p*-value of .02. What can you conclude about the finding? List two other pieces of information that you would need to know to fully interpret the finding.

4. Consider two researchers who are interested in testing the effects of new programs of psychotherapy. One program is relatively inexpensive to administer because it is conducted in groups by a social worker. The other program is more expensive because it is conducted in individual sessions by a trained psychiatrist. How would the expense of the therapy be likely to influence how the researcher sets alpha and beta in testing the effectiveness of the therapies?

5. Consider a research design in which alpha might be set at less than $\alpha = .05$ and a research design in which alpha might be set at greater than $\alpha = .05$. Indicate why these decisions might be made in these cases.

6. Researcher Smith has found a Pearson correlation coefficient between two variables that has a *p*-value of .01 and an N of 1,000. Researcher Jones has found a correlation between the same two variables, with a *p*-value of .01 and an N of 100. Which researcher has found a larger correlation between the two variables, and why?

CHAPTER NINE
Correlational Research Designs

STUDY QUESTIONS

- What are correlational research designs, and why are they used in behavioral research?

- What patterns of association can occur between two quantitative variables?

- What is the Pearson product-moment correlation coefficient? What are its uses and limitations?

- How does the chi-square statistic assess association?

- What is multiple regression, and what are its uses in correlational research designs?

- How can correlational data be used to make inferences about the causal relationships among measured variables? What are the limitations of correlational designs in doing so?

- What are the best uses for correlational designs?

Correlational research designs are used to search for and describe relationships among measured variables. For instance, a researcher might be interested in looking for a relationship between family background and career choice, between diet and disease, or between the physical attractiveness of a person and how much help she or he receives from strangers. There are many patterns of relationships that can occur between two measured variables, and an even greater number of patterns can occur when more than two variables are assessed. It is exactly this complexity, which is also part of everyday life, that correlational research designs attempt to capture.

In this chapter we will first consider the patterns of association that can be found between one predictor and one outcome variable and the statistical techniques used to summarize these associations. Then we will consider techniques for simultaneously assessing the relationships among more than two measured variables. We will also discuss when and how correlational data can be used to learn about the causal relationships among measured variables.

Associations Among Quantitative Variables

Let's begin our study of patterns of association by looking at the raw data from a sample of twenty college students, presented in Table 9.1. Each person has

TABLE 9.1 Raw Data from a Correlational Study

Participant #	Optimism Scale	Reported Health Behavior
1	6	13
2	7	24
3	2	8
4	5	7
5	2	11
6	3	6
7	7	21
8	9	12
9	8	14
10	9	21
11	6	10
12	1	15
13	9	8
14	2	7
15	4	9
16	2	6
17	6	9
18	2	6
19	6	12
20	3	5

a score on both a Likert scale measure of optimism (such as the Life Orientation Test; Scheier, Carver, & Bridges, 1994) and a measure that assesses the extent to which he or she reports performing healthy behaviors such as going for regular physical examinations and eating low-fat foods. The optimism scale ranges from 1 to 9, where higher numbers indicate a more optimistic personality, and the health scale ranges from 1 to 25, where higher numbers indicate that the individual reports engaging in more healthy activities.

At this point the goal of the researcher is to assess the strength and direction of the relationship between the variables. It is difficult to do so by looking at the raw data itself because there are too many scores and they are not organized in any meaningful way. One way of organizing the data is to graph the variables using a scatterplot. As shown in Figure 9.1, a **scatterplot** uses a standard coordinate system in which the horizontal axis indicates the scores on the predictor variable and the vertical axis represents the scores on the outcome variable. A point is plotted for each individual at the intersection of his or her scores on the two variables.

Scatterplots provide a visual image of the relationship between the variables. In this example you can see that the points fall in a fairly regular pattern in which most of the individuals are located in the lower left corner, in the center, or in the upper right corner of the scatterplot. You can also see that a straight line, known as the **regression line,** has been drawn through the points. The regression line is sometimes called the line of "best fit" because it

FIGURE 9.1   Scatterplot of Optimism by Health Behavior

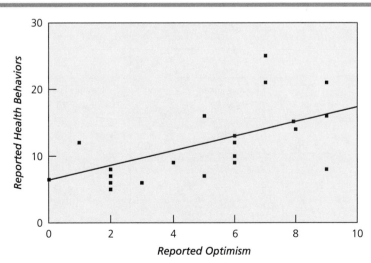

In this scatterplot of the data in Table 9.1, the predictor variable (optimism) is plotted on the horizontal axis and the dependent variable (health behaviors) is plotted on the vertical axis. The regression line, which minimizes the squared distances of the points from the line, is drawn. You can see that the relationship between the variables is positive linear.

is the line that minimizes the squared distance of the points from the line. The regression line is discussed in more detail in Appendix C.

Linear Relationships

When the association between the variables on the scatterplot can be easily approximated with a straight line, as in Figure 9.1, the variables are said to have a **linear relationship.** Figure 9.2 shows two examples of scatterplots of linear relationships. When the straight line indicates that individuals who have above-average values on one variable also tend to have above-average values on the other variable, as in Figure 9.2(a), the relationship is said to be *positive linear. Negative linear* relationships, in contrast, occur when above-average values on one variable tend to be associated with below-average values on the other variable, such as in Figure 9.2(b).

Nonlinear Relationships

Not all relationships between variables can be well described with a straight line, and those that are not are known as **nonlinear relationships.** Figure 9.2(c) shows a common pattern in which the distribution of the points is essentially random. In this case there is no relationship at all between the

FIGURE 9.2   Patterns of Relationships Between Two Variables

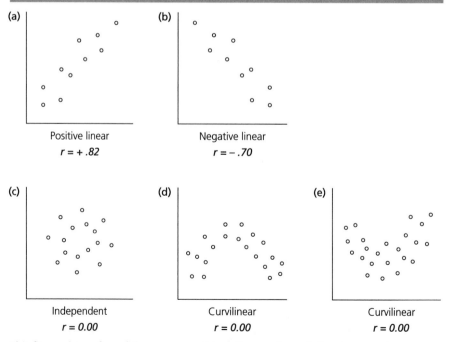

This figure shows five of the many possible patterns of association between two quantitative variables.

two variables, and they are said to be **independent.** When the two variables are independent, it means that we cannot use one variable to predict the other.

Figures 9.2(d) and 9.2(e) show patterns of association in which, although there is an association, the points are not well described by a single straight line. For instance, Figure 9.2(d) shows the type of relationship that frequently occurs between anxiety and performance. Increases in anxiety from low to moderate levels are associated with performance increases, whereas increases in anxiety from moderate to high levels are associated with decreases in performance. Relationships that change in direction and thus are not described by a single straight line are called **curvilinear relationships.**

Statistical Assessment of Relationships

Although the scatterplot gives a pictorial image, the relationship between variables is frequently difficult to detect visually. As a result, descriptive statistics are normally used to provide a numerical index of the relationship between or among two or more variables. The descriptive statistic is in essence a shorthand for the graphic image.

The Pearson Correlation Coefficient

As we have seen in Chapter 1, a descriptive statistic known as the Pearson product-moment correlation coefficient is normally used to summarize and communicate the strength and direction of the association between two quantitative variables. The Pearson correlation coefficient, frequently referred to simply as the correlation coefficient, is designated by the letter r. The correlation coefficient is a number that indicates both the direction and the magnitude of association. Values of the correlation coefficient range from $r = -1.00$ to $r = +1.00$.

The direction of the relationship is indicated by the sign of the correlation coefficient. Positive values of r (such as $r = .54$ or $r = .67$) indicate that the relationship is positive linear (that is, that the regression line runs from the lower left to the upper right), whereas negative values of r (such as $r = -.3$ or $r = -.72$) indicate negative linear relationships (that is, that the regression line runs from the upper left to the lower right). The strength or effect size (see Chapter 8) of the linear relationship is indexed by the distance of the correlation coefficient from zero (its absolute value). For instance, $r = .54$ is a stronger relationship than $r = -.30$, whereas $r = -.72$ is a stronger relationship than $r = .57$.

Interpretation of r.   The calculation of the correlation coefficient is described in Appendix C, and you may wish to verify that the correlation between optimism and health behavior in the sample data in Table 9.1 is $r = .52$. This confirms what we have seen in the scatterplot in Figure 9.1—that the relationship is positive linear. The p-value associated with r can be calculated as described in Appendix C, and in this case r is significant at $p < .01$.

A significant r indicates that there is a linear association between the variables and thus that it is possible to use knowledge about a person's score on one variable to predict his or her score on the other variable. For instance, because optimism and health behavior are significantly positively correlated, we can use optimism to predict health behavior. The extent to which we can predict is indexed by the effect size of the correlation, and the effect size for the Pearson correlation coefficient is r, the correlation coefficient itself. The proportion of variance measure is r^2, which is known as the **coefficient of determination.**

When the correlation coefficient is not statistically significant, this indicates that there is not a positive linear or a negative linear relationship between the variables. However, a nonsignificant r does not necessarily mean that there is no systematic relationship between the variables. As we have seen in Figure 9.2(d) and 9.2(e), the correlation between two variables that have curvilinear relationships is likely to be about zero. What this means is that although one variable can be used to predict the other, the Pearson correlation coefficient does not provide a good estimate of the extent to which this is possible. This represents a limitation of the correlation coefficient because, as we have seen, some important relationships are curvilinear.

Restriction of Range.   The size of the correlation coefficient may be reduced if there is a restriction of range in the variables being correlated. **Restriction of range** occurs when most participants have similar scores on one of the variables being correlated. This may occur, for instance, when the sample under study does not cover the full range of the variable. One example of this problem occurs in the use of the Scholastic Aptitude Test (SAT) as a predictor of college performance. It turns out that the correlation between SAT scores and measures of college performance such as grade-point average (GPA) is only about $r = .30$. However, the size of the correlation is probably greatly reduced by the fact that only students with relatively high SAT scores are admitted to college, and thus there is restriction of range in the SAT measure among students who also have college GPAs. When there is a smaller than normal range on one or both of the measured variables, the value of the correlation coefficient will be reduced and thus will not represent an accurate picture of the true relationship between the variables. The effect of restriction of range on the correlation coefficient is shown in Figure 9.3.

The Chi-Square Statistic

Although the correlation coefficient is used to assess the relationship between two quantitative variables, an alternative statistic, known as the **chi-square (χ^2) statistic,** must be used to assess the relationship between two nominal variables (the statistical test is technically known as the *chi-square test of independence*). Consider as an example a researcher who is interested in studying the relationship between a person's ethnicity and his or her attitude

FIGURE 9.3 Restriction of Range and the Correlation Coefficient

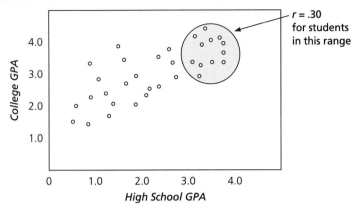

The correlation between high school GPA and college GPA across all students is about $r = .80$. However, since only the students with high school GPAs above about 2.5 are admitted to college, data are only available on both variables for the students who fall within the circled area. The correlation for these students is much lower ($r = .30$). This phenomenon is know as *restriction of range*.

toward a new low-income housing project in the neighborhood. A random sample of 300 individuals from the neighborhood is asked to express opinions about the housing project.

Calculating the Chi-Square Statistic. To calculate χ^2, the researcher first constructs a **contingency table,** which displays the number of individuals in each of the combinations of the two nominal variables. The contingency table in Table 9.2 shows the number of individuals from each ethnic group who favor or oppose the housing project. The next step is to calculate the number of people who would be expected to fall into each of the entries in the table given the number of individuals with each value on the original two variables. If the number of people actually falling into the entries is substantially different from the expected values, then there is an association between the variables, and if this relationship is strong enough the chi-square test will be statistically significant and the null hypothesis that the two variables are independent can be rejected. In our example χ^2 is equal to 45.78, which is highly significant, $p < .001$. The associated effect size statistic for χ^2 is discussed in Appendix C.

Although a statistically significant chi square indicates that there is an association between the two variables, the specific pattern of the association is usually determined through inspection of the contingency table. In our example the pattern of relationship is very clear—African Americans and Hispanics are more likely to favor the project, whereas whites and Asians are more likely to be opposed to it.

TABLE 9.2   Contingency Table and Chi-Square Analysis

	Opinion		
Ethnicity	Favor	Oppose	Total
White	56	104	160
African American	51	11	62
Asian	31	29	60
Hispanic	14	4	18
Total	152	148	300

This contingency table presents the opinions of a sample of 300 community residents about the construction of a new neighborhood center in their area. The numbers in the lighter-shaded cells indicate the number of each ethnic group who favor or oppose the project. The data are analyzed using the chi statistic, which evaluates whether the different ethnic groups differ in terms of their opinions. In this case the test is statistically significant, chi ($N = 300$) = 45.78, $p < .001$, indicating that the null hypothesis of no relationship between the two variables can be rejected.

Reporting Correlations and Chi-Square Statistics.   As we have seen, when the research hypothesis involves the relationship between two quantitative variables, the correlation coefficient is the appropriate statistic. The null hypothesis is that the variables are independent ($r = 0$), and the research hypothesis is that the variables are not independent (either $r > 0$ or $r < 0$). In some cases the correlation between the variables can be reported in the text of the research report—for instance, "As predicted by the research hypothesis, the variables of optimism and reported health behavior were significantly positively correlated in the sample, $r(20) = .52, p < .01$." In this case the correlation coefficient is .52, 20 refers to the sample size (N), and .01 is the p-value of the observed correlation.

When there are many correlations to be reported at the same time, they can be presented in a **correlation matrix,** which is a table showing the correlations of many variables with each other. An example of a correlation matrix printed out by the statistical software program SPSS® is presented in Table 9.3. The variables that have been correlated are SAT, Social Support, Study Hours, and College GPA, although these names have been abbreviated by SPSS into shorter labels. The printout contains sixteen cells, each indicating the correlation between two of these variables. Within each box are the appropriate correlations (r) on the first line, the p-value on the second line, and the sample size (N) on the third line. Note that SPSS indicates the (two-tailed) p-values as "sig."

Because any variable correlates at $r = 1.00$ with itself, the correlations on the diagonal of a correlation matrix are all 1.00. The correlation matrix is also symmetrical in the sense that each of the correlations above the diagonal is also represented below the diagonal. Because the information on the diagonal is not particularly useful, and the information below the diagonal is redundant with the information above the diagonal, it is general practice to report only the upper triangle of the correlation matrix in the research report. An example of a correlation matrix based on the output in Table 9.3 as reported using APA format is shown in Table 9.4. You can see that only the upper triangle of correlations has been presented, and that rather than reporting the exact p-values, they are instead indicated using a legend of asterisks. Because the sample size for each of the correlations is the same, it is only presented once, in a note at the bottom of the table.

TABLE 9.3   A Correlation Matrix as an SPPS Output

		SAT	Support	Hours	GPA
SAT	Pearson Correlation	1	−.020	.240**	.250**
	Sig. (2-tailed)	.	.810	.003	.002
	N	155	155	155	155
SUPPORT	Pearson Correlation	−.020	1	.020	.140
	Sig. (2-tailed)	.810	.	.806	.084
	N	155	155	155	155
HOURS	Pearson Correlation	.240**	.020	1	.240**
	Sig. (2-tailed)	.003	.806	.	.003
	N	155	155	155	155
GPA	Pearson Correlation	.250**	.140	.240**	1
	Sig. (2-tailed)	.002	.084	.003	.
	N	155	155	155	155

**Correlation is significant at the 0.01 level (2-tailed).

TABLE 9.4   A Correlation Matrix as Reported in APA Format

Predictor Variables	1	2	3	4
1. Rated social support	—	−.02	.24*	.25*
2. High school SAT score		—	.02	.14
3. Rated social support			—	.24*
4. Weekly reported hours of study				—

Note: Correlations indicated with an asterisk are significant at $p < .05$. All correlations are based on $N = 155$.

When the chi-square statistic has been used, the results are usually reported in the text of the research report. For instance, the analysis shown in Table 9.2 would be reported as χ^2 (3, N = 300) = 45.78, p < .001, where 300 represents the sample size, 45.78 is the value of the chi-square statistic, and .001 is the p-value. The number 3 refers to the *degrees of freedom* of the chi square, a statistic discussed in Appendix C.

Multiple Regression

Although the goal of correlational research is frequently to study the relationship between two measured variables, it is also possible to study relationships among more than two measures at the same time. Consider, for example, a scientist whose goal is to predict the grade-point averages of a sample of college students. As shown in Figure 9.4, the scientist uses three predictor variables (perceived social support, number of study hours per week, and SAT score) to do so. Such a research design, in which more than one predictor variable is used to predict a single outcome variable, is analyzed through **multiple regression.** Multiple regression is a statistical technique based on Pearson correlation coefficients both between each of the predictor variables and the outcome variable and among the predictor variables themselves. In this case the original correlations that form the input to the regression analysis are shown in the correlation matrix in Table 9.3.[1]

If you look at Table 9.3 carefully, you will see that the correlations between the three predictor variables and the outcome variable range from r = .14 (for the correlation between social support and college GPA) to r = .25 (for the correlation between SAT and college GPA). These correlations, which serve as the input to a multiple regression analysis, are known as *zero-order correlations*. The advantage of a multiple regression approach is that it allows the researcher to simultaneously consider the influence of all of the predictor variables on the outcome variable. And if each of the predictor variables has some (perhaps only a very small) correlation with the outcome variable, then the ability to predict the outcome variable will generally be even greater if all of the predictor variables are used to predict at the same time.

Because multiple regression requires an extensive set of calculations, it is always conducted on a computer. The outcome of our researcher's multiple regression analysis is shown in Figure 9.4. There are two pieces of information. First, the ability of all of the predictor variables together to predict the outcome variable is indicated by a statistic known as the **multiple correlation coefficient,** symbolized by the letter **R.** For the data in Figure 9.4, R = .34. The statistical significance of R is tested with a statistic known as F, described in Appendix D. In our case the R is significant, p < .05. Because R is the effect size statistic for a multiple regression analysis, and R^2 is the proportion of variance measure, R and R^2 can be directly compared to r and r^2, respectively. You can

---

[1]As described more fully in Appendix D, multiple regression can also be used to examine the relationships between nominal predictor variables and a quantitative outcome variable.

FIGURE 9.4   Multiple Regression

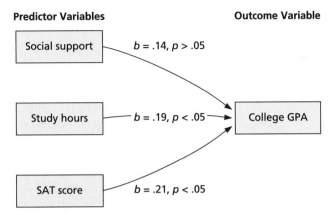

This figure represents the simultaneous impact of three measured independent variables (perceived social support, hours of study per week, and SAT score) as predictors of college GPA based on a hypothetical study of 155 college students. The numbers on the arrows indicate the regression coefficients of each of the predictor variables with the outcome variable. The ability of the three predictor variables to predict the outcome variable is indexed by the multiple correlation, *R,* which in this case equals .34.

see that, as expected, the ability to predict the outcome measure using all three predictor variables at the same time ($R = .34$) is better than that of any of the zero-order correlations (which ranged from $r = .14$ to $r = .25$).

Second, the regression analysis shows statistics that indicate the relationship between each of the predictor variables and the outcome variable. These statistics are known as the **regression coefficients**[2] or **beta weights.** Each regression coefficient can be tested for statistical significance, and both the regression coefficients and their *p*-values are indicated on the arrows connecting the predictor variables and outcome variable in Figure 9.4.

The regression coefficients are not exactly the same as the zero-order correlations because they represent the effects of each of the predictor measures in the regression analysis, holding constant or *controlling for* the effects of the other predictor variables. This control is accomplished statistically. The result is that the regression coefficients can be used to indicate the relative contributions of each of the predictor variables. For instance, the regression coefficient of .19 indicates the relationship between study hours and college GPA, controlling for both social support and SAT. In this case the regression coefficient is statistically significant, and the relevant conclusion is that estimated study hours predicts GPA even when the influence of social support and SAT is controlled. Furthermore, we can see that SAT ($b = .21$) is somewhat more predictive

---

[2]As we will see in Appendix D, these are technically *standardized* regression coefficients.

of GPA than is social support (b = .14). As we will see in the next section, one of the important uses of multiple regression is to assess the relationship between a predictor and an outcome variable when the influence of other predictor variables on the outcome variable is statistically controlled.

Correlation and Causality

As we have seen in Chapter 1, an important limitation of correlational research designs is that they cannot be used to draw conclusions about the causal relationships among the measured variables. An observed correlation between two variables does not necessarily indicate that either one of the variables caused the other. Thus even though the research hypothesis may have specified a predictor and an outcome variable, and the researcher may believe that the predictor variable is causing the outcome variable, the correlation between the two variables does not provide support for this hypothesis.

Interpreting Correlations

Consider, for instance, a researcher who has hypothesized that viewing violent behavior will cause increased aggressive play in children. He has collected, from a sample of fourth-grade children, a measure of how many violent TV shows the child views per week, as well as a measure of how aggressively each child plays on the school playground. Furthermore, the researcher has found a significant positive correlation between the two measured variables. Although this positive correlation appears to support the researcher's hypothesis, because there are alternative ways to explain the correlation it *cannot* be taken to indicate that viewing violent television causes aggressive behavior.

Reverse Causation. One possibility is that the causal direction is exactly opposite from what has been hypothesized. Perhaps children who have behaved aggressively at school develop residual excitement that leads them to want to watch violent TV shows at home:

Although the possibility that aggressive play causes increased viewing of violent television, rather than vice versa, may seem less likely to you, there is no way to rule out the possibility of such **reverse causation** on the basis of this observed correlation. It is also possible that both causal directions are operating and that the two variables cause each other. Such cases are known as **reciprocal causation:**

Common-Causal Variables.   Still another possible explanation for the observed correlation is that it has been produced by the presence of a common-causal variable (sometimes known as a *third variable*). **Common-causal variables** are variables that are not part of the research hypothesis but that cause both the predictor and the outcome variable and thus produce the observed correlation between them. In our example a potential common-causal variable is the discipline style of the children's parents. For instance, parents who use a harsh and punitive discipline style may produce children who both like to watch violent TV and behave aggressively in comparison to children whose parents use less harsh discipline:

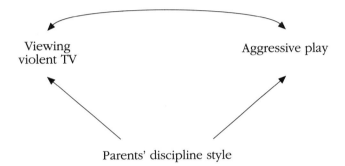

In this case, TV viewing and aggressive play would be positively correlated (as indicated by the curved arrow), even though neither one caused the other but they were both caused by the discipline style of the parents (the straight arrows).

When the predictor and outcome variables are both caused by a common-causal variable, the observed relationship between them is said to be spurious. In a **spurious relationship,** the common-causal variable produces and "explains away" the relationship between the predictor and outcome variables. If effects of the common-causal variable were taken away, or controlled for, the relationship between the predictor and outcome variables would disappear. In our example the relationship between aggression and TV viewing might be spurious because if we were to control for the effect of the parents' disciplining style, the relationship between TV viewing and aggressive behavior might go away. You can see that if a common-causal variable such as parental discipline was operating, this would lead to a very different interpretation of the data. And the identification of the true cause of the relationship would also lead to a very different plan to reduce aggressive behavior—a focus on parenting style rather than the presence of violent television.

I like to think of common-causal variables in correlational research designs as "mystery" variables because, since they have not been measured, their presence and identity are usually unknown to the researcher. Since it is not possible to measure every variable that could cause both the predictor and outcome variables, the existence of an unknown common-causal variable is always a possibility. For this reason, we are left with the basic limitation of correlational research: "Correlation does not demonstrate causation." And, of course, this is exactly why, when possible, it is desirable to conduct experimental research designs.

When you read about correlational research projects, keep in mind the possibility of spurious relationships, and be sure to interpret the findings appropriately. Although correlational research is sometimes reported as demonstrating causality without any mention being made of the possibility of common-causal variables, informed consumers of research, like you, are aware of these interpretational problems.

Extraneous Variables. Although common-causal variables are the most problematic because they can produce spurious relationships, correlational research designs are also likely to have other variables that are not part of the research hypothesis and that cause one or more of the measured variables. For instance, how aggressively a child plays at school is probably caused to some extent by the disciplining style of the child's teacher, but TV watching at home is probably not:

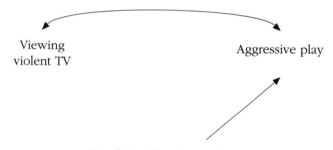

Variables other than the predictor variable that cause the outcome variable *but that do not cause the predictor variable* are called **extraneous variables.** The distinction between extraneous variables and common-causal variables is an important one because they lead to substantially different interpretations of observed correlations. Extraneous variables may reduce the likelihood of finding a significant correlation between the predictor variable and outcome variable because they cause changes in the outcome variable. However, because they do not cause the predictor variable, extraneous variables cannot produce a spurious correlation.

Mediating Variables. Another type of variable that can appear in a correlational research design and that is relevant for gaining a full understanding of the causal relationships among measured variables is known as a *mediating variable* or **mediator.** In a correlational design, a **mediating variable** is a variable that is caused by the predictor variable and that in turn causes the outcome variable. For instance, we might expect that the level of arousal of the child might mediate the relationship between viewing violent material and displaying aggressive behavior:

Violent TV $\longrightarrow$ Arousal $\longrightarrow$ Aggressive play

In this case, the expected causal relationship is that violent TV causes arousal and that arousal causes aggressive play. Other examples of mediating variables would include:

Failure on a task $\longrightarrow$ Low self-esteem $\longrightarrow$ Less interest in the task

and

More study time $\longrightarrow$ Greater retention of material in long-term memory $\longrightarrow$ Better task performance

Mediating variables are important because they explain *why* a relationship between two variables occurs. For instance, we can say that viewing violent material increases aggression *because* it increases arousal, and that failure on a task leads to less interest in the task *because* it decreases self-esteem. Of course, there are usually many possible mediating variables in relationships. Viewing violent material might increase aggression because it reduces inhibitions against behaving aggressively:

Violent TV $\longrightarrow$ Fewer inhibitions $\longrightarrow$ Aggressive play

or because it provides new ideas about how to be aggressive:

Violent TV $\longrightarrow$ Violence-related ideas $\longrightarrow$ Aggressive play

rather than (or in addition to) its effects on arousal. Mediating variables are often measured in correlational research as well as in experimental research to help the researcher better understand why variables are related to each other.

Using Correlational Data to Test Causal Models

Although correlational research designs are limited in these ways, they can in some cases provide at least some information about the likely causal relationships among measured variables. This evidence is greater to the extent that the data allow the researcher to rule out the possibility of reverse causation and to control for common-causal variables.

Conducting Longitudinal Research. One approach to ruling out reverse causation is to use a longitudinal research design (also known as a **panel study**). **Longitudinal research designs** are those in which the same individuals are measured more than one time and the time period between the measurements is long enough that changes in the variables of interest could occur. Consider, for instance, research conducted by Eron, Huesman, Lefkowitz, and Walder (1972). They measured both violent television viewing and aggressive play behavior in a group of children when they were eight years old, but they also waited and measured these two variables again when the children were

FIGURE 9.5   Path Diagram

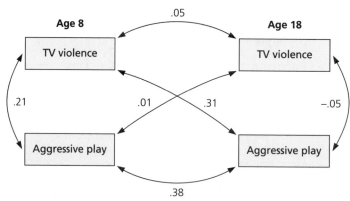

Source: From L. D. Eron, L. R. Huesman, M. M. Lefkowitz, and D. O. Walder, "Does Television Watching Cause Aggression?" *American Psychologist,* 1972, Vol. 27, 254–263. Copyright © 1972 by the American Psychological Association. Adapted with permission.

This figure presents data from a longitudinal study in which children's viewing of violent television and their displayed aggressive behavior at school were measured at two separate occasions spaced ten years apart. Each path shows the regression coefficient between two variables. The relevant finding is that the regression coefficient between TV viewing at time 1 and aggressive behavior at time 2 ($b = .31$) is significantly greater than the regression coefficient between aggressive behavior at time 1 and television viewing at time 2 ($b = .01$). The data are thus more supportive of the hypothesis that television viewing causes aggressive behavior than vice versa.

eighteen years old. The resulting data were a set of correlation coefficients among the two variables, each measured at each time period.

Correlational data from longitudinal research designs are often analyzed through a form of multiple regression that assesses the relationships among a number of measured variables, known as a **path analysis.** The results of the path analysis can be displayed visually in the form of a **path diagram,** which represents the associations among a set of variables, as shown for the data from the Eron et al. study in Figure 9.5. As in multiple regression, in a path diagram the paths between the variables represent the regression coefficients, and each regression coefficient again has an associated significance test.

Recall that Eron and his colleagues wished to test the hypothesis that viewing violent television causes aggressive behavior, while ruling out the possibility of reverse causation—namely, that aggression causes increased television viewing. To do so, they compared the regression coefficient linking television viewing at age eight with aggression at age eighteen ($b = .31$) with the regression coefficient linking aggression at age eight with television viewing at age eighteen ($b = .01$). Because the former turns out to be significantly greater than the latter, the data are more consistent with the hypothesis that viewing violent television causes aggressive behavior than the reverse. However, although this longitudinal research helps rule out reverse causation, it does not rule out the possibility that the observed relationship is spurious.[3]

As you can imagine, one limitation of longitudinal research designs is that they take a long time to conduct. Eron and his colleagues, for instance, had to wait ten years before they could draw their conclusions about the effect of violent TV viewing on aggression! Despite this difficulty, longitudinal designs are essential for providing knowledge about causal relationships. The problem is that research designs that measure people from different age groups at the same time—they are known as **cross-sectional research designs**—are very limited in their ability to rule out reverse causation. For instance, if we found that older children were more aggressive than younger children in a cross-sectional study, we could effectively rule out reverse causation because the age of the child could not logically be caused by the child's aggressive play. We could not, however, use a cross-sectional design to draw conclusions about what other variables caused these changes. A longitudinal design in which both the predictor and the outcome variables are measured repeatedly over time can be informative about these questions.

Controlling for Common-Causal Variables. In addition to helping rule out the possibility of reverse causation, correlational data can in some cases be used to rule out, at least to some extent, the influence of common-causal variables. Consider again our researcher who is interested in testing the hypothesis that viewing violent television causes aggressive behavior in elementary school children. And imagine that she or he has measured not only television viewing and aggressive behavior in the sample of children but also the discipline style of the children's parents. Because the researcher has measured this potential common-causal variable, she or he can attempt to control for its effects statistically using multiple regression.

The idea is to use both the predictor variable (viewing violent TV) and the potential common-causal variable (parental discipline) to predict the outcome variable (aggressive play):

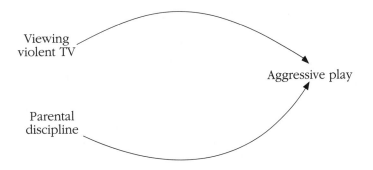

---

[3]The procedures for conducting a path analysis, including the significance test that compares the regression coefficients, can be found in Kenny (1979, p. 239).

If the predictor variable still significantly relates to the outcome variable when the common-causal variable is controlled (that is, if the regression coefficient between violent TV and aggressive play is significant), we have more confidence that parental discipline is not causing a spurious relationship. However, this conclusion assumes that the measured common-causal variable really measures parental discipline (that is, that the measure has construct validity), and it does not rule out the possibility of reverse causation. Furthermore, there are still other potential common-causal variables that have not been measured and that could produce a spurious relationship between the predictor and the outcome variables.

Assessing the Role of Mediating Variables.   Multiple regression techniques can also be used to test whether hypotheses about proposed mediators are likely to be valid. As we have seen, mediational relationships can be expressed in the form of a path diagram:

Viewing
violent ⟶ Arousal ⟶ Aggressive play
TV

If arousal is actually a mediator of the relationship, then the effects of viewing violent material on aggression are expected to occur because they influence arousal, and not directly. On the other hand, if arousal is *not* a mediator, then violent TV should have a direct effect on aggressive play, which is not mediated through arousal:

Viewing violent TV   Arousal   Aggressive play

To test whether arousal is a likely mediator, we again enter both the predictor variable (in this case, viewing violent TV) as well as the proposed mediating variable (in this case, arousal) as predictors of the outcome variable in a regression equation. If arousal is a mediator, then when its effects are controlled in the analysis, the predictor variable (viewing violent TV) should no longer correlate with the outcome variable (that is, the regression coefficient for viewing violent TV should no longer be significant). If this is the case, then we have at least some support for the proposed mediational variable.

Structural Equation Analysis.   Over the past decades, new statistical procedures have been developed that allow researchers to draw even more conclusions about the likely causal relationships among measured variables using correlational data. One of these techniques is known as structural equation analysis. A **structural equation analysis** is a statistical procedure that tests whether the observed relationships among a set of variables conform to a theoretical prediction about how those variables should be causally related.

One advantage of structural equation analysis over other techniques is that it is designed to represent both the conceptual variables as well as the meas-

FIGURE 9.6   Structural Equation Model

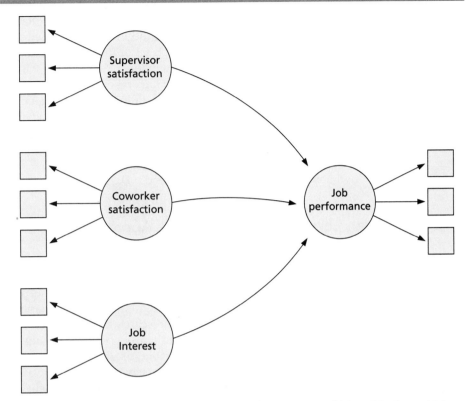

This hypothetical structural equation analysis uses nine measures of job satisfaction, which are combined into three latent variables, to predict a single latent variable of job performance, as measured by three dependent variables. The value of the overall fit of the model to the collected data can be estimated. The structural equation analysis tests both the measurement of the latent variables and the relationships among them.

ured variables in the statistical analysis. Normally, each conceptual variable is assessed using more than one measured variable, which allows the analysis to also calculate the reliability of the measures. When conducting a structural equation analysis, the scientist enters the variables that have been used to assess each of the conceptual variables. The conceptual variables are usually called **latent variables** in a structural equation analysis, and the analysis is designed to assess both the relationships between the measured and the conceptual variables and the relationships among the conceptual variables. The conceptual variables can include both independent and dependent variables.

Consider as an example an industrial psychologist who has conducted a correlational study designed to predict the conceptual variable of "job performance" from three conceptual variables of "supervisor satisfaction," "coworker satisfaction," and "job interest." As shown in Figure 9.6, the researcher has used three measured variables (represented as squares) to assess each of the four conceptual variables (supervisor satisfaction, coworker satisfaction, job interest, and job performance), represented as circles. Rather than computing a separate reliability analysis on the three independent variables and the dependent variable, combining each set of three scores together, and then using a regression analysis with three independent variables and one dependent variable, the scientist could use a structural equation analysis to test the entire set of relationships at the same time. In the structural equation analysis all of the relationships among the variables—some of which involve the relationship between the measured variables and the conceptual variables and others of which involve the relationships among the conceptual variables themselves—are simultaneously tested. More information about the use of structural equation analyses can be found in Appendix D.

When Correlational Designs Are Appropriate

We have seen in this chapter that correlational research designs have both strengths and limitations. Their greatest strength may be that they can be used when experimental research is not possible because the predictor variables cannot be manipulated. For instance, it would be impossible to test, except through a correlational design, the research hypothesis that people who go to church regularly are more helpful than people who do not go to church. An experimental design is not possible because we cannot randomly assign some people to go to church and others to stay at home. Correlational designs also have the advantage of allowing the researcher to study behavior as it occurs in everyday life.

Scientists also frequently use correlational research designs in applied research when they want to predict scores on an outcome variable from knowledge about a predictor variable but do not need to know exactly what causal relationships are involved. For instance, a researcher may use a personality test to determine which employees will do well on a job but may not care whether the relation is produced by the personality variable or another common-causal variable.

However, although sometimes used to provide at least some information about which patterns of causal relationships are most likely, correlational studies cannot provide conclusive information about causal relationships among variables. Only experimental research designs in which the independent variable is manipulated by the experimenter can do this. And it is to such designs that we now turn.

SUMMARY

Correlational research is designed to test research hypotheses in cases where it is not possible or desirable to experimentally manipulate the independent variable of interest. It is also desirable because it allows the investigation of behavior in naturally occurring situations. Correlational methods range from analysis of correlations between a predictor and an outcome variable to multiple regression and path analyses assessing the patterns of relationships among many measured variables.

Two quantitative variables can be found to be related in either linear or nonlinear patterns. The type of relationship can be ascertained graphically with a scatterplot. If the relationships are linear, they can be statistically measured with the Pearson correlation coefficient (r). Associations between two nominal variables are assessed with the χ^2 test of independence.

Multiple regression uses more than one predictor variable to predict a single outcome variable. The analysis includes a test of the statistical significance between the predictor and outcome variables collectively (the multiple R) and individually (the regression coefficients).

Correlational research can in some cases be used to make at least some inferences about the likely causal relationships among variables if reverse causation and the presence of common-causal variables can be ruled out. In general, the approach is to examine the pattern of correlations among the variables using either multiple regression or structural equation analysis. Correlational data can also be used to assess whether hypotheses about proposed mediating variables are likely to be valid. However, because even the most sophisticated path analyses cannot be used to make definitive statements about causal relations, researchers often rely, at least in part, on experimental research designs.

KEY TERMS

beta weights 165
chi-square (χ^2) statistic 160
coefficient of determination (r^2) 160
common-causal variables 167
contingency table 161
correlation matrix 162
cross-sectional research designs 171
curvilinear relationships 159
extraneous variables 168
independent 159
latent variables 173
linear relationship 158
longitudinal research designs 169
mediating variable (mediator) 168

multiple correlation coefficient (R) 164
multiple regression 164
nonlinear relationship 158
panel study 169
path analysis 170
path diagram 170
reciprocal causation 166
regression coefficients 165
regression line 157
restriction of range 160
reverse causation 166
scatterplot 157
spurious relationship 167
structural equation analysis 172

REVIEW AND DISCUSSION QUESTIONS

1. When are correlational research designs used in behavioral research? What are their advantages and disadvantages?

2. What are a linear relationship and a curvilinear relationship? What does it mean if two variables are independent?

3. Interpret the meanings of, and differentiate between, the two Pearson correlation coefficients $r = .85$ and $r = -.85$.

4. What is multiple regression, and how is it used in behavioral science research?

5. What is a spurious relationship?

6. What is the difference between a common-causal variable, an extraneous variable, and a mediating variable?

7. In what ways can correlational data provide information about the likely causal relationships among variables?

HANDS-ON EXPERIENCE

1. List an example of each of the following:
   a. Two quantitative variables that are likely to have a positive linear relationship
   b. Two quantitative variables that are likely to have a negative linear relationship
   c. Two quantitative variables that are likely to be independent
   d. Two quantitative variables that are likely to have a curvilinear relationship
   e. Two nominal variables that are likely to be associated
   f. Two nominal variables that are likely to be independent

2. Consider potential common-causal variables that might make each of the following correlational relationships spurious:
   a. Height and intelligence in children
   b. Handgun ownership and violent crime in a city
   c. The number of firefighters at a fire and the damage done by the fire
   d. The number of ice cream cones sold and the number of drownings

3. Develop your own example of a correlation that is likely to be spurious.

4. Develop five examples of conceptual variables that cannot be studied through experimental research designs and for which correlational designs must be used.

5. What is meant by a spurious relationship, and how do spurious relationships limit the ability of the researcher to draw conclusions about the causal relationships among variables?

6. List three variables that might be used to predict each of the following outcome variables in a regression analysis:
   a. Level of anxiety
   b. Job satisfaction
   c. Degree of self-esteem

7. For each of the following, order the variables according to the likely predictor, mediator, and dependent variables:
   a. Viewing a comedy film, helping, a positive mood state
   b. Number of bystanders, diffusion of responsibility, helping
   c. Anxiety, importance of test to self-esteem, task performance
   d. Job satisfaction, job performance, current salary

8. Answer Hands-on Experience problems 1 through 5 in Appendix C and Hands-on Experience problem 1 in Appendix D.

CHAPTER TEN
Experimental Research: One-Way Designs

STUDY QUESTIONS

- What types of evidence allow us to conclude that one variable causes another variable?

- How do experimental research designs allow us to demonstrate causal relationships between independent and dependent variables?

- How is equivalence among the levels of the independent variable created in experiments?

- How does the Analysis of Variance test hypotheses about differences between the experimental conditions?

- What are repeated-measures experimental designs?

- How are the results of experimental research designs presented in the research report?

- What are the advantages and disadvantages of experimental designs versus correlational research?

Because most scientists are particularly interested in answering questions about how and when changes in independent variables cause changes in dependent variables, they frequently employ experimental research designs. In contrast to correlational research in which the independent and dependent variables are measured, in an experiment the investigator manipulates the independent variable or variables by arranging different experiences for the research participants and then assesses the impact of these different experiences on one or more measured dependent variables.[1]

As we will see in this chapter and in Chapter 11, there are many different varieties of experimental designs. Furthermore, as we will see in Chapter 12, to be used to make inferences about causality, experiments must be conducted very carefully and with great attention to how the research participants are treated and how they are responding to the experimental situation. However, when experiments are conducted properly, the fact that the independent variable is manipulated rather than measured allows us to be more confident that any observed changes on the dependent measure were caused by the independent variable.

Demonstration of Causality

How can we tell when one event causes another event to occur? For instance, how would we determine whether watching violent cartoons on TV causes aggressive play in children or whether participating in a program of psychotherapy causes a reduction in anxiety? To answer such questions—that is, to make inferences of causality—we must consider three factors: association, temporal priority, and control of common-causal variables. These form the basis of experimental research (Mill, 1930).

Association

Before we can infer that the former causes the latter, there must first be an association, or correlation, between an independent and a dependent variable. If viewing violent television programs causes aggressive behavior, for instance, there must be a positive correlation between television viewing and aggression. Of course, the correlation between the two variables will not be perfect. That is, we cannot expect that every time the independent variable (viewing a violent TV show) occurs, the dependent variable (acting aggressively) will also occur or that acting aggressively will occur only after viewing violent TV.

Rather than being perfect, the causal relationships between variables in behavioral science, as well as in many other fields, are *probabilistic*. To take

---

[1]Although the word *experiment* is often used in everyday language to refer to any type of scientific study, the term should really only be used for research designs in which the independent variable is manipulated.

another well-known example, consider the statement "Cigarette smoking causes lung cancer." Because there are lots of other causes of cancer, and because precise specification of these causes is not currently possible, this causal statement is also probabilistic. Thus, although we can state that when smoking occurs, lung cancer is more likely to occur than if no smoking had occurred, we cannot say exactly when or for whom smoking will cause cancer. The same holds true for causal statements in the behavioral sciences.

Temporal Priority

A second factor that allows us to draw inferences about causality is the temporal relation between the two associated variables. If event A occurs before event B, then A could be causing B. However, if event A occurs after event B, it cannot be causing that event. For instance, if children view a violent television show before they act aggressively, the viewing may have caused the behavior. But the viewing cannot have been the causal variable if it occurred only after the aggressive behavior. The difficulty in determining the temporal ordering of events in everyday life makes the use of correlational research to draw causal inferences problematic.

Control of Common-Causal Variables

Although association and temporal priority are required for making inferences about causality, they are not sufficient. As we have seen in Chapter 9, to make causal statements also requires the ability to rule out the influence of common-causal variables that may have produced spurious relationships between the independent and dependent variables. As we will see in the following sections, one of the major strengths of experimental designs is that through the use of **experimental manipulations,** the researcher can rule out the possibility that the relationship between the independent and dependent variables is spurious.

One-Way Experimental Designs

Let us consider the experimental research design diagrammed in Figure 10.1. The experiment is known as a **one-way experimental design** because it has one independent variable. In the experiment twenty fourth-grade boys and girls watched a sequence of five cartoons that had been selected by a panel of experts to be extremely violent, and another twenty children watched a series of nonviolent cartoons. After viewing the cartoons, the children were taken to a play area where they were allowed to play with toys, while a team of observers (who did not know which cartoons the children had seen) coded the aggressiveness of the children's play. The research hypothesis was that the children who had viewed the violent cartoons would play more aggressively than those who had viewed the nonviolent cartoons.

FIGURE 10.1   One-Way Between-Participants Experimental Design Using Random Assignment to Conditions

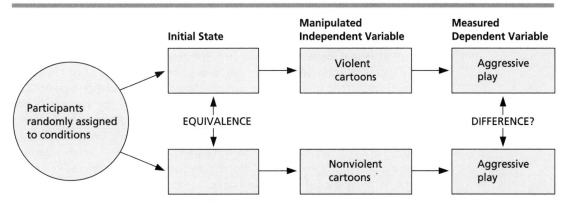

This is a one-way experimental design with two levels of the independent variable. Equivalence has been created through random assignment to conditions. The research hypothesis is that there will be a significant difference in aggressive play between the two experimental conditions such that children who have viewed the violent cartoons will play more aggressively than children who have viewed the nonviolent cartoons.

The Experimental Manipulation

To guarantee that the independent variable occurs prior to the dependent variable, in experimental designs the independent variable or variables are cre-ated or, in experimental terms, **manipulated.** In an experiment the manipula-tion becomes the independent variable, and it is given a name that reflects the different situations that have been created. In this experiment the independent variable refers to the type of cartoons that the children have viewed. The in-dependent variable is called *cartoon type* to indicate that the manipulation in-volved children viewing either violent or nonviolent cartoons. The term **levels** refers to the specific situations that are created within the manipulation. In our example the manipulated independent variable (cartoon type) has two levels: "violent cartoons" and "nonviolent cartoons." In one-way designs the levels of the independent variable are frequently called the experimental **conditions.**

Equivalence and Control.   In addition to guaranteeing that the independent variable occurs prior to measurement of the dependent variable, an experi-mental manipulation also allows the researcher to rule out the possibility of common-causal variables—variables that cause both the independent and the dependent variable. In experimental designs the influence of common-causal variables is eliminated (or *controlled*) through creation of equivalence among the participants in each of the experimental conditions before the manipula-tion occurs. As we will see in the sections to come, equivalence can be created either through using different but equivalent participants in each level of the experiment (**between-participants designs**) or through using the same people in each of the experimental conditions (**repeated-measures designs**).

Random Assignment to Conditions.   In a between-participants experimental design such as that shown in Figure 10.1, the researcher compares the scores on the dependent variable between different groups of participants. However, the participants in the groups are equated before the manipulation occurs. The most common method of creating equivalence among the experimental conditions is through **random assignment to conditions.**[2] Random assignment involves the researcher determining separately for each participant which level of the independent variable she or he will experience; the researcher does this through a random process such as flipping a coin, drawing numbers out of an envelope, or using a random number table. In essence, random assignment involves the researcher drawing separate simple random samples of participants to be in each of the levels of the independent variable. And because the samples are drawn from the same population, we can be confident that before the manipulation occurs, the participants in the different levels of the independent variable are, on average, equivalent in every respect except for differences that are due to chance.

In our case, because the children have been randomly assigned to conditions, those who are going to view the violent cartoons will, on average, be equivalent to those who are going to view the nonviolent cartoons in terms of every possible variable, including variables that are expected to be related to aggression, such as hormones and parental discipline. This does not, of course, mean that the children do not differ on the variables. There are some children who are more aggressive than others, who are in better moods than others, and who have stricter parents. These variables are (as we have discussed in Chapter 9) extraneous variables. However, random assignment to conditions ensures that the average score on all of these variables will be the same for the participants in each of the conditions. Although random assignment does not guarantee that the participants in the different conditions are *exactly* equivalent before the experiment begins, it does greatly reduce the likelihood of differences. And the likelihood of chance differences between or among the conditions is reduced even further as the sample size in each condition increases.

Selection of the Dependent Variable

Experiments have one or more measured dependent variables designed to assess the state of the participants after the experimental manipulation has occurred. In our example the dependent variable is a behavioral measure of ag-

---

[2]Be careful not to confuse *random assignment,* which involves assignment of participants to levels of an independent variable, with *random sampling,* which (as described in Chapter 6) is used to draw a representative sample from a population.

gressive play, but any of the many types of measures discussed in Chapter 4 could serve as a dependent variable. It is necessary, as in all research, to ensure that the dependent measures are reliable and valid indicators of the conceptual variable of interest (see Chapter 5).

The research hypothesis in an experimental design is that *after* the manipulation occurs, the mean scores on the dependent variable will be significantly different between the participants in the different levels of the independent variable. And if the experimenter does observe significant differences between the conditions, then he or she can conclude that the manipulation, rather than any other variable, caused these differences. Since equivalence was created before the manipulation occurred, common-causal variables could not have produced the differences. In short, except for random error, the *only* difference between the participants in the different conditions is that they experienced different levels of the experimental manipulation.

Variety and Number of Levels

Experiments differ in both the number of levels of the independent variable and the type of manipulation used. In the simplest experimental design there are only two levels. In many cases one of the two levels involves the presence of a certain situation (for instance, viewing violent cartoons), whereas the other level involves the absence of that situation (for instance, viewing nonviolent cartoons). In such a case the level in which the situation of interest was created is often called the **experimental condition,** and the level in which the situation was not created is called the **control condition.**

Adding Control Conditions.   There are many different types of control conditions, and the experimenter must think carefully about which one to use. As we will discuss more fully in Chapter 12, the control condition is normally designed to be the same as the experimental condition except for the experimental manipulation; thus the control condition provides a comparison for the experimental condition. For instance, in our example the children in the control condition watched nonviolent, rather than violent, cartoons. Not all experiments have or need control conditions. In some cases the manipulation might involve changes in the level of intensity of the independent variable. For instance, an experiment could be conducted in which some children viewed ten violent cartoons and other children viewed only five violent cartoons. Differences between the conditions would still be predicted, but neither condition would be considered a control condition.

Adding More Levels.   While satisfactory for testing some hypotheses, experimental designs with only two levels have some limitations. One is that it can sometimes be difficult to tell which of the two levels is causing a change in the dependent measure. For instance, if our research showed that children behaved more aggressively after viewing the violent cartoons than they did after viewing the nonviolent cartoons, we could conclude that the nonviolent cartoons *decreased* aggression rather than that the violent cartoons increased aggression. Perhaps the children who watched the nonviolent cartoons got bored and were just too tired to play aggressively. One possibility in such a case would be to include a control condition in which no cartoons are viewed at all. In this case we could compare aggressive behavior in the two cartoon conditions with that in the no-cartoon control condition to determine which cartoon has made a difference.

Detecting Nonlinear Relationships.   Another limitation of experiments with only two levels is that in cases where the manipulation varies the strength of the independent variable, it is difficult to draw conclusions about the pattern of the relationship between the independent and dependent variables. The problem is that some relationships are *curvilinear* such that increases in the independent variable cause increases in the dependent variable at some points but cause decreases at other points. As we have seen in Chapter 9, one such example involves the expected relationship between anxiety and performance. As anxiety rises from low to moderate levels, task performance tends to increase. However, once the level of anxiety gets too high, further increases in anxiety cause performance decreases. Thus the relationship between anxiety and performance is curvilinear.

As shown in Figure 10.2, a two-level experiment could conclude that anxiety improved performance, that it decreased performance, or that it did not

FIGURE 10.2   Detecting Curvilinear Relationships

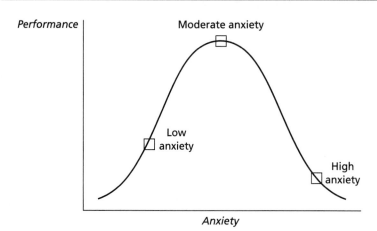

The relationship between anxiety and performance is curvilinear. An experimental design that used only two levels of anxiety could conclude that anxiety increased, decreased, or had no effect on performance, depending on whether the levels of anxiety that were created were low and medium, medium and high, or low and high. However, only a three-level experiment that included all three levels of anxiety (low, medium, and high) could determine that the true relationship between anxiety and performance is curvilinear.

change performance at all, *depending on what specific levels of anxiety were induced by the manipulation*. But an experiment with only two levels would never be able to demonstrate the true, curvilinear relationship between the variables. However, an experiment that used three or more levels of the independent variable would be able to demonstrate that the relationship between anxiety and performance was curvilinear. Although experiments with more than two levels may provide a more complete picture of the relationship between the independent and dependent variables, they also require more participants. Therefore, they should be used only when they are likely to provide specific information that would not be available in a two-level experiment.

Analysis of Variance

We have now seen that experimental designs help us determine causality by ensuring that the independent variable occurs prior to the dependent variable and by creating equivalence among the levels of the independent variable before the manipulation occurs. But how do we determine if there is an association between the independent and the dependent variable—that is, whether there are differences on the dependent measure across the levels? This question is answered through the use of a statistical procedure, known as the **Analysis of Variance (ANOVA),** that is specifically designed to compare the means of the dependent variable across the levels of an experimental research design. The ANOVA can be used for one-way research designs and, as we will see in Chapter 11, for research designs with more than one independent variable.[3]

Hypothesis Testing in Experimental Designs

Recall from our discussion in Chapter 8 that hypothesis testing always begins with a null hypothesis. In experimental designs the null hypothesis is that the mean score on the dependent variable is the same at all levels of the independent variable except for differences due to chance and thus that the manipulation has had no effect on the dependent variable. In our example the null hypothesis is

$$\text{Mean}_{\text{Violent cartoons}} = \text{Mean}_{\text{Nonviolent cartoons}}$$

The research hypothesis states that there is a difference among the conditions and normally states the specific direction of those differences. For instance, in our example the research hypothesis is that the children in the

---

[3]Just as the correlation coefficient (r) tests the association between two quantitative variables and the chi-square test for independence tests the association between two nominal variables, the one-way ANOVA tests the relationship between one nominal (independent) variable and one quantitative (dependent) variable.

violent-cartoon condition will show more aggression than the children in the nonviolent-cartoon condition:

$$\text{Mean}_{\text{Violent cartoons}} > \text{Mean}_{\text{Nonviolent cartoons}}$$

Although the goal of the ANOVA is to compare the means on the dependent variable across the different levels of the independent variable, it actually accomplishes this by analyzing the variability of the dependent variable. The ANOVA treats the null hypothesis in terms of the absence of variability among the condition means. That is, if all of the means are equivalent, then there should be no differences among them except those due to chance. But if the experimental manipulation has influenced the dependent variable, then the condition means should not all be the same, and thus there will be significantly more variability (that is, more differences) among them than would be expected by chance.

Between-Groups and Within-Groups Variance Estimates

As described in Chapter 7, the variance (s^2) is a measure of the dispersion of the scores on a variable. The ANOVA compares the variance of the means of the dependent variable *between* the different levels to the variance of individuals on the dependent variable *within* each of the conditions. The variance among the condition means is known as the **between-groups variance,** and the variance within the conditions is known as the **within-groups variance.** If the between-groups variance is significantly greater than the within-groups variance, then we conclude that the manipulation has influenced the dependent measure because the influence of the manipulation across the levels is greater than the random fluctuation among individuals within the levels. A statistic called ***F*** is calculated as the ratio of the two variances:

$$F = \frac{\text{Between-groups variance}}{\text{Within-groups variance}}$$

As the condition means differ more among each other in comparison to the variance within the conditions, F increases. F has an associated p-value, which is compared to alpha. If the p-value is less than alpha, then the null hypothesis (that all the condition means are the same) is rejected. The effect size measure for F is known as **eta (η),** and the proportion of variance in the dependent variable accounted for by the experimental manipulation is η^2. The formula for computing a one-way Analysis of Variance is presented in Appendix B.

The ANOVA Summary Table

The ANOVA calculations are summarized in an **ANOVA summary table,** as shown in Figure 10.3. The summary table includes the between-groups and the within-groups variances (usually labeled the "mean squares"), as well as F and the p-value ("Sig."). In our case the F (10.98) is statistically significant ($p = .01$). The summary table also indicates the number of levels of the independent variable as well as the number of research participants in the entire

FIGURE 10.3   ANOVA Summary Table

ANOVA

		Sum of Squares	df	Mean Square	F	Sig.
DV	Between groups	14.40	1*	14.400	10.980	.010
	Within groups	49.78	38†	1.310		
	Total	64.18	39			

$*df_{between\ groups}$ = number of conditions (2) minus 1.

$†df_{within\ groups}$ = number of participants (N) minus number of conditions, $40 - 2 = 38$.

$\bar{X}_{violent\ cartoons} = 2.89$. $\bar{X}_{nonviolent\ cartoons} = 1.52$.

study. This information is presented in the form of statistics known as **degrees of freedom (df).** The between-groups degrees of freedom are equal to the number of levels in the independent variable minus 1, and the within-groups degrees of freedom are equal to the number of participants minus the number of conditions. In the case of Figure 10.3, the degrees of freedom indicate that there are two levels of the independent variable and forty participants.

The first step in interpreting the results of an experiment is to inspect the ANOVA summary table to determine whether the condition means are signifi- cantly different from each other. If the F is statistically significant, and thus the null hypothesis of no differences among the levels can be rejected, the next step is to look at the means of the dependent variable in the different condi- tions. The results in the summary table are only meaningful in conjunction with an inspection of the condition means. The means for our example ex- periment are presented at the bottom of Figure 10.3.

In a one-way experiment with only two levels, a statistically significant F tells us that the means in the two conditions are significantly different.[4] However, the significant F only means that the null hypothesis can be rejected. To determine if the research hypothesis is supported, the experimenter must then examine the particular pattern of the condition means to see if it supports the research hy- pothesis. For instance, although the means in Figure 10.3 show that the research hypothesis was supported, a significant F could also have occurred if aggres- sion had been found to be significantly *lower* in the violent-cartoons condition.

When there are more than two levels of the independent variable, interpre- tation of a significant F is more complicated. The significant F again indicates that there are differences on the dependent variable among the levels and thus

---

[4]A statistic known as the ***t* test** may be used to compare two group means using either a between-participants design (an *independent samples t test*) or a repeated-measures design (a *paired-samples t test*). However, the *t* test is a special case of the *F* test that is used only for comparison of two means. Because the *F* test is more general, allowing the comparison of differences among any number of means, it is more useful.

that the null hypothesis (that all of the means are the same) can be rejected. But a significant *F* does not tell us which means differ from each other. For instance, if our study had included three levels, including a condition in which no cartoons were viewed at all, we would need to make further statistical tests to determine whether aggression was greater in the violent-cartoons condition than in either of the other two conditions. We will look at how to statistically compare the means of experimental conditions in Chapter 11.

Repeated-Measures Designs

As you read about between-participant designs, you might have wondered why random assignment to conditions is necessary. You might have realized that there is no better way to ensure that participants are the same in each experimental condition than to actually have the *same* people participate in each condition! When equivalence is created in this manner, the design is known as a **within-participants (within-subjects) design** because the differences across the different levels are assessed within the same participants. Within-participants designs are also called repeated-measures designs because the dependent measure is assessed more than one time for each person.

In most cases the same research hypothesis can be tested with a between-participants or a repeated-measures research design. Consider, for instance, that the repeated-measures experimental design shown in Figure 10.4 tests ex-

FIGURE 10.4 One-Way Repeated-Measures Experimental Design

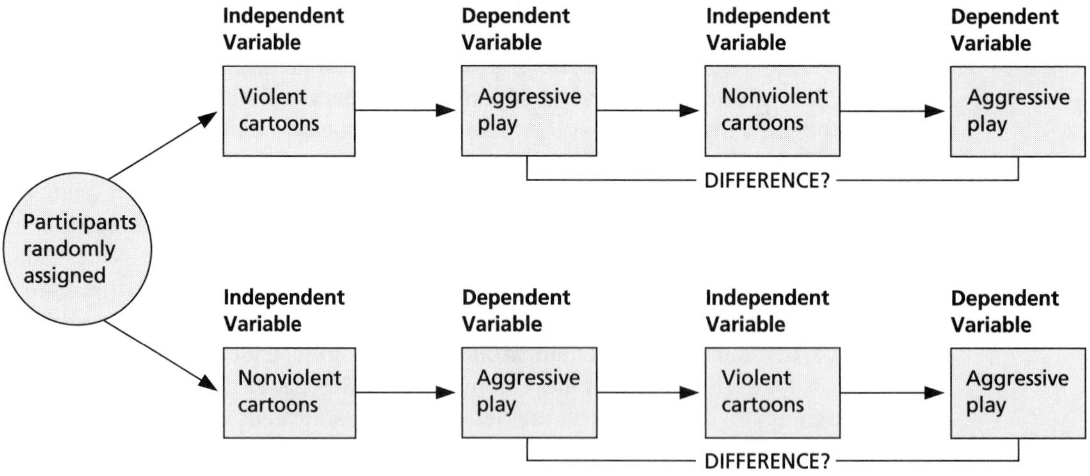

This is a one-way experimental design where equivalence has been created through use of the same participants in both levels of the independent variable. It tests the same hypothesis as the between-subjects design shown in Figure 10.1. The experiment is counterbalanced, such that one half of the participants view the violent cartoons first and the other half view the nonviolent cartoons first.

actly the same hypothesis as the between-participants design shown in Figure 10.1. The difference is that in the repeated-measures design each child views both the violent cartoons and the nonviolent cartoons and aggression is measured two times, once after the child has viewed each set of cartoons. Repeated-measures designs are also evaluated through Analysis of Variance, and the ANOVA summary table in a repeated-measures design is very similar to that in a between-participants design except for changes in the degrees of freedom. The interpretation of the effect size statistic, η, is also the same.

Advantages of Repeated-Measures Designs

Repeated-measures designs have advantages in comparison to between-participants designs using random assignment to conditions.

Increased Statistical Power.   One major advantage of repeated-measures designs is that they have greater statistical power than between-participants designs. Consider, for instance, a child in our experiment who happens to be in a particularly bad mood on the day of the experiment, and assume that this negative mood state increases his or her aggressive play. Because the child would have been assigned to either the violent-cartoon condition or the nonviolent-cartoon condition in a between-participants design, the mean aggression in whichever group the child had been assigned to would have been increased. The researcher, however, would have no way of knowing that the child's mood state influenced his or her aggressive play.

In a repeated-measures design, however, the child's aggressive play after viewing the violent cartoons is compared to his or her aggressive play after viewing the nonviolent cartoons. In this case, although the bad mood might increase aggressive play, it would be expected to increase it on both aggression measures equally. In short, because the responses of an individual in one condition (for instance, after seeing nonviolent cartoons) can be directly compared to the same person's responses in another condition (after seeing violent cartoons), the statistical power of a repeated-measures design is greater than the power of a between-participants design in which different people are being compared across conditions.

Economy of Participants.   A related advantage of repeated-measures designs is that they are more efficient because they require fewer participants. For instance, to have twenty participants in each of the two levels of a one-way design, forty participants are required in a between-participants design. Only twenty participants are needed in a repeated-measures design, however, because each participant is measured in both of the levels.

Disadvantages of Repeated-Measures Designs

Despite the advantages of power and economy, repeated-measures designs also have some major disadvantages that may in some cases make them inappropriate. These difficulties arise because the same individuals participate in more than one condition of the experiment and the dependent measure is assessed more than once.

Carryover.   One problem is that it is sometimes difficult to ensure that each measure of the dependent variable is being influenced only by the level it is designed to assess. For instance, consider the diagram at the top half of Figure 10.4 in which the children are first shown violent cartoons and then shown nonviolent cartoons. If the effects of viewing the violent cartoons last for a period of time, they may still be present when the children are measured after viewing the nonviolent cartoons. Thus the second measure of aggression may be influenced by both the nonviolent cartoons and the violent cartoons seen earlier. When effects of one level of the manipulation are still present when the dependent measure is assessed for another level of the manipulation, we say that **carryover** has occurred.

Practice and Fatigue.   In addition to carryover, the fact that participants must be measured more than once may also be problematic. For instance, if the dependent measure involved the assessment of physical skills such as typing into a computer, an individual might improve on the task over time through practice, or she or he might become fatigued and perform more poorly over time. In this case, the scores on the dependent variable would change over time for reasons unrelated to the experimental manipulation. One solution to carryover, practice, and fatigue effects is to increase the time period between the measurement of the dependent measures. For instance, the children might view the violent cartoons on one day and be observed and then be brought back a week later to view the nonviolent cartoons and be observed again. Although separation of the measures may reduce carryover, practice, and fatigue effects, it also has the disadvantage of increasing the cost of the experiment (the participants have to come on two different days), and the children themselves may change over time, reducing equivalence.

Counterbalancing.   One approach to problematic carryover, practice, or fatigue effects is **counterbalancing.** Counterbalancing involves arranging the order in which the conditions of a repeated-measures design are experienced so that each condition occurs equally often in each position. For instance, as shown in Figure 10.4, in our experiment the conditions would be arranged such that one half of the children viewed the violent cartoons first and the other half viewed the nonviolent cartoons first, with the order of viewing determined randomly. This would ensure that carryover from the nonviolent cartoons occurred just as often as did carryover from the violent cartoons. Although counterbalancing does not reduce carryover, it does allow the researcher to estimate its effects by comparing the scores on the dependent variable for the participants who were in the two different orders.

In repeated-measures designs with more than two levels, there are several possible approaches to counterbalancing. The best approach, when possible, is to use each possible order of conditions. Although this technique works well when there are two or three conditions, it becomes problematic as the number of conditions increases. Consider, for instance, a researcher who is interested in testing the ability of workers to type on a computer keyboard under six different lighting conditions: blue light, green light, orange light, red light, yellow light, and white light. Because of the possibility of practice or fatigue effects on the typing task, counterbalancing the conditions is desirable.

Latin Square Designs.   The problem in this case is that when there are six conditions, there are 720 possible orders of conditions! Because each order should be used an equal number of times, at least 720 participants would be needed. An alternative approach is to use a subset of all of the possible orders, but to ensure that each condition appears in each order. A **Latin square design** is a method of counterbalancing the order of conditions so that each condition appears in each order but also follows equally often after each of the other conditions.

The Latin square is made as follows: First, label each of the conditions with a letter (ABC for three conditions, ABCDEF for six conditions, and so forth) and then use the following ordering to create the first row of the square (A, B, L, C, L-1, D, L-2, E . . .) where L is the letter of the last condition. In other words, the order for the first row when there are four conditions will be ABDC and the order for the first row when there are six conditions will be ABFCED.

At this point the rest of the rows in the Latin square are constructed by increasing by one each letter in the row above. The last letter (in our case F) cannot be increased, of course, so it is changed to the letter A. If there is an odd number of conditions, you must make an additional Latin square that is a reversal of the first one, such that in each row the first condition becomes the last condition, the second condition is next to last, and so on. In this case you will use both Latin squares equally often in your research design (that is, you will have twice as many orders as experimental conditions). Once the Latin square or squares are made, each participant is assigned to one of the rows. In the case with six conditions, the Latin square is:

ABFCED

BCADFE

CDBEAF

DECFBA

EFDACB

FAEBDC

When to Use a Repeated-Measures Design

Although carryover, practice, and fatigue effects pose problems for repeated-measures designs, they can be alleviated to a great extent through counterbalancing. There are, however, some cases in which a repeated-measures design is simply out of the question—for example, when the participants, because they are in each of the experimental conditions, are able to guess the research hypothesis and change their responses according to what they think the researcher is studying. You can imagine that children who are first shown a violent film, observed, and then shown a control film and observed again might become suspicious that the experiment is studying their reactions to the cartoons. In such cases repeated-measures designs are not possible.

In other cases counterbalancing cannot be done effectively because something that occurs in one level of the independent variable will always influence behavior in any conditions that follow it. For instance, in an experiment testing whether creation of a mental image of an event will help people remember it, the individuals given this memory strategy will probably continue using it in a later control condition.

Nevertheless, the problems caused by a repeated-measures strategy do not occur equally in all research. With unobtrusive behavioral measures, for instance, the problem of guessing the hypothesis might not be severe. And some measures may be more likely than others to produce practice or fatigue effects. It is up to the researcher to determine the likelihood of a given problem occurring before deciding whether to use a repeated-measures design. In short, repeated-measures research designs represent a useful alternative to standard between-participants designs in cases where carryover effects are likely to be minimal and where repeated administration of the dependent measure does not seem problematic.

Presentation of Experiment Results

Once the experiment has been conducted and the results analyzed, it will be necessary to report the findings in the research report. Although the F and the p-value will be presented, the discussion of the results will be focused on the interpretation of the pattern of the condition means. Because the condition means are so important, they must be presented in a format that is easy for the reader to see and to understand. The means may be reported in a table, in a figure, or in the research report itself, but each mean should be reported using only one of these methods. Figure 10.5 presents the means from our hypothetical experiment, reported first as they would be in a table and then as they would be in a bar chart. You can see that one advantage to using a table format is that it is easy to report the standard deviations and the sample size of each of the experimental conditions. On the other hand, the use of a figure makes the pattern of the data easily visible.

In addition to the condition means, the research report must also present F and the p-value. Generally, a reporting of the entire ANOVA summary table is not necessary. Rather, the information is reported in the text, as in the following example:

> There were significant differences on rated aggression across the levels of the cartoon condition, $F(1, 38) = 10.98$, $p < .01$. Children who viewed the violent cartoons ($M = 2.89$) were rated as playing more aggressively than children who had viewed the nonviolent cartoons ($M = 1.52$).

FIGURE 10.5   Presenting Means in Experimental Designs

(a) Table format

Aggressive play as a function of cartoons viewed

Cartoons viewed	$\bar{x}$	s	N
Violent	2.89	1.61	20
Nonviolent	1.52	.91	20

(b) Figure format (bar chart)

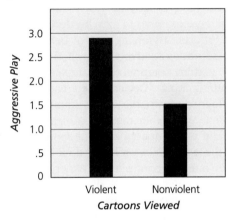

The results of experiments include both the ANOVA summary table and the condition means. This figure shows how the condition means from a one-way experimental design would be reported in a table (a) or in the form of a bar chart in a figure (b).

In addition to the F value (10.98) and the p-value ($< .01$), the within-groups (1) and between-groups (38) degrees of freedom are also reported. When the variable means are presented in the text, they are labeled with an "M." If the condition means are reported in the text, as they are in the preceding paragraph, they should not also be reported in a table or a figure.

When Experiments Are Appropriate

In comparison to correlational research designs, experiments have both advantages and disadvantages. Their most important advantage is that they maximize the experimenter's ability to draw conclusions about the causal relationship between the independent and dependent variables. This is the result of the use of an experimental manipulation and the creation of equivalence. In experiments we can be more confident that the relationship between the independent and dependent variables is not spurious than we can in correlational designs because equivalence has made it unlikely that there are differences among the participants in the different conditions except for the effects of the manipulation itself.

A first disadvantage to experimental research is that many of the most interesting behavioral variables cannot be experimentally manipulated. We cannot manipulate a person's sex, race, intelligence, family background, or religious practice, and such variables must be studied through correlational research designs.[5] A second disadvantage is that because experiments are usually conducted in a laboratory situation, and because the experimental manipulation never provides a perfect match to what would occur in everyday life, we can be virtually certain that participants who participate in experiments will not behave exactly as they would behave if observed outside of the lab. Although experiments may be designed to test real-world phenomena, such as the effects of viewing violent behavior on displaying aggression, they always do so under relatively controlled and artificial conditions.

A third potential disadvantage of experiments is that they necessarily oversimplify things. Because the creation of equivalence is designed to reduce the influence of variables other than the independent variable, it is not possible to ascertain whether these variables would have influenced the dependent variable if their impact had not been controlled. Of course, in everyday life many of these variables probably do influence the dependent variable, which is why they must be controlled in experiments. Thus, although the goal of a one-way experimental research design is to demonstrate that a given independent variable can cause a change in the measured dependent variable, we can never assume that it is the only causal variable. We learn about causation by eliminating common-causal variables, but this also necessarily oversimplifies reality. However, not all experiments are limited to testing the effects of a single independent variable, and it is to experimental designs that involve more than one independent variable that we now turn.

SUMMARY

Experimental research designs enable the researcher to draw conclusions about the causal relationship between the independent variable and the dependent variable. The researcher accomplishes this by manipulating, rather than measuring, the independent variable. The manipulation guarantees that the independent variable occurs prior to the dependent variable.

The creation of equivalence among the conditions in experiments rules out the possibility of a spurious relationship. In between-participants research designs, equivalence is created through random assignment to conditions, whereas in repeated-measures designs equivalence is created through the

---

[5]This does not mean that such questions cannot be studied, however; we will discuss methods of doing so in Chapter 14.

presence of the same participants in each of the experimental conditions. In experiments we can be more confident that the relationship between the independent and dependent variables is not due to common-causal variables than we can in correlational designs because equivalence makes it unlikely that there are any differences among the participants in the different conditions before the experimental manipulation occurred.

Repeated-measures designs have the advantages of increased statistical power and economy of participants, but these designs can be influenced by carryover, practice, and fatigue. These difficulties can, however, be eliminated to some extent through counterbalancing. When there are many conditions to be counterbalanced, a Latin square design may be used. The Analysis of Variance tests whether the mean scores on the dependent variable are different in the different levels of the independent variable, and the results of the ANOVA are presented in the ANOVA summary table.

Although experiments do allow researchers to make inferences about causality, they also have limitations. Perhaps the most important of these is that many of the most interesting behavioral variables cannot, for ethical or practical reasons, be experimentally manipulated.

KEY TERMS

Analysis of Variance (ANOVA) 185
ANOVA summary table 186
between-groups variance 186
between-participants designs 182
carryover 190
conditions 181
control condition 183
counterbalancing 190
degrees of freedom (df) 187
eta (η) 186
experimental condition 183
experimental manipulations 180

F 186
Latin square design 191
levels 181
manipulated 181
one-way experimental design 180
random assignment to conditions 182
repeated-measures designs 182
t test 187
within-groups variance 186
within-participants (within-subjects) design 188

REVIEW AND DISCUSSION QUESTIONS

1. In what ways are experimental research designs preferable to correlational or descriptive designs? What are the limitations of experimental designs?

2. What is the purpose of random assignment to conditions?

3. Describe how the ANOVA tests for differences among condition means.

4. Consider the circumstances under which a repeated-measures experimental research design, rather than a between-participants experimental design, might be more or less appropriate.

5. Explain what *counterbalancing* refers to and which potential problems it can and cannot solve.

6. Why is it important in experimental designs to examine both the condition means and the ANOVA summary table?

7. What are the advantages and disadvantages of using (a) figures, (b) tables, and (c) text to report the results of experiments in the research report?

8. Differentiate between random sampling and random assignment. Which is the most important in survey research, and why? Which is the most important in experimental research, and why?

HANDS-ON EXPERIENCE

1. Read and study the following experimental research designs. For each:
   a. Identify and provide a label for the independent and dependent variables.
   b. Indicate the number of levels in the independent variable, and provide a label for each level.
   c. Indicate whether the research used a between-participants or a within-participants research design.
   - The researchers are interested in the effectiveness of a particular treatment for insomnia. Fifty adult insomnia sufferers are contacted from a newspaper ad, and each is given a pill with instructions to take it before going to sleep that night. The pill actually contains milk powder (a placebo). The participants are randomly assigned to receive one of two instructions about the pill: One half are told that the pill will make them feel "sleepy," and the other half are told that the pill will make them feel "awake and alert." The next day the patients return to the lab and are asked to indicate how long it took them to fall asleep the night before after taking the pill. The individuals who were told the pill would make them feel alert report having fallen asleep significantly faster than the patients who were told the pill would make them feel sleepy.
   - An experimenter wishes to examine the effects of massed versus distributed practice on the learning of nonsense syllables. He uses three randomly assigned conditions of college students. Group 1 practices a twenty nonsense-syllable list for ninety minutes on one day. Group 2 practices the same list for forty-five minutes per day for two successive days. Group 3 practices the same list for thirty minutes per day for three successive days. The experimenter assesses each condition's performance with a free recall test after each condition completes the designated number of sessions. The mean recall of the twenty syllables for condition 1 is 5.2; for condition 2, 10.0; and for condition 3, 14.6. These means are significantly different from one another, and the experimenter concludes that distributed practice is superior to massed practice.

- Saywitz and Snyder (1996) studied whether practice would help second-through sixth-grade children recall more accurately events that happened to them. During one of their art classes, a person entered the classroom and accused the teacher of stealing the markers that the children were using. The intruder and the teacher argued at first, but then developed a plan to share the markers. Two weeks after the incident, the children were asked to recall as much as they could about the event. Before they did so, the children were separated into three groups. One was given instructions, such as noting who were the people involved and what each said and did, to help recall what happened. The second group was given both instructions and practice in recalling the event, while the third group was given no specific instructions at all. The results showed that the instructions-plus-practice group was able to recall significantly more information about the original incident than either of the other groups.
- Ratcliff and McKoon (1996) studied how having previously seen an image of an object may influence one's ability to name it again when it reappears later. Participants were first shown pictures of common objects—a purse, a loaf of bread, etc.—on a computer screen. The participants then left and returned one week later. At this time, they were shown some of the original pictures they had seen in the first session, some similar but not identical images, and some entirely new ones, and then were asked to name the objects as quickly as possible. The researchers found that the original objects were named significantly faster than the new objects, but that the similar objects were named more slowly than the new ones.

2. Design a one-way experiment to test each of the following research hypotheses:
   a. The more a person tries *not* to think of something, the more he or she will actually end up thinking about it.
   b. People are more helpful when they are in a good mood than when they are in a bad mood.
   c. Consumption of caffeine makes people better at solving mathematics problems.
   d. People learn faster before they eat a big meal than after they eat a big meal.

3. Perform the following test to determine the effectiveness of random assignment to conditions. Use random assignment to divide your class into two halves. Then calculate the mean of the two halves on (a) the following three variables and (b) three other variables of your own choice.

   Number of sporting events attended last year
   Number of different restaurants eaten at in the past month
   Number of hours of study per week

   Compare the means of the two halves using a one-way ANOVA. Was random assignment to conditions successful in creating equivalence?

4. Consider whether and why a within-participants, rather than a between-participants, research design would be appropriate in each of the following cases:

   a. Comparing memory when one is in a happy mood versus a sad mood
   b. Comparing performance on a simulated driving test before and after having smoked marijuana
   c. Comparing the ability to distinguish colors in bright versus dim lighting conditions
   d. Comparing helping behavior after viewing a helpful or a nonhelpful model
   e. Comparing memory for material presented early in a list versus memory for material presented late in a list
   f. Comparing performance on tests after receiving failure feedback versus after receiving success feedback
   g. Comparing ability to identify shapes when displayed in color versus in black and white

5. Consider the following means and the ANOVA summary table for an experiment that compared the food intake per hour in grams for four groups of rats that had been deprived of sleep for five, ten, fifteen, or twenty-five hours.

   a. Indicate the F value.
   b. How many rats were used in the experiment?
   c. Is the F test statistically significant?
   d. What can be said about the effects of sleep deprivation on food intake?

Sleep Deprivation in Hours	Mean Food Intake in Grams
5	11.17
10	10.50
15	7.33
25	4.83

ANOVA

		Sum of Squares	df	Mean Square	F	Sig.
DV	Between groups	155.46	3	51.82	5.07	.009
	Within groups	204.50	20	10.23		
	Total	359.96	23			

6. Complete Hands-on Experience problems 7 to 8 in Appendix C.

PART FOUR

Designing and Interpreting Research

CHAPTER ELEVEN
Experimental Research: Factorial Designs

STUDY QUESTIONS

- What are factorial experimental designs, and what advantages do they have over one-way experiments?

- What is meant by crossing the factors in a factorial design?

- What are main effects, interactions, and simple effects?

- What are some of the possible patterns that interactions can take?

- How are the data from a factorial design presented in the research report?

- What is a mixed factorial design?

- What is the purpose of means comparisons, and what statistical techniques are used to compare means?

Although one-way experiments are used to assess the causal relationship between a single independent and a dependent variable, in everyday life behavior is simultaneously influenced by many different independent variables. For instance, aggressive behavior is probably influenced by the amount of violent behavior that a child has recently watched, the disciplining style of the child's parents, his or her current mood state, and so forth. Similarly, the ability to memorize new information is probably influenced by both the type of material to be learned and the study method used to learn it. To try capturing some of this complexity, most experimental research designs include more than one independent variable, and it is these designs that are the topic of this chapter.

Factorial Experimental Designs

Experimental designs with more than one independent (manipulated) variable are known as **factorial experimental designs.** The term **factor** refers to each of the manipulated independent variables. Just as experiments using one independent variable are frequently called one-way designs, so experiments with two independent variables are called two-way designs, those with three factors are called three-way designs, and so forth.

Factorial research designs are described with a notational system that concisely indicates both how many factors there are in the design and how many levels there are in each factor. This is accomplished through a listing of the number of levels of each factor, separated by "×" signs. Thus a two-way design with two levels of each factor is described as a 2 × 2 (read as "2 by 2") design. This notation indicates that because there are two numerals, there are two factors, and that each factor has two levels. A 2 × 3 design also has two factors, one with two levels and one with three levels, whereas a 2 × 2 × 2 design has three factors, each with two levels. The total number of conditions (the conditions in factorial designs are sometimes known as the **cells**) can always be found through multiplication of the number of levels in each factor. In the case of a 2 × 2 design, there are four conditions, in a 3 × 3 design there are nine conditions, and in a 2 × 4 × 2 design there are sixteen conditions.[1]

As we will see, the use of more than one independent variable in a single experiment increases the amount of information that can be gained from the experimental design. And it is also always cheaper in terms of the number of research participants needed to include two or more factors within a single experiment rather than running separate one-way experiments. This is because the factorial design provides all of the information that would be gained from two separate one-way designs, as well as other information that would not have been available if the experiments had been run separately. Because factorial

---

[1]Whereas in a one-way ANOVA the number of levels is the same as the number of conditions (and thus either term can be used to describe them), in a factorial design there is a difference. *Levels* refer to the number of groups in each of the factors, whereas *conditions* refer to the total number of groups in the experiment.

designs also begin with the creation of initial equivalence among the participants in the different conditions (see Chapter 10), these designs (like one-way designs) also help researchers draw conclusions about the causal effects of the independent variables on the dependent variable.

The Two-Way Design

In many cases factorial designs involve the addition of new independent variables to one-way experiments, often with the goal of finding out whether the original results will hold up in new situations. Consider, for instance, a one-way experiment that has demonstrated that children who have viewed violent cartoons subsequently play more aggressively than those who have viewed nonviolent cartoons. And consider a possible extension of this research design that has as its goal a test of the conditions under which this previously demonstrated relationship might or might not be observed. In this case the researcher is interested in testing whether the relationship between the viewing of violent cartoons and aggression will hold up in all situations or whether the pattern might be different for children who have previously been frustrated.

As shown in Figure 11.1, a researcher could accomplish such a test using a two-way factorial experimental design by manipulating two factors in the same experiment. The first factor is the same as that in the one-way experiment—the type of cartoons viewed (violent versus nonviolent). In addition, the researcher also manipulates a second variable—the state of the children before viewing the cartoons (frustrated versus nonfrustrated). In the experiment all of the children are allowed to play with some relatively uninteresting toys in a play session before they view the cartoons. However, for half of the

FIGURE 11.1 Two-Way Factorial Design: Assignment to Conditions

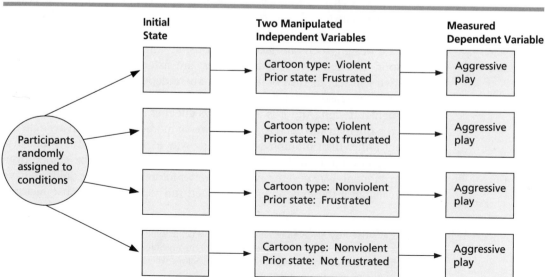

children (the frustration condition) the experimenter places some really fun toys in the room but does not allow the children to play with them. The other half of the children (the no-frustration condition) are not shown the fun toys. Then the children view the cartoons before their behavior is observed in a subsequent play session.

In factorial designs the conditions are arranged such that each level of each independent variable occurs with each level of the other independent variables. This is known as *crossing* the factors. It is important in factorial designs that the conditions be equated before the manipulations occur. This is usually accomplished through random assignment of participants to one of the conditions, although, as we will see later, it is also possible to use repeated-measure factors. Figure 11.1 shows the process of assigning participants to our between-participants factorial design and the four resulting conditions. You can see that crossing two factors, each with two levels, results in four different conditions, each specified by one level of the cartoon factor and one level of the prior state factor. Specifically, the four conditions are "violent cartoons–frustrated," "violent cartoons–not frustrated," "nonviolent cartoons–frustrated," and "nonviolent cartoons–not frustrated." In the research report, the design of the experiment would be described (using both the names and the levels of the factors) as a "2 (cartoon type: violent, nonviolent) × 2 (prior state: frustrated, not frustrated) design."

The research hypothesis in a factorial design normally makes a very specific prediction about the pattern of means that is expected to be observed on the dependent measure. In this case the researcher has predicted that the effect of viewing violent cartoons would be reversed for the frustrated children because for these children the act of viewing the violent cartoons would release their frustration and thus *reduce* subsequent aggressive behavior. The research hypothesis is: "For nonfrustrated children, those who view the violent cartoons will behave more aggressively than those who view the nonviolent cartoons. However, for frustrated children, those who view the violent cartoons will behave less aggressively than those who view the nonviolent cartoons."

Figure 11.2 presents a *schematic diagram* of the factorial design in which the specific predictions of the research hypothesis are notated. In the schematic diagram, greater than (>) and less than (<) signs are used to show the expected relative values of the means.

Main Effects

Let us now pretend for a moment that the 2 × 2 experiment we have been discussing has now been conducted, and let us consider for a moment one possible outcome of the research. You can see that in Figure 11.3 the schematic diagram of the experiment has now been filled in with the observed means on the aggression dependent variable in each of the four conditions.

Pretend for a moment that the prior state variable (frustration versus no frustration) had not been included in the design, and consider the means of the dependent variable in the two levels of the cartoon condition. These

FIGURE 11.2 Two-Way Factorial Design: Predictions

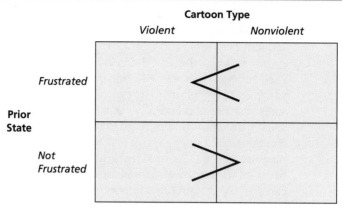

Dependent Measure: Aggressive play

means are shown at the bottom of Figure 11.3. The mean of 4.15 is the average aggression score for all of the children (both frustrated and nonfrustrated) who viewed the violent cartoons, and the mean of 2.71 is the mean of all of the children (both frustrated and nonfrustrated) who viewed the nonviolent cartoons.

When means are combined across the levels of another factor in this way, they are said to *control for* or to *collapse across* the effects of the other factor and are called **marginal means.** Differences on the dependent measure across the levels of any one factor, controlling for all other factors in the experiment, are known as the **main effect** of that factor. As we will see, in this

FIGURE 11.3 Observed Condition Means from a Two-Way Factorial Design

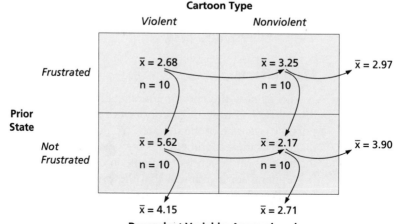

Dependent Variable: Aggressive play

experiment the difference between the two marginal means at the bottom of the figure is statistically significant—the children who viewed the violent cartoons behaved significantly more aggressively (M = 4.15) than did those who viewed the nonviolent cartoons (M = 2.71).

The main effect of the prior state factor can also be tested, this time controlling for the conditions of the cartoon variable. The two marginal means on the right side of Figure 11.3, which control for the influence of cartoon, provide a test of the main effect of prior state. You can see that the children who had been frustrated (M = 2.97) behaved somewhat less aggressively than children who had not been frustrated (M = 3.90), although, as we will see, this difference is not statistically significant.

Interactions and Simple Effects

The two main effects in this experiment give the researcher all of the information that would have been provided if she or he had conducted two different one-way experiments, one of which manipulated the cartoon variable and one of which manipulated the prior state variable. The two main effects test the influence of each of the independent variables, controlling for the influence of the other variable. However, the purpose of factorial designs is not only to assess main effects. It is also to make predictions about interactions between or among the factors. An **interaction** is a pattern of means that may occur in a factorial experimental design when the influence of one independent variable on the dependent variable is different at different levels of another independent variable or variables.

You will recall that in our experiment the researcher's hypothesis was in the form of an interaction. The hypothesis predicted that the effect on children of viewing violent cartoons would be different for those children who had previously been frustrated than it would be for those children who had not already been frustrated. The effect of one factor within a level of another factor (for instance, the effect of viewing violent versus nonviolent cartoons for frustrated children) is known as a **simple effect** of the first factor.

The observed means for the four conditions in our experiment, as shown in Figure 11.3, demonstrate that there is indeed an interaction between the cartoon variable and the frustration variable because the simple effect of cartoon type is different in each level of the prior state variable. For the children who had not been frustrated, the simple effect of cartoon viewed is such that those who viewed the violent cartoons showed *more* aggression (M = 5.62) than those who viewed the nonviolent cartoons (M = 2.17). But the simple effect was reversed for the children who had been frustrated. For the frustrated children, those who had viewed the violent cartoons actually behaved somewhat *less* aggressively (M = 2.68) than those who had viewed the nonviolent cartoons (M = 3.25).

The ANOVA Summary Table

Factorial designs are very popular in behavioral research because they provide so much information. Although two separate experiments manipulating the cartoon variable and the frustration variable, respectively, would have provided information about the main effects of each variable, because the two variables were crossed in a single experiment, the interaction between them can also be tested statistically. In a factorial design the statistical tests for the main effects and the significance test of the interaction may each be significant or nonsignificant. For instance, in a 2 × 2 design there may or may not be a significant main effect of the first factor, there may or may not be a significant main effect of the second factor, and there may or may not be a significant interaction between the first and second factor.

As in one-way experimental designs, the *F* values and significance tests in factorial designs are presented in an ANOVA summary table. The ANOVA summary table for the data shown in Figure 11.3 is presented in Figure 11.4, along with a bar chart showing the means. As you can see, this table is very similar

FIGURE 11.4   ANOVA Summary Table

(a) Factorial Design

		Sum of Squares	df	Mean Square	F	Sig.
Dependent	Cartoon viewed	23.56	1	23.56	4.56	.04*
variable:	Prior state	11.33	1	11.33	2.00	.17
Aggressive play	Cartoon viewed by prior state	29.45	1	29.45	5.87	.03†
	Residual	41.33	36	5.17		
	Total	94.67	39	59.51		

*Main effect of cartoon viewed is significant.
†Interaction between cartoon viewed and prior state is significant.

(b) Bar Chart of Means

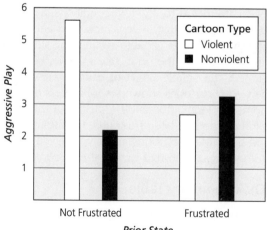

to that in a one-way design except that there are *F* values for each of the main effects and interactions and the within-groups sum of squares, degrees of freedom, and mean squares are labeled as "residual" rather than "within-groups."

In factorial designs each main effect and each interaction has its own *F* test, as well as its own associated degrees of freedom and *p*-value. The first df (numerator) for the *F* test is always printed on the same line as the name of the variable, whereas the second df (denominator) is on the line labeled "residual." Thus in this table the main effect of cartoons viewed is significant, $F(1, 36) = 4.56$, $p < .05$, whereas the main effect of prior state is not, $F(1, 36) = 2.00$, $p > .05$. The interaction is also significant, $F(1, 36) = 3.76$, $p < .05$. It is also possible to compute, for each main effect and interaction, an associated effect size statistic, η. This statistic indicates the size of the relationship between the manipulated independent variable (or the interaction) and the dependent variable.

The presentation of the results of factorial designs in the research report is similar to that of one-way designs except that more means and *F* tests need to be reported. We first inspect the ANOVA summary table to determine which *F* tests are significant, and we then study the condition means to see if they are in the direction predicted by the research hypothesis. Because of the large number of condition means in factorial designs, it is usually better to report them in a chart (for instance, in the form of a bar chart, as shown in Figure 11.4), or in a table. However, each mean should be reported only once using only one of these methods.

Understanding Interactions

Because there are many conditions in factorial research designs, it is often useful to visualize the relationships among the variables using a line chart. In a two-way design, the levels of one of the factors are indicated on the horizontal axis at the bottom of the chart, and the dependent variable is represented and labeled on the vertical axis. Points are drawn to represent the value of the observed mean on the dependent variable in each of the experimental conditions. To make clear which point is which, lines are connected between the points that indicate each level of the second independent variable.

Patterns of Observed Means

Figure 11.5 presents some of the many possible patterns of main effects and interactions that might have been observed in our sample experiment. In these line charts the main effects and interactions are interpreted as follows:

- A main effect of the cartoon variable is present when the average height of the two points above the violent cartoon condition is greater than or less than the average height of the two points above the nonviolent cartoon condition.

- A main effect of the prior state variable is present when the average height of the line representing the frustration condition (the solid line) is

FIGURE 11.5 Hypothetical Outcomes of a Two-Way Factorial Design

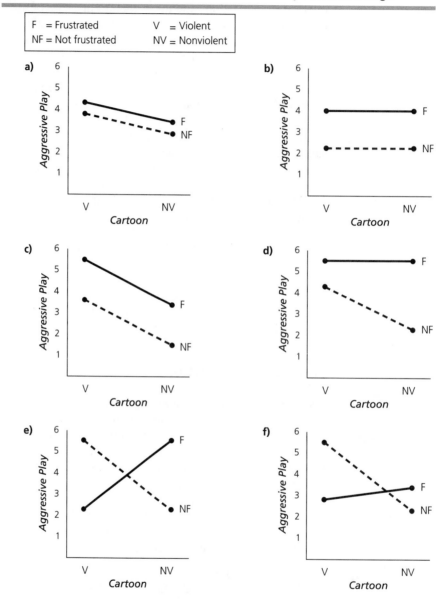

greater than or less than the average height of the line representing the no-frustration condition (the dashed line).

- An interaction is present when the two lines are not parallel. The fact that they are not parallel demonstrates that the simple effect of cartoons (across the bottom) is different in the frustration condition (the solid line) than it is in the no-frustration condition (the dashed line).

Patterns with Main Effects Only.   In Figure 11.5(a) there is only a main effect of the cartoon variable, but no interaction. In this case the proposed research hypothesis in our sample experiment is clearly incorrect—the children showed more aggression after viewing violent (versus nonviolent) cartoons regardless of whether they were frustrated. Figure 11.5(b) shows another possible (but unexpected) pattern—a main effect of the prior state variable only, demonstrating that frustrated children were more aggressive than nonfrustrated children. Figure 11.5(c) shows two main effects, but no interaction. In this case both violent cartoons and frustration increased aggression.

Patterns with Main Effects and Interactions.   You can see in Figure 11.5(d) that the lines are not parallel, indicating that there is an interaction. But if you look closely, you will see that the interaction is not exactly in the form predicted by the research hypothesis. Part of the hypothesis seems to have been supported because the viewing of violent (versus nonviolent) cartoons increased aggression for children in the nonfrustrated condition. However, the type of cartoon made no difference for the children who were frustrated. In this case the main effect of prior state is also significant—the solid line is higher than the dashed line.

Figure 11.5(e) shows the pattern of means originally predicted by the research hypothesis. In a case such as this, when the interaction is such that the simple effect in one level of the second variable is *opposite,* rather than just *different,* from the simple effect in the other level of the second variable, the interaction is called a **crossover interaction.** Finally, Figure 11.5(f) shows the actual pattern found (these means correspond exactly to those presented in Figure 11.3). Here, the research hypothesis is supported because the predicted crossover interaction is observed, but there is also an unanticipated main effect of the cartoon factor (the mean in the violent cartoon condition is greater than the mean in the nonviolent cartoon condition).

Interpretation of Main Effects When Interactions Are Present

As you design or interpret a factorial experiment, keep in mind that the predictions are always stated in the form of expected main effects and interactions. Furthermore, once the data are collected, it is the exact pattern of condition means that provides support (or lack of support) for the research hypothesis. There is rarely a perfect correspondence between the pattern of means that is predicted by the research hypothesis and the actual pattern of observed means. For instance, in our example the predictions (shown in Figure 11.2) do not exactly match the observed results of the experiment (shown in Figure 11.3), even though there is a significant interaction and thus the research hypothesis is supported. Nevertheless, even a significant interaction will not provide support for the research hypothesis if the means are not in the predicted pattern.

Although each of the three statistical tests in a two-way factorial design may or may not be significant, whether the interaction test is significant will influence how the main effects are interpreted. When there is a statistically significant interaction between the two factors, the main effects of each factor must be interpreted with caution. This is true precisely because the presence of an interaction indicates that the influence of each of the two independent variables cannot be understood alone. Rather, the main effects of each of the two factors are said to be *qualified* by the presence of the other factor. To return to Figure 11.3, because there is an interaction, it would be inappropriate to conclude on the basis of this experiment that the viewing of violent cartoons increases aggressive behavior, even though the main effect of the cartoon variable is significant, because the interaction demonstrates that this pattern is true only for nonfrustrated children. For the frustrated children, viewing violent cartoons tended to decrease aggression.

More Factorial Designs

The factorial design is the most common of all experimental designs, and the 2 × 2 design represents the simplest form of the factorial experiment. However, the factorial design can come in many forms, and in this section we will discuss some of these possibilities.

The Three-Way Design

Although many factorial designs involve two independent variables, it is not uncommon for experimental designs to have even more. Consider, for instance, the 2 × 2 experimental design we have been discussing. Because the research used both boys and girls as participants, you can imagine that the researcher might be interested in knowing if there were any differences in how boys and girls reacted to the cartoons and to frustration. Because both boys and girls participated in each of the original four conditions, we can treat the sex of the child as a third factor and conduct a three-way ANOVA.[2] The experimental design now has three independent variables, each of which has two levels. The design is a 2 (cartoon viewed: violent, nonviolent) × 2 (prior state: frustrated, not frustrated) × 2 (sex of child: male, female) design. The ANOVA summary table is shown in Table 11.1, along with the condition means.

The ANOVA Summary Table.   In addition to a greater number of means (there are now eight), the number of main effects and interactions has also increased in the three-way design. There is now a significance test of the main effect for each of the three factors. You can see in Table 11.1 that both the main effect of the cartoon factor and the main effect of the sex of child factor are statistically significant. Interpreting the main effects requires collapsing

---

[2]Because the sex of the child was not, of course, manipulated by the experimenters, it is technically a *participant variable*. We will discuss such variables more fully in Chapter 14.

TABLE 11.1 Observed Condition Means and ANOVA Summary Table from a Three-Way Factorial Design

(a) Means

Aggressive Play as a Function of Cartoon Viewed and Prior State

	Boys	Girls
Violent cartoon		
Frustrated	2.91	2.45
Nonfrustrated	6.69	4.55
Nonviolent cartoon		
Frustrated	4.39	2.11
Nonfrustrated	1.68	2.66

(b) ANOVA Summary Table

Source	Sum of Squares	df	Mean Square	F	Sig.
Main effects					
Cartoon	23.56	1	23.56	4.56	.05
Prior state	11.33	1	11.33	2.00	.34
Sex of child	28.55	1	28.55	5.52	.05
2-way interactions					
Cartoon × prior state	17.32	1	17.32	3.35	.01
Cartoon × sex of child	5.25	1	5.25	1.02	.93
Sex of child × prior state	7.73	1	7.73	1.50	.52
3-way interaction					
Cartoon × prior state × sex of child	32.11	1	32.11	6.21	.01
Residual	41.33	32	5.17		
Total	94.67	39			

over the other two factors in the design. If you average the top four means and the bottom four means in Table 11.1(a), you will find that the appropriate interpretation of the cartoon viewed main effect is that more aggression was observed after violent than after nonviolent cartoons. You can collapse the means across cartoon viewed and prior state to discover the direction of the main effect of sex of child.

There are also three *two-way interactions* (that is, interactions that involve the relationship between two variables, controlling for the third variable). The two-way interaction between cartoon and prior state tests the same hypothesis as it did in the original 2 × 2 analysis because it collapses over sex of child.

You can see that this interaction is still statistically significant even though the exact F value has changed slightly from the two-way interaction shown in Figure 11.4. This change reflects the fact that the residual variance estimate has changed because the addition of sex of child as a factor results in eight, rather than four, conditions.

The sex of child by cartoon type interaction tests whether boys and girls were differentially affected by the cartoon viewed (controlling for prior state), and the sex of child by prior state interaction considers whether boys and girls were differentially affected by prior state (controlling for cartoon viewed). Neither of these interactions is significant.

The Three-Way Interaction.   The three-way interaction tests whether all three variables simultaneously influence the dependent measure. In a three-way interaction, the null hypothesis is that the two-way interactions are the same at the different levels of the third variable. In this case the three-way interaction F test is significant, which demonstrates that the interaction between cartoon and prior state is different for boys than it is for girls. If you look at the means carefully (you may wish to create line charts), you will see that the original crossover interaction pattern is found much more strongly for boys than it is for girls.

When a three-way interaction is found, the two-way interactions and the main effects must be interpreted with caution. We saw in the two-way analysis that it would be inappropriate to conclude that viewing violent material always increases aggression because this was true only for nonfrustrated children. The three-way analysis shows that even this conclusion is incorrect because the crossover interaction between cartoon and prior state is found only for boys.

You can see that interpretation of a three-way interaction is complicated. Thus, although the addition of factors to a research design is likely to be informative about the relationships among the variables, it is also costly. As the number of conditions increases, so does the number of research participants needed, and it also becomes more difficult to interpret the patterns of the means. There is thus a practical limit to the number of factors that can profitably be used. Generally, ANOVA designs will have two or three factors.

Factorial Designs Using Repeated Measures

Although the most common way to create equivalence in factorial research designs is through random assignment to conditions, it is also possible to use repeated-measures designs in which individuals participate in more than one condition of the experiment. Any or all of the factors may involve repeated measures. Thus factorial designs may be entirely between participants (random assignment is used on all of the factors), may be entirely repeated measures (the same individuals participate in all of the conditions), or may be some of each. Designs in which some factors are between participants and some are repeated measures are known as **mixed factorial designs.** Figure 11.6 shows

FIGURE 11.6 Repeated-Measures and Mixed Factorial Designs

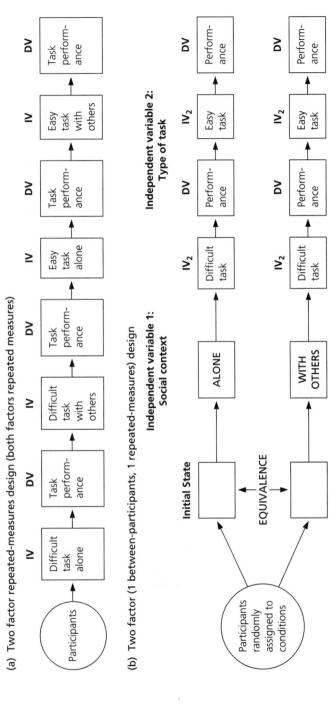

(a) Two factor repeated-measures design (both factors repeated measures)

(b) Two factor (1 between-participants, 1 repeated-measures) design

This figure shows two methods of conducting a 2 × 2 factorial experiment including type of task (easy versus difficult) as the first factor and social context (alone versus with others) as the second factor. In Figure (a) both factors are repeated measures and the participant is in all four of the conditions. In this design the order that the participants experience each of the four conditions would be counterbalanced. Figure (b) shows a mixed factorial design in which the social context factor is between participants and the task factor is repeated measures.

how the same research hypothesis could be tested with both a repeated-measures design and a mixed design. As we discussed in Chapter 10, the use of repeated-measures designs has both advantages and disadvantages, and the researcher needs to weigh these before making a decision about whether to use these designs.

Comparison of the Condition Means in Experimental Designs

One of the complexities in interpreting the results of the ANOVA is that when more than two groups are being compared, a significant F does not indicate which groups are significantly different from each other. For instance, although the significant interaction test shown in Figure 11.4 for the means in Figure 11.3 tells us that the effect of viewing violent cartoons is significantly different for frustrated than for nonfrustrated children, it does not tell us which means are significantly different from each other. To fully understand the results, we may want more specific information about the significance of the simple effects. That is, we may want to know whether viewing violent cartoons caused significantly more aggression for children who were not frustrated and whether viewing the violent cartoons significantly decreased aggression for children in the frustration condition.

Because a significant F value does not provide answers to these specific questions, further statistical tests known as **means comparisons** are normally conducted to discover which group means are significantly different from each other. These comparisons are used both in one-way designs with more than two levels and in factorial designs.

Pairwise Comparisons

The most common type of means comparison is a **pairwise comparison** in which any one condition mean is compared with any other condition mean. One problem with pairwise comparisons is that there can be a lot of them. For instance, in a 2 × 2 factorial design there are six possible pairwise comparisons:

Violent cartoons–frustrated with violent cartoons–not frustrated
Violent cartoons–frustrated with nonviolent cartoons–frustrated
Violent cartoons–frustrated with nonviolent cartoons–not frustrated
Violent cartoons–not frustrated with nonviolent cartoons–frustrated
Violent cartoons–not frustrated with nonviolent cartoons–not frustrated
Nonviolent cartoons–frustrated with nonviolent cartoons–not frustrated

In the three-way factorial design shown in Table 11.1 there are twenty-eight possible pairwise comparisons!

Because there are so many possible pairwise comparisons, it is normally not appropriate to conduct a statistical test on each pair of condition means because each possible comparison involves a statistical test and each test has a probability of a Type 1 error equivalent to alpha (normally .05). As each comparison is made, the likelihood of a Type 1 error increases by alpha. As a result, the **experimentwise alpha**—that is, the probability of the experimenter having made a Type 1 error in at least one of the comparisons—also increases. When six comparisons are made, the experimentwise alpha is .30 (.05 × 6), whereas when twenty comparisons are made, the experimentwise alpha is 1.00, indicating that one significant comparison would be expected by chance alone.

Planned Comparisons. There are three ways to reduce the experimentwise alpha in means comparison tests. The first approach is to compare only the means in which specific differences were predicted by the research hypothesis. Such tests are called **planned comparisons** or **a priori comparisons.** For instance, because in our experiment we explicitly predicted ahead of time that the viewing of violent cartoons would cause more aggression than the viewing of nonviolent cartoons for the nonfrustrated children, we could use a planned comparison to test this simple effect. However, because we had not explicitly predicted a difference, we would not compare the level of aggression for the children who saw the violent cartoons between the frustration and the no-frustration conditions. In this case the planned comparison test (as described in Appendix D) indicates that for the nonfrustrated children aggression was significantly greater in the violent-cartoon condition (M = 5.62) than in the nonviolent cartoon condition (M = 2.17), $F(1, 36)$ = 4.21, $p < .05$.

Post Hoc Comparisons. When specific comparisons have not been planned ahead of time, increases in experimentwise alpha can be reduced through the use of a second approach: **post hoc comparisons.** These are means comparisons that, by taking into consideration that many comparisons are being made and that these comparisons were not planned ahead of time, help control for increases in the experimentwise alpha. One way that post hoc tests are able to prevent increases in experimentwise alpha is that in some cases they only allow the researchers to conduct them if the F test is significant. Examples of popular post hoc tests include the *Least Significant Difference (LSD) Test,* the *Tukey Honestly Significant Difference (HSD) Test,* and the *Scheffé Test.* These tests are discussed in more detail in Appendix D.

Complex Comparisons

The third approach to dealing with increases in experimentwise alpha is to conduct **complex comparisons** in which more than two means are compared at the same time. For instance, we could use a complex comparison to compare aggression in the violent cartoon–frustration condition to the average aggression in the two no-frustration conditions. Or we could use a complex comparison to study the four means that produce the interaction between cartoon viewed and prior state for boys only in Table 11.1(a), while ignoring the data from the girls. Complex comparisons are usually conducted with **contrast tests;** this procedure is discussed in Appendix D.

SUMMARY

In most cases one-way experimental designs are too limited because they do not capture much of the complexity of real-world behavior. Factorial experimental designs are usually preferable because they assess the simultaneous impact of more than one manipulated independent variable on the dependent variable of interest. Each of the factors in a factorial experimental design may be either between participants or repeated measures. Mixed experimental designs are those that contain both between-participants and repeated-measures factors.

In factorial experimental designs the independent variables are usually crossed with each other such that each level of each variable occurs with each level of each other independent variable. This is economical because it allows tests, conducted with the Analysis of Variance, of the influence of each of the independent variables separately (main effects), as well as tests of the interaction between or among the independent variables.

All of the main effect and interaction significance tests are completely independent of each other, and an accurate interpretation of the observed pattern of means must consider all the tests together. It is useful to create a schematic diagram of the condition means to help in this regard. In many cases it is desirable to use means comparisons to compare specific sets of condition means with each other within the experimental design. These comparisons can be either planned before the experiment is conducted (a priori comparisons) or chosen after the data are collected (post hoc comparisons).

KEY TERMS

a priori comparisons 215
cells 201
complex comparisons 215
contrast tests 215
crossover interaction 209
experimentwise alpha 215
factor 201
factorial experimental designs 201
interaction 205

main effect 204
marginal means 204
means comparisons 214
mixed factorial designs 212
pairwise comparisons 214
planned comparisons 215
post hoc comparisons 215
simple effect 205

REVIEW AND DISCUSSION QUESTIONS

1. What are three advantages of factorial experimental designs over one-way experimental designs?

2. What are main effects, simple effects, and interactions? How should significant main effects be interpreted when one or more of the interactions are significant?

3. For each of the following research designs, indicate the number of factors, the number of levels within each factor, the number of main effects, the number of interactions, and the number of conditions:
   a. $2 \times 3 \times 2$
   b. 3×4
   c. $3 \times 5 \times 7$
   d. 2×5

4. How are the results of factorial experimental designs reported in the research report?

5. What is the purpose of means comparisons, and what different types of means comparisons are there? What do they tell the researcher that the significance test for F cannot?

HANDS-ON EXPERIENCE

1. Read and study the following experimental designs. For each:
   a. Identify the number of factors and the number of levels within each of the factors. Identify whether each of the factors is between participants or repeated measures.
   b. Indicate the format of the research design. How many conditions are in the design?
   c. Identify the dependent variable.
   d. Draw a schematic diagram of the experiment. Indicate the name of each of the factors, the levels of each of the factors, and the dependent variable.
   e. State the research hypothesis or hypotheses in everyday language, and diagram the hypothesis using correlational operators ($<$, $>$, $=$) in the schematic diagram.

   - The principle of social facilitation states that people perform well-learned tasks faster when they work with others but perform difficult tasks better when they work alone. To test this idea, Markus (1978) brought 144 participants to a lab. Some of them were randomly assigned to work in a room by themselves. Others were randomly assigned to work in a room with other people. Each person performed two tasks: taking off his or her shoes and socks (an easy task) and putting on a lab coat that ties in the back (a difficult task). Results show that people working alone performed the difficult task *faster* than people working with others but performed the easy task *slower* than people working with others. The results thus support the social facilitation model.
   - A study explores the hypothesis that attitude change will be more likely to occur on the basis of salient but actually very uninformative characteristics of the communicator when individuals listening to the message are distracted from carefully processing it. College students are randomly assigned to hear a persuasive message given either by an attractive or an

unattractive person and to hear this message either when there is a lot of construction noise in the next room or when conditions are quiet. Results show that students who were exposed to the attractive communicator showed significantly more attitude change than the participants who saw the unattractive communicator, but that this difference occurred only in the distraction conditions.

- Kassin and Kiechel (1996) researched whether presenting false incriminating evidence leads people to accept guilt for a crime they did not commit. Participants began the experiment by typing letters on a computer keyboard while another person dictated. The letters were read at either a slow pace (43 letters per minute) or a fast pace (67 letters per minute). Before they began, the participants were warned not to press the "ALT" key positioned near the space bar, because doing so would cause the computer program to crash and data would be lost. After one minute of typing, the computer supposedly crashed, and the experimenter then accused the participant of having touched the "ALT" key. All of the participants were in fact innocent and initially denied the charge. The person who had been reading the letters (a confederate of the experimenter) then said that either he or she hadn't seen anything or that he or she had seen the participant hit the "ALT" key. The participant was then asked to sign a false confession stating: "I hit the 'ALT' key and caused the program to crash. Data were lost." The predictions for the experiment were that more participants would sign the confession when they had been accused by a witness, and particularly when the letters had been read at a fast pace, leading the participant to believe the validity of the (false) accusation. You may want to look up the surprising results of this experiment!

2. Locate a research report that uses a factorial design. Identify the independent and dependent variables and the levels of each of the factors, and indicate whether each factor is between participants or repeated measures.

3. Make predictions about what patterns of main effects and interactions you would expect to observe in each of the following factorial designs:
   a. The influence of study time and sleep time on exam performance
   b. The effects of exposure time and word difficulty on memory

4. Create some examples of two-way factorial experimental designs, and make predictions about what patterns of main effects and interactions you would expect to observe.

5. A researcher is testing the variables that influence the performance of high school students on a mathematics test. Using a two-way experimental design, the experimenter manipulates both the actual difficulty of the math questions (hard versus easy) and the students' expectations about the difficulty of the questions (the students are told to expect the questions to be either easy or difficult). The dependent variable is the number of questions

out of fifty possible questions that the students answer correctly on the math test. The following represent the means and the ANOVA summary table from this researcher's analysis.

ANOVA Summary Table

		Sum of Squares	df	Mean Square	F	Sig.
Main Effects	Actual difficulty	7.90	1	7.89	4.13	<.05
	Expected difficulty	7.78	1	7.78	4.07	<.05
2-Way Interaction	Actual difficulty by expected difficulty	.06	1	.06	.03	>.05
Residual		103.20	54	1.91		

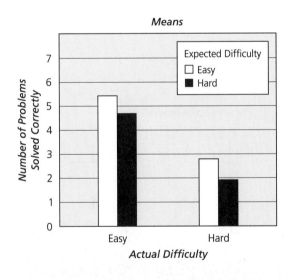

Means

a. Write a paragraph that reports the results of the research, including the *F* values, *df,* and *p*-values.
b. In your own words, describe how the scientist should interpret the results of the experiment.
c. Create a table showing the means of the dependent variable in the experimental conditions.

6. For each of the following hypothetical outcomes of two-way factorial designs,
    a. Calculate the marginal means for each factor, and indicate if it appears that there is a main effect for the factor.
    b. Draw a bar chart of the means, and indicate if it appears that there is an interaction.

Factor B

		Level 1	Level 2	Marginal Means
	Level 1	4	9	_____
1) Factor A				
	Level 2	3	10	_____
	Marginal Means	_____	_____	

Factor B

		Level 1	Level 2	Marginal Means
	Level 1	3	9	_____
2) Factor A				
	Level 2	10	4	_____
	Marginal Means	_____	_____	

Factor A

		Level 1	Level 2	Marginal Means
	Level 1	17	19	_____
3) Factor A				
	Level 2	18	3	_____
	Marginal Means	_____	_____	

Factor A

		Level 1	Level 2	Marginal Means
	Level 1	33	19	_____
4) Factor A	Level 2	24	23	_____
	Level 3	18	36	_____
	Marginal Means	_____	_____	

7. Consider the following hypothetical outcome of a three-way factorial design.
   a. Calculate the marginal means for each factor, and indicate if there appears to be a main effect for each factor.
   b. Draw a bar chart of the means for each of the two-way interactions (Factor A × Factor B, Factor A × Factor C, and Factor B × Factor C), and indicate if they appear to be significant.
   c. Indicate if the three-way interaction appears to be significant. That is, does it appear that the A × B interaction and the A × C interaction have different forms?

		Factor C		
		Level 1		Level 2	
		Factor B, Level 1	Factor B, Level 2	Factor B, Level 1	Factor B, Level 2
	Level 1	7	9	6	2
Factor A					
	Level 2	3	12	8	1

Experimental Control and Internal Validity

STUDY QUESTIONS

- What are the potential threats to the validity of research?

- What is experimental control?

- What effects do extraneous variables have on the validity of research?

- What is meant by confounding? Why does confounding reduce an experiment's internal validity?

- What are some methods of controlling for extraneous variables in experimental research designs?

- What are some methods for increasing the validity of experimental manipulations?

- What are manipulation checks and confound checks, and what can they tell us?

- What are some common artifacts in experimental research, and how can they produce confounding?

We have now completed our discussion of the goals and the logic of descriptive, correlational, and experimental research designs. And we have seen that each of these three research approaches is useful for answering some types of research questions. Understanding the basics of research designs is the first step in becoming a proficient consumer and practitioner of research in the behavioral sciences. But research that looks good on the surface may sometimes, when scrutinized carefully, be found to have serious flaws. We will consider potential threats to the validity of research in this chapter, as well as in Chapters 13 and 14. These chapters are perhaps the most important in the entire book, for it is here that you will learn how to evaluate the quality of research that you read about and how to design experiments that are able to fully answer your research questions.

Threats to the Validity of Research

Good research is *valid* research. By *valid,* we mean that the conclusions drawn by the researcher are correct. For instance, if a researcher concludes that a new drug reduces headaches, or that people prefer Coca-Cola over Pepsi, the research is valid only if the new drug really works or if people really do prefer Coke. Unfortunately, there are many threats to the validity of research, and these threats may sometimes lead to unwarranted conclusions. Of course, researchers do not attempt to conduct invalid research—that is, they do not attempt to draw inaccurate conclusions about their data. Yet often, despite researchers' best intentions, some of the research reported in newspapers, magazines, and even scientific journals is invalid. Validity is not an all-or-none phenomenon, and yet some research is better than other research in the sense that it is more valid. Only by understanding the potential threats to validity will you be able to make knowledgeable decisions about the conclusions that can or cannot be drawn from a research project.

As shown in Table 12.1, there are four major types of threats to the validity of research. The first is one that should be familiar to you, as we have already discussed it in Chapter 5. A threat to *construct validity* occurs when the measured variables used in the research are invalid because they do not adequately assess the conceptual variables they were designed to measure. In this chapter we will see that in experimental research, in addition to being certain that the dependent measure is construct valid, the experimenter must also be certain that the manipulation of the independent variable is construct valid in the sense that it appropriately creates the conceptual variable of interest.

In Chapter 8 we considered a second type of potential threat, which can be referred to as a threat to the *statistical conclusion validity* of the research. This type of invalidity occurs when the conclusions that the researcher draws about the research hypothesis are incorrect because either a Type 1 error or a Type 2 error has occurred. A Type 1 error occurs when the researcher mistakenly rejects the null hypothesis, and a Type 2 error occurs when the researcher mistakenly fails to reject the null hypothesis. We have already discussed the

TABLE 12.1   Four Threats to the Validity of Research

1. **Threats to construct validity.**   Although it is claimed that the measured variables or the experimental manipulations relate to the conceptual variables of interest, they actually may not. (Chapters 5 and 12)
2. **Threats to statistical conclusion validity.**   Conclusions regarding the research may be incorrect because a Type 1 or Type 2 error was made. (Chapter 8)
3. **Threats to internal validity.**   Although it is claimed that the independent variable caused the dependent variable, the dependent variable may have actually been caused by a confounding variable. (Chapter 12)
4. **Threats to external validity.**   Although it is claimed that the results are more general, the observed effects may actually only be found under limited conditions or for specific groups of people. (Chapter 13)

These four threats to the validity of research are discussed in the indicated chapters of this book.

use of alpha as a method for reducing Type 1 errors and have considered statistical power as a measure of the likelihood of avoiding Type 2 errors. In this chapter we will more fully discuss ways to increase the power of research designs and thus reduce the likelihood of the researcher making Type 2 errors.

In addition to threats to construct validity and statistical conclusion validity, there are two other major threats to the validity of research. These threats are present even when the research is statistically valid and the construct validity of the manipulations and measures is ensured. Behavioral scientists refer to these two potential problems as threats to the *internal validity* and to the *external validity* of the research design (Campbell & Stanley, 1963). As we will see, *internal validity* refers to the extent to which we can trust the conclusions that have been drawn about the causal relationship between the independent and dependent variable, whereas *external validity* refers to the extent to which the results of a research design can be generalized beyond the specific settings and participants used in the experiment to other places, people, and times.

Experimental Control

One of the important aspects of a good experiment is that it has **experimental control,** which occurs to the extent that the experimenter is able to eliminate effects on the dependent variable other than the effects of the independent variable. The greater the experimental control is, the more confident we can be that it is the independent variable, rather than something else, that caused changes in the dependent variable. We have already discussed in Chapter 10 how experimental control is created in part through the establishment of initial equivalence across the experimental conditions. In this chapter we will expand our discussion of experimental control by considering how control is reduced through the introduction into the research of *extraneous variables* and *confounding variables*. Then we will turn to ways to reduce the influence of these variables.

Extraneous Variables

One of the greatest disappointments for a researcher occurs when the statistical test of his or her research hypothesis proves to be nonsignificant. Unfortunately, the probabilistic nature of hypothesis testing makes it impossible to determine exactly why the results were not significant. Although the research hypothesis may have been incorrect and thus the null hypothesis should not have been rejected, it is also possible that a Type 2 error was made. In the latter case the research hypothesis was correct and the null hypothesis should have been rejected, but the researcher was not able to appropriately do so.

One cause of Type 2 errors is the presence of extraneous variables in the research. As we have seen in Chapter 9, extraneous variables are variables other than the independent variable that cause changes in the dependent variable. In experiments extraneous variables include both initial differences among the research participants in such things as ability, mood, and motivation, and differences in how the experimenter treats the participants or how they react to the experimental setting. Because these variables are not normally measured by the experimenter, their presence increases the within-groups variability in an experimental research design, thus making it more difficult to find differences among the experimental conditions on the dependent measure. Because extraneous variables constitute random error or noise, they reduce power and increase the likelihood of a Type 2 error.

Confounding Variables

In contrast to extraneous variables, which constitute random error, **confounding variables** are variables other than the independent variable on which the participants in one experimental condition differ *systematically* or on average from those in other conditions. As we have seen in Chapter 10, although random assignment to conditions is designed to prevent such systematic differences among the participants in the different conditions before the experiment begins, confounding variables are those that are created during the experiment itself.

Consider, for instance, a researcher who uses an experimental research design to determine whether working in groups, rather than alone, causes people to perform better on mathematics problems. Because lab space is at a premium, the experimenter has the participants working alone complete the problems in a small room with no windows in the basement of the building, whereas the groups complete the task in a large classroom with big windows on the top floor of the building. You can see that even if the groups did perform better than the individuals, it would not be possible to tell what caused them to do so. Because the two conditions differ in terms of the presence or absence of windows as well as in terms of the presence or absence of other people, it is not possible to tell whether it was the windows or the other people who changed performance.

Confounding and Internal Validity.   When another variable in addition to the independent variable of interest differs systematically across the experimental conditions, we say that the other variable is confounded with the independent variable. **Confounding** means that the other variable is mixed up with the independent variable, making it impossible to determine which of the variables has produced changes in the dependent variable. The extent to which changes in the dependent variable can confidently be attributed to the effect of the independent variable, rather than to the potential effects of confounding variables, is known as the **internal validity** of the experiment. Internal validity is ensured only when there are no confounding variables.

Alternative Explanations.   The presence of a confounding variable does not necessarily mean that the independent variable did not cause the changes in the dependent variable. Perhaps the effects on task performance in our experiment really were due to group size, and the windows did not influence performance. The problem is that the confounding variable always produces potential **alternative explanations** for the results. The alternative explanation is that differences in the confounding variable (the windows), rather than the independent variable of interest (group size), caused changes on the dependent measure. To the extent that there are one or more confounding variables, and to the extent that these confounding variables provide plausible alternative explanations for the results, the confidence with which we can be sure that the experimental manipulation really produced the differences in the dependent measure, and thus the internal validity of the experiment, is reduced.

Control of Extraneous Variables

Now that we have seen the difference between extraneous and confounding variables, we will turn to a consideration of how they can be recognized and controlled in research designs. Keep in mind that both types of variables are problematic in research and that good experiments will attempt to control each.

Limited-Population Designs

We have seen that one type of extraneous variable involves initial differences among the research participants within the experimental conditions. To the extent that these differences produce changes in the dependent variable, they constitute random error, and because they undermine the power of the research, they should be reduced as much as possible. One approach to controlling variability among participants is to select them from a limited, and therefore relatively homogeneous, population. One type of limited population that behavioral scientists frequently use is college students. Although this practice is used partially because of convenience (there are many college students available to researchers on college campuses), there is another advantage that comes from the relative homogeneity of college students in comparison to human beings at large.

Consider a psychologist who is interested in studying the performance of mice in mazes. Rather than capturing mice at the local landfill, he or she is more likely to purchase white mice that have been bred to be highly similar to each other in terms of genetic makeup. The psychologist does this to reduce variability among the mice on such things as intelligence and physical strength, which would constitute random error in the research. For similar reasons, behavioral scientists may prefer to use college students in research because students are, on average, more homogeneous than a group of people that included both college students and other types of people. College students are of approximately the same age, live in similar environments, have relatively similar socioeconomic status, and have similar educational background. This does not mean that there is no variability among college students, but it does mean that many sources of random error are controlled. Of course, using only college students has a potential disadvantage—there is no way to know whether the findings are specific to college students or would also hold up for other groups of people (see Sears, 1986). We will discuss this problem more fully in Chapter 13 when we consider the external validity of research designs.

Before-After Designs

A second approach to controlling for differences among the participants is the use of **before-after research designs.** Imagine an experiment in which the research hypothesis is that participants who are given instructions to learn a list of words by creating a sentence using each one will remember more of the words on a subsequent memory test than will participants who are not given any specific method for how to learn the words. To test this hypothesis, an experimental design is used in which college students are given a list of words to remember. One half of the students are randomly assigned to a condition in which they construct sentences using each of the words, and the other half are just told to remember the words the best they can. After a brief delay all participants are asked to remember the words.

You can well imagine that there are many differences, even without the manipulation, in the ability of the students to remember the words on the memory test. These differences would include IQ and verbal skills, current mood, and motivation to take the experiment seriously. As shown in Figure 12.1, in a before-after design the dependent measure (in this case, memory) is assessed both before and after the experimental manipulation. In this design the students memorize and are tested on one set of words (list A). Then they are randomly assigned to one of the two memory instructions before learning the second set of words (list B) and being tested again. The first memory test is known as a **baseline measure,** and the second memory test is the dependent variable.

FIGURE 12.1 Controlling Extraneous Variables: Multiple-Group Before-After Design

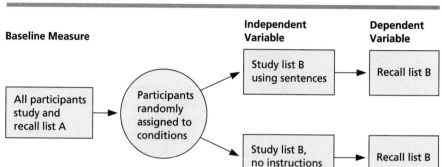

Advantages. The logic of the before-after design is that any differences among the participants will influence both the baseline memory measure and the memory measure that serves as the dependent variable. For instance, a student with a particularly good memory would score better than average on both list A and list B. Thus we can compare each individual's memory performance on list A to his or her performance on list B.[1]

You may have noticed that before-after research designs share some similarities with repeated-measures designs in the sense that the dependent variable (in this case, memory) is measured more than one time. And both repeated-measures and before-after designs increase the power of an experiment by controlling for variability among the research participants. The difference is that in repeated-measures designs each individual is in more than one condition of the experiment. In our before-after design each person is in only one condition, but the dependent variable is measured more than one time, with the first measurement serving as a baseline measure.

Disadvantages. Although completion of the dependent measure more than once in a before-after design helps reduce random error, as you will recall from Chapter 4, doing so also creates the possibility of retesting effects. For instance, fatigue may occur, or the participants who are given an initial memory test may begin to develop their own memory strategies for doing better on the second test, and these strategies may conflict with the strategies being experimentally manipulated. In addition, having participants complete the same or similar measures more than one time increases the likelihood that they will be able to guess the research hypothesis.

---

[1]This comparison can be made either through statistical control of performance on the baseline memory measure (that is, by including it, along with a variable indicating the participant's experimental condition, as a predictor variable in a multiple regression analysis) or through treatment of the two memory measures as two levels of a repeated-measures factor in a mixed-model ANOVA.

Matched-Group Designs

In cases where retesting seems a potential problem, one approach is not to control for differences by measuring the dependent measure more than once, but to collect, either before or after the experiment, a different measure that is expected to influence the dependent measure. For instance, in a memory experiment if there is concern about similar memory measures being taken twice, we might measure participants' intelligence on the basis of an IQ test, with the assumption that IQ is correlated with memory skills and that controlling for IQ will reduce between-person variability.

A researcher who wanted to conduct such a design might administer the intelligence test before the experimental session and select participants on the basis of their scores. As shown in Figure 12.2, in a **matched-group research design,** participants are measured on the variable of interest (for instance, IQ) before the experiment begins and then are assigned to conditions on the basis of their scores on that variable. For instance, during assignment of participants to conditions in the memory experiment, the two individuals with the two highest IQs would be randomly assigned to the sentence-creation condition and the no-instructions conditions, respectively. Then the two participants with the next highest IQs would be randomly assigned to the two conditions, and so on. Because this procedure reduces differences between the conditions on the matching variable, it increases the power of the statistical tests. Participants can also be matched through the use of more than one variable, although it is difficult to find participants who are similar on all of the measured characteristics.

In some cases it is only possible to obtain the participants' scores on the matching variable after the experiment has been completed. For instance, if the participants cannot be selected on the basis of their IQ, they might nevertheless be asked to complete a short IQ test at the end of the memory experiment. In such cases it is obviously not possible to assign participants to

FIGURE 12.2   Controlling Extraneous Variables: Matched-Group Design

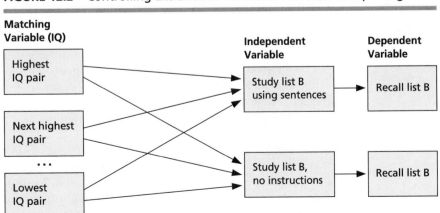

conditions based on their scores. Rather, differences among people on the matching variable are controlled statistically through multiple regression analysis. As long as the matching variable (for instance, IQ) actually correlates with the dependent measure (memory), the use of a matched-group design will reduce random error and increase the statistical power of the research design.

It should be kept in mind that the use of matched-group designs is not normally necessary in experimental research. Random assignment is sufficient to ensure that there are no differences *between* the experimental conditions—matching is used only if one feels that it is necessary to attempt to reduce variability among participants *within* the experimental conditions. Matching is most useful when there are measures that are known to be correlated with the dependent measure that can be used to match the participants, when there are expected to be large differences among the participants on the measure, and when sample sizes are small and thus reducing within-conditions variability is critical.

Standardization of Conditions

In addition to minimizing extraneous variables that come from differences among the experimental participants, an experimenter should also try to minimize any differences that might occur within the experiment itself. **Standardization of conditions** is accomplished when, as much as is possible, all participants in all levels of the independent variable are treated in exactly the same way, with the single exception of the manipulation itself. The idea is to hold constant every other possible variable that could potentially influence the dependent measure.

To help ensure standardization, a researcher contacts all participants in all of the experimental conditions in the same manner, provides the exact same consent form and instructions, ensures interaction with the same experimenters in the same room, and, if possible, runs the experiment at the same time of day. Furthermore, as the experiment proceeds, the activities of the groups are kept the same. In an ideal experiment, all participants take the same amount of time, interact with the same people, learn the same amount of information, and complete the same activities except for the changes in the experimental manipulation.

The Experimental Script. The most useful tool for ensuring standardization of conditions is the **experimental script** or **protocol.** The script is just like a script in a stage play—it contains all the information about what the experimenter says and does during the experiment, beginning with the greeting of the participants and ending with the debriefing.

Automated Experiments. One potential method of producing standardization is to use automated devices, such as tape recorders or computers, to run the experiment. The machine presents all of the instructions and in the case of the computer may also record responses to questions, reaction times, or physiological responses. In some cases all the experimenter has to do is turn on the machine—the rest of the experiment is completely standardized. Although automated techniques ensure standardization because exactly the same instructions are given to each and every participant, they also have some disadvantages. If the participant is daydreaming or coughing and thus misses an important part of the instructions, there is no way to know about or correct this omission. These techniques also do not allow the participants to ask questions and thus may reduce the impact of the experimental manipulation in comparison to interaction with a human experimenter. It is often better, therefore, when using computers, for the experimenter to be present for one or more initial practice trials to enable the participant to ask questions and ensure that he or she understands the procedure. The experimenter then leaves the room once the experimental trials begin.

Creation of Valid Manipulations

You may recall from our discussion in Chapter 5 that *construct validity* refers to the extent to which the operational definition of a measured variable proves to be an adequate measure of the conceptual variable it is designed to assess. But construct validity can also refer to the effectiveness of an experimental manipulation. The manipulation has construct validity to the extent that it produces the hoped-for changes in the conceptual variable it is designed to manipulate, but at the same time does not create confounding by simultaneously changing other conceptual variables.

Impact and Experimental Realism

The manipulations used in experimental designs must be strong enough to cause changes in the dependent variable despite the presence of extraneous variables. When the manipulation creates the hoped-for changes in the conceptual variable, we say that it has had **impact.** Because the types of manipulations used in behavioral science research are highly varied, what is meant by an "impactful" manipulation also varies from experiment to experiment. In some cases the manipulation is rather straightforward, such as when participants are asked to memorize a list of words that appear at either a fast or a slow pace. In this case the trick is to vary the speed of presentation enough to make a difference.

In other cases the effectiveness of the manipulation requires that the experimenter get the participants to believe that the experiment is important and to attend to, believe in, and take seriously the manipulation. For instance, in research designed to assess how changes in the type of arguments used by a speaker influence persuasion, the research participants must be given a reason to pay attention to the speaker's message and must actually do so, or these changes will not have impact. To create this interest, researchers frequently use topics that are relevant to students, such as proposed changes in the curriculum requirements or increases in tuition at their college or university

(Cacioppo, Petty, & Morris, 1983). And if participants are told that they have failed at a task, the feedback must be given in such a way that the participants actually believe it.

The extent to which the experimental manipulation involves the participants in the research is known as **experimental realism.** This is increased when the participants take the experiment seriously and thus are likely to be influenced by the manipulations. For instance, in a well-known experiment on obedience by Milgram (1974), male participants were induced to punish another person by administering heavy doses of what they thought was electrical shock. The reactions of the participants clearly showed that they were experiencing a large amount of stress. These reactions raise questions about the ethics of conducting such an experiment but leave no doubt that the manipulation had experimental realism and impact.

In general we can say that, particularly when you are first creating a new experimental manipulation, it is best to make the manipulation as strong as you possibly can, subject to constraints on ethics and practicality. For instance, if you are studying variation in speed of exposure to words, then make the slow condition very slow, and the fast condition very fast. Similarly, if your manipulation involves changes in exposure to violent versus nonviolent material, then choose material that is extremely violent to use as the stimuli in the violence condition. Using strong manipulations as well as attempting to involve the participants in the research by increasing experimental realism will increase the likelihood of your manipulation being successful.

Manipulation Checks

Experimenters often rely on the face validity of an experimental manipulation to determine its construct validity—that is, does the manipulation appear to create the conceptual variable of interest? But it is also possible to directly measure whether the manipulation is having the hoped-for impact on the participants. **Manipulation checks** are measures used to determine whether the experimental manipulation has had the intended impact on the conceptual variable of interest (Sigall & Mills, 1998).

Designing and Interpreting Manipulation Checks. Manipulation checks are sometimes used simply to ensure that the participants notice the manipulation. For instance, in an experiment designed to measure whether people respond differently to requests for help from older versus younger people, the participants might be asked when the experiment was over to estimate the age of the person who had asked them for help. The manipulation could be considered successful if the participants in the older helper condition estimated a higher age than those in the younger helper condition. Although in this case it might seem unlikely that they would not have noticed the age of the person, participants are likely to be distracted by many other things during the experiment, and thus it is easier than you might think for them to entirely miss or ignore experimental manipulations.

In most cases, however, manipulation checks are designed not to assess whether the participants noticed the manipulation but to see if the manipulation had the expected impact on them. For instance, in an experiment designed to manipulate mood state, the participants might be asked to indicate their current mood using a couple of Likert scales.

Manipulation checks are usually given after the dependent variables have been collected because if given earlier, these checks may influence responses on the dependent measures. For instance, if the goal of an experiment was to assess the effects of mood state on decision making, but people were asked to report on their mood before they completed the decision-making task, they might realize that the experiment concerned the influence of mood on decision making. Of course, there is also a potential difficulty if the manipulation checks are given at the end of the experiment because by then the impact of the manipulation (in this case, the mood induction) may have worn off. Giving the manipulation check at the end of the experiment may thus underestimate the true impact of the experimental manipulation.

Manipulation checks turn out to be particularly important when no significant relationship is found between the independent and dependent variables. Without manipulation checks, the experimenter is left in the awkward position of not knowing whether the participants did not notice the manipulation; whether they noticed the manipulation, but it did not have the expected impact; or whether the manipulation actually had the hoped-for impact but nevertheless did not have the expected effect on the dependent variable. Because it is usually very easy to include one or more manipulation checks, they should almost always be used. Inspecting the scores on the manipulation checks can help the experimenter determine exactly what impact the experimental manipulation had on the participants.

Internal Analyses. One other potential advantage of a manipulation check is that it can be used to make alternative tests of the research hypothesis in cases where the experimental manipulation does not have the expected effect on the dependent measure. Consider, for instance, an experiment in which the independent variable (a manipulation of a positive versus a neutral mood state) did not have the expected effect on the dependent variable (helping behavior). However, on the basis of a manipulation check, it is also clear that the manipulation did not have the expected impact. That is, the positive mood manipulation did not produce positive mood for all of the participants in the positive-mood condition and some of the participants in the neutral-mood condition reported being in very positive moods anyway.

Although one option at this point would be to conduct an analysis including only those participants in the positive-mood condition who reported being in a positive mood, and only those in the control condition who did not report being in a positive mood, this procedure would require deleting many participants from the analysis and would result in a loss in statistical power. An alternative approach is to conduct an **internal analysis,** which involves computing a correlation of the scores on the manipulation check measure with the scores on the dependent variable as an alternative test of the research hypothesis. In our case we would correlate reported mood state with helping, and we would predict that participants who were in more positive moods (regardless of their experimental condition) would help more frequently. However, because an internal analysis negates much of the advantage of experimental research by turning an experimental design into a correlational study, this procedure is used only when no significant relationship between the experimental manipulation and the dependent variable is initially found.

Confound Checks

In addition to having impact by causing differences on the independent variable of interest, the manipulation must avoid changing other, confounding conceptual variables. Consider, for instance, an experiment designed to test the hypothesis that people will make fewer errors in detecting misspellings in an interesting text than in a boring one. The researcher manipulates interest in the experiment by having one half of the participants look for errors in a text on molecular biology (a boring task), while the other half searches for errors in the script of a popular movie (an interesting task).

You can see that even if the participants who read the biology text did detect fewer spelling errors, it would be difficult to conclude that these differences were caused by differences in the interest value of the task. There is a threat to the internal validity of the research because, in addition to being less interesting, the biology text might also have been more difficult to spell-check. If so, task difficulty would have been confounded with task interest, making it impossible to determine whether performance differences were caused by task interest or task difficulty.

In such a case we might use a manipulation check (asking the participants how interesting they found the proofreading task) to confirm that those who read the movie script, rather than the passage from the biology text, would report having found it more interesting. But we might also want to use one or more confound checks to see if the manipulation also had any unintended effects. **Confound checks** are measures used to determine whether the manipulation has unwittingly caused differences on confounding variables. In this study, as a confound check the participants might also be asked to indicate how difficult they had found the proofreading task, with the hope that the rated difficulty would *not* have differed between the biology and the movie texts.

How to Turn Confounding Variables into Factors

Although one of the goals of valid experiments is to be certain that everything stays the same for all participants except the experimental manipulation, this may not always be possible. For example, it may not be possible to use the same experimenter for each participant or to run all of the participants in the same room. This is not usually a great problem as long as these differences occur such that they are *crossed with,* rather than *confounded with,* the levels of the manipulation. That is, the experiment should be designed such that rather than having the different experimenters each run different conditions, each experimenter runs an equal number of participants in each of the conditions. And rather than running all of one condition in one room and all of the other condition in another room, the experimenter should run each condition the same number of times in each of the rooms. Furthermore, if a record is kept of which experimenter and which room were used, it is even possible for the experimenter to determine if these variables actually influenced the dependent variable by including them as factors in the data analysis.

Although confounding variables are sometimes nuisance variables such as room size and experimenter, in other cases the potential confounds are more meaningful conceptual variables. Consider again the experiment described previously in which the interest value and the difficulty of a text passage could have been confounded. Perhaps the best solution to this potential problem would be to conduct the experiment as a 2 × 2 factorial design in which task difficulty and task interest were separately manipulated. In short, participants would proofread a difficult but interesting text, a difficult but boring text, an easy but interesting text, or an easy but boring text. This design would allow the researcher to separate out the effects of interest value and task difficulty on the dependent measure.

Pilot Testing

It takes practice to create an experimental manipulation that produces at the same time an impactful manipulation and a lack of confounding variables. Such difficulties are particularly likely in cases where it is not certain that the participants will believe the manipulation or where they might be able to guess the research hypothesis.

One strategy that can be useful when you are not sure that a manipulation is going to be successful is to conduct a **pilot test** of the manipulation on a few participants before you begin the experiment itself. Participants are brought to the lab, administered the manipulation, and then given the manipulation checks and perhaps some confound checks. A postexperimental interview (see Chapter 3) can also be used to help determine how the participants interpreted the experimental manipulation and whether they were suspicious of the manipulations or able to guess the hypothesis.

Pilot testing before the experiment helps to ensure that the manipulation checks and confound checks administered in the experiment will show the expected patterns. For example, the experimenters in our proofreading experiment could pilot-test the passages on participants who were not going to participate in the experiment until they had found two passages rated equally difficult, but varying in the degree of interest. This would help eliminate the potential confound of task difficulty before the experiment was to begin.

Sometimes pilot testing can take quite a bit of time. For instance, in some of the research that I and my colleagues recently conducted, we were interested in getting our research participants to believe that they were either very good at a task or that their skills were more average (Stangor & Carr, 2002). We had to pilot-test for a whole semester before we were able to find a task that the participants did not already think that they were very good at, so that the half of them who received feedback suggesting that they were only average would believe it. Pilot testing can also be useful for helping determine the effectiveness of your dependent variable or variables. It will help you ensure that there is variability in the measure (that the memory test is not too easy or too hard, for instance), and you can do a preliminary check on the reliability of the measure using the data from the pilot study. If necessary, the dependent measures can be altered before the experiment is run.

Although pilot testing takes time and uses up participants, it may be worthwhile if it allows you to determine whether the manipulation is working as you hope it will. Careful reading about other experiments in the area may also give you ideas of what types of manipulations and dependent variables have been successful in the past, and in many cases it is better to use these previously tested variables than try to develop new ones of your own.

Threats to Internal Validity

Although there are many potential threats to the internal validity of an experimental design, some are common enough that they deserve to be investigated here.[2] In this section we will consider how to recognize and avoid three common threats to internal validity in behavioral research: placebo effects, demand characteristics, and experimenter bias. We will also consider how to most effectively assign participants to conditions to avoid confounding. These threats to internal validity are sometimes known as **artifacts**—aspects of the research methodology that may go unnoticed and that may inadvertently produce confounding.

Placebo Effects

Consider an experimental design in which a researcher tests the hypothesis that drinking alcohol makes members of the opposite sex look more attractive. Participants over the age of twenty-one are randomly assigned either to drink orange juice mixed with vodka or to drink orange juice alone. However, to reduce deception, the participants are told whether their drink contains vodka. After enough time has passed for the alcohol to take effect, the participants are asked to rate the attractiveness of a set of pictures of members of the opposite sex. The results of the experiment show that, as predicted, the participants who have had vodka rate the photos as significantly more attractive.

If you think about this experiment for a minute, it may occur to you that

---

[2]Many of these threats are summarized in important books by Campbell and Stanley (1963) and Cook and Campbell (1979). Because some of the threats to internal validity discussed by these authors are more likely to occur in quasi-experimental, rather than in experimental, research, they will be discussed in Chapter 14.

although the researcher wants to draw the conclusion that alcohol is causing the differences in perceived attractiveness, the expectation of having consumed alcohol is confounded with the presence of alcohol. That is, the people who drank alcohol also knew they drank alcohol, and those who did not drink alcohol knew they did not. Just knowing that they were drinking alcohol, rather than the alcohol itself, may have caused the differences. Whenever participants' expectations about what effect an experimental manipulation is supposed to have influences the dependent measure independently of the actual effect of the manipulation, we call the change in the dependent measure a **placebo effect.**

Placebo effects are particularly problematic in medical research, where it is commonly found that patients who receive placebos (that is, medications that have no actual physiological effect) can frequently experience a large reduction in symptoms (Price, 1984). Thus the researcher cannot give some patients a medication and other patients no medication because the first group's knowledge of having taken the medication would then be confounded with its potential effect. The solution in medical research is to give a medication to all of the patients in the research, but to arrange it so that a randomly selected half of the participants gets the true medication, whereas the other half gets a drug that has no real effect (a placebo). The participants do not know which they have received. This procedure does not prevent placebo effects, but it controls for them by making sure that, because all of the participants now think they have received a medication, the effects occur equally in each condition.

Similar procedures can be used in behavioral research. For instance, because it turns out that it is very difficult to tell whether vodka has been mixed with orange juice, our experimenter might tell both groups that they are drinking orange juice and vodka but really give alcohol to only half of the participants. If differences in perceived attractiveness were found, the experimenter could then confidently attribute them to the alcohol rather than to a placebo effect. Notice that this use of an appropriate control group is one example of standardization of conditions—making sure that everything (in this case, including expectations about having consumed alcohol) is the same in all conditions except for the changes in the independent variable of interest. These techniques are frequently used in research studying the effects of alcohol (see, for instance, Knight, Barbaree, & Boland, 1986).

Demand Characteristics

Another common threat to internal validity in behavioral research occurs when the research participant is able to guess the research hypothesis. The ability to do so is increased by the presence of **demand characteristics**—aspects of the research that allow participants to guess the research hypothesis. For instance, in an experiment designed to study the effects of mood states on helping behavior, participants might be shown either a comedy film or a control, nonhumorous film before being given an opportunity to help, such as by volunteering to participate in another experiment without compensation. It might not be too difficult in such an situation for an observant participant in the comedy film condition to guess that the experiment is testing the effects of mood on helping and that the research hypothesis is that people will be more helpful when they are in a positive mood.

Demand characteristics are potentially problematic because, as we have seen in Chapter 4, participants who have been able to guess the research hypothesis may frequently behave cooperatively, attempting to act in ways that they think will help confirm the hypothesis. Thus when demand characteristics are present, the internal validity of the study is threatened because changes in the dependent measure might be due to the participants' desire to please the experimenter and confirm the hypothesis rather than to any actual impact of the experimental manipulation. In the following sections we will consider some of the most common approaches to reducing the likelihood of demand characteristics.

Cover Stories. In some cases a cover story can be used to prevent the participants from guessing the research hypothesis. The **cover story** is a false or misleading statement about what is being studied. For instance, in experiments designed to study the effects of mood states on helping, participants might view either a comedy film or a control film. The cover story might be that the goal of the research is to learn about what specific aspects of films lead people to like them. This cover story might be enhanced by having the participants complete a questionnaire on which they rate how much they liked each of the actors, whether the dialogue and story line were clear, and so forth. Providing a cover story might help keep the participants from guessing that the real goal of the film was to change mood.

Although the use of a cover story means that the participants are not told until the debriefing what the researcher is really studying, the cover story does not have to be completely untrue. For instance, in research in my lab we often tell participants that the research is studying how individuals perform tasks when in groups versus when alone. Although this information is completely true, we do not mention that we are specifically interested in how initial confidence in one's task ability affects this performance (Stangor & Carr, 2002).

The Unrelated-Experiments Technique. In some cases the cover story involves the use of the **unrelated-experiments technique.** In this technique participants are told that they will be participating in two separate experiments conducted by two separate experimenters. In reality, the experimental manipulation is presented in the first experiment, and the dependent measure is collected in the second experiment. For instance, in an experiment testing the effects of mood states on decision making, participants might first be asked to participate in an experiment concerning what leads people to enjoy a film. They would then be placed in either a positive or a neutral mood by their viewing one of two films and, as part of the cover story, would make some ratings of the film they had viewed; debriefing would follow. At this point the participants would be asked to move to another room where another experiment on decision making was being run. They would meet a new experimenter who has them sign a new consent form before they work on a decision-making task that serves as the dependent measure. You can see that this technique will reduce the likelihood of the participants being able to guess the hypothesis because they will think that the two experiments are unrelated.

Because cover stories involve deception, they should be used only when necessary, and the participants must be fully debriefed at the end of the second experiment. In some cases other approaches to avoidance of demand characteristics are possible, such as simulation studies (see Chapter 3). In cases where demand characteristics are likely to be a problem, suspicion checks (see Chapter 3) should also be used to help determine whether the participants might have guessed the research hypothesis.

Use of Nonreactive Measures.   Another approach to avoiding demand characteristics, and one that can in some cases avoid the deception involved in a cover story, is to use nonreactive dependent measures. As we have discussed in Chapter 4, nonreactive measures are those in which the participants do not realize what is being measured or cannot control responding on them. For instance, in the experiment by Macrae and his colleagues described in Chapter 1, the dependent measure was how far the participants sat from the chair on which the skinhead had supposedly left his belongings. It is unlikely that any of the participants in that study could have guessed the hypothesis that the chair that they sat down on was a nonreactive measure of their attitudes toward the skinhead. As another example, in the study of the effects of mood on helping, the helping task might be presented in the form of a nonreactive behavioral measure, such as having a confederate drop some books and measuring whether the participants helped pick them up (Isen & Levin, 1972).

Although nonreactive measures are frequently used to assess the dependent variable, in some cases the manipulation can itself be nonreactive in the sense that it appears to have occurred by accident or is very subtle. For instance, in studies of the effects of mood on helping and decision making, Isen and her colleagues have used subtle mood manipulations such as finding a coin in a phone booth or receiving a small gift such as a bag of candy (Isen & Levin, 1972; Isen, Nygren, & Ashby, 1988). These manipulations were able to induce a positive mood state as assessed by manipulation checks, and yet they were so unobtrusive that it is unlikely that the participants had any idea what was being studied. Although I have argued earlier that it is generally useful, at least in initial stages of research, to use manipulations that are likely to produce a large impact, when subtle manipulations are found to have an influence on the dependent measures, we can often be sure that the participants were not able to guess the research hypothesis and thus that demand characteristics are not a problem (Prentice & Miller, 1992).

Taken together, there are many approaches to reducing the potential of demand characteristics, and one of the important aspects of experimentation is figuring out how to do so. Also, keep in mind that demand characteristics can influence the results of research, without the experimenter ever being aware of it, if the participants discuss the research with future participants after they leave the experiment. In this case new participants may arrive at the experiment having already learned about the research hypothesis. This is why it is usual to ask participants not to discuss the nature of the research with other people until the experiment is completed (for instance, at the end of the academic semester).

Experimenter Bias

Experimenter bias is an artifact that is due to the simple fact that the experimenter usually knows the research hypothesis. Although this may seem to be a relatively trivial matter, it can in fact pose a grave danger to the internal validity of research. The danger is that when the experimenter is aware of the research hypothesis, and also knows which condition the participants he or she is running are in, the experimenter may treat the research participants in the different conditions differently, such that an invalid confirmation of the research hypothesis is created.

In a remarkable demonstration of the possibility of experimenter bias, Rosenthal and Fode (1963) sent twelve students to test a research hypothesis concerning maze learning in rats. Although the students were not initially told so, they were actually the participants in an experiment. Six of the students were randomly told that the rats they would be testing had been bred to be highly intelligent, whereas the other six students were led to believe that the rats had been bred to be unintelligent. But there were actually no differences among the rats given to the two groups of students.

When the students returned with their data, a startling result emerged. The rats run by students who expected them to be intelligent showed significantly better maze learning than the rats run by students who expected them to be unintelligent. Somehow the students' expectations influenced their data. They evidently did something different when they tested the rats, perhaps subtly changing how they timed the maze running or how they treated the rats. And this experimenter bias probably occurred entirely out of their awareness.

Naive Experimenters.   Results such as these make it clear that experimenters may themselves influence the performance of their participants if they know the research hypothesis and also know which condition the participants are in. One obvious solution to the problem is to use experimenters who do not know the research hypothesis—we call them **naive experimenters.** Although in some cases this strategy may be possible (for instance, if we were to pay people to conduct the experiment), in most cases the use of naive experimenters is not practical. The person who developed the research hypothesis will often also need to run the experiment, and it is important to fully inform those working on a project about the predictions of the research so that they can answer questions and fully debrief the participants.

Blind Experimenters.   Although it is not usually practical or desirable to use naive experimenters, experimenters may be kept *blind to condition*. In this case the experimenter may be fully aware of the research hypothesis, but his or her behavior cannot influence the results because he or she does not know what condition each of the research participants is in. In terms of Rosenthal's experiments, the students, even though they might have known that the study involved intelligent versus unintelligent rats, could have remained blind to condition if they had not been told ahead of time which rats were expected to have which characteristic.

One way of keeping experimenters blind to condition is to use automated experiments or tape recordings. In an automated experiment the computer can randomly determine which condition the participant is in without the experimenter being aware of this. Or the experimenter might create two tape recordings, one containing the instructions for one condition and another containing instructions for the other condition. Then these two tapes (which look identical) are marked by a person who is not involved in running the experiment with the letter "A" and the letter "B," respectively, but without the experimenter running the experiment being told which tape is which. The experimenter starts the tape for each participant but leaves the room before the critical part of the tape that differs between conditions is played. Then the experimenter reenters, collects the dependent measures, and records which tape was played. Only later, after all the participants have been run, does the experimenter learn which tape was which.

Another method of keeping experimenters blind to condition is to use two experimenters. In this procedure one experimenter creates the levels of the independent variable, whereas the other experimenter collects the dependent variable. The behavior of the second experimenter cannot influence the results because he or she is blind to the condition created by the first experimenter. In still other cases it is not feasible to keep the experimenter blind to condition, but it is possible to wait until the last minute to effect the manipulation. For instance, the experimenter might pick up a card that indicates which condition the participant is to be in only at the last minute before the manipulation occurs. This ensures that the experimenter cannot differentially influence the participants before that time.

Random Assignment Artifacts

Before leaving the discussion of confounding, we must consider one more potential artifact that can cause internal invalidity. Although random assignment to conditions is used to ensure equivalence across the experimental conditions, it must be done correctly, or it may itself result in confounds. To understand how this might occur, imagine that we had a 2 × 2 between-participants experimental design, that we desired during the course of a semester to run fifteen students in each condition, and that the conditions were labeled as "A," "B," "C," and "D." The question is, "How do we determine which participants are assigned to which of the four conditions?"

One approach would be to place sixty pieces of paper in a jar, fifteen labeled with each of the four letters, and to draw one of the letters at random for each arriving participant. There is, however, a potential problem with this approach because it does not guarantee which conditions will be run at which time of the semester. It could happen by chance that the letter A was drawn more frequently than the letter D in the beginning of the semester and that the letter D was drawn more often near the end of the semester. The problem if this were to happen is that because condition A has been run, on average, earlier in the semester than condition D, there is now a confound between condition and time of the semester. The students in the different conditions might no longer have been equivalent before the experimental manipulation occurred if, for instance, the students who participated earlier in the semester were more intelligent or more motivated than the students who participated later, or if those who participated near the end of the semester were more knowledgeable about the material or more suspicious.

When considering this problem, you might decide to take another approach, which is simply to run the conditions sequentially, beginning with condition A and continuing through condition D and then beginning again with condition A. Although this reduces the problem somewhat, it also has the unwanted outcome of guaranteeing that condition A will be run, on average, earlier in the semester than condition D.

The preferred method of assigning participants to conditions, known as **blocked random assignment,** has the advantages of each of the two previous approaches. An example of this approach is shown in Table 12.2. Four letters are put into a jar and then randomly selected until all four conditions have

TABLE 12.2   Blocked Random Assignment

Blocks	Participants	Order of Conditions
1	1, 2, 3, 4	A, C, D, B
2	5, 6, 7, 8	B, A, D, C
3	9, 10, 11, 12	D, A, C, B
4	13, 14, 15, 16	A, B, C, D
5	17, 18, 19, 20	B, C, A, D
6	21, 22, 23, 24	D, A, C, B
7	25, 26, 27, 28	C, A, D, B
8	29, 30, 31, 32	A, C, D, B
9	33, 34, 35, 36	B, C, D, A
10	37, 38, 39, 40	A, B, D, C

In an experimental design, it is important to avoid confounding by being very careful about the order in which participants are run. The blocked random design is the best solution. In this case there are four conditions in the experiment, indicated as "A," "B," "C," and "D." Each set of four participants are treated as a block and are assigned to the four conditions randomly within the block. Because it is desired to have 40 participants in total, 10 blocks are used.

been used. Then all four letters are replaced in the jar, and the process is repeated fifteen times. This creates a series of blocks of four letters, each block containing all four conditions, but the order of the conditions within each of the blocks is random.

A randomized block procedure can also be used to help reduce confounding in experiments. Consider a situation in which different experimenters (or experimental rooms or computers) have to be used in the research. In general, it will be desirable to turn these potential confounding variables into extraneous variables by being certain that each experimenter is assigned to each experimental condition an equal number of times. An easy solution to this problem is to assign participants to experimenter by blocks. Ideally each experimenter will run an equal number of blocks in the end, but this is not absolutely necessary. As long as each experimenter completes running an entire block of participants before beginning a new block, he or she will end up running each condition an equal number of times.

SUMMARY

Although experimental research designs are used to maximize the experimenter's ability to draw conclusions about the causal effects of the independent variable on the dependent variable, even experimental research contains threats to validity and thus the possibility of the experimenter drawing invalid conclusions about these relationships.

One potential problem is that the presence of extraneous variables may threaten the statistical conclusion validity of the research because these variables make it more difficult to find associations between the independent and dependent variables. Researchers therefore attempt to reduce extraneous variables within the experimental conditions through the use of such techniques as limited-population, before-after, or matched-group designs, as well as through standardization of conditions.

Although extraneous variables may lead to Type 2 errors, the presence of confounding variables leads to internal invalidity, in which it is no longer possible to be certain whether the independent variable or the other confounding variables produced observed differences in the dependent measure. To avoid internal invalidity, researchers use appropriate control groups, cover stories, and blocked random assignment to conditions.

Some of the most common threats to the internal validity of experiments include placebo effects, demand characteristics, and experimenter bias. Creating valid experiments involves thinking carefully about these potential threats to internal validity and designing experiments that take them into consideration. Blocked random assignment is used to avoid artifacts when assigning participants to conditions in an experiment.

KEY TERMS

alternative explanations 226
artifacts 236
baseline measure 227
before-after research designs 227
blocked random assignment 242
confound checks 234
confounding 226
confounding variables 225
cover story 238
demand characteristics 237
experimental control 224
experimental realism 232
experimental script 230

experimenter bias 240
impact 231
internal analysis 233
internal validity 226
manipulation checks 232
matched-group research design 229
naive experimenters 240
pilot test 235
placebo effect 237
protocol 230
standardization of conditions 230
unrelated-experiments technique 238

REVIEW AND DISCUSSION QUESTIONS

1. Describe four types of invalidity that can be found in experimental research designs.

2. What are extraneous and confounding variables? Which type of variable is most dangerous to the statistical conclusion validity and the internal validity of experimental research, and why?

3. What is confounding, and how does confounding produce alternative explanations?

4. What are the techniques by which experimenters attempt to control extraneous variables within an experimental design?

5. What methods are used to help ensure that experiments are internally valid?

6. How are manipulation checks and confound checks used to help interpret the results of an experiment?

7. What are placebo effects, and how can they be avoided?

8. What are demand characteristics, and how can they be avoided?

9. In what ways may experimenters unwittingly communicate their expectations to research participants, and what techniques can they use to avoid doing so?

HANDS-ON EXPERIENCE

1. Each of the following research designs has a potential threat to the internal validity of the research. For each, indicate what the confounding variable is and how it might have been eliminated.

a. The Pepsi-Cola Company conducted the "Pepsi Challenge" by randomly assigning individuals to taste either a Pepsi or a Coke. The researchers labeled the glasses with only an "M" (Pepsi) or a "Q" (Coke) and asked the participants to indicate which they preferred. The research showed that subjects overwhelmingly preferred glass "M" over glass "Q." Why can't the researchers conclude that Pepsi was preferred to Coke?

b. Researchers gave white college students two résumés in an experiment in which they were asked to play the role of an employment officer. The résumés were designed to have equal qualifications, but one had a photo of an African-American applicant attached, and the other had a photo of a white applicant. The researcher found that there were no significant differences between the evaluations of the black applicant and the white applicant. Why can't the researcher conclude that the student's judgments were not influenced by the race of the applicant?

c. In a study of helping behavior, Ellsworth and Langer (1976) predicted that when the person who needed help made eye contact with the potential helper, situations in which the need for help was clear and unambiguous would produce more helping than would situations in which the need for help was less clear. To manipulate the ambiguity of the need for help, participants were randomly assigned to discover a person who had lost a contact lens, whereas in the other condition the person in need of help was apparently ill. Even if more help was given in the latter condition than the former, why should the researchers not conclude that it is the ambiguity of the situation that caused the difference?

d. McCann and Holmes (1984) tested the hypothesis that exercise reduces depression. They randomly assigned depressed undergraduate women either to an exercise condition (attending an aerobics class a couple of times a week for ten weeks) or to a relaxation training condition (the individuals relaxed at home by watching a videotape over the same period of time). Although the results showed that the exercise group reported less depression at the end of the ten-week period than did the relaxation group, why can't the researchers conclude that exercise reduces depression?

e. Ekman, Friesen, and Scherer (1976) tested whether lying influenced one's voice quality. Participants were randomly assigned to view either a pleasant film or an unpleasant film, but all of the participants were asked to describe the film they saw as being pleasant. (Thus the subjects who watched the unpleasant film had to lie about what they saw.) An analysis of voice quality showed that participants used significantly higher voices when they were describing the unpleasant film rather than the pleasant film. Why can't the authors conclude that lying produced the differences in voice quality?

f. A researcher studying the "mere exposure" phenomenon (Zajonc, 1980) wants to show that people like things more if they have seen them more often. He shows a group of participants a list of twenty words at an experimental session. One week later, the participants return for a second session in which they are randomly assigned to view either the same words again or a different set of twenty words, before indicating how much they like the twenty words that everyone had seen during the first session. The results show that the participants who have now seen the words twice like the words better than the group that only saw the words once. Why can't the researcher conclude that people like the words more because they have seen them more often?

g. A researcher wants to show that people with soft voices are more persuasive than people with harsh voices. She has a male actor with a loud voice give an appeal to one set of participants and a woman with a soft voice give the exact same appeal to another set of participants. The researcher finds that the soft voice is indeed more persuasive because people change their attitudes more after hearing the appeal from the female. Why can't the researcher conclude that soft voices are more persuasive?

h. An elementary school teacher wants to show that parents' involvement helps their children learn. She randomly chooses one half of the boys and one half of the girls in her class and sends a note home with them. The note asks the parents to spend more time each day working with the child on his or her math homework. The other half of the children do not receive a note. At the end of the school year, the teacher finds that the children whose parents she sent notes to have significantly better final math grades. Why can't the researcher conclude that parental involvement increased the students' scores?

i. Employees in a large factory are studied to determine the influence of providing incentives on task performance. Two similar assembly rooms are chosen for the study. In one room, the experimenters talk about the research project that is being conducted and explain that the employees will receive a reward for increased performance: Each worker will receive a weekly bonus if he or she increases his or her performance by 10 percent. In the other room, no mention is made of any research. If the reward is found to increase the performance in the first assembly room, why can't the researchers conclude that it was the financial bonus that increased production?

2. View the film of Milgram's research on obedience (*Obedience,* available from the Pennsylvania State University) or the *Stanford Prison Experiment* (available from Philip Zimbardo at Stanford University). Comment on the experimental realism of the research.

3. Study some or all of the many examples of confounding variables that are presented in the book *Rival Hypotheses* by Huck and Sandler (1979).

CHAPTER THIRTEEN
External Validity

STUDY QUESTIONS

- What is meant by the external validity of a research design?

- How is research limited in regard to generalization to other groups of people?

- How does ecological validity help increase confidence that an experiment will generalize to other research settings?

- What is the purpose of replication? What are the differences among exact, conceptual, and constructive replications?

- What is a participant replication, and when is it used?

- What is the purpose of review papers and meta-analyses? What are the differences between the two?

In Chapter 12 we considered the internal validity of experiments. In this chapter we will consider a second major set of potential threats to the validity of research. These threats are known collectively as threats to *external validity* because they concern the extent to which the experiment allows conclusions to be drawn about what might occur outside of or beyond the existing research.

Understanding External Validity

Imagine for a moment that you are reading a research report that describes an experiment that used a sample of children from an elementary school in Bloomington, Indiana. These children were randomly assigned to watch either a series of very violent Bugs Bunny cartoons or a series of less violent cartoons before their aggressive behavior was assessed during a play session. The results showed that children who viewed the violent cartoons displayed significantly more physical aggression in a subsequent free play period than did the children who watched the less violent cartoons. You can find no apparent alternative explanations for the results, and you believe that the researcher has drawn the appropriate conclusion—in this case, the viewing of violent cartoons caused increased aggressive behavior.

What implications do you think that such a study should have on public policy? Should it be interpreted as indicating that violent television shows are likely to increase aggression in children and thus that violent network programming should be removed from the airwaves? If you think about this question a bit, you may well decide that you are not impressed enough by the results of the scientist's experiment to suggest basing a new social policy on it. For one, you might reasonably conclude that since the result has been found only once, it may be statistically invalid, and thus the finding really represents a Type 1 error. You might also note that although the experiment did show the expected relationship, there may have been many other experiments that you do not know about that showed no relationship between viewing violence and displaying aggressive behavior.

Thinking about it further, you could develop even more arguments concerning the research. For one, the results were found in a laboratory setting, where the children were subjected to unusual conditions—they were forced to watch a cartoon that they might not have watched in everyday life. Furthermore, they watched only cartoons and not other types of aggressive TV shows, and only one measure of aggression was used. In short, perhaps there is something unique about the particular experiment conducted by this scientist that produced the observed results, and the same finding wouldn't be found in other experiments, much less in everyday life.

You might also argue that the observed results might not hold up for other children. Bloomington, Indiana, is a small university town where many children are likely to have college professors as parents, and these children may react differently to violent television shows than would other children. You might wonder whether the results would hold up for other children, such as those living in large urban areas.

Arguments of the type just presented relate to the external validity of an experiment. **External validity** refers to the extent to which the results of a research design can be generalized beyond the specific way the original experiment was conducted. For instance, these might include questions about the specific participants, experimenters, methods, and stimuli used in the experiment. The important point here is that any research, even if it has high internal validity, may be externally invalid if its findings cannot be expected to or cannot be shown to hold up in other tests of the research hypothesis.

Generalization

The major issue underlying external validity is that of **generalization.** *Generalization* refers to the extent to which relationships among conceptual variables can be demonstrated in a wide variety of people and a wide variety of manipulated or measured variables. Because any research project is normally conducted in a single laboratory, uses a small number of participants, and employs only a limited number of manipulations or measurements of each conceptual variable, it is inherently limited. Yet the results of research are only truly important to the extent that they can be shown to hold up across a wide variety of people and across a wide variety of operational definitions of the independent and dependent variables. The extent to which this occurs can only be known through further research.

Generalization Across Participants

When conducting experimental research, behavioral scientists are frequently not particularly concerned about the specific characteristics of the sample of people they use to test their research hypotheses. In fact, as we have seen in Chapter 12, experiments in the behavioral sciences frequently use convenience samples of college students as research participants. This is advantageous to researchers, both because it is efficient and because it helps minimize variability within the conditions of the experiment and thus provides more powerful tests of the research hypothesis. But the use of college students also has a potential disadvantage because it may not be possible to generalize the results of a study that included only college students from one university to college students at another university or to people who are not college students. However, although the use of college students poses some limitations, it must be realized that *any* sample of research participants, no matter who they are, will be limited in some sense. Let us consider this problem in more detail.

As we have seen, the goal of experimental research is not to use the sample to provide accurate descriptive statistics about the characteristics of a specific population of people. Rather, the goal of experimental research is to elucidate underlying causal relationships among conceptual variables. And in many cases these hypothesized relationships are expected to be so encompassing that they will hold for every human being at every time and every place. For instance, the principle of distributed versus massed practice suggests that the same amount of study will produce greater learning if it is done in several shorter time periods (distributed) rather than in one longer time period (massed). And there is much research evidence to support this hypothesis (Baddeley, 1990). Of course, the principle does not state that this should be true only for college students or only for Americans. Rather, the theory predicts that learning will be better for all people under distributed versus massed practice no matter who they are, where they live, and whether they went to college. In fact, we can assume that this theory predicts that people who are already dead would have learned better under distributed versus massed practice, and so will people who are not yet born once they are alive!

Although the assumption of many theories in the behavioral sciences is that they will hold, on average, for all human beings, it is obviously impossible to ever be completely sure about this. Naturally, it is not possible to test every human being. And because the population that the relationship is assumed to apply to consists of every human being, in every place and every time, it is also impossible to take a representative sample of the population of interest. People who are not yet born, who live in unexplored territories, or who have already died simply cannot be included in the scientist's sample.

Because of the impossibility of the scientist drawing a representative sample of all human beings, true generalization across people is not possible. No researcher will ever be able to know that his or her favorite theory applies to all people, in all cultures and places, and at all times because he or she can never test or even sample from all of those people. For this reason, we frequently make the simplifying assumption that unless there is a specific reason to believe otherwise, relationships between conceptual variables that are observed in one group of people will also generally be observed in other groups of people.

Because the assumed relationships are expected to hold for everyone, behavioral scientists are often content to use college students as research participants. In short, they frequently assume that college students have the same basic characteristics as all other human beings, that college students will interpret the meaning of the experimental conditions the same way as any other group of human beings, and thus that the relationships among conceptual variables that are found for college students will also be found in other groups of people.

Of course, this basic assumption may, at least in some cases, be incorrect. There may be certain characteristics of college students that make them different. For instance, college students may be more impressionable than are older people because they are still developing their attitudes and their self-identity. As a result, college students may be particularly likely to listen to those in positions of authority. College students may also be more cognitively (rather than emotionally) driven than the average person and have a higher need for peer approval than most people (Sears, 1986). And there are some theories that are only expected to hold for certain groups of people—such as young children or those with an anxiety disorder.

In some cases, then, there may be a compelling reason to suspect that a relationship found in college students would not be found in other populations. And whenever there is reason to suspect that a result found for college students (or for any specific sample that has been used in research) would not hold up for other types of people, then research should be conducted with these other populations to test for generalization. However, unless the researcher has a specific reason to believe that generalization will not hold, it is appropriate to assume that a result found in one population (even if that population is college students) *will* generalize to other populations. In short, because the researcher can never demonstrate that his or her results generalize to all populations, it is not expected that he or she will attempt to do so. Rather, the burden of proof rests on those who claim that a result will *not* generalize to demonstrate that this is indeed the case.

Generalization Across Settings

Although most people learning about behavioral research immediately realize the potential dangers of generalizing from college students to "people at large," expert researchers are generally at least, if not more, concerned with the extent to which a research finding will generalize beyond the specific settings and techniques used in the original test of the hypothesis. The problem is that a single experiment usually uses only one or two experimenters and is conducted in a specific place. Furthermore, an experiment uses only one of the many possible manipulations of the independent variable and at most a few of the many possible measured dependent variables. The uniqueness of any one experiment makes it possible that the findings are limited in some way to the specific settings, experimenters, manipulations, or measured variables used in the research.

Although these concerns may seem less real to you than concerns about generalization to other people, they can actually be quite important. For instance, it is sometimes found that different researchers may produce different behaviors in their research participants. Researchers who act in a warm and engaging manner may capture the interest of their participants and thus produce different research findings than do cold researchers to whom people are not attracted. It is also the case that the sex, age, and ethnicity of the experimenter may also influence whether a relationship is or is not found (Ickes, 1984).

Ecological Validity.   As we will discuss later in this chapter, repeating the experiment in different places and with different experimenters and different operationalizations of the variables is the best method of demonstrating generalization across settings. But it is also possible to increase the potential generalization of a single experiment by increasing its ecological validity.[1] As

---

[1]When referring to experimental designs, ecological validity is sometimes referred to as *mundane realism*.

we have seen in Chapter 7, the ecological validity of a research design refers to the extent to which the research is conducted in situations that are similar to the everyday life experiences of the participants (Aronson & Carlsmith, 1968). For instance, a research design that deals with how children learn to read will have higher ecological validity if the children read a paragraph taken from one of their textbooks than it would if they read a list of sentences taken from adult magazines.

Field Experiments.   One approach that can be used to increase the ecological validity of experiments in some cases is to actually conduct them in natural situations. **Field experiments** are experimental research designs that are conducted in a natural environment such as a library, a factory, or a school rather than in a research laboratory. Because field experiments are true experiments, they have a manipulation, the creation of equivalence, and a measured dependent variable.

Because field experiments are conducted in the natural environment of the participants, they will generally have higher ecological validity than laboratory experiments. Furthermore, they may also have an advantage in the sense that research participants may act more naturally than they would in a lab setting. However, there are also some potential costs to the use of field experiments. For one, it is not always possible to get permission from the institution to conduct them, and even if access is gained, it may not be feasible to use random assignment. Children often cannot be randomly assigned to specific teaching methods or workers to specific tasks. Furthermore, in field settings there is usually a greater potential for systematic and random error because unexpected events may occur that could have been controlled for in the lab.

In general, we have more confidence that a finding will generalize if it is tested in an experiment that has high ecological validity, such as a field experiment. However, field experiments are not *necessarily* more externally valid than are laboratory experiments. An experiment conducted in one particular factory may not generalize to work in other factories in other places any more than the data collected in one laboratory would be expected to generalize to other laboratories or to everyday life. And lab experiments can frequently provide a very good idea of what will happen in real life (Banaji & Crowder, 1989; Berkowitz & Donnerstein, 1982). Field experiments, just like laboratory experiments, are limited because they involve one sample of people at one place at one particular time. In short, no matter how well an experiment is designed, there will always be threats to its external validity. Just as it is impossible to show generalization across all people, it is equally impossible to ever show that an observed relationship holds up in every possible situation.

Replications

Because any single test of a research hypothesis will always be limited in terms of what it can show, important advances in science are never the result of a single research project. Rather, advances occur through the accumulation of knowledge that comes from many different tests of the same theory or research hypothesis, made by different researchers using different research designs, participants, and operationalizations of the independent and dependent variables. The process of repeating previous research, which forms the basis of all scientific inquiry, is known as **replication.** Although replications of previous experiments are conducted for many different purposes, they can be classified into four general types, as discussed in the following sections.

Exact Replications

Not surprisingly, the goal of an **exact replication** is to repeat a previous research design as exactly as possible, keeping almost everything about the experiment the same as it was the first time around. Of course, there really is no such thing as an *exact* replication—when a new experiment replicates an old one, new research participants will have to be used, and the experiment will be conducted at a later date. It is also likely that the research will also occur in a new setting and with new experimenters, and in fact the most common reason for attempting to conduct an exact replication is to see if an effect that has been found in one laboratory or by one researcher can be found in another lab by another researcher.

Although exact replications may be used in some cases to test whether a finding can be discovered again, they are actually not that common in behavioral science. This is partly due to the fact that even if the exact replication does not reproduce the findings from the original experiment, this does not necessarily mean that the original experiment was invalid. It is always possible that the experimenter who conducted the replication did not create the appropriate conditions or did not measure the dependent variable properly. However, to help others who wish to replicate your research (and it is a great honor if they do because this means they have found it interesting), you must specify in the research report the procedures you followed in enough detail that another researcher would be able to follow your procedures and conduct an exact replication of your study.

Conceptual Replications

In general, other types of replication are more useful than exact replications because in addition to demonstrating that a result can be found again, they provide information about the specific conditions under which the original relationship might or might not be found. In a **conceptual replication** the scientist investigates the relationship between the same conceptual variables that were studied in previous research, but she or he tests the hypothesis using different operational definitions of the independent variable and/or the measured dependent variable. For example, when studying the effects of exposure to violence on aggression, the researcher might use clips from feature films, rather than cartoons, to manipulate the content of the viewed stimuli, and he or she might measure verbal aggression, rather than physical aggression, as a dependent variable.

If the same relationship can be demonstrated again with different manipulations or different dependent measures, the confidence that the observed relationship is not specific to the original measures is increased. And if the conceptual replication does *not* find the relationship that was observed in the original research, it may nevertheless provide information about the situations in and measures for which the effect does or does not occur. For example, if the same results of viewing violent material were found on a measure of verbal aggression (such as shouting or swearing) as had earlier been found on physical aggression (such as hitting or pushing), we would learn that the relationship between exposure to aggressive material generalizes. But if the same results were not found, this might suggest that the original relationship was limited to physical, rather than verbal, aggression.

Although generally more useful than exact replications, conceptual replications are themselves limited in the sense that it is difficult to draw conclusions about exactly what changes between the original experiment and the replication experiment might have produced differences in the observed relationships. For instance, if a conceptual replication fails to replicate the original finding, this suggests that something that has been changed is important, but it does not conclusively demonstrate what that something is.

Constructive Replications

Because it is important to know exactly how changes in the operational definitions of the independent and dependent variables in the research change the observed relationships between them, the most popular form of replication is known as a constructive replication. In a **constructive replication** the researcher tests the same hypothesis as the original experiment (in the form of either an exact or a conceptual replication), but also adds new conditions to the original experiment to assess the specific variables that might change the previously observed relationship. In general, the purpose of a constructive replication is to rule out alternative explanations or to add new information about the variables of interest.

Some Examples.   We have already considered some examples of constructive replications. For one, in Chapter 10 we considered a case in which the constructive replication involved adding a new control condition to a one-way experimental design. In this case, adding a condition in which participants did not view any films at all allowed us to test the possibility that the nonviolent cartoons were reducing aggressive behavior rather than that the violent cartoons were increasing aggressive behavior. In this case the goal of the constructive replication is to rule out an alternative explanation for the initial experiment.

In Chapter 11 we looked at another type of constructive replication—a study designed to test limitations on the effects of viewing violence on aggressive behavior. The predictions of this experiment are shown in Figure 11.2 in Chapter 11. The goal of the experiment was to replicate the finding that exposure to violent behavior increased aggression in the nonfrustrated condition, but then to show that this relationship reverses if the children have previously been frustrated. Notice that in this constructive replication the original conditions of the experiment have been retained (the no-frustration conditions), but new conditions have been added (the frustration conditions).

Moderator Variables.   As in this case, constructive replications are often factorial experimental designs where a new variable (in this case, the prior state of the children) is added to the variable that was manipulated in the original experiment (violent or nonviolent cartoons). One level of the new variable represents an exact or a conceptual replication of the original experiment, whereas the other level represents a condition where it is expected that the original relationship does not hold or reverses. The prediction is that there will be an observed interaction between the original variable and the new variable.

When the interaction in a constructive replication is found to be statistically significant, the new variable is called a moderator variable, and the new variable can be said to *moderate* the initial relationship. A **moderator variable** is a variable that produces an interaction of the relationship between two other variables such that the relationship between them is different at different levels of the moderator variable (Baron & Kenny, 1986).

You might wonder why it is necessary to include the conditions that replicate the previous experiment when it is the new conditions, in which a different relationship is expected, that are of interest. That is, why not just test the children under the frustration condition rather than including the original nonfrustration condition as well? The reason is that if the original conditions are not included, there is no guarantee that the new experiment has adequately recreated the original experimental situation. Thus, because constructive replications create both conditions designed to demonstrate that the original pattern of results can be replicated and conditions where the original pattern of results is changed, these replications can provide important information about exactly what changes influence the original relationship.

Participant Replications

Although the previous types of replication have dealt with generalization across settings, in cases where there is reason to believe that an observed relationship found with one set of participants will not generalize to or will be different in another population of people, it may be useful to conduct replications using new types of participants. To be most effective, a **participant replication** should not simply repeat the original experiment with a new population. As we have previously discussed, such repetition is problematic because if a different relationship between the independent and dependent variables is found, the experimenter cannot know if that difference is due to the use of different participants or to other potentially unknown changes in the experimental setting. Rather, the experiment should be designed as a constructive replication in which both the original population and the new one are used. Again, if the original result generalizes, then only a main effect of the original variable will be observed, but if the result does not generalize, an interaction between the original variable and the participant population will be observed.

One type of participant replication involves testing people from different cultures. For instance, a researcher might test whether the effects on aggression of viewing violent cartoons are the same for Japanese children as they are for U.S. children by showing violent and nonviolent films to a sample of both U.S. and Japanese schoolchildren. Interpreting the results of cross-cultural replications can be difficult, however, because it is hard to know if the manipulation is conceptually equivalent for the new participants. For instance, the cartoons must be translated into Japanese, and although the experimenter may have attempted to adequately translate the materials, children in the new culture may interpret the cartoons differently than the children in the United States did. The same cartoons may have appeared more (or less) aggressive to the Japanese children. Of course, the different interpretations may themselves be of interest, but there is likely to be ambiguity regarding whether differences in aggression are due to cultural differences in the effects of the independent variable on the dependent variable or to different interpretations of the independent variable.

Summarizing and Integrating Research Results

If you have been carefully following the topics in the last two chapters, you will have realized by now that every test of a research hypothesis, regardless of how well it is conducted or how strong its findings, is limited in some sense. For instance, some experiments are conducted in such specific settings that they seem unlikely to generalize to other tests of the research hypothesis. Other experiments are undermined by potential alternative explanations that result from the confounding of other variables with the independent variable of interest. And, of course, every significant result may be invalid because it represents a Type 1 error.

In addition to the potential of invalidity, the drawing of conclusions about research findings is made difficult because the results of individual experiments testing the same or similar research hypotheses are never quite consistent among one another. Some studies find relationships, whereas others do not. Of those that do, some show stronger relationships, some show weaker relationships, and still others may find relationships that are in the opposite direction from what most of the other studies show. Other studies suggest that the observed relationship is stronger or weaker under certain conditions or with the use of certain experimental manipulations or measured variables.

Research Programs

The natural inconsistency among different tests of the same hypothesis and the fact that any one study is potentially invalid make it clear why science is never built on the results of single experiments but rather is cumulative—building on itself over time through replication. Because scientists are aware of the limitations of any one experiment, they frequently conduct collections of experiments, known as **research programs,** in which they systematically study a topic of interest through conceptual and constructive replications over a period of time. The advantage of the research program is that the scientists are able to increase their confidence in the validity and the strength of a relationship, as well as the conditions under which it occurs or does not occur, by testing the hypothesis using different operationalizations of the independent and dependent variables, different research designs, and different participants.

Review Papers

The results of research programs are routinely reviewed and summarized in review papers, which appear in scientific books and journals. A **review paper** is a document that discusses the research in a given area with the goals of summarizing the existing findings, drawing conclusions about the conditions under which relationships may or may not occur, linking the research findings to other areas of research, and making suggestions for further research. In a review paper a scientist might draw conclusions about which experimental manipulations and dependent variables seem to have been most successful or seem to have been the most valid, attempt to explain contradictory findings in the literature, and perhaps propose new theories to account for observed findings.

Meta-analysis

Many review papers use a procedure known as meta-analysis to summarize research findings. A **meta-analysis** is a statistical technique that uses the results of existing studies to integrate and draw conclusions about those studies. Because meta-analyses provide so much information, they are very popular ways of summarizing research literatures. Table 13.1 presents the findings of some recent meta-analyses in the behavioral sciences.

A meta-analysis provides a relatively objective method of reviewing research findings because it (1) specifies **inclusion criteria** that indicate exactly which studies will or will not be included in the analysis, (2) systematically searches for all studies that meet the inclusion criteria, and (3) uses the effect size statistic to provide an objective measure of the strength of observed relationships.

One example of the use of meta-analysis involves the summarizing of the effects of psychotherapy on the mental health of clients. Over the years hundreds of studies have been conducted addressing this question, but they differ among each other in virtually every imaginable way. These studies include many different types of psychological disorders (for instance, anxiety, depression, and schizophrenia) and different types of therapies (for instance, hypnosis, behavioral therapy, and Freudian therapy). Furthermore, the dependent measures used in the research have varied from self-report measures of mood or anxiety to behavioral measures such as amount of time before release from

TABLE 13.1   Examples of Meta-analyses

Meta-analysis	Findings
Twenge and Nolen-Hoeksema (2002)	Compared levels of depression among children at different ages and of different ethnic groups
Hardy and Hinkin (2002)	Studied the effect of HIV infection on cognition by comparing reaction times of infected and noninfected patients
Gully, Incalcaterra, Joshi, and Beaubien (2002)	Studied the relationship between group interdependence and task performance in teams
Schmitt (2002)	Found that different social contexts (for instance, mixed- versus single-sex interactions) influenced our perceptions of others' physical attractiveness
Dowden and Brown (2002)	Found that different patterns of drug and alcohol use predicted criminal recidivism
Brierley, Shaw, and David (2002)	Measured the normal size of the amygdala in humans, and studied how it changes with age

This table presents examples of some of the more than 300 meta-analyses published in 2002.

psychological institutions. And the research has used both correlational and experimental research designs.

Defining Inclusion Criteria.   Despite what might have appeared to be a virtually impossible task, Smith, Glass, and Miller (1980) summarized these studies and drew important conclusions about the effects of psychotherapy through the use of a meta-analysis. The researchers first set up their inclusion criteria to be studies in which two or more types of psychotherapy were compared or in which one type of psychotherapy was compared against a control group. They further defined psychotherapy to include situations in which the clients had an emotional or behavioral problem, they sought or were referred for treatment, and the person delivering the treatment was identified as a psychotherapist by virtue of training or professional affiliation.

The researchers then systematically searched computer databases and the reference sections of previous research reports to locate every single study that met the inclusion criteria. Over 475 studies were located, and these studies used over 10,000 research participants.

Coding the Studies.   At this point each of these studies was systematically coded and analyzed. As you will recall from our discussion in Chapter 8, the *effect size* is a statistical measure of the strength of a relationship. In a meta-analysis one or more effect size statistics are recorded from each of the studies, and it is these effect sizes that are analyzed in the meta-analysis. In some cases the effect size itself is reported in the research report, and in other cases it must be calculated from other reported statistics.

Analyzing the Effect Size.   One of the important uses of meta-analysis is to combine many different types of studies into a single analysis. The meta-analysis can provide an index of the overall strength of a relationship within a research literature. In the case of psychotherapy, for instance, Smith and her colleagues found that the average effect size for the effect of therapy was +.85, indicating that psychotherapy had a relatively large positive effect on recovery (recall from Chapter 8 that in the behavioral sciences a "large" effect size is usually considered to be about .40). In addition to overall statements, the meta-analysis allows the scientist to study whether other coded variables moderate the relationship of interest. For instance, Smith et al. found that the strength of the relationship between therapy and recovery (as indexed by the effect size) was different for different types of therapies and on different types of recovery measures.

Benefits and Limitations of Meta-analyses.   Meta-analyses have both benefits and limitations in comparison to narrative literature reviews. On the positive side, the use of explicit inclusion criteria and an in-depth search for all studies that meet these ensures objectivity in what is and what is not included in the analysis. Readers can be certain that *all* of the relevant studies have been included, rather than just a subset of these, which is likely in a paper that does not use meta-analysis. Second, the use of the effect size statistic provides an objective measure of the strength of observed relationships.

As a result of these features, meta-analyses are therefore more accurate than narrative research reviews. In fact, it has been found that narrative reviews tend to underestimate the magnitude of the true relationships between variables in comparison to meta-analyses (Cooper & Rosenthal, 1980; Mann, 1994). This seems to occur in part because, since research is normally at least in part contradictory, the narrative reviews tend to reach correct, but potentially misleading conclusions such as "some evidence supports the hypothesis whereas other evidence contradicts it." Meta-analyses, in contrast, frequently tend to show that, although there is of course some contradiction across studies, the underlying tendency is much stronger in one direction than in the other.

However, because meta-analyses are based on archival research, the conclusions that can be drawn will always be limited by the data that have been published. This can be problematic if the published studies have not measured or manipulated all of the important variables or are not representative of all of the studies that have been conducted. For instance, because studies that have significant results are more likely to be published than those that are nonsignificant, the published studies may overestimate the size of a relationship between variables.

In the end, meta-analyses are really just another type of research project. They can provide a substantial amount of knowledge about the magnitude and generality of relationships. And as with any research, they have both strengths and limitations, and the ability to adequately interpret them involves being aware of these.

Interpretation of Research Literatures

The primary goal of replication is to determine the extent to which an observed relationship generalizes across different tests of the research hypothesis. However, just because a finding does not generalize does not mean it is not interesting or important. Indeed, science proceeds by discovering limiting conditions for previously demonstrated relationships. Few relationships hold in all settings and for all people. Scientific theories are modified over time as more information about their limitations is discovered. As an example, one of the interesting questions in research investigating the effects of exposure to violent material on aggression concerns the fact that although it is well known that the viewing of violence tends to increase aggression on average, this does not happen for all people. So it is extremely important to conduct participant replications to determine which people will, and which will not, be influenced by exposure to violent material.

The cumulative knowledge base of a scientific literature, gained through replication and reported in review papers and meta-analysis, is much more informative and accurate than is any individual test of a research hypothesis. However, the skilled consumer of research must learn to evaluate the results of research programs to get an overall feel for what the data in a given domain are showing. There is usually no clear-cut right or wrong answer to these questions, but the individual reader has to be the judge of the quality of a research result.

Finally, it is worth mentioning that replication also serves to keep the process of scientific inquiry honest. If the results of a scientist's research are important, then other scientists will want to try to replicate them to test for generalizability of the findings. Still other scientists will attempt to apply the research results to make constructive advances. If a scientist has fabricated or altered data, the results will not be replicable, and the research will not contribute to the advancement of science.

SUMMARY

External validity refers to the extent to which relationships between independent and dependent variables that are found in a test of a research hypothesis can be expected to be found again when tested with other research designs, other operationalizations of the variables, other participants, other experimenters, or other times and settings.

A research design has high external validity if the results can be expected to generalize to other participants and to other tests of the relationship. External validity can be enhanced by increasing the ecological validity of an experiment by making it similar to what might occur in everyday life or by conducting field experiments.

Science relies primarily on replications to test the external validity of research findings. Sometimes the original research is replicated exactly, but more often conceptual replications with new operationalizations of the independent or dependent variables, or constructive replications with new conditions added to the original design, are employed. Replication allows scientists to test both the generalization and the limitations of research findings.

Because each individual research project is limited in some way, scientists conduct research programs in which many different studies are conducted. These programs are often summarized in review papers. Meta-analysis represents a relatively objective method of summarizing the results of existing research that involves a systematic method of selecting studies for review and coding and analyzing their results.

KEY TERMS

conceptual replication 253	meta-analysis 257
constructive replication 254	moderator variable 255
exact replication 253	participant replication 255
external validity 249	replication 253
field experiments 252	research programs 257
generalization 249	review paper 257
inclusion criteria 257	

REVIEW AND DISCUSSION QUESTIONS

1. Define *external validity,* and indicate its importance to scientific progress.

2. Why is it never possible to know whether a research finding will generalize to all populations of individuals? How do behavioral scientists deal with this problem?

3. What are the four different types of replication, and what is the purpose of each?

4. Explain how replication can be conceptualized as a factorial experimental design.

5. Why are research programs more important to the advancement of science than are single experiments?

6. Define a meta-analysis, and explain its strengths and limitations.

HANDS-ON EXPERIENCE

1. In each of the following cases, the first article presents a study that has a confound and the second article represents a constructive replication designed to eliminate the confound. Report on one or more of the pairs of articles:

   a. Aronson, E., & Mills, J. (1959). The effect of severity of initiation on liking for a group. *Journal of Abnormal and Social Psychology, 59,* 177–181.
   Gerard, H. B., & Matthewson, G. C. (1966). The effects of severity of initiation on liking for a group: A replication. *Journal of Experimental Social Psychology, 2,* 278–287.

   b. Zimbardo, P. G. (1970). The human choice: Individuation, reason, and order versus deindividuation, impulse, and chaos. In W. J. Arnold and D. Levine (Eds.), *Nebraska Symposium on Motivation, 1969.* Lincoln: University of Nebraska Press.
   Johnson, R. D., & Downing, L. L. (1979). Deindividuation and the valence of cues: Effects on prosocial and antisocial behavior. *Journal of Personality and Social Psychology, 37,* 1532–1538.

   c. Pennebaker, J. W., Dyer, M. A., Caulkins, R. S., Litowitz, D. L., Ackerman, P. L., & Anderson, D. B. (1979). Don't the girls get prettier at closing time: A country and western application to psychology. *Personality and Social Psychology Bulletin, 5,* 122–125.
   Madey, S. F., Simo, M., Dillworth, D., & Kemper, D. (1996). They do get more attractive at closing time, but only when you are not in a relationship. *Basic and Applied Social Psychology, 18,* 387–393.

   d. Baron, R. A., & Ransberger, V. M. (1978). Ambient temperature and the occurrence of collective violence: The "long, hot summer" revisited. *Journal of Personality and Social Psychology, 36,* 351–360.
   Carlsmith, J. M., & Anderson, C. A. (1979). Ambient temperature and the occurrence of collective violence: A new analysis. *Journal of Personality and Social Psychology, 37,* 337–344.

2. Locate a research report that contains a replication of previous research. Identify the purpose of the replication and the type of replication that was used. What are the important findings of the research?

3. Develop a research hypothesis, and propose a specific test of it. Then develop a conceptual replication and a constructive replication that investigate the expected boundary conditions for the original relationship.

4. Prepare a report summarizing a research program conducted by a scientist or a group of scientists, as recommended by your instructor.

5. Locate a review paper that does not use a meta-analysis, and comment on its findings. Compare the objectivity of these findings with those in the meta-analysis you read in problem 6.

6. Locate a meta-analysis (for instance, one of those found in Table 13.1), and review its findings.

CHAPTER **FOURTEEN**
Quasi-experimental Research Designs

STUDY QUESTIONS

• What is program evaluation research, and when is it used?

• What is a quasi-experimental research design? When are such designs used, and why?

• Why do quasi-experimental designs generally have lower internal validity than true experiments?

• What are the most common quasi-experimental research designs?

• What are the major threats to internal validity in quasi-experimental designs?

• What is regression to the mean, and what problems does it pose in research?

• What is a participant-variable research design?

• What is a single-participant research design?

We have seen in Chapter 10 that the strength of experimental research lies in the ability to maximize internal validity. However, a basic limitation of experimental research is that, for practical or ethical reasons, the independent variables of interest cannot always be experimentally manipulated. In this chapter we will consider research designs that are frequently used by researchers who want to make comparisons among different groups of individuals but cannot randomly assign the individuals to the groups. These comparisons can be either between participants (for instance, a comparison of the scholastic achievement of autistic versus nonautistic children) or repeated measures (for instance, a comparison of the mental health of individuals before and after they have participated in a program of psychotherapy). These research designs are an essential avenue of investigation in domains such as education, human development, social work, and clinical psychology because they are frequently the only possible approach to studying the variables of interest.

Program Evaluation Research

As we have seen in Chapter 1, one type of applied research that involves the use of existing groups is program evaluation research (Campbell, 1969; Rossi & Freeman, 1993). Program evaluation research is research designed to study intervention programs, such as after-school programs, clinical therapies, or prenatal care clinics, with the goal of determining whether the programs are effective in helping the people who make use of them.

Consider as an example a researcher who is interested in determining the effects on college students of participation in a study abroad program. The researcher expects that one outcome of such programs, in which students spend a semester or a year studying in a foreign country, is that the students will develop more positive attitudes toward immigrants to their own country than students who do not participate in exchange programs.

You can see that it is not going to be possible for the researcher to exert much control in the research, and thus there are going to be threats to its internal validity. For one, the students cannot be randomly assigned to the conditions. Some students spend time studying abroad, and others do not, but whether they do or do not is determined by them, not by the experimenter. And there are many variables that may determine whether a student does or does not participate, including his or her interests, financial resources, and cultural background. These variables are potential common-causal variables in the sense that they may cause both the independent variable (participation in the program) and the dependent variable (attitudes toward immigrants). Their presence will thus limit the researcher's ability to make causal statements about the effectiveness of the program.

In addition to the lack of random assignment, because the research uses a longitudinal design in which measurements are taken over a period of time, the researcher will have difficulty controlling what occurs during that time. Other changes are likely to take place, both within the participants and in their environment, and these changes become extraneous or confounding variables within the research design. These variables may threaten the validity of the research.

Quasi-experimental Designs

Despite such difficulties, with creative planning a researcher may be able to create a research design that is able to rule out at least some of the threats to the internal validity of the research, thus allowing conclusions about the causal effects of the independent variable on the dependent variable to be drawn. Because the independent variable or variables are measured, rather than manipulated, these research designs are correlational, not experimental. Nevertheless, the designs also have some similarity to experimental research because the independent variable involves a grouping and the data are usually analyzed with ANOVA. For these reasons, such studies have been called **quasi-experimental research designs.**[1]

In the following sections, we will consider some of the most important research designs that involve the study of naturally occurring groups of individuals, as well as the particular threats to internal validity that are likely to occur when these designs are used. Figure 14.1 summarizes these designs as they would apply to the study abroad research example, and Table 14.1 summarizes the potential threats to the internal validity of each design.

Single-Group Design

One approach that our scientist might take is to simply locate a group of students who have spent the past year studying abroad and have now returned to their home university, set up an interview with each student, and assess some dependent measures, including students' attitudes toward immigrants in the United States.

Research that uses a single group of participants who are measured after they have had the experience of interest is known as a **single-group design.**[2] You can see, however, that there is a major limitation to this approach—since there is no control group, there is no way to determine what the attitudes of these students would have been if they hadn't studied abroad. As a result, our researcher cannot use the single-group design to draw conclusions about the effect of study abroad on attitudes toward immigrants.

Despite these limitations, single-group research designs are frequently reported in the popular literature, and they may be misinterpreted by those who

[1]For further information about the research designs discussed in this chapter, as well as about other types of quasi-experimental designs, you may wish to look at books by Campbell and Stanley (1963) and Cook and Campbell (1979).

[2]Campbell and Stanley (1963) called these "one-shot case studies."

FIGURE 14.1 Summary of Quasi-experimental Research Designs

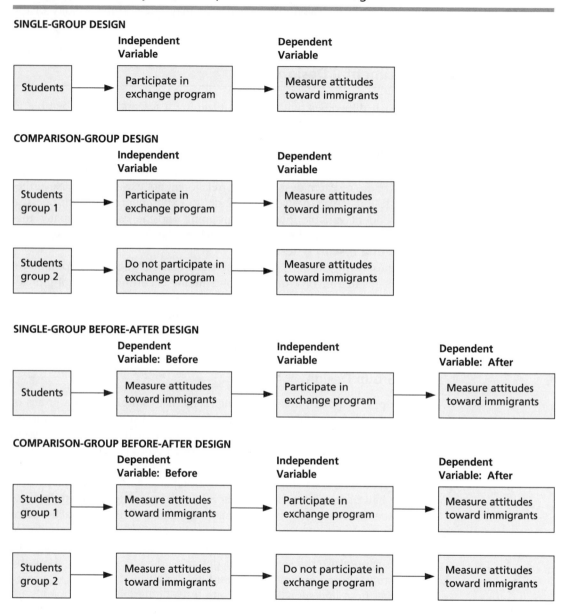

read them. Examples include books reporting the experiences of people who have survived stressful experiences such as wars or natural disasters or those who have lived through traumatic childhood experiences. If the goal of the research is simply to describe the experiences that individuals have had or their reactions to them (for instance, to document the reactions of the residents of

TABLE 14.1　Threats to the Internal Validity of Quasi-experimental Designs

Research Design	Threat to Validity						Interpretational Difficulties
	Selection	Attrition	Maturation	History	Retesting	Regression	
Single group	✓						No causal interpretation is possible because there is no comparison group.
Comparison group	✓						Comparisons are possible only to the extent that the comparison group is equivalent to the experimental group.
Single group before-after		✓	✓	✓	✓		Selection is not a problem because the same participants are measured both times. Attrition, maturation, history, and retesting cause problems.
Comparison group before-after		✓				✓	Maturation, history, and retesting should be controlled because the comparison group has experienced the same changes. Regression to mean is still problematic, as is the potential for differential attrition.

California to an earthquake), the data represent naturalistic descriptive research, as we have discussed in Chapter 7. In these cases we may be able to learn something about the experience itself by studying how the individuals experienced these events and reacted to them.

Single-group studies can never, however, be used to draw conclusions about how an experience has affected the individuals involved. For instance, research showing that children whose parents were alcoholics have certain psychological problems cannot be interpreted to mean that their parents' alcoholism caused these problems. Because there is no control group, we can never know what the individuals would have been like if they had not experienced this stressful situation, and it is quite possible that other variables, rather than their parents' alcoholism, caused these difficulties. As an informed consumer of scientific research, you must be aware that although single-group studies may be informative about the current characteristics of the individuals who have had the experiences, these studies cannot be used to draw conclusions about how the experiences affected them.

Comparison-Group Design

You can see that if our researcher wishes to draw any definitive conclusions about the effects of study abroad on attitudes toward immigrants, he or she will need one or more groups for comparison. A **comparison group** is a group that is expected to be similar but not equivalent to the experimental group (random assignment has not been used). One possibility is to include a second group of students who did not participate in the student exchange program. Ideally, this comparison group would be equivalent to the group that did participate on all characteristics except the participation itself. For instance, we could use as a comparison group students from the same university who had the same major but did not participate in the study abroad program. Even better would be a group of students who had an alternative study experience, such as spending a year at another university in the United States, but who did not travel abroad. The prediction is that if study abroad changes attitudes toward immigrants, then the students in this group should express more tolerance than the group that did not study abroad. This prediction would be tested with a one-way between-participants ANOVA with two levels of the independent variable.

Although the **comparison-group design** provides more information than a single-group design, you can see that there are still some serious threats to internal validity. These arise because it is possible that any observed differences on the dependent measure were due not to the effects of the study abroad program but to differences between the groups that existed before the sojourn began. Threats to internal validity that occur because individuals select themselves into groups, rather than being randomly assigned to groups, are called **selection threats.** In our case the major selection threat is that students who were interested in studying abroad were more tolerant of immigrants to begin with.

The more similar the two groups are to each other before they participate in the exchange program, the less problematic will be selection threats, and the stronger will be the conclusions drawn about the effects of the independent variable on the dependent variable. But even if the comparison group had been selected to be as equivalent as possible to the study group, it would almost certainly differ to some extent on at least some variables. In some cases potential differences between the groups can be statistically controlled, as we have discussed in Chapter 9.

Single-Group Before-After Design

Because the addition of one or more comparison groups in a comparison-group design involves recruiting another group of students, and because this design does not allow us to know how those groups differed before the experience occurred, you can imagine that it might be preferable in some cases to take a longitudinal approach. In this case the scientist would measure the attitudes of a group of students before they went abroad and then measure the attitudes again after the students returned home. Comparisons would be made over time, with the expectation that the students would express more tolerance toward immigrants after they returned home than they did before they left. The statistical comparison would be a one-way repeated-measures ANOVA with two levels.

One obvious advantage of the **single-group before-after design** is in terms of equivalence. The individuals who complete the measures after their exchange program are equivalent to those who completed them before they left because they are the same people. However, a before-after approach has its own set of potential threats to internal validity.

Retesting Threats.   One such threat involves the danger of retesting. As we have seen in Chapter 5, whenever the dependent measures are assessed more than once, participants may be able to guess the research hypothesis, and this may lead them to respond differently to the second set of measures than they otherwise would have. In our case an astute and cooperative student might guess that the researcher expected a positive change in attitudes over time and might therefore complete the questionnaire in a manner that would support this prediction.

Attrition Threats.   Another problem with the before-after approach in this case is that some of the students may drop out of college, transfer to another university, or stay abroad rather than returning home and thus never complete the second measure. This problem, known as **attrition** or **mortality,** poses a threat to internal validity in longitudinal research designs because the students who stay with the program may be different from those who drop out. In our example, for instance, the influence of the exchange program on attitudes may be overestimated if those students who had the most positive attitudes in the beginning are also the most likely to stay in the program.

Maturation and History Threats.   The addition of a time delay in a before-after design also introduces other extraneous variables into the research design. While the students were abroad, other things may have happened that were not related to the research hypothesis and yet may have caused changes in the dependent variable. One obvious change is that when the students return home, they are one year older than they were when they left. Since older students may be less prejudiced than younger students, the students might have become more tolerant toward immigrants over the time period even if they hadn't gone abroad. Threats to internal validity that involve potential changes in the research participants over time but that are unrelated to the independent variable are called **maturation threats.**

In addition to changes in the individuals themselves, other events unrelated to the exchange program that occur over the time period might influence the dependent variable. For instance, political events in the United States during the time under study might have caused changes in attitudes toward immigrants in the students. Threats to internal validity that occur due to the potential influence of changes in the social climate during the course of a study are called **history threats.**

Comparison-Group Before-After Design

Because both comparison-group and before-after designs have their unique sets of threats to internal validity, it is often desirable, when possible, to combine them, making use of a **comparison-group before-after design.**

In this design more than one group of individuals is studied, and the dependent measure is assessed for both groups before and after the intervening event. The comparison group either engages in other comparable activities during this time or else does not engage in any activity. If we used a group of students who did not study abroad as a comparison group, for instance, they would also be measured both before and after the study group visited abroad. In this case the appropriate statistical test would be a two-way ANOVA with one between-participants factor (group) and one repeated-measures factor (time of measurement). The prediction is for an interaction such that the group that studies abroad shows more change over time than does the comparison group.

The use of a comparison group allows the scientist to control for some of the threats to validity that occur in before-after studies that last over a period of time. For one, maturation is less likely to provide a threat to internal validity because the students in the comparison group also mature to the same extent over the time period. This design also controls for history threats when these events influence both groups equally. It is still possible, however, that if the two groups are in different locations, they may be differentially affected by history. For instance, if the U.S. government made important decisions about immigration policy during the time period of the study, this may have had a different impact on students in the United States (who were more likely to know about the decision) than it did for those who were abroad (who may have been more likely not to have known about the decision). This design also controls for attrition, unless the amount of attrition is different in the two groups.

Regression to the Mean as a Threat to Internal Validity

In short, measurement of the dependent variable before the experience in the comparison-group before-after design has the advantage of allowing the researcher to know if and how the groups differed before the differences in the independent variable occurred. Although this knowledge is helpful, whenever participants in different groups differ on the dependent variable before the independent variable occurs, the researcher cannot be certain that it was the independent variable, rather than something else, that caused differences on the measurements made after the independent variable occurred.

One threat to validity that occurs whenever there is not initial equivalence between the groups results from a statistical artifact known as *regression to the mean*. One way to understand why this artifact occurs is to recall that a regression equation can be used to predict a person's score on the outcome variable if the score on the predictor variable is known (see Chapter 9). If variables are first converted to standard (z) scores, the following equation holds:

$$z_y = r \times z_x$$

where r is the Pearson correlation coefficient between the two variables.

You will see from this equation that whenever the correlation between the independent variable (z_x) and the dependent variable (z_y) is less than $r = 1.00$

or greater than $r = -1.00$, a given score on the independent variable will always result in a prediction for the dependent variable that is nearer the mean (that is, less extreme). For instance, if $r = .30$, then a person who received a score of $z_x = 2$ on the independent variable would be expected to receive a score of $z_y = .67$ on the dependent variable, and a person who received a score of $z_x = -2$ on the independent variable would be expected, by chance, to receive a score of $z_y = -.67$.

What this means for the interpretation of quasi experiments is that whenever the same variable is measured more than once, to the extent that the correlation between the two measures is less than $r = 1.00$ or greater than $r = -1.00$, individuals will tend to score more toward the average score of the group on the second measure than they did on the first measure, even if nothing has changed between the two measures. This change is known as **regression to the mean.**

Misinterpreting Results as a Result of Regression to the Mean.

When regression to the mean occurs in everyday life, people often attribute a meaning to the change that it does not deserve. For instance, the first recordings produced by a musical group are frequently the best recordings it ever makes. Although people may interpret this pattern to mean that the group got worse, such effects can be easily explained by regression to the mean—extremely good outcomes at one time point tend to be followed by more average ones later. Another example is that athletes who, because of an exceptional athletic performance, are pictured on the cover of *Sports Illustrated* generally do not perform as well afterward as they did before they received the honor. Although it is commonly thought that being featured in the magazine causes the players to do more poorly (perhaps because they then experience more pressure to do well), a more likely explanation is regression to the mean. Just as very intelligent parents tend to have less intelligent children, and very short parents tend to have taller children, most things tend to become more average over time.

Regression to the mean causes interpretational difficulties whenever there is initial nonequivalence between the groups in a quasi-experimental research design. And these difficulties are enhanced under two conditions. First, regression to the mean is more problematic to the extent that the groups have extreme scores on the initial measure because the farther a group is from the mean, the greater the regression to the mean will be. Second, as you will recall from Chapter 5, one reason that scores on the same measured variable might not correlate highly over time is that the measure is unreliable. Thus we can say that unreliable measures are more likely to produce regression to the mean.

Consider as an example a comparison-group before-after design that compares the reading skills of a group of children before and after they complete a reading-skill training program with another group of children who do not participate in the program. However, because the program is offered only to very poor readers, the group that received the training had much lower reading scores to begin with than did the comparison group. Even if the reading skills of the children in the training program increased significantly more than the skills of the comparison group over time, this does not necessarily indicate that the program was effective. Because the poor readers initially scored extremely low on the reading test, they would be expected to show more improvement over time than the comparison group even without the benefit of instruction.

In some cases the effect of regression to the mean is to make it more difficult to demonstrate that programs had the expected effect. To return to our example testing whether study abroad programs increase tolerance, it would be difficult to know how to interpret a result showing that the students did not develop more positive attitudes over time. Because students who enroll in such programs are likely to initially be very positive toward foreigners, their scores will tend to decrease over time through regression to the mean, and this change will tend to cancel out any positive effects of the program. In fact, some research findings show that students who volunteer for foreign exchange programs often develop *less* favorable attitudes toward foreigners over the course of their experience, but this is probably due, at least in part, to regression to the mean. Because students who participate in study abroad programs probably have very positive attitudes toward foreigners to begin with, their attitudes may become more neutral over time (cf. Stangor, Jonas, Stroebe, & Hewstone, 1996).

Avoiding Problems Associated with Regression to the Mean.   Difficulties such as regression to the mean make it clear why, whenever possible, experimental research designs, rather than quasi-experimental research designs, should be used. For instance, in some cases a treatment program is implemented, but there are not enough places in the program for everyone who wishes to participate. In this case participants may be put on a waiting list, and participants can be randomly assigned to be allowed into the program. Those who are able to get into the program would then be equivalent to those who did not.

In many cases, however, practical considerations of time, money, and the cooperation of those in charge of the program limit the researcher to a quasi-experimental approach. Of course, the ability to control for threats to internal validity in quasi-experimental research is dependent on the type of research design, and some designs allow at least some of the many threats to internal validity to be ruled out. Furthermore, no research is perfectly valid. As in other research, the evidence for a relationship between variables accumulates over time as more and more studies, each using different research designs, are conducted. Because different research projects have different threats to internal validity, they may, when taken together, allow strong conclusions about the causal relationships among variables to be drawn.

Time-Series Designs

The basic logic of the before-after research design can be taken a step further through the use of longitudinal research designs in which the dependent measure is assessed for one or more groups more than twice, at regular intervals, both before and after the experience of interest occurs. Such research designs are collectively known as **time-series designs,** and they may in some cases be able to rule out more threats to internal validity than can the designs we have investigated to this point.

Consider, for instance, a hypothetical time-series design that uses archival data to investigate the incidence of street robberies in a large U.S. city at regular, one-month intervals over a period of three years. The goal of the research is to investigate the effects on crime of the institution of a "cop on the streets" program in which a substantial number of police officers moved out of their cruisers and began walking street beats.

You can see from the data in Figure 14.2 that there was a consistent trend of increasing street robberies in the years preceding the enactment of the new program, but that this trend leveled off and even began to decrease slightly after the enactment of the program. The advantage of the time-series approach in this case is that it allows us to see trends in the data over time, something that would not have been possible if we had measured the crime rate only twice—once before and once after the program was initiated.

Although the results of this time-series study are consistent with the hypothesis that the police on the streets program reduced the incidence of robberies, something else occurring at the same time as the initiative may have caused the difference. However, time-series designs can be even more conclusive if the events of interest produce changes in the dependent variable

FIGURE 14.2 Hypothetical Results of a Time-Series Study

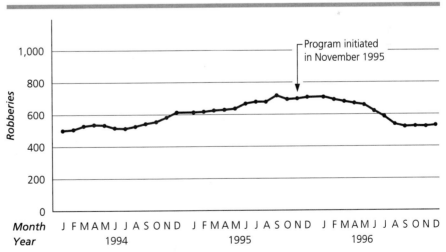

These are the results of a hypothetical study that uses archival data to track the incidence of street robberies in a large U.S. city at regular, one-month intervals over a period of three years, before and after the institution of a "cop on the street" program in which a substantial number of police officers moved out of their cruisers and began walking street beats.

more than once over the series. For instance, in a classic study of the effects of violent crimes on aggression, Berkowitz and Macaulay (1971) found that the number of murders in the United States increased dramatically in the months following the assassination of President John Kennedy in 1963 and also increased after the highly publicized mass murders by Richard Speck in 1966. Because homicides increased after *both* events, it is less likely (but not impossible) that something else unrelated to the crimes might have been the causal variable.

Participant-Variable Designs

Although to this point we have considered comparisons across groups of people who have had different experiences, perhaps the most common type of quasi-experimental research design is one in which one or more of the independent variables is a naturally occurring characteristic of individuals—for instance, a demographic variable such as sex or ethnicity or a personality variable such as parenting style, anxiety, or level of prejudice. When the grouping variable involves preexisting characteristics of the participants, the design is known as a **participant-variable design** and the variable that differs across the participants is known as a **participant variable.**

Demographic Variables

We have already considered in Chapter 11 the use of a participant-variable research design where the participant variable is a demographic characteristic—namely, the sex of the participant. The research described in Table 11.1 found that the relationship between viewing violent cartoons and behaving aggressively was different for boys than it was for girls. Similar comparisons could also be made on the basis of the race or the religion of the children, or on any other demographic variable.

Perhaps the most commonly studied demographic variable within the behavioral sciences is age. The fields of developmental psychology and human development are based to a large extent on participant-variable studies that compare the cognitive and social skills of individuals, particularly children, across different age levels. As we have discussed in Chapter 9, these comparisons can be made either between groups (**cross-sectional designs**) or by observing the children repeatedly over time (longitudinal designs). For instance, to study differences in children's memory skills, we could compare kindergarten, second-grade, and fourth-grade children at one time point (a cross-sectional approach), or we could follow the same children as they progress from kindergarten to fourth grade. Because each type of approach has some advantages, both types of designs are sometimes used together (see Applebaum & McCall, 1983).

Personality Variables

In other cases the participant variable of interest is a trait rather than a demographic characteristic. For instance, a clinical psychologist might compare the social skills of a group of highly anxious individuals (as determined by an anxiety test) with those of a group of less anxious individuals, or a health psychologist might compare the health behaviors of individuals with optimistic personalities with those who have less optimistic personalities.

In some cases the researcher may be able to select, from a large pool of individuals who have completed the personality test, two groups who have scored high and low. In other cases, when it is not possible to select people ahead of time, the personality measure may be given at the experimental session, and the participants may be divided into those who are above and below the median score on the measure to represent two levels of the personality variable. In other cases, rather than creating groups of individuals, the original quantitative personality variable can be used to predict the dependent variable using a regression analysis (Bissonnette, Ickes, Bernstein, & Knowles, 1990).

Interpretational Difficulties

Because the participant variable is measured, rather than manipulated, causal conclusions about the effect of the participant variable on the dependent variable are difficult to draw. For instance, if participants in a research project are selected on the basis of their scores on an anxiety measure, they are likely to differ as well on many other characteristics. One of these other characteristics, rather than anxiety, may have caused the differences on the dependent measure.

Single-Participant Designs

We have seen that participant-variable studies are used to compare groups of people, whereas time-series designs are used to study behavior over a period of time. However, the ability to track the behavior of individuals over time makes it possible in some cases to draw conclusions about the changes in behavior of a single person. Such studies are called **single-participant research designs.** Consider, for instance, a study designed to assess the effectiveness of a reinforcement therapy program on the speech behavior of an autistic child. As shown in Figure 14.3, the number of speech vocalizations that the child displayed in school was recorded by the child's teachers over a period of three months, both before and after the therapy program was instituted.

Although the goal of this study was to determine the impact of the reinforcement therapy program, the program was not immediately initiated when the study began. Rather, the behavior of the child was tracked for one month to observe the baseline level of vocalization. As you can see, the number of vocalizations during the baseline period is highly stable—the child had almost an equal number of vocalizations every day. The reinforcement therapy intervention, begun in the second month, caused a very large increase in vocalization in comparison to the variability before the experience. Furthermore, when the reinforcement was removed at the end of the second month, the child's

FIGURE 14.3   Results from a Single-Participant Design

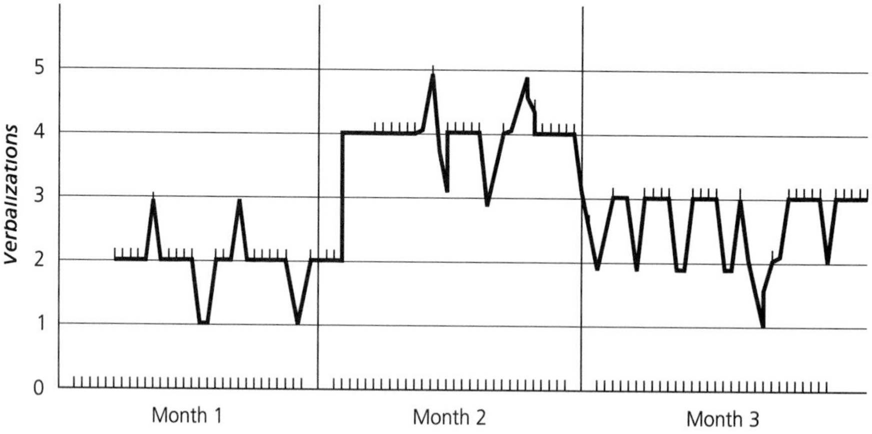

These are the results of a hypothetical study designed to assess the effectiveness of a reinforcement therapy program on the verbal behavior of an autistic child. The data report the number of verbalizations that the child displays in school, as recorded by the child's teacher over a period of three months, both before and after a reinforcement therapy program was instituted.

vocalizations again decreased dramatically, although they remained at a somewhat higher level than before the intervention.

You can see that this study is a type of repeated-measures experimental design where behavior is initially measured during a baseline period, measured again after the intervention of interest begins, and then measured once more after the intervention is removed. Such a design is frequently called an **A-B-A design** or a **reversal design** because the condition of interest is first created and then reversed or taken away. It was possible in this case to use the A-B-A design to study only one child because behavior during the baseline period was very stable over time and because the therapy intervention had a relatively large effect. Furthermore, despite the fact that only one participant was used, because the experimenter was able to control the occurrence of the intervention, the internal validity of the study was high. It was clearly the introduction of the reinforcement therapy that caused the changes in the child's behavior.

Although single-participant designs are useful when the researcher wants to investigate the effects of a particular intervention on a specific individual, they are not common in the behavioral sciences. For one, they can be used only where the effect size of the intervention is relatively large and there is a stable baseline period. But in most cases in the behavioral sciences the effect size is relatively small in comparison to the amount of random error. Furthermore, there are no statistical tests for assessing the effectiveness of the intervention in a single-participant design. In some cases the effects of the intervention are so large that no statistical analysis is necessary and the results can be seen visually. For example, it is clear that the reinforcement therapy increased verbalizations in our example. In other cases, however, the effects are not so clear. For instance, it is difficult to tell whether the rate of verbalizations for our child was meaningfully higher in the third month, after the therapy was over, than it had been in the first month baseline period. Finally, single-participant designs also suffer from threats to external validity because there is little guarantee that the results found for one individual will generalize to others.

SUMMARY

Quasi-experimental research designs are used when it is not possible to randomly assign individuals to groups. Such studies are common in program evaluation research, which involves assessing the effects of training and therapy programs. In other cases the research involves comparisons among individuals who differ on demographic or personality variables.

There are several common quasi-experimental research designs, including the single-group design, the comparison-group design, the before-after design, and the comparison-group before-after design. In general, because participants have not been randomly assigned to the groups, quasi-experimental research has more threats to internal validity than do true experiments. Since the participants select whether to participate in a given treatment, the individuals in the different groups are not equivalent before the differences in the independent variable occur. Furthermore, the participants may decide to drop out of the research before it is over. Other threats result from the presence of extraneous variables, such as changes in the individuals (maturation) or in the experimental setting (history) that occur over time and that influence the dependent measure.

Time-series designs involve the measurement of behavior more than twice over a period of time. Such designs allow the researcher to get a good idea about what changes occur over the time period being studied. When the initial rate of a behavior is very stable, it is sometimes possible to draw inferences about the behavior of a single participant by observing him or her over time.

KEY TERMS

A-B-A design 276
attrition 269
comparison group 267
comparison-group before-after
  design 269
comparison-group design 268
cross-sectional designs 274
history threats 269
maturation threats 269
mortality 269
participant variable 274
participant-variable design 274

quasi-experimental research designs
  265
regression to the mean 271
reversal design 276
selection threats 268
single-group before-after design
  268
single-group design 265
single-participant research designs
  275
time-series designs 273

REVIEW AND DISCUSSION QUESTIONS

1. What are quasi-experimental research designs, and when are they used in behavioral research? What advantages and disadvantages do they have in comparison to experimental research?

2. What are the most important threats to validity that occur in quasi-experimental research designs when individuals are not randomly assigned to groups? What techniques can be used to minimize these potential interpretive problems?

3. What are the most important threats to validity that occur in quasi-experimental research designs when the research is conducted over a period of time? What techniques can be used to minimize these potential interpretive problems?

4. What is regression to the mean, and why is it a threat to the validity of research designs in which random assignment has not been used?

5. What are time-series research designs, and how are they used to learn about changes in behavior over time?

6. What types of independent variables can be used in participant-variable research designs, and what conclusions can and cannot be drawn from their use?

7. What are single-participant research designs? When are they used, and what are their limitations?

HANDS-ON EXPERIENCE

1. A researcher has developed the hypothesis that teenagers are better able to learn about and remember technological information than are older adults, whereas older adults are better able to remember information about historical events than are teenagers. Develop a 2 × 2 factorial design that could test this research hypothesis. What type of design is the research? What pattern of data is expected, and what conclusions could be drawn if the data come out as expected?

2. Make up an example, other than those used in the text, of an everyday phenomenon that might be explained in terms of regression to the mean but that people might believe had another cause.

3. For each of the following research examples:
   a. Indicate the independent and dependent variables and which type of quasi-experimental research design was used.
   b. Consider what conclusions can be drawn about the effects of the independent variable on the dependent variable, and mention any specific threats to internal validity that you find.

c. Consider whether any other research designs might have been used to gain more information about the relationship between the independent and dependent variable.

- A study finds that the veterans of the Gulf War report being frequently anxious and depressed.

- A study demonstrates that women perform more poorly, on average, than do men on the mathematics section of the SAT.

- A study demonstrates that lower-socioeconomic-status students benefit more over time from an academic tutoring program than do higher-socioeconomic-status students.

- A researcher compares the job performance of a group of employees before and after they complete a training course. The employees perform better after the program than before.

- A researcher tests the effects of a new therapy program by comparing the mental functioning, both before and after therapy, of a group of patients who had participated in a therapy program against an equivalent group of patients who had not participated in any therapy. The patients who went through the program showed significantly greater increases in mental functioning over time.

- A researcher compares the self-esteem scores of a group of students who dropped out of college with another group that remained in school.

- Two different teaching techniques are in use at two different high schools in a large community. The proportion of students who continue on to college is greater at one high school than at the other.

- Using a cross-sectional study, a researcher measures the IQ of individuals who are twenty years old, forty-five years old, and seventy years old. The mean IQ for the three groups is 103, 100, and 90, respectively, a highly statistically significant difference. Can the researcher conclude that people lose intelligence in old age?

- An experimenter decides to test the effects of a new training program by comparing the motivation of twenty employees who had volunteered to participate in the program against an equivalent group of twenty employees who had not gone through any training at all. The employees were measured when they had completed the program, and it was found that those who had gone through the program had much greater on-the-job motivation than those who had not. The experimenter concludes that the difference in motivation was due to the content of the training program.

- An experimenter wants to know whether taking a one-semester-long test-preparation course affects one's performance on the Scholastic Aptitude Test (SAT). She contacts high school students who had and who had not taken the course and compares their scores on the SAT exam. She finds that the students who took the course scored significantly higher on the test.

- The German experimental psychologist Hermann Ebbinghaus studied learning and memory by using himself as a research participant. In one study he first learned a list of words until he knew them perfectly, and then tested himself on his memory for the words after one hour, after one day, and after three days. On the basis of these data he was able to construct a picture of the rate of forgetting over time.

4. Find an example of a quasi-experimental research design in a journal article. Describe the study in your own words, and indicate the exact research design that was used. Provide a citation for the article.

APPENDICES

A
Reporting Research Results

STUDY QUESTIONS

- How do scientists share their research findings with others?

- Through what stages does a research report go as it is considered for publication in a scientific journal?

- What are the major sections of a research report, and what information is contained in each section?

- What are the important goals to keep in mind when writing a research report?

To this point we have discussed how researchers develop and test their research hypotheses and analyze and interpret the data they collect. Having accomplished these steps, the researcher may be in the enviable position of having collected data that support the proposed research hypothesis or that produce other unexpected but interesting results. In such cases the researcher will naturally want to communicate these findings to others. This is the ultimate goal of every scientist—contributing to the accumulation of scientific knowledge. In this chapter we will consider how research is shared, with a particular emphasis on the practical aspects of writing a research report using American Psychological Association format.

Communication of Scientific Knowledge

Although a written research report will almost always be the final and definitive description of a scientific research project, the results of research are also shared through other media. Science is inherently a social enterprise, and information is often shared with other scientists in whatever ways are most convenient, enjoyable, fastest, and cheapest. This appendix will consider some of the ways that researchers share their ideas and their findings with others and will then discuss the format and style of written research reports.

Face-to-Face Contact

One way that scientists share their ideas is through direct contact with each other. It is a rather strange experience being a researcher working at a university because, unlike large corporations that have a corporate headquarters where many employees work together, the scientific colleagues of university professors are spread out around the world at different universities.

Professional Collaboration.   Scientists often collaborate with others on their research projects even when these colleagues are not nearby. Collaboration is efficient in the sense that more resources can be brought to bear on the problem of interest. Researchers working together share ideas, lab space, research funds, and their own time. However, because research collaborators are often located in different places around the world, communication is critical. The conduct of scientific research has been made much more efficient through recent technological advances in information transmission such as fax machines and e-mail. Because these sources of communication are inexpensive, quick, and readily available to researchers, they are used heavily. Although hard copies of journals are not yet out of date, much communication among scientists now occurs informally through electronic media, and many journals are now available electronically through libraries.

Scientific Meetings.   In addition to electronic communications, most researchers regularly attend professional meetings and conferences where they share their ideas and their research results in person with other scientists, both formally and informally. Formal presentations are made at conferences in the form of talks as well as at poster presentations in which the researcher displays data in a public forum and conference participants come around to look at and discuss them. These exchanges are extremely important to the advancement of science because they provide a forum in which colleagues can respond to and critique a scientist's work on the spot and while it is in progress. This feedback, which usually occurs in a friendly and helpful manner, can be extremely valuable in helping the scientist develop new ideas and determine new directions for future research. Informally, scientists spend time at conferences in restaurants and cafés, conversing and relaxing. These exchanges provide a chance to share ideas, and many important scientific ideas have been generated in such settings. Scientific meetings are particularly useful because they allow scientists to share the most up-to-date information about their research with each other.

Professional Organizations.   Most researchers belong to one or more professional organizations that hold annual conferences. Within the field of psychology, these include the meetings of the *American Psychological Society (APS)* and the *American Psychological Association (APA)*. Sociologists attend the meetings of the *American Sociological Association (ASA)*. These meetings are large conferences, held during the summer months in major cities in the United States or Canada, where students and faculty members from all over North America present their latest research findings. The APA, APS, and ASA conventions, as well as many local conventions in your area, are open to undergraduate and graduate students.

If you are interested in a career in behavioral research, consider attending a scientific conference and perhaps submitting your research for potential inclusion in the program. Although attendance can sometimes be costly (you must pay for transportation, food, and lodging as well as a registration fee, although the latter is usually reduced for students), there is no substitute for learning what research is about and what types of people conduct it and for making contacts with these people.

Publication in Scientific Journals

Even though the avenues through which scientific knowledge is communicated are always changing, most research is still ultimately published in scientific journals, either in traditional book format or online. Scientists consider the publication of journal articles to be the ultimate test of success. If their work is published in important journals, and if other scientists read this work and cite it, they rightly feel that their work has had an impact on the field.

The process that leads to the ultimate publication of research results in a scientific journal involves a series of stages and takes a substantial amount of time. The first step is to write the research report—known at this stage as the "manuscript." It is not easy to write a research report. The work is painstaking and involves much specific knowledge and many skills. Because there are so many things to be done, problems can develop. It will probably take you at least twice as long to write your first research report as you think it will.

Scientists spend a good portion of their time writing professional papers, painstakingly going over every detail to make sure each report is accurate, complete, persuasive, and fair. I often spend several months working on a manuscript, verifying that everything is correct. I read the paper again and again, checking the report with the data I have collected and making changes that I think result in a more informative and easier-to-read paper.

APA Format.   Research reports in the behavioral sciences are written in one or more standard formats, as specified by the basic conventions of the scientific method. Before beginning to write a report, you should determine the appropriate guidelines for the journal or other outlet that you plan to use for your paper. Journal editors and publishers are quite serious about following the appropriate format. If you submit a manuscript that does not follow the guidelines, they may not read it at all.

One formal set of guidelines that has been used almost exclusively in psychological research, and frequently in other areas of behavioral science research, is the format outlined in the fifth edition of the *Publication Manual of the American Psychological Association* (2001). If you are planning to submit a research report to a journal, and if that journal requests that submitted manuscripts use APA format, it is well worth the investment to purchase a copy of this paperback. Because of its popularity and extensive use in social science journals, the APA format will form the basis of this discussion of the format of research reports. Other formats will be very similar. In addition to the publication manual, the APA also publishes a computer program called *APA-Style Helper.* This program works with your word processor to help you format an APA-style paper. There is also a workbook and training guide for the *APA Publication Manual* (Gelfand & Walker, 2001). These materials can be purchased from the APA Web site: *www.apa.org.*

You may think that following the details of the APA format makes for a lot of work and results in boring reading. It is true that the rules specified in the APA manual do not allow the researcher much leeway—writing a journal article is not like writing poetry. As we have seen, science is an organized discipline, and just as the scientific method determines how data are collected, analyzed, and interpreted, it also determines how they are reported. Everyone does reporting in the same way, and this makes for regularity and objectivity, if some monotony. Use of the standard format is thus one part of the scientific process and makes it easy for readers to quickly find the information they are looking for in your report. Furthermore, many aspects of the APA format are designed to help typesetters and proofreaders as the manuscript is prepared for publication.

Submission of the Manuscript.   Once the research manuscript is completed, it is sent to a scientific journal for consideration for publication. There are many different journals that publish behavioral science research, and the decision of which journal to send a manuscript to is made on the basis of both the content and the quality of the research. In terms of content, an article on child development would be sent to a developmental psychology journal, whereas a paper on organizational behavior would be suited for an industrial organizational journal. Sometimes the data have not worked out as well as the researcher might have hoped, or maybe the researcher decides that the research hypothesis was not as interesting as he or she had thought when data collection began. If this is the case, then the researcher might choose to send the manuscript to a journal that publishes shorter articles or those of lesser quality. Other times the data have worked out well, and the researcher believes the paper is suitable for publication in a top-notch journal.

After having chosen a journal, the researcher will locate the name and address of the journal's editor in a recent edition of the journal. The editor is a senior scientist in the area who serves as the final decision maker regarding which articles are suitable for publication in the journal. Once the manuscript is submitted to the editor (and this is often done electronically now), the researcher may just as well forget about the paper for about three months while the paper is under peer review.

Peer Review.   When the journal editor receives the submitted manuscript, he or she will choose three or four scientists to serve as peer reviewers. **Peer review** is the process by which the people who can best judge the quality of the research—other people in the scientist's field—read and comment on the manuscript. Often these people come from the group of scientists who constitute the editorial board of the journal. The submitted manuscript is sent to each of these reviewers, who read and study the paper and return their comments to the editor. Among other things, the reviewers assess the importance of the research, its scientific rigor, and the writing style. Usually reviewers are fair and objective, but just as in any other stage of the research process, personal values and biases may at times come into play.

Once the editor has received two or three reviews of the manuscript and has read it carefully, he or she writes an "action letter" to the author. In this letter the editor summarizes his or her own reactions to the paper, informed by the comments of the reviewers, and also communicates a decision about the fate of the paper. In most cases the author also receives copies of the reviewers' comments, although the identities of the reviewers are usually withheld from the author. In the best case the editor will decide that the paper makes an important enough contribution to be accepted for publication. Even in this happy case, the author will usually have to make some revisions first. More likely, the editor will not be happy with the manuscript as it stands and will require the author to make many revisions before publication. Sometimes the editor will request the author to collect more data to rule out potential alternative explanations of the results or to further demonstrate the findings. This revision may be sent out for further peer review.

Unfortunately, the most common outcome of the peer review process is rejection. The editor has decided that the manuscript is not suitable for publication in the journal. He or she may have found alternative explanations for the results or may have decided that the results are not strong enough or interesting enough to warrant publication. The problem is not always only one of quality. There are a limited number of journal pages available, and often even high-quality research cannot be published for lack of space. At this point the author may decide to submit the manuscript to another journal, where the entire peer review process begins over again, or to collect new data. Although sending the manuscript to another journal after it has been rejected from one is entirely appropriate, the author should submit the manuscript to only one journal at a time. In every case, however, the author should carefully consider the comments of the editor and reviewers and thoroughly revise the manuscript before resubmitting it.

Publication Lag.   You probably now realize why scientists rely so much on e-mail and personal communication to share their research results with others. By the time a paper is published in a journal (even if it is accepted on the first round), over a year will likely have elapsed since the manuscript was first submitted. Publishing research in scientific journals is a long and arduous process, which is frequently rewarded with rejection and infrequently rewarded with publication. Although the peer review process takes a long time, it helps ensure that high-quality papers are published and that these papers are improved before publication through the input from knowledgeable experts in the field. The rewards of publication include a personal sense of achievement and the knowledge that you have contributed to the accumulation of scientific knowledge. With this glad news in mind, let's turn to the details of the research report.

The Research Report

Developing an idea for research, collecting the data, and analyzing them to draw appropriate conclusions are only one part of the research process. It is safe to say that most researchers struggle over writing up their research as much as they do over designing or conducting it. Writing research reports takes plenty of effort and practice—it is not something that comes naturally to most people. As you write your first research report, you will struggle to organize the information in a coherent manner, to make sure that the reader can understand your procedures, and to present your data accurately and fairly. Becoming proficient requires perseverance.

In the next sections I will outline APA publication format, consider some issues of style, and then present some suggestions for writing good research reports.[1] As summarized in the figure on the inside of the front cover of this book, there are five major sections to the research report written in APA format:

---

[1]For even more information, you might want to look at an article by Bem (1987) and a book by Sternberg (1993), as well as the American Psychological Association's manual (2001).

Abstract

Introduction

Methods

Results

Discussion

Although these five sections form the bulk of the report, there are also four other sections that contain important information:

Title Page

References

Endnotes and Author Notes

Tables and Figures

Although the major goal of the format is to allow efficient presentation of the data, the format can also facilitate the writing of an interesting and informative story in the sense that all of the pieces of the research report fit together to create a coherent whole. One method of helping accomplish this is to write the manuscript in an "hourglass" shape in which the report begins at a general level, progresses to more specific details, and then returns to a broad level in the final section. The hourglass approach is diagrammed in Figure A.1.

There are many specific details of the APA format, and one of the most useful ways to learn about these details is to carefully study a draft manuscript that has already been written in APA style. An annotated sample of a manuscript is provided at the end of this chapter, and a checklist for avoiding some common errors is shown in Table A.1.

Although the APA format provides many details about how the research report is to be written, it cannot be used to make every decision for you. There are no absolute rules for writing research reports, only general guidelines, and thus you will have to use your own good sense to create a high-quality report. You must strive for clarity and organization, but you will also need to be concise. The latter will involve making many decisions about what is important enough to include and what needs to be left out.

Headings in APA Format

One of the important aspects of the APA format is that it arranges all of the information in the report in a logical manner. The sections follow in a specified order, and each section contains a certain set of information. Each section should contain only the information appropriate to that section.

To help organize the paper, APA format makes use of a system of headings. First, the research report has a *page heading* that is printed at the top of each page, along with the page number. This heading normally is the first two or three words of the title of the research report. Furthermore, each section, and subsection, of the research report has its own heading. As shown here, in

FIGURE A.1   Using the "Hourglass Shape" to Write an Effective
Research Report

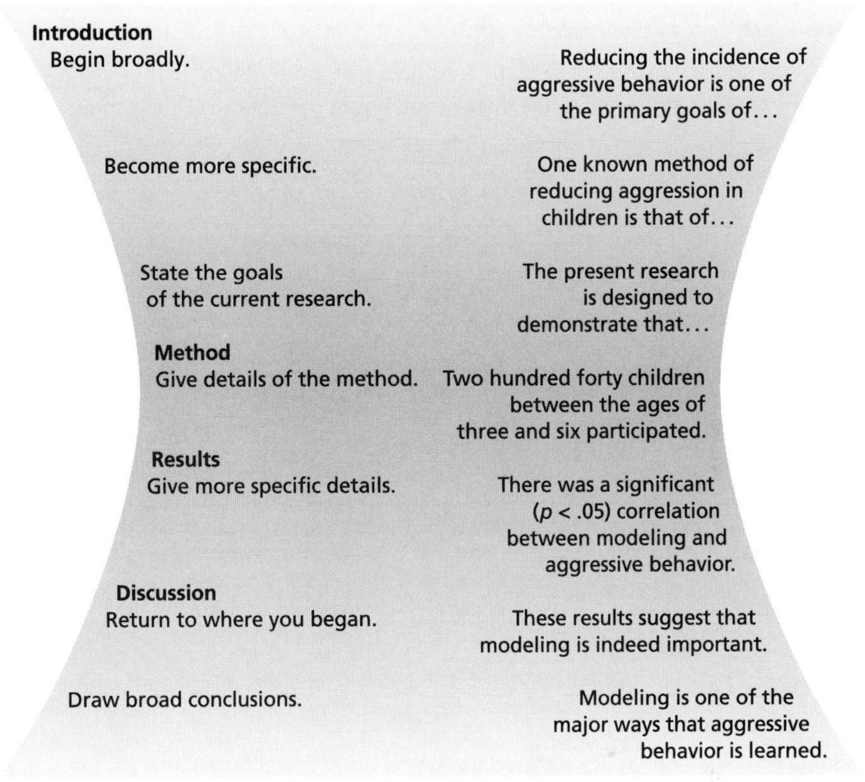

Introduction
    Begin broadly.

        Reducing the incidence of
        aggressive behavior is one of
        the primary goals of...

    Become more specific.

        One known method of
        reducing aggression in
        children is that of...

    State the goals
    of the current research.

        The present research
        is designed to
        demonstrate that...

    Method
    Give details of the method.   Two hundred forty children
                                    between the ages of
                                    three and six participated.

    Results
    Give more specific details.

        There was a significant
        ($p < .05$) correlation
        between modeling and
        aggressive behavior.

    Discussion
    Return to where you began.

        These results suggest that
        modeling is indeed important.

    Draw broad conclusions.

        Modeling is one of the
        major ways that aggressive
        behavior is learned.

most cases three or four levels of headings are sufficient. If you need only two, use the Level 1 and Level 3 headings. If you need only three, use Levels 1, 3, and 4. If you need more than four, consult the APA publication manual.

(Level 1) Centered Uppercase and Lowercase Heading

(Level 2) *Centered, Italicized, Uppercase and Lowercase Heading*

(Level 3) *Flush Left, Italicized, Upper and Lowercase Side Heading*

(Level 4) *Indented, italicized, lowercase paragraph heading ending with a period.*

Figure A.2 shows a schematic diagram of a sample research report with the appropriate headings.

TABLE A.1   APA Format Checklist

Overall

Use 1-inch margins on all sides.

Use left justification on your word processor, not full justification.

Place footnotes at the end of the manuscript, not at the bottom of the page.

Place figures and tables at the end of the manuscript.

Title Page

The running head should be left justified and typed in capitals.

Number the title page as page 1.

Abstract

The first line of the abstract is *not* indented.

Introduction

Begin the Introduction section on a new page. Center the title of the manuscript (upper and lower case) at the top of the first page. Do *not* label this section as Introduction.

Method

Do *not* begin on a new page.

Use the past tense to describe a study that has already been completed (e.g., "I ran 100 participants.")

Results

Do *not* begin on a new page.

Some common abbreviations should always be used. The abbreviations are the same in singular and plural, and do not have periods after them:

cm = centimeter	dB = decibel
g = gram	hr = hour
m = meter	mg = milligram
min = minutes	ml = milliliter
mm = millimeter	ms = millisecond
s = seconds	

References in the Text

Use the word *and* to separate authors when the reference is not in parentheses, but use the symbol & to separate authors when the reference is in parentheses.

Use only the last name, not the initials, of the authors.

List of references are alphabetized by the last name of the author, and separated by semicolons.

Indicate the year of publication every time you cite the work.

Reference List

Begin the reference list on a new page.

FIGURE A.2 Page Sequence for a Report in APA Format

Page Heading 1	Page Heading 2	Page Heading 3	Page Heading 4
Running head: ____	Abstract	Title	
Title Author Name Affiliation			
Author Name Affiliation	(not more than 150 words)		

Page Heading 5	Page Heading 6	Page Heading 7	Page Heading 8
Method Overview	*Participants*	*Procedure*	
	Stimulus Materials		Results

Page Heading 9	Page Heading 10	Page Heading 11	Page Heading 12
Discussion		References	Author Note

Page Heading 13	Page Heading 14	Page Heading 15	
Footnotes	Table 1 *Table Title*	Figure Caption(s) Figure 1. ____	(Figures are placed last, one per page. Indicate figure number on back.)
		Figure 2. ____	
	Table Notes ____		

The abstract, introduction, references, author notes, footnotes, table, figure captions, and figures each start on a new page.

Title Page

The research report begins with a title page, numbered as page 1 of the manuscript. Along with the title of the paper, this page also contains the names and the institutional affiliations of the author or authors, as well as a **running head** of not more than fifty characters. The running head identifies the research topic and will appear on the top of the pages of the journal article when it is published, just as the running head "Appendix A   REPORTING RE-SEARCH RESULTS" is printed at the top of this page.

Describing the Nature of the Research.   The title of the research report should accurately describe the nature of the research in about ten to twelve words. Because most research hypotheses involve an independent and dependent variable and the finding of a specific relationship between them, this relationship can usually be the basis of the title. Consider the following titles:

"Positive Mood Makes Judgments of Others' Emotions More Positive"

"Saccharine Enhances Concept Learning in Pigeons"

These titles are precise because they specify the independent and dependent variables as well as the specific relationship found between them. In contrast, the title "A Study of Learning and Forgetting" is poor because it wastes space by stating the obvious (that the research report describes a study) and because it does not say much about how learning and forgetting are measured or about how they are found to be related.

Listing the Authors.   A decision must also be made regarding who should be an author on the paper and what order the authors' names should follow if there are more than one. These decisions are made in terms of the magnitude of each person's contribution to the research project, and only those individuals who have made substantial contributions are listed as authors. The American Psychological Association publication manual offers some guidelines in this regard, but there are no hard and fast rules. When there is more than one author and each has contributed equally, the order of authorship may be determined randomly.

Abstract

The second page of the research report contains the Abstract, which provides a short summary of the entire research report. The Abstract is limited to a maximum of 120 words. Particular care should be taken in writing the Abstract because it, along with the title, will be contained in computer databases, such as those discussed in Chapter 2, and thus will be used by those deciding whether to read the entire paper.

I usually write the Abstract last after I know what I have to summarize. I try to take one or two sentences each from the Introduction, Methods, and Results sections to form the Abstract. Because the Abstract should use similar words to describe the research as are used in the research report itself, it is relatively easy to write. It is not usually a good idea to review the Discussion section in the Abstract—there is not enough space, and the Method and Results are more important.

Introduction

The body of the research report begins on the third page of the manuscript with the Introduction section. The title of the research report is centered at the top of this page. The general tasks of this section are to outline the goals and purposes of your research, to inform the reader about past research that is relevant to your research, and to link your research to those earlier findings. You must also explain why your research is interesting and important and try to get readers interested in the research project.

Engaging the Reader. In many ways the Introduction serves as the warm-up band for the headliner show that is going to follow—the Introduction is designed to get people's attention and prepare them for the research. One of my favorite examples of an opening paragraph in a research report is the following, from a paper by Lord and Gilbert (1983, p. 751):

A graduate student and a professor were discussing evidence that California sunshine puts people in a good mood. "When I moved across the country," said the graduate student, "I noticed that the people who waited on me in stores and restaurants in California were more pleasant than those on the East Coast." "I have a better story than that," countered the professor. "When the moving men picked up our furniture on the East Coast they were thoroughly obnoxious. We drove across the country to California and arrived to find the moving men sitting on the front lawn in the sunshine, eating fried chicken. They greeted us warmly and were quite genial and accommodating in delivering our furniture. These were the *same men,* mind you." The graduate student and the professor agreed that the latter evidence was more compelling.

Who wouldn't be interested in reading such a paper?

Highlighting Relevant Existing Research. Once the general problem being investigated has been presented, the existing literature relevant to the current project is discussed, with an emphasis on how the present research is designed to build on the earlier findings and thus contribute to the accumulation of scientific knowledge. Only literature that is relevant to the current hypothesis is cited. The reader doesn't need a whole lot of information about this existing literature, only enough to indicate what it has shown, how it is limited, and how the new research is going to relate to it. The literature review must not stand separate from your research; rather, it becomes an integral part of the story that your research is designed to relate. The literature is always presented in a way that sets up your project as a logical extension of previous work.

After reviewing the literature, you can tie it into your research with sentences such as the following:

"Although the results of the previous research are consistent with the proposed hypothesis, an alternative explanation is still possible."

"Despite this research, very little is known about . . ."

"One basic limitation with this research is that it has not . . ."

Stating the Research Hypothesis.   Another major goal of the Introduction section is to explicitly define the conceptual variables that you will be investigating (see Chapter 4). For instance, if the study involves the assessment of "concept formation," you must be certain to define what concept formation is. Relating the conceptual variable to definitions used in past research can be useful in this regard.

By the end of the Introduction section, the writing begins to become more focused. We are now reaching the narrow part of the hourglass in Figure A.1. At this point the general ideas and limitations of previous work have been clearly made, and the goals of the present research have been outlined. The goal now is to give the reader more specifics about the research that is to follow. The general ideas are refined into the specific operational definitions of the independent and dependent variables, and the research hypothesis is stated. At this point it may be useful to consider potential problems that might be encountered in the research, as well as discuss how you hope to avoid them.

"Rewriting the Introduction."   One problem that frequently occurs in research is that the collected data do not exactly support the original research hypothesis that led to the creation of the research design. Perhaps the data only confirmed one part of the predictions and not another part, or maybe the researcher has discovered other interesting but unexpected relationships between the variables. In these cases the question becomes whether to write the Introduction section in terms of the original predictions, and then explain in the discussion the ways in which the results were unexpected, or to "rewrite" the Introduction as if the results that were found had been predicted all along.

It may seem that reframing and rewriting the research hypothesis are not very scientific, but this is not true. Although research is always designed to test a specific research hypothesis, that hypothesis is only one of the many possible hypotheses that could have been proposed, and in the end the observed data are more important than the original hypothesis. In fact, it can be argued that collected data are really no more important when they support a predicted research hypothesis than when they support an equally interesting but completely unexpected hypothesis. Of course, if your research has tested but failed to support a hypothesis derived from an important theory, it will be of interest to readers to mention this.

Because the collected data almost never exactly support the original research hypothesis, it is frequently useful to reframe or recast the Introduction of the report in terms of the findings that were actually significant. In some cases this may even involve reformulating the original research hypothesis. Although you may not find this procedure to be elegant, it has the inherent advantage of making the research report easier to understand and reducing the complexity of the paper. In the long run, rest assured that what is important is that the data you report be interesting and replicable, not necessarily that they exactly support your original research hypothesis.

Method

The goal of the Method section is to precisely describe how the research was conducted from beginning to end. Precision is required in this regard so that the readers can follow exactly what was done, allowing them to draw appropriate conclusions about the data and to conduct an exact replication of the study should they so desire. At the same time, however, the Method section must also be concise, and only those details that are important need to be reported. In contrast to the other sections, which normally stand on their own, the Method section is normally made up of several subsections. The most common of these are reviewed here, although you may decide to use others as well, depending on the needs of your research report.

Participants.   This subsection provides a detailed description of the individuals who participated in the research, including the population from which the individuals were drawn, the sample size (N), and the sampling techniques used to select the sample (see Chapter 7). If any participants were deleted before the statistical analyses were conducted, this should be mentioned (see Appendix B). Any other information that you think is relevant to the research should also be included. For instance, if the research project involves college students, it is probably not necessary to report their average age or IQ. But if the participants were drawn from a special population, such as those with a particular personality disorder, the characteristics of the population and the sample will need to be described in detail. If the research is a survey study, then detailed information about the sampling procedures is necessary, whereas if it is an experimental study involving a convenience sample of college students, only this needs to be mentioned.

It is standard practice to indicate the number of men and women who participated in the research, but other potential differences among participants, such as age, race, or ethnicity, are not normally reported unless they are deemed relevant. What you report will also depend on whether you choose to look for or to report any differences you may have found between men and women or among different ethnic groups.

Materials and Apparatus.   This subsection provides details about the stimulus materials used as the independent and dependent variables. Stimulus materials may include videotapes, transparencies, computer programs, or questionnaires. In the latter case the procedures used to develop the items in the scale would be described, as well as the number of questions and the response format. In many cases details about the scale have been reported in previous research reports, and it is only necessary to direct the reader to these existing papers. Again, the goal is to provide enough information to allow an exact replication but to avoid irrelevant details.

If you have used any special equipment, such as for collecting physiological responses or reaction times, you will need to describe the equipment. Appropriate descriptions will allow another person who wants to run the study to use the same or equivalent equipment.

Procedure.   The Procedure subsection is designed to completely describe the experience of being a participant in the research project and should include enough details that the reader can understand exactly what happened to the participant and conduct an exact replication of the research. The depth and length of this description will vary depending on the research design. In survey research, for instance, it may only be necessary in the Procedure to briefly describe when and where the measures were completed. Experimental designs, in contrast, will generally involve a longer description.

In a laboratory experiment involving the manipulation of the independent variable, the Procedure will provide details about the order in which all of the events occurred, beginning with the greeting of the participants by the experimenter and ending with the mention of their debriefing (see Chapter 3). It is usually most convenient to describe the Procedure following the order in which the events occurred, but in some cases it is more efficient to first describe the parts of the research that were common to all of the participants (for instance, the greeting, instructions, dependent measures, and debriefing) and then later to specify the changes that produced the different levels of the independent variable.

Results

The Results section presents the statistical analyses of the data. It is the most fine-grained of all of the sections and is therefore a place where the flow of the research report can bog down. The writer needs to think carefully about how to keep the paper smoothly moving along in a concise manner, while being certain to include all of the necessary statistical tests. This flow of the results can usually be enhanced if the order in which they are presented is arranged either in terms of (1) importance, (2) what the researcher expected to find, or (3) the sequence in which the variables were collected.

One technique is to write the Results section first without any statistics and then to add the statistical tests. You should try to write this section so that it would be understandable for someone who didn't read the rest of the report. You can do this by beginning the Results section with a brief restatement of the experimental hypothesis and the names of the independent and dependent variables (for instance, "The reader will recall that this research tested the hypothesis that reaction times would be influenced by both previous exposure and word content").

Determining What to Include.   One of the major difficulties at this point is to determine what information should be put in the Results and what must be saved for the Discussion. Although the Results section should formally include only the statistical analyses of the data, it is often tempting and frequently useful to briefly discuss the meaning of the results as they are presented rather than waiting to do so. One solution that can be used if the paper is relatively short is to combine the Results and Discussion sections into a single section entitled "Results and Discussion."

In most cases an initial goal of the Results section will be to document the effectiveness of the manipulated and measured variables. The reliability of the measured variables and the outcomes of any manipulation checks that were collected should be reported. Only after the measurement issues have been addressed are the results of the tests of the research hypothesis presented. Generally, it is friendlier to the reader if the findings are first stated in everyday language and then the statistical tests are reported. For instance, we might state, "The expected differences were found: 94 percent of animals who had ingested saccharine completed the task, whereas only 71 percent of those who had ingested the placebo did so." Then we would continue on to report the statistical test that confirmed the significance of the difference between the groups.

Knowing what *not* to include in the Results can be just as important as knowing what to include. For instance, you do not need to include statistical formulas or the name of the statistical software used to analyze the data unless these are new or likely to be unknown. You do need to make clear what statistical tests you used in the analysis, but you can assume that readers are familiar with these tests, and you do not have to describe what they are or how they are to be used. The appropriate results of the statistical tests, such as Ns or degrees of freedom, means and standard deviations, p-values and effect sizes, must of course be reported.

Deciding Whether to Use Tables and Figures.   Another decision concerns whether to use tables and figures to present the data. If the analysis is relatively simple, they are not necessary, and the means and the statistical tests can be reported in the text. However, if there are a large number of correlations or means to report, then a table should be used. A general rule is that any information should be placed either in the text or in a figure or table but not in more than one place. When tables or figures are used, the reader should always be referred to them (for instance, "The mean ratings in each of the experimental conditions are shown in Table 1").

Discussion

In the Discussion section you will (1) review your major findings and provide your own interpretation of their meaning, (2) attempt to integrate the findings with other research, and (3) note possible qualifications and limitations of the results. The Discussion also presents an opportunity to focus on the unique responses of the participants. A description, for instance, of how specific individuals responded to the suspicion check or debriefing procedure might be appropriate.

The Discussion normally begins with a brief summary of the major findings. Because the findings have usually been stated in a piecemeal fashion in the Results, this is an opportunity to integrate them into a coherent whole. This summary section should be brief, however, and no new statistical tests should be reported either here or anywhere in the Discussion.

After the summary, the Discussion will turn to your interpretation of the results and your attempt to integrate them with those of previous research. Because your expectations in this regard have already been framed in the Introduction, the discussion can frequently be organized in a way that systematically answers the questions that have been proposed in the Introduction and that your research has (at least partially) answered. It is a good idea to check that every claim that you make about how the data have supported your research hypothesis is supported by an appropriate statistic, as reported in the Results.

Interpreting the Data. In interpreting your data, emphasize what is new and important about the findings. It is entirely appropriate, and indeed expected, that you will use the Discussion section to draw the most interesting and positive conclusions about the data. It is not appropriate to be overly negative about the importance of the research. Just because there are some limitations in the findings, or because not all of the predictions were supported, this does not mean that the data are uninteresting. Indeed, all research has both strengths and weaknesses, and the Discussion should be focused on the strengths.

Framing the discussion positively does not, however, mean either that the importance of the findings should be overstated or that their limitations should be ignored. Rather, you must attempt to make sure that the conclusions match the true import of the data. It is not appropriate to state that the research is the definitive study in an area, showing all others to be in error, or to proclaim that the findings are going to change the world. To do so ignores the basic principle that science proceeds through the gradual accumulation of knowledge. Any weaknesses or limitations of the research that you may be aware of should be mentioned. The general goal is fairness, and being honest about these limitations may reduce the likelihood that less scientifically sophisticated readers will draw erroneous conclusions about the data.

In general, the better the results have worked out, the shorter the Discussion needs to be. If the predictions were entirely confirmed, all you really need to do is to say that they were and then briefly discuss their implications. If, however, the research hypotheses have not been supported, the Discussion section needs to consider why this might have been. Although interpreting data that do not allow rejection of the null hypothesis is always difficult, keep in mind that even nonsignificant results can contribute to the advancement of scientific knowledge.

If it has turned out that the measured variables were not reliable or construct valid, the appropriate conclusion will necessarily be to question the operational definitions of the conceptual variables. If the measured variables seem to have adequately assessed the conceptual variables, the relevant conclusion is either that the research hypothesis was incorrect or that a Type 2 error was made. Although the latter is always a possibility when results are nonsignificant (see Chapter 8), it should never be made the primary focus of the discussion of the limitations of a research report.

Considering the Broader Implications. After considering both the strengths and weaknesses of the research in some detail, you may be tempted to end the research report with a call for further research on the topic area, potentially with some suggestions in this regard. Although it is not inappropriate to do so, it is usually even better to end the paper where it began—with a discussion of the implication of the results for the topic area in the broadest possible context. The last paragraphs, which again represent the broad end of the hourglass format, present a chance for you to make some general statements about the impact of the research.

References

APA style uses the "author-year" format in which the last name of the author or authors and the year of publication of the research report are placed in parentheses within the body of the text. The information in the text is sufficient to allow the reader to locate the full citation of the paper in the References section of the article. The entries in the References section are formatted according to APA guidelines. There is a specific format for virtually any type of article, book, book chapter, software package, or other information that needs to be listed in the References. The most frequently used of these text and reference formats are shown in Table A.2.

The References section is a list of all of the literature cited in your paper, alphabetized by the last name of the author. When the same person is the first author on more than one publication, those in which he or she is the only author come first. When two publications have exactly the same author or authors, the ordering is by the year of publication, with earlier publications first.

Footnotes and Author Notes

Footnotes are numbered consecutively in the text and are placed on one or more pages immediately after the References. Footnotes are not placed at the bottom of the pages in the manuscript copy. Footnotes should be kept to a minimum, but are sometimes used to report important information that would bog down the flow of the story if included in the text itself.

Author Notes include the mailing address, telephone number, and e-mail address of one of the authors for future correspondence. The Author Notes may also include any other information that the author wishes to communicate, including the sources of any funds that were obtained to conduct the

TABLE A.2   APA Reference Format

The following are the most commonly used reference formats from the fifth edition of the *Publication Manual of the American Psychological Association* (American Psychological Association, 2001).

Single-Author Journal Article

Cited in text as (Stangor, 1988).

Listed in references as:

Stangor, C. (1988). Stereotype accessibility and information processing. *Personality and Social Psychology Bulletin, 14,* 694–708.

Journal Article with Two Authors

Cited in text as (Stangor & Duan, 1991).

Listed in references as:

Stangor, C., & Duan, C. (1991). Effects of multiple task demands upon memory for information about social groups. *Journal of Experimental Social Psychology, 27,* 357–378.

Journal Article with More Than Two Authors

Cited in text as (Stangor, Sullivan, & Ford, 1992) the first time the work is cited, and as (Stangor et al., 1992) every other time.

Listed in references as:

Stangor, C., Sullivan, L. S., & Ford, T. E. (1992). Affective and cognitive determinants of prejudice. *Social Cognition, 9,* 359–380.

Written Book

Cited in text as (Stangor, 2003).

Listed in references as:

Stangor, C. (2003). *Research methods for the behavioral sciences* (2nd ed.). Boston: Houghton Mifflin.

Edited Book

Cited in text as (Macrae, Stangor, & Hewstone, 1996).

Listed in references as:

Macrae, C. N., Stangor, C., & Hewstone, M. (Eds.). (1996). *Foundations of stereotypes and stereotyping.* New York: Guilford Press.

Book Chapter in an Edited Book

Cited in text as (Stangor & Schaller, 1996).

Listed in references as:

Stangor, C., & Schaller, M. (1996). Stereotypes as individual and collective representations. In C. N. Macrae, C. Stangor, & M. Hewstone (Eds.), *Foundations of stereotypes and stereotyping* (pp. 3–37). New York: Guilford Press.

research, collaborators who are not included as authors, and thanks to individuals who contributed to the project but who are not authors. The Author Notes are placed in the manuscript on a separate page following the Footnotes and will be printed on the first page of the journal article.

Tables and Figures

The tables and figures are numbered consecutively in the text (for instance, Figure 1 and Table 1) and are themselves included as the last pages of the manuscript rather than being inserted within the text. Although this may seem inconvenient to the reader, the procedure groups them together and contributes to the ease of preparing the manuscript for publication. The formats for tables are detailed in the APA publication manual. Each table has a brief title that explains what is included in it, and figures also have captions explaining them, which are printed on a separate page with the heading "Figure Captions" at the top. Write the figure number on the back of each figure to identify it.

Tips on Writing the Research Report

Writing a research report is not something that can easily be taught—it must be learned through experience. However, there are a few basic rules that may be useful to you.

1. *Be organized.* Think about what you're going to say before you start. Organize both across and within the sections of the report. Before you start writing, make an outline of what you plan to say and where you plan to say it. Be sure that the Discussion addresses all of the questions that were raised in the Introduction.

2. *Be precise.* Say exactly what you mean and exactly what you did. Define your conceptual variables exactly, so that readers know what you are studying, and describe the operational definitions in enough detail that an exact replication is possible. Use the most specific word you can think of to describe the participants and procedures (for instance, *three* rather than *some* and *college students* rather than *people*). Be careful to say only what you know happened to the participants, not what you think happened. For instance, unless you know for sure that they did, do not say that the participants "experienced a good mood." Say instead that they were "exposed to information designed to place them in a good mood." Use accepted scientific terminology wherever possible.

3. *Be concise.* Do not cite literature that is not directly relevant to your research. Assume that the reader has a basic knowledge of statistical principles. For instance, you don't need to explain why your results need to be reliable, only that they are reliable. Remember that you may not have space to tell

everything. However, all information that is relevant to the research *must* be mentioned. You need to decide what is relevant.

4. *Be compulsive.* Follow APA format exactly. Check everything two or three times. Proofread the manuscript carefully yourself, and use the spell-checker on your word processor before you print it. Be prepared to rewrite the manuscript many times, moving paragraphs around and even starting over if you need to. Read the paper out loud to yourself, and ask others to read it, too. Allow yourself plenty of time, so that you have the opportunity to put the paper away for a day or two and then read it again. This break will often allow you to see things in a new light and to find new ways of expressing your ideas.

5. *Be clear and interesting.* Although your readers will be most interested in your data, you must try to frame those data in a compelling and interesting manner. Explain why what you did is important and why readers should care about what you are doing. Readers prefer simple, rather than complex, writing. Write your report so that an intelligent friend who is a major in art history, or perhaps even your grandmother, could understand what you did and why.

Use the active voice when possible (e.g., "I demonstrated" rather than "It was found" or "This study demonstrated"). If you feel that the reader may have lost the thread of your story, repeat crucial aspects ("Recall from the Introduction that it was expected . . ."). The use of examples can be helpful, as can tables and figures if there would otherwise be too many numbers in the text. Make sure your points flow in an orderly fashion from section to section. Transition words, such as *furthermore, nevertheless,* and *however,* can help in this regard.

6. *Be fair.* In addition to being nice to your readers, be fair to them. Avoid language that may be offensive, and do not be overly harsh in your critique of the work of others. It is better (and almost always more accurate) to say that you have "added" to previous work than to say that you've "destroyed" it or "proved it wrong." Also be particularly careful that the ideas you express are your own. If you have borrowed from others, be sure to give them credit by referencing their work.

SUMMARY

Communicating scientific ideas and research findings is one of the most important aspects of scientific progress because it contributes to the accumulation of scientific knowledge. Scientists share information with each other in person at scientific conventions, through electronic communication such as fax and e-mail, and through the publication of written research reports.

Research reports, many of which are eventually published in a scientific journal, are the definitive descriptions of a research project. The research report is prepared according to a formal set of guidelines, such as that provided by the American Psychological Association. The goals for writing the research report include being organized, precise, concise, compulsive, interesting, and fair.

There are five major sections within the APA format: Abstract, Introduction, Methods, Results, and Discussion, as well as other sections that contain supplementary information. Each section contains important information about the research, but only the information appropriate to that section. Although constrained to follow a specific format, the research report must also read smoothly and be interesting to the reader. Creating a research report that is both technically informative and easy to read takes a substantial amount of work and will generally require much rewriting.

KEY TERMS

peer review 286   running head 292

REVIEW AND DISCUSSION QUESTIONS

1. Why is it important for scientists to share their ideas and research findings with each other, and how do they do so?

2. Why is scientific knowledge communicated at scientific conventions and through electronic communications in addition to the formal publication of research reports in scientific journals?

3. Describe the progress of the research manuscript as it is considered for publication in a scientific journal. What are the strengths and weaknesses of the peer review process?

4. Describe the basic objectives of the research report written in APA style. What information goes in each of the five major sections?

5. What information is contained in each of the supplementary sections of the research report?

6. How are the levels of the headings of a research report determined?

7. Summarize the writing and stylistic goals that can help a person write an effective research report.

HANDS-ON EXPERIENCE

1. Each of the following sentences violates a basic rule of report writing. Indicate the relevant difficulty in each case.
   a. "The scale was coded to assess optimism, or lack thereof, in the participants."
   b. "Seven of the twenty-one participants were male, and fourteen of the twenty-one were female."

    c. "To be significant, the p-value of the test had to be less than the alpha level of .05."

    d. "The majority of students were between twenty and twenty-six years old."

    e. "The professor required that we code the independent variables two different ways."

    f. "Results of the correlational analysis are presented in Table A."

    g. "The procedure in Experiment 2 was just about the same as in Experiment 1."

2. Read a research report, and write a critique of it. Consider the extent to which the information that should be contained in the report (as outlined inside the front cover of this book) is actually presented, as well as how effectively the report meets the general goals of report writing.

Sample Research Report

The Title Page includes the title, the name of author/authors and their institutional affiliations, and the running head. The title page is numbered as page 1.

Running head is typed flush with left margin.

Title is centered, double-spaced, upper and lower case.

Solo Status and Task Feedback   1

Running Head: SOLO STATUS AND TASK FEEDBACK

Influence of Solo Status and Task Feedback on

Expectations About Task Performance in Groups

Charles Stangor and Christine Carr

University of Maryland College Park

The manuscript should be double-spaced on 8½-by-11-inch paper. Preferred fonts are 12-point Times New Roman or Courier.

Use the "header" function in your word processor to have the header printed on each page.

The Abstract appears on page 2. The first line of the Abstract is not indented.

Abstract is a single paragraph not exceeding 120 words.

Abstract

Two studies investigated men and women's predictions of their performance on a word-finding task in groups in which they expected to be either the only member of their sex and major or in which the other group members were also of the same sex and had similar majors. The data supported a feedback-undermining hypothesis: Individuals who were led to expect that they had high (versus ambiguous) abilities on a task expected to perform better in the future when working on the task alone and in similar groups but not in dissimilar groups. These differences seem to have occurred because working in a dissimilar group undermined an individual's task confidence rather than because of expected negative affective reactions in the groups.

Solo Status and Task Feedback   3

Influence of Solo Status and Task Feedback on

Expectations About Task Performance in Groups

Social psychologists have recently begun to expand their study of stereotyping and prejudice from a more traditional interest in how majority or power-ful groups perceive and respond to minorities or less powerful groups, to an interest in how members of stigmatized groups perceive, interpret, cope, and attempt to change the stereotyping, prejudice, and discrimination they encounter or expect to encounter (cf. Cohen & Swim, 1995; Crocker, Major, & Steel, 1998; Miller & Kaiser, 1991; Saenz, 1994; Steele & Aronson, 1994; Swim & Stangor, 1998). Such an interest is driven not only by the theoretical goal of provid-ing a more complete understanding of the nature of intergroup relations, but also by the practical goal of better understanding the potential outcomes of prejudice on the everyday life of stigmatized group members.

Although the target individual's experience of prejudice and discrimination may in some cases be direct (such as employment and housing discrimina-tion, sexual harassment, or racial slurs), in other cases potential targets of stereotyping, prejudice, or discrimination may be indirectly affected by their own perceptions of how likely they are to be the victim of stereotyping, prejudice, or discrimina-

The Introduction starts on page 3. The title of the paper is centered at the top of the page.

Begin with a general introduc-tion to the topic of the manuscript.

c.f. is a Latin abbreviation meaning "to compare" and is used only in parentheses.

References are in the author/year format (see Table A.2). Full refer-ences are found in the References section at the end of the manuscript.

References in lists are ordered by the last name of the first author and separated by semicolons in the list.

tion (e.g., Kleck & Strenta, 1980), even in the absence of such behavior.

Such perceptions may lead an individual to alter his or her task choices or task interests. He or she may avoid engaging in certain tasks, expect to have difficulty performing those tasks, or attempt to change the task situation before entering it. For instance, women concerned about being stereotyped by instructors or other students in mathematics, engineering, and science courses may be particularly unlikely to enroll in them (cf. Eccles, 1994), or African Americans with similar concerns may avoid academic pursuits altogether (Crocker et al., 1998).

The present research studies one particular situation in which individuals might expect to be vulnerable to stereotyping--namely, when they find themselves as the only member of their social group (for instance, the only woman within a larger group of men). In this case, the lone woman is known as a solo (Heilman, 1979; Kanter, 1977). Our general expectation is that individuals will be less certain about their abilities to perform well on relevant tasks when they are solos. This prediction is derived from the results of several existing lines of research. For one, there is literature to suggest that solos are likely to be stereotyped by other group members. For instance, Taylor, Fiske, Etcoff,

---

e.g. is a Latin abbreviation meaning "for example."

Provide more specific information about what is being studied.

Use et al. (not italicized) to indicate multiple authors in second and later citations of a paper with more than two authors.

Here is a general overview of the research.

Solo Status and Task Feedback 5

Cite only refer-
ences that relate
to the proposed
hypothesis.

and Ruderman (1978) had perceivers view discussion
groups in which a solo man or woman interacted within
a larger group of women or men. Taylor et al. found
that the observers paid disproportionate attention to
the solos, preferentially recalled their contributions
to the discussion, and frequently described them using
stereotypical traits.

Research showing that solos *expect* to be stereotyped is even more relevant to the present thesis. In
one study, Cohen and Swim (1995) told male and female
participants that they would be working with a group
of students who were either of the same sex as they
were or of the other sex. Cohen and Swim found that
their participants reported expecting to be stereotyped by the other group members to a greater degree
when they were to be a solo.

Taken together, then, there is at least some evidence to suggest that solos are aware that they may
be stereotyped and that being a solo can impact task
performance. However, a question not heretofore addressed concerns whether such individuals are aware
of the potential impact that being in solo status
may have on their task performance prior to engaging
in the task. This question is important from a practical perspective because if individuals realize that
being in solo status can have a negative impact on
task performance, they may expect to perform more
poorly than they would as majority group members,

Discuss how your
research is differ-
ent and what it is
expected to add.

and this perception may lead them to avoid such situations.

We expected that perceived task ability would have an impact in the form of *feedback undermining*, such that for individuals who expected to work with similar others, those who received positive feedback would predict better performance than those who received ambiguous feedback, but that individuals expecting to be solos would predict poor task performance regardless of feedback. In short, this possibility suggests that solo status would create so much uncertainty about future task performance that it would undermine any effects of positive feedback on expectancies about task performance.

Method

Overview

We approached our research question by providing our participants with evaluative feedback about their skills on a word-finding task that suggested either that they were clearly good at the task or that their skills were ambiguous. Furthermore, we manipulated the group with which they expected to subsequently work on the task to be either very similar to or very different from them. We then asked the participants to estimate their likely performance on the task on which they had been given feedback and

State the research hypothesis.

Heading is centered, upper case and lower case. Do not start these headings on a new page.

Heading is flush left, italicized, upper case and lower case.

The Overview section is a common (but not required) way to set up the goals of the research and to let the reader know what to expect.

their preferences for working on the same task again (or changing the task).

We expected that solos would be aware of the potential negative impact of being in minority status on task performance and that this knowledge would make them unsure of their future performance. As a result, we expected that judgments about future performance in dissimilar groups would be different from those about future performance in similar groups. As another control, we also asked participants to predict their likely future performance on the task were they to work on it alone.

Participants

Participants were 63 white female and 31 white male undergraduates between the ages of 18 and 23 who participated in exchange for course credit in an introductory psychology course.[1] Participants were recruited by telephone on the basis of their college major to allow us to create potential work groups of either similar or dissimilar others. No individuals who did not have a declared college major were selected for participation. Participants were randomly assigned to one of four conditions: similar group, positive feedback; similar group, ambiguous feedback; dissimilar group, positive feedback; and dissimilar group, ambiguous feedback.

See page 295 for information about what to include in the Participants section.

Use digits for numbers 10 and greater.

Place text of the footnotes at the end of the manuscript, not at the bottom of the page.

Solo Status and Task Feedback   8

Procedure and Stimulus Materials

In this case, because they are relatively short, two sections are combined together.

Participants were greeted by a female experimenter and told that they would be participating in research comparing task performance in individual versus group situations. They were told that they would take part in four sessions during which they would be working alone, in groups, or in both. It was further explained that in each session they would be working on a word-finding task. They were asked if they had any questions, and they then signed an experimental consent form.

The Procedure must provide sufficient information for a reader to be able to conduct an exact replication.

At this point participants were told that before the experiment could continue, the researchers needed to have an initial baseline measure of their performance, and they completed the word-finding task for the first time. The task consisted of three puzzles, each of which contained letters displayed in blocks of 13 columns and 16 rows. The experimenter showed the task to the participants and explained that the goal was to find as many words as possible in any direction. The experimenter left the room for 7 minutes while the participants worked on the three puzzles. The experimenter then returned and, explaining to the participants that their words would now be scored by an assistant in the next room, again left the room. The experimenter returned in 4 minutes to give the feedback, which consisted of a sheet that indicated ratings in four categories:

number of words, diversity of words, originality of words, and length of words, each rated on a scale from 1 = *poor* to 7 = *excellent*.

Use digits for numbers less than 10 if they refer to scores or times.

Participants in the positive-feedback condition received scores of 6 or 7 on each of the four dimensions and were told by the experimenter that they had done "very well on all aspects of the task" and that they were "in the top 10% of the students who had previously done the task." Participants in the ambiguous-feedback condition received scores of 2, 6, 6, and 1 on the four respective dimensions and were told that they had done "very well on some aspects of the task and not so well on others." These participants were also told that, although they had scored "in the top 10% of the students who had previously done the task on two dimensions, they had scored in the bottom 10% of the students who had previously done the task" on the other two dimensions.

Participants were then told that there would be three more sessions of similar tasks and that we needed volunteers to work both alone and in groups. Furthermore, they were told that for the next session the researchers were attempting to place individuals in the environment of their choice and that we would need to get some information from them about their preferences for working both alone and in groups.

We manipulated the supposed group that participants might be joining to be either similar or dissimilar by providing a sheet of demographic information about each of the potential group members. In the similar conditions, the participants learned that the group members were two men and two women of college age who had (as determined via pretesting) a very similar major to the participant. For instance, similar majors for psychology majors were sociology and criminal justice. In the dissimilar condition, all four of the other group members were described as being college-age men who had majors that were (again on the basis of pretesting) known to be perceived as very different to those of the participant (for instance, dissimilar majors for psychology students were engineering and physics).

At this point participants completed questionnaires assessing their estimated performance on the task if they were to work in the group and alone (1 = *poor*, 8 = *excellent*) and their desire to change the task before the next session began (1 = *not at all*, 8 = *very much*). Participants also indicated how well they had performed on the task in the last session (1 = *poor*, 7 = *excellent*) and rated the similarity of the people in the group they might be joining (1 = *different from me*, 7 = *like me*). At this point the experimenter asked the participants to write any thoughts that they had about the experiment so far, and the participants were debriefed.

Results

Manipulation Checks

We tested the effectiveness of the feedback manipulation and whether the students had indeed perceived the group as similar or dissimilar to them. The manipulation checks were analyzed in terms of 2 (task feedback: positive, ambiguous) x 2 (group composition: similar, dissimilar) ANOVAs. Both manipulations were successful. Those who had received ambiguous feedback (M = 4.61) rated their performance on the original task as having been significantly less positive than those who had received positive feedback (M = 5.96), F (1,86) = 22.25, p < .001. Furthermore, the participants who expected to join the similar group rated the group members as being significantly more similar to them (M = 5.32) in comparison to those who expected to join a dissimilar group (M = 2.26), F (1,86) = 146.73, p < .001. There were no other significant effects in these analyses.

Estimated Task Performance

We investigated estimated task performance while working alone and in groups using a 2 (task feedback: positive, ambiguous) x 2 (group composition:

Report first the results of the manipulation checks (and reliability of measures).

Round numbers to two digits to the right of the decimal, except for very small *p*-values. See Chapter 8 for information on reporting *p*-values.

In this case, headers are used to order the results according to which dependent variable is being analyzed.

Mention the specific data analysis.

Report the results of the *F* tests and the condition means.

similar, dissimilar) x 2 (judgments: alone, group)
ANOVA with repeated measures on the last factor. The
expected 3-way interaction was significant F (1,84) =
4.68, p < .05, and the means, as shown in Table 1,
were in exactly the predicted direction. When the
alone judgments were analyzed separately, only a main
effect of feedback was observed, F (1,84) = 16.61,
p < .001. Participants who received positive feedback
(M = 5.60) estimated that they would perform better
while working alone than did those who received
ambiguous feedback (M = 4.40) regardless of group
similarity. The simple interaction between
feedback and group composition was not significant,
F (1,84) = 1.62. On the group judgments the pattern
was different. As shown in Table 1, the impact of
feedback was stronger in the similar-group condition
than in the dissimilar-group condition, although this
simple interaction did not quite reach significance,
F (1,84) = 3.46, p < .07.

Attempt to explain unexpected results.

There was one other significant effect--a main effect of judgment, F (1,84) = 11.39, p < .001, such
that participants predicted better performance in
the group conditions (M = 5.91) than they did in the
alone conditions (M = 5.06). Although this was not
expected, it seems reasonable to assume that this
effect was due to the fact that the group sessions

were expected to be public. It is possible, for instance, that the participants expected to receive help
from the other group members.

Desire to Change the Task

We next looked at the influence of the manipulations on the desire to change the task. This analysis produced a significant interaction F (1,83) = 5.66,
p < .05. The means took the form of a cross-over interaction. As shown in Figure 1, for individuals in
the dissimilar-group condition ambiguous feedback
increased the desire to change the task--it would
be undesirable to be in a situation in which failure could be seen by dissimilar others. For
those in the similar-group condition, positive
feedback slightly increased the desire to change
the task.

Discussion

The basic finding of this study is that
participants made different judgments about
their likely performance on and their desire to
engage again in the same word-finding task depending on their expectations about their ability
at the task and the type of group with which
they expected to work. In their estimation of
their future performance on the task while
working alone, prior feedback had the expected

> Begin the Discus-
> sion with a short
> overview of the
> research findings.

effect. Those who received positive feedback predicted
better performance. On ratings of group performance,
however, feedback and group composition produced
an interactive effect, such that the impact of
positive feedback was undermined in prediction of
performance in dissimilar groups. Although those
expecting to work in similar groups expected better
performance when they had received positive feedback,
those who expected to work in a dissimilar group
predicted relatively poor performance regardless of
feedback.

In terms of desire to change the task, we found
that, as expected, individuals who were unsure of
their expected task performance were more likely to
want to change the task when they expected to work in
a dissimilar group. However, individuals who had received positive feedback and who expected to work in a
similar group were also more likely to want to change
the task than those who received negative feedback and
expected to work in a similar group. Although the latter was not expected, this might suggest that the participants found it undesirable to perform extremely
well in the company of similar others--perhaps because
doing so would seem embarrassing.

Our findings are consistent with the idea that
performance expectations are simply more uncertain
when an individual is expecting to work with others

Solo Status and Task Feedback   15

Compare the current results to other research findings, and relate the results to the questions raised in the Introduction.

who are dissimilar. As a result, generalization from past performance to future performance is thus less sure and more influenced by other factors. We are not completely sure that these other factors include the perceived likelihood of being stereotyped by others, but past research suggests that solos do expect to be stereotyped, and this perception could contribute to the observed differences.

The present research has a few limitations. First, our manipulation, in which both the sex of the group members and their major were simultaneously varied to create similar and dissimilar groups, has some problems. Although this approach provides a strong manipulation of similar or dissimilar groups, we cannot know for sure whether it was changes in sex or in major that produced the observed differences. Future research could vary each dimension separately. Also, it might be informative to vary the task itself to be either stereotypical of men or women.

Discuss the potential limitations of the research.

Second, it is not clear whether the present results, which were found for solos, would be the same for numerical minorities. We used solo status because it produces a strong manipulation of being different. Whether being in minority status, meaning individuals have at least one other member of their group, would prevent the effects from occurring could be studied in future research.

In any case, the present results suggest that individuals are aware of the composition of the groups
in which they are likely to work and that this awareness can influence their perceptions of their own
likely task performance and their desire to engage in
the task. Such effects may account, in part, for how
individuals choose college majors and occupations.

Close very broadly, addressing the issues that began the paper.

Solo Status and Task Feedback 17

References

Cohen, L. L., & Swim, J. K. (1995). The differential
impact of gender ratios on women and men: Token-
ism, self-confidence, and expectations. *Personality
and Social Psychology Bulletin, 21,* 876-884.

Crocker, J., Major, B., & Steele, C. M. (1998). Social
stigma. In S. T. Fiske, D. Gilbert, & G. Lindzey
(Eds.), *Handbook of social psychology* (4th ed.).
Boston: McGraw-Hill.

Eccles, J. S. (1994). Understanding women's
educational and occupational choices. *Psychology
of Women Quarterly, 18,* 585-609.

Heilman, M. E. (1979). High school students' occupational interest as a function of projected sex ratios in male-dominated occupations. *Journal of
Applied Psychology, 64,* 275-279.

Kanter, R. M. (1977). Some effects of proportions on
group life: Skewed sex ratios and responses to token women. *American Journal of Sociology, 82,*
965-990.

Kleck, R., & Strenta, A. (1980). Perceptions of the
impact of negatively valued physical characteristics on social interaction. *Journal of Personality
and Social Psychology, 39,* 861-873.

Miller, C. T., & Kaiser, C. R. (2001). A theoretical
perspective on coping with stigma. *Journal of Social Issues, 56,* 73-92.

See page 299 for information about the References section.

Saenz, D. S. (1994). Token status and problem-solving deficits: Detrimental effects of distinctiveness and performance monitoring. *Social Cognition, 12,* 61-74.

Steele, C. M., & Aronson, J. (1994). Stereotype threat and the intellectual test performance of African Americans. *Journal of Personality and Social Psychology, 69,* 797-811.

Swim, J. T., & Stangor, C. (Eds.). (1998). *Prejudice from the target's perspective.* Santa Barbara, CA: Academic Press.

Taylor, S. E., Fiske, S. T., Etcoff, N. L., & Ruderman, A. J. (1978). Categorical and contextual bases of person memory and stereotyping. *Journal of Personality and Social Psychology, 36,* 778-793.

Author Note

This is an edited version of a manuscript that has been submitted for publication.

Correspondence concerning this article should be addressed to Charles Stangor, Department of Psychology, University of Maryland, College Park, MD 20742. Electronic mail: Stangor@psyc.umd.edu.

Author Note appears on a separate page after the References. Author Note is not numbered or referenced in the text.

Solo Status and Task Feedback   20

Footnotes

[1]Ninety-nine participants were originally run. However, five of these were deleted from analysis because they expressed suspicion about the validity of the task feedback.

Footnotes are listed together, starting on a new page.

Solo Status and Task Feedback   21

Table 1

Estimated Task Performance as a Function of Task

Feedback and Group Composition

Task feedback	Alone judgments		Group judgments	
	Similar	Different	Similar	Different
Positive	6.06	5.92	6.75	5.23
Ambiguous	4.14	4.53	4.86	4.53
Difference	1.92	1.39	1.89	0.70

Tables are inserted at the end of the manuscript, each on a separate page. The table number and a descriptive title are listed flush left. Notes can be added to explain information included in the table.

Figure Caption

Figure 1. Desire to change task as a function of task feedback and group composition.

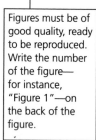

Figures must be of good quality, ready to be reproduced. Write the number of the figure— for instance, "Figure 1"—on the back of the figure.

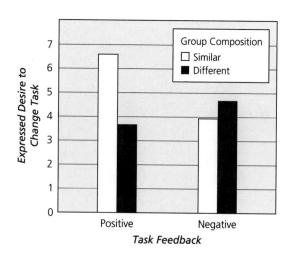

B

Data Preparation and Univariate Statistics

STUDY QUESTIONS

- How are computers used in data collection and analysis?

- How are collected data prepared for statistical analysis?

- How are missing data treated in statistical analyses?

- When is it appropriate to delete data before they are analyzed?

- What are descriptive statistics and inferential statistics?

- What determines how well the data in a sample can be used to predict population parameters?

Appendices B, C, and D are designed as a guide to the practical use of statistical procedures used to understand the implications of collected data. In most cases these statistics will be computed with statistical software programs. The use of computers is encouraged not only because it saves time but also because it reduces computational errors. Nevertheless, understanding how the statistical tests are computed and computing at least some by hand are essential for a full understanding of their underlying logic.

Appendices B and C will serve as a review of elementary statistical calculations for students who have previously had an introductory statistics course and are familiar with statistical methods. These appendices provide many formulas for computing these statistics by hand. Appendix D provides information about more advanced statistical procedures, and since these procedures are normally conducted on computers, we will focus on interpreting computer printouts. Together the three appendices will serve as a basic research reference.

We will begin our discussion of statistical techniques in this appendix by considering the selection of statistical software programs to analyze data and the preparation of data for statistical analysis. We will also discuss methods for graphically and numerically studying the distributions of scores on sample variables, as well as reviewing the elementary concepts of statistical inference.

Preparing Data for Analysis

An adequate discussion of data analysis necessarily involves a consideration of the role of computers. They are increasingly being used both to collect data from participants and to analyze data. The dramatic recent increases in computing power have provided new ways of collecting data and have also encouraged the development of many statistical analyses that were not heretofore available.

Collecting the Data

In many cases the individuals who participate in behavioral science research can directly enter their data into a computer using data collection software packages. These programs allow the researcher to create displays of stimulus information, including text, charts, and graphic images, for presentation to the research participants. The software can be programmed to select and present displays and can record responses from a keyboard, a mouse, or other devices such as physiological recording equipment; the software can also record reaction times. The use of computers to collect data can both save time and reduce errors. For instance, when the responses to a questionnaire are completed on a paper copy, the data must later be entered into the computer for analysis. This takes time and may result in errors. Appendix F considers the use of computers to collect data in more detail.

Analyzing the Data

In addition to providing new ways of collecting data, the increased use of computers has resulted in dramatic changes in how data are analyzed. Up until the 1970s, every statistical analysis was calculated by hand with a mechanical adding machine. These calculations often took days to complete and check. In the 1970s and 1980s, analyses were computed by large mainframe computers, which reduced the processing time to hours. Today, data are entered into the computer, the relevant statistical analyses and variables are selected, and the results of most analyses are calculated within seconds.

There are many statistical software packages available for analyzing behavioral science data. Which one you use will depend on the availability of different programs and the requirements of your research project. We will focus our discussion in Appendices B, C, and D on the program that is most commonly used in the behavioral sciences—the *Statistical Package for the Social Sciences* (*SPSS*). This program can be used to compute all of the statistical analyses that we will be discussing and is available for student use at many colleges and universities. A student version is available for purchase at a moderate price.

Like any good statistical program, SPSS contains a spreadsheet data editor, the ability to easily make transformations on the variables (such as adding them together or reverse-scoring them), and subprograms to compute the statistical analyses that you will need. SPSS contains, among many others, the following subprograms:

Frequency distributions
Descriptive statistics
Correlations
Regression
Analysis of variance
Reliability
Loglinear analysis
Factor analysis

Entering the Data into the Computer

The raw data are normally entered in a matrix format into the data editor of the statistical software package. In this format the data can be saved and edited. In most cases the data matrix is arranged so that the participants make up the rows of the matrix, the variables are represented in the columns, and the entries are the scores on the variables.

Figure B.1 shows the data from the first fifteen participants in Table 6.1 after they have been entered into the SPSS data editor. The variables are listed across the top of the matrix and have names of up to eight letters. The first variable, labeled "id," provides a unique identification number for each participant.

Using Coding Systems.   The two nominal variables ("sex" and "ethnic") are listed next. These variables are coded with numbers. The coding system is arbitrary, but consecutive integers are normally used. In this case, sex is coded as follows:

FIGURE B.1   Data in the SPSS Data Editor

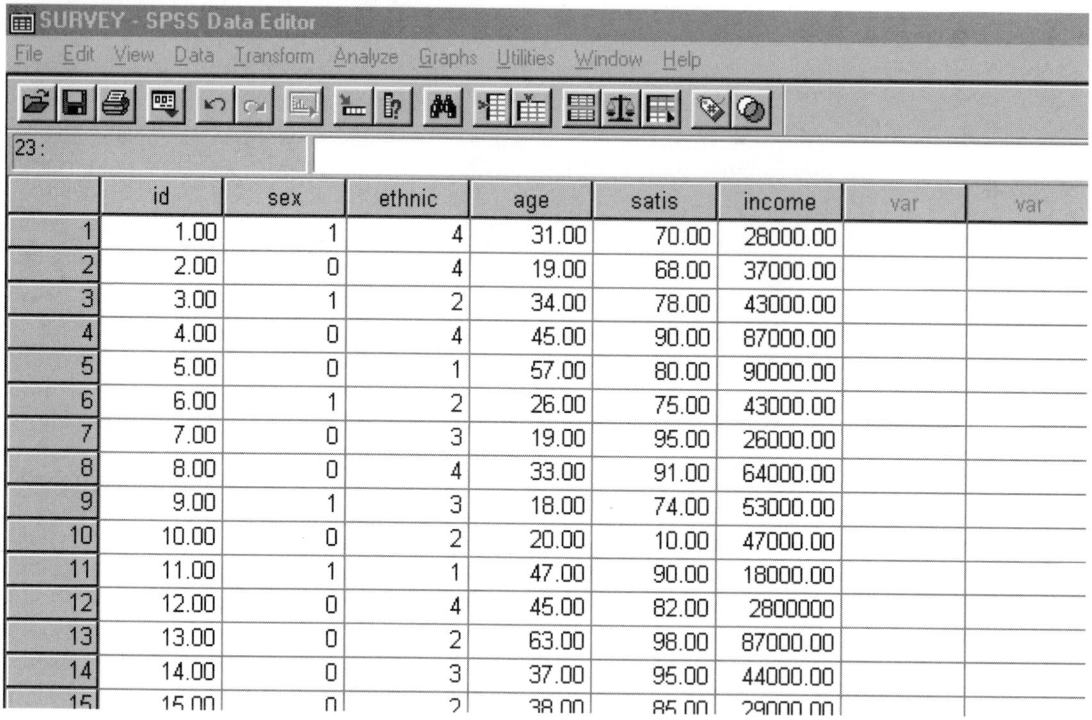

	id	sex	ethnic	age	satis	income	var	var
1	1.00	1	4	31.00	70.00	28000.00		
2	2.00	0	4	19.00	68.00	37000.00		
3	3.00	1	2	34.00	78.00	43000.00		
4	4.00	0	4	45.00	90.00	87000.00		
5	5.00	0	1	57.00	80.00	90000.00		
6	6.00	1	2	26.00	75.00	43000.00		
7	7.00	0	3	19.00	95.00	26000.00		
8	8.00	0	4	33.00	91.00	64000.00		
9	9.00	1	3	18.00	74.00	53000.00		
10	10.00	0	2	20.00	10.00	47000.00		
11	11.00	1	1	47.00	90.00	18000.00		
12	12.00	0	4	45.00	82.00	2800000		
13	13.00	0	2	63.00	98.00	87000.00		
14	14.00	0	3	37.00	95.00	44000.00		
15	15.00	0	2	38.00	85.00	29000.00		

0 = female

1 = male

Ethnic is coded according to the following scheme:

1 = African American

2 = Asian

3 = Hispanic

4 = White

5 = Other

The experimental conditions in an experimental research design would also be coded with integers—for instance:

1 = experimental condition

0 = control condition

Three quantitative variables are also entered: "age," "satis," and "income."

The participants are listed down the left side of the matrix, and the data for each person take up one row of the matrix. The variable "id" provides a unique number for each participant, and this number can be used to match the data matrix with the original questionnaires if need be. It does not matter in which order the variables or the participants are entered. It may be convenient, however, to enter all of the independent variables first, followed by the dependent variables.

Keeping Notes.   It is important to keep good notes about how the data were entered into the computer. Although you may think you will be able to remember which variable name refers to which variable and how you coded each of the variables, it is easy to forget important details (for instance, did the code number 2 indicate African Americans or Asian Americans?). In most statistical packages, including SPSS, it is possible to enter labels to indicate what the numbers used to code the nominal variables refer to.

Saving the Data.   As you enter the data into the data editor, save them regularly to disk in case there is a computer problem. Also be sure to have at least one backup copy of your data files. It is also a good idea to enter all of the data that you have collected into the computer, even if you do not plan to use them in the analysis. It does take some work to enter each variable, but it takes even more work later to find and enter the data for a variable that you thought you wouldn't need but then decided you did.

It is extremely easy to make mistakes when you are entering data. Work slowly and carefully, being sure to guard against every conceivable error. If the data were originally recorded on paper, you should save the original questionnaires at least until the analyses are completed. If you plan to publish the research, some publishers will require you to save all of your data for at least five years after the article is published.

Checking and Cleaning the Data

Once the data have been entered, the first goal is always to check that they have been entered properly. One approach is to compare all of the entered data with the original questionnaires. This is time-consuming and may not always be necessary. It is always, however, a good idea to spot-check a small sample of the data. For instance, you might compare the entered data for the first participant, the last participant, and a couple of the participants in the middle with their original questionnaires. If you find many mistakes, this will indicate that the whole data set should be checked.

The most basic procedure for checking the accuracy of data coding is to search for obvious errors. Begin (as we have discussed in Chapter 6) by calculating descriptive statistics and printing a frequency distribution or a stem and leaf plot for each of the variables. Inspecting the mean, N, and the maximum and minimum values of the variables is a helpful check on the data coding. For instance, for the variable *sex* in our data set, the minimum and maximum values should be 0 and 1 and N should equal 25, the total number of participants. Once the data are checked, any errors should be corrected.

Even though these actions seem obvious, and even though you can't imagine making such mistakes, you would be surprised how many errors are made by experimenters failing to initially check the data once they have been entered. Generally, statistical analyses are not affected to a great extent if one or two data points within a data set are off by a number or two. For instance, if a coder mistakenly enters a "2" instead of a "3" on a seven-point Likert scale for one participant, the data analysis will not be greatly affected. However, if the coder enters "22" instead of "2" or "+6" instead of "–6," the statistical tests can be dramatically changed. Checking the maximum and minimum values of all the variables before beginning other analyses can help you avoid many of these problems.

Dealing with Missing Data

One of the most commonly occurring headaches in data analysis occurs when some of the data are not available. In general, the basic rule is to avoid missing data at all costs because they can pose a threat to the validity of the research and may lead to the necessity of additional data collection.

When data are missing, the entry in the data matrix that would contain the value is usually left blank. This means that not all analyses can be performed on all participants. In some cases, such as when the information about the individual's experimental condition is missing, it will mean that the individual cannot be used in any analyses. In other cases (for instance, when data are missing only on some dependent measures), the data from the individual can be used, but not in analyses involving that variable. Statistical software packages usually allow the user to specify how missing values should be treated in the statistical analyses, and it is worth becoming familiar with these procedures.

Reasons for Missing Data.   There are two types of missing data, and they will usually be treated differently. One type occurs when the respondent has decided not to answer a question, perhaps because it is inappropriate or because the respondent has other, personal reasons for not doing so. For instance, if a questionnaire asks an individual to rate the attractiveness of his or her boyfriend or girlfriend, a person who doesn't currently have a partner will have to leave the question blank. Thinking carefully about whether all questions are appropriate ahead of time can help you alleviate this type of missing data, as well as potentially saving respondents from embarrassing situations.

A second and more serious problem occurs when data are missing because although the information could and should be available, it is for some other reason not there. Perhaps the individual forgot to answer the question or completely missed an entire page of the questionnaire. Data can also be missing because equipment failed, pertinent information about the respondent (such as his or her demographic information) was not recorded by the experimenter, or it cannot be determined which person contributed the data. Many of these problems can be avoided through careful data collection and pilot testing. When questionnaires are completed in the presence of the experimenter, their completeness can be checked before the respondent leaves. If more than one page of dependent measures are used, it is a good idea to staple them together when they are collected and to mark each page with a code number to avoid confusion. Equipment problems can often be reduced through pilot testing.

Attrition Problems.   When the research requires that data be collected from the respondents at more than one time, it is virtually certain that some of them will drop out. This represents the basic problem of participant attrition, as we have discussed in Chapter 14. In this case the question becomes not only what to do with those who are missing at later sessions (they may have to be discarded from the study altogether) but also how to determine whether those who did not return are somehow different from those who did.

Although there is no good solution to this problem, one possibility is to create a variable that indicates whether the person returned for the second session or not. Then this variable can be used as an independent variable in an analysis that compares the scores from the first session of the participants who did return to the later session with those who did not return. If there are no differences, the researcher can be more certain that there are no important differences between the two groups and thus that differential attrition is not a problem.

Deleting and Retaining Data

One of the more difficult decisions in data analysis concerns the possibility of deleting some data from the final statistical analyses. In general, the researcher is obligated to use all of the data that have been collected unless there is a valid reason to discard any. Thus a decision to discard data must always be carefully considered before it is made. Discarding of data might occur for several reasons and at various levels of analysis. We might, for instance, wish to delete variables that do not seem to be measuring what they were expected to measure. Or we might want to discard the responses from one or more individuals because they are extreme or unusual, because they did not follow or understand the directions, or because they did not take the task seriously. Let us consider each of these possibilities.

Deleting Variables.   We have already considered in Chapter 5 cases in which although they were designed to measure the same conceptual variable, one or more variables are deleted because a reliability analysis indicates that they do not measure the same thing that other variables are measuring. Doing so is usually acceptable, particularly when a new measured variable is being developed. The decision to delete a variable is more difficult, however, in cases where one variable (for instance, a self-report measure) shows the expected relationship with the independent variable but another variable (for instance, a behavioral measure) does not. In such cases it is usually not appropriate to delete a variable simply because it does not show the expected results. Rather, the results of both variables should be reported, but the researcher should try to explain in the Discussion section of the research report why the different variables might have shown different relationships.

Deleting Responses.   Another reason for deleting data is because one or more responses given by one or more participants are considered to be outliers. As we have seen in Chapter 6, an *outlier* is a very extreme score on a variable. Consider as an example a scientist who is testing the hypothesis that because anxiety-related words are highly emotionally charged, they will be pronounced more slowly. A computer program is designed to show participants a series of words, some of which are related to anxiety and some of which are comparable neutral words, and to measure how long it takes the participants to pronounce them. The scientist determines that the average pronunciation time across the participants was 765 milliseconds for the high-anxiety words, but only 634 milliseconds for the control words, a statistically significant difference. However, there is one individual who took over 10 seconds (that is, 10,000 milliseconds) to make a response to one of the high-anxiety words, and this response clearly contributed to the observed difference.

The difficult question the researcher faces in this situation is whether to keep or delete the outlier. In such a case the scientist would probably first question the measurement or coding of the data. Perhaps the computer failed to record the response correctly, or a mistake was made when the score was entered into the data matrix. If this does not appear to be the case, the possibility that something unique happened on this response for this person must be considered. Perhaps she or he was not paying attention, or maybe this person could not see or comprehend the word. Although these possibilities all suggest that the score should be deleted, it is also possible that the participant may simply have taken that long to pronounce the word.

Trimming the Data.   Although there are no hard and fast rules for determining whether a score should or should not be deleted, one common approach is to delete scores that are more than 3 standard deviations above or below the variable's mean. In this case the 10,000 milliseconds score would probably be found to be extreme enough to be deleted. However, deletion of extreme responses from only one end of the distribution is usually considered inappropriate. Rather, with a procedure known as **trimming** (Tukey, 1977), the most extreme response given by the individual on the other end of the distribution (even if it is not an outlier) is also removed before analysis.

Deleting Participants.   In some cases the participant may have contributed such a large number of unusual scores that the researcher decides to delete all of that participant's data. This might occur, for instance, if the average response time for the individual across all of the responses is very extreme, which might be taken to indicate that the person was not able to perform the task or did not understand the instructions. It is also advisable to delete individuals who have failed a suspicion check (see Chapter 3) from further analysis. Any person who has guessed the research hypothesis or who did not take the research seriously may contribute invalid data.

Whenever variables, scores, or participants have been deleted from analysis, these deletions must be notated in the research report. One exception to this rule involves cases where whole studies might not be reported, perhaps because the initial first tests of the research hypothesis were unsuccessful. Perhaps the best guideline in these cases is to report all decisions that would affect a reader's interpretation of the reported data, either in a footnote or in the text of the research report. In general, whenever data are deleted for any reason, some doubt is cast on the research itself. As a result, it is always better to try avoiding problems ahead of time.

Transforming the Data

Once the data have been entered and cleaned and decisions have been made about deleting and retaining them, the data often have to be transformed before the statistical analyses are conducted. For instance, on a Likert scale some of the variables must be reverse-scored, and then a mean or a sum across the items must be taken. In other cases the experimenter may want to create composite measures by summing or averaging variables together. Statistical software packages allow the user to take averages and sums among variables and to make other transformations as desired.

In general, a good rule of thumb is to always let the computer make the transformations for you rather than doing them yourself by hand. The computer is less likely to make errors, and once you learn how to use it to make the transformations, you will find this technique is also much faster.

Conducting Statistical Analysis

Once the data have been entered into the data editor, you will want to begin conducting statistical analyses on them. **Statistics** are mathematical methods for systematically organizing and analyzing data.

Descriptive Statistics, Parameters, and Inferential Statistics

A **descriptive statistic** is a number that represents the characteristics of the data in a sample, whereas a **parameter** is a number that represents the characteristics of a population.[1] Each descriptive statistic has an associated parameter. Descriptive statistics are symbolized with Arabic letters, whereas parameters are symbolized with Greek letters. For instance:

	Descriptive Statistic	Population Parameter
Mean	$\bar{x}$	μ (mu)
Standard deviation	s	σ (sigma)
Correlation coeficient	r	ρ (rho)

[1]Samples and populations are discussed in detail in Chapter 6 of this book.

One important difference between a descriptive statistic and a parameter is that a descriptive statistic can be calculated exactly because it is based on the data collected from a sample, whereas a parameter can only be estimated because it describes a population and the entire population cannot be measured. However, as we will see later, we can use descriptive statistics to estimate population parameters. For instance, we can use $\bar{x}$ to estimate μ and r to estimate ρ.

An **inferential statistic** is a number, such as a *p*-value or a *confidence interval,* that is used to estimate the value of a parameter on the basis of a descriptive statistic. For instance, we can use inferential statistics to make statements about the probability that $\rho > 0$ or that $\mu = 100$. The techniques of statistical inference are discussed in detail in Chapter 8. In this appendix we will cover the mathematical computations of some inferential statistics.

Statistical Notation

The following notational system is used in Appendices B, C, and D:

X and *Y* refer to the names of measured variables in a sample.

N refers to the sample size (usually the number of participants from whom data have been collected).

Subscripts on variable names refer to the score of a given individual on a given variable. For instance, X_1 refers to the score of the first person on variable *X,* and Y_N refers to the score of the *N*th (that is, the last) person on variable *Y.*

Summation Notation.   The summation sign (Σ) indicates that a set of scores should be summed. For instance, consider the following five scores on a variable, *X:*

$$X_1 = 6$$
$$X_2 = 5$$
$$X_3 = 2$$
$$X_4 = 7$$
$$X_5 = 3$$

$\Sigma(X_1, X_2, X_3, X_4, X_5)$ indicates the sum of the five scores, that is, $(6 + 5 + 2 + 7 + 3) = 23$. We can represent these operations in *summation notation* as follows:

$$\sum_{i=1}^{N} X_i = 23$$

The notations above and below the summation sign indicate that *i* takes on the values from 1 (X_1) to *N* (X_N). For convenience, because the summation is usually across the whole sample (from 1 to *N*), the subscript notation is often dropped, and the following simplification is used:

$$\sum X = 23$$

Rounding. A common practice in the reporting of the results of statistical analysis is to round the presented figures (including both descriptive and inferential statistics) to two decimal places. This rounding should be done only when the computation is complete. Intermediate stages in hand calculations should not be rounded.

Computing Descriptive Statistics

The goal of statistics is to summarize a set of scores. As we have seen in Chapter 6, perhaps the most straightforward method of doing so is to indicate how frequently each score occurred in the sample.

Frequency Distributions

When the variables are nominal, a presentation of the frequency of the scores is accomplished with a *frequency distribution,* and the data can be shown graphically in a *bar chart*. An example of each can be found in Table 6.1. For quantitative variables, there are often so many values that listing the frequency of each one in a frequency distribution would not provide a very useful summary. One solution, as we have discussed in Chapter 6, is to create a *grouped frequency distribution*. The adjacent values are grouped into a set of categories, and the frequencies of the categories are examined. A grouped frequency distribution is shown in Figure 6.2. In this case the ages have been grouped into five categories: "Less than 21," "21–30," "31–40," "41–50," "greater than 50."

The grouped frequency distribution may be displayed visually in the form of a *histogram,* as shown in Figure 6.2(b). A histogram is slightly different from a bar chart because the bars touch each other to indicate that the original variable is continuous. If the frequencies of the groups are indicated with a line, rather than bars, as shown in Figure 6.2(c), the display is called a frequency curve. Another alternative to the display of continuous data, as shown in Figure 6.3, is the stem and leaf plot. However, although frequency distributions can provide important information about the distributions of quantitative variables, it is also useful to describe these distributions with descriptive statistics.

Measures of Central Tendency

Central tendency refers to the point in the distribution of a variable on which the data are centered. There are three primary measures of central tendency—the *mean,* the *median,* and the *mode*—and the uses of each are discussed in Chapter 6. Let us consider how these measures would be calculated for the following ten scores on a variable X:

$$X_1 = 6$$
$$X_2 = 5$$
$$X_3 = 2$$

$$X_4 = 7$$
$$X_5 = 3$$
$$X_6 = 4$$
$$X_7 = 6$$
$$X_8 = 2$$
$$X_9 = 1$$
$$X_{10} = 8$$

The Mean.   The mean (also known as the arithmetic average) is symbolized as $\overline{X}$ (read "X-bar") and is calculated as the sum of all of the scores divided by the sample size.

$$\overline{X} = \frac{X_1 + X_2 + X_3 \ldots X_N}{N} = \frac{\Sigma X}{N}$$

In our case the mean of X is

$$\overline{X} = \frac{6 + 5 + 2 + 7 + 3 + 4 + 6 + 2 + 1 + 8}{10} = \frac{44}{10} = 4.4$$

The Median.   The sample median represents the score at which half of the observations are greater and half are smaller. Another way of saying this is that the median is the score at the fiftieth percentile rank, where **percentile rank** refers to the percentage of scores on the variable that are lower than the score itself. To calculate the median, the scores are first ranked from lowest to highest. If the sample size is odd, the median is the middle number. If the sample size is even, the median is the mean of the two center numbers. In our case the ranked scores are 1, 2, 2, 3, 4, 5, 6, 6, 7, 8, and the median is the average of 4 and 5, or 4.5.

The Mode.   The mode is the most frequently occurring value in a variable and can be obtained by visual inspection of the scores themselves or a frequency distribution of the scores. In some cases the distribution is **multimodal** (having more than one mode). This is true in our case, where (because there are two of each score) the modes are 2 and 6.

Measures of Dispersion

Dispersion refers to the extent to which the observations are spread out around the measure of central tendency.

The Range.   One simple measure of dispersion is to find the largest (the *maximum*) and the smallest (the *minimum*) observed values of the variable and to compute the *range* of the variable as the maximum score minus the minimum score. In our case the range of X is the maximum value (8) minus the minimum value (1) = 7.

TABLE B.1 Calculation of Descriptive Statistics

X	$(X - \overline{X})$	$(X - \overline{X})^2$	X^2	z
1	−3.40	11.56	1	−1.43
2	−2.40	5.76	4	−1.01
2	−2.40	5.76	4	−1.01
3	−1.40	1.96	9	−.59
4	−0.40	0.16	16	−.17
5	0.60	0.36	25	.25
6	1.60	2.56	36	.68
6	1.60	2.56	36	.68
7	2.60	6.76	49	1.10
8	3.60	12.96	64	1.52
$\Sigma = 44$	$\Sigma = 0.00$	$\Sigma = 50.40$	$\Sigma = 244$	$\overline{X} = 4.4$

The Variance and the Standard Deviation.   Dispersion can also be measured through calculation of the distance of each of the scores from a measure of central tendency, such as the mean. Let us consider the calculation of a measure of central tendency known as the *standard deviation,* as shown in Table B.1. The first column in Table B.1 represents the scores on X, and the second column, labeled $X - \overline{X}$, represents the mean deviation scores.

The **mean deviation scores** are calculated for each individual as the person's score (X) minus the mean ($\overline{X}$ = 4.4). If the score is above the mean, the mean deviation is positive, and if the score is below the mean, the mean deviation is negative. It turns out that the sum of the mean deviation scores is always zero:

$$\sum(X - \overline{X}) = 0$$

Not only is this particular property true only for the mean (and no other value), but it also provides a convenient way to check your calculations.

Next, the deviation scores are each squared, as shown in the column in Table B.1 marked $(X - \overline{X})^2$. The sum of the squared deviations is known as the **sum of squares,** symbolized as **SS.**

$$SS = \sum(X - \overline{X})^2 = 50.4$$

The variance (symbolized as s^2) is the sum of squares divided by N:

$$s^2 = \frac{SS}{N} = \frac{50.4}{10} = 5.04$$

TABLE B.2   Descriptive Statistics: SPSS Output

	N					Std.				
	Valid	Missing	Mean	Median	Mode	Deviation	Variance	Range	Minimum	Maximum
AGE	25	0	33.5200	32.0000	18.00[a]	12.5104	156.5100	45.00	18.00	63.00
SATIS	25	0	74.1600	80.0000	80.00[a]	23.4462	549.7233	89.00	10.00	99.00
INCOME	25	0	159920	43000.0	43000.00	550480.2	3.0E+11	2782000	18000.00	2800000

a. Multiple modes exist. The smallest value is shown.

This is a printout from the Frequencies Procedure in SPSS. (See footnote below for an explanation of scientific notation.)

The standard deviation (s) is the square root of the variance:

$$s = \sqrt{s^2} = 2.24$$

There is a shortcut to computing the sum of squares that does not involve creating the mean deviation scores:

$$SS = \Sigma(X^2) - \frac{(\Sigma X^2)}{N} = 244 - \frac{1{,}936}{10} = 50.4$$

Note in this case that $\Sigma(X^2)$ is the sum of the X^2 scores (as shown in the fourth column in Table B.1), whereas $(\Sigma X)^2$ is the sum of the scores squared ($44^2 = 1{,}936$).

Computer Output

When the sample size is large, it will be easier to use a computer to calculate the descriptive statistics. A sample printout from SPSS is shown in Table B.2.[2]

Standard Scores

As we have discussed in Chapter 6, most distributions of quantitative variables, regardless of whether they are the heights of individuals, intelligence test scores, memory errors, or ratings of supervisor satisfaction, are found to

_____

[2]SPSS and other statistical programs often use scientific notation when they print their results. If you see a printout that includes a notation such as "8.6E + 02" or 8.6E – 02," this means that the number is in scientific notation. To convert the figure to decimal notation, first write the number to the *left* of the E (in this case it is 8.6). Then use the number on the *right* side of the E to indicate which way to move the decimal point. If the number is positive, move the decimal point the indicated number of positions to the right. If the number is negative, move the decimal point the indicated number of positions to the left. Examples:

8.6 – 02 = .086   9.4E – 04 = .00094
8.6 + 02 = 860   9.4E + 04 = 94,000

fall into a bell-shaped curve known as the *normal distribution* (there are some exceptions to this general rule, as we have discussed in Chapter 6). Nevertheless, even though the shape of the distributions of many variables is normal, these distributions will usually have different means and standard deviations. This presents a difficulty if we wish to compare the scores on different variables with each other.

For instance, consider Bill and Susan, who were taking a research methods class but had different instructors who gave different exams. Susan and Bill wanted to know who had done better:

Susan had received a score of 80 on a test with $\overline{X}$ = 50 and s = 15.

Bill had received a score of 75 on a test with $\overline{X}$ = 60 and s = 10.

The solution to this problem is to transform each of the scores into a standard score or a z score using the following formula:

$$z = \frac{X - \overline{X}}{s}$$

A **standard score (z score)** represents the distance of a score from the mean of the variable (the mean deviation) expressed in standard deviation units. The last column in Table B.1 presents the standard scores for the variable X that we have been using as an example. One important property of standard scores is that once all of the original scores have been converted to standard scores, the mean of the standard scores will always be zero and the standard deviation of the standard scores will always be equal to 1.

The advantage of standard scores is that because the scores from each of the variables now have the same mean and standard deviation, we can compare the scores:

$$z_{\text{Susan}} = \frac{X - \overline{X}}{s} = \frac{80 - 50}{10} = 2.0$$

$$z_{\text{Bill}} = \frac{X - \overline{X}}{s} = \frac{75 - 60}{10} = 1.5$$

On the basis of these calculations, we can see that Susan (z = 2.0) did better than Bill (z = 1.5) because she has a higher standard score.

The Standard Normal Distribution

If we assume that the original scores are normally distributed, once they have been converted to standard scores, they will approximate the shape of a hypothetical population distribution of standard scores known as the **standard normal distribution.** Because the standard normal distribution is made up of standard scores, it will have a mean (μ) = 0 and a standard deviation (σ) = 1. Furthermore, because the standard normal distribution is so well defined, we can calculate the proportion of scores that will fall at each point in the distribution. And we can use this information to calculate the percentile

FIGURE B.2   The Standard Normal Distribution

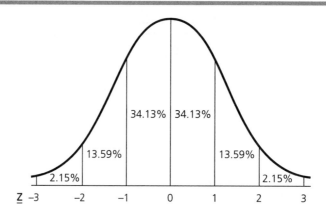

rank of a person with a given standard score (as we have seen, the percentile rank of a score refers to the percentage of scores that are lower than it is).

The standard normal distribution is shown in Figure B.2, along with the percentage of scores falling in various areas under the frequency curve. You can see that in the hypothetical distribution, 34.13 percent of the scores lie between $z = 0$ and $z = 1$, 13.59 percent of the scores lie between $z = 1$ and $z = 2$, and 2.15 percent of the scores lie between $z = 2$ and $z = 3$. There are also some scores greater than $z = 3$, but not very many. In fact, only .13 percent of the scores are greater than $z = 3$.

Keep in mind that because the standard normal distribution is symmetrical, the percentage of scores that lie between the mean and a positive z score is exactly the same as the percentage of scores between the mean and the same negative z score. Furthermore, exactly 50 percent of the scores are less than the mean (0), and 50 percent are greater than the mean.

The exact percentile rank of a given standard score can be found with Statistical Table B in Appendix E. The table gives the proportion of scores within the standard normal distribution that fall between the mean (0) and a given z value. For instance, consider Bill, who had a standard score of $z = 1.5$ on his test. The table indicates that 43.32 percent of the scores lie between $z = 0$ and $z = 1.5$. Therefore, Bill's score is higher than all of the scores below the mean (50 percent) and also higher than the 43.32 percent of the scores that lie between $z = 0$ and $z = 1.5$. Bill's percentile rank is thus $50.00 + 43.32 = 93.32$. Similarly, Susan's percentile rank is 97.72.

Working with Inferential Statistics

Consider for a moment a researcher who is interested in estimating the average grade-point average (GPA) of all of the psychology majors at a large university. He begins by taking a simple random sample of one hundred psychology majors and calculates the following descriptive statistics:

$$\overline{X} = 3.40$$
$$s = 2.23$$

Although the sample mean ($\overline{X}$) and standard deviation (s) can be calculated exactly, the corresponding population parameters μ and σ can only be estimated. This estimation is accomplished through probabilistic statements about the likelihood that the parameters fall within a given range.

Unbiased Estimators

It can be demonstrated mathematically that the sample mean ($\overline{X}$) is an **unbiased estimator** of the population mean (μ). By unbiased, we mean that $\overline{X}$ will not consistently overestimate or underestimate the population mean and thus that it represents the best guess of μ.

The sample standard deviation (s), however, is not an unbiased estimator of the population standard deviation, sigma (σ). However, an unbiased estimate of sigma, known as "sigma-hat" ($\hat{s}$), can be derived with the following formula:

$$\hat{s} = \sqrt{\frac{SS}{N-1}}$$

The Central Limit Theorem

Although these estimates of μ and σ are unbiased, and thus provide the best guess of the parameter values, they are not likely to be precise estimates. It is possible, however, through the use of a mathematical statement known as the central limit theorem, to determine how precisely the sample mean, $\overline{X}$, estimates the population mean, μ.[3] The **central limit theorem** shows that descriptive statistics calculated on larger samples provide more precise estimates of population parameters than do descriptive statistics calculated on smaller samples. This is true because small samples are more likely to be unusual than are larger samples and thus are less likely to provide an accurate description of the population.

The Standard Error

It can be demonstrated that if one were to take all possible samples of $N = 100$ from a given population, not only would the resulting distribution of the sample means (known as the **sampling distribution of the mean**) have $\overline{X} = \mu$, but also that the distribution would be normally distributed with a standard deviation known as the **standard error of the mean** (or simply the

---

[3]It is also possible to estimate how well s estimates σ, but because that estimate is not frequently needed, we will not discuss that procedure here.

standard error). The standard error is symbolized as $s_{\bar{x}}$ and calculated as follows:

$$s_{\bar{x}} = \frac{s}{\sqrt{N-1}} = \frac{2.23}{\sqrt{99}} = .22$$

Confidence Intervals

Because we can specify the sampling distribution of the mean, we can also specify a range of scores, known as a **confidence interval,** within which the population mean is likely to fall. However, this statement is probabilistic, and the exact width of the confidence interval is determined with a statistic known as **Student's *t*.** The exact distribution of the *t* statistic changes depending on the sample size, and these changes are specified with the degrees of freedom associated with the *t* statistic. The confidence interval is specified as the range between a lower limit:

$$\text{Lower limit } \mu = \bar{X} - t(s_{\bar{x}}) = 3.40 - 1.99(.22) = 2.96$$

and an upper limit:

$$\text{Upper limit } \mu = \bar{X} + t(s_{\bar{x}}) = 3.40 + 1.99(.22) = 3.84$$

where *t* is the value of the *t* statistic for a given alpha as found in Statistical Table C in Appendix E, with $df = N - 1$. In our case if we set alpha = .05, then the appropriate *t* value (with $df = 99$) is $t = 1.99$. The confidence interval allows us to state with 95 percent certainty that the GPA in the college population, as estimated by our sample, is between 2.96 and 3.84.

SUMMARY

Once the data from a research project have been collected, they must be prepared for statistical analysis. Normally this is accomplished by the user entering the data into a computer software program. Once they are entered and saved, the data are checked for accuracy. Decisions must also be made about how to deal with any missing values and whether it is appropriate to delete any of the data.

Statistical analyses of the sample data are based on descriptive statistics, whereas population parameters are estimated using inferential statistics. Frequency distributions are normally used to summarize nominal variables, whereas measures of central tendency and dispersion are normally used to summarize quantitative variables.

Use of inferential statistics involves making estimates about the values of population parameters based on the sampling distribution of the sample statistics. Although the sample mean ($\bar{X}$) is an unbiased estimator of the population mean (μ), the sample standard deviation (s) must be corrected to provide an unbiased estimator of the population mean (σ).

The ability to accurately predict population parameters is based to a large extent on the size of the sample that has been collected, since larger samples provide more precise estimates. Statistics such as the standard error of the mean and confidence intervals around the mean are used to specify how precisely the parameters have been estimated.

KEY TERMS

central limit theorem 345
confidence interval 346
descriptive statistic 337
inferential statistic 338
mean deviation scores 341
multimodal 340
parameter 337
percentile rank 340
sampling distribution of the mean
    345
standard error 346

standard error of the mean 345
standard normal distribution
    343
standard score (z score) 343
statistics 337
Student's t 346
sum of squares (SS) 341
trimming 336
unbiased estimator 345
z score 343

REVIEW AND DISCUSSION QUESTIONS

1. What aspects of data analysis can be performed by computers, and what are the advantages of using them to do so?

2. Review the procedures used to verify that collected data are coded and entered correctly before they are analyzed through statistical software packages. What mistakes can be made when these steps are not properly followed?

3. What are the most common causes of missing data, and what difficulties do missing data cause? What can be done if data are missing?

4. Comment on the circumstances under which a researcher would consider deleting one or more responses, participants, or variables from analysis.

5. What is the difference between descriptive and inferential statistics?

6. Describe the most common descriptive statistics.

7. What are standard scores, and how are they calculated?

8. What is meant by an unbiased estimator of a population parameter?

9. How does the sample size influence the extent to which the sample data can be used to accurately estimate population parameters?

10. What statistics are used to indicate how accurately the sample data can predict population parameters?

HANDS-ON EXPERIENCE

1. Compute a frequency distribution and draw by hand a bar chart for the variable *sex* using the data in Table 6.1. If you have access to a computer program, enter the data and compute the same statistics using the computer.

2. With a computer program, compute a grouped frequency distribution, a histogram, and a frequency curve for the life satisfaction variable in Table 6.1.

3. Compute by hand the mean, median, mode, range, variance, and standard deviation for the quantitative variables in Table 6.1. Check your calculations with the printout in Table B.2.

4. Calculate the mean deviation scores for the life satisfaction variable in Table 6.1. Check that they sum to zero (within rounding error), as they should. Now calculate the sum of squares from the mean deviations.

5. Calculate the SS and the mean deviation scores as you did in problem 4, but use the median and the mode instead of the mean. (You may wish to try other numbers.) Note that the mean is the *only* value that produces $\Sigma(X - \overline{X}) = 0$ and that the SS calculated with any other number than the mean will always be greater or equal to the SS calculated with the mean.

6. Compute standard (*z*) scores for Susan and Bill, who obtained the following scores (*X*) on two tests with the listed means and standard deviations:

   Susan: $X = 80$, where $\overline{X} = 71$ and $s = 13$
   Bill: $X = 74$, where $\overline{X} = 68$ and $s = 12$

   Who did better on the test? Compute the percentile rank for each student's score.

7. The Scholastic Aptitude Test has a population mean of 500 and a population standard deviation of 100. Calculate the percentile rank of students who score 350, 600, and 800.

C

Bivariate Statistics

STUDY QUESTIONS

- What statistical tests are used to assess the relationships between two nominal variables, two quantitative variables, and one nominal and one quantitative variable?

- How is the Pearson correlation coefficient calculated and tested for significance?

- How is the relationship between two nominal variables in a contingency table statistically measured with χ^2?

- How is Cohen's kappa computed?

- How is bivariate regression used to predict the scores on an outcome variable given knowledge of scores on a predictor variable?

- What do the regression equation, the regression line, and the sum of squares refer to in bivariate regression?

- How is the One-Way Analysis of Variance computed?

In this appendix we continue with discussion of statistical analysis by considering **bivariate statistics**—statistical methods used to measure the relationships between two variables. These statistical tests allow assessment of the relationships between two quantitative variables (the Pearson correlation coefficient and bivariate regression), between two nominal variables (the analysis of contingency tables), and between a nominal independent and a quantitative dependent variable (the One-Way Analysis of Variance).

The Pearson Correlation Coefficient

The *Pearson product-moment correlation coefficient* (Pearson's *r*) is used to specify the direction and magnitude of linear association between two quantitative variables. The correlation coefficient can range from $r = -1.00$ to $r = +1.00$. Positive values of r indicate that the relationship is positive linear, and negative values indicate that it is negative linear. The strength of the correlation coefficient (the effect size) is indexed by the absolute value of the correlation coefficient. The use and interpretation of *r* are discussed in detail in Chapter 9.

Let us consider the calculation of *r* on the basis of mean deviation scores using the data in Table C.1 (the data are the same as in Table 9.1). Each of twenty individuals has contributed scores on both a Likert scale measure of optimism that ranges from 1 to 9 where higher numbers indicate greater optimism and a measure of health behavior that ranges from 1 to 25 where higher numbers indicate healthier behaviors. The third and fourth columns in the table present the standard (*z*) scores for the two variables.

Calculating *r*

We can calculate an index of the direction of relationship between the two variables (referred to as *x* and *y*) by multiplying the standard scores for each individual. The results, known as the cross-products, are shown in the fifth column. The cross-products will be mostly positive if most of the students have either two positive or two negative mean deviation scores. In this case the relationship is positive linear. If most students have a positive mean deviation on one variable and a negative mean deviation on the other variable, the cross-products will be mostly negative, indicating that the relationship is negative linear.

Pearson's *r* is computed as the sum of the cross-products divided by the sample size minus 1:

$$r = \frac{\Sigma(Z_x Z_y)}{N - 1} = \frac{9.88}{19} = .52$$

In essence, *r* represents the extent to which the participants have, on average, the same *z* score on each of the two variables. In fact, the correlation between the two variables will be $r = 1.00$ if and only if each individual has

TABLE C.1   Computation of Pearson's r

Optimism	Health	$z_{Optimism}$	z_{Health}	$z_{Optimism} \times z_{Health}$
6	13	.39	.33	.13
7	24	.76	2.34	1.77
2	8	−1.09	−.58	.64
5	7	.02	−.77	−.01
2	11	−1.09	−.04	.04
3	6	−.72	−.95	.69
7	21	.76	1.79	1.36
9	12	1.50	.15	.22
8	14	1.13	.51	.58
9	21	1.50	1.79	2.68
6	10	.39	−.22	−.09
1	15	−1.46	.69	−1.01
9	8	1.50	−.58	−.88
2	7	−1.09	−.77	.84
4	9	−.35	−.40	.14
2	6	−1.09	−.95	1.04
6	9	.39	−.40	−.16
2	6	−1.09	−.95	1.04
6	12	.39	.15	.06
3	5	−.72	−1.13	.82

$\bar{X} = 4.95$ $\bar{X} = 11.20$
$s = .86$ $s = 2.70$
The sum of the cross-products is 9.88; $r = .52$.

identical z scores on each variable. In this case the sum of the cross-products is equal to $N - 1$ and $r = 1.00$.

Because r involves the relationship between the standard scores, the original variables being correlated do not need to have the same response format. For instance, we can correlate a Likert scale that ranges from 1 to 9 with a measure of health behavior that ranges from 1 to 25.

We can also calculate Pearson's r without first computing standard scores using the following formula:

$$r = \frac{\Sigma XY - \dfrac{(\Sigma X)(\Sigma Y)}{N}}{\sqrt{\left[\Sigma X^2 - \dfrac{(\Sigma X)^2}{N}\right]\left[\Sigma Y^2 - \dfrac{(\Sigma Y)^2}{N}\right]}}$$

In our example the calculation is:

$$r = \frac{1255 - \dfrac{(99)(224)}{20}}{\sqrt{\left[629 - \dfrac{(99)^2}{20}\right]\left[3{,}078 - \dfrac{(224)^2}{20}\right]}} = .52$$

Obtaining the *p*-value

The significance of a calculated *r* can be obtained using the critical values of *r* as shown in Statistical Table D in Appendix E. Because the distribution of *r* varies depending on the sample size, the critical *r* ($r_{critical}$) is found with the degrees of freedom (*df*) for the correlation coefficient. The *df* are always $N-2$. In our case it can be determined that the observed *r* (.52), with *df* = 18, is greater than the $r_{critical}$ of .444, and therefore we can reject the null hypothesis that $r = 0$, at $p < .05$.

The effect size for the Pearson correlation coefficient is *r*, the correlation coefficient itself, and the proportion of variance measure is r^2, which is frequently referred to as the *coefficient of determination.*

As you will recall from Chapter 9, when there are more than two correlation coefficients to be reported, it is common to place them in a *correlation ma-*

TABLE C.2   Correlations: SPSS Output

		SAT	SUPPORT	STUDY	GPA
Pearson Correlation	SAT	1.000	-.015	.243**	.254**
	SUPPORT	-.015	1.000	.020	.138
	STUDY	.243**	.020	1.000	.241**
	GPA	.254**	.138	.241**	1.000
Sig. (2-tailed)	SAT		.852	.002	.001
	SUPPORT	.852		.804	.087
	STUDY	.002	.804		.003
	GPA	.001	.087	.003	
N	SAT	155	155	155	155
	SUPPORT	155	155	155	155
	STUDY	155	155	155	155
	GPA	155	155	155	155

**. Correlation is significant at the 0.01 level (2-tailed).

This is a printout from the Bivariate Correlation Procedure in SPSS. It includes the Pearson *r*, the sample size (*N*), and the *p*-value. Different printouts will place these values in different places.

trix. Table C.2 presents a computer printout of the correlation matrix shown in Table 9.3. Note that in addition to the correlation coefficient, r, the two-tailed significance level (p-value) and the sample size (N) are also printed.

Contingency Tables

As you will recall from Chapter 9, *contingency tables* display the number of individuals who have each value on each of two nominal variables. The size of the contingency table is determined by the number of values on the variable that represents the rows of the matrix and the number of values on the variable that represents the columns of the matrix. For instance, if there are two values of the row variable and three values of the column variable, the table is a 2×3 contingency table.

Although there are many different statistics that can be used to analyze contingency tables, in the following sections we will consider two of the most commonly used measures—the *chi-square test for independence* and a measure of interrater reliability known as *Cohen's kappa.*

The Chi-Square Test for Independence

As we have seen in Chapter 9, the *chi-square statistic,* symbolized as χ^2, is used to assess the degree of association between two nominal variables. The null hypothesis is that there is no relationship between the two variables. Table C.3 presents a Statistical Package for the Social Sciences (SPSS) computer output of the χ^2 analysis of the study shown in Table 9.2. The data are from a study assessing the attitudes of 300 community residents toward construction of a new community center in their neighborhood. The 4×2 contingency table displays the number of individuals in each of the combinations of the two nominal variables.

The number of individuals in each of the ethnic groups (for instance, 160 whites and 62 African Americans) is indicated to the right of the contingency table, and the numbers who favor and oppose the project are indicated at the bottom of the table. These numbers are known as the *row marginal frequencies* and the *column marginal frequencies,* respectively. The contingency table also indicates, within each of the boxes (they are called the *cells*), the *observed frequencies* or *counts* (that is, the number of each ethnic group who favor or oppose the project).

Calculating χ^2. Calculation of the chi-square statistic begins with a determination, for each cell of the contingency table, of the number of each ethnic group who would be expected to favor or oppose the project if the null hypothesis were true. These *expected frequencies,* or f_e, are calculated on the expectation that if there were no relationship between the variables, the number

TABLE C.3   Contingency Table: SPSS Output

ETHNIC * OPINION Crosstabulation

| | | | OPINION | | |
			Favor	Oppose	Total
ETHNIC	African American	Count	51	11	62
		Expected Count	31.4	30.6	62.0
	Asian	Count	31	29	60
		Expected Count	30.4	29.6	60.0
	Hispanic	Count	14	4	18
		Expected Count	9.1	8.9	18.0
	White	Count	56	104	160
		Expected Count	81.1	78.9	160.0
Total		Count	152	148	300
		Expected Count	152.0	148.0	300.0

Chi-Square Tests

	Value	df	Asymp. Sig. (2-tailed)
Pearson Chi-Square	45.780	3	.000

This is a printout from the Crosstabs procedure in SPSS. Notice that on computer output, a p-value such as p = .000 means that the p-value is very small and thus highly significant!

in each of the categories would be determined by the marginal frequencies. For instance, since 152 out of the 300 total respondents favored the project, we would expect that 152/300 of the 62 African-American respondents would agree. So the expected frequency in the African American/agree cell is 152 × 62/300 = 31.4. More generally:

$$f_e = \frac{\text{Row Marginal} \times \text{Column Marginal}}{N}$$

The expected frequencies (counts) are also listed in Table C.3.

Once the f_e have been computed, the chi-square statistic can be, too:

$$\chi^2 = \sum \frac{(f_o - f_e)^2}{f_e}$$

where the summation is across all of the cells in the contingency table, f_o is the observed frequency in the cell, and f_e is the expected frequency for the cell. In our case, the calculation is

$$\chi^2 = \frac{(51 - 31.40)^2}{31.40} + \frac{(11 - 30.60)^2}{30.60} \cdots + \frac{(104 - 78.90)^2}{78.90} = 45.78$$

Calculating the p-value. Because the sampling distributions of χ^2 differ depending on the number of cells in the contingency table, the appropriate p-value is obtained with the use of the degrees of freedom (df) associated with χ^2, which are calculated as follows:

$$f = (\text{Number of rows} - 1) \times (\text{Number of columns} - 1) = (4 - 1) \times (2 - 1) =$$

Statistical Table E in Appendix E presents a listing of the critical values of χ^2 with df from 1 to 30 for different values of α. If the observed χ^2 is greater than the critical χ^2 as listed in the table at the appropriate df, the test is statistically significant. In our case $\chi^2_{observed}$ (45.78) is greater than the $\chi^2_{critical}$ (11.341) at alpha = .01.

Calculating the Effect Size Statistics. The chi-square test has a different associated effect size statistic depending on the number of rows and columns in the table. For 2 × 2 tables, the appropriate effect size statistic is **phi (ϕ).** Phi is calculated as:

$$\phi = \sqrt{\frac{\chi^2}{N}} = \sqrt{\frac{45.78}{300}} = .39$$

For tables other than 2 × 2, the associated effect size statistic is **Cramer's statistic (V_c),** calculated as

$$V_c = \sqrt{\frac{\chi^2}{N(L - 1)}}$$

where L is the lesser of either $r - 1$ or $c - 1$.

Kappa

As we have discussed in Chapter 5, in some cases the variables that form the basis of a reliability analysis are nominal rather than quantitative, and in these cases a statistic known as kappa (κ) is the appropriate test for reliability. Because in this situation the data are represented as a contingency table, and because the calculation of κ is quite similar to the calculation of χ^2, we consider it here.

TABLE C.4   Coding of Two Raters

Eva's Coding	Ana's Coding			
	Alone	Pair	Group	Total
Alone	18 (7.25)	4	7	29
Pair	5	25 (12.87)	9	39
Group	2	4	26 (13.44)	32
Total	25	33	42	100

Let us take as an example a case where two trained judges (Ana and Eva) have observed a set of children for a period of time and categorized their play behavior into one of the following three categories:

Plays alone

Plays in a pair

Plays in a group

We can create a contingency table indicating the coding of each judge for each child's behavior, as shown in Table C.4 (ignore the values in the parentheses for a moment).

We are interested in how often the two judges agree with each other. Agreements are represented on the diagonal. For instance, we can see that Ana and Eva agreed on "alone" judgments eighteen times; "pair" judgments, twenty-five times; and "group" judgments, twenty-six times. We can calculate the frequency that the two coders agreed with each other as the number of codings that fall on the diagonal:

$$\sum f_o = 18 + 25 + 26 = 69$$

Thus the *proportion of agreement* between Eva and Ana is 69/100 = .69. Although this might suggest that agreement was quite good, this estimate inflates the actual agreement between the judges because it does not take into consideration that the coders would have agreed on some of the codings by chance.

One approach to correcting for chance agreement is to correct the observed frequency of agreement by the frequency of agreement that would have been expected by chance (see Cohen, 1960). As in a chi-square analysis, we compute f_e (but only for the cells on the diagonal) as

$$f_e = \frac{\text{Row Marginal} \times \text{Column Marginal}}{N}$$

where N is the total number of judgments. We can then calculate the sum of the expected frequencies:

$$\sum f_e = \frac{(29 \times 25)}{100} + \frac{(33 \times 39)}{100} + \frac{(32 \times 42)}{100} = 7.25 + 12.87 + 13.44 = 33.56$$

and compute κ:

$$\kappa = \frac{\sum f_o - \sum f_e}{N - \sum f_e} = \frac{69 - 33.56}{100 - 33.56} = .53$$

Notice that the observed kappa (.53), which corrects for chance agreement, is considerably lower than the proportion of agreement that we calculated previously (.69), which does not. Although there is no statistical test, in general kappa values greater than .7 are considered satisfactory. In this case the computed value, $\kappa = .53$, suggests that the coders will wish to improve their coding methods.

Bivariate Regression

We have seen that the correlation coefficient indexes the linear relationship between two quantitative variables, and we have seen that the coefficient of determination (r^2) indicates the extent to which we can predict for a person from the same population but who is not in the sample the likely score on the dependent variable given that we know that person's score on the independent variable. Larger values of r (and thus r^2) indicate a better ability to predict. Bivariate regression allows us to create an equation to make the prediction.

The Regression Equation

The actual prediction of the dependent variable from knowledge of one or more independent variables is accomplished through the creation of a **regression equation.** When there is only a single predictor (independent) variable, the formula for the regression equation is as follows:

$$\hat{Y} = \overline{Y} + r\frac{s_Y}{s_X}(X - \overline{X})$$

Of course, r is the Pearson correlation coefficient, and s_X and s_Y are the standard deviations of X and Y, respectively. $\hat{Y}$ ("Y hat") is the predicted score of an individual on the dependent variable, Y, given that person's score on the independent variable, X.

Let us return for a moment to the data in Table C.1. We can create a regression equation that can be used to predict the likely health behavior of a person with a given optimism score. Using the knowledge that the correlation between the two variables is $r = .52$, as well as information from Table C.1, we can predict that a person with an optimism score of 6 ($X = 6.0$) will have a health behavior score of $\hat{Y} = 12.91$.

FIGURE C.1   Scatterplot

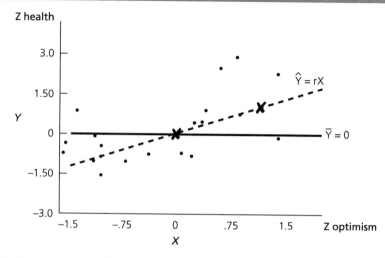

This figure is a scatterplot of the standard scores of optimism and health behavior. The data are from Table C.1. The correlation between the two variables is $r = .52$. In addition to the points, two lines have been plotted on the graph. The solid line represents $X = \bar{Y}$, our best guess of Y if we did not know X. The dashed line is the regression line or line of best fit: $\hat{Y} = rX$.

The line of best fit is drawn by plotting a line between two points that are on the line. We substitute two values of X:

$$\text{If } X = 0, \text{ then } \hat{Y} = .52 \times 0 = 0$$
$$\text{If } X = 1, \text{ then } \hat{Y} = .52 \times 1 = .52$$

The deviation of the points around the line of best fit $\Sigma(Y - \hat{Y})^2$ is less than the deviation of the points around the mean of $Y \Sigma(Y - \bar{Y})^2$.

$$\hat{Y} = 11.20 + .52 \frac{2.70}{.86} (6 - 4.95) = 12.91$$

As discussed in Chapter 9, the regression equation has many applied uses. For instance, an employer may predict a job candidate's likely job performance ($\hat{Y}$) on the basis of his or her score on a job screening test (X).

The Regression Line

Unless the correlation between X and Y is either $r = 1.00$ or $r = -1.00$, we will not be able to perfectly predict the score on the dependent measure for an individual who is not in the sample. However, the regression equation does produce the *best possible* prediction of $\hat{Y}$ in the sense that it minimizes the sum of squared deviations (the sum of squares) around the line described by the regression equation—the regression line or line of best fit.

Figure C.1 presents a scatterplot of the standard scores of the optimism and health behavior variables using the scores from Table C.1. Two lines have also been plotted. The solid line is the equation $X = \bar{Y}$. This line indicates that the best guess of the value of Y (health behavior) *if we didn't have any knowledge of X* (optimism) would be $\bar{Y}$. The dashed line represents the line of best fit, which is our best guess of health behavior *given that we know the individual's optimism score.*

Partitioning of the Sum of Squares

Unless $r = 1.00$ or $r = -1.00$, the points on the scatterplot will not fall exactly on the line of best fit, indicating that we cannot predict the $\hat{Y}$ scores exactly. We can calculate the extent to which the points deviate from the line by summing the squared distances of the points from the line. It can be shown that whenever r is not equal to 0, the sum of the squared deviations of the points from the line of best fit (known as the *unexplained or residual sum of squares*) will always be smaller than the sum of the squared deviations of the points from the line that represents $\bar{Y}$ (this is, the *total sum of squares*). Thus the total SS of Y can be broken up into two parts—Total SS = Unexplained SS + Explained SS—or more formally:

$$\sum (Y - \bar{Y})^2 = \sum (Y - \hat{Y})^2 + \sum (\hat{Y} - \bar{Y})^2$$

Thus the improvement in prediction that comes from use of the regression equation to predict $\hat{Y}$, rather than simply predicting the mean of Y, is the explained SS divided by the total SS:

$$r^2 = \frac{\text{Explained } SS}{\text{Total } SS}$$

Of course, we won't ever need to calculate r^2 this way because r^2 is the correlation coefficient squared (the coefficient of determination)!

If X and Y are first converted to standard scores, the regression equation takes a simpler form and also becomes symmetrical. That is:

$$Z_{\hat{y}} = rz_x$$

and

$$Z_{\hat{x}} = rz_y$$

One-Way Analysis of Variance

As discussed in Chapter 10, One-Way Analysis of Variance (ANOVA) is used to compare the means on a dependent variable between two or more groups of participants who differ on a single independent variable.[1] The number of groups is symbolized by k. The k groups may represent the different conditions in an experimental research design, or they may represent naturally occurring groupings in a quasi-experimental study. In each case the null hypothesis is that the groups have been drawn from the same population and thus that the mean on the dependent variable is the same for all of the groups except for differences due to random error:

$$H_0 : \mu_1 = \mu_2 = \mu_3 \ldots = \mu_k$$

The ANOVA is based on the assumption that if the means of the k groups are equal, then there should be no variability among them except that due to chance. If the groups differ, then the group means should not all be the same, and thus there will be significantly more variability among them than would be expected by chance.

ANOVA compares two estimates of variance. One comes from differences among the scores within each group. This estimate, known as the within-group variance, is considered random error. The second estimate, known as the between-groups variance, comes from differences among the group means. If these two estimates do not differ appreciably, we conclude that all of the group means come from the same population and that the differences among them are due to random error. If the group means differ more than expected, the null hypothesis that the differences are due only to chance is rejected.

---

[1]As we have seen in Chapter 10, the t test is a specialized case of the ANOVA that can be used to compare the means of two groups. The formula for the t test in a between-participants design is:

$$t = \frac{\bar{x}_1 - \bar{x}_2}{s_p \sqrt{\frac{1}{n_1} + \frac{1}{n_2}}}$$

where x_1 and x_2 are the means of groups 1 and 2, respectively, n_1 and n_2 are the sample sizes in groups 1 and 2, and s_p is the pooled variance estimate, calculated as:

$$s^2_p = \frac{(n_1 - 1)s^2_1 + (n_2 - 1)s^2_2}{n_1 + n_2 - 2}$$

where s^2_1 is the variance of group 1 and s^2_2 is the variance of group 2. The significance of the t test is calculated using Statistical Table C in Appendix E. The degrees of freedom are $n_1 + n_2 - 2$. The test is significant if the obtained t value is equal to or greater than the tabled critical value.

Computation of a One-Way Between-Participants ANOVA

Let us consider the use of the ANOVA to analyze a hypothetical experi-mental research design in which scores on a dependent measure of aggressive behavior are compared for fifteen children, five of whom have previously viewed a set of violent cartoons, five of whom have viewed a set of nonvio-lent cartoons, and five of whom have viewed no cartoons.

Cartoons Viewed

Violent	Nonviolent	None
9	5	3
7	8	6
9	7	3
8	4	5
8	5	5

$\overline{X}_{violent} = 8.20$ $\overline{X}_{nonviolent} = 5.80$ $\overline{X}_{none} = 4.40$

$\overline{X}_{total} = 6.13$

We first calculate the *grand mean* $(\overline{X}_{total})$, which is the mean across all fif-teen participants, as well as the means within each of the three groups. We then calculate the sum of squares of the scores for the participants within each of the three groups using the equation on page 342. The *SS* for the nonviolent cartoon group is

$$SS_{within(nonviolent\ cartoons)} = \left(179 - \frac{841}{5}\right) = 10.80$$

and the *SS* for the other two groups are

$$SS_{within(no\ cartoons)} = 7.20$$
$$SS_{within(violent\ cartoons)} = 2.80$$

The within-group sum of squares, or SS_{within}, is the total *SS* across the three groups:

$$SS_{within} = SS_1 + SS_2 \ldots + SS_k = 10.8 + 7.2 + 2.8 = 20.80$$

The SS_{within} is converted to an estimate of the within-group variability through division of it by a number that relates to the number of scores on which it is based. In the ANOVA the division is by the degrees of freedom. The within-group degrees of freedom (df_{within}) are equal to $N - k$ where N is the to-tal number of participants and k is the number of groups. In our case the

$df_{within} = 15 - 3 = 12$. This variability estimate is called the within-group mean square, or MS_{within}:

$$MS_{within} = \frac{SS_{within}}{df_{within}} = \frac{20.80}{12} = 1.73$$

The next step is to estimate the variability of the means of the k groups around the grand mean, the between-groups sum of squares, or $SS_{between}$. We subtract each condition mean from the grand mean and square these deviations. Then we multiply each by the number of participants in the condition and sum them all together:

$$SS_{between} = \sum N_i (\overline{X}_i - \overline{X}_{total})^2$$

where N_i is the number of participants in each group and $\overline{X}_i$ represents the means of each group. In our example

$$SS_{between} = 5(5.8 - 6.13)^2 + 5(4.4 - 6.13)^2 + 5(8.2 - 6.13)^2 = 36.93$$

The between-conditions sum of squares is then divided by the between-groups degrees of freedom ($df_{between}$), which are $k - 1$. The result is the between-conditions variability estimate, the between-groups mean square ($MS_{between}$):

$$MS_{between} = \frac{SS_{between}}{df_{between}} = \frac{36.93}{2} = 18.47$$

The ANOVA Summary Table

The following is a summary of all of the calculations:

$SS_{within} = 20.80$
$df_{within} = N - k = 12$
$MS_{within} = SS_{within}/df_{within} = 1.73$
$SS_{between} = 36.93$
$df_{between} = k - 1 = 2$
$MS_{between} = SS_{between}/df_{between} = 18.47$

These calculations are summarized in the ANOVA summary table, as shown in Table C.5.

The F Statistic. Also included in the table is the F value, which is the ratio of the between- to the within-variability estimates:

$$F_{obtained} = \frac{MS_{between}}{MS_{within}} = \frac{18.47}{1.73} = 10.65$$

The $F_{obtained}$ is compared to the sampling distribution of the F statistic, which indicates the expected F value if the null hypothesis of no differences among the group means was true. Because the sampling distribution of F takes

TABLE C.5   One-Way ANOVA: SPSS Output

Descriptives					
			N	Mean	Std. Deviation
AGGRESS CARTOON	1.00		5	8.2000	.8367
	2.00		5	5.8000	1.6432
	3.00		5	4.4000	1.3416
	Total		15	6.1333	2.0307

ANOVA		Sum of Squares	df	Mean Square	F	Sig.
AGGRESS	Between Groups	36.933	2	18.467	10.654	.002
	Within Groups	20.800	12	1.733		
	Total	57.733	14			

This is a printout from the One-Way ANOVA Procedure in SPSS.

on different shapes depending on the $df_{between}$ and the df_{within}, the $F_{critical}$ is found through Statistical Table F in Appendix E with these two values. The $F_{obtained}$ is compared to the $F_{critical}$ value from the table. If $F_{obtained}$ is greater than or equal to $F_{critical}$ at the chosen alpha, the null hypothesis (that all the condition means are the same) is rejected. The means must then be examined to see if they are in the direction predicted by the research hypothesis.

The p-value.   In our case, because $F_{obtained}$ (10.65) is greater than the $F_{critical}$ with $df_{between} = 2$ and $df_{within} = 12$ as found in Statistical Table F at alpha = .05 (6.93), the null hypothesis is rejected.

Eta

The effect size for the one-way ANOVA is eta (η), and the proportion of variance statistic is η^2. The former can be calculated from the information in the ANOVA summary table:

$$\eta^2 = \frac{SS_{between}}{(SS_{between} + SS_{within})} = \frac{36.93}{(36.93 + 20.80)} = .80$$

Because eta is not always given in research reports, it is useful to know that it can be calculated from the degrees of freedom and the F value as follows:

$$\eta = \sqrt{\frac{F(df_{\text{between}})}{F(df_{\text{between}}) + df_{\text{within}}}} = \sqrt{\frac{10.65(2)}{10.65(2) + 12}} = .80$$

SUMMARY

Bivariate statistics are used to assess the relationships between two nominal variables (the χ^2 test for independence), between two quantitative variables (the Pearson correlation coefficient and bivariate regression), or between a nominal and a quantitative variable (one-way ANOVA).

KEY TERMS

bivariate statistics 350
Cramer's statistic (V_c) 355

phi (ϕ) 355
regression equation 357

REVIEW AND DISCUSSION QUESTIONS

1. List all of the different bivariate statistical tests covered in this chapter, and indicate how they are used.

2. How is Statistical Table D used to assess the significance of the correlation coefficient? What are the appropriate df?

3. Interpret in your own words the meaning of the computer printout in Table C.2.

4. Interpret in your own words the meaning of the computer printout in Table C.3.

5. Explain the meaning of the regression equation and the regression line as shown in Figure C.1.

6. What is meant by "partitioning the sum of squares" in a regression analysis?

7. Interpret in your own words the meaning of the computer printout in Table C.5.

HANDS-ON EXPERIENCE

1. Compute Pearson's r between the life satisfaction variable and the family income variable in Table 6.1. Test the r for statistical significance, and draw conclusions about the meaning of the test.

2. Compute a Pearson correlation coefficient between the age and the family income variable using the data in Table 6.1. Then compute the correlation again, deleting the individual with the very extreme income of $2,800,000. Notice how the presence of outliers can influence the correlation coefficient.

3. Compute the correlation between age and family income again using only the individuals in Table 6.1 who have an income less than $30,000. Again, notice how the correlation coefficient changes.

4. Create a scatterplot and calculate the Pearson correlation coefficient for the following data set. Determine whether the correlation is statistically significant. Explain the meaning of the correlation coefficient in this case (you may wish to refer to Chapter 9).

Variable A	Variable B
1	1
1.5	2
2	3
2.5	4
3	5
3.5	5
4	5
4.5	4
5	3
5.5	2
6	1

5. Construct the regression equation for predicting life satisfaction (Y) from knowledge of family income (X) using the data in Table B.1. Calculate the predicted life satisfaction variable for a person with a family income of $38,000.

6. The following data represent a contingency table showing the relationship between sex of student and declared major. Answer the following questions using the data in the contingency table:
   a. How many respondents are in the sample?
   b. What percentage of the sample is men?
   c. What percentage of the sample is psychology majors?
   d. What percentage of the sample is male sociology majors?
   e. Calculate the expected frequencies (f_e) for each of the cells.
   f. Calculate the χ^2 statistic and test it for statistical significance. Report the statistics as they would be reported in a research report.

Declared College Major

	Biology	Chemistry	English	Psychology	Physics	Sociology	Total
Men	155	140	111	131	112	71	720
Women	56	50	260	227	53	134	780
Total	211	190	371	358	165	205	1500

7. The following are the data from an experimental research design in which mice who had either received training or not received training searched for a food box in a maze. The dependent variable is the number of seconds it took them to find the food. The independent variable is coded as 0 (no training) or 1 (training). The dependent variable is performance. Compare the means of the two conditions using a one-way ANOVA.

Training Condition	Food Box Performance
0	78
0	91
0	35
0	46
0	13
0	56
0	23
0	13
1	14
1	53
1	23
1	66
1	23
1	13
1	25
1	23

8. The following are data from an experiment in which vision has been tested for twelve individuals, four of whom performed the test under white light, four under green light, and four under red light. The dependent measure represents the number of seconds needed to locate a visual image. Compare the means using a one-way ANOVA. What can be concluded about the effects of the light on performance? Write a brief report of the findings. Create either a table or a figure showing the means.

Condition	Performance
White	9.8
White	6.5
White	7.5
White	9.6
Green	4.3
Green	5.6
Green	2.3
Green	1.3
Red	1.4
Red	6.3
Red	7.3
Red	8.6

D

Multivariate Statistics

Multiple Regression
Regression Coefficients
The Multiple Correlation Coefficient (R)
Hierarchical and Stepwise Analyses
Multiple Regression and ANOVA

Loglinear Analysis

Means Comparisons
A Priori Contrast Analysis
Post Hoc Means Comparisons

Multivariate Statistics
Coefficient Alpha

Exploratory Factor Analysis
Canonical Correlation and MANOVA
Structural Equation Analysis

How to Choose the Appropriate Statistical Test

Summary

Key Terms

Review and Discussion Questions

Hands-on Experience

STUDY QUESTIONS

- What are simultaneous, hierarchical, and stepwise multiple regression analyses?

- What is a loglinear analysis?

- Which statistical procedures are used to compare group means?

- What are multivariate statistics?

- How are factor analyses used in research?

- What are the Multivariate Analysis of Variance (MANOVA) and canonical correlation?

- What is structural equation analysis?

- What procedures are used to choose the appropriate statistical test for a given research design?

As we have discussed at many points throughout this book, most research designs in the behavioral sciences involve a study of the relationships among more than two variables. In this appendix we will consider statistical techniques that are used to analyze such designs. The first part of the appendix will review analyses in which there is more than one independent variable. These designs are primarily analyzed through multiple regression analysis and factorial ANOVA. We will also consider the selection and computation of means comparisons tests as well as the use of *loglinear analyses* to analyze factorial designs in which the dependent measure is nominal rather than quantitative. In the second part of the appendix we will consider cases where there is more than one dependent variable. These analyses include the Multivariate Analysis of Variance (MANOVA), canonical correlation analysis, factor analysis, and structural equation analysis. Finally, we will also address another fundamental aspect of data analysis—determining which statistical procedures are most appropriate for analyzing which types of data.

Multiple Regression

As we have discussed in Chapter 9, many relational research designs take the form of multiple regression, in which more than one independent variable is used to predict a single dependent variable. Like bivariate regression (discussed in Appendix C), the goal of multiple regression is to create a mathematical equation that allows us to make the best prediction of a person's score on a dependent or outcome variable given knowledge of that person's scores on a set of independent or predictor variables.

Multiple regression is perhaps the most useful and flexible of all of the statistical procedures that we discuss in this book, and it has many applications in behavioral science research. For instance, as we have seen in Chapter 12, multiple regression can be used to reduce error by controlling for scores on baseline measures in before-after research designs. Multiple regression is also used to create path-analytic diagrams that allow specifying causal relationships among variables (see Chapter 9).

The goal of a multiple regression analysis is to find a linear combination of independent variables that makes the best prediction of a single quantitative dependent variable in the sense that it minimizes the squared deviations around a line of best fit. The general form of the multiple regression equation is

$$\hat{Y} = A + B_1 X_1 + B_2 X_2 + B_3 X_3 \ldots + B_i X_i$$

where the X's represent scores on independent variables, A is a constant known as the *intercept,* and the B's, known as the *regression coefficients,* represent the linear relationship between each independent variable and the dependent variable, taking into consideration or *controlling for* each of the other independent variables.

If the predictor variables are first converted to standard (z) scores, the regression equation can be written as

$$\hat{Y}_z = \beta_1 z_1 + \beta_2 z_2 + \beta_3 z_3 \ldots \beta_i z_i$$

In the standardized equation the intercept is always zero and is therefore no longer in the equation. The betas (β_1, β_2, and β_3), which are not the same as the B's in the previous equation, are known as the *standardized regression coefficients* or *beta weights*.

Regression Coefficients

Consider as an example the multiple regression analysis that was presented in Chapter 9 and displayed in Figure 9.4. The goal of the analysis is to predict the current grade-point average (GPA) of a group of 155 college students using knowledge about their scores on three predictor variables—Scholastic Aptitude Test (SAT) score, study time, and rated social support. The input to the regression analysis is the correlation matrix among the predictor and outcome variables, as shown in Table 9.3. Because the actual calculation of the regression coefficients involves many mathematical calculations, it is best performed by computer. The computer printout from the Statistical Package for the Social Sciences (SPSS) is shown in Table D.1.

The unstandardized regression coefficients and the intercept are listed in the bottom panel of the printout, in the column labeled "B." This information can be used to create a regression equation that would allow us to predict the college GPA of a student who is not in the sample if we know his or her scores on the predictor variables. For instance, a student who was known to have the following scores on the predictor variables:

Study hours = 12
SAT = 1120
Social support = 7

would be expected to have a college GPA of 2.51:

GPA = .428 + .00086 × 1120 + .086 × 7 + .043 × 12 = 2.51

Unless the goal is to actually make the prediction of an individual's score, the standardized regression coefficients are more commonly used and are usually presented in the research report (see as an example Figure 9.4). In our case the solution to the standardized regression comes from the column labeled "beta" in the bottom panel of Table D.1:

$$\hat{z}_{GPA} = .210 \times z_{SAT} + .137 \times z_{SUPPORT} + .187 \times z_{STUDY}$$

As discussed in Chapter 9, the standardized regression coefficients indicate the extent to which any one independent variable predicts the dependent variable, taking account of or controlling for the effects of all of the other independent variables.

Each of the regression coefficients can be tested for statistical significance (the test is the same for the unstandardized and the standardized coefficient). The appropriate statistical test is a t statistic, along with an associated p-value, as shown in the right-most two columns in the coefficients section of Table D.1.

TABLE D.1 Output from a Multiple Regression Analysis

Model Summary[a,b]

	Variables				Adjusted	Std. Error of the
Model	Entered	Removed	R	R Square	R Square	Estimate
1	STUDY, SUPPORT, SAT[c,d]	.	.342	.117	.100	.6256

a. Dependent Variable: GPA

b. Method: Enter

c. Independent Variables: (Constant), STUDY, SUPPORT, SAT

d. All requested variables entered.

ANOVA[a]

Model		Sum of Squares	df	Mean Square	F	Sig.
1	Regression	7.841	3	2.614	6.679	.000[b]
	Residual	59.089	151	.391		
	Total	66.930	154			

a. Dependent Variable: GPA

b. Independent Variables: (Constant), STUDY, SUPPORT, SAT

Coefficients[a]

Model		Unstandardized Coefficients		Standardized Coefficients		
		B	Std. Error	Beta	t	Sig.
1	(Constant)	.428	.533		.804	.423
	SAT	8.6E-04	.000	.210	2.666	.009
	SUPPORT	8.6E-02	.048	.137	1.795	.075
	STUDY	4.3E-02	.018	.187	2.368	.019

a. Dependent Variable: GPA

This is a printout from the multiple regression procedure in SPSS (see footnote on page 342 for an explanation of scientific notation).

The Multiple Correlation Coefficient (*R*)

The *multiple correlation coefficient, R,* indicates the extent to which the predictor variables as a group predict the outcome variable. *R* is thus the effect size for the multiple regression analysis, and R^2 indicates the proportion of variance in the outcome variable that is accounted for by all of the predictor variables together. The multiple *R* is printed in the first section of the printout in Table D.1. The statistical test for the significance of *R* is an *F* ratio, and this is also found on the computer printout. As shown in the middle section of Table D.1, the *F* value in our example is highly statistically significant. The *F* value should be reported in the research report, much as it would be in an ANOVA, but with the "regression" and the "residual" degrees of freedom. In this case the appropriate way to report the *F* value is: $F(3, 151) = 6.68, p < .01$.

Hierarchical and Stepwise Analyses

To this point we have considered the case in which all of the predictor variables are simultaneously used to predict the outcome variable and the multiple *R* is used to indicate how well they do so. This procedure is known as **simultaneous multiple regression.** In other cases, however, it is possible to enter the predictor variables into the multiple regression analysis in steps or stages. The goal is to examine the extent to which the entering of a new set of variables increases the multiple correlation coefficient.

In some cases the variables are entered in a predetermined theoretical order. For instance, when predicting job satisfaction, the researcher might first enter demographic variables such as the employee's salary, age, and number of years on the job. Then, in a second stage the researcher might enter the individual's ratings of his or her supervisors and work environment. This approach would allow the researcher to see if the set of variables that measured the person's perceptions of the job (set 2) increased the ability to predict satisfaction above and beyond the demographic variables (set 1). When the predictor variables are added in a predetermined order, the analysis is known as a **hierarchical multiple regression.**

In other cases there is no particular order selected ahead of time, but the variables are entered into the analysis such that those that produce the biggest increase in the multiple *R* are entered first. For instance, if our researcher did not have a particular theory, but only wanted to see what variables predicted job satisfaction, she or he might let the computer determine which of the variables best predicted according to the extent to which they increased the multiple *R*. This approach is known as a **stepwise multiple regression.** A fuller discussion of these procedures can be found in Cohen and Cohen (1983), and in Aiken and West (1991).

Multiple Regression and ANOVA

Although we have only considered the use of quantitative predictor variables to this point, it is also possible to use nominal variables as the predictors in either bivariate or multiple regression analyses. Consider, for instance, an experimental research design in which there were two levels of the independent variable. Instead of conducting a one-way ANOVA on the dependent variable, we could analyze the data using regression. Individuals who were in one condition of the experiment would receive a score of 0 on the predictor variable, and those who were in the other condition would receive a score of 1 (it does not matter which score is assigned to which group).

This predictor variable would be entered into a bivariate regression analysis along with the measured dependent variable from the experiment. It turns out that the associated p-value of the regression equation will be exactly the same as the p-value associated with the F in a one-way between-participants ANOVA (you can test this yourself—see Hands-on Experience problem 1 at the end of this appendix).

Although the relationship between correlation and the means tests in ANOVA analysis is clear from this example, in cases of factorial ANOVA the coding of the different levels of the independent variables and the interaction tests is more complicated (see Cohen & Cohen, 1983). However, any test that can be conducted as an ANOVA can also be conducted as a multiple regression analysis. In fact, both multiple regression and ANOVA are special cases of a set of mathematical procedures called the **general linear model (GLM).** Because the GLM is almost always used by computer programs to compute ANOVAs, you may find this term listed in your statistical software package.

When the prediction involves both nominal and quantitative variables, the analysis allows the means of the dependent variable in the different experimental conditions to be adjusted or controlled for the influence of the quantitative variables. This procedure, called the **Analysis of Covariance,** can be used in some cases to control for the effects of potential confounding variables (see Cohen & Cohen, 1983).

Loglinear Analysis

As we have discussed the use of factorial ANOVA in detail in Chapter 11, including the interpretation of the ANOVA summary table, we will not review these procedures here. However, one limitation of factorial ANOVA is that it should be used only when the dependent variable is approximately normally distributed. Although this can usually be assumed for quantitative dependent measures, the ANOVA should never be used to analyze nominal dependent measures. For instance, if the dependent measure is a dichotomous response, such as a "yes" or a "no" decision or an indication of whether someone "helped" or "did not help," an ANOVA analysis is not appropriate.

As we have seen in Appendix C, if there is only one nominal independent-variable and one nominal dependent variable, the χ^2 test for independence is the appropriate test of association. However, when more than one nominal variable is used to predict a nominal dependent variable, a statistical analysis known as loglinear analysis can be used. The **loglinear analysis** basically represents a χ^2 analysis in which contingency tables that include more than two variables are created and the association among them is tested. A full discussion of loglinear analysis can be found in statistical textbooks such as Hays (1988).

Means Comparisons

As we have discussed in Chapter 11, whenever there are more than two conditions in an ANOVA analysis, the F value or values alone do not provide enough information for the scientist to fully understand the differences among the condition means. For instance, a significant main effect of a variable that has more than two levels indicates that the group means are not all the same but does not indicate which means are statistically different from each other. Similarly, a significant F value can indicate that an interaction is significant, but it cannot indicate which means are different from each other.

In these cases *means comparisons* are used to test the differences between and among particular group means. As we have discussed in Chapter 11, means comparisons can be either *pairwise comparisons* in which any two means are compared or *complex comparisons* in which more than two means are simultaneously compared. Furthermore, the approach to comparing means is different depending on whether the specific means comparisons were planned ahead of time (*a priori means comparisons*) or are chosen after the data have been collected (*post hoc means comparisons*). There are a variety of different statistical tests that can be used to compare means, and in this section we will consider some of the most popular means comparison statistics (see Keppel & Zedeck, 1989, for more information).

A Priori Contrast Analysis

The most general method of conducting means comparisons that have been planned a priori (this method can be used for either pairwise or complex comparisons) is known as **contrast analysis** (see Rosenthal & Rosnow, 1985, for a detailed investigation of this topic). A contrast analysis involves computing an F value, which is the ratio of two variance estimates (mean squares). The mean square that is entered into the numerator of the F ratio is known as the $MS_{comparison}$ and is calculated as follows:

$$MS_{comparison} = n(c_1\bar{X}_1 + c_2\bar{X}_2c = \ldots c_k\bar{X}_k)^2$$

where n is the number of participants in each of the k groups, the $\bar{X}_1$ are the group means for each of the groups, and the c_i are the contrast weights.

Setting the Contrast Weights. The **contrast weights** are set by the researcher to indicate how the group means are to be compared. The following rules apply in the setting of contrast weights:

Means that are not being compared are given contrast weights of $c_i = 0$.

The sum of the contrast weights (Σc_i) must equal 0.

The F involves a ratio between the $MS_{comparison}$ and the MS_{within} from the ANOVA analysis:

$$F = \frac{MS_{comparison}}{MS_{within}}$$

The significance of F is tested with $df_{comparison} = 1$ and the df_{within} from the ANOVA analysis.

Computing the Contrasts. To take a specific example, let us return for a moment to the ANOVA summary table and the observed group means from the data in Table C.5. Assume that the researcher wishes to compare aggressive play behavior in the violent-cartoon condition with aggressive play in the nonviolent-cartoon condition. He or she therefore sets the following contrast weights:

$$c_{violent} = 1$$
$$c_{nonviolent} = -1$$
$$c_{none} = 0$$

and then calculates the $MS_{comparison}$:

$$MS_{comparison} = \frac{5[(1)8.20 + (-1)5.80 + (0)4.44]^2}{(1)^2 + (-1)^2(0)^2} = \frac{28.80}{2.00} = 14.40$$

and the associated F value:

$$F_{comparison} = \frac{MS_{comparison}}{MS_{within}} = \frac{14.4}{1.78} = 8.24$$

The critical F value $(F_{critical})$ is found from Statistical Table F in Appendix E with $df_{numerator} = 1$ and $df_{denominator} = 12$. This value is 4.75. Because the $F_{comparison}$ (8.24) is greater than the $F_{critical}$ (4.75), we conclude that aggressive play for the children in the violent-cartoon condition is significantly greater than that in the nonviolent-cartoon condition.

It is also possible to use contrast analysis to conduct complex comparisons in which more than two means are compared at the same time. For instance, if the researcher wished to compare aggressive play in the violent-cartoon condition with aggressive play in the nonviolent and no-film conditions combined, the following contrast weights would be used:

$$c_{violent} = 1$$
$$c_{nonviolent} = -1/2$$
$$c_{none} = -1/2$$

Note that (as it should be) the sum of the comparison weights is zero. In this case the $F_{comparison}$ (18.28) is again greater than $F_{critical}$ (4.75) and thus is significant. Contrast analysis can also be used to compare means from factorial and repeated measures experimental designs.

Post Hoc Means Comparisons

As we have discussed in Chapter 11, one of the dangers of means comparisons is that there can be a lot of them, and each test increases the likelihood of a Type 1 error. The increases in experimentwise alpha are particularly problematic when the researcher desires to make pairwise comparisons that have not been planned ahead of time. *Post hoc means comparisons tests* are designed to control the experimentwise alpha level in means comparisons that are made after the data have been conducted.

The Fisher LSD Test.   One approach to reducing the probability of a Type 1 error is to use the overall F test as a type of initial filter on the significance of the mean differences. In this procedure, known as the **Fisher Least Significant Difference (LSD) Test,** regular contrast analyses (as discussed previously) are used, but with the following provisos:

1. Only pairwise comparisons are allowed.
2. Pairwise comparisons can be made only if the initial ANOVA F value is significant.

The Fisher test thus protects to some extent against increases in Type 1 errors by limiting the number of comparisons that can be made, and only allowing them to be made after an initially significant F test.

The Scheffé Test.   A second approach to conducting post hoc means comparisons, and one that can be used for either pairwise or complex comparisons, is to reduce the alpha level to statistically reduce the likelihood of a Type 1 error. One such approach is known as the **Scheffé Means Comparison Test.** The Scheffé test involves comparing the $F_{comparison}$ to a critical F value that is adjusted to take into consideration the number of possible comparisons. This is done through computation of a Scheffé F value:

$$F_{Scheffé} = (k - 1)F_{critical}$$

where k is the number of groups in the research design being compared. The contrast test is considered significant only if the $F_{comparison}$ is greater than or equal to $F_{Scheffé}$. In our example the contrast analysis comparing aggression in the violent versus the nonviolent films would not be considered significant because the $F_{comparison}$ (8.24) is less than $F_{Scheffé}$ ($2 \times 4.75 = 9.50$).

The Tukey HSD Test.   One disadvantage of the Scheffé test is that it is very conservative, and thus although it reduces the probability of Type 1 errors, it also increases the possibility of Type 2 errors. However, many researchers do not feel that the Fisher LSD Test sufficiently protects against the possibility of

Type 1 errors. Therefore, alternative means comparisons tests are sometimes used. One popular alternative, which is often considered to be the most appropriate for post hoc comparisons, is the **Tukey Honestly Significant Difference (HSD) Test.** This means comparison statistic can be calculated by most statistical software programs (see Keppel & Zedeck, 1989).

Multivariate Statistics

To this point in the book we have primarily considered cases in which data have been collected on more than one independent variable but there is only a single dependent variable. Such statistical procedures are called **univariate statistics.** However, in many research projects more than one dependent variable is collected. Inclusion of a combination of variables that measure the same or similar things together increases the reliability of measurement and thus the likelihood that significant relationships will be found.

Multivariate statistics are data analysis procedures that are specifically designed to analyze more than one dependent variable at the same time.[1] Most basically, the goal of multivariate statistics is to reduce the number of measured variables by analyzing the correlations among them and combining them together to create a smaller number of new variables that adequately summarize the original variables and can be used in their place in subsequent statistical analyses (see Harris, 1985; Stevens, 1996; Tabachnick & Fidell, 1989).

The decisions about which variables to combine together in multivariate statistical procedures can be made both on the basis of theoretical expectations about which variables should be measuring the same conceptual variables and on an empirical analysis of how the measures actually correlate among one another. These procedures are mathematically complex and are calculated by computers.

Coefficient Alpha

We have already discussed one type of multivariate statistical analysis in Chapter 5. Measures that are expected to be assessing the same conceptual variable are usually entered into a *reliability analysis,* and if they are found to be intercorrelated, they are combined together into a single score. And we have seen that the most frequently used measure of reliability among a set of quantitative variables is *coefficient alpha*. Although it is usually better to compute coefficient alpha using a computer program (a sample computer output

---

[1]Although we will focus on the case in which the multiple measures are dependent variables, multivariate statistics can actually be used whenever there are multiple measured variables. They are therefore appropriate for descriptive, correlational, or experimental research designs, depending on the specific needs of the research project.

TABLE D.2   Output from a Reliability Analysis

```
R E L I A B I L I T Y   A N A L Y S I S   -   S C A L E   (A L P H A)

Item-total Statistics

                 Scale        Scale      Corrected
                 Mean        Variance      Item-           Alpha
               if Item      if Item       Total          if Item
               Deleted      Deleted     Correlation      Deleted

ESTEEM1        30.7309      39.0992        .3330           .8289
ESTEEM2        30.5785      39.3036        .4272           .8191
ESTEEM3        31.5998      38.0226        .5548           .8087
ESTEEM4        30.8318      39.2916        .4105           .8204
ESTEEM5        31.7253      37.3330        .5043           .8119
ESTEEM6        30.9731      35.8242        .6625           .7967
ESTEEM7        31.0908      35.9659        .6256           .7999
ESTEEM8        32.6143      34.9959        .5133           .8128
ESTEEM9        32.6973      35.1990        .5426           .8084
ESTEEM10       32.2287      34.4056        .6031           .8011


Reliability Coefficients

N of Cases =     892.0                    N of Items = 10


Alpha =    .8268
```

This is a printout from the reliability procedure in SPSS. The data represent the scores from 892 students who completed the ten-item Rosenberg self-esteem scale, as shown in Figure 4.2. Items 3, 5, 8, 9, and 10 have been reverse-scored before analysis. As shown at the bottom of the printout, coefficient alpha, based on all ten items, is .83. The last column, labeled "Alpha if item deleted," is particularly useful because it indicates the coefficient alpha that the scale would have if the item on that line was deleted. This information can be used to delete some items from the scale in order to increase alpha (see Chapter 5).

is shown in Table D.2), it is also possible to do so by hand using the following formula:

$$\text{Coefficient alpha} = \frac{k}{k-1} \times \left(\frac{\sigma^2_y - \Sigma\sigma^2_i}{\sigma^2_y} \right)$$

where k is the number of items, σ^2_y is the variance of the scale sum, and σ^2_i are the variances of the k items. (The interpretation of coefficient alpha is discussed in Chapter 5.)

Exploratory Factor Analysis

When the measured dependent variables are all designed to assess the same conceptual variable, reliability analysis is most appropriate. In other cases, however, the measured variables might be expected to assess similar but not necessarily identical conceptual variables. Consider, for instance, a researcher who is interested in assessing the effects of a therapy program on the mood states of a sample of patients who have just completed the therapy in comparison to a control group of patients who have not had therapy. Both groups are asked to rate, using seven-point Likert scales, how much they have experienced each of the twenty-one emotions listed in Table D.3 over the past week. The researcher's hypothesis is that the group that has completed therapy will report more positive emotion. However, because the ratings measure a variety of different emotional responses, the researcher does not think that it would be appropriate to combine all of the twenty-one emotion ratings into a single score. Instead, she or he decides to conduct an exploratory factor analysis.

Exploratory factor analysis is a multivariate statistical technique used to analyze the underlying pattern of correlations among a set of measured variables and to develop a simplified picture of the relationships among these variables. This approach is generally used when the researcher does not already have an expectation about which variables will be associated with each other but rather wishes to learn about the associations by examining the collected data.

Creation of the Factors.   In our example the researcher begins with the correlation matrix among the sixteen emotion variables. The factor analysis is used to reduce the number of variables by creating or *extracting* a smaller set of **factors,**[2] each of which is a linear combination of the scores on the original variables. In the first stage of the factor analysis the number of factors needed to adequately summarize the original variables is determined. In this part of the analysis the factors are ordered such that the first factor is the combination of the original variables that does the best job of summarizing the data and each subsequent factor does less well in doing so.

In the second stage the linear combinations of the original variables are created through a process known as *rotation*. The goal of the rotation is to achieve a set of factors where, as much as possible, each of the original variables contributes to only one of the underlying factors. In practice there are a number of different techniques for determining the number of factors and developing the linear combinations. For instance, the factors themselves may be constrained to be either correlated or uncorrelated (see Tabachnick & Fidell, 1989).

The Factor Loading Matrix.   The primary output of an exploratory factor analysis, as shown in Table D.3, is a matrix indicating how each of the original measured variables contributes to each of the factors after the extraction and rotation. In our example four factors, represented in the four columns, were extracted from the correlation matrix. The numbers in the columns are called the *factor loadings* of the twenty-one original emotion variables on each

---

[2]Be careful not to confuse the use of the term *factor* in a factor analysis with the term *factor* as an independent variable in a factorial experimental design. They are not the same.

TABLE D.3   Output from a Factor Analysis: The Rotated Factor Matrix

	Factor 1	Factor 2	Factor 3	Factor 4
Happy	.87	—	—	—
Satisfied	.85	—	—	—
Pleased	.84	—	—	—
Delighted	.83	—	—	—
Glad	.83	—	—	—
Content	.77	—	—	—
Excited	.71	—	—	—
Sad	−.68	.41		
Droopy	—	.84	—	—
Gloomy	—	.79	—	—
Depressed	—	.75	—	—
Miserable	—	.67	—	—
Distressed	—	.60	—	—
Tired	—	.58	—	—
Sleepy	—	.58	—	—
Angry	—	—	.69	—
Frustrated	—	—	.65	—
Tense	—	—	.63	—
Annoyed	—	—	.62	—
Relaxed	—	−.48	—	.74
Calm	—	—	—	.63

This rotated factor matrix presents the loadings of each of the original twenty-one emotion variables on each of the four factors. Negative loadings indicate that the variable is negatively related to the factor. Loadings less than .30 are not reported. The four factors seem to indicate the emotions of "satisfaction," "depression," "anger," and "relaxation," respectively. The factor rotation is satisfactory because, with only a few exceptions, each of the original variables loads on only one of the factors. The factor analysis has successfully reduced the twenty-one original items to only four factors.

of the four factors. Factor loadings range from −1.00 to + 1.00 and are interpreted in the same manner as a correlation coefficient would be. Higher loadings (either positive or negative) indicate that the variable is more strongly associated with the factor. The variables that correlate most highly with each other, because they have something in common with each other, end up loading on the same factor.

One important limitation of an exploratory factor analysis is that it does not provide an interpretation of what the factors mean—this must be done by the scientist. However, a "good" factor analysis is one that is interpretable in the sense that the factors seem to comprise theoretically meaningful variables.

The factor analysis in Table D.3 is interpretable because the four factors appear to represent the broader emotions of "satisfaction," "depression," "anger," and "relaxation," respectively.

Factor Scores.   Once the factors have been extracted, a new set of variables, one for each factor, can be created. The participants' scores on each of these variables are known as the **factor scores.** Each factor score is a combination of the participants' scores on all of the variables that load on the factor and represents, in essence, what the person would have scored if it had been possible to directly measure the factor. The advantage of the factor analysis is that the factor scores can be used as dependent variables in subsequent analyses to substitute, often without much loss of information, for the original variables.

In our example the researcher could then compare the therapy group with the control group not on each of the twenty-one original variables but on the four factor scores representing satisfaction, depression, anger, and relaxation. You can see that great economy has been gained through the factor analysis because the original twenty-one variables have now been reduced to the four factor score variables. Although some information is lost, there is a great savings in the number of variables that need to be analyzed.

Canonical Correlation and MANOVA

Although exploratory factor analysis is frequently used to create a simplified picture of the relationships among the dependent measures, and the factor scores are then used as dependent measures in subsequent analyses, there is another method of analyzing data that can be used when there is a set of dependent variables to be analyzed. This approach involves computing statistical associations between the independent variable or variables in the research design and the set of dependent variables, taken as a group.

When the independent variable or variables in the research design are nominal, the **Multivariate Analysis of Variance (MANOVA)** can be used. The MANOVA is essentially an ANOVA that assesses the significance of the relationship between one or more nominal independent variables and a set of dependent variables. For instance, rather than computing an exploratory factor analysis, our researcher could have used a MANOVA analysis to directly test whether there was a significant difference between the therapy group and the control group on all of the sixteen emotion variables taken together.

The statistical test in a MANOVA analysis is known as a *multivariate F*. Like an F test in an ANOVA, the multivariate F has associated degrees of freedom as well as a p-value. If the multivariate F is significant, the researcher can draw the conclusion that the groups are different on some linear combination of the dependent variables.

Canonical correlation is a statistical procedure similar to a MANOVA that is used when the independent variable or variables are quantitative rather than nominal. The **canonical correlation** assesses the association between either a single independent variable and a set of dependent variables or between sets of independent and dependent variables. The goal of the statistical analysis is to determine whether there is an overall relationship between the two sets of variables. The resulting statistical test is significant if there is a linear combination that results in a significant association between the independent and the dependent variables.

Practical Uses.   The major advantages of MANOVA and canonical correlation is that they allow the researcher to make a single statistical test of the relationship between the independent and dependent variables. Thus these tests are frequently used as a preliminary step to control the likelihood of Type 1 errors— if the multivariate statistical test is significant, then other follow-up tests (ANOVAs, correlations, or regressions) are made on the individual dependent variables, but if the multivariate statistic is not significant, the null hypothesis is not rejected and no further analyses are made.

Disadvantages.   Although MANOVA and canonical correlation are sometimes used as initial tests in cases where there is a set of dependent variables, they do not provide information about how the independent and dependent variables are associated. For instance, a significant multivariate F test in a MANOVA analysis means that there is some pattern of differences across the groups on the dependent variables, but it does not provide any information about what these differences are. For this reason, many researchers avoid using MANOVA and canonical correlation and rely on factor analysis instead.

Structural Equation Analysis

In the preceding examples, because there was no preexisting hypothesis about the expected relationships among the variables, the researcher used multivariate statistical tests to help determine this relationship. In other cases, however, the expected relationships among the dependent variables and between the independent and dependent variables can be specified ahead of time. In these cases another multivariate approach, known as structural equation analysis, can be used. As we have seen in Chapter 9, a **structural equation analysis** is a multivariate statistical procedure that tests whether the observed relationships among a set of variables conform to a theoretical prediction about how those variables should be related.

Confirmatory Factor Analysis.   One type of structural equation analysis is known as a confirmatory factor analysis. Like exploratory factor analysis, the goal of **confirmatory factor analysis** is to explore the correlations among a set of measured variables. In a structural equation analysis, however, the summary variables are called **latent variables** rather than factors.

Consider, for instance, a scientist who has developed a new thirty-item scale to assess creativity. However, the items were designed to assess different conceptual variables, each of which represents a subcomponent of creativity. For instance, some of the items were designed to measure "musical creativity," some were designed to measure "artistic creativity," and still others were designed to assess "social creativity," such as having a good sense of humor.

Because there is an expected relationship among the measured variables, confirmatory factor analysis can be used to test whether the actual correlations among the items conform to the theoretical expectations about how the items should be correlated. In a confirmatory factor analysis an expected theoretical relationship among the variables, in the form of a hypothesized factor loading matrix, is inputted into the program. In our case the scientist would specify that three factors (musical creativity, artistic creativity, and social creativity) were expected, as well as indicating which of the items were expected to load on each of the factors. As we will see in a moment, the confirmatory factor analysis would be used to test whether the observed relationships among the items on the creativity scale matched the relationships that were expected to be observed among them.

Testing of Relationships Among Variables. One particular advantage of structural equation analyses is that, in addition to the relationships between the measured variables and the latent variables (the factor loadings), the relationships among the latent variables can be studied. And the latent variables can include both independent and dependent variables. Consider as an example an industrial psychologist who has conducted a correlational study designed to predict the conceptual variable of "job performance" from three conceptual variables of "supervisor satisfaction," "coworker satisfaction," and "job interest."

As shown in Figure D.1, the researcher has used three measured variables (represented as squares) to assess each of the four latent variables (supervisor satisfaction, coworker satisfaction, job interest, and job performance). Rather than computing a separate reliability analysis on the three independent variables and the dependent variable, combining each set of three scores together, and then using a regression analysis with three independent variables and one dependent variable, the scientist could use a structural equation analysis to test the entire set of relationships at the same time. In the structural equation analysis all of the relationships among the variables—some of which involve the relationship between the measured variables and the latent variables and others of which involve the relationships among the latent variables themselves—are simultaneously tested.

The Goodness of Fit Index. In addition to estimating the actual relationships among the variables, the structural equation analysis tests whether these observed relationships fit a proposed set of theoretical relationships among the variables. A measure known as a **goodness of fit statistic** is used to test how well the collected data fit the hypothesized relationship, and in many cases the fit of the data is also tested with a chi-square test of statistical significance. If the pattern of observed relationships among the measured variables matches the pattern of expected relationships, then the goodness of fit statistic is large (usually above .90) and the chi-square test is small and nonsignificant. In this case the data are said to "fit" the hypothesized model.

In summary, structural equation analysis, of which confirmatory factor

FIGURE D.1   Structural Equation Model

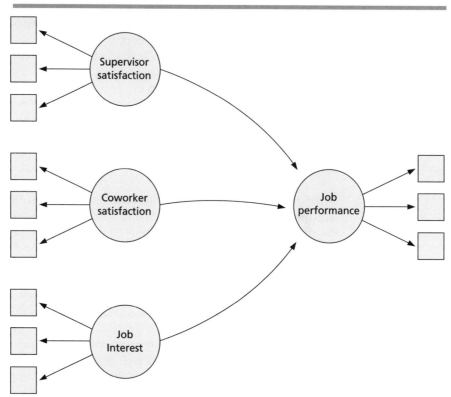

This hypothetical structural equation analysis uses nine measures of job satisfaction, which are combined into three latent variables, to predict a single latent variable of job performance, as measured by three dependent variables. The value of the overall fit of the model to the collected data can be estimated. The structural equation analysis tests both the measurement of the latent variables and the relationships among them.

analysis is one example, is a procedure used to test hypotheses about the relationships among variables. If the observed relationships among the variables fit the proposed relationships among the variables, the data can be taken as supporting the research hypothesis. Although most often used in correlational designs, structural equation modeling can also be used in experimental research designs where there is more than one measured dependent variable.

How to Choose the Appropriate Statistical Test

This book has been devoted to outlining the general procedures for creating research designs, collecting data, and analyzing those data to draw appropriate conclusions. In many cases the research design itself specifies which set of

FIGURE D.2   Choosing a Statistical Analysis

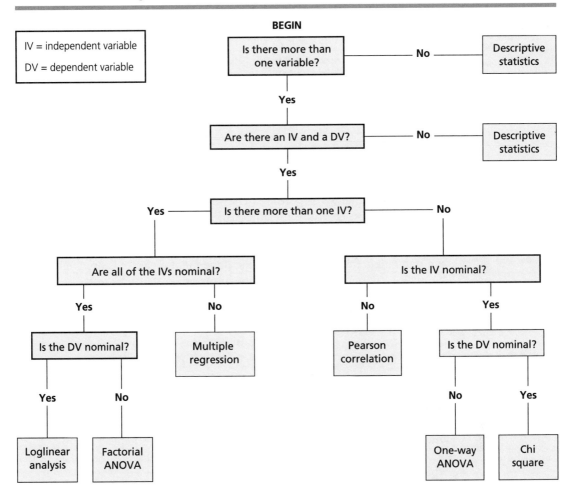

statistical techniques will be used to analyze the collected data. For instance, experimental designs are usually analyzed with ANOVA, and correlational research designs are best analyzed with correlational techniques such as multiple regression analysis. Nevertheless, these basic rules are virtually always limited in some sense because the collected data are almost always more complicated than was expected, and therefore creative application of statistical techniques to the data is required to fully understand them. Thus the art of data analysis goes beyond a mere understanding of research designs and statistical analysis and involves the creative selection of statistical tools to better understand collected data.

Experts in data analysis are able to get a "feel" for the data, and this understanding leads them to try different approaches to data analysis. One approach that can help get you started when you are considering a data analysis strategy is to determine the format of the independent and dependent variables in the research design and then to choose an appropriate statistical technique by following the flow chart shown in Figure D.2. Nevertheless, experience with data analysis will be your best teacher when you are learning the complex art of data analysis.

SUMMARY

In most research projects the relationships among more than two variables are assessed at the same time. When there are more than two independent variables but only a single dependent variable, multiple regression is the most appropriate data analysis procedure. The independent variables in a multiple regression can be entered simultaneously, hierarchically, or by using a stepwise approach. The factorial Analysis of Variance is really a type of regression analysis in which the independent variables are nominal. When there is more than one independent variable and the dependent measure is nominal, loglinear analysis, rather than ANOVA, is the appropriate statistical test.

One difficulty in ANOVA designs that have more than two conditions is that the F values do not always provide information about which groups are significantly different from each other. A number of means comparison procedures, including contrast analysis, the Fisher LSD test, the Scheffé test, and the Tukey HSD test, can be used to help make this determination.

In cases where more than one dependent measure has been assessed, multivariate statistics may be used to analyze the relationships among the variables and to reduce their complexity. Examples of multivariate procedures include exploratory factor analysis, MANOVA, and canonical correlation. When a theoretical relationship among the variables is specified ahead of time, structural equation modeling can be used to test whether the observed data fit the expected pattern of relationships.

One of the important aspects of research is learning how to use the complex array of available statistical procedures to analyze the data that have been collected. There is no substitute for experience in learning to do so.

KEY TERMS

Analysis of Covariance 373
canonical correlation 381
confirmatory factor analysis 382
contrast analysis 374
contrast weights 374
exploratory factor analysis 379
factor scores 381
factors 379
Fisher Least Significant Difference
    (LSD) Test 376
general linear model (GLM) 373
goodness of fit statistic 383
hierarchical multiple regression 372
latent variables 382

loglinear analysis 373
Multivariate Analysis of Variance
    (MANOVA) 381
multivariate statistics 377
Scheffé Means Comparison Test
    376
simultaneous multiple regression
    372
stepwise multiple regression 372
structural equation analysis 382
Tukey Honestly Significant
    Difference (HSD) Test 377
univariate statistics 377

REVIEW AND DISCUSSION QUESTIONS

1. Why is it possible to consider ANOVA as a special case of regression?

2. Give an example of when simultaneous, hierarchical, and stepwise multiple regression analyses might be used in research.

3. How is a loglinear analysis used?

4. Consider the various means comparison procedures that have been discussed in this appendix, and indicate the advantages and disadvantages of each.

5. What is the difference between exploratory factor analysis and confirmatory factor analysis, and under what conditions would each be used?

6. What are the Multivariate Analysis of Variance (MANOVA) and canonical correlation, and what are their advantages and disadvantages?

7. How is structural equation analysis used to test the measurement of, and the relationships among, conceptual variables?

8. Interpret in your own words the meaning of the computer printouts in Tables D.1, D.2, and D.3.

HANDS-ON EXPERIENCE

1. Compute a Pearson correlation coefficient between the independent variable and the dependent variable in Hands-on Experience problem 7 in Appendix C. If you have access to a computer software package, demonstrate that the p-value for the correlation coefficient is exactly the same as that for a one-way ANOVA on the data.

2. The following data set contains the raw data from 20 people who have completed the Rosenberg self-esteem scale, as shown in Table 4.2. The variables are entered exactly as the respondents answered the questions (be sure to reverse-score the appropriate variables before continuing):

Participant

#	Q1	Q2	Q3	Q4	Q5	Q6	Q7	Q8	Q9	Q10
1	1	1	1	2	1	2	2	1	1	1
2	1	1	1	2	2	2	2	3	2	2
3	1	1	1	2	4	1	1	1	2	1
4	1	1	1	1	2	2	2	3	3	1
5	1	1	1	1	1	1	1	1	1	1
6	1	1	1	2	1	2	1	2	2	2
7	1	1	1	1	1	1	1	1	1	1
8	2	2	1	1	2	2	2	2	3	1
9	1	1	2	2	1	2	2	2	3	3
10	1	2	2	2	1	2	2	2	3	2
11	1	1	1	1	1	1	1	1	1	1
12	1	2	1	2	2	2	2	2	3	3
13	2	2	2	2	2	3	2	3	3	3
14	1	1	2	2	1	2	1	3	2	2
15	1	1	2	1	1	1	2	1	1	1
16	1	1	2	1	1	1	1	1	2	2
17	1	1	1	1	1	1	1	4	3	2
18	2	2	2	2	2	2	2	2	2	2
19	2	2	1	2	2	2	2	3	3	2
20	2	4	2	4	3	3	4	4	1	2

a. Use the data to calculate split-half reliability with the odd-even method (see Chapter 5).

b. Calculate Cronbach's coefficient alpha.

c. If you have access to a computer software package, determine which item has the highest and which item has the lowest item-to-total correlation.

3. Consider the means and the ANOVA summary table from the one-way ANOVA in Hands-on Experience problem 5 in Chapter 10.
   a. Use a contrast analysis to compare the performance of the group that had been deprived of sleep for five hours with the group that had been deprived of sleep for twenty-five hours.
   b. Use a contrast analysis to compare the performance of the group that had been deprived of sleep for twenty-five hours against the performance of the other three groups.
   c. Test each of these comparisons again using a Scheffé comparison.

4. For each of the following research examples, determine what type of research design was used, what the independent and dependent variables are, and what statistical analysis is most appropriate. You may wish to use Figure D.2 to help you.
   a. A study was conducted in which high school children were asked about their drug use. The researchers recorded the percentage of students who indicated they had used each of a number of drugs, including cigarettes, marijuana, and cocaine.
   b. A group of researchers asked residents in a suburban housing development if they were interested in reducing electric consumption by decreasing their use of air-conditioning. Those who agreed to participate were randomly assigned to a control or an experimental condition. The participants in the experimental condition received feedback several times a week on the amount of electricity they used, whereas this information was not provided to the individuals in the control condition. The major finding was that those who received feedback consumed less electricity than those in the control condition.
   c. A survey was conducted to determine the predictors of success in the work force. It was found that parents' education, parents' earnings, family size, number of years of school completed, and personality characteristics as a teenager (such as leadership) were all related to both occupational status and earnings.
   d. Newborn rats were randomly assigned to one of four rearing conditions, so that researchers could assess the effects of social deprivation on behavior. One group was reared with mother and peers; a second group was reared with mother but without peers; a third group was raised in incubators (which provided food needs) without mother but with peers; a fourth group was raised without mother or peers. Several measures of emotionality (heart rate, frequency of urination, and so on) were obtained when the rats were sixty-five days old. The general finding was that maternally deprived rats showed less adaptive behavior, regardless of whether peers were present or absent.
   e. A researcher studied people's reactions to having someone stand very close to them at bus stops. The basic procedure consisted of having a male or a female confederate of the investigator approach and stand very close to a pedestrian waiting for a bus. Both male and female pedes-

trians were approached, and the extent to which each moved away from the confederate was recorded. It was found that male confederates induced more movement than female confederates and that female pedestrians tended to move more than male pedestrians.

f. Researchers compared college students who reported they had smoked marijuana at least fifteen days a month with similar students who said they had smoked five days a month at most. A day after going without marijuana, the heavy users performed significantly worse on tasks that involved paying attention to complex stimuli.

5. Read a journal article, and report on the statistical tests used to analyze the data.

E

Statistical Tables

Statistical Table A: Random Numbers

Statistical Table A contains a list of random numbers that can be used to draw random samples from populations or to make random assignment to conditions. Consider the table as a list of single digits ranging from 0 to 9 (the numbers are spaced in pairs to make them easier to read).

Selecting a Random Sample

To select a simple random sample, you must first number the participants in your population (the sampling frame). Let's say that there are 7,000 people in the frame, numbered from 0001 to 7000, and assume you wish to draw a sample 100 of these individuals.

Beginning anywhere in the table, you will create 100 four-digit numbers. For instance, let's say that you began at the top of the second column and worked down that column. The numbers would be:

6065
~~7106~~
4821
5963
3166 . . .

If the number that you select is above 7,000, just ignore it and move on. Continue this process until you have obtained 100 numbers. These 100 individuals will be in your sample.

Selecting Orders for Random Assignment Conditions

The table can also be used to create the orders for running participants in experiments that use random assignment to conditions. Assume, for instance, that you needed to order four conditions.

First, number the conditions from 1 to 4 in any order. Then, begin somewhere in the table, and go through the numbers until you find either a 1, a 2, a 3, or a 4. This condition will go first. Then, continue through the table until you find a number that you haven't already found, and so on. For instance, if I began in the third row and worked across, I would first find a 1, a 3, a 2, and then a 4.

STATISTICAL TABLE A　Random Number Table

75 60 37 09 88	08 94 46 87 98	60 11 49 68 29	91 68 93 79 29
74 65 24 12 93	82 38 69 43 63	99 07 95 72 56	39 27 34 09 41
05 71 83 25 48	22 98 16 44 51	33 60 93 47 94	34 26 06 81 28
00 06 63 57 92	74 03 53 71 47	86 47 28 55 92	33 20 28 45 49
82 48 75 70 05	42 06 73 76 39	95 68 12 12 01	59 25 42 51 61
91 21 86 40 18	55 13 72 51 93	40 26 32 64 47	67 55 89 27 34
68 59 86 51 28	44 32 21 90 74	32 89 56 87 22	42 62 27 52 03
37 63 58 24 60	57 57 56 05 07	48 01 24 05 70	13 45 34 83 41
64 31 87 14 42	52 53 04 64 62	21 03 47 63 08	09 65 62 98 61
10 66 04 59 46	77 32 46 82 73	49 79 75 78 34	84 20 95 32 74
42 61 10 93 15	80 48 50 52 28	00 64 88 81 30	53 60 33 40 72
46 39 66 23 15	74 45 72 13 08	81 84 55 86 49	32 59 63 73 08
95 38 26 74 33	89 63 67 85 47	33 47 51 29 92	07 92 69 22 69
72 63 08 33 81	67 51 98 65 17	81 43 55 10 13	41 63 46 10 53
11 89 89 53 65	34 44 29 19 66	74 32 87 32 97	45 42 63 22 11
31 08 04 92 30	72 42 89 30 41	97 03 48 61 04	40 42 22 25 28
85 54 58 35 98	48 60 52 31 93	94 86 13 25 14	01 57 23 18 67
50 14 24 78 20	34 23 56 61 98	35 93 50 30 12	52 39 75 24 49
47 07 98 78 06	75 19 03 89 17	06 92 78 16 83	16 13 55 22 63
57 35 95 84 44	40 29 90 96 96	38 83 83 55 14	98 75 15 58 25
28 26 38 44 81	19 26 99 74 29	84 40 58 35 71	58 04 95 86 74
69 94 40 62 70	15 60 93 22 79	40 81 62 56 66	35 89 17 25 62
99 39 31 18 56	11 13 76 48 26	33 36 24 20 97	03 83 22 75 83
64 60 67 78 86	17 75 04 93 28	19 82 55 21 43	07 73 24 85 87
53 04 78 98 41	53 93 98 05 30	51 37 24 13 10	48 13 15 04 06
21 34 59 88 31	48 65 00 09 44	34 44 99 98 40	07 72 44 25 32
46 42 92 66 20	13 36 41 57 25	47 01 45 32 30	61 51 33 16 51
06 23 75 56 43	90 71 23 98 01	74 43 81 52 73	37 95 48 58 58
94 94 28 25 52	18 16 04 27 72	49 82 48 79 21	31 48 80 37 75
34 37 97 77 31	10 07 46 68 85	83 30 69 01 34	51 31 00 22 44
91 54 65 30 10	10 55 48 87 61	14 47 69 60 09	74 89 13 00 69
60 38 19 14 13	42 90 06 60 66	31 42 02 86 83	09 05 42 83 76
20 95 74 36 04	82 92 97 80 68	11 84 97 74 07	67 30 76 38 89
83 66 13 27 42	70 54 97 51 25	92 50 60 96 83	70 28 77 83 14
87 31 13 51 04	66 11 59 84 87	47 68 00 74 66	45 82 04 00 84
16 49 57 88 27	42 15 84 12 62	25 75 13 98 55	45 98 71 12 05
74 57 52 70 10	79 70 25 97 51	67 80 36 56 52	20 41 69 75 71
19 53 80 24 06	15 14 04 26 67	94 17 91 58 24	00 16 80 65 01
31 14 50 02 91	93 11 59 73 33	41 69 50 85 58	34 68 42 01 36
29 26 11 72 42	81 40 46 42 03	76 27 03 83 69	73 14 76 44 21
55 46 22 40 67	36 12 92 27 00	12 80 53 13 33	82 21 91 49 30
28 90 15 49 26	42 02 11 58 82	42 38 74 47 27	48 50 20 84 16
42 62 49 73 33	77 25 67 06 66	38 04 98 66 44	72 26 92 07 28
35 86 42 40 36	91 41 43 50 24	42 23 04 09 02	44 76 04 34 99
45 62 85 78 11	33 52 35 24 87	72 15 63 59 10	00 94 57 10 94
42 39 38 74 05	78 91 43 88 95	06 99 11 78 17	17 77 10 52 71
11 17 55 73 83	41 60 28 81 15	73 15 22 48 94	86 69 72 21 68

Statistical Table B: Distribution of *z* in the Standard Normal Distribution

This table represents the proportion of the area under the standard normal distribution. The distribution has a mean of 0 and a standard deviation of 1.00. The total area under the curve is also equal to 1.00. (You can convert the listed proportions to percentages by multiplying by 100.)

Because the distribution is symmetrical, only the areas corresponding to positive *z* values are listed. Negative *z* values will have exactly the same areas.

Column B represents the percentage of the distribution that falls between the mean and the tabled *z* value:

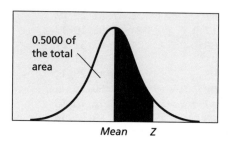
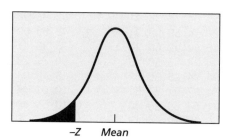

Column C represents the proportion of area beyond *z*:

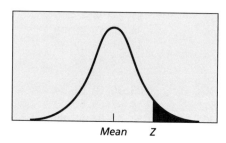
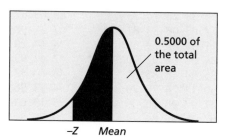

When you calculate proportions with positive *z* scores, remember that .50 of the scores lie below the mean.

STATISTICAL TABLE B   Distribution of z in the Standard Normal Distribution

(A) z	(B) Area Between Mean and z	(C) Area Beyond z	(A) z	(B) Area Between Mean and z	(C) Area Beyond z	(A) z	(B) Area Between Mean and z	(C) Area Beyond z
0.00	.0000	.5000	0.40	.1554	.3446	0.80	.2881	.2119
0.01	.0040	.4960	0.41	.1591	.3409	0.81	.2910	.2090
0.02	.0080	.4920	0.42	.1628	.3372	0.82	.2939	.2061
0.03	.0120	.4880	0.43	.1664	.3336	0.83	.2967	.2033
0.04	.0160	.4840	0.44	.1700	.3300	0.84	.2995	.2005
0.05	.0199	.4801	0.45	.1736	.3264	0.85	.3023	.1977
0.06	.0239	.4761	0.46	.1772	.3228	0.86	.3051	.1949
0.07	.0279	.4721	0.47	.1808	.3192	0.87	.3078	.1922
0.08	.0319	.4681	0.48	.1844	.3156	0.88	.3106	.1894
0.09	.0359	.4641	0.49	.1879	.3121	0.89	.3133	.1867
0.10	.0398	.4602	0.50	.1915	.3085	0.90	.3159	.1841
0.11	.0438	.4562	0.51	.1950	.3050	0.91	.3186	.1814
0.12	.0478	.4522	0.52	.1985	.3015	0.92	.3212	.1788
0.13	.0517	.4483	0.53	.2019	.2981	0.93	.3238	.1762
0.14	.0557	.4443	0.54	.2054	.2946	0.94	.3264	.1736
0.15	.0596	.4404	0.55	.2088	.2912	0.95	.3289	.1711
0.16	.0636	.4364	0.56	.2123	.2877	0.96	.3315	.1685
0.17	.0675	.4325	0.57	.2157	.2843	0.97	.3340	.1660
0.18	.0714	.4286	0.58	.2190	.2810	0.98	.3365	.1635
0.19	.0753	.4247	0.59	.2224	.2776	0.99	.3389	.1611
0.20	.0793	.4207	0.60	.2257	.2743	1.00	.3413	.1587
0.21	.0832	.4168	0.61	.2291	.2709	1.01	.3438	.1562
0.22	.0871	.4129	0.62	.2324	.2676	1.02	.3461	.1539
0.23	.0910	.4090	0.63	.2357	.2643	1.03	.3485	.1515
0.24	.0948	.4052	0.64	.2389	.2611	1.04	.3508	.1492
0.25	.0987	.4013	0.65	.2422	.2578	1.05	.3531	.1469
0.26	.1026	.3974	0.66	.2454	.2546	1.06	.3554	.1446
0.27	.1064	.3936	0.67	.2486	.2514	1.07	.3577	.1423
0.28	.1103	.3897	0.68	.2517	.2483	1.08	.3599	.1401
0.29	.1141	.3859	0.69	.2549	.2451	1.09	.3621	.1379
0.30	.1179	.3821	0.70	.2580	.2420	1.10	.3643	.1357
0.31	.1217	.3783	0.71	.2611	.2389	1.11	.3665	.1335
0.32	.1255	.3745	0.72	.2642	.2358	1.12	.3686	.1314
0.33	.1293	.3707	0.73	.2673	.2327	1.13	.3708	.1292
0.34	.1331	.3669	0.74	.2704	.2296	1.14	.3729	.1271
0.35	.1368	.3632	0.75	.2734	.2266	1.15	.3749	.1251
0.36	.1406	.3594	0.76	.2764	.2236	1.16	.3770	.1230
0.37	.1443	.3557	0.77	.2794	.2206	1.17	.3790	.1210
0.38	.1480	.3520	0.78	.2823	.2177	1.18	.3810	.1190
0.39	.1517	.3483	0.79	.2852	.2148	1.19	.3830	.1170

STATISTICAL TABLE B   (continued)

(A) z	(B) Area Between Mean and z	(C) Area Beyond z	(A) z	(B) Area Between Mean and z	(C) Area Beyond z	(A) z	(B) Area Between Mean and z	(C) Area Beyond z
1.20	.3849	.1151	1.60	.4452	.0548	2.00	.4772	.0228
1.21	.3869	.1131	1.61	.4463	.0537	2.01	.4778	.0222
1.22	.3888	.1112	1.62	.4474	.0526	2.02	.4783	.0217
1.23	.3907	.1093	1.63	.4484	.0516	2.03	.4788	.0212
1.24	.3925	.1075	1.64	.4495	.0505	2.04	.4793	.0207
1.25	.3944	.1056	1.65	.4505	.0495	2.05	.4798	.0202
1.26	.3962	.1038	1.66	.4515	.0485	2.06	.4803	.0197
1.27	.3980	.1020	1.67	.4525	.0475	2.07	.4808	.0192
1.28	.3997	.1003	1.68	.4535	.0465	2.08	.4812	.0188
1.29	.4015	.0985	1.69	.4545	.0455	2.09	.4817	.0183
1.30	.4032	.0968	1.70	.4554	.0446	2.10	.4821	.0179
1.31	.4049	.0951	1.71	.4564	.0436	2.11	.4826	.0174
1.32	.4066	.0934	1.72	.4573	.0427	2.12	.4830	.0170
1.33	.4082	.0918	1.73	.4582	.0418	2.13	.4834	.0166
1.34	.4099	.0901	1.74	.4591	.0409	2.14	.4838	.0162
1.35	.4115	.0885	1.75	.4599	.0401	2.15	.4842	.0158
1.36	.4131	.0869	1.76	.4608	.0392	2.16	.4846	.0154
1.37	.4147	.0853	1.77	.4616	.0384	2.17	.4850	.0150
1.38	.4162	.0838	1.78	.4625	.0375	2.18	.4854	.0146
1.39	.4177	.0823	1.79	.4633	.0367	2.19	.4857	.0143
1.40	.4192	.0808	1.80	.4641	.0359	2.20	.4861	.0139
1.41	.4207	.0793	1.81	.4649	.0351	2.21	.4864	.0136
1.42	.4222	.0778	1.82	.4656	.0344	2.22	.4868	.0132
1.43	.4236	.0764	1.83	.4664	.0336	2.23	.4871	.0129
1.44	.4251	.0749	1.84	.4671	.0329	2.24	.4875	.0125
1.45	.4265	.0735	1.85	.4678	.0322	2.25	.4878	.0122
1.46	.4279	.0721	1.86	.4686	.0314	2.26	.4881	.0119
1.47	.4292	.0708	1.87	.4693	.0307	2.27	.4884	.0116
1.48	.4306	.0694	1.88	.4699	.0301	2.28	.4887	.0113
1.49	.4319	.0681	1.89	.4706	.0294	2.29	.4890	.0110
1.50	.4332	.0668	1.90	.4713	.0287	2.30	.4893	.0107
1.51	.4345	.0655	1.91	.4719	.0281	2.31	.4896	.0104
1.52	.4357	.0643	1.92	.4726	.0274	2.32	.4898	.0102
1.53	.4370	.0630	1.93	.4732	.0268	2.33	.4901	.0099
1.54	.4382	.0618	1.94	.4738	.0262	2.34	.4904	.0096
1.55	.4394	.0606	1.95	.4744	.0256	2.35	.4906	.0094
1.56	.4406	.0594	1.96	.4750	.0250	2.36	.4909	.0091
1.57	.4418	.0582	1.97	.4756	.0244	2.37	.4911	.0089
1.58	.4429	.0571	1.98	.4761	.0239	2.38	.4913	.0087
1.59	.4441	.0559	1.99	.4767	.0233	2.39	.4916	.0084

STATISTICAL TABLE B   (continued)

(A) z	(B) Area Between Mean and z	(C) Area Beyond z	(A) z	(B) Area Between Mean and z	(C) Area Beyond z	(A) z	(B) Area Between Mean and z	(C) Area Beyond z
2.40	.4918	.0082	2.72	.4967	.0033	3.04	.4988	.0012
2.41	.4920	.0080	2.73	.4968	.0032	3.05	.4989	.0011
2.42	.4922	.0078	2.74	.4969	.0031	3.06	.4989	.0011
2.43	.4925	.0075	2.75	.4970	.0030	3.07	.4989	.0011
2.44	.4927	.0073	2.76	.4971	.0029	3.08	.4990	.0010
2.45	.4929	.0071	2.77	.4972	.0028	3.09	.4990	.0010
2.46	.4931	.0069	2.78	.4973	.0027	3.10	.4990	.0010
2.47	.4932	.0068	2.79	.4974	.0026	3.11	.4991	.0009
2.48	.4934	.0066	2.80	.4974	.0026	3.12	.4991	.0009
2.49	.4936	.0064	2.81	.4975	.0025	3.13	.4991	.0009
2.50	.4938	.0062	2.82	.4976	.0024	3.14	.4992	.0008
2.51	.4940	.0060	2.83	.4977	.0023	3.15	.4992	.0008
2.52	.4941	.0059	2.84	.4977	.0023	3.16	.4992	.0008
2.53	.4943	.0057	2.85	.4978	.0022	3.17	.4992	.0008
2.54	.4945	.0055	2.86	.4979	.0021	3.18	.4993	.0007
2.55	.4946	.0054	2.87	.4979	.0021	3.19	.4993	.0007
2.56	.4948	.0052	2.88	.4980	.0020	3.20	.4993	.0007
2.57	.4949	.0051	2.89	.4981	.0019	3.21	.4993	.0007
2.58	.4951	.0049	2.90	.4981	.0019	3.22	.4994	.0006
2.59	.4952	.0048	2.91	.4982	.0018	3.23	.4994	.0006
2.60	.4953	.0047	2.92	.4982	.0018	3.24	.4994	.0006
2.61	.4955	.0045	2.93	.4983	.0017	3.25	.4994	.0006
2.62	.4956	.0044	2.94	.4984	.0016	3.30	.4995	.0005
2.63	.4957	.0043	2.95	.4984	.0016	3.35	.4996	.0004
2.64	.4959	.0041	2.96	.4985	.0015	3.40	.4997	.0003
2.65	.4960	.0040	2.97	.4985	.0015	3.45	.4997	.0003
2.66	.4961	.0039	2.98	.4986	.0014	3.50	.4998	.0002
2.67	.4962	.0038	2.99	.4986	.0014	3.60	.4998	.0002
2.68	.4963	.0037	3.00	.4987	.0013	3.70	.4999	.0001
2.69	.4964	.0036	3.01	.4987	.0013	3.80	.4999	.0001
2.70	.4965	.0035	3.02	.4987	.0013	3.90	.49995	.00005
2.71	.4966	.0034	3.03	.4988	.0012	4.00	.49997	.00003

Source: From R. A. Fisher and F. Yates (1974). *Statistical Tables for Biological, Agricultural and Medical Research* (6th ed.). Edinburgh Gate, Harlow, Essex: Addison Wesley Longman. Copyright © 1963 R. A. Fisher and F. Yates. Reprinted by permission of Pearson Education Limited.

Statistical Table C: Critical Values of *t*

The obtained *t* value with the listed degrees of freedom (down the side) is significant at the listed alpha (across the top) if it is equal to or greater than the value shown in the table. Negative *t* values have the equivalent *p*-values as their positive counterparts.

STATISTICAL TABLE C   Critical Values of *t*

df	$\alpha = .10$	$\alpha = .05$	$\alpha = .02$	$\alpha = .01$	$\alpha = .001$
1	6.314	12.706	31.821	63.657	636.619
2	2.920	4.303	6.965	9.925	31.598
3	2.353	3.182	4.541	5.841	12.941
4	2.132	2.776	3.747	4.604	8.610
5	2.015	2.571	3.365	4.032	6.859
6	1.943	2.447	3.143	3.707	5.959
7	1.895	2.365	2.998	3.499	5.405
8	1.860	2.306	2.896	3.355	5.041
9	1.833	2.262	2.821	3.250	4.781
10	1.812	2.228	2.764	3.169	4.587
11	1.796	2.201	2.718	3.106	4.437
12	1.782	2.179	2.681	3.055	4.318
13	1.771	2.160	2.650	3.012	4.221
14	1.761	2.145	2.624	2.977	4.140
15	1.753	2.131	2.602	2.947	4.073
16	1.746	2.120	2.583	2.921	4.015
17	1.740	2.110	2.567	2.898	3.965
18	1.734	2.101	2.552	2.878	3.922
19	1.729	2.093	2.539	2.861	3.883
20	1.725	2.086	2.528	2.845	3.850
21	1.721	2.080	2.518	2.831	3.819
22	1.717	2.074	2.508	2.819	3.792
23	1.714	2.069	2.500	2.807	3.767
24	1.711	2.064	2.492	2.797	3.745
25	1.708	2.060	2.485	2.787	3.725
26	1.706	2.056	2.479	2.779	3.707
27	1.703	2.052	2.473	2.771	3.690
28	1.701	2.048	2.467	2.763	3.674
29	1.699	2.045	2.462	2.756	3.659
30	1.697	2.042	2.457	2.750	3.646
40	1.684	2.021	2.423	2.704	3.551
60	1.671	2.000	2.390	2.660	3.460
120	1.658	1.980	2.358	2.617	3.373
∞	1.645	1.960	2.326	2.576	3.291

Note: All *p*-values in this table are two-sided.
Source: From R. A. Fisher and F. Yates (1974). *Statistical Tables for Biological, Agricultural and Medical Research* (6th ed.). Edinburgh Gate, Harlow, Essex: Addison Wesley Longman. Copyright © 1963 R. A. Fisher and F. Yates. Reprinted by permission of Pearson Education Limited.

Statistical Table D: Critical Values of *r*

The obtained *r* value with the listed degrees of freedom (down the side) is significant at the listed alpha (across the top) if it is equal to or greater than the value shown in the table. The appropriate *df* for testing the significance of *r* is $N - 2$.

STATISTICAL TABLE D   Critical Values of *r*

$(N - 2)$	$\alpha = .10$	$\alpha = .05$	$\alpha = .02$	$\alpha = .01$	$\alpha = .001$
1	.988	.997	.9995	.9999	1.000
2	.900	.950	.980	.990	.999
3	.805	.878	.934	.959	.991
4	.729	.811	.882	.917	.974
5	.669	.754	.833	.874	.951
6	.622	.707	.789	.834	.925
7	.582	.666	.750	.798	.898
8	.550	.632	.716	.765	.872
9	.521	.602	.685	.735	.847
10	.497	.576	.658	.708	.823
11	.476	.553	.634	.684	.801
12	.458	.532	.612	.661	.780
13	.441	.514	.592	.641	.760
14	.426	.497	.574	.623	.742
15	.412	.482	.558	.606	.725
16	.400	.468	.542	.590	.708
17	.389	.456	.528	.575	.693
18	.378	.444	.516	.561	.679
19	.369	.433	.503	.549	.665
20	.360	.423	.492	.537	.652
22	.344	.404	.472	.515	.629
24	.330	.388	.453	.496	.607
25	.323	.381	.445	.487	.597
30	.296	.349	.409	.449	.554
35	.275	.325	.381	.418	.519
40	.257	.304	.358	.393	.490
45	.243	.288	.338	.372	.465
50	.231	.273	.322	.354	.443
55	.220	.261	.307	.338	.424
60	.211	.250	.295	.325	.408

STATISTICAL TABLE D (continued)

($N - 2$)	$\alpha = .10$	$\alpha = .05$	$\alpha = .02$	$\alpha = .01$	$\alpha = .001$
65	.203	.240	.284	.312	.393
70	.195	.232	.274	.302	.380
75	.189	.224	.264	.292	.368
80	.183	.217	.256	.283	.357
85	.178	.211	.249	.275	.347
90	.173	.205	.242	.267	.338
95	.168	.200	.236	.260	.329
100	.164	.195	.230	.254	.321
125	.147	.174	.206	.228	.288
150	.134	.159	.189	.208	.264
175	.124	.148	.174	.194	.248
200	.116	.138	.164	.181	.235
300	.095	.113	.134	.148	.188
500	.074	.088	.104	.115	.148
1000	.052	.062	.073	.081	.104
2000	.037	.044	.052	.058	.074

Note: All *p*-values in this table are two-sided.
Source: From R. A. Fisher and F. Yates (1974). *Statistical Tables for Biological, Agricultural and Medical Research* (6th ed.). Edinburgh Gate, Harlow, Essex: Addison Wesley Longman. Copyright © 1963 R. A. Fisher and F. Yates. Reprinted by permission of Pearson Education Limited.

Statistical Table E: Critical Values of Chi Square

The obtained χ^2 value with the listed degrees of freedom (down the side) is significant at the listed alpha (across the top) if it is equal to or greater than the value shown in the table.

STATISTICAL TABLE E   Critical Values of Chi Square

df	$\alpha = .10$	$\alpha = .05$	$\alpha = .02$	$\alpha = .01$
1	2.706	3.841	5.412	6.635
2	4.605	5.991	7.824	9.210
3	6.251	7.815	9.837	11.341
4	7.779	9.488	11.668	13.277
5	9.236	11.070	13.388	15.086
6	10.645	12.592	15.033	16.812
7	12.017	14.067	16.622	18.475
8	13.362	15.507	18.168	20.090
9	14.684	16.919	19.679	21.666
10	15.987	18.307	21.161	23.209
11	17.275	19.675	22.618	24.725
12	18.549	21.026	24.054	26.217
13	19.812	22.362	25.472	27.688
14	21.064	23.685	26.873	29.141
15	22.307	24.996	28.259	30.578
16	23.542	26.296	29.633	32.000
17	24.769	27.587	30.995	33.409
18	25.989	28.869	32.346	34.805
19	27.204	30.144	33.687	36.191
20	28.412	31.410	35.020	37.566
21	29.615	32.671	36.343	38.932
22	30.813	33.924	37.659	40.289
23	32.007	35.172	38.968	41.638
24	33.196	36.415	40.270	42.980
25	34.382	37.652	41.566	44.314
26	35.563	38.885	42.856	45.642
27	36.741	40.113	44.140	46.963
28	37.916	41.337	45.419	48.278
29	39.087	42.557	46.693	49.588
30	40.256	43.773	47.962	50.892

Source: From R. A. Fisher and F. Yates (1974). *Statistical Tables for Biological, Agricultural and Medical Research* (6th ed.). Edinburgh Gate, Harlow, Essex: Addison Wesley Longman. Copyright © 1963 R. A. Fisher and F. Yates. Reprinted by permission of Pearson Education Limited.

Statistical Table F: Critical Values of *F*

The obtained *F* value with the listed numerator and denominator degrees of freedom is significant at alpha = .05 if it is equal to or greater than the value shown in the light row of the table. The obtained *F* value is significant at alpha = .01 if it is equal to or greater than the value shown in the dark row of the table.

STATISTICAL TABLE F Critical Values of *F*

Degrees of Freedom

	1	2	3	4	5	6	7	8	9	10	11
1	161	200	216	225	230	234	237	239	241	242	243
	4052	4999	5403	5625	5764	5859	5928	5981	6022	6056	6082
2	18.51	19.00	19.16	19.25	19.30	19.33	19.36	19.37	19.38	19.39	19.40
	98.49	99.01	99.17	99.25	99.30	99.33	99.34	99.36	99.38	99.40	99.41
3	10.13	9.55	9.28	9.12	9.01	8.94	8.88	8.84	8.81	8.78	8.76
	34.12	30.81	29.46	28.71	28.34	27.91	27.67	27.49	27.34	27.23	27.13
4	7.71	6.94	6.59	6.39	6.26	6.16	6.09	6.04	6.00	5.96	5.93
	21.20	18.0	16.69	15.98	15.52	15.21	14.98	14.80	14.66	14.54	14.45
5	6.61	5.79	5.41	5.19	5.05	4.95	4.88	4.82	4.78	4.74	4.70
	16.26	13.27	12.06	11.39	10.97	10.67	10.45	10.27	10.15	10.05	9.96
6	5.99	5.14	4.76	4.53	4.39	4.28	4.21	4.15	4.10	4.06	4.03
	13.74	10.92	9.78	9.15	8.75	8.47	8.26	8.10	7.98	7.87	7.79
7	5.59	4.74	4.35	4.12	3.97	3.87	3.79	3.73	3.68	3.63	3.60
	12.25	9.55	8.45	7.85	7.46	7.19	7.00	6.84	6.71	6.62	6.54
8	5.32	4.46	4.07	3.84	3.69	3.58	3.50	3.44	3.39	3.34	3.31
	11.26	8.65	7.59	7.01	6.63	6.37	6.19	6.03	5.91	5.82	5.74
9	5.12	4.26	3.86	3.63	3.48	3.37	3.29	3.23	3.18	3.13	3.10
	10.56	8.02	6.99	6.42	6.06	5.80	5.62	5.47	5.35	5.26	5.18
10	4.96	4.10	3.71	3.48	3.33	3.22	3.14	3.07	3.02	2.97	2.94
	10.04	7.56	6.55	5.99	5.64	5.39	5.21	5.06	4.95	4.85	4.78
11	4.84	3.98	3.59	3.36	3.20	3.09	3.01	2.95	2.90	2.86	2.82
	9.65	7.20	6.22	5.67	5.32	5.07	4.88	4.74	4.63	4.54	4.46
12	4.75	3.88	3.49	3.26	3.11	3.00	2.92	2.85	2.80	2.76	2.72
	9.33	6.93	5.95	5.41	5.06	4.82	4.65	4.50	4.39	4.30	4.22
13	4.67	3.80	3.41	3.18	3.02	2.92	2.84	2.77	2.72	2.67	2.63
	9.07	6.70	5.74	5.20	4.86	4.62	4.44	4.30	4.19	4.10	4.02

Degrees of Freedom for Denominator

for Numerator

12	14	16	20	24	30	40	50	75	100	200	500	∞
244	245	246	248	249	250	251	252	253	253	254	254	254
6106	6142	6169	6208	6234	6258	6286	6302	6323	6334	6352	6361	6336
19.41	19.42	19.43	19.44	19.45	19.46	19.47	19.47	19.48	19.49	19.49	19.50	19.50
99.42	99.43	99.44	99.45	99.46	99.47	99.48	99.48	99.49	99.49	99.49	99.50	99.50
8.74	8.71	8.69	8.66	8.64	8.62	8.60	8.58	8.57	8.56	8.54	8.54	8.53
27.05	26.92	26.83	26.69	26.60	26.50	26.41	26.30	26.27	26.23	26.18	26.14	26.12
5.91	5.87	5.84	5.80	5.77	5.74	5.71	5.70	5.68	5.66	5.65	5.64	5.63
14.37	14.24	14.15	14.02	13.93	13.83	13.74	13.69	13.61	13.57	13.52	13.48	13.46
4.68	4.64	4.60	4.56	4.53	4.50	4.46	4.44	4.42	4.40	4.38	4.37	4.36
9.89	9.77	9.68	9.55	9.47	9.38	9.29	9.24	9.17	9.13	9.07	9.04	9.02
4.00	3.96	3.92	3.87	3.84	3.81	3.77	3.75	3.72	3.71	3.69	3.68	3.67
7.72	7.60	7.52	7.39	7.31	7.23	7.14	7.09	7.02	6.99	6.94	6.90	6.88
3.57	3.52	3.49	3.44	3.41	3.38	3.34	3.32	3.29	3.28	3.25	3.24	3.23
6.47	6.35	6.27	6.15	6.07	5.98	5.90	5.85	5.78	5.75	5.70	5.67	5.65
3.28	3.23	3.20	3.15	3.12	3.08	3.05	3.03	3.00	2.98	2.96	2.94	2.93
5.67	5.56	5.48	5.36	5.28	5.20	5.11	5.06	5.00	4.96	4.91	4.88	4.86
3.07	3.02	2.98	2.93	2.90	2.86	2.82	2.80	2.77	2.76	2.73	2.72	2.71
5.11	5.00	4.92	4.80	4.73	4.64	4.56	4.51	4.45	4.41	4.36	4.33	4.31
2.91	2.86	2.82	2.77	2.74	2.70	2.67	2.64	2.61	2.59	2.56	2.55	2.54
4.71	4.60	4.52	4.41	4.33	4.25	4.17	4.12	4.05	4.01	3.96	3.93	3.91
2.79	2.74	2.70	2.65	2.61	2.57	2.53	2.50	2.47	2.45	2.42	2.41	2.40
4.40	4.29	4.21	4.10	4.02	3.94	3.86	3.80	3.74	3.70	3.66	3.62	3.60
2.69	2.64	2.60	2.54	2.50	2.46	2.42	2.40	2.36	2.35	2.32	2.31	2.30
4.16	4.05	3.98	3.86	3.78	3.70	3.61	3.56	3.49	3.46	3.41	3.38	3.36
2.60	2.55	2.51	2.46	2.42	2.38	2.34	2.32	2.28	2.26	2.22	2.22	2.21
3.96	3.85	3.78	3.67	3.59	3.51	3.42	3.37	3.30	3.27	3.18	3.18	3.16

STATISTICAL TABLE F (continued)

Degrees of Freedom

	1	2	3	4	5	6	7	8	9	10	11
14	4.60	3.74	3.34	3.11	2.96	2.85	2.77	2.70	2.65	2.60	2.56
	8.86	6.51	5.56	5.03	4.69	4.46	4.28	4.14	4.03	3.94	3.86
15	4.54	3.68	3.29	3.06	2.90	2.79	2.70	2.64	2.59	2.55	2.51
	8.68	6.36	5.42	4.89	4.56	4.32	4.14	4.00	3.89	3.80	3.73
16	4.49	3.63	3.24	3.01	2.85	2.74	2.66	2.59	2.54	2.49	2.45
	8.53	6.23	5.29	4.77	4.44	4.20	4.03	3.89	3.78	3.69	3.61
17	4.45	3.59	3.20	2.96	2.81	2.70	2.62	2.55	2.50	2.45	2.41
	8.40	6.11	5.18	4.67	4.34	4.10	3.93	3.79	3.68	3.59	3.52
18	4.41	3.55	3.16	2.93	2.77	2.66	2.58	2.51	2.46	2.41	2.37
	8.28	6.01	5.09	4.58	4.25	4.01	3.85	3.71	3.60	3.51	3.44
19	4.38	3.52	3.13	2.90	2.74	2.63	2.55	2.48	2.43	2.38	2.34
	8.18	5.93	5.01	4.50	4.17	3.94	3.77	3.63	3.52	3.43	3.36
20	4.35	3.49	3.10	2.87	2.71	2.60	2.52	2.45	2.40	2.35	2.31
	8.10	5.85	4.94	4.43	4.10	3.87	3.71	3.56	3.45	3.37	3.30
21	4.32	3.47	3.07	2.84	2.68	2.57	2.49	2.42	2.37	2.32	2.28
	8.02	5.78	4.87	4.37	4.04	3.81	3.65	3.51	3.40	3.31	3.24
22	4.30	3.44	3.05	2.82	2.66	2.55	2.47	2.40	2.35	2.30	2.26
	7.94	5.72	4.82	4.31	3.99	3.76	3.59	3.45	3.35	3.26	3.18
23	4.28	3.42	3.03	2.80	2.64	2.53	2.45	2.38	2.32	2.28	2.24
	7.88	5.66	4.76	4.26	3.94	3.71	3.54	3.41	3.30	3.21	3.14
24	4.26	3.40	3.01	2.78	2.62	2.51	2.43	2.36	2.30	2.26	2.22
	7.82	5.61	4.72	4.22	3.90	3.67	3.50	3.36	3.25	3.17	3.09
25	4.24	3.38	2.99	2.76	2.60	2.49	2.41	2.34	2.28	2.24	2.20
	7.77	5.57	4.68	4.18	3.86	3.63	3.46	3.32	3.21	3.13	3.05
26	4.22	3.37	2.89	2.74	2.59	2.47	2.39	2.32	2.27	2.22	2.18
	7.72	5.53	4.64	4.14	3.82	3.59	3.42	3.29	3.17	3.09	3.02
27	4.21	3.35	2.96	2.73	2.57	2.46	2.37	2.30	2.25	2.20	2.16
	7.68	5.49	4.60	4.11	3.79	3.56	3.39	3.26	3.14	3.06	2.98
28	4.20	3.34	2.95	2.71	2.56	2.44	2.36	2.29	3.24	2.19	2.15
	7.64	5.45	4.57	4.07	3.76	3.53	3.36	3.23	3.11	3.03	2.95
29	4.18	3.33	2.93	2.70	2.54	2.43	2.35	2.28	2.22	2.18	2.14
	7.60	5.52	4.54	4.04	3.73	3.50	3.32	3.20	3.08	3.00	2.92

Degrees of Freedom for Denominator

for Numerator

12	14	16	20	24	30	40	50	75	100	200	500	∞
2.53	2.48	2.44	2.39	2.35	2.31	2.27	2.24	2.21	2.19	2.16	2.14	2.13
3.80	3.70	3.62	3.51	3.43	3.34	3.26	3.21	3.14	3.11	3.06	3.02	3.00
2.48	2.43	2.39	2.33	2.29	2.25	2.21	2.18	2.15	2.12	2.10	2.08	2.07
3.67	3.56	3.48	3.36	3.29	3.20	3.12	3.07	3.00	2.97	2.92	2.89	2.87
2.42	2.37	2.33	2.28	2.24	2.20	2.16	2.13	2.09	2.07	2.04	2.02	2.01
3.55	3.45	3.37	3.25	3.18	3.10	3.01	2.96	2.89	2.86	2.80	2.77	2.75
2.38	2.33	2.29	2.23	2.19	2.15	2.11	2.08	2.04	2.02	1.99	1.97	1.96
3.45	3.35	3.27	3.16	3.08	3.00	2.92	2.86	2.79	2.76	2.70	2.67	2.65
2.34	2.29	2.25	2.19	2.15	2.11	2.07	2.04	2.00	1.98	1.95	1.93	1.92
3.37	3.27	3.19	3.07	3.00	2.91	2.83	2.78	2.71	2.68	2.62	2.59	2.57
2.31	2.26	2.21	2.15	2.11	2.07	2.02	2.00	1.96	1.94	1.91	1.90	1.88
3.30	3.19	3.12	3.00	2.92	2.84	2.76	2.70	2.63	2.60	2.54	2.51	2.49
2.28	2.23	2.18	2.12	2.08	2.04	1.99	1.96	1.92	1.90	1.87	1.85	1.84
3.23	3.13	3.05	2.94	2.86	2.77	2.69	2.63	2.56	2.53	2.47	2.44	2.42
2.25	2.20	2.15	2.09	2.05	2.00	1.96	1.93	1.80	1.87	1.84	1.82	1.81
3.17	3.07	2.99	2.88	2.80	2.72	2.63	2.58	2.51	2.47	2.42	2.38	2.36
2.23	2.18	2.13	2.07	2.03	1.98	1.93	1.91	1.87	1.84	1 81	1 80	1.78
3.12	3.02	2.94	2.83	2.75	2.67	2.58	2.53	2.46	2.42	2.37	2.33	2.31
2.20	2.14	2.10	2.04	2.00	1.96	1.91	1.88	1.84	1.82	1.79	1.77	1.76
3.07	2.97	2.89	2.78	2.70	2.62	2.53	2.48	2.41	2.37	2.32	2.28	2.26
2.18	2.13	2.09	2.02	1.98	1.94	1.89	1.86	1.82	1.80	1.76	1.74	1.73
3.03	2.93	2.85	2.74	2.66	2.58	2.49	2.44	2.36	2.33	2.27	2.23	2.21
2.16	2.11	2.06	2.00	1.96	1.92	1.87	1.84	1.80	1.77	1.74	1.72	1.71
2.99	2.89	2.81	2.70	2.62	2.54	2.45	2.40	2.32	2.29	2.23	2.19	2.17
2.15	2.10	2.05	1.99	1.95	1.90	1.85	1.82	1.78	1.76	1.72	1.70	1.69
2.96	2.86	2.77	2.66	2.58	2.50	2.41	2.36	2.28	2.25	2.19	2.15	2.13
2.13	2.08	2.03	1.97	1.93	1.88	1.84	1.80	1.76	1.74	1.71	1.68	1.67
2.93	2.83	2.74	2.63	2.55	2.47	2.38	2.33	2.25	2.21	2.16	2.12	2.10
2.12	2.06	2.02	1.96	1.91	1.87	1.81	1.78	1.75	1.72	1.69	1.67	1.65
2.90	2.80	2.71	2.60	2.52	2.44	2.35	2.30	2.22	2.18	2.13	2.09	2.06
2.10	2.05	2.00	1.94	1.90	1.85	1.80	1.77	1.73	1.71	1.68	1.65	1.64
2.87	2.77	2.68	2.57	2.49	2.41	2.32	2.27	2.19	2.15	2.10	2.06	2.03

STATISTICAL TABLE F   (continued)

						Degrees of Freedom					
	1	**2**	**3**	**4**	**5**	**6**	**7**	**8**	**9**	**10**	**11**
30	4.17	3.32	2.92	2.69	2.53	2.42	2.34	2.27	2.21	2.16	2.12
	7.56	5.39	4.51	4.02	3.70	3.47	3.30	3.17	3.06	2.98	2.90
32	4.15	3.30	2.90	2.67	2.51	2.40	2.32	2.25	2.19	2.14	2.10
	7.50	5.34	4.46	3.97	3.66	3.42	3.25	3.12	3.01	2.94	2.86
34	4.13	3.28	2.88	2.65	2.49	2.38	2.30	2.23	2.17	2.12	2.08
	7.44	5.29	4.42	3.93	3.61	3.38	3.21	3.08	2.97	2.89	2.82
36	4.11	3.26	2.86	2.63	2.48	2.36	2.28	2.21	2.15	2.10	2.06
	7.39	5.25	4.38	3.89	3.58	3.35	3.18	3.04	2.94	2.86	2.78
38	4.10	3.25	2.85	2.62	2.46	2.35	2.26	2.19	2.14	2.09	2.05
	7.35	5.21	4.34	3.86	3.54	3.32	3.15	3.02	2.91	2.82	2.75
40	4.08	3.23	2.84	2.61	2.45	2.34	2.25	2.18	2.12	2.07	2.04
	7.31	5.18	4.31	3.83	3.51	3.29	3.12	2.99	2.88	2.80	2.73
42	4.07	3.22	2.83	2.59	2.44	2.32	2.24	2.17	2.11	2.06	2.02
	7.27	5.15	4.29	3.80	3.49	3.26	3.10	2.96	2.86	2.77	2.70
44	4.06	3.21	2.82	2.58	2.43	2.31	2.23	2.16	2.10	2.05	2.01
	7.24	5.12	4.26	3.78	3.46	3.24	3.07	2.94	2.84	2.75	2.68
46	4.05	3.20	2.81	2.57	2.42	2.30	2.22	2.14	2.09	2.04	2.00
	7.21	5.10	4.24	3.76	3.44	3.22	3.05	2.92	2.82	2.73	2.66
48	4.04	3.19	2.80	2.56	2.41	2.30	2.21	2.14	2.08	2.03	1.99
	7.19	5.08	4.22	3.74	3.42	3.20	3.04	2.90	2.80	2.71	2.64
50	4.03	3.18	2.79	2.56	2.40	2.29	2.20	2.13	2.07	2.02	1.98
	7.17	5.06	4.20	3.72	3.41	3.18	3.02	2.88	2.78	2.70	2.62
55	4.02	3.17	2.78	2.54	2.38	2.27	2.18	2.11	2.05	2.00	1.97
	7.12	5.01	4.16	3.68	3.37	3.15	2.98	2.85	2.75	2.66	2.59
60	4.00	3.15	2.76	2.52	2.37	2.25	2.17	2.10	2.04	1.99	1.95
	7.08	4.98	4.13	3.65	3.34	3.12	2.95	2.82	2.75	2.63	2.56
65	3.99	3.14	2.75	2.51	2.36	2.24	2.15	2.08	2.02	1.98	1.94
	7.04	4.95	4.10	3.62	3.31	3.09	2.93	2.79	2.70	2.61	2.54
70	3.98	3.13	2.74	2.50	2.35	2.32	2.14	2.07	2.01	1.97	1.93
	7.01	4.92	4.08	3.60	3.29	3.07	2.91	2.77	2.67	2.59	2.51
80	3.96	3.11	2.72	2.48	2.33	2.21	2.12	2.05	1.99	1.95	1.91
	6.96	4.88	4.04	3.56	3.25	3.04	2.87	2.74	2.64	2.55	2.48

Degrees of Freedom for Denominator

for Numerator

12	14	16	20	24	30	40	50	75	100	200	500	∞
2.09	2.04	1.99	1.93	1.89	1.84	1.79	1.76	1.72	1.69	1.66	1.64	1.62
2.84	2.74	2.66	2.55	2.47	2.38	2.29	2.24	2.16	2.13	2.07	2.03	2.01
2.07	2.02	1.97	1.91	1.86	1.82	1.76	1.74	1.69	1.67	1.64	1.61	1.59
2.80	2.70	2.62	2.51	2.42	2.34	2.25	2.20	2.12	2.08	2.02	1.98	1.96
2.05	2.00	1.95	1.89	1.84	1.80	1.74	1.71	1.67	1.64	1.61	1.59	1.57
2.76	2.66	2.58	2.47	2.38	2.30	2.21	2.15	2.08	2.04	1.98	1.94	1.91
2.03	1.89	1.93	1.87	1.82	1.78	1.72	1.69	1.65	1.62	1.59	1.56	1.55
2.72	2.62	2.54	2.43	2.35	2.26	2.17	2.12	2.04	2.00	1.94	1.90	1.87
2.02	1.96	1.92	1.85	1.80	1.76	1.71	1.67	1.63	1.60	1.57	1.54	1.53
2.69	2.59	2.51	2.40	2.32	2.22	2.14	2.08	2.00	1.97	1.90	1.86	1.84
2.00	1.95	1.90	1.84	1.79	1.74	1.69	1.66	1.61	1.59	1.55	1.53	1.51
2.66	2.56	2.49	2.37	2.29	2.20	2.11	2.05	1.97	1.94	1.88	1.84	1.81
1.90	1.94	1.89	1.82	1.78	1.73	1.68	1.64	1.60	1.57	1.54	1.51	1.49
2.64	2.54	2.46	2.35	2.26	2.17	2.08	2.02	1.94	1.91	1.85	1.80	1.78
1.98	1.92	1.88	1.81	1.76	1.72	1.66	1.63	1.58	1.56	1.52	1.50	1.48
2.62	2.52	2.44	2.32	2.24	2.15	2.06	2.09	1.92	1.88	1.82	1.78	1.75
1.97	1.91	1.87	1.80	1.75	1.71	1.65	1.62	1.57	1.54	1.51	1.48	1.46
2.60	2.50	2.42	2.30	2.22	2.13	2.04	1.98	1.90	1.86	1.80	1.76	1.72
1.96	1.90	1.86	1.79	1.74	1.70	1.64	1.61	1.56	1.53	1.50	1.47	1.45
2.58	2.48	2.40	2.28	2.20	2.11	2.02	1.96	1.88	1.84	1.78	1.73	1.70
1.95	1.90	1.85	1.78	1.74	1.69	1.63	1.60	1.55	1.52	1.48	1.46	1.44
2.56	2.46	2.39	2.26	2.18	2.10	2.00	1.94	1.86	1.82	1.76	1.71	1.68
1.93	1.88	1.83	1.76	1.72	1.67	1.61	1.58	1.52	1.50	1.46	1.43	1.41
2.53	2.43	2.35	2.23	2.15	2.06	1.96	1.90	1.82	1.78	1.71	1.66	1.64
1.92	1.86	1.81	1.75	1.70	1.65	1.59	1.56	1.50	1.48	1.44	1.41	1.39
2.50	2.40	2.32	2.20	2.12	2.03	1.93	1.87	1.79	1.74	1.68	1.63	1.60
1.90	1.85	1.80	1.73	1.68	1.63	1.57	1.54	1.49	1.46	1.42	1.39	1.37
2.47	2.37	2.30	2.18	2.09	2.00	1.90	1.84	1.76	1.71	1.64	1.60	1.56
1.89	1.84	1.79	1.72	1.67	1.62	1.56	1.53	1.47	1.45	1.40	1.37	1.35
2.45	2.35	2.28	2.15	2.07	1.98	1.88	1.82	1.74	1.69	1.62	1.56	1.53
1.88	1.82	1.77	1.70	1.65	1.60	1.54	1.51	1.45	1.42	1.38	1.35	1.32
2.41	2.32	2.24	2.11	2.03	1.94	1.84	1.78	1.70	1.65	1.57	1.52	1.49

STATISTICAL TABLE F   (continued)

Degrees of Freedom

Degrees of Freedom for Denominator	1	2	3	4	5	6	7	8	9	10	11
100	3.94	3.09	2.70	2.46	2.30	2.19	2.10	2.03	1.97	1.92	1.88
	6.90	4.82	3.98	3.51	3.20	2.99	2.82	2.69	2.59	2.51	2.43
125	3.92	3.07	2.68	2.44	2.29	2.17	2.08	2.01	1.95	1.90	1.86
	6.84	4.78	3.94	3.47	3.17	2.95	2.79	2.65	2.56	2.47	2.40
150	3.91	3.06	2.67	2.43	2.27	2.16	2.07	2.00	1.94	1.89	1.85
	6.81	4.75	3.91	3.44	3.13	2.92	2.76	2.62	2.53	2.44	2.37
200	3.89	3.04	2.65	2.41	2.26	2.14	2.05	1.98	1.92	1.87	1.83
	6.76	4.71	3.38	3.41	3.11	2.90	2.73	2.60	2.50	2.41	2.34
400	3.86	3.02	2.62	2.39	2.23	2.12	2.03	1.96	1.90	1.85	1.81
	6.70	4.66	3.83	3.36	3.06	2.85	2.69	2.55	2.46	2.37	2.29
1000	3.85	3.00	2.61	2.38	2.22	2.10	2.02	1.95	1.89	1.84	1.80
	6.66	4.62	3.80	3.34	3.04	2.82	2.66	2.53	2.43	2.34	2.26
∞	3.84	2.99	2.60	2.37	2.21	2.09	2.01	1.94	1.88	1.83	1.79
	6.64	4.60	3.78	3.32	3.02	2.80	2.64	2.51	2.41	2.32	2.24

Source: From R. A. Fisher and F. Yates (1974). *Statistical Tables for Biological, Agricultural and Medical Research* (6th ed.). Edinburgh Gate, Harlow, Essex: Addison Wesley Longman. Copyright © 1963 R. A. Fisher and F. Yates. Reprinted by permission of Pearson Education Limited.

for Numerator

12	14	16	20	24	30	40	50	75	100	200	500	∞
1.85	1.79	1.75	1.68	1.63	1.57	1.51	1.48	1.42	1.39	1.34	1.30	1.28
2.36	2.26	2.19	2.06	1.98	1.89	1.79	1.73	1.64	1.59	1.51	1.46	1.43
1.83	1.77	1.72	1.65	1.60	1.55	1.49	1.45	1.39	1.36	1.31	1.27	1.25
2.33	2.23	2.15	2.03	1.94	1.85	1.75	1.68	1.59	1.54	1.46	1.40	1.37
1.82	1.76	1.71	1.64	1.59	1.54	1.47	1.44	1.37	1.34	1.29	1.25	1.22
2.30	2.20	2.12	2.00	1.91	1.83	1.72	1.66	1.56	1.51	1.43	1.37	1.33
1.80	1.74	1.69	1.62	1.57	1.52	1.45	1.42	1.35	1.32	1.26	1.22	1.19
2.28	1.17	2.09	1.97	1.88	1.79	1.69	1.62	1.53	1.48	1.39	1.33	1.28
1.78	1.72	1.67	1.60	1.54	1.49	1.42	1.38	1.32	1.28	1.22	1.16	1.13
2.23	2.12	2.04	1.92	1.84	1.74	1.64	1.57	1.47	1.42	1.32	1.24	1.19
1.76	1.70	1.65	1.58	1.53	1.47	1.41	1.36	1.30	1.26	1.19	1.13	1.08
2.20	2.09	2.01	1.89	1.81	1.71	1.61	1.54	1.44	1.38	1.28	1.19	1.11
1.75	1.69	1.64	1.57	1.52	1.46	1.40	1.35	1.28	1.24	1.17	1.11	1.00
2.18	2.07	1.99	1.87	1.79	1.69	1.59	1.52	1.41	1.36	1.25	1.15	1.00

Statistical Table G: Statistical Power

This table represents the number of participants needed in various research designs to produce a power of .80 with alpha = .05. For ANOVA designs, the number of participants per condition is the tabled number divided by the number of conditions in the design. Small, medium, and large effect sizes are .10, .30 and .50, except for one-way and factorial ANOVA, where they are .10, .25, and .40, respectively.

STATISTICAL TABLE G   Statistical Power

	Estimated Effect Size		
	Small	Medium	Large
Correlation coefficient (r)			
	783	85	28
One-way (between participants) ANOVA (F)			
2 groups	786	128	52
3 groups	966	156	63
6 groups	1290	210	84
Factorial (between-participants) ANOVA (F)			
2 × 2	788	132	56
2 × 3	972	162	66
3 × 3	1206	198	90
2 × 2 × 2	792	136	64
Contingency table (χ^2)			
1 df	785	87	31
2 df	964	107	39
3 df	1090	121	44
4 df	1194	133	48
Multiple regression (R)			
2 IVs	481	67	30
3 IVs	547	76	34
5 IVs	645	91	42
8 IVs	757	107	50

Source: From Cohen, J. (1992). A power primer. *Psychological Bulletin, 112,* 155–159. Copyright © 1992 by the American Psychological Association. Adapted with permission.

F
Using Computers to Collect Data

As we have seen throughout this book, computers are commonly used in the behavioral sciences to perform statistical analyses and to write and edit research reports. But computers are also being used to a greater and greater extent to collect data from research participants. This Appendix presents a brief summary of the use of computers to collect data, both in the lab and over the Internet.

Collecting data with computers has several important advantages. For one, computers can help standardize conditions by ensuring that each participant receives the exact same stimuli, in the exact same order, and for the exact same amount of time. The computer can also be programmed to automatically assign participants to experimental conditions—for instance, by using blocked random assignment—and to present different information to the participants in the different conditions. In many cases this allows the experimenter to leave the lab room after the research participant starts the procedure, thereby reducing the possibility of distraction, demand characteristics, and experimenter bias.

Another advantage of computers is that they allow researchers to present and collect information in ways that would be difficult or impossible to do without them. In terms of presenting information, computers can randomly select stimuli from lists, allowing counterbalancing across research participants. They can also keep track of which stimuli have been presented, and in which order. Moreover, computers can present a wide variety of stimuli, including text, graphics, audio, and video. Computers also allow researchers to present stimuli at exactly timed durations, which may be extremely short. For instance, in priming experiments, it may desired that the stimulus (such as an image) be presented for exactly 50 milliseconds (1/20 of a second), so that although participants may react to it at an unconscious level, they are not aware of seeing it.

In terms of the dependent variables, computers can collect virtually any data that could be collected in other ways, including free- and fixed-format responses, reaction times, and even in some cases physiological measures. Furthermore, the computer can be programmed so that the participant must answer each item before he or she continues, thus reducing the amount of missing data. When participants complete measures on computers, the data can normally be transferred directly to the statistical software package, alleviating the need to enter the data manually.

Despite these many advantages, using computers also has some disadvantages. For one, although they become cheaper every year, computers are still more expensive than paper-and-pencil measures. Furthermore, because each participant mush have his or her own computer, the number of participants that can be run at the same time will be limited. It is also possible that some people will not pay attention to or will not follow the instructions given by the computer, and the experimenter may not be able to check up on whether they have. In some cases the computer may malfunction.

A number of software packages are available for use in collecting data; these are summarized in Table F.1. All of these packages perform the following basic functions:

1. Allow the experimenter to indicate which stimuli are to be presented, in which order, and which measures are to be collected. In some cases the experimental setup uses a graphical interface; in other cases the setup is more like a programming language.

2. Randomly assign participants to experimental conditions and present different instructions and stimuli in the different conditions.

3. Present a variety of stimuli, including text, graphics, video, and audio. These stimuli can be chosen randomly from lists, grouped into blocks, and placed in specific locations on the screen.

4. Collecting responses, including free- and fixed-format self-report measures. These responses can be assessed through keyboard, mouse, voice, or button-box input.

5. Precisely time the duration at which stimuli are displayed as well as the elapsed time between the presentation of a stimulus and the participant's response.

6. Write all collected data to a file suitable for importing into software packages.

Other functions that are available on some packages are the ability to collect visual and physiological data and to collect data over the Internet. If you are planning to use computers to conduct research, you may wish to check with your instructor to see if any of these programs are available at your college or university.

STATISTICAL TABLE F.1   Some Computer Software Packages for Collecting Data from Research Participants

Program	Platforms/Comments	Web Site
DirectRT	Windows	*www.empirisoft.com/directrt*
E-prime	Windows	*www.pstnet.com/e-prime/ default.htm*
Inquisit	Windows	*www.millisecond.com*
Matlab	Windows & Mac	*www.mathworks.com/products/ matlab/*
Medialab	Windows	*www.empirisoft.com/medialab*
Presentation	Windows freeware; collects physiological measures	*www.neurobehavioralsystems.com*
Psyctoolbox	Works with Matlab to collect visual data such as gaze tracking	*http://psychtoolbox.org*
PsyScope	Mac freeware	*http://psyscope.psy.cmu.edu*
RSVP	Mac freeware	*www.cog.brown.edu/~tarr/rsvp.html*
Superlab	Windows & Mac	*www.superlab.com*
Perseus Survey Solutions	Windows; Web-based survey collection	*www.perseus.com*

Glossary

A priori comparisons See *planned comparisons*.

A-B-A design A research design in which measurements are made before, during, and after the change in the independent variable occurs.

Abstracts Written summaries of research reports.

Acquiescent responding (yeah-saying bias) A form of reactivity in which people tend to agree with whatever questions they are asked.

Alpha (α) The probability of making a Type 1 error.

Alternative explanations The possibility that a confounding variable, rather than the independent variable, caused the differences in the dependent measure.

Analysis of Covariance (ANCOVA) An analysis in which the means of the dependent variable in the different experimental conditions are adjusted or controlled for the influence of one or more quantitative variables on the dependent variable.

Analysis of Variance (ANOVA) A statistical procedure designed to compare the means of the dependent variable across the conditions of an experimental research design.

ANCOVA See *Analysis of Covariance*.

ANOVA See *Analysis of Variance*.

ANOVA summary table A table that displays the ANOVA calculations including F and its associated p-value.

Applied research Research designed to investigate issues that have implications for everyday life and to provide solutions to real-world problems.

Archival research Research that uses existing records of public behavior as data.

Arithmetic mean ($\bar{x}$) A measure of central tendency equal to the sum of the scores on the variable divided by the sample size (N).

Artifacts Aspects of the research methodology that may produce confounding.

Attrition A threat to internal validity in longitudinal research when participants who stay in the research are different from those who drop out.

Bar chart A visual display of a frequency distribution.

Baseline measure An initial measurement of the dependent variable in a before-after research design.

Basic research Research designed to answer fundamental questions rather than to address a specific real-world problem.

Before-after research designs Designs in which the dependent measure is assessed both prior to and after the experimental manipulation has occurred.

Behavioral categories The specific set of observations that are recorded in systematic observational research.

Behavioral measures Measured variables designed to directly measure an individual's actions.

Behavioral research Research designed to study the thoughts, feelings, and behavior of human beings and animals.

Beta (β) The probability of making a Type 2 error.

Beta weights See *regression coefficients*.

Between-groups variance In ANOVA, a measure of the variability of the dependent variable across the experimental conditions.

Between-participants designs Experiments in which the comparison of the scores on the dependent variable is between the participants in the different levels of the independent variable and each individual is in only one level.

Binomial distribution The sampling distribution of events that have two equally likely outcomes.

Bivariate statistics Statistical procedures used to analyze the relationship between two variables.

Blocked random assignment A method of random assignment in which participants are assigned to conditions in sequential blocks, each of which contains all of the conditions.

Canonical correlation A statistical procedure used to assess the relationships between one or more quantitative independent variables and a set of quantitative dependent variables.

Carryover A situation that can occur in a repeated-measures design when the effects of one level of the manipulation are still present when the dependent measure is assessed for another level of the manipulation.

Case studies Descriptive records of one or more individual's experiences and behavior.

Cells The conditions in factorial designs.

Census A survey of an entire population.

Central limit theorem A mathematical statement that demonstrates that as the sample size increases, the sample mean provides a more precise estimate of the population mean.

Central tendency The point in the distribution of a quantitative variable around which the scores are centered.

Chi-square (χ^2) statistic A statistic used to assess the relationship between two nominal variables.

Cluster sampling A probability sampling technique in which a population is divided into groups (called *clusters*) for which there are sampling frames and then some of the clusters are chosen to be sampled.

Coefficient of determination (r^2) The proportion of variance accounted for by the correlation coefficient.

Common-causal variables In a correlational research design, variables that are not part of the research hypothesis but that cause both the predictor and the outcome variable and thus produce a spurious correlation between them.

Comparison group A group that is expected to be similar to the experimental group but that (because random assignment has not been used) is not expected to be equivalent to the experimental group.

Comparison-group before-after design Research in which more than one group of individuals is studied and the dependent measure is assessed for all groups before and after the intervening event.

Comparison-group design Research that uses more than one group of individuals that differ in terms of whether they have had or have not had the experience of interest.

Complex comparisons Means comparisons in which more than two means are compared at the same time.

Conceptual replication A replication that investigates the relationship between the same conceptual variables that were studied in previous research but tests the hypothesis using different operational definitions of the independent variable and/or the dependent variable.

Conceptual variables Abstract ideas that form the basis of research designs and that are measured by measured variables.

Concurrent validity A form of criterion validity that involves evaluation of the relationship between a self-report and a behavioral measure that are assessed at the same time.

Conditions A term used to describe the levels of an experimental manipulation in one-way experimental designs, or the cells in a factorial design.

Confidence interval A range of scores within which a population parameter is likely to fall.

Confirmatory factor analysis A type of structural equation analysis that tests whether a set of collected data is consistent with a hypothesized set of factor loadings.

Confound checks Measures used to determine whether the manipulation has unwittingly caused differences on confounding variables.

Confounding A situation that occurs when one or more variables are mixed up with the independent variable, thereby making it impossible to determine which of the variables has produced changes in the dependent variable.

Confounding variables Variables other than the independent variable on which the participants in one experimental condition differ systematically from those in other conditions.

Construct validity The extent to which a measured variable actually measures the conceptual variable that it is designed to assess.

Constructive replication A replication that investigates the same hypothesis as the original experiment (either in the form of an exact or a conceptual replication) but also adds new conditions to the original experiment to assess the specific variables that might change the previously observed relationship.

Content analysis The systematic coding of free-format data.

Content validity The degree to which a measured variable appears to have adequately sampled from the potential domain of topics that might relate to the conceptual variable of interest.

Contingency table A table that displays the number of individuals who have each value on each of two nominal variables.

Contrast analysis A method of conducting a priori means comparisons that can be used for either pairwise or complex comparisons.

Contrast tests Statistical procedures used to make complex means comparisons.

Contrast weights Numbers set by the researcher in a contrast analysis that indicate how the group means are to be compared.

Control condition The level of the independent variable in which the situation of interest was not created. (Compare with *experimental condition.*)

Convenience samples Nonprobability samples containing whatever individuals are readily available, with no attempt to make the samples representative of a population.

Convergent validity The extent to which a measured variable is found to be related to other measured variables designed to measure the same conceptual variable.

Converging operations Using more than one measurement or research approach to study a given topic, with the hope that all of the approaches will produce similar results.

Correlation matrix A table showing the correlations of many variables with each other.

Correlational research Research that involves the measurement of two or more relevant variables and an assessment of the relationship between or among those variables.

Counterbalancing A procedure in which the order of the conditions in a repeated-measures design is arranged so that each condition occurs equally often in each order.

Cover story A false or misleading statement by the experimenter about what is being studied that is used to reduce the possibility of demand characteristics.

Cramer's statistic (V_c) The effect size statistic in contingency tables other than 2 × 2.

Criterion validity An assessment of validity calculated though the correlation of a self-report measure with a behavioral measured (criterion) variable.

Criterion variable The behavioral variable that is predicted when testing for criterion validity.

Cronbach's coefficient alpha (α) A measure of internal consistency that estimates the average correlation among all of the items on a scale.

Cross-sectional research designs Research in which comparisons are made across different age groups, but all groups are measured at the same time (compare with *longitudinal research designs*).

Crossover interaction An interaction in a 2 × 2 factorial design in which the two simple effects are opposite in direction.

Curvilinear relationships Nonlinear relationships that change in direction and, thus, cannot be described with a single straight line.

Data Information collected through formal observation or measurement.

Debriefing Information given to a participant immediately after an experiment has ended that is designed to both explain the purposes and procedures of the research and remove any harmful aftereffects of participation.

Deception The practice of not completely and fully informing research participants about the nature of a research project before they participate in it; sometimes used when the research could not be conducted if participants knew what was really being studied.

Deductive method The use of a theory to generate specific ideas that can be tested through research.

Degrees of freedom (df) The number of values that are free to vary given restrictions that have been placed on the data.

Demand characteristics Aspects of the research that allow participants to guess the research hypothesis.

Dependent variable In an experiment, the variable that is caused by the independent variable.

Descriptive research Research designed to answer questions about the current state of affairs.

Descriptive statistics Numbers, such as the *mean,* the *median,* the *mode,* the *standard deviation,* and the *variance,* that summarize the distribution of a measured variable.

Discriminant validity The extent to which a measured variable is found to be unrelated to other measured variables designed to assess different conceptual variables.

Dispersion The extent to which the scores in a sample are all tightly clustered around the central tendency or are more spread out away from it. Dispersion is normally measured using the *standard deviation* and the *variance*.

Distribution The pattern of scores observed on a measured variable.

Ecological validity The extent to which research is conducted in situations that are similar to the everyday life experiences of the participants.

Effect size A statistic that indexes the size of a relationship.

Empirical Based on systematic collection of data.

Equivalent-forms reliability A form of test-retest reliability in which two different but equivalent versions of the same measure are given at different times and the correlation between the scores on the two versions is assessed.

Eta (η) The effect size measure in the ANOVA.

Event sampling In systematic observation, the act of focusing in on specific behaviors to be observed.

Exact replication Research that repeats a previous research design as exactly as possible, keeping almost everything about the research the same as it was the first time around.

Experimental condition The level of the independent variable in which the situation of interest was created. (Compare with *control condition*.)

Experimental control The extent to which the experiment has eliminated effects on the dependent variable other than the effects of the independent variable.

Experimental manipulations The independent variable, created by the experimenter, in an experimental design.

Experimental realism The extent to which the experimental manipulation involves the participants in the research.

Experimental research Research that includes the manipulation of a given situation or experience for two or more groups of individuals who are initially created to be equivalent, followed by a measurement of the effect of that experience.

Experimental script A precise description of all aspects of the research procedure.

Experimenter bias A source of internal validity that occurs when an experimenter who knows the research hypothesis unknowingly communicates his or her expectations to the research participants.

Experimentwise alpha The probability of the researcher having made a Type 1 error in at least one of the statistical tests conducted during the research.

Exploratory factor analysis A multivariate statistical technique used to analyze the underlying pattern of correlations among a set of measured variables and to develop a simplified picture of the relationships among these variables.

External validity The extent to which the results of a research design can be generalized beyond the specific settings and participants used in the experiment to other places, people, and times.

Extraneous variables Variables other than the predictor variable that cause the outcome variable but that do not cause the predictor variable.

F In the ANOVA, a statistic that assesses the extent to which the means of the experimental conditions differ more than would be expected by chance.

Face validity The extent to which a measured variable appears to be an adequate measure of the conceptual variable.

Factor An independent variable in a factorial experimental design.

Factor scores In a factor analysis, the new summarizing variables that are created out of the original variables.

Factorial experimental designs Experimental research designs that have more than one independent variable.

Factors In a factor analysis, the sets of variables that are found to be correlated with each other.

Facts Information that is objectively true.

Falsifiable A characteristic of a theory or research hypothesis such that the variables of interest can be adequately measured and the expected relationship between the variables can be shown through research to be incorrect.

Field experiments Experimental research designs that are conducted in a natural environment such as a library, a factory, or a school rather than in a research laboratory.

Fisher Least Significant Difference (LSD) Test A post hoc means comparison test in which pairwise means comparisons are made only if the initial ANOVA F value is significant.

Fixed-format self-report measures Measured variables in which the respondent indicates his or her thoughts or feelings by answering a structured set of questions.

Focus group A type of unstructured interview in which a number of people are interviewed at the same time and share ideas with the interviewer and with each other.

Free-format self-report measures Measured variables in which respondents are asked to freely list their thoughts or feelings as they come to mind.

Frequency curve A visual display of a grouped or ungrouped frequency distribution that uses a line to indicate the frequencies.

Frequency distribution A statistical table that indicates how many individuals in a sample fall into each of a set of categories.

General In relation to a theory, summarizing many different outcomes.

General linear model (GLM) A set of mathematical procedures used by computer programs to compute multiple regression and ANOVA.

Generalization The extent to which relationships among conceptual variables can be demonstrated in a wide variety of people and with a wide variety of manipulated or measured variables.

Goodness of fit statistic In a structural equation analysis, a test that indicates how well the collected data fit the hypothesized relationships among the variables.

Grouped frequency distribution A statistical table that indicates how many individuals in a sample fall into each of a set of categories on a quantitative variable.

Guttman scale A fixed-format self-report scale in which the items are arranged in a cumulative order such that it is assumed that if a respondent answers one item correctly, he or she will also answer all previous items correctly.

Hierarchical multiple regression A multiple regression analysis in which the predictor variables are added into the regression equation in a predetermined order.

Hindsight bias The tendency to think that we could have predicted something that we probably could not have predicted.

Histogram A visual display of a grouped frequency distribution that uses bars to indicate the frequencies.

History threats Threats to internal validity that result from the potential influence of changes in the social climate during the course of a study.

Impact The extent to which the experimental manipulation creates the hoped-for changes in the conceptual independent variable.

Inclusion criteria The rules that determine whether a study is to be included in a meta-analysis.

Independent Two variables are said to be independent if there is no association between them.

Independent variable In an experiment, the variable that is manipulated by the researcher.

Individual sampling In systematic observation, the act of choosing which individuals will be observed.

Inductive method The observation of specific facts to get ideas about more general relationships among variables.

Inferential statistics Numbers, such as a p-value, that are used to specify the characteristics of a population on the basis of the data in a sample.

Informed consent The practice of providing research participants with information about the nature of the research project before they make a decision about whether to participate.

Institutional Review Board (IRB) A panel of at least five individuals, including at least one whose primary interest is in nonscientific domains, that determines the ethics of proposed research.

Interaction A pattern of means that may occur in a factorial experimental design when the influence of one independent variable on the dependent variable is different at different levels of another independent variable or variables.

Internal analysis In an experiment, an analysis in which the scores on the manipulation check measure are correlated with the scores on the dependent variable as an alternative test of the research hypothesis.

Internal consistency The extent to which the scores on the items of a scale correlate with each other and thus are all measuring true score rather than random error.

Internal validity   The extent to which changes in the dependent variable can confidently be attributed to the influence of the independent variable rather than to the potential influence of confounding variables.

Interrater reliability   The internal consistency of the ratings made by a group of judges.

Interval scale   A measured variable in which equal changes in the measured variable are known to correspond to equal changes in the conceptual variable being measured.

Interview   A survey that is read to a respondent either in person or over the telephone.

Items   Questions on a scale.

kappa (κ)   A statistic used to measure interrater reliability.

Latent variables   The conceptual variables or factors in a structural equation analysis.

Latin square design   A repeated-measures research design that is counterbalanced such that each condition appears equally often in each order and also follows equally often after each of the other conditions.

Laws   Principles that are so general that they are assumed to apply to all situations.

Levels   The specific situations created by the experimental manipulation.

Likert scale   A fixed-format self-report scale that consists of a series of items that indicate agreement or disagreement with the issue that is to be measured, each with a set of responses on which the respondents indicate their opinions.

Linear relationship   A relationship between two quantitative variables that can be approximated with a straight line.

Loglinear analysis   A statistical analysis that assesses the relationship between more than one nominal predictor variable and a nominal dependent variable.

Longitudinal research designs (panel studies)   Research in which the same individuals are measured more than one time and the time period between the measurements is long enough that changes in the variables of interest could occur (compare with *cross-sectional research designs*).

Main effect   Differences on the dependent measure across the levels of any one factor when all other factors in the experiment are controlled for.

Manipulated   See *experimental manipulation*.

Manipulation checks   Measures used to determine whether the experimental manipulation has had the intended impact on the conceptual independent variable of interest.

Margin of error   See *confidence interval*.

Marginal means   The means of the dependent variable within the levels of any one factor, which are combined across the levels of one or more other factors in the design.

Matched-group research design   A research design in which participants are measured on a variable of interest before the experiment begins and are then assigned to conditions on the basis of their scores on that variable.

Maturation threats   Threats to internal validity that involve potential changes in the research participants over time that are unrelated to the independent variable.

Mean   See *arithmetic mean*.

Mean deviation   See *mean deviation scores*.

Mean deviation scores   People's scores on the variable (X) minus the mean of the variable ($X - \bar{x}$).

Means comparisons   Statistical tests used when there are more than two condition means to determine which condition means are significantly different from each other.

Measured variables   Numbers that represent conceptual variables and that can be used in data analysis.

Measurement   The assignment of numbers to objects or events according to specific rules.

Measures   See *measured variables*.

Median   A measure of central tendency equal to the score at which half of the scores are higher and half of the scores are lower.

Mediating variable (mediator)   A variable that is caused by one variable and that in turn causes another variable.

Mediator   See *mediating variable*.

Meta-analysis   A statistical technique that uses the results of existing studies to integrate and draw conclusions about those studies.

Mixed factorial designs   Experimental designs that use both between-participants and repeated-measures factors.

Mode A measure of central tendency equal to the score or scores that occur most frequently on the variable.

Moderator variable A variable that produces an interaction of the relationship between two other variables such that the relationship between them is different at different levels of the moderator variable.

Mortality See *attrition*.

Multimodal A distribution that has more than one mode.

Multiple correlation coefficient (*R*) A statistic that indicates the extent to which all of the predictor variables in a regression analysis are able together to predict the outcome variable.

Multiple regression A statistical technique for analyzing a research design in which more than one predictor variable is used to predict a single outcome variable.

Multivariate Analysis of Variance (MANOVA) A statistical procedure used to assess the relationships between one or more nominal independent variables and a set of quantitative dependent variables.

Multivariate statistics Data analysis procedures designed to analyze more than one dependent variable at the same time.

Mundane realism. See *ecological validity*.

Naive experimenters Researchers who do not know the research hypothesis.

Naturalistic research Research designed to study the behavior of people or animals in their everyday lives.

Nominal variable A variable that names or identifies a particular characteristic.

Nomological net The pattern of correlations among a group of measured variables that provides evidence for the convergent and discriminant validity of the measures.

Nonlinear relationships Relationships between two quantitative variables that cannot be approximated with a straight line.

Nonreactive behavioral measures Behavioral measures that are designed to avoid reactivity because the respondent is not aware that the measurement is occurring, does not realize what the measure is designed to assess, or cannot change his or her responses.

Normal distribution Bell-shaped and symmetrical pattern of scores that is expected to be observed on most measured quantitative variables.

Null hypothesis (H_0) The assumption that observed data reflect only what would be expected from the sampling distribution.

Objective Free from personal bias or emotion.

Observational research Research that involves observing behavior and recording those observations objectively.

One-sided *p*-values *P*-values that consider only the likelihood that a relationship occurs in the predicted direction.

One-way experimental design An experiment that has one independent variable.

Operational definition A precise statement of how a conceptual variable is measured or manipulated.

Ordinal scale A measured variable in which the numbers indicate whether there is more or less of the conceptual variable but do not indicate the exact interval between the individuals on the conceptual variable.

Outliers Scores that are so extreme that their validity is questioned.

Oversampling A procedure used in stratified sampling in which a greater proportion of individuals are sampled from some strata than from others.

Pairwise comparisons Means comparisons in which any one condition mean is compared with any other condition mean.

Panel study See *longitudinal research designs*.

Parameter A number that represents the characteristics of a population. (Compare *descriptive statistic*.)

Parsimonious In relation to a theory, providing the simplest possible account of an outcome or outcomes.

Participant replication A replication that tests whether the findings of an existing study will hold up in a different population of research participants.

Participant variable A variable that represents differences among individuals on a demographic characteristic or a personality trait.

Participant-variable design A research design in which one of the variables represents measured differences among the research participants, such as demographic characteristics or personality traits.

Path analysis A form of multiple regression that assesses the relationships among a number of variables.

Path diagram A graphic display of the relationships among a number of variables.

Pearson product-moment correlation coefficient (r) A statistic used to assess the direction and the size of the relationship between two variables.

Peer review The process by which experts in a field judge whether a research report is suitable for publication in a scientific journal.

Percentile rank The percentage of scores on the variable that are lower than the score itself.

Phi (φ) The effect size statistic for 2 × 2 contingency tables.

Pilot test An initial practice test of a research procedure to see if it is working as expected.

Placebo effect An artifact that occurs when participants' expectations about what effect an experimental manipulation is supposed to have influence the dependent measure independently of the actual effect of the manipulation.

Planned comparisons Means comparisons in which specific differences between means, as predicted by the research hypothesis, are analyzed.

Population The entire group of people about whom a researcher wants to learn.

Post hoc comparisons Means comparisons that were not planned ahead of time. Usually these comparisons take into consideration that many comparisons are being made and thus control the experimentwise alpha.

Postexperimental interview Questions asked of participants after research has ended to probe for the effectiveness of the experimental manipulation and for suspicion.

Power The probability that the researcher will, on the basis of the observed data, be able to reject the null hypothesis given that the null hypothesis is actually false and thus should be rejected. Power is equal to $1 - \beta$.

Predictive validity A form of criterion validity in which a self-report measure is used to predict future behavior.

Probability sampling A sampling procedure used to ensure that each person in a population has a known chance of being selected to be part of the sample.

Probability value (p-value) The statistical likelihood of an observed pattern of data, calculated on the basis of the sampling distribution of the statistic.

Process debriefing A debriefing that involves an active attempt by an experimenter to undo any changes that might have occurred in participants during the research.

Program evaluation research Research designed to study intervention programs, such as after-school programs or prenatal care clinics, with the goal of determining whether the programs are effective in helping the people who make use of them.

Projective measure A measure of personalities in which an unstructured image, such as an inkblot, is shown to participants, who are asked to list what comes to mind as they view the image.

Proportion of explained variability The amount of the dependent (or outcome) variable accounted for by the independent (or predictor) variable.

Protocol See *experimental script.*

Psychophysiological measures Measured variables designed to assess the physiological functioning of the nervous or endocrine system.

Qualitative research Descriptive research that is focused on observing and describing events as they occur, with the goal of capturing all of the richness of everyday behavior.

Quantitative research Descriptive research in which the collected data are subjected to formal statistical analysis.

Quantitative variable A variable that is used to indicate the extent to which a person possesses a characteristic.

Quasi-experimental research designs Research designs in which the independent variable involves a grouping but in which equivalence has not been created between the groups.

Questionnaire A set of self-report items that is completed by respondents at their own pace, often without supervision.

Random assignment to conditions A method of ensuring that the participants in the different levels of the independent variable are equivalent before the experimental manipulation occurs.

Random error Chance fluctuations in measurement that influence scores on measured variables.

Range A measure of dispersion equal to the maximum observed score minus the minimum observed score on a variable.

Ratio scales Interval scales in which there is a zero point that is known to represent the complete lack of the conceptual variable.

Raw data The original collected data in a research project.

Reactivity Changes in responding that occur as a result of measurement.

Reciprocal causation In a correlational research design, the possibility that the predictor variable causes the outcome variable and the outcome variable also causes the predictor variable.

Regression coefficients Statistics that indicate the relationship between one of the predictor variables and the outcome variable in a multiple regression analysis.

Regression equation The equation that makes the best possible prediction of scores on the outcome variable using scores on one or more predictor variables.

Regression line On a scatterplot, the line that minimizes the squared distance of the points from the line.

Regression to the mean A statistical artifact such that whenever the same variable is measured more than once, if the correlation between the two measures is less than $r = 1.00$ or greater than $r = -1.00$, then the individuals will tend to score more toward the average score of the group on the second measure than they did on the first measure, even if nothing has changed between the two measures.

Reliability The extent to which a measured variable is free from random error.

Repeated-measures designs Experiments in which the same people participate in more than one condition of an experiment, thereby creating equivalence, and the differences across the various levels are assessed within the same participants.

Replication The repeating of research, either exactly or with modifications.

Representative sample A sample that is approximately the same as the population in every respect.

Research design A specific method used to collect, analyze, and interpret data.

Research hypothesis A specific and falsifiable prediction regarding the relationship between or among two or more variables.

Research programs Collections of experiments in which a topic of interest is systematically studied through conceptual and constructive replications over a period of time.

Research report A document that presents scientific findings using a standardized written format.

Response rate The percentage of people who actually complete a questionnaire and return it to the investigator.

Restriction of range A circumstance that occurs when most participants have similar scores on a variable that is being correlated with another variable. Restriction of range reduces the absolute value of the correlation coefficient.

Retesting effects Reactivity that occurs when the responses on the second administration are influenced by respondents having been given the same or similar measures before.

Reversal design See *A-B-A design*.

Reverse causation In a correlational research design, the possibility that the outcome variable causes the predictor variable rather than vice versa.

Review paper A document that discusses the research in a given area with the goals of summarizing the existing findings, drawing conclusions about the conditions under which relationships may or may not occur, linking the research findings to other areas of research, and making suggestions for further research.

Running head A short label that identifies the research topic and that appears at the top of the pages of a journal article.

Sample The group of people who actually participate in a research project.

Sampling Methods of selecting people to participate in a research project, usually with the goal of being able to use these people to make inferences about a population.

Sampling bias What occurs when a sample is not actually representative of the population because the probability with which members of the population have been selected for participation is not known.

Sampling distribution The distribution of all the possible values of a statistic.

Sampling distribution of the mean The set of all possible means of samples of a given size taken from a population.

Sampling frame A list indicating an entire population.

Scales Fixed-format self-report measures that contain more than one item (such as an intelligence test or a measure of self-esteem).

Scaling Specification of the relationship between the numbers on the measured variable and the values of the conceptual variable.

Scatterplot A graph showing the relationship between two quantitative variables in which a point for each individual is plotted at the intersection of their scores on the predictor and the outcome variables.

Scheffé Means Comparison Test A post hoc means comparison test in which the critical F value is adjusted to take into consideration the number of possible comparisons.

Scientific fraud The intentional alteration or fabrication of scientific data.

Scientific method The set of assumptions, rules, and procedures that scientists use when conducting research.

Selection threats Threats to internal validity that occur whenever individuals select themselves into groups rather than being randomly assigned to the groups.

Self-promotion A type of reactivity in which the research participants respond in a way that they think will make them look intelligent, knowledgeable, caring, healthy, and nonprejudiced.

Self-report measures Measures in which individuals are asked to respond to questions posed by an interviewer or on a questionnaire.

Semantic differential A fixed-format self-report scale in which the topic being evaluated is presented once at the top of the page and the items consist of pairs of adjectives located at the two endpoints of a standard response format.

Significance level See *alpha*.

Simple effect The effect of one factor within one level of another factor.

Simple random sampling A probabilistic sampling technique in which each person in the population has an equal chance of being included in the sample.

Simulation study Research in which participants are fully informed about the nature of the research and asked to behave "as if" they were in a social setting of interest.

Simultaneous multiple regression A multiple regression analysis in which all of the predictor variables are simultaneously used to predict the outcome variable.

Single-group before-after design Research that uses a single group of participants who are measured before and after they have had the experience of interest.

Single-group design Research that uses a single group of participants who are measured after they have had the experience of interest.

Single-participant research designs Research in which a single individual, or a small group of individuals, is studied over a period of time.

Skewed In relation to a distribution of scores, not symmetrical.

Snowball sampling A nonprobabilistic sampling technique in which one or more members of a population are located and used to lead the researchers to other members of the population.

Social desirability A type of reactivity in which research participants present themselves in a positive or socially acceptable way to the researcher.

Split-half reliability A measure of internal consistency that involves correlating the respondents' scores on one half of the items with their scores on the other half of the items.

Spurious relationship A relationship between two variables that is produced by a common-causal variable.

Standard deviation (*s*) A measure of dispersion equal to the square root of the variance.

Standard error See *standard error of the mean*.

Standard error of the mean The theoretical standard deviation of the means in the sampling distribution of the mean.

Standard normal distribution A hypothetical population distribution of standard scores.

Standard score A number that represents the distance of a score from the mean of the variable (the mean deviation) expressed in standard deviation units:

$$\left(\frac{x - \bar{x}}{s}\right)$$

Standardization of conditions The goal of treating all experimental participants in exactly the same way, with the single exception of the manipulation itself.

States Personality variables that are expected to change within the same person over a short period of time.

Statistically nonsignificant The conclusion to not reject the null hypothesis, made when the p-value is greater than alpha ($p > .05$).

Statistically significant The conclusion to reject the null hypothesis, made when the p-value is smaller than alpha ($p < .05$).

Statistics Mathematical methods used to systematically organize and analyze data.

Stem and leaf plot A method of graphically summarizing raw data such that the original data values can still be seen.

Stepwise multiple regression A multiple regression analysis in which the predictor variables are entered into the analysis according to the extent to which they increase the multiple R.

Strata Population subgroups used in stratified sampling.

Stratified sampling A probability sampling technique that involves dividing a sample into subgroups (or *strata*) and then selecting samples from each of these groups.

Structural equation analysis A multivariate statistical procedure that tests whether the actual relationships among a set of collected variables conform to a theoretical prediction about how those variables should be related.

Structured interview An interview that uses fixed-format, self-report questions.

Student's *t* A statistic, derived from a theoretical set of sampling distributions that become smaller as the degrees of freedom increase, that is used in testing differences between means and in creating confidence intervals.

Sum of squares (*SS*) The sum of the squared mean deviations of a variable: $\Sigma(X - \bar{x})^2$.

Survey A series of self-report measures administered through either an interview or a written questionnaire.

Suspicion check One or more questions asked of participants at the end of research to determine whether they believed the experimental manipulation or guessed the research hypothesis.

Systematic error The influence on a measured variable of other conceptual variables that are not part of the conceptual variable of interest.

Systematic observation Observation following a fixed set of decisions about which observations are to be made on which people and in which times and places.

Systematic random sampling A probability sampling technique that involves selecting every nth person from a sampling frame.

***T* test** A statistical test used to determine whether two observed means are statistically different. T is a special case of the F statistic.

Tautological A characteristic of a theory or research hypothesis such that it cannot be disconfirmed.

Test-retest reliability The extent to which scores on the same measured variable correlate with each other on two different measurements given at two different times.

Theory An integrated set of principles that explains and predicts many, but not all, observed relationships within a given domain of inquiry.

Think-aloud protocol A free-response measure in which participants verbalize the thoughts they are having as they complete a task.

Time sampling In systematic observation, the act of observing individuals for certain amounts of time.

Time-series designs Longitudinal research designs in which the dependent measure is assessed for one or more groups more than twice, at regular intervals, both before and after the experience of interest occurs.

Traits Personality variables that are not expected to vary (or at most to vary only slowly) within people over time.

Trimming A method of deleting outliers from the distribution of a variable in which the most extreme scores on each end of the distribution are simultaneously deleted.

True score The part of a scale score that is not random error.

Tukey Honestly Significant Difference (HSD) Test A post hoc means comparison test that controls for experimentwise alpha.

Two-sided *p*-values P-values that consider the likelihood that a relationship can occur either in the expected or the unexpected direction.

Type 1 error Rejection of the null hypothesis when it is really true; Type 1 errors occur with probability equal to alpha.

Type 2 error Failure to reject the null hypothesis

when the null hypothesis is really false. Type 2 errors occur with probability equal to beta.

Unbiased estimator   A statistic, such as the sample mean, that does not consistently overestimate or underestimate the population parameter.

Univariate statistics   Data analysis procedures that use one dependent variable.

Unrelated-experiments technique   An experimental technique in which participants are told that they will be participating in two separate experiments. In reality, there is only one experiment, and the experimental manipulation is created in the "first experiment," and the dependent measure is collected in the "second experiment."

Unstructured interview   An interview that uses free-format, self-report questions.

Values   Personal beliefs of an individual.

Variable   Any attribute that can assume different values—for instance, among different people or across different times or places.

Variance (s^2)   A measure of dispersion equal to the sum of squares divided by the sample size (N).

Within-groups variance   A measure of the variability of the dependent variable across the participants within the experimental conditions in ANOVA.

Within-participants (within-subjects) design   See *repeated-measures designs.*

Z score   See *standard score.*

References

Adair, J. G., Dushenko, T. W., & Lindsay, R. C. L. (1985). Ethical regulations and their impact on research practice. *American Psychologist, 40,* 59–72.

Aiken, L. S., & West, S. G. (1991). *Multiple regression: Testing and interpreting interactions.* Newbury Park, CA: Sage.

Ainsworth, M. D. S., Blehar, M. C., Waters, E., & Wall, S. (1978). *Patterns of Attachment.* Hillsdale, NJ: Lawrence Erlbaum.

American Psychological Association (2002). Ethical principles of psychologists. *American Psychologist, 57,* 1060–1073.

American Psychological Association (2001). *Publication manual of the American Psychological Association* (5th ed.). Washington, DC: American Psychological Association.

American Psychological Association (1995). *Psychology: Scientific problem solvers, careers for the 21st century* (Package of information about careers in psychology). Washington, DC: American Psychological Association (800-374-2741 to order).

Anderson, C. A. (1989). Temperature and aggression: Ubiquitous effects of heat on occurrence of human violence. *Psychological Bulletin, 106,* 74–96.

Applebaum, M. I., & McCall, R. B. (1983). Design and analysis in developmental psychology. In P. H. Mussen & W. Kessen (Eds.), *Handbook of child psychology: Vol. 1. History, theory and methods* (pp. 415–476). New York: Wiley.

Aronson, E., & Carlsmith, J. M. (1968). Experimentation in social psychology. In G. Lindzey & E. Aronson (Eds.), *Handbook of social psychology* (2nd ed., Vol. 2, pp. 1–79). Reading, MA: Addison-Wesley.

Aronson, E., & Mills, J. (1959). The effect of severity of initiation on liking for a group. *Journal of Abnormal and Social Psychology, 59,* 177–181.

Baddeley, A. D. (1990). *Human memory: Theory and practice.* Boston: Allyn and Bacon.

Bakeman, R., & Gottman, J. M. (1986). *Observing interaction.* Cambridge: Cambridge University Press.

Banaji, M. R., & Crowder, R. G. (1989). The bankruptcy of everyday memory. *American Psychologist, 44,* 1185–1193.

Baron, R. M., & Kenny, D. A. (1986). The moderator-mediator variable distinction in social psychological research: Conceptual, strategic and statistical considerations. *Journal of Personality and Social Psychology, 51,* 1173–1182.

Baron, R. A., & Ransberger, V. M. (1978). Ambient temperature and the occurrence of collective violence: The "long, hot summer" revisited. *Journal of Personality and Social Psychology, 36,* 351–360.

Bartholow, B. D., Fabiana, M., Gratton, G., & Battencourt, B. A. (2001). A psychophysiological examination of cognitive processing of and affective responses to social expectancy violations. *Psychological Science, 12,* 197–204.

Baumrind, D. (1985). Research using intentional deception: Ethical issues revisited. *American Psychologist, 40,* 165–174.

Bem, D. J. (1987). Writing the empirical journal article. In M. P. Zanna & J. M. Darley (Eds.), *The compleat academic: A practical guide for the beginning social scientist.* New York: Random House.

Berkowitz, L., & Donnerstein, E. (1982). External validity is more than skin deep: Some answers to criticisms of laboratory experiments. *American Psychologist, 37,* 245–257.

Berkowitz, L., & Macaulay, J. (1971). The contagion of criminal violence. *Sociometry, 34,* 238–260.

Berscheid, E., Baron, K. S., Dermer, M., & Libman, M. (1973). Anticipating informed consent: An empirical approach. *American Psychologist, 28,* 913–925.

Bissonnette, V., Ickes, W., Bernstein, I., & Knowles, E. (1990). Personality moderating variables: A warning about statistical artifacts and a comparison of analytic techniques. *Journal of Personality, 58,* 567–587.

Bower, G. H. (1981). Mood and memory. *American Psychologist, 36,* 129–148.

Bramel, D. (1962). A dissonance theory approach to defensive projection. *Journal of Abnormal and Social Psychology, 64,* 121–129.

Brierley, B., Shaw, P., & David, A. S. (2002). The human amygdala: A systematic review and meta-analyses of volumetric magnetic resonance imaging. *Brain Research Reviews, 39,* 84–105.

Cacioppo, J. T., & Petty, R. E. (1983). *Social psychophysiology: A sourcebook.* New York: Guilford.

Cacioppo, J. T., Petty, R. E., & Morris, K. J. (1983). Effects of need for cognition on message evaluation, recall, and persuasion. *Journal of Personality and Social Psychology, 45,* 805–818.

Cacioppo, J. T., Tassinary, L. G., & Berntson, G. G. (Eds.). (2000). *Handbook of psychophysiology* (2nd ed.). Cambridge, England: Cambridge University Press.

Campbell, D. T. (1969). Reforms as experiments. *American Psychologist, 24,* 409–429.

Campbell, D. T., & Stanley, J. C. (1963). *Experimental and quasi-experimental designs for research.* Chicago: Rand McNally.

Carlsmith, J. M., & Anderson, C. A. (1979). Ambient temperature and the occurrence of collective violence: A new analysis. *Journal of Personality and Social Psychology, 37,* 337–344.

Clubb, J. M., Austin, E. W., Geda, C. L., & Traugott, M. W. (1985). Sharing research data in the social sciences. In S. E. Fienber, M. E. Martin, & M. L. Straff (Eds.), *Sharing Research Data.* Washington, DC: National Academy Press.

Cohen, J. (1977). *Statistical power analysis for the behavioral sciences.* New York: Academic Press.

Cohen, J., & Cohen, P. (1983). *Applied multiple regression/correlation analysis for the behavioral sciences* (2nd ed.). Hillsdale, NJ: Lawrence Erlbaum.

Cohen, S., Tyrrell, D. A. J., & Smith, A. P. (1993). Negative life events, perceived stress, negative affect and susceptibility to the common cold. *Journal of Personality and Social Psychology, 64,* 131–140.

Cook, T. D., & Campbell, D. T. (1979). *Quasi-experimentation: Design and analysis issues for field settings.* Chicago: Rand McNally.

Coombs, C. H. (1964). *A theory of data.* New York: Wiley.

Cooper, H. M., & Rosenthal, R. (1980). Statistical versus traditional procedures for summarizing research findings. *Psychological Bulletin, 87*(3), 442–449.

Crowne, D. P., & Marlowe, D. (1964). *Studies in evaluative dependence.* New York: Wiley.

Davis, J. A., & Smith, T. W. (1994). *General Social Surveys, 1972–1994: Cumulative Codebook.* Chicago: National Opinion Research Center.

Denzin, N. K., & Lincoln, Y. S. (Eds.). (2000). *Handbook of qualitative research* (2nd ed.). Thousand Oaks, CA: Sage.

Dickerson, C. A., Thibodeau, R., Aronson, E., & Miller, D. (1992). Using cognitive dissonance to encourage water conservation. *Journal of Applied Social Psychology, 22*(11), 841–854.

Diener, E., & Crandall, R. (1978). *Ethics in social and behavioral research.* Chicago: University of Chicago Press.

Diener, E., Fraser, S. C., Beaman, A. L., & Kelem, R. T. (1976). Effects of deindividuation variables on stealing among stealing Halloween trick-or-treaters. *Journal of Personality and Social Psychology, 33,* 178–183.

Dillman, D. A. (1978). *Mail and telephone surveys: The total design method.* New York: Wiley.

DiMatteo, M. R., Morton, S. C., Lepper, H. S., & Damush, T. M. (1996). Cesarean childbirth and psychosocial outcomes: A meta-analysis. *Health Psychology, 15,* 303–314.

Dowden, C., & Brown, S. L. (2002). The role of substance abuse factors in predicting recidivism: A meta-analysis. *Psychology, Crime and Law, 8,* 243–264.

Durkheim, E. (1951). Suicide. (J. A. Spaudling & G. Simpson, Trans.). New York: Free Press.

Eagly, A. H., & Chravala, C. (1986). Sex differences in conformity: Status and gender-role interpretations. *Psychology of Women Quarterly, 10,* 203–220.

Eisenberger, R., & Cameron, J. (1996). Detrimental effects of reward: Reality or myth? *American Psychologist, 51,* 1151–1166.

Ekman, P., Friesen, W. V., & Scherer, K. R. (1976). Body movement and voice pitch in deceptive interaction. *Semiotica, 16,* 23–27.

Ellsworth, P. C., & Langer, E. J. (1976). Staring and approach: An interpretation of the stare as a nonspecific activator. *Journal of Personality and Social Psychology, 33,* 117–122.

Ericsson, K. A., & Simon, H. A. (1980). Verbal reports as data. *Psychological Review, 87,* 215–251.

Eron, L. D., Huesman, L. R., Lefkowitz, M. M., & Walder, L. O. (1972). Does television watching cause aggression? *American Psychologist, 27,* 253–263.

Fagio, R. H., Effrein, E. A., & Falender, V. J. (1981). Self-perceptions following social interaction. *Journal of Personality and Social Psychology, 41*(2), 232–242.

Festinger, L., Riecken, H. W., & Schachter, S. (1956). *When prophecy fails: A social and psychological study of a modern group that predicted the destruction of the world.* Minneapolis: University of Minnesota Press.

Fiske, S. T., Bersoff, D. N., Borgida, E., Deaux, K., & Heilman, M. E. (1991). Social science research on trial: The use of sex stereotyping research in *Price Waterhouse* vs. *Hopkins. American Psychologist, 46,* 1049–1060.

Fiske, S. T., Neuberg, S. L., Beattie, A. E., & Milberg, S. J. (1987). Category-based and attribute-based reactions to others: Some informational conditions of stereotyping and individuating processes. *Journal of Experimental Social Psychology, 23,* 399–427.

Freud, S. (1959). Analysis of a phobia in a 5-year-old boy. In A. Strachey & J. Strachey (Eds.), *Collected Papers* (Vol. 3). New York: Basic Books.

Gelfand, H., & Walker, C. (Eds.). (2001). *Mastering APA style: Instructor's resource guide.* Washington, DC: American Psychological Association.

Gerard, H. B., & Matthewson, G. C. (1966). The effects of severity of initiation on liking for a group: A replication. *Journal of Experimental Social Psychology, 2,* 278–287.

Gosling, S., Ko, S. J., Mannarelli, T., & Morris, M. (2002). A room with a cue: Personality judgments based on offices and bedrooms. *Journal of Personality and Social Psychology, 82,* 379–398.

Greenberg, B. S. (1980). *Life on television: Current analyses of U.S. TV drama.* Norwood, NJ: Ablex.

Gully, S. M., Incalcaterra, K. A., Joshi, A., & Beaubien, J. M. (2002). A meta-analysis of team-efficacy, potency, and performance: Inter-dependence and level of analysis as moderators of observed relationships. *Journal of Applied Psychology, 87,* 819–832.

Guttman, L. (1944). A basis of scaling quantitative data. *American Sociological Review, 9,* 139–150.

Haney, C., Banks, C., & Zimbardo, P. (1973). Interpersonal dynamics in a simulated prison. *International Journal of Criminology and Penology, 1,* 69–87.

Harackiewicz, J. M., Manderlink, G., & Sansone, C. (1984). Rewarding pinball wizardry: Effects of evaluation and cue value on intrinsic interest. *Journal of Personality and Social Psychology, 47,* 287–300.

Hardy, D. J., & Hinkin, C. H. (2002). Reaction time slowing in adults with HIV: Results of a meta-analysis using brinley plots. *Brain and Cognition, 50,* 25–34.

Harmon-Jones, E., & Sigelman, J. (2001). State anger and prefrontal brain activity: Evidence that insult-related relative left prefrontal activation is associated with experienced anger and aggression. *Journal of Personality and Social Psychology, 80,* 797–803.

Harris, R. J. (1985). *A primer of multivariate statistics* (2nd ed.). Orlando, FL: Academic Press.

Hays, W. L. (1988). *Statistics* (4th ed.). New York: Holt, Rinehart and Winston.

Heider, F. (1958). *The psychology of interpersonal relations.* Hillsdale, NJ: Lawrence Erlbaum.

Herrnstein, R. J., & Murray, C. (1994). *The bell curve: Intelligence and class structure in American life.* New York: Free Press.

Huck, S. W., & Sandler, H. M. (1979). *Rival hypotheses: Alternative interpretations of data-based conclusions.* New York: Harper and Row.

Hull, J. G., & Young, R. D. (1983). Self-consciousness, self-esteem, and success-failure as determinants of alcohol consumption in male social drinkers. *Journal of Personality and Social Psychology, 44* 1097–1109.

Humphreys, L. (1975). *Tearoom trade: Impersonal sex in public places* (Enl. ed.). Chicago: Aldine.

Ickes, W. (1984). Compositions in black and white: Determinants of interaction in interracial dyads. *Journal of Personality and Social Psychology, 47,* 330–341.

Isen, A. M., & Levin, P. F. (1972). The effect of feeling good on helping: Cookies and kindness. *Journal of Personality and Social Psychology, 21,* 384–388.

Isen, A. M., Nygren, T. E., & Ashby, F. G. (1988). Influence of positive affect on the subjective utility of gains and losses: It is just not worth the risk. *Journal of Personality and Social Psychology, 55,* 710–717.

Johnson, R. D., & Downing, L. L. (1979). Deindividuation and the valence of cues: Effects on prosocial and antisocial behavior. *Journal of Personality and Social Psychology, 37,* 1532–1538.

Jorgensen, R. S., Johnson, B. T., Kolodziej, M. E., & Schreer, G. E. (1996). Elevated blood pressure and personality: A meta-analytic review. *Psychological Bulletin, 120,* 293–320.

Kahle, L. R. (1980). Stimulus condition self-selection by males in the interaction of locus of control and skill-chance situations. *Journal of Personality and Social Psychology, 38,* 50–56.

Kassin, S. M., & Kiechel, K. L. (1996). The social psychology of false confessions: Compliance, internalization and confabulation. *Psychological Science, 7,* 125–128.

Kelley, H. H. (1967). Attribution theory in social psychology. In D. Levine (Ed.), *Nebraska symposium on motivation* (Vol. 15, pp. 192–238). Lincoln: University of Nebraska Press.

Kenny, D. A. (1979). *Correlation and causality.* New York: Wiley-Interscience.

Keppel, G., & Zedeck, S. (1989). *Data analysis for research designs.* New York: Freeman.

Kim, H., & Marcus, H. (1999). Deviance or uniqueness, harmony or conformity: A cultural analysis. *Journal of Personality and Social Psychology, 77,* 785–800.

Kimmel, A. (1998). In defense of deception. *American Psychologist, 53,* 803–805.

Kish, L. (1965). *Survey sampling.* New York: Wiley.

Knight, L. J., Barbaree, H. E., & Boland, F. J. (1986). Alcohol and the balanced-placebo design: The role of experimenter demands in expectancy. *Journal of Abnormal Psychology, 95,* 335–340.

Kohlberg, L. (1969). Stage and sequence: The cognitive-developmental approach to socialization. In D. A. Goslin (Ed.), *Handbook of socialization theory and research* (pp. 347–480). Chicago: Rand McNally.

Lewin, K. (1944). Constructs in psychology and psychological ecology. *University of Iowa Studies in Child Welfare, 20,* 23–27.

Lieberman, J., Solomon, S., Greenberg, J., & McGregor, H. (1999). A hot new way to measure aggression: Hot sauce allocation. *Aggressive Behavior, 25,* 331–348.

Likert, R. (1932). A technique for the measurement of attitudes. *Archives of Psychology, 140,* 5–53.

Lord, C. G., & Gilbert, D. T. (1983). The "same person" heuristic: An attributional procedure based on an assumption about person similarity. *Journal of Personality and Social Psychology, 45,* 751–762.

Macrae, C. N., Bodenhausen, G. V., Milne, A. B., & Jetten, J. (1994). Out of mind but back in sight: Stereotypes on the rebound. *Journal of Personality and Social Psychology, 67,* 808–817.

Madey, S. F., Simo, M., Dillworth, D., & Kemper, D. (1996). They do get more attractive at closing time, but only when you are not in a relationship. *Basic and Applied Social Psychology, 18,* 387–393.

Mann, C. (1994). Can meta-analysis make policy? *Science, 266,* 960–962.

Markus, H. (1978). The effect of mere presence on social facilitation: An unobtrusive test. *Journal of Experimental Social Psychology, 4, 14,* 389–397.

McCann, I. L., & Holmes, D. S. (1984). Influence of aerobic exercise on depression. *Journal of Personality and Social Psychology, 46,* 1142–1147.

Milgram, S. (1974). *Obedience to authority: An experimental view.* New York: Harper and Row.

Mill, J. S. (1930). *A system of logic.* London: Longmans Green.

Miller, N. E. (1985). The value of behavioral research on animals. *American Psychologist, 40,* 423–440.

Mills, J. (1976). A procedure for explaining experiments involving deception. *Personality and Social Psychology Bulletin, 2,* 3–13.

Modin, B. (2002). Birth order and mortality: A lifelong follow-up of 14,200 boys and girls born in early 20th century Sweden. *Social Science and Medicine, 54,* 1051–1064.

Morgan, C. D., & Murray, H. A. (1935). A method for investigating fantasies: The thematic apperception test. *Archives of Neurological Psychiatry, 34,* 289–306.

Mori, D., Chaiken, S., & Pliner, P. (1987). "Eating lightly" and the self-presentation of femininity. *Journal of Personality and Social Psychology, 53*(4), 693–702.

Nettles, M. T., Thoeny, A. R., & Gosman, E. J. (1986). Comparative and predictive analyses of black and white students' college achievement and experiences. *Journal of Higher Education, 57*, 289–318.

Nisbett, R. E., & Ross, L. (1980). *Human inference: Strategies and shortcomings of social judgment*. Englewood Cliffs, NJ: Prentice-Hall.

Nisbett, R. E., & Wilson, T. D. (1977). Telling more than we can know: Verbal reports on mental processes. *Psychological Review, 84*, 231–259.

Nunnally, J. C. (1978). *Psychometric theory*. New York: McGraw-Hill.

Orne, M. T. (1962). On the social psychology of the psychological experiment. *American Psychologist, 17*, 776–783.

Ortmann, A., & Hertwig, R. (1997). Is deception acceptable? *American Psychologist, 52*, 746–747.

Osgood, C. E., Suci, G. J., & Tannenbaum, P. H. (1957). *The measurement of meaning*. Urbana: University of Illinois Press.

Pennebaker, J. W., Dyer, M. A., Caulkins, R. S., Litowitz, D. L., Ackerman, P. L., & Anderson, D. B. (1979). Don't the girls get prettier at closing time: A country and western application to psychology. *Personality and Social Psychology Bulletin, 5*, 122–125.

Piaget, J. (1952). *The origins of intelligence in children*. New York: International University Press.

Piliavin, I. M., Rodin, J., & Piliavin, J. A. (1969). Good samaritanism: An underground phenomenon? *Journal of Personality and Social Psychology, 8*, 121–133.

Plous, S. (1996). Attitudes toward the use of animals in psychological research and education. *Psychological Science, 7*, 352–358.

Pomerantz, E. M., Ruble, D. N., Frey, K. S., & Greulich, F. (1995). Meeting goals and confronting conflict: Children's changing perceptions of social comparison. *Child Development, 66*, 723–738.

Popper, K. R. (1959). *The logic of scientific discovery*. New York: Basic Books.

Prentice, D. A., & Miller, D. T. (1992). When small effects are impressive. *Psychological Bulletin, 112*, 160–164.

Price, L. (1984). Art, science, faith, and medicine: The implications of the placebo effect. *Sociology of Health and Illness, 6*, 61–73.

Ratcliff, R., & McKoon, G. (1996). Bias effects in implicit memory tasks. *Journal of Experimental Psychology: General, 125*, 403–421.

Reed, J. G., & Baxter, P. M. (1983). *Library use: A handbook for psychology*. Washington, DC: American Psychological Association.

Robinson, J. P., Shaver, P. R., & Wrightsman, L. S. (1991). *Measures of personality and social psychological attitudes*. San Diego, CA: Academic Press.

Rokeach, M. (1964). *The three Christs of Ypsilanti: A psychological study*. New York: Knopf.

Rosenberg, M. (1965). *Society and the adolescent self-image*. Princeton, NJ: Princeton University Press.

Rosenhan, D. L. (1973). On being sane in insane places. *Science, 179*, 250–258.

Rosenthal, R. (1994). Science and ethics in conducting, analyzing, and reporting psychological research. *Psychological Science, 5*, 127–134.

Rosenthal, R., & Fode, K. L. (1963). The effect of experimenter bias on the performance of the albino rat. *Behavioral Science, 8*, 183–189.

Rosenthal, R., & Rosnow, R. L. (1975). *The volunteer subject*. New York: Wiley.

Rosenthal, R., & Rosnow, R. L. (1985). *Contrast analysis: Focused comparison in the Analysis of Variance*. Cambridge: Cambridge University Press.

Rosenthal, R., & Rosnow, R. L. (1991). *Essentials of behavioral research: Methods and data analysis* (2nd ed.). New York: McGraw-Hill.

Ross, L., Lepper, M. R., & Hubbard, M. (1975). Perseverance in self-perception and social perception: Biased attributional processes in the debriefing paradigm. *Journal of Personality and Social Psychology, 32*, 880–892.

Rossi, P. H., & Freeman, H. E. (1993). *Evaluation: A systematic approach* (5th ed.). Newbury Park, CA: Sage.

Roy, D. F. (1959–1960). Banana time. *Human Organization, 18*, 158–168.

Rubin, Z. (1973). Designing honest experiments. *American Psychologist, 28*, 445–448.

Saxe, L., Dougherty, D., & Cross, T. (1985). The validity of polygraph testing: Scientific analysis and public controversy. *American Psychologist, 40*, 355–366.

Saywitz, K. J., & Snyder, L. (1996). Narrative elaboration: Test of a new procedure for interviewing children. *Journal of Constructive and Clinical Research, 64,* 1347–1357.

Scheier, M. F., Carver, C. S., & Bridges, M. W. (1994). Distinguishing optimism from neuroticism (and trait anxiety, self-mastery, and self-esteem): A reevaluation of the Life Orientation Test. *Journal of Personality, 67,* 1063–1078.

Schlenker, B. R., & Forsyth, D. R. (1977). On the ethics of psychological research. *Journal of Experimental Social Psychology, 13,* 369–396.

Schmitt, D. P. (2000). A meta-analysis of sex differences in romantic attraction: Do rating contests moderate tactic effectiveness judgments? *British Journal of Social Psychology, 41,* 387–402.

Schuman, H., & Presser, S. (1981). *Questions and answers: Experiments on question form, wordings, and content in surveys.* New York: Academic Press.

Schwarz, N., & Strack, F. (1991). Context effects in attitude surveys: Applying cognitive theory to social research. In W. Stroebe & M. Hewstone (Eds.), *European review of social psychology* (Vol. 2, pp. 31–50). New York: Wiley and Sons.

Sears, D. O. (1986). College sophomores in the laboratory: Influences of a narrow data base on social psychology's view of human nature. *Journal of Personality and Social Psychology, 51,* 515–530.

Selltiz, C., Jahoda, M., Deutsch, M., & Cook, S. W. (1966). *Research methods in social relations.* New York: Holt, Rinehart and Winston.

Serketich, W. J., & Dumas, J. E. (1996). The effectiveness of behavioral parent training to modify antisocial behavior in children. A meta-analysis. *Behavior Therapy, 27,* 171–186.

Shrout, P. E. (1997). Should significance tests be banned? Introduction to a special section exploring the pros and cons. *Psychological Science, 8,* 1–2.

Sigall, H., & Mills, J. (1998). Measures of independent variables and mediators are useful in social psychology experiments: But are they necessary? *Personality and Social Psychology Review, 2,* 218–226.

Simonton, D. K. (1988). Presidential style: Personality, biography, and performance. *Journal of Personality and Social Psychology, 55,* 928–936.

Slaby, R. G., & Frey, K. S. (1975). Development of gender constancy and selective attention to same-sex models. *Child Development, 46,* 849–856.

Smith, M. L., Glass, G. V., & Miller, R. L. (1980). *The benefits of psychotherapy.* Baltimore, MD: Johns Hopkins University Press.

Smith, S. S., & Richardson, D. (1983). Amelioration of deception and harm in psychological research. *Journal of Personality and Social Psychology, 44,* 1075–1082.

Snyder, M. (1974). Self-monitoring of expressive behavior. *Journal of Personality and Social Psychology, 30,* 526–537.

Sperry, R. W. (1982). Some effects of disconnecting the cerebral hemispheres. *Science, 217,* 1223–1226.

Stangor, C., & Carr, C. (2002). Influence of solo status and task performance feedback on expectations about task performance in groups. Manuscript submitted for publication.

Stangor, C., Jonas, K., Stroebe, W., & Hewstone, M. (1996). Development and change of national stereotypes and attitudes. *European Journal of Social Psychology, 26,* 663–675.

Stangor, C., & Ruble, D. N. (1987). Development of gender-role knowledge and gender constancy. In L. Liben & M. Signorella (Eds.), *Children's gender schemata* (pp. 5–22). San Francisco: Jossey-Bass. ´

Stangor, C., Sullivan, L. A., & Ford, T. E. (1991). Affective and cognitive determinants of prejudice. *Social Cognition, 9,* 359–380.

Sternberg, R. J. (1993). *The psychologist's companion* (3rd ed.). New York: Cambridge University Press.

Stevens, J. (1996). *Applied multivariate statistics for the social sciences.* Matwah, NJ: Lawrence Erlbaum.

Sullivan, G. L., & O'Connor, P. J. (1988). Women's role portrayals in magazine advertising: 1958–1983. *Sex Roles, 18,* 181–188.

Tabachnick, B. G., & Fidell, L. S. (1989). *Using multivariate statistics* (2nd ed.). New York: Harper and Row.

Thomas, G., & Blackman, D. (1992). The future of animal studies in psychology. *American Psychologist, 47,* 1678.

Trappey, C. (1996). A meta-analysis of consumer choice and subliminal advertising. *Psychology and Marketing, 13,* 517–530.

Tukey, J. W. (1977). *Exploratory data analysis.* Reading, MA: Addison-Wesley.

Twenge, J. M., & Nolen-Hoeksema, S. (2002). Age,

gender, race, socioeconomic status, and birth cohort difference on the children's depression inventory: A meta-analysis. *Journal of Abnormal Psychology, 111,* 578–588.

U.S. Department of Health and Human Services. (2001). OPRR Reports: Protection of human subjects, Title 45, Code of Federal Regulations Part 46, as amended December 13, 2001. Washington, DC: Government Printing Office.

Vaughan, T. R. (1967). Governmental intervention in social research: Political and ethical dimensions in the Wichita jury recordings. In G. Sjoberg (Ed.), *Ethics, politics, and social research* (pp. 50–77). Cambridge, MA: Schenkman.

Webb, E. J., Campbell, D. T., Schwartz, R. D., Sechrest, L., & Grove, J. B. (1981). *Unobtrusive measures: Nonreactive research in the social sciences* (2nd ed.). Boston: Houghton Mifflin.

Weber, S. J., & Cook, T. D. (1972). Subject effects in laboratory research: An examination of subject roles, demand characteristics, and valid inference. *Psychological Bulletin, 77,* 273–295.

Weick, K. E. (1985). Systematic observational methods. In G. Lindzey & E. Aronson (Eds.), *Handbook of social psychology* (3rd ed., Vol. 1, pp. 567–634). New York: Random House.

Wells, G. L., Leippe, M. R., & Ostrom, T. M. (1979). Guidelines for empirically assessing the fairness of a line-up. *Law and Human Behavior, 11,* 113–130.

Whyte, W. F. (1993). *Street corner society: The social structure of an Italian slum* (4th ed.). Chicago: University of Chicago Press.

Word, C. O., Zanna, M. P., & Cooper, J. (1974). The nonverbal mediation of self-fulfilling prophecies in interracial interaction. *Journal of Experimental Social Psychology, 10,* 109–120.

Zajonc, R. B. (1965). Social facilitation. *Science, 149,* 269–274.

Zajonc, R. B. (1980). Compresence. In P. B. Paulus (Ed.), *Psychology of group influence* (pp. 35–60). Hillsdale, NJ: Lawrence Erlbaum.

Zimbardo, P. G. (1970). The human choice: Individuation, reason, and order versus deindividuation, impulse, and chaos. In W. J. Arnold & D. Levine (Eds.), *Nebraska Symposium on Motivation, 1969.* Lincoln: University of Nebraska Press.

Name Index

Subject Index

Mindfulness

Mindfulness

3rd Edition

by Shamash Alidina

Mindfulness For Dummies®, 3rd Edition

Published by: **John Wiley & Sons, Inc.,** 111 River Street, Hoboken, NJ 07030-5774, www.wiley.com

Copyright © 2020 by John Wiley & Sons, Inc., Hoboken, New Jersey

Published simultaneously in Canada

No part of this publication may be reproduced, stored in a retrieval system or transmitted in any form or by any means, electronic, mechanical, photocopying, recording, scanning or otherwise, except as permitted under Sections 107 or 108 of the 1976 United States Copyright Act, without the prior written permission of the Publisher. Requests to the Publisher for permission should be addressed to the Permissions Department, John Wiley & Sons, Inc., 111 River Street, Hoboken, NJ 07030, (201) 748-6011, fax (201) 748-6008, or online at http://www.wiley.com/go/permissions.

Trademarks: Wiley, For Dummies, the Dummies Man logo, Dummies.com, Making Everything Easier, and related trade dress are trademarks or registered trademarks of John Wiley & Sons, Inc., and may not be used without written permission. All other trademarks are the property of their respective owners. John Wiley & Sons, Inc., is not associated with any product or vendor mentioned in this book.

For general information on our other products and services, please contact our Customer Care Department within the U.S. at 877-762-2974, outside the U.S. at 317-572-3993, or fax 317-572-4002. For technical support, please visit https://hub.wiley.com/community/support/dummies.

Wiley publishes in a variety of print and electronic formats and by print-on-demand. Some material included with standard print versions of this book may not be included in e-books or in print-on-demand. If this book refers to media such as a CD or DVD that is not included in the version you purchased, you may download this material at http://booksupport.wiley.com. For more information about Wiley products, visit www.wiley.com.

Library of Congress Control Number: 2019956698

ISBN 978-1-119-64156-8 (pbk); ISBN 978-1-119-64160-5 (ebk); ISBN 978-1-119-64161-2 (ebk)

Manufactured in the United States of America

V10016681_010720

Contents at a Glance

Table of Contents

Introduction

L ife can be wonderful. Laughing with friends or family, achieving something meaningful or spending quality time with a partner can all feel great. And life can also be very difficult. Dealing with a breakup, facing challenges at work, discovering health problems or grieving the loss of a loved one all cause much suffering.

And even if you have a healthy mind, great relationships and plenty of money, you will unfortunately still suffer. We all suffer. We all come to planet Earth with a mind, and minds can feel shame and guilt about the past and get anxious and worried about the future. No matter how great your external surroundings, your mind can easily visit many painful places.

So how are you supposed to deal with life's suffering and tap into its joys? *Mindfulness* offers a radical, powerful, evidence-based way.

This book will show you some ways you can ease the suffering and find more joy in your life. You'll discover how to relate to your inner and outer difficulties in a healthy way. You will find out how to practise mindfulness in a way that works for you, so you can integrate a new way of being into your everyday life, helping you to cope with managing stress, challenging emotions, and increasing your general sense of wellbeing in a rich variety of different ways. You will find out how to re-ignite your perception of this mystery called life, so you aren't just existing to complete to-do lists but are actually living a rich and meaningful life.

About This Book

Mindfulness For Dummies provides you with the tools to practise mindfulness on your own. Each chapter is brimming with insights about what mindfulness is, how to practise mindfulness quickly and easily, and how to deepen your experience. I wrote this book with the beginner in mind, but the knowledge goes far deeper, and experienced mindfulness practitioners will find lots of new aspects to ponder. As the research on mindfulness continues to develop rapidly, I've chosen to explain in detail the core mindfulness practices and approaches that have been tested many times before and found to be effective.

Foolish Assumptions

In writing this book, I made a few assumptions about who you are:

>> You're keen to learn more about mindfulness, but don't know exactly what it is and how to practise it.

>> You are willing to have a good go at trying out the various mindfulness exercises before judging if they'll work for you.

>> You're interested in the many different applications of mindfulness.

>> You're not afraid of a bit of mindfulness meditation.

Beyond those, I've not assumed too much, I hope. This book is for you whether you're male or female, 8 or 88.

Icons Used in This Book

Sprinkled throughout the book you'll see various icons to guide you on your way. Icons are a *For Dummies* way of drawing your attention to important stuff, interesting stuff, and stuff you really need to know how to do.

The audio tracks that accompany this book (found at www.dummies.com/go/mindfulnessuk3e) include a selection of guided mindfulness exercises for you to try. Find these exercises by looking for this icon.

This is stuff you need to know. Whatever else you carry away from this book, note these bits with care.

Have a go at different mindfulness exercises and tips with this icon.

Take careful note of the advice under this icon, and you'll avoid unnecessary problems. Ignore at your peril.

Find some precious pearls of wisdom and meaningful stories next to this icon.

Beyond the Book

In addition to the content in the print or e-book you're reading right now, this book also comes with some access-anywhere goodies on the web.

Cheat Sheet

Check out the free online Cheat Sheet for a simple summary of all the key points contained in this book. Simply go to at www.dummies.com and type "*Mindfulness For Dummies* cheat sheet" in the search box. This really handy reference can be printed out for you to carry with you throughout the day, so you can dip into it for some mindfulness anytime you need to.

Guided mindfulness

And last but most important, this book also includes lots of high quality, down-loadable mindfulness exercises. These exercises are available online as audio tracks. They are referred to through the book, as marked with the icon Play This, and vary in lengths from 3 minutes to 25 minutes.

To download the audio tracks to your device, go to www.dummies.com/go/mindfulnessuk3e.

Alternatively, you could even play them straight from your smartphone when you have Wi-Fi access. Be sure to bookmark the link so that you can easily access the mindfulness audio tracks anytime you need them. Listening to the guided mindfulness exercises is the easiest way most people practise mindfulness as beginners.

Where to Go from Here

I've put this book together so that you can dip in and out as you please. I invite you to make good use of the Table of Contents – or the index – and jump straight into the section you fancy. You're in charge and it's up to you of course. If you're a total beginner, or not sure where to start, take a traditional approach and begin with Part 1.

I wish you all the best in your mindfulness quest and hope you find something of use within these pages. Good luck! I'm rooting for you!

1
Getting Started with Mindfulness

Discover what mindfulness is and explore its meaning.

Take a journey into the benefits of mindfulness living.

Find out just what makes mindfulness so popular.

Chapter **1**

Discovering Mindfulness

Mindfulness means flexibly paying attention on purpose, in the present moment, infused with qualities like kindness, curiosity, acceptance and openness.

Through being mindful, you discover how to live in the present moment in an enjoyable way rather than worrying about the past or being concerned about the future. The past has already gone and can't be changed. The future is yet to arrive and is completely unknown. The present moment, this very moment now, is ultimately the only moment you have. Mindfulness shows you how to live in this moment in a harmonious way. You find out how to make the present moment a more wonderful moment to be in – the only place in which you can create, decide, listen, think, smile, act or live.

You can develop and deepen mindfulness through doing mindfulness meditation on a daily basis, from a few minutes to as long as you want. This chapter introduces you to mindfulness and mindfulness meditation and welcomes you aboard a fascinating journey.

Understanding the Meaning of Mindfulness

Mindfulness was originally developed in ancient times, and can be found in Eastern and Western cultures. Mindfulness is a translation of the ancient Indian word *Sati*, which means awareness, attention and remembering.

» **Awareness.** This is an aspect of being human that makes you conscious of your experiences. Without awareness, nothing would exist for you.

» **Attention.** Attention is a focused awareness; mindfulness training develops your ability to move and sustain your attention wherever and however you choose.

» **Remembering.** This aspect of mindfulness is about remembering to pay attention to your experience from moment to moment. Being mindful is easy to forget. The word 'remember' originally comes from the Latin *re* 'again' and *memorari* 'be mindful of.'

Say that you want to practise mindfulness to help you cope with stress. At work, you think about your forthcoming presentation and begin to feel stressed and nervous. By becoming *aware* of this, you *remember* to focus your mindful *attention* to your own breathing rather than constantly worrying. Feeling your breath with a sense of warmth and gentleness helps slowly to calm you down. See Chapter 6 for more about mindful breathing.

Dr Jon Kabat–Zinn, who first developed mindfulness in a therapeutic setting, says:

'Mindfulness can be cultivated by paying attention in a specific way, that is, in the present moment, and as non-reactively, non-judgementally and openheartedly as possible.'

You can break down the meaning even further:

» **Paying attention.** To be mindful, you need to pay attention, whatever you choose to attend to.

» **Present moment.** The reality of being in the here and now means you just need to be aware of the way things are, *as they are now*. Your experience is valid and correct just as it is.

» **Non-reactively.** Normally, when you experience something, you automatically react to that experience according to your past conditioning. For example, if you think, 'I still haven't finished my work,' you react with thoughts, words and actions in some shape or form.

Mindfulness encourages you to *respond* to your experience rather than *react* to thoughts. A reaction is automatic and gives you no choice; a response is deliberate and considered action. (Chapter 12 delves deeper into mindful responses.)

AWARENESS FROM THE HEART

The Japanese character for mindfulness is illustrated below:

This Japanese character combines the words for 'mind' and 'heart' and beautifully captures the essence of mindfulness as not just awareness, but awareness from the heart.

>> **Non-judgementally.** The temptation is to judge experience as good or bad, something you like or dislike. I want to feel bliss; I don't like feeling afraid. Letting go of judgements helps you to see things as they are rather than through the filter of your personal judgements based on past conditioning.

>> **Openheartedly.** Mindfulness isn't just an aspect of mind. Mindfulness is of the heart as well. To be open-hearted is to bring a quality of kindness, compassion, warmth and friendliness to your experience. For example, if you notice yourself thinking, 'I'm useless at meditation,' you discover how to let go of this critical thought and gently turn your attention back to the focus of your meditation, whatever that may be. For more on attitudes to cultivate for mindfulness, see Chapter 4.

WISE WORDS

World-renouned monk, Ajahn Brahm, says the word mindfulness doesn't capture the importance of kindness in the practise. So what word does he recommend? *Kindfulness.* And I fully agree! I usually tell my students to practise 'kindfulness' rather than just mindfulness. This helps to remind them to bring a warm, friendly awareness when practising mindfulness – and usually makes them smile too! Remember to practise being kindful, not just mindful.

Looking at Mindfulness Meditation

Mindfulness meditation is a particular type of meditation that's been well researched and tested in clinical settings.

Meditation isn't thinking about nothing. Meditation is kindly paying attention in a systematic way to whatever you decide to focus on, which can include awareness of your thoughts. By listening to your thoughts, you discover their habitual patterns. Your thoughts have a massive impact on your emotions and the decisions you make, so being more aware of them is helpful.

In mindfulness meditation, you typically focus on one, or a combination, of the following:

>> The feeling of your own breathing

>> Any one of your senses

>> Your body

>> Your thoughts or emotions

>> Your intentions

>> Whatever is most predominant in your awareness

This book and accompanying downloadable audio (MP3s) include guided meditations.

Mindfulness meditation comes in two distinct types:

>> **Formal meditation.** This is a meditation where you intentionally take time out in your day to embark on a meditative practise. Time out gives you an opportunity to deepen your mindfulness practise and understand more about your mind, its habitual tendencies and how to be mindful for a sustained period of time, with a sense of kindness and curiosity towards yourself and your experience. Formal meditation is mind training. Chapter 6 contains more about formal meditation.

>> **Informal meditation.** This is where you go into a focused and meditative state of mind as you go about your daily activities such as cooking, cleaning, walking to work, talking to a friend, driving – anything at all. Think of it as everyday mindfulness. In this way, you continue to deepen your ability to be mindful, and train your mind to stay in the present moment more often rather than habitually straying into the past or future. Informal mindfulness meditation means you can rest in a mindful awareness at any time of day, whatever you're doing. See Chapter 8 for more ways to be mindful informally.

When I say 'practise' with regard to meditation, I don't mean a rehearsal. To practise meditation means to engage in the meditation exercise – not practising in the sense of aiming one day to get the meditation perfect. You don't need to judge your meditation or perfect it in any way. Your experience is your experience.

Mindfulness is not just about having your attention caught – it's about cultivating a flexible attention. Flexible attention means you can choose where to focus your attention. For example, when a child (or adult!) is playing a computer game, they may have their full attention on the game, but the attention is usually not flexible. Their attention is caught by the game. That's not mindfulness. As you become more mindful, you're able to move your attention from one place to the other more in a flexible way.

Using Mindfulness to Help You

You know how you get lost in thought? Most of the day, as you go about your daily activities, your mind is left to think whatever it wants. You're operating on 'automatic pilot' (explained more fully in Chapter 5). But some of your automatic thoughts may be unhelpful to you, or perhaps you're so stuck in those thoughts you don't actually experience the world around you. For example, you go for a walk in the park to relax, but your mind is lost in thoughts about your next project.

First, you're not really living in the present moment, and second, you're making yourself more stressed, anxious or depressed if your thoughts are unhelpful. (Chapters 12 and 13 explore overcoming unhelpful thoughts.)

Mindfulness isn't focused on fixing problems. Mindfulness emphasises acceptance first, and change may or may not come later. So if you suffer from anxiety, mindfulness shows you how to accept the feeling of anxiety rather than denying or fighting the feeling, and through this approach change naturally comes about.

I like to say, 'What you resist, persists. What you accept, transforms.'

This section explores the many ways in which mindfulness can help you.

WARNING

In mindfulness, acceptance means to *acknowledge* your present-moment experience, whether pleasant or unpleasant, is already here. You're discoverering how to 'make peace' with your present moment experience rather than fighting it. Acceptance doesn't mean resignation or giving up. Acceptance is an active and empowering state of mind.

Allowing space to heal

When you have a physical illness, it can be a distressing time. Your condition may be painful or even life-threatening. Perhaps your illness means you're no longer able to do the simple things in life you took for granted before, like run up the stairs or look after yourself in an independent way. Illness can shake you to your very core. How can you cope with this? How can you build your inner strength to manage the changes that take place, without being overwhelmed and losing all hope?

High levels of stress, particularly over a long period of time, have been clearly shown to reduce the strength of your immune system. Perhaps you went down with flu after a period of high stress. The scientific evidence strongly agrees. For example, research on care-givers who experience high levels of stress for long periods of time shows that they have a weaker immune system in response to diseases like flu.

Mindfulness reduces stress, and for this reason is one way of managing illness. By reducing your stress you improve the effectiveness of your immune system, and this may help increase the rate of healing from the illness you suffer, especially if the illness is stress-related.

REMEMBER

Mindfulness can reduce stress, anxiety, pain and depression, and boost energy, creativity, the quality of relationships and your overall sense of wellbeing. The more you engage in mindfulness, the better: monks who've practised mindfulness all their lives have levels of wellbeing, measured in their brains, way above anything scientists thought was possible. Sometimes their happiness levels are so high, they think there's something wrong with their brain scanners!

Chapter 14 is all about how mindfulness can help to heal the body.

Enjoying greater relaxation

Mindfulness can be a very relaxing experience. As you discover how to rest with an awareness of your breathing or the sounds around you, you may begin to feel calmer.

However, *the aim of mindfulness is not relaxation*. Relaxation is one of the welcome by-products. In clinical studies comparing the benefits of mindfulness and relaxation, there's often little beneficial effect in the relaxation exercises but significant benefits in practising mindfulness. This shows how different they are.

Mindfulness is the development of awareness of your inner and outer experiences, whatever they are, with a sense of kindness, curiosity and acceptance. You may experience very deep states of relaxation when practising mindfulness, or you may not. If you don't, this certainly doesn't mean you're practising mindfulness incorrectly.

Why is relaxation and mindfulness so different? Mindfulness is about cultivating greater awareness of what's going on within or around you. It's a state of wakefulness. Whereas relaxation is associated with falling asleep, letting go and reducing your level of awareness. Mindfulness is about moving towards challenging experiences to help you learn from difficult thoughts, feelings, urges and sensations. Relaxation is often about moving away from such challenges – which means you can't learn from them.

REMEMBER

When you first begin practising mindfulness, you may not find it relaxing at all. This is totally normal and nothing to worry about. Try shortening your practises and take a break whenever you wish. Be kind to yourself and let the process of mindfulness be unforced and gentle.

Table 1-1 shows the difference between relaxation and mindfulness exercises.

Improving focus and feeling happier

To be mindful, you usually need to do one thing at a time. When walking, you just walk. When listening, you just listen. When writing, you just write. By practising formal and informal mindfulness meditation, you're training your brain, with mindful attitudes like kindness, curiosity and acceptance.

TABLE 1-1   **Relaxation versus Mindfulness**

Exercise	Aim	Method
Mindfulness	To pay attention to your experience from moment to moment, as best you can, with kindness, curiosity, acceptance and openness	To observe your experience and shift your attention back to its focus if you drift into thought, without self-criticism if you can
Relaxation	To make muscles relaxed and to feel calm	Various, such as tightening and letting go of muscles

So, if you're writing a report, you focus on that activity as much as you can, without overly straining yourself. Each time your mind wanders off to another thought, you notice what you were thinking about (curiosity), and then without criticising (remember you're being kind to yourself), you guide your attention back to the writing. So, you finish your report sooner (less time spent thinking about other stuff) and the work is probably of better quality (because you gave the report your full attention). The more you can focus on what you're doing, the more you can get done. So mindfulness can help you finish your work early – yippee!

REMEMBER

You can't suddenly decide to focus on your work and then become focused. The power of attention isn't just a snap decision you make. You can train attention, just as you can train your biceps in a gym. Mindfulness is gym for the mind. However, you don't need to make a huge effort as you do when working out. When training the mind to be attentive, you need to be gentle or the mind becomes less attentive. This is why mindfulness requires kindness. If you're too harsh with yourself, your mind rebels. Be mindful with your mind, not against your mind.

Your work also becomes more enjoyable if you're mindful and when you're enjoying something you're more creative and focused. If you're training your mind to be curious about experience rather than bored, you can be curious about whatever you engage in.

Eventually, through experience, you begin to notice that work flows through you, rather than you doing the work. You find yourself feeding the children or making that presentation. You lose the sense of 'me' doing this and become more relaxed and at ease. When this happens, the work is effortless, often of a very high quality and thoroughly enjoyable – which sounds like a nice kind of focus, don't you think? In psychology, this is called being in a state of flow, and it is strongly associated with greater wellbeing and happiness – yay! (More on going with the flow in Chapter 5.)

Developing greater wisdom

Wisdom is regarded highly in Eastern and Western traditions. Socrates and Plato considered philosophy as literally the love of wisdom (*philo-sophia*). According to

Eastern traditions, wisdom is your essential nature and leads to a deep happiness for yourself and to helping others to find that happiness within themselves too.

You can access greater wisdom. Mindfulness leads to wisdom, because you learn to handle your own thoughts and emotions skilfully. Just because you have a negative thought, you don't believe the thought to be true. And when you experience tricky emotions like sadness, anxiety or frustration, you're able to process them using mindfulness rather than being overwhelmed by them.

With your greater emotional balance, you're able to listen deeply to others and create fulfilling, lasting relationships. With your clear mind, you're able to make better decisions. With your open heart, you can be happier and healthier.

Mindfulness leads to wisdom because of your greater level of awareness. You become aware of how you relate to yourself, others and the world around you. With this heightened awareness, you're in a much better place to make informed choices. Rather than living automatically like a robot, you're consciously awake and you take action based on reflection and what's in the best interest of everyone, including yourself.

I consider the Dalai Lama as an example of a wise person. He's kind and compassionate, and thinks about the welfare of others. He seeks to reduce suffering and increase happiness in humanity as a whole. He isn't egocentric, laughs a lot and doesn't seem overwhelmed with all his duties and the significant losses he's experienced. People seem to thoroughly enjoy spending time with him. He certainly seems to live in a mindful way.

Think about who you consider to be wise people. What are their qualities? I'd guess you find them to be conscious and aware of their actions, rather than habitual and lost in their own thoughts – in other words, they're mindful!

Discovering your true self

Mindfulness can lead to an interesting journey of personal discovery. The word *person* comes from the Latin word *persona*, originally meaning a character in a drama, or a mask. The word *discovery* means to dis-cover or to uncover. So in this sense, personal discovery is about uncovering your mask.

As Shakespeare said: 'All the world's a stage, and all the men and women merely players.' Through mindfulness practise, you begin to see your roles, your persona or mask(s) as part of what it means to be you. You still do everything you did before: you can keep helping people or making money or whatever you like doing, but you know that this is only one way of seeing things, one dimension of your being.

You probably wear all sorts of different masks for different roles that you play. You may be a parent, daughter or son, partner, employee. Each of these roles asks you to fulfil certain obligations. You may not be aware that it's possible to put all the masks down through mindfulness practise.

REMEMBER

Mindfulness is an opportunity to just be yourself. When practising mindfulness meditation, you sometimes have clear experiences of a sense of being. You may feel a deep, undivided sense of peace, of stillness and calm. Your physical body, which usually feels so solid, sometimes fades into the background of your awareness or may feel like it disappears altogether, and you can have a deep sense of connection and oneness with your surroundings.

Some people become very attached to these positive experiences in meditation and try hard to repeat them, as if they're 'getting closer' to something. However, over time you come to realise that even these seemingly blissful experiences also come and go. Enjoy them when they come, and then let them go.

Through the practise of mindfulness, you may come to discover that you're a witness to life's experiences. Thoughts, emotions, and bodily sensations come and go in your mindfulness practise, and yet a part of you is just observing this all happening – awareness itself. This is something very simple that everyone can see and experience. In fact, being naturally yourself is so simple, you easily overlook it.

In research into the latest form of mindfulness therapy called Acceptance and Commitment Therapy (ACT), becoming aware of this sense of self that is beyond your thoughts, emotions, sensations and urges is a key part of mindfulness. Through identifying with this 'Observer Self' you become more psychologically flexible and resilient against the challenges of life.

According to Eastern philosophy, as this witness, you're perfect, whole and complete just as you are. You may not feel as if you're perfect, because you identify with your thoughts, emotions and body, which are changing over time. Ultimately you don't need to do anything to attain this natural state, because you are this natural state all the time – right here and right now.

For these reasons, mindfulness is not about self-improvement. At the core of your being, you're perfect just the way you are! Mindfulness exercises and meditations are just to help gently train your brain to be more focused and calm, and your heart to be warm and open. Mindfulness is not about changing you: it's about realising that you're perfectly beautiful within, just the way you are.

WISE WORDS

Consider what Eckhart Tolle, author of *A New Earth: Create a Better Life*, says:

'What a liberation to realize that the "voice in my head" is not who I am. Who am I then? The one who sees that.'

Once you spend more time being the witness of your internal experiences, you're less disturbed by the ups and downs of life. This understanding offers you a way to a happier life. It's that little bit easier to go with the flow and see life as an adventure rather than just a series of struggles.

Starting the Mindfulness Adventure

Mindfulness isn't a quick fix, but the adventure of a lifetime. Imagine mindfulness as being like a journey on a boat. You're an explorer looking for new and undiscovered land. Along the way I'll explain how mindfulness mirrors such a journey.

Beginning the voyage

The journey begins, and you set sail. You're not sure what you're going to find, and you may not be too sure why you're going in the first place, but that's part of the excitement and adventure. You may think that you're finally doing something you really enjoy and can gain from. This is what you wanted to do, and you're on the boat now. At the same time, you're a bit anxious about what may happen – what if things don't work out?

The beginning of the mindfulness journey may feel like this for you. You may be thinking, 'Finally, I've found what I need to do,' and you're keen to find out how to do it, being curious and in anticipation. At the same time, you may feel unsure that you can 'do' mindfulness: you suspect you don't have the patience/focus/discipline/inner strength. You have *ideas* about the journey of mindfulness. At the moment you may suffer from x and y, and after reading this book you want to have reduced those painful feelings. You may have clear goals you want to achieve and hope mindfulness is going to help you to achieve those goals.

REMEMBER

Having a long-term vision as to what you hope to achieve from mindfulness is helpful, but concentrating too much on goals is unhelpful. Mindfulness is ultimately a goalless activity. Mindfulness is process-oriented rather than goal-oriented. You're not actually going anywhere. This is the paradox of mindfulness. If you get overly obsessed with the goals, you focus on the goal rather than the process. However, mindfulness is the journey itself. You aren't going to reach the present moment sometime in the future: you can only be in the present moment *now*. More important than anything else is how you meet this moment. If you can train yourself to be open, curious, accepting, kind and aware of this moment, the future takes care of itself. So, as you steer your boat, keep aware and awake. See Chapter 3 for more about vision in mindfulness.

Overcoming challenges

As you continue your mindfulness journey, before long the initial excitement begins to wear off. You experience rough seas and pirates! Some days, you wish you hadn't started this journey in the first place. Perhaps you should have just stayed at home.

Regularly practising mindfulness can be challenging. What was new and exciting to begin with no longer feels fresh. You may sense a resistance to sit down and meditate, even for a short period, but without knowing why. Don't worry: this is very common. When you overcome the initial resistance, you may discover the practise isn't as bad as you imagined meditating to be. As soon as you start, you feel okay and even enjoy it. You also feel great afterwards, because you managed to overcome the initial resistance of your mind to do something for your own health and wellbeing.

Each time you struggle with the thoughts and feelings in your mindfulness practise, you're probably not accepting or acknowledging them as the natural state of your mind. You're aiming to achieve a certain state of mind rather than being present to what's arising in your mind. Lack of acceptance usually means criticism of yourself or of the whole process of mindfulness. If you persevere, you discover slowly but surely the importance of accepting your thoughts and emotions and the situation you're in and not blaming anyone for that situation, including yourself. In mindfulness, acceptance always comes first; change follows.

Another common challenge is understanding the right attitude to bring to your mindfulness practise. Unhelpful but common attitudes include:

>> I'm going do this and must get it right.

>> I should focus 100 per cent.

>> I'm going to try extremely hard.

Having done a bit of mindfulness meditation, you get thoughts like 'I can't focus at all' or 'My mind was all over the place. I can't do it' or 'That was a bad meditation.' However, as you continue your journey of mindfulness, your attitudes begin to shift towards thoughts such as:

>> I'm going to bring an attitude of kindness and curiosity, and acknowledge whatever my experience is, as best I can.

>> I won't try too hard, nor will I give up. I'll stay somewhere in the middle.

>> My mind is bound to wander off. That's okay and part of being mindful.

>> There's no such thing as a bad meditation. Every meditation is an opportunity to learn and grow.

REACHING THE OTHER SIDE

WISE WORDS

One day, a young man was going for a walk when he reached a wide river. He spent a long time wondering how he would cross such a gushing current. Just when he was about to give up his journey, he saw his teacher on the other side. The young man shouted from the bank: 'Can you tell me how to get to the other side of this river?'

The teacher smiled and replied: 'My friend, you are on the other side.'

You may feel that you have to change, when actually you just have to realise that perhaps you're fine just the way you are. You're running to achieve goals so that you can be peaceful and happy, but actually you're running away from the peace and happiness. Mindfulness is an invitation to stop running and rest. You're already on the other side.

As your attitudes change, mindful exercises and meditations becomes easier, because you're bombarded by fewer judgemental thoughts during and after the practise. And even if you do have judgemental thoughts, you treat them like all the other thoughts you experience and let them go as best you can.

Exploring the journey of a lifetime

After sailing for a long time, you finally see some land in the distance that's more beautiful than anything you've seen in your exploration. You decide to stop when you get there. The land looks so new and fresh, but at the same time very familiar and cosy. As you draw closer, you discover that you're approaching your own house. Of all the places you've been and all the adventures you've had, you feel most at home here, the place you left! However, the journey hasn't been fruitless. You've discovered much along the way and had to travel that journey to discover what you most treasure.

Ultimately in mindfulness, you realise that you don't need to search for anything at all. Everything is okay just the way things are. You're already home. Each moment is magical, new and fresh. Each moment is a treasure never to be repeated again, ever. Your awareness is always shining, lighting up the world around you and inside you effortlessly. Awareness has no off or on switch: awareness is always effortlessly on. Although you experience ups and downs, pleasures and pain, you no longer hang onto things as much, and you therefore suffer less. This isn't so much a final goal as an ongoing journey of a lifetime. Life continues to unfold in its own way, and you begin to grasp how to flow with life.

In this context, think about the following quote from Buddha:

'The secret of health for both mind and body is not to mourn for the past, worry about the future, or anticipate troubles, but to live in the present moment wisely and earnestly.'

The journey of mindfulness is to discover how to live this way.

A TASTE OF MINDFULNESS: MINDFULNESS OF SENSES

PLAY THIS

You may like to experience a little mindfulness. You could read endlessly about what a coconut tastes like, but you won't really know till you taste it yourself. The same goes for mindfulness.

The beauty of this simple mindfulness exercise is that it covers everything you need to know about mindfulness. I have adapted the exercise from a technique I discovered at a 'school of practical philosophy' many years ago. I would like to pass on the gift to you.

This exercise is best done by listing to Track 2 from the audio. Find a comfortable posture for you. You can sit up in a chair, a couch or lie down on a mat – whatever you prefer. Begin by noticing the colours entering your eyes. Notice the tones, shades and hues. Enjoy the miracle of sight that some people don't have. Then, gently close your eyes and be aware of the sense of touch. The sensations of your body. The feeling of your body naturally and automatically breathing. Feel areas of tension and relaxation. Next, be aware of scent. Then move on to any taste in your mouth. Next, become aware of sounds. Sounds near and far. Listen to the sound itself, not so much your thoughts about the sounds. Let go of all effort when listening – allow the sounds to come to you. Finally drop into your observer self – the awareness that lights up all your senses. Rest in that background awareness, whatever that means for you. The feeling of 'being'. The feeling of 'I am' that we all have. Just let go of all effort to do something, and just be . . . and when you're ready, bring this mindful exercise to a close and stretch your body if you wish.

Consider these questions:

What effect did that exercise have on your body and mind? What did you discover?

If you want to become more mindful, you could simply practise this exercise a few times a day. The exercise is simple but powerful and transformative when practised regularly.

Chapter **2**

Enjoying the Benefits of Mindfulness

The enjoyment that comes from mindfulness is a bit like the enjoyment that comes from dancing. Yes, it's only the second chapter and we are already hitting the dance floor! Do you dance just because of the cardiovascular benefits or for boosting your brain by following a tricky dance routine? When you dance but are overfixated on a goal or motive, it kind of spoils it a bit, right? Dancing for the sake of dancing is far more fun. But of course, dancing for the sheer pleasure of it doesn't reduce the benefits on your mind and body of dancing – they're just the icing on the cake. Yummy!

In the same way, be mindful for the sake of being mindful. Mindfulness is about connecting with your senses, being curious, exploring the inner workings of the human mind. If you're too concerned about reaping the benefits of mindfulness, you spoil the fun of it. The journey of mindfulness isn't to reach a certain destination: the journey *is* the destination. Keep this in mind as you read about the various benefits of mindfulness described in this chapter, and let the dance of mindfulness unfold within you. The benefits of mindfulness – relaxation, better mental and emotional health, and an improved relationship with yourself and others – are just the added bonuses along the way. Read on to discover how mindfulness can help you.

Relaxing the Body

The body and mind are almost one entity. If your mind is tense with anxious thoughts, your body automatically tenses as well. They go together, hand in hand.

Why does your body become tense when you experience high levels of stress? The reason is mechanical and wired in the human body. When you experience stress, a chain reaction starts in your body, and your whole being prepares to fight or flee the situation. This is very helpful in dangerous situations when you need to fight or run away, but not so useful when chatting to your boss. So a lot of energy surges through your body; because your body doesn't know what to do with this energy, you tense up.

The aim of mindfulness isn't to make you more relaxed. Mindfulness goes far deeper than that. Mindfulness – a mindful awareness – is about becoming aware and exploring your moment-by-moment experience, in a joyful way if at all possible.

So if you're tense, mindfulness means becoming aware of that tension. Which part of your body feels tense? Does the tension have an associated shape, colour and texture? What's your reaction to the tension; what are your thoughts? Mindfulness is about bringing curiosity to your experience. Then you can begin breathing into the tense part of your body, bringing kindness and accepting your present moment experience – again, not trying to change or get rid of the tension. And that's it. Rest assured, doing this often leads to relaxation – just don't make that your aim. See Chapter 12 for more on stress reduction.

Getting back in touch

As a baby, you were probably very much in touch with your body. You noticed subtle sensations, and may have enjoyed feeling different textures in the world around you. As you grew up, you learnt to use your head more and your body less. You probably aren't as in touch with your body as you were as a young child. You may not notice subtle messages that the body gives you through the mind. I'm sure that some people see the body as simply a vehicle for carrying the brain from one meeting to another!

In fact, the messages between your mind and body are a two-way process. Your mind gives signals to your body, and your body gives signals to your mind. You think, 'I fancy reading that mindfulness book,' and your body picks it up. You feel hungry, and your body signals to your mind that it's time to eat. What about the feeling of stress? If you notice the tension in your shoulders, the twitch in your eye, or the rapid beating of your heart, again your body is sending signals to your mind.

THE CRACKED POT

Once upon a time there was a water bearer who carried two pots of water to his teacher each day. Each day he would walk to the nearest stream, fill both pots with water, and walk back, one pot on each side of a pole he carried across his neck. One pot was cracked, and so by the time the water bearer reached his teacher, it was only half full. This continued for two years, with the water bearer only bringing one and a half pots of water. The perfect pot was proud of its achievements. The cracked pot was sad that it could only do half the job it was supposed to do. One day, the cracked pot said to the water bearer, 'I feel so upset and ashamed. I'm imperfect and I can't hold a full pot of water. What use am I to anyone?' The water bearer told the cracked pot to look on the ground as he carried it. The cracked pot noticed the most beautiful wild flowers and plants on its side of the path. The water bearer explained, 'When I realised you were cracked, I decided to plant seeds on one side of the path, and every day, as you leak, you water that side of the path. If you weren't cracked, these gorgeous flowers wouldn't be here for all to enjoy.'

Sometimes you may think you're not perfect, or your mindfulness practise is not perfect, but how do you know? This story goes to show that even a cracked pot can be seen as perfect just as it is. In the same way, you're perfect just the way you are, with all your imperfections – they're what make you unique.

What if your mind is so busy with its own thoughts that it doesn't even notice the signals from your body? When this happens, you're no longer in touch with or looking after your body. Hunger and thirst, tiredness and stress – you're no longer hearing clearly your instinctual messages. This leads to a further disconnection between bodily signals and your mind, so things can get worse. Stress can spiral out of control through this lack of awareness.

Mindfulness emphasises awareness of your body. An important mindfulness meditation is the body scan (described in full in Chapter 6). In this meditation, you spend 10–30 minutes simply being guided to pay attention to different parts of your body, from the tips of your toes to the top of your head. Some people's reaction is, 'Wow, I've never paid so much attention to my body; that was interesting!' or 'I now feel I'm moving back into my body.' I loved what one of my students said: 'That was like have a massage from the inside out!'

The body scan meditation can offer a healing experience. Emotions you experienced in the past but weren't ready to feel, perhaps because you were too young, can be suppressed and trapped in the body. Sometimes, people suffer for years from a particular physical ailment, but doctors are unable to explain the cause of it. Then, through counselling or meditation, the suppressed emotion arises into consciousness, which releases the emotion. The tightness in the body or the unexplained 'dis-ease' sometimes disappear with the release of the emotion. This is another example of how interconnected mind and body really are, and of the benefits of getting back in touch with the body. Chapter 14 has more on healing the body through mindfulness.

Boosting your immune system

If something's wrong with your body, normally your immune system fights it. Unfortunately, one aspect of the stress response is your immune system not working as hard. When threatened, your body puts all its resources into surviving that threat; energy required for digestion or immunity is turned off temporarily.

REMEMBER

Stress isn't necessarily bad for you. If your stress levels are too low, you're unable to perform effectively and get bored easily. However, if you're stressed for sustained periods of time at high levels, your body's natural immune system is going to stop working properly.

The latest research has found that if you have a positive attitude towards stress, seeing stress as energising and uplifting, the stress seems to have no negative effect on your body. So even your attitude towards stress has a huge effect on your wellbeing.

Mindfulness enables you to notice subtle changes in your body. At the first sign of excessive stress, you can bring a mindful awareness to the situation and discover how to dissipate the stress rather than exacerbate it. By being mindful, you can also remember to see the positive, energising benefits of stress rather than just its negatives. In this way, mindfulness can really benefit your immune system.

Reducing pain

Amazingly, mindfulness has been proven to actually reduce the level of pain experienced by people practising it over a period of eight weeks. I've had clients who couldn't find anything to help them manage and cope with their pain until they began using mindfulness meditation.

When you experience pain, you quite naturally want to block that pain out. You tighten your muscles around the region and make an effort to distract yourself. Another approach is that you want the pain to stop, so you react towards the pain in an angry way. This creates greater tension, not only in the painful region but in other areas of the body. Sometimes you may feel like fighting the pain. This creates a duality between you and your pain, and you burn energy to battle with it. Or perhaps you react with resignation: the pain has got the better of you and you feel helpless.

TIP

Mindfulness takes a radically different approach. In mindfulness, you're encouraged to pay attention to the sensation of pain, as far as you can. So, if your knee is hurting, rather than distracting yourself or reacting in any other way, you actually focus on the area of physical pain with a mindful awareness. This means you bring attitudes like kindness, curiosity and acknowledgment towards the area of pain, as best you can. This isn't easy at first, but you can get better with practise. You can then consider the difference between the sensation of the physical pain itself and all the other stuff you bring to the pain. You begin to understand the difference between *physical* pain and *psychological* pain. The physical pain is the actual raw sensation of pain in the body, whereas the psychological pain is the stress, anxiety, and frustration generated. Through mindfulness, you begin to let go of psychological pain so that only the physical pain is left. When the psychological pain begins to dissolve, the muscle tension around the physical pain begins to loosen, further reducing the perception of pain. You begin to be able to accept the pain as it is in this present moment. Read Chapter 14 for more about mindfulness and physical healing.

Slowing down the ageing process

Have you ever wondered why people die of old age? What exactly is the ageing process? Scientists have discovered that ageing occurs quite naturally in your cells. The scientists (Elizabeth Blackburn and colleagues) who discovered this won the Nobel Prize in medicine back in 2009 for this finding.

All your cells contain *DNA* – the information needed to reproduce each cell. These bundles of DNA are protected with small caps called *telomeres*, which are like the protective ends of shoelaces. The caps prevent the chains of DNA from fraying.

The older you get, the more these caps shorten. Eventually they disappear completely and your cells are unable to reproduce. That's called dying of old age.

This wearing out of the caps at the ends of DNA bundles is associated with many diseases of old age like cancer, heart disease, diabetes and arthritis. Previously, scientists thought that this shortening of telomeres was inevitable.

The good news, however, is that the healthier your levels of stress, the slower these telomeres wear out. Research on groups that practise mindfulness meditation has shown that telomeres can actually be lengthened. This is an incredible finding. A mental discipline of mindfulness affected the microscopic genes in the bodies of those in the study and effectively reduced the rate of ageing. Those mindful meditators who felt the most positive benefit were the ones with the most improved telomere lengths.

WISE WORDS

DON'T TRY HARDER

A martial arts student went to his teacher and said earnestly: 'I'm devoted to studying your martial system. How long will it take me to master it?' The teacher's reply was casual: 'Ten years.' Impatiently, the student answered: 'But I want to master it faster than that. I'll work very hard. I'll practise every day – ten or more hours a day if I have to. How long will it take then?' The teacher thought for a moment and replied: 'Twenty years.'

What does this story mean to you? To me, it shows that hard work and attaining a goal don't necessarily go together. Sometimes, especially when practising something like mindfulness, you need simply to let things unfold in their own time. If you're anxious, you may just block your understanding. Mindfulness is about letting go, not trying harder.

So, no more need for Botox, anti-ageing cream or plastic surgery. Just practise mindfulness – it's cheaper and you'll probably look more beautiful and live to a ripe old age!

Calming the Mind

Your mind is like the ocean: occasionally wild, and at other times calm. Sometimes your mind goes from thought to thought without stopping to rest. At other times, your thoughts come more slowly and have more space between them.

Mindfulness isn't so much about changing the rate of your thoughts, but about noticing the thoughts arising in the first place. By taking a step back from thoughts, you can hover above the waves. The waves are still there, but you have more possibility of watching the show rather than being controlled by the thoughts themselves.

REMEMBER

Think of your mind like a good friend. If you invited your friend to your home, how do you treat her? Should you force her to drink coffee, eat three chocolate biscuits, and listen to you talk about your day even if she doesn't want to? She may prefer tea and plain biscuits, and want to talk about her day too. You *ask* her what she'd like, in a kind and friendly manner. In the same way, treat your mind like a friend. Invite your mind to pay attention to your breath or the work you're doing. When you notice that your mind is restless, acknowledge this. Smile and gently ask your mind to re-focus. The gentle approach is the only way. If you currently treat your mind like your enemy, this shift in attitude could make a significant difference.

Listening to your thoughts

Everything man-made around you was originally a thought in someone's head. Many people consider thought to be all-powerful. All your words, all your actions and activities – everything is motivated by thought. So, being aware of the kind of thoughts going through your mind makes sense.

Have you ever noticed how you have the same sort of thoughts going around and around in your head? The brain easily gets into habitual patterns as your thoughts travel their paths within your brain. *Neurons that fire together, wire together.* Each time you have a particular thought or carry out a particular action, you slightly increase the chance of having the same thought again. Through repeated thinking or action, the connection between neurons strengthens. If you aren't mindful of these thoughts or actions, you may have all sorts of negative, untrue, unhelpful thoughts or behaviours that influence your life without you even being aware of them or questioning the truth or validity of them.

YOUR BRAIN IS TELLING YOU STORIES

Scientists are interested in how the sense of self is created in your brain. You know that you're alive, but how? That's what scientists are studying.

Researchers discovered that your brain is constantly telling you stories. Stories about who you are, what your relationship is to the people you're with, where you're going, what you're going to do this week, and so on. Let's call this your story-telling self. But what if you're telling yourself negative stories? Stories about how you're not good enough and that you're undeserving of happiness and success. It can become a real energy drain.

Fortunately, I've got good news for you. The story-telling self isn't always in operation. There's also a present-moment self. When this part of your brain is activated, you're living in the here and now, connected with your senses. People who practise mindfulness exercises can increase the amount of time they operate with this present-moment self, and can help themselves to become happier people!

So watch out when your mind is telling stories about you, especially discouraging stories, and then smile and turn your attention to one of your senses. By smiling, you're helping yourself see the positive side of your situation rather that setting up a battle in your mind. And connecting with your senses helps to disengage the ruminative, story-telling brain from taking over your mind.

For example, let's say a client gives you negative feedback for some work you did. The thought 'I'm not good enough for this job' or 'That person is so stupid' may keep going around and around your head. You feel rough, your sleep is impacted and you can't properly focus on today's tasks. That's not a great help. But fret not: mindfulness to the rescue!

Mindfulness encourages you to watch your thoughts, emotions, and actions; then you're better able to notice unhelpful thoughts and question their truth. Additionally, just being mindful of thoughts and emotions with a sense of warmth seems to naturally dissipate them. They become far less of a problem. Turn to Chapter 6 for a sitting meditation that includes mindfulness of thoughts and emotions.

Making better decisions

Every moment of every day you make decisions, whether you're aware of them or not. You made a decision to read this chapter. At some point, you'll decide to stop and do something else. Even if you decide to make no decisions, that's a decision too! More significant decisions you have to make have a bigger impact, and a 'good' decision is highly desirable. All you do and have at the moment is mostly due to the decisions you made in the past.

REMEMBER

Awareness of your body can help you make better decisions: a gut feeling, sometimes called intuition, is a signal from your belly telling you what to do, and has been found in some experiments to be faster and more accurate than logical thinking, especially for more complex decisions involving lots of factors. Research shows that there's a mass of nerves in the gut, and some euphemistically call it the gut brain. Tapping into intuition is routinely used by top entrepreneurs and CEOs of corporations to make critical decisions with great success. Other research has found people who tend to be luckier often practise mindfulness and use their intuition to make decisions about work, home or their relationships. So be more mindful and make luckier choices in your life.

Richard Branson, founder of the Virgin Group, says he makes most of his decisions based on gut instinct. If he relied on pure logical thinking and advice from accountants, he wouldn't have started Virgin Atlantic, Virgin Galactic or many of his other ventures. Relying on his feelings, and not just pure reason, has made him both a multi-billionaire and great philanthropist.

Why is gut feeling so effective? Your unconscious mind has far more information than your conscious mind can handle. Making decisions just based on conscious logical thought misses out on the huge capacity of the unconscious brain. Mindfulness helps to deepen your level of awareness and helps you to begin to tap into your intuitive side.

Coming to your senses

One of the key ways of becoming more mindful and of calming the mind is to connect with your senses: sight, sound, touch, smell and taste. Consider the expressions, 'That was *sensible*,' 'I *sense* something's wrong,' and 'She's come to her *senses*.' People's use of the word 'sense' shows we appreciate and value being in touch with our organs of perception. You know innately the value of connecting to your senses if you want to make a *sensible* decision.

What's the benefit of purposefully connecting with your senses? Well, if you aren't paying attention to the stimulation coming through your five senses, you're only paying attention to your thoughts and emotions. You're not aware of anything else. Your thoughts are mainly based on your experiences from the past – from memory. You may imagine something new, but on the whole your mind reworks past experiences or projects ideas into the future based on your past experiences. Emotions are also influenced by your thoughts. So, without paying attention to your senses, you're stuck with your own thoughts and emotions based on the past instead of the present.

By purposefully connecting with one of your senses – say, touch – you begin naturally to calm your mind a little. In mindfulness you can begin by focusing on your breathing. Focus on your belly stretching or your chest expanding, or perhaps the movement of the air as it enters and leaves your body. By focusing on a particular sense, in this case the sense of touch, you're focusing your attention. Rather than your mind wandering wherever it pleases, you're gently training it to stay on one object, namely your breathing. And in the same way as you train a puppy to walk along a path and not keep running off, each time your attention strays, you bring it back, just as you would gently pull the puppy back to the path. You're discovering how to be gentle with yourself, as well as finding out how to focus your attention. See Chapter 6 for a short mindful breathing meditation.

By coming to your senses mindfully, you are doing the following:

>> Training your attention to focus

>> Being kind to yourself when your mind wanders off

>> Realising that you have a certain amount of choice about what you pay attention to

>> Understanding that you can deliberately choose to shift attention away from thinking and into the senses

>> Calming your mind and developing a sense of clarity

Creating an attentive mind

Attention is essential in achieving anything. If you can't pay attention, you can't get the job done, whatever the job is. Mindfulness trains your attention by sustaining your attention on one thing, or by switching the type of attention from time to time.

Daniel Goleman, author of the book *Emotional Intelligence: Why It Can Matter More Than IQ*, recently published a book called *Focus: The Hidden Driver of Excellence*. He explains just how important focus is in every domain of our lives. He also identified a research study that imaged the brains of people practising mindfulness of breath (try it yourself in Chapter 6). Researchers found four different stages while the brain went through the following mental workout:

1. **Focus on your breathing.** The part of the brain that deals with focus is activated.

2. **Notice that your brain is on a train of thought.** The part of the brain that notices that your attention has drifted off into a train of thought is activated.

3. **Let go of that train of thought.** The part of the brain that enables you to let go of your thoughts is activated.

4. **Refocus on your breathing.** The part of the brain used to re-focus on the object you wish to focus on is re-activated.

The parts of the brain dedicated to each of these processes were strengthened through repeated mindfulness practise.

If you do this exercise regularly, you'll become more adept at focusing on whatever you need to pay attention to – whether it's writing an email, listening to a loved one or watching a sunset.

Your attention can be focused in different ways (shown in Figure 2-1):

- » Narrow attention is focused and sharp, like the beam of a laser. You may use this type of attention when chopping vegetables or writing a letter.

- » Wide attention is more open and spacious, like a floodlight. When you're driving, ideally your attention is open so you notice if a car moves closer to you from the side, or if children are playing farther ahead.

- » Outer attention is attention to the outer world through your senses.

- » Inner attention is an awareness of your thoughts and feelings.

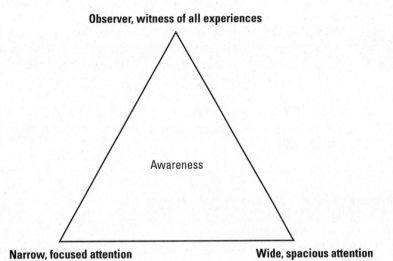

FIGURE 2-1:
The different types of attention.

Observer, witness of all experiences

Awareness

Narrow, focused attention   Wide, spacious attention

© John Wiley & Sons, Inc.

>> Observer or witness awareness is your capacity to know what type of attention you're using. For example, if you're drawing a picture, you're aware that your attention is narrow. If you're walking through the countryside, you're aware that your attention is wide. For more on witness awareness, see the section 'Becoming Aware: Discovering Yourself' below.

WISE WORDS

EMPTY YOUR CUP

A professor once went to visit a teacher of mindfulness. The professor was a world-famous scholar of mindfulness and had studied all the different methods. He knew all the Eastern scriptures and Western science on the subject. He could answer any question on mindfulness with ease and a sense of pride.

The teacher asked if he would like a cup of tea, and the professor said yes. The teacher began filling the cup until it was full, and kept going. The tea was overflowing, and the teacher continued to pour. 'What are you doing! The cup is already full!' exclaimed the professor, panicking. 'You are like this cup,' said the teacher calmly. 'How can I teach you anything of real value until you empty your cup?'

If you want to benefit from mindfulness, you need to put aside all your ideas about it, especially if you think you know what mindfulness is all about. Opinions, ideas, and beliefs block the beauty and simplicity of mindfulness.

Mindfulness is about cultivating a *flexible* attention – not just a focused attention on one thing. So try and practise different mindful exercises so that you're training your mind to be able to both focus narrowly, widely and move attention from one place to another at will.

All the different mindfulness exercises you read about in this book train your mind to be able to sustain attention in the various different ways mentioned in the preceding list.

Soothing Your Emotions

Emotions are tremendously influential on your behaviour and thoughts. If you're feeling low, you're probably far more reluctant to go out with friends, or laugh at a joke, or work with zest. If you're feeling great, you're on top of things; everything feels easy, and life flows easily.

How do you deal with emotions? Are you swept up by them, and do you just hope for the best? Mindfulness offers the opportunity to soothe yourself and step back from emotional ups and downs.

Understanding your emotions

What's an emotion, a feeling, or mood?

You experience emotion partly from a survival point of view. If you don't feel scared when faced with a raging bull, you'll find yourself in lots of trouble. Other emotions, like happiness, help to create social ties with those around you, increasing your security. Even depression is thought to have evolved for your protection, reducing motivation and therefore the chance of experiencing harm or wasting energy through pursuing an unattainable goal.

Emotion comes from a Latin word meaning 'to move out'. If you observe emotions, you can discover certain important characteristics:

>> Emotions are always changing. You aren't stuck with one emotion all your life, at the same intensity.

» Emotions are a very physical experience. If you're feeling anxious, you may feel a tingling in your stomach. If you're feeling angry, you may feel your breathing and heart rate go up.

» You can observe your own emotions. You can sense the difference between yourself and your emotions. You're not your emotions, you're the observer of your emotions.

» Emotions make a huge impact on your thoughts. When you're feeling down, you're likely to predict negative things about yourself or other people. When you're feeling happy, you're more likely to think positive thoughts, predict positive outcomes, and look upon the past in a positive light too.

» You tend to perceive emotions as pleasant, unpleasant, or neutral.

Managing feelings differently

Take a few minutes to consider the following emotions and how you deal with them:

» Anger

» Anxiety

» Fear

» Depression

Your approach may be to either avoid the emotion and pretend it isn't there, or to express your feelings to whoever is nearby. Mindfulness offers an alternative – a way of meeting emotions that enables you to see them in a different light. The idea is to acknowledge and give mindful attention to difficult feelings, rather than avoid or react to them. Surprisingly, this tends to dissipate the strength and the pain of the emotion. See Chapters 12 and 13 for ways of dealing with a variety of different emotions.

My first experience of mindfulness was exciting, because my emotional state was quickly changed to a sense of calmness and joy. In fact, I didn't even know I was previously stressed! The feeling of stress was just my normal state of mind. I was amazed that such a short mindfulness exercise could have such a powerful effect. I immediately had a desire to share this new-found technique with others.

THE GUESTHOUSE

This superb poem by Rumi (1207–1273) captures the attitude you're moving towards when dealing with emotions mindfully.

This being human is a guesthouse.

Every morning a new arrival.

A joy, a depression, a meanness,

some momentary awareness comes

as an unexpected visitor.

Welcome and entertain them all!

Even if they're a crowd of sorrows

who violently sweep your house

empty of its furniture,

still, treat each guest honourably.

He may be clearing you out

for some new delight.

The dark thought, the shame, the malice,

meet them at the door laughing,

and invite them in.

Be grateful for whoever comes,

because each has been sent

as a guide from beyond.

Uplifting Your Spirit

You may wish to practise mindfulness just for your body or mind – and that's totally fine. But you may be interested in how mindfulness offers a greater sense of purpose in your life, or how it relates to spirituality, whatever that means to you. If that sounds worthwhile, this section is for you.

Everyone defines spirituality differently, which I respect. For me, to be spiritual means to value a deeper sense of connection between yourself and something bigger. And that could be your connection with nature, your love for your friends or family, the Universe or even your love for God, if that's your belief.

Mindfulness offers you a way to deepen your connection with yourself and whatever is most meaningful for you – a connection that comes from both your head and heart. And having a deeper sense of meaning is really important – vital infact.

Victor Frankl, in his incredibly moving book, *Man's Search for Meaning,* showed how having a deeper sense of meaning helped him survive the hellish conditions of a concentration camp. He was a psychotherapist and observed that others in the concentration camp also survived if they had something deeper worth living for, whether that was a loved one or belief in something greater than themselves. He ended up creating a whole new therapy based on helping people find greater meaning in their lives.

TIP

Take a few moments to reflect or write down what's most important for you. Is it your friends, family or a loved one? Do you love nature and yearn to spend time with her? Do you have certain values that are most meaningful for you? Perhaps you believe in a God? Or maybe you're a fan of the *Star Wars* movies and want to be one with 'The Force.' (Sorry, no lightsabers are included with this current edition of the book!)

Whatever you find most meaningful in your life, once you start practising mindfulness, your connection may deepen. And as your sense of meaning and connection grows, you're likely to have a greater resilience and stability from the challenges that life throws at you.

This is a healthy development and one I hope you'll consider exploring and enjoying at a pace that feels right for you.

Knowing Thyself: Discovering Your Observer Self

Before examining my sense of self and relationship with the world, I used to believe that I was a tiny, isolated human being living in the corner of a city on a planet called Earth, fighting to survive on my own. However, through mindfulness I began to discover a totally different and satisfying dimension of myself that I'd overlooked. Mindfulness helps you to see things from a more holistic perspective. Having a sense of a deeper dimension and connection with the world around you puts the waves of life's challenges into a much bigger context. If you feel interconnected with other people, nature or even the Universe, you're part of something bigger. If you're the ocean, what trouble do waves give you?

This journey begins with a deeper connection with youself. Inscribed above the ancient Greek temple of Apollo at Delphi is the phrase 'Know thyself,' a vitally important concept for Greek philosophers like Socrates. But self-reflection isn't advocated so much in the twenty-first century!

WISE WORDS

THE LION AND THE SHEEP

Mindfulness naturally leads to self-examination – examination of who's doing the mindfulness in the first place. The following story may help to illustrate the realisation that can take place.

A lion cub accidentally strayed away from its mother and ended up with a flock of sheep. The lion cub grew up with the other sheep, ate what the other sheep ate and behaved like them too. As the lion grew up he continued to behave in the same way, frightened of the subtlest sounds. However, something just didn't feel right. One day, he looked into a still pool of water and saw a beautifully clear reflection of himself. He was a lion, not a sheep. Because he'd believed himself to be like the other sheep, he behaved and thought like one. Now that he saw who he truly was, everything changed, and yet he was just the same as he always was. He returned to his pride and lived according to his true nature.

In the same way, if you identify yourself with thoughts like 'I can never talk to her!' or emotions like 'I am depressed,' you're like the lion identifying itself as a sheep. Mindfulness shows you that you're much bigger that fleeting thoughts and emotions; you're also awareness itself. Then you see thoughts as just thoughts and emotions as just emotions. They're not reality: they're just a passing experience.

Who are you? What is this incredible thing called life? These are the questions I've often grappled with. While making money and spending time with friends was fun, it lacked any sense of depth. My life had its pleasures but was lacking in purpose. So I found myself in a mindfulness class. Life was too wonderful and mysterious to be lived without meaning or purpose.

Mindfulness helps you to put things in perspective. If you go from place to place, rushing to finish all that stuff on your to-do list, and when you're done are so exhausted that you just collapse in front of the television, you may have a bit of a problem discovering who you truly are in the meantime. By taking some time to be mindful, you're giving yourself the opportunity to stop and look at all these incessant thoughts and emotions that come and go, and discover the sense of being that's behind the mind chatter. A part of yourself that's peaceful, joyous and whole.

This book describes one approach to discovering your sense of self that I've found immensely liberating and fascinating. Self-discovery is a personal journey, so you may have a totally different way of understanding your deep, inner being.

TIP

Here's one interesting way to explore your sense of self and awareness: read each of these paragraphs as slowly as you can. Notice your judgements and desire to agree or disagree with the statements. Try doing neither, and instead just read and reflect.

>> **Are you just your body?** Your body is made up of hundreds of millions of cells. Cells are dying and re-forming all the time. Every few years, pretty much all the cells in your body are replaced with new ones – so your body is completely different to the one you had as a baby. Right now, you're digesting food, your nails and hair are growing, and your immune system is fighting any diseases within you. It's all just happening – you're not doing it. Even if your body becomes totally paralysed, the sense of you being here will still be present. The very fact that you say 'my body' suggests that the body is something you *have*, rather than your core self.

>> **Are you just your thoughts?** Thoughts keep coming, no matter how mindful you are. The fact that you can be aware of your thoughts means that you are separate from them. If you were your thoughts, you wouldn't be able to notice them. The fact that you can observe your thoughts means they're separate and a space lies between you and what you think. In mindfulness practise, you can step back from your thoughts from time to time, but you can't control thoughts. Do you even know what you're going to think in the next few minutes? No. But can you be *aware* of your thoughts? Yes.

>> **Are you just your emotions?** Just as you can observe thoughts, you can also observe your emotions. Doesn't this mean you're separate from your emotions? Emotions arise and eventually pass away. If you were your emotions, then your emotions would never pose any problem at all. You would be able to control emotions and wouldn't choose to have negative feelings.

REMEMBER

So what are you? What's left? Let's call it the observer self. There's no specific word in the English language for this. If you're the observer, you can't be that which you observe. In this sense you can say *you are awareness*. Thoughts and ideas, emotions and images, desires, fears and actions arise *in you* but you're aware of them all. Everything arises *in awareness*, in being. That's what you are. You aren't just the thought 'I'm Shamash' or 'I'm Jane;' you're that sense of presence that underlies experience.

These are some of the attributes of awareness or the observer self:

>> **You're always aware.** Sometimes that awareness is lost in thoughts and dreams; sometimes it's connected with the senses.

>> **Awareness happens by itself.** Awareness is different to attention. Attention or *mindful* awareness is something to be cultivated and trained, which is what most of this book is about, but *pure* awareness is your inner self. To be aware takes no effort. You don't need to *do* awareness. Awareness is effortlessly operating right now as you read. You can't turn off or run away from awareness!

>> **Awareness comes before thought.** As a baby, you had awareness without words and ideas. Thoughts and concepts come after awareness.

>> **In terms of awareness, you're both 'no-thing' and everything.** Without awareness, nothing would exist for you. With awareness, you're a part of every experience you have. This sounds contradictory, but look into these concepts yourself. Ask yourself what your daily experience would be like without awareness.

Having read all these attributes of awareness, what's your reaction? Whether you believe these ideas or not isn't important; what *is* important is examining and exploring these ideas for yourself. As Socrates said, 'The unexamined life is not worth living.' I've personally found looking deeper into my identity to be completely transformative and liberating – mindful self-discovery is the ultimate exploration for me!

TIP

Spend a few minutes resting as an observer of your moment-to-moment experience. This can turn out to be an incredibly peaceful experience. That's a meditation in itself. No need to react to your thoughts, emotions, or any other sensations. Just watch the experiences arise and fall again. Be the observer self. And if you find yourself trying too hard, don't forget to smile! That'll remind you that this is a non-doing process – not just another thing that requires a lot of effort. To experience this further, see the sitting mediation in Chapter 6. It's called 'open awareness.'

THE STORY OF THE STONEMASON

Once upon a time a stonemason paused to rest from his hard work for a few minutes at the side of an enormous rock. He saw a lord and his servants pass underneath the shade of the trees nearby.

When the stonemason saw this rich lord with all his luxuries and comfort, his work suddenly felt much harder. 'Oh, if only I were a rich man,' he thought, 'I'd be so happy!' Suddenly a voice answered from the mountain: 'Your wish shall become reality; a rich man you shall be!'

When the stonemason returned home, he found a beautiful palace where his simple home had stood. The poor man was overflowing with joy, and before long his old life was completely forgotten. One day, when he was walking in the marketplace, he felt the Sun burn on his face, and he wished he was as mighty as the Sun itself. Immediately he became the Sun.

As the Sun, he felt all-powerful. His light shone around the entire world, and his rays beamed on kings and cobblers alike. But before long, a cloud moved in front of him and obscured his light. 'What's this?' he wondered. 'A cloud is mightier than me! Oh, how I wish I were a cloud.'

And a cloud he became. He blocked the Sun's beams, and for weeks he poured rain until the rivers overflowed their banks and the crops of rice stood in water. Towns and villages were destroyed by the sheer power of the rain, but he noticed that only the great rock on the mountainside remained unmoved. 'What's this?' he cried. 'A rock is mightier than me! Oh how I wish I were a rock.'

And the rock he became, and he gloried in the power. Proudly he stood, and neither the heat of the Sun nor the force of rain could move him. 'This is the best!' he said to himself. But soon he heard a strange noise at his feet, and when he looked down he saw a stonemason breaking him up, piece by piece. Then he cried in his anger: 'Oh, if only I were a stonemason!'

In that instant, he became the stonemason once again, and remained content as he was for the rest of his life.

2

Preparing the Ground for Mindful Living

Create a solid foundation on which to build a life filled with everyday mindfulness.

Explore how cultivating the habit of daily mindfulness to benefit your life.

Learn to enjoy the moment by going with the flow.

Chapter **3**

Making Mindfulness a Daily Habit

O ne of the best ways of boosting your capacity to be mindful is to practise mindfulness every day. Establishing a daily habit of mindfulness isn't always easy, but it's well worth the effort. With a clear understanding of how behaviour change works, you can engage in practising mindfulness regularly. Once the habit of daily mindfulness is created, the routine becomes as natural as having a shower – you now have a way of training and 'cleansing' your mind every day, not just your body.

This chapter explores how best to change your behaviour effectively, discover the science of habits, find out what your intentions of mindfulness are and how to develop a long-term daily mindfulness practise.

Discovering the Secret to Change

Every year millions of people make new year resolutions. 'I will go to the gym several times a week.' 'I'll stop eating chocolate cake.' And you'll even hear 'I'll practise mindfulness every day this year.' And yet within just a couple of weeks, most people fail to stick to their resolutions and give up. Have you had that experience to? I certainly have!

New year resolutions are attempts to change behaviour. You may not have been successful because you haven't learnt *how* to change your behaviour. Behaviour change is actually a skill – not an innate talent. The good new is you can learn how to change. And with that skill, you can make lots of positive changes in your life, including daily mindfulness!

Although most people consider changing their daily habits to be hard, it's actually not as difficult as you think – once you know how. Learning to change your behaviour is like learning to swim – it looks really difficult at first, but it's easy once you know how! And then it gets really exciting to put your new skills to work.

In this section, you're going to learn how to change your behaviour so that you're able to make time to practise mindfulness in some form or another every day – however you choose.

Designing your life for mindfulness

As you've picked up this book, I'm guessing you are curious about the power of mindfulness and wish to apply it in your daily life.

If you dive in without a well designed plan, you're unlikely to succeed in practising mindfulness long term. Why? Because you're relying on your motivation. And your motivation doesn't stay high all the time: It goes up and down as shown in Figure 3-1.

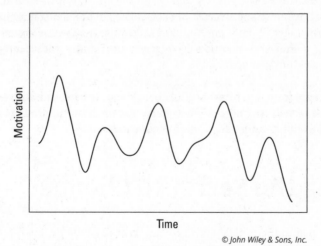

FIGURE 3-1: The ups and downs of motivation.

© John Wiley & Sons, Inc.

For example, after reading some chapters of this book, you may feel highly motivated to practise mindfulness every day. You may say to yourself, 'This is brilliant stuff. I'm going to do some mindfulness meditation for half an hour every day. This is going to be my new habit. I can do this!'

This is an example of what most people do. They use determination and sheer will-power to try to drive change into their life. The first few days go fine: you remember to do your mindful meditation and are pleased with yourself. Then a few days in and you wake up with a headache. No way do you feel like practising mindfulness. That's out of the question! You're not motivated to be mindful. You'd rather stay in bed and sleep. The next day you wake up late. Motivation is still down. Then the next day you forget. A few days pass and you realise you haven't practised mindfulness, so you give up.

How do you think you'd feel? Probably not that great. Perhaps you may even think of yourself as a failure – someone who can't stick to new habits. Next time you realise you need to create a new habit, you'll be less likely to have a go because you don't want to fail again and think of yourself as a failure.

Most people, at this point, blame themselves. You may think, 'If only I tried harder' or 'If only I was more disciplined.'

Blaming yourself doesn't help you; nor does just giving up. So what's the solution?

Starting small: The secret to creating new habits

As motivation goes up and down in humans, rather than starting habits with a big commitment and requiring lots of willpower, why not start small – really small? What if you just began with a mindfulness practise that takes less than 30 seconds?

If you start small, you don't need lots of motivation to stick to the new habit. Even if you wake up with a headache, or oversleep or whatever other excuse you may have, you always have 30 seconds to do some mindfulness. And you get that sense of success each time you manage the short practise.

In this way, you have a much better chance of success. After a week or so, you can gradually increase the length of time you practise mindfulness.

Over time, you don't need to worry about motivation because your mindfulness practise becomes a habit. Once an action becomes a habit in your daily life, high levels of motivation are no longer necessary. The new activity becomes almost automatic – like brushing your teeth or having a shower. You've cleverly side-stepped the need for motivation.

Mindfulness is about living more consciously, not automatically. So making mindfulness into an automatic habit may sound counterintuitive. But actually, the opposite is true. If you don't put mindfulness practise as part of your routine, you're much less likely to remember to be mindful, and your whole day could pass by automatically. So make the practise of mindfulness a daily habit and look for-ward to a more mindful life!

To create a new habit, in this case the habit of practising mindfulness every day, there are three steps:

1. Decide what your daily mindfulness practise will be, which shouldn't take more than 30 seconds.

2. Find a suitable spot in your daily schedule to do your short mindfulness practise.

3. Celebrate your success!

In the following subsections, I'll go through each of these important steps in turn.

Deciding on your daily mindfulness practise

You can do any mindfulness practise you wish. To help you decide, here are a few options:

>> Mindfulness of breath (see Chapter 11)

>> Mindfully feeling your feet on the floor

>> Drinking a cup of tea or coffee mindfully

>> Mindfully stretching

>> Reflecting on three things you're grateful for (see Chapter 11)

These are just some of my suggestions. You can pick one of these practises, or if you have some other practise that you'd like to try, go for it!

I recommend a short mindfulness practise every day rather than once every few days or once a week, because that way it's much easier to make it a habit. Habits generally don't form if they are practised every few days, and short daily practise is far more powerful than long practises done haphazardly.

Don't think about it too much. Just pick one, have a go and let's see what happens. You're experimenting. If it works, great. If not, no problem at all. That's feedback. Try a different one. If you have the attitude of an experimenter trying new things, you won't fear failure so much. You'll see that as part and parcel of your process of learning something new about yourself.

» Pick something you *want* to do, not something you feel you *have* to do.

» Remember to keep the mindfulness practise to approximately 30 seconds. This is the hard bit as you may feel that's not enough and want to do more. We humans are over-ambitious at the beginning and then end up giving up. Slow and steady wins the race. Just stick to roughly 30 seconds for now. There's a reason for it. And it doesn't matter if it's a bit more or less. You don't need to use a timer.

Choosing a suitable spot for your daily mindfulness practise

Ok, you've hopefully chosen a *short* mindfulness practise you *want* to experiment with trying every single day.

The next step is to find a suitable spot for your mindfulness practise to grow.

Why do you need a suitable spot rather than just randomly practising whenever you have time? To understand why, you need to learn how habits work. To form a habit, you need to start with a cue – a trigger to tell your brain to carry out the habit.

For example, if you see some chocolate, that can be a cue for you to grab the chocolate bar. (I'm speaking for myself here!) An alarm clock going off can be a cue for you to get out of bed (or hit the snooze button). Feelings can also be cues. Feeling tired can be a cue for you to go to bed, or perhaps reach for another cup of coffee. Our lives are filled with cues for our habits, so look out for them.

THE POWER OF SMALL STEPS – LITERALLY!

This is an amazing experiment has been repeated from the U.S. to Ireland. Researchers pick two random groups of people in an office, that don't exercise regularly. With one group, they give them gift vouchers to buy gym shoes and clothes and offer them free access to a gym for six month. They get everything they need to get started at the gym. With the other group, they just say 'On Monday, walk up one flight of stairs. On Tuesday, do the same but add just one extra step. On Wednesday, one more step again. In the same way, keep adding an extra step every single day.'

Which group do you think were fitter, happier, and had healthier blood pressure three years later? The walking group.

This experiment shows you the power of taking small steps – literally! Big change happens through taking small, consistent steps every day.

In the same way, if you wish to create the habit of mindfulness every day, you need a reliable cue. The ideal cue for a new daily habit would be a part of your routine that you already have. You sit up in your bed every day. Sitting up in your bed can be your cue to do your mindfulness practise. (That's mine actually.) Or if you start your day with a shower in the morning, you can do your mindfulness practise after getting dressed.

Giving yourself a reward for practising mindfulness

To complete your habit loop, you need to have a reward. Without a reward, you don't create a habit. The reward tells your brain that you had a pleasant experience that's worth having again. So here are the three steps required for a habit to form:

1. **Cue:** A prompt to remind you to practise mindfulness. For example, your alarm clock in the morning or when you sit on your bed after getting dressed.

2. **Action:** The practise of mindfulness itself. For example, feeling 10 mindful breaths or mindful listening to the sounds in your surroundings.

3. **Reward:** A positive experience. Fore example, the feeling of being grounded or saying something positive in your mind.

You can remember the acronym CAR to remind you of these three steps in habit formation shown in Figure 3-2.

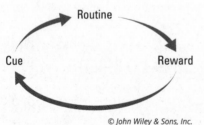

FIGURE 3-2: To create a habit you need a cue, the action, and a sense of reward.

© John Wiley & Sons, Inc.

Going back to the example of chocolate, the reward is obviously the delicious taste. The reward for, say, checking your mobile phone is a sense of satisfaction that someone has contacted you.

So what's the reward for practising mindfulness. There are three ways of rewarding yourself, to increase your chance of the mindfulness action becoming a regular habit:

» Enjoy your practise of mindfulness if you can.

» Smile during and at the end of your mindfulness practise.

> » Celebrate at the end of your mindfulness practise by saying something
> positive, fun or uplifting to yourself like 'Yes!' or 'Yipee!' or 'Go me!' or even 'Yes,
> I managed to practise 30 seconds of mindfulness yet again. I'm doing so well!'

The more you are able to celebrate your success at completing the short new mindfulness exercise, the higher the likelihood that you'll practise again, resulting in the activity turning into a habit and becoming part of your new daily routine.

Being playful with your new habit

Your new habit will probably not take root straight away. And that's okay! In fact, that's normal. The idea is to experiment with trying to be mindful in different spots to find the right place for you.

For example, you may try a mindful exercise straight after your alarm goes off, but you're too sleepy. So then you may try after coming home from work, but find you're distracted by your kids. Then you experiment with a mindful meditation after getting dressed in the morning, and that's perfect. You feel refreshed and love being mindful then.

Of course, your mindfulness habit doesn't have to be meditation. It could be an everyday mindful practise like mindful tea drinking, or taking ten mindful breaths as you smile, or noticing five new things you can see, hear, smell, taste or touch. Experiment with any activity that unlocks you from your automatic thoughts and brings you into the moment.

Watering the seeds of your mindful habits

How do you grow your mindfulness habit? The secret is not to rush to grow it.

I'm reminded of a story of a little child who planted a seed. Every day the child watered the seed and watched the soil intensely, waiting for a shoot to come out. After two days, the child decided to dig the seed out to see how was doing. Of course, the child damaged the tiny seedling that was growing. If the child was a bit more patient, he would have been rewarded with a beautiful new plant.

In the same way, once you find your spot to do your daily mindfulness practise, stick with it for a bit. No need to lengthen the practise. Just stick with the 30 seconds or so until it becomes a habitual part of your day.

After a week or so, increase the length of the habit gradually – maybe 45 seconds or one minute. Keep practising consistently and increase the length of the habit in such a way that it seems almost too easy. If you do this, you'll find forming your new habit happens with almost no effort. After a month or two, you may find yourself up to 10 minutes or more of daily practise, if that's your aim. You decide what's right for your lifestyle.

Scattering seeds of mindfulness throughout the day

After you have played around with your first habit of mindfulness, perhaps a short mindfulness meditation, you can use cues throughout the day to remind you to practise mindfulness.

Here's some ideas for cues that you can use throughout the day:

>> The sound of a phone ringing or a text message

>> Sitting down on some form of public transport

>> Stepping outside in the morning

>> The sound of your doorbell

>> Opening your journal

These are all examples of cues you can use to do short mindfulness practises:

>> Taking a few deep, conscious breaths

>> Holding a gentle smile on your face

>> Checking in with how your body or mind feels

>> Noticing what thoughts are arising in your head and imagining placing them on clouds in the sky of awareness

>> Asking yourself: 'How can I best take care of myself right now?'

REMEMBER

Each time you practise mindfulness, you increase the chance of being mindful again on another day because any new activity you take on, whether physical or mental, creates a new pathway in the brain. It's a bit like creating a new pathway through a forest. At first, walking through all the overgrowth is a bit difficult. You need to push the overhanging branches out of the way and tread on the long grass under your feet. However, if you keep walking on that path, it becomes easier and easier. Soon enough, you don't need to work hard any more or think about which way to go next. The path is clear. It's the same with pathways in the brain. In fact, that's what a new activity creates in the brain: a pathway to greater mindfulness, awareness and 'aliveness.'

NOTHING BEATS THE REAL THING

I find that all the time I spend talking, writing or teaching mindfulness makes almost no difference to how mindful I am. The only thing that deepens my mindfulness is regular practise of mindfulness meditation itself, which can be mindful walking, mindful body scan meditation or the mindful sitting meditation.

You may spend every waking hour reading, writing, studying and talking about mindfulness but hardly ever practise it. And just as describing a mango isn't the same as tasting one, so talking or reading about mindfulness isn't the same as practising it. Reading about and discussing mindfulness may seem much more comfortable and easy than doing it, but unfortunately, it makes no difference to your mind or body. So I recommend you aim at doing 'non-doing' every day, for however long you decide and in whatever form that works for you.

Exploring Your Intentions

The word 'intention' comes from the Latin *intendere*, meaning to direct attention. Intention is purpose – what you hope to achieve from a certain action. If you're driving to work and your intention is to get there on time no matter what happens, you may drive recklessly and dangerously. If you're driving to work and your intention is to get there safely, you try to drive with a more focused attention, and at a safe and reasonable speed. Here's a more startling example. Imagine someone cutting you with a knife – such as a surgeon who has to insert a blade and cut you open. Because the intention of the surgeon is to help restore your health, you're probably willing to undergo this seemingly horrendous procedure. However, a murderer may also use a blade, but with a far less positive intention and you're unlikely to be so willing!

Intention shapes the nature of the whole action itself. Although the action may be the same (as with the example of cutting someone open), the intention itself strongly influences your moment-by-moment experience and state of mind. For this reason, the right intention is vitally important in mindfulness meditation. I'd go so far as to say that the nature of the intention itself strongly influences the quality of your mindful practise.

Clarifying intention in mindfulness

Dr Shauna Shapiro of Santa Clara University, together with several colleagues, came up with a helpful model to suggest how mindfulness works. The researchers identified three key components: *intention*, *attention* and *attitude*. The components are required together and feed into each other when you engage in mindfulness.

The components link in well with the often-used definition of mindfulness, which is *paying attention in a particular way: on purpose, in the present moment and non-judgementally*. Let's break down this definition:

>> Paying attention – *attention*

>> On purpose – *intention*

>> In a particular way – *attitude*

These three components work together seamlessly to create the moment-to-moment experience that is mindfulness. Figure 3-3 shows the components of mindfulness working together.

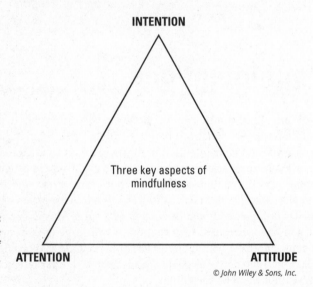

INTENTION

Three key aspects of
mindfulness

FIGURE 3-3:
The three
components of
mindfulness.

ATTENTION   ATTITUDE

Intention is a component that often gets lost when people consider mindfulness, and yet it's vitally important. Intention sets the scene for what unfolds in the practise itself.

Intention evolves. One study has shown that people's intention in mindfulness is usually stress reduction, and moves on to greater understanding of their thoughts and emotions, and finally towards greater compassion. For example, you may begin practising mindfulness to reduce your anxiety and when that subsides, you practise to attain greater control over your emotions and eventually to be a more compassionate and kind person to your family and friends. What's *your* intention?

REMEMBER

Mindfulness is being developed to relieve the suffering caused by a whole host of different conditions, from eating disorders to anxiety in pregnancy, from reducing students' stress to speeding up the healing process for psoriasis. These are all a wonderful flowering of applications of mindfulness, but keep in mind the original purpose and vision of mindfulness as a way of relieving *all* suffering, both yours and others', and developing a greater sense of compassion. Such a large and positive vision enlarges the practise of mindfulness for those who share those possibilities.

Finding what you're looking for

The following exercise – what I call a 'mindful visualisation' – can give you great insight into your true and deep intentions in practising mindfulness. When I first used this exercise, I was surprised and fascinated by the insights into my own deep motives.

Afterwards, do the writing exercise described in the next section.

Discovering your intention: Mindful visualisation

PLAY THIS

This exercise is best done by listing to Track 3 from the audio. Find a comfortable position: seated in a chair or sofa, or lying down. Choose a position in which you feel cosy and comfortable. Close your eyes.

> Imagine that you're sitting by the side of a beautiful lake. The place can be somewhere you've been before or seen before, or may be completely created in your imagination – it doesn't matter which. Find a place where you feel calm and relaxed. The lake may have majestic trees around one side and stunning mountains in the distance. The temperature is just about perfect for you, and a gentle breeze ensures that you feel refreshed. A flock of birds are flying across the horizon, and you can sense a freshness in the air. Your body feels relaxed and at ease.
>
> You look down and notice a pebble. You pick it up and look at it. It has a question engraved on it. The question is: 'What do I hope to get from mindfulness?' You look carefully at the question as you hold the pebble gently in your hand.
>
> You throw the pebble out into the lake. You watch the pebble as it soars through the air in an arc, almost in slow motion, and eventually makes contact with the surface of the water. You see the circular ripples radiate out. As the pebble contacts with the water, you continue to reflect on the question: 'What do I hope to get from mindfulness?'
>
> The pebble moves down into the water. You're able to see the pebble as it sinks deeper and deeper into the water. As it continues to smoothly fall downwards in the deep water, you continue to watch it, and you continue to reflect on the question: 'What do I hope to get from mindfulness?' You keep watching as the pebble falls, and you keep reflecting on the question.

Eventually, the pebble softly makes contact with the bottom and settles there. The question 'What do I hope to get from mindfulness?' is still visible. Reflect on that question for a few more moments.

Bring the exercise to a close, noticing the physical sensations of your body, taking a slightly deeper breath and, when you're ready, slowly opening your eyes. If you keep a journal, record what you discovered in it. This may help to reveal further insights as you write.

No right or wrong answers exist for this 'intention' meditation. Some people get clear answers about what they hope to get out of practising mindfulness, and others reflect on the question, yet no answers arise. Some people find that the answers they get at the surface of the lake are the more obvious ones but, as the pebble falls deeper, their reasons to practise clarify and deepen too. If the exercise was helpful, great; if not, don't be concerned – there are other exercises to do later in this chapter.

Discovering your intention: Sentence completion

Take a piece of paper or your journal, and write as many answers as you can to the following questions in one minute, without thinking about them too much:

I want to practise mindfulness because . . .

I'm hoping mindfulness will give me . . .

If I'm more mindful I'll . . .

The real reasons I want to practise mindfulness are to . . .

Ultimately mindfulness will give me . . .

Mindfulness is . . .

These sentence-completion exercises may help to clarify your motivation and intentions for mindfulness.

Now read and reflect on your answers. Did any of your answers surprise you? Why is that? You may like to come back to these answers when you're struggling to motivate yourself to be mindful; reading your answers then can be a way of empowering yourself to practise some mindfulness.

Developing a vision

A *vision* is a long-term aspiration: something you're willing to work towards. By having a clear vision, you have an idea of where you need to get to. Think of it in terms of any journey you make, for which you need to know two things: where you are now, and where you need to get to.

Mindfulness is about being in the present moment and letting go of goals. Why think about visions and intentions? Why not just be in the here and now and forget about aspirations? Well, the vision gives you the energy, the motivation and the strength to practise mindfulness, especially when you really don't feel like practising.

For example, your mind may be jam-packed with thoughts, ideas and opinions to such an extent that you can't easily calm down. Your vision may be to be a calm and collected person, someone who never really worries about things too much, and who others come to for advice. With this in mind, you know why you're practising mindfulness and *are committed* to sticking at it. This doesn't mean that the goal of each and every mindful meditation is calmness, and that if you're not calm you've failed; a vision is bigger than that – a long-term objective rather than a short-term goal.

If you're not too sure what your vision is, come back to this section after doing some mindfulness exercises or after dipping into other areas of this book. Doing this may give you a clearer idea of a vision to work towards. The practise of mindfulness itself helps to develop an unambiguous vision as you begin to experience some benefits.

Try the following two exercises to help clarify your vision.

Writing a letter to your future self

This is a wonderful way to develop a long-term vision of what you hope to achieve through mindfulness.

Reflect on your future self in five or ten years. This is your chance to let go and dream. How will you feel? What sort of person do you hope to be? How do you cope with challenges in your life?

Write a letter to yourself about it, or if you're a visual person, draw pictures. This vision gives your brain something to work towards, and the opportunity to begin discovering a path for you to tread to get there.

Pin the letter up on the wall at home, or ask a good friend to post the letter back to you any time in the next year. Most people feel great receiving a letter from themselves dropping through the post, and the self-reflection always seems to arrive at the right time in your life.

You can even send an email to yourself from your future self. The website www.futureme.org allows you to do this for free.

Attending your own funeral

Try to overcome any reluctance about this exercise, because it's very moving and powerful. Imagine being at your own funeral service. You're aware of family and friends around you. Consider each person and imagine everyone saying what you'd *like* them to say about you. Really hear the positive things they're saying about you and your life. What do they value about you? What sort of aspects of your personality would you like them to talk about? What have they admired about you? After the exercise, think about it. How did you feel? What did people say about you?

The exercise helps to put things into context and clarifies your values – what's really important to you. How can you use what was said to create a vision of the kind of person you want to become? How can that vision help motivate your mindfulness practise?

Ask yourself the following question every day for a couple of weeks: 'If today were the last day of my life, would I want to do what I'm about to do today?' Whenever the answer is no for too many days in a row, you know that you need to change something. Even if you don't explicitly ask this question, you get a flavour of the value of considering death in order to help you wake up and focus on what's most important in life.

Practising mindfulness for everyone's benefit

If you're clear about the personal benefits of mindfulness, and practise mindfulness for your own benefit, that's great. However, you can also experiment with practising mindfulness for others. Shifting your intention can make the experience more enjoyable. Just like if you do some volunteer work, you're doing the work to help others, so you can practise mindfulness meditation in a way that's of service to others.

How does mindfulness benefit others? Well, the more you practise mindfulness, the more likely you are to be kind, attentive and helpful to others. You'll probably be less snappy and irritable. You'll be in control of your temper and have the energy and willingness to help others with their difficulties. All these qualities are not just great for you – they're great for anyone you come into contact with.

Here are a few people you can think of who may benefit from your mindfulness practise:

>> Your partner or close family

>> Your friends

THE DONKEY AND THE WELL

Once upon a time, a farmer's donkey fell into a well. The farmer tried all sorts of different ways to get the donkey out, to no avail. Eventually and regrettably he gave up. The well needed filling up anyway, so he decided to bury the donkey. He convinced himself that the donkey wouldn't suffer any longer. He began shovelling soil into the well.

At first the donkey was scared and brayed loudly, but then calmed down and was silent. After shovelling for a while, the farmer decided to take a closer look inside, using a torch. The donkey was alive, and closer to the top of the well. Each time the farmer threw mud onto the donkey, he shook it off his back and stepped up onto the soil. Before long the donkey was able to step out of the well and into safety, as if nothing had happened.

The donkey took small, easy steps to stay alive. If the donkey had thought, 'Oh no, I have no hope, I'm going to die,' then the donkey would have been buried. With small daily steps in practising mindfulness, you can come up with creative solutions to life's challenges too.

>> Your colleagues at work

>> The village, town or city where you live

Pick one group that resonates with you. See if you can practise your mindfulness from the perspective of helping that particular group of people through your increased mindful awareness and friendly demeanour.

This approach works for all activities. For example, when I remember that I'm writing this book for your benefit, I feel far more motivated. I want to write it as best I can to help you to be healthier, happier and more peaceful. It feels great! If I was writing and *just* thinking about how it may make me more popular or wealthy, the action becomes far less joyous.

Preparing Yourself for Mindfulness

Having an open attitude towards mindfulness is helpful, especially when you're starting off. You're probably new to mindfulness, therefore you don't know whether it'll work for you. But being curious to the possibility that you'll find value in mindfulness helps, just like when learning any new skill like golf, French or flower arranging!

If you go into mindfulness thinking 'This isn't going to help me,' as you practise and meet obstacles, you may just give up.

As Henry Ford said, 'Whether you think you can or you think you can't, you're right.'

So think you can! It's worth listening to Henry Ford: he revolutionised the car industry. You may not agree with Ford's invention, but he achieved what many thought was impossible. Mindfulness can be just as revolutionary in your own life, if you have the right attitude. By having an open and curious attitude, you're giving yourself permission to find more awareness, compassion and wisdom in your life.

TIP

When you cultivate a long-term vision for why you want to practise mindfulness, let it be just that: long term. Let go in the here and now as you engage in the practise. Don't worry too much about whether you're moving towards your goal. Trust that the process of mindfulness meditation, practised by millions of people and supported scientifically by thousands of research papers, will take care of itself if you give it time, and stop questioning its value as far as you can.

Looking beyond problem-solving

Mindfulness isn't a quick fix. You need to practise mindfulness on the good days and the bad ones – on days when you feel things are going okay, as well as when you feel anxious, stressed or depressed. Mindfulness is best cultivated slowly and steadily, day by day, so that when things become difficult or challenging for you, you can remember and use mindful awareness to bring your attention to your breathing and soothe your mind.

WISE
WORDS

Think of regular mindfulness like putting on a safety belt in a car. You put the belt on every time you travel just in case you're in an accident. You don't put the belt on just before you crash – you'd be too late. The car journey is the same, whether you have a belt on or not, but the main difference is the preparation for what may happen. The safety belt of mindfulness helps to slow things down, so you can enjoy the view and come to a safe stop when things become challenging.

Dealing with resistance to practise

Before long, you may get a sense of resistance in practising mindfulness. Don't worry, you're not alone. People often ask me, both in person and on social media, how to overcome the resistance to practising mindfulness. They know it's good for them, but for some reason they just can't make themselves sit down and practise mindfulness. I think it's a common experience for many people.

Here are some tips I suggest:

>> **Make peace with the resistance.** If you really don't feel like being mindful or meditating, that's okay. You don't need to set up a battle within yourself! Instead, take a break. Let go of the inner fight to practise. Come back to it when you're ready to do so.

>> **Feel the resistance.** Notice when you feel the resistance in your body. Is the feeling in the pit of your stomach, your chest or somewhere else? Feel the sensation together with your breathing. Now you're already practising some mindfulness without knowing it – sneaky, but cool!

>> **Boost your informal mindfulness practise.** This means just being more conscious of whatever your daily activities are. If you need to walk to the bus stop, really feel the sensations in your feet and the breeze against your skin. If you're drying clothes on the washing line, make an extra effort to notice the fresh scent of the clothes and the stretch in your body as you peg the clothes up. Give your mind a break from your usual recurring thoughts.

Chapter **4**

Growing Healthy Attitudes

T he three important aspects to mindfulness are intention, attitude and attention (explained fully in Chapter 3). This chapter focuses on attitude.

Attitudes colour your experience of life. Even if you're living the ideal life, if you're always looking for what's not good enough, that's what you'll find. On the flip side, you could be living with just the bare minimum to feed and clothe you and your family, but if you're focusing on what you do have, life becomes a joy.

When it comes to attitude, you have a choice. If you're aware of your outlook, you can begin to choose to change it for the better. Attitude isn't about what happens in your life, how successful you are or even how you feel. You can be feeling the emotion of frustration but think, 'Hey, at least I'm aware of it' or 'This is just a feeling' or 'This is a chance for me to understand the feeling of frustration.'

Changing your attitude isn't always easy. Be kind to yourself, and if you notice you need to change your attitude, begin slowly and gently. By choosing mindful attitudes towards your moment-to-moment inner and outer experiences, you begin to release self-limiting beliefs and live life with greater fluidity.

Think about singing. What's your attitude towards singing? Maybe you love it and can't wait to jump up on the stage. If you don't care what other people think, or think you're a great singer, then belting out your favourite song isn't a problem. However, if you think you must do it right or worry about what others think, you may be more hesitant to sing and this affects your feelings, mood and how you actually sound.

TIP

Choosing your actions in any given moment is even easier than controlling your attitude. So, in the above example, even if your mind tells you can't sing and you feel anxious, you can still go ahead and sing. And over time, you may find your attitude, thoughts and feelings beginning to shift too. So if you feel stuck with a negative attitude, that's okay. Try taking a small, positive action like going for a walk or texting a friend.

Knowing How Attitude Affects Outcome

WISE WORDS

A school once had six different ability groups for maths. Each year, the same maths teachers taught the same ability level in the subject. One year the head teacher decided to experiment. She picked a teacher at random, who turned out to be the teacher of the second from bottom set. The head told the teacher how good she was and that she'd give her the top set for maths next year. The teacher's attitude and expectations for the class totally changed when she received her new class. She knew that the top set should get the top grades as they always had. She taught them accordingly and, sure enough, the pupils achieved straight A grades. The amazing thing was that the class wasn't really the top set at all, but was the second from bottom set. Because the teacher had changed her attitude and expectations for the class, the students rose to the challenge and produced outstanding results. This experiment goes to show the power of attitude.

How does attitude affect the quality of mindfulness? Well, if your attitude is 'Mindfulness is really hard,' then you try very hard to get somewhere. If your attitude is 'Mindfulness is easy' and you then struggle, you may begin to get frustrated. If your attitude is 'I don't know how it'll go. I'm going to give it a good go and see what happens,' you're prepared for whatever arises.

REMEMBER

Attitudes are the soil in which your mindfulness practises grow tall and strong. A rich, nutritious soil nourishes the seed of mindfulness and ensures that it grows well. Each time you practise mindfulness, you water the seed, giving it care and attention. However, if that soil deteriorates through unhelpful attitudes, then the young seedling will begin to wither. A plant needs regular watering to grow– a lack of care and attention results in it perishing.

Discovering Your Attitudes to Mindfulness

Attitudes can become habits – both good and bad. And attitudes, like habits, aren't always easy to change. You need to work to improve your attitude. Begin by discovering your current attitudes towards mindfulness, stillness, silence and non-doing. Then, through understanding and effort, you can develop attitudes that are more conducive to a regular mindfulness practise.

TIP

Get pen and paper and answer the following ten questions to help you discover what your attitudes towards mindfulness are:

1. What do you hope to get out of practising mindfulness?

2. Why are you practising mindfulness?

3. What experiences do you expect to arrive at through practising mindfulness?

4. How long do you think it'll take before you notice the benefits of mindfulness?

5. What physical sensations do you expect during or after a mindfulness meditation?

6. What are your past experiences of mindfulness? Do you continue to hold onto them or have you let them go?

7. How much effort are you willing to put into the practise? Will you practise mindfulness several times a day, once a day, once a week or whenever you feel like it?

8. When you hear the word 'meditation' or 'mindfulness,' what sort of thoughts and feelings arise?

9. How will you know that you're doing your mindfulness practise correctly?

10. What's the best thing about mindfulness?

Now, look at your answers. Do you notice any patterns? Are you very positive about the potential benefits of mindfulness? Are you negative about mindfulness? Or are you indifferent and do you just want to experiment, like being a scientist of your own mind?

Try to be non-judgemental towards your answers. See them as just the way things are. If you can't help being caught up in thinking, 'That's good' or 'Oh, that's a really bad attitude, what's wrong with me?,' notice that too. Your mind is simply coming up with judgements.

Developing Helpful Attitudes

This section contains the key foundational attitudes that provide a base from which you can build a strong mindfulness practise. These attitudes help you to handle difficult sensations and emotions, overcome feelings of lethargy and generate energy for taking action. Without these attitudes your practise may become stale and your intention may weaken, along with your power to pay attention in the present moment. Some helpful ways of approaching your practise are developed through experience; others are available right from the start.

Think of these key attitudes like strawberry seeds. If you're hoping to taste the delicious strawberries, you need to plant the seeds and water them regularly. In the same way, you need to water your attitudes regularly, by giving them your mindful attention. Then you can enjoy the fruit of your efforts in the form of a sweet, delicious strawberry. I'm a sucker for strawberries.

Although the attitudes identified in this section seem separate, they feed into and support each other. Any one of these attitudes, pursued and encouraged to grow, inadvertently supports the others.

TIP

Here's a different approach that often works well. It's called the 'Acting As If' principle. Maybe you don't feel like shifting your attitude. Perhaps you're having a hard time practising mindfulness. Maybe you feel annoyed, sad or angry. What can you do? Another very powerful approach is to use your facial expression or body to shift your attitude. So you can 'act as if' you're feeling accepting, calm or happy. For example, lots of research shows how holding a smile on your face or walking as if you have a bounce in your step can lift your mood and shift your attitude within just a minute. As Shakespeare said, 'Assume a virtue, if you have it not.'

Understanding acceptance

Acceptance turns out to be one of the most helpful attitudes to bring to mindfulness. Acceptance means perceiving your experience and simply acknowledging it rather than judging it as good or bad. You let go of the battle with your present-moment experience. For some people, the word 'acceptance' is off-putting– replace it with the word 'acknowledgement,' if you prefer.

WARNING

By acceptance, I don't mean resignation. I don't mean, 'If you think you can't do something, accept it' – that would be giving up rather than accepting. I'm talking about your experience from moment to moment.

For example, when you feel pain, whether it's physical, such as a painful shoulder, or mental, such as depression or anxiety, the natural reaction is to try to avoid feeling the pain. This seems very sensible, because the sensation of physical or mental pain is unpleasant. You ignore it, distract yourself, or perhaps even go so far as turning to recreational drugs or alcohol to numb the discomfort. This avoidance may work in the immediate short term, but before long, avoidance fails in the mental and emotional realm.

By fighting the pain, you still feel the pain, but on top of that, you feel the emotional hurt and struggle with the pain itself. Buddha called this the 'second arrow.' If a warrior is injured by an arrow and unleashes a series of thoughts like, 'Why did this happen to me?' or 'What if I can never walk again?' that's a 'second arrow.' You may inflict this on yourself each time you feel some form of pain or even just a bit of discomfort, rather than accepting what has happened and taking the next step. Avoidance – running away – is an aspect of the 'second arrow' and compounds the suffering. Acceptance means stopping fighting with your moment-to-moment experience. Acceptance removes that second arrow of blame, criticism or denial.

A useful formula to remember is

Suffering = Pain x Resistance

The more your resist the pain you're experiencing, the more you suffer. The pain is already there. Resisting the pain compounds your difficulties. Acceptance teaches you to let go of the resistance and therefore ease your suffering.

Perhaps when you're mindful, you feel bombarded by thoughts dragging you away again and again. If you don't accept the fact that your mind likes thinking, you become more and more frustrated, upset and annoyed with yourself. You want to focus on your mindfulness practise, but you just can't.

In the above example:

>> **First arrow:** Lots of thoughts entering your mind during mindfulness practise.

>> **Second arrow:** Not accepting that thoughts are bound to come up in mindfulness; criticising yourself for having too many thoughts.

>> **Solution:** Acknowledge and accept that thoughts are part and parcel of mindfulness practise. Let go of your resistance. You can do this by gently saying to yourself, 'Thinking is happening' or 'It's natural to think' or simply labelling it as 'thinking . . . thinking.'

By *acknowledging* the feeling, thought or sensation and going into it, the experience changes. Even with physical pain, try experimenting by actually feeling it. Research has found that the pain reduces.

But remember, you're not acknowledging it to get rid of the feeling. That's not acceptance. You need to try to acknowledge the sensation, feeling or thought *without trying to change it* at all – pure acceptance of it, just as it is.

Maybe even relax into the discomfort. One way to relax into the discomfort is by courageously turning to the sensation of discomfort and simultaneously feeling the sensation of your own breath. With each out-breath, allow yourself to move closer and soften the tension around the discomfort.

If all this acceptance or acknowledgement of your pain seems impossible, just try getting a sense of it and make the tiniest step towards it. The smallest step towards acceptance can set up a chain of events ultimately leading towards transformation. Any tiny amount of acceptance is better than none at all.

Another aspect of acceptance is to come to terms with your current situation. If you're lost, even if you have a map of where you want to get to, you have no hope of getting there *if you don't know where you are to start with*. You need to know and accept where you are. Then you can begin working out how to get to where you want to be. Paradoxically, acceptance is the first step for any radical change. If you don't acknowledge where you are and what's currently happening, you can't move on appropriately from that point.

TIP

Here are some ways you can try to cultivate acceptance:

>> Gently state the label of the experience you aren't accepting. For example, if you're not accepting that you're angry, state in your mind, to yourself, 'I'm feeling angry at the moment . . . I'm feeling angry.' In this way, you begin to acknowledge your feeling.

>> Notice which part of your body feels tense and imagine your breath going into and out of the area of tightness. As you breathe in and out, say to yourself, 'It's okay. It's already here . . . It's already here.' Allow the muscles around the sensation to soften and release if you can.

>> Consider how much you accept or acknowledge your current thoughts/feelings/sensation on a scale of 1 to 10. Ask yourself what you need to do to increase your acceptance by 1, and then do it as best you can.

>> Become really curious about your experience. Consider, 'Where did this feeling come from? Where do I feel it? What's interesting about it? What can I learn from it?' In this way, the curiosity leads you to a little more acceptance.

REMEMBER

In the realm of emotions, the quickest way to get from A to B isn't to try and force yourself to get to B, but to accept A. Wholehearted acceptance leads to change automatically.

Discovering patience

Helen Keller, the American deaf-blind political activist, is quoted as saying: 'We could never learn to be brave and patient if there were only joy in the world.' The quote makes a valid point. If every time you practised mindfulness, you were filled with joy and peace, you wouldn't need that wonderful attitude of patience. The reality is that challenging thoughts and emotions sometimes arise in mindfulness, like in any activity. The important thing is how you meet and welcome those feelings.

Although you can experience the benefits of mindfulness after a short period of time, research shows that the more time you dedicate to cultivating mindfulness, the more effective the result. Mindfulness meditation is a training of the mind and training takes time.

REMEMBER

If you're a naturally rather impatient person, mindfulness meditation is the perfect training for you. Patience, like all the attitudes I talk about in this section, is a state you can develop through regular effort. Attitudes are muscles you can train in the gym of the mind.

TIP

Here are some ways you can develop your patience:

>> Whenever you're in any situation where you begin to experience impatience, see this as an opportunity to practise mindfulness of thoughts. This means becoming fascinated by the kind of thoughts that are popping into your head. Are they all true? What effect are the thoughts having on your emotional state? What are the thoughts all about?

>> The next time you're driving and see an amber light, stop safely rather than speeding through it. See how that makes you feel. Repeat this several times and notice if it becomes easier or more difficult to be patient.

>> Rather than frantically choosing the shortest queue at the supermarket checkout, just choose the nearest one. Connect with any feelings of impatience that arise and bring a sense of curiosity to your experience, rather than immediately reacting to your impatience.

When having a conversation with someone, spend more time listening rather than speaking. Let go of your initial urge to speak, and listen more. Listening can take tremendous effort, and is excellent patience training. Each time you practise, you train your brain to become slightly more patient.

Seeing afresh

Seeing afresh is normally referred to as the *beginner's mind*, a term that was first used by the Zen master Suzuki Roshi. He once said: 'In the beginner's mind there are many possibilities, but in the expert's there are few.' What does that mean?

Consider a young child. Children, if they're fortunate enough to be brought up lovingly, are the greatest mindfulness teachers in the world! They're amazed by the simplest thing. Give babies a set of keys, and they stare at them, notice the wide range of colours reflected in them, shake them and listen to the sound – and probably giggle too. Then, of course, they taste the keys!

Children epitomise the beginner's mind. They see things as if for the first time, because they're not filled with ideas, concepts, beliefs, names or thoughts about the right or wrong thing to do. Babies don't intellectualise. They connect with the raw sensory data entering their minds and they love it. Young children are naturally mindful, and that mindfulness is a true joy for them.

TIP

You can see life in a similar way. You can cultivate this attitude of the beginner's mind, of seeing things afresh – you just need to make a little effort. Try this exercise:

1. Sit or lie down in a relaxed and comfortable posture and close your eyes.

2. Now imagine you've been blind from birth. You've never experienced colour before. You've heard people talking about it, but you can't even imagine colour. Spend at least five minutes doing this. When you find your mind wandering off into thoughts, gently guide it back to this exercise.

3. When you're ready, gently open your eyes as if you're seeing for the first time. See with the beginner's mind. Enjoy the range of colours and forms in front of you. Notice how your mind automatically names different objects. Bring your attention back to the awareness of the variety of colours, shadows and reflections. You may even begin to notice things you've never noticed before; that's a sign that you're engaging with the beginner's mind and seeing things anew.

4. Continue with this beginner's mind attitude as you go about your activities today, and be with each experience as if for the first time.

When you experience the state of the beginner's mind, you live in a world of fascination, curiosity, creativity, attention and fun. You're continuously discovering and looking out with the eyes of a child. You're in 'don't know' mind. When you think, 'I know what's going to happen' or 'I know what the breath feels like,' you stop looking. You don't know what's going to happen; you just think you do. Each moment is fresh. Each moment is different and unique. Each moment is the only moment you have.

If you're a beginner at mindfulness, you're in an enviable position. You really are in the beginner's mind! However, by the time you practise your second mindfulness meditation, you may begin comparing it with your first one and think, 'It was better last time' or 'Why can't I concentrate now?' or 'This is it. I've got it!' You start to compare, conceptualise or condemn. When this happens, try to let it go – as much as you can – and bring your attention back to the here and now, as if you're engaging in this for the very first time. I'm not saying that the beginner's mind is an easy attitude, but it's fundamental to sustaining a long-term mindfulness practise.

Mindful living is about living life afresh. One cool way to do this is to reduce the amount of planning you do. Leave some days unplanned. That way, you make space for new and exciting things to emerge. Most of the time, life doesn't go to plan anyway – so don't try too hard to stick to a schedule. You can even try letting go of planning your work occasionally. When I give a talk without planning, I don't know what I'll say, and it's more fun both for my audience and me. I'm forced to live in the present and respond to the moment; mindfulness arises spontaneously.

Finding trust

Without a certain degree of trust, mindfulness is challenging. This is because trust helps you to continue believing in the process of mindfulness when you feel that nothing's happening or something 'wrong' is happening. For example, if you're doing a mindfulness exercise and you suddenly feel bored, you need to trust that this is just another feeling, and that by continuing to practise mindfulness, that feeling may go away or it may not. Or, you may find that by the end of a mindfulness practise, you feel a bit worse than when you started. Without trust, you won't be able to see that this is just a temporary experience which, like all experiences, won't last forever.

Trust takes time to develop in relationships. You can't expect to meet people and immediately trust them. You need to see how they behave, what they say, and how they treat you and others. With time, with patience, trust grows. And with that growing trust, the relationships deepen, mature and become more meaningful. A relationship that lacks in trust has little beauty. With trust comes warmth, friendship and a feeling of connection – you feel at ease and comfortable in a trusting relationship. Your relationship with mindfulness is similar. You may not trust in the process to begin with, but with patience, dedicated and regular practise, you may begin to trust it. The more you trust in its power to heal and restore you, the more you relax into it and allow mindfulness to *happen* to you, in a sense, rather than trying to *do* mindfulness. Mindfulness is an act of non-doing, or being, which arises out of the security of trust.

TIP

Here are some ways of building your trust:

>> **Decide how long you're going to try mindfulness for and stick to it.** So, if you want to try practising mindfulness for four weeks, for 20 minutes a day, just do it. Be prepared to find it harder to practise on some days than others, and begin to trust in the process.

>> **If you're scientifically minded, look up all the research on mindfulness available, in this book or elsewhere.** This may help to convince you to stick to the discipline.

>> **If you know someone else who regularly practises mindfulness, ask her about her relationship with it.** Consider meditating with her to help you.

>> **Give mindfulness time.** Be patient with it as far as you can, and your trust will naturally grow with time.

>> **Try trusting your own experience, in the here and now.** What is your intuition trying to tell you?

Cultivating curiosity

Einstein was a master of curiosity. He thought that curiosity was an essential part of a fulfilling life. Einstein is quoted as saying the following:

> *The important thing is not to stop questioning. Curiosity has its own reason for existing. One cannot help but be in awe when he contemplates the mysteries of eternity, of life, of the marvellous structure of reality. It is enough if one tries merely to comprehend a little of this mystery every day. Never lose a holy curiosity.*

Curiosity is the basis of all true learning. If you're curious, you want to find out something new: you want to gain some new knowledge. A curious person is fully connected with her senses. If you're curious, you look around intently and earnestly to see something you haven't seen before. You ask lots of questions, both of yourself and others. These can be questions like, 'Why is the sky blue?' or 'Why is that shadow over there faint, whereas this one is much darker?' Or it may be questions about yourself, like 'I wonder why I feel tired after eating X?' or 'Where do thoughts come from?' or 'What happens to the feeling of frustration if I try to feel it in my body and breathe into it?'

Bringing curiosity to your mindfulness practise is especially helpful. In fact, with curiosity, mindfulness automatically arises: you naturally begin to pay attention and, with a sense of wonder, to notice what's happening. Take the example of thought: if you're really curious about the types of thoughts that you have over a period of ten minutes, you pay attention and watch thoughts in your mind as best you can. That's mindfulness. If your curiosity is genuine, you'll probably keep watching those thoughts until that curiosity is satisfied.

TIP

How can you develop curiosity in mindfulness? I say, by asking questions. Here are some questions you can ask yourself before a mindfulness practise, to get you started:

>> What happens if I practise mindfulness every day for 20 minutes for four weeks, whether I feel like it or not?

>> What occurs if I put more effort into my mindfulness practise? What if I put in less effort?

>> What if I sit or lie down really still, even if I have the urge to move. What happens then?

>> Where in the body do I feel positive emotions? Where do I feel negative ones? What shape and colour do the emotions have, if any?

>> What effect does having a gentle smile while being mindful have on my practise?

I could go on and on with thousands of questions to ask. Try to come up with some of your own; your own curiosity is more powerful than anything I give you.

Ask yourself a question and investigate. Feed your curiosity and see what you discover. Allow your curiosity to spread from your mindfulness practise to your day-to-day living. Become curious about your thoughts, emotions and physical sensations rather than just ignoring them or trying to instantly change them.

Experimenting with doing things differently is a great way to fuel your curiosity and increase your mindfulness. For example, today I thought, 'How can I brush my teeth in a different way, just for fun?' The answer came: stand on one leg. So I brushed my teeth while balancing on one leg. I was surprised at how much more mindful I was. Rather than automatically brushing and letting my mind wander, I was conscious of keeping my balance. You probably think I'm mad – perhaps you're right! But the point I'm trying to make is that if you do things differently that immediately makes life a bit more fun and a bit more mindful too. What can you do differently today?

REMEMBER

Mindfulness is like a laboratory, where you come up with ideas, observe, watch, see what happens and perhaps draw conclusions. Keep asking yourself questions, and keep going in that way. Mindfulness gives you the opportunity to find out more about yourself and the workings of your own mind and heart, and when you understand that, you understand not only yourself, but everyone else, because everyone has essentially the same processes going on. Humans are far more similar than you may think.

Letting go

Imagine I told you to hold a glass of water absolutely still. In fact, imagine I said that I'd give you whatever you wanted if you held the glass of water perfectly still. You'd probably try very hard and the glass might look quite still, but if you or anyone else looked really carefully at the water, you'd notice that it was still moving. I suspect that the harder you tried to hold the glass still, the more you'd shake it as you felt more worried or nervous about being 100 per cent still. The best way for the glass of water to be still would be for you to *let it go* and put it down on a solid surface. Then the water would stop moving.

Nature has many beautiful examples of letting go. Apple trees need to let go of their fruit so that the seeds inside can germinate. Animals need to let go of their young so they can find out how to fend for themselves. Young birds need to let go of any fear they feel when they first jump off a branch to begin to fly. You're always letting go of each breath of air to make room for the next one. This last example shows that you naturally know how to let go all the time, in one sense. Remember this the next time you're struggling to let go.

Letting go is the essence of mindfulness. Thoughts, emotions, ideas, opinions, beliefs, emotions and sensations are all to be observed, explored and then let go. If you're struggling to understand or practise mindfulness, try letting go. Just gently practise as best you can and see what you discover – you'll be on the right track.

How do you let go? Imagine you're holding a tennis ball in your hands, and you're asking me how to let go. Letting go isn't something you do. Letting go is about stopping the doing. To let go of something, you stop holding onto it. The first step is to realise you're holding onto the object in the first place. If you're walking around holding a tennis ball, you can't let go if you don't know that the ball is in your hands. Once you know that the ball is there and feel the tension in your hands, you automatically let go.

PLAY THIS

Here's a short mindfulness exercise on the practise of letting go. Have a go and see what arises for you. You can use the accompanying guided audio (MP3 Track 5) if you wish.

1. **Find a comfortable posture.** You don't even need to close your eyes if you don't want to.

2. **Notice, right now, the position of your body.** Can you feel any physical tension in your body? Which parts feel warm and which ones cold? Does the

tension have a shape, a colour, a texture? Be aware of what they are. What happens to the tension and tightness as you become aware of them? Do they release or stay there?

3. **Become aware of any emotions that are touching you at the moment.** What happens when you observe them? Get a sense of how strong the emotion is. Don't *try* to let go. Putting effort into letting go just creates more tension. Instead, become aware of it and allow the emotion to take its own course. Let the emotion let go of itself if it wants to. If the feeling lingers on, can you be okay with that and accept it as it is?

4. **At the end of this short exercise, see whether you're willing to let go of anything that you found out** – anything that you're holding onto, trusting that you have within you all that needs to be known.

Developing kindness

Kindness is my religion.

Dalai Lama

This is one of the most important of all attitudes you can bring to your mindfulness practise. Your awareness of your breath, or your body or sounds, or whatever you're paying attention to, can have a quality to it. The quality can be cold, harsh and incisive, or it can be warm, kind, friendly, forgiving, caring, gentle – in other words, loving. By bringing a sense of friendliness to your experience, the experience – whether it's pleasant, unpleasant or neutral – is transformed.

Because kindness is such an important attitude, I go into this in more detail in the next section.

Figure 4-1 is the tree of mindfulness. The growth and development of the tree of mindfulness represents your own inner capacity to be mindful. Watering the roots represents the effort you make to cultivate the mindful attitudes and practise mindfulness. The fruit represent the benefits you naturally gain from the effort you put into being mindful. 'As you sow, so shall you reap' is the essence of mindfulness; this is why the fruit from your own tree of mindfulness is the same as the roots.

Over time, as you continue to look after the tree of mindfulness within you, the tree strengthens and matures. Your roots grow deep into the earth and your tree stands firmly earthed to the ground, offering shade to those around quite naturally. Mindfulness is firmly established within your being.

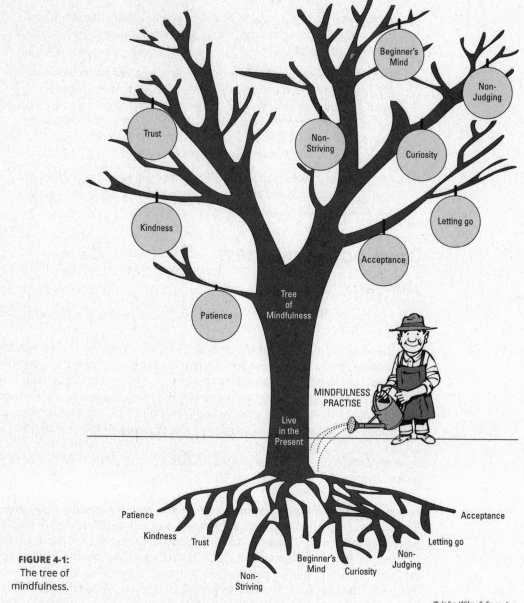

FIGURE 4-1:
The tree of
mindfulness.

© John Wiley & Sons, Inc.

Appreciating 'Heartfulness'

With attentiveness, a marksman can shoot an innocent person, a thief can plot a
bank robbery, and a drug baron can count his money. But this isn't true
mindfulness – mindfulness isn't pure attention alone. In Eastern language, the

word for mind and heart is often the same, which is *heartfulness*. Instead of *Mind-fulness For Dummies*, this book could just as easily be called *Heartfulness For Dummies*. Heartfulness is giving attention to anything that you can perceive with a sense of warmth, kindliness and friendliness, and thereby avoid self-criticism and blame.

Here are some ways of specifically generating warmth and friendliness, along with attention. You need to give each of these exercises at least five minutes for best effect. Try to generate an intention rather than a feeling.

>> Look at something in front of you in the same way as you may look into the eyes of a beautiful child, or at a flower. Bring a sense of affection to your visual perception, whatever that may be, for a few minutes. Note what happens.

>> Listen to your favourite piece of relaxing music. This may be a piece of classical music, New Age music, or perhaps it's the sounds of nature, such as birds singing or the wind rustling through the trees.

>> Smell the aroma in the room around you or of the food on your plate, in the same way that you smell the most beautiful scent of a perfume.

>> When you next eat, take a few moments to feel your breath. You may find this difficult, because the habit is to dive in and munch, but hold back if you can. Now remember how lucky you are to have food to eat at all. Chew each morsel fully before you tuck into your next helping. Savour the taste.

>> Notice the sense of touch as you walk from one place to another. Slow down as much as you can and feel the sensations in the feet. Imagine that your feet are kissing the earth with each step you take. Visualise yourself walking on precious ground, and allow yourself to be fully immersed in the sense of contact.

>> As you walk around, notice other people and wish them happiness. Think 'May you be happy.' See whether you can make your wish genuine, from your heart.

>> Listen to any negative thoughts or emotions in yourself. Perhaps you're habitually critical of yourself for having these feelings. Try a radically different approach: befriend your negative thoughts. Bring a sense of warmth and kindness to your anger, jealousy or frustration. Listen to yourself compassion-ately as you would to a good friend – with care and understanding. What happens?

Developing an Attitude of Gratitude

Gratitude is considered by some as the greatest of all emotions that can be culti-vated. Recent studies are beginning to show that gratitude has a unique relation-ship with wellbeing, and can explain aspects of wellbeing that other personality traits cannot. An attitude of gratitude goes hand in hand with mindfulness.

You're grateful when you're aware of what you *do* have rather than what you don't. The effect of this is an opening of the heart. When you're aware with an open heart, you're in a deeper mindful mode.

TIP

Gratitude is a skill that you can develop. If you're bad at tennis or playing the piano, with practise you get better. The same is true of gratitude. Through repeated effort you can develop, strengthen and intensify gratitude. Flex your gratitude muscle by trying this exercise, which is almost guaranteed to make you more grateful:

1. **Think of something you're not grateful for.** Perhaps you're not grateful for your job, a relationship or your place of residence.

2. **Now think of all the things that are good about it.** Give yourself two minutes, and challenge yourself to come up with as many good things as possible. For example, if you're not happy with your job: Does it pay you good money? How much time do you get off? Is there a pension or medical plan with the job? Do you like any of your colleagues? Do you get breaks? Does working make being at home more pleasurable? Think of as many positive aspects for which you're grateful. To supercharge this exercise rather than just thinking about it, write down your answers. Be aware that you may have to overcome some resistance to doing this, especially if you're very ungrateful about the situation.

3. **Try this exercise again for other areas of your life.** See what effect that has on them. Again, remember that the exercise takes some effort, but the rewards make it worthwhile.

4. **Commit to doing this regularly for a week or a month on a daily basis.** You may find yourself being naturally more grateful for all sorts of other things too, including mindfulness.

Letting go through forgiveness

Life has its difficulties. And you're bound to get hurt by others, often wrongly so. The danger comes when you carry this hurt around with you. If you don't let the emotional pain go, the next time something hurts you, the suffering accumulates. Over a period of years, the hurt can feel like you're walking around carrying a heavy sack everywhere you go. Your shoulders feel tense. Your face is screwed up. You're tense and uptight.

This harmful state of mind requires forgiveness for you to feel happier. Being annoyed with someone else hurts you rather than anyone else. You may admire hearing about others forgiving in situations of hatred, but when you're called upon to do so yourself, you're stuck. You may find yourself feeling angry, depressed or hateful. Many studies now show that releasing and letting go of past hurts through forgiveness leads to a longer and happier life.

Forgiveness doesn't mean what the other person did to you was right or okay. It means you're willing to let that go so you can move on and live a happier life. Forgiveness is an act of kindness towards yourself. And through that self-kindness, you naturally become a nicer person to be with for others too.

TIP

Try this approach to begin to allow yourself to forgive:

>> Understand that hating someone else doesn't actually hurt that person at all.

>> List all the beneficial things that have emerged from a situation. Try to see the situation from a totally different perspective. Ask a trusted friend to help you if you'd like to.

>> Be compassionate with yourself. If you've been ruminating over a problem for some time, perhaps now's the time to let it go. You don't deserve all this hurt you're carrying around with you.

>> Understand that the story you're telling yourself is just that: a story. This pain and hurt may be repeating itself in your mind through a story. Try letting go of the story, or seeing the story from another person's perspective. Something may shift that will help you forgive.

>> Wish the person well. If someone has hurt you, counteract that with some loving-kindness meditation. Wish the person well, just as you may wish yourself or a friend well. Use the loving-kindness meditations in Chapter 6 to help you.

PLAY THIS

An alternative practise is to do a forgiveness meditation. You can choose to listen to the guided audio (MP3 Track 4) that comes with this book. The steps are:

1. **Sit in a comfortable and relaxed position.** Let your eyes close, if that feels comfortable, and allow your breath to find a natural rhythm.

2. **Imagine or feel the breath going into your heart.** Become aware of and feel the obstructions you've created in your heart due to a lack of forgiveness, whether for yourself or others. Become mindful of the heartache from a lack of forgiveness in your core.

3. **Now you can *ask forgiveness of others*.** Say to yourself: 'Let me become aware of the many ways that knowingly or unknowingly I've caused others pain and suffering though my own fear, pain or anger.' Visualise each person who comes to mind – feel the sorrow and pain they feel due to your words and actions. Now, finally, release this sadness, sorrow and heartache by asking for forgiveness. As you imagine or feel each person's presence, say: 'I ask for your forgiveness. Forgive me.' Repeat this slowly as many times as you feel appropriate, speaking from the heart.

4. **Now you can move on to *forgiving yourself*.** You've hurt yourself in many ways through thoughts, words or actions. You may have done this consciously – or unconsciously, without even knowing it. Allow yourself to become mindful of any unkindness you've directed towards yourself. Feel the suffering you've caused yourself and begin to release this by saying: 'For all the ways I have been causing suffering to myself through thoughts, words or actions, consciously or unconsciously, I forgive myself. I forgive myself as far as I can.'

5. **Now you can move on to *forgive other people*** who've hurt you. You've been hurt by many people through their words or actions, knowingly or unknowingly. They've caused you suffering in your being to different degrees. Imagine the ways they've done this. Become aware, feel the pain others have caused you, and allow yourself to let go of this sadness from your heart with the words: 'I've been hurt by others many times, in many ways, due to the pain, sorrow, anger or misunderstanding of others. I've carried this suffering in my being for long enough. As far as I'm ready to, I offer my forgiveness. To those who've hurt me, I forgive you.' Repeat these phrases if you want.

With time and practise, you may feel a shift in your heart and be able to forgive. If the shift doesn't happen, notice how you feel, and be soft and kind with yourself. Let the forgiveness be genuine. Forgiveness takes time, so be patient and practise the meditation regularly. With regular commitment, you'll be able to release yourself from the sorrow you're carrying, through gentle forgiveness.

Tackling Unhelpful Attitudes

Just as you have helpful attitudes to cultivate in your mindfulness practise, you also have unhelpful attitudes that you'd be better off staying away from. For example, if you're a bit of a perfectionist and are worried you're going to fall asleep in your mindfulness practise, you don't need to start panicking, or worrying when you start struggling to stay awake. You just need to become aware of the perfectionist mindset and, as best you can, let the unhelpful approach go.

REMEMBER

The most unhelpful thing you can do with mindfulness is not to practise. Once you begin practising regularly, in no matter how small a way, you may begin to discover which attitudes to nurture, and which are unhelpful.

Avoiding quick-fix solutions

If you want a quick fix for all your problems, you've come to the wrong place. *Mindfulness is simple but not easy.* Mindfulness is a powerful process that takes time, and a certain type of effort, energy and discipline. You can find quick fixes in the domain of television advertising, billboards and the Internet. I know these temptations are great, and marketing companies spend billions to work out how to convince you to part with your hard-earned cash. Unfortunately, however, in my limited experience of instant happiness, that form of happiness is just that: instantly present and instantly gone.

What you can do is integrate mindfulness practises into your life in short bursts. You don't have to sit for hours and hours in the lotus posture. One minute of mindful attention on your breath on a daily basis can begin to shift something within you. The more you put in, the more you get out. Five minutes is better than one minute. You need to decide what's right for you: trust in yourself to make a decision and stick to that choice for a period of time.

REMEMBER

Mindfulness is not about how long you can sit still for. If that was the case, roosting chickens would be Zen masters. What really matters is the quality of your intention, attention and attitude.

Overcoming perfectionism

'I'll meditate as soon as I've sorted my life out.' 'I'll do the course when things are totally settled.' 'I'll practise mindfulness when I have no more problems in my life.' These excuses are common and, on the whole, unconstructive. Sometimes you do need to allow major events in your life to settle before you work on a new skill like mindfulness. However, you can't wait for life to become perfect. You don't have time to waste. If you've found a way to systematically and thoroughly create a meaningful way of producing further health and wellbeing in your life, why not take the first step? Yes, you may get it wrong and make mistakes, but imperfection, mistakes and stumbles are an integrated part of the process of finding out about anything. No child ever began to walk without falling. No driver ever learns to drive without stalling. Take the first step today.

Finding out from failure

Failures are finger posts on the road to achievement.

CS Lewis

REMEMBER

There's no such thing as a bad mindfulness practise. There's no failure in meditation. If mindfulness was about success and failure, it'd be like any other activity in life. But mindfulness is different – that's the beauty of it. I list here some experiences that people *think* made them fail at being mindful, and reasons why they aren't 'failures':

>> **'I couldn't concentrate. My mind was all over the place.'** You can't concentrate continuously. Sooner or later your mind goes into thoughts, dreams, ideas or problems. The nature of the mind is to wander off. Lack of concentration is an integral part of mindfulness. Expect your mind to wander and be pleased when you've noticed, then gently bring your attention back.

>> **'I couldn't sit still.'** Your body is designed to move. If sitting really isn't for you, remember you can do mindfulness while you move. Try walking meditation (Chapter 6), exercises that integrate awareness, like yoga or tai chi, or any other action you choose, in a mindful and therefore meditative way. You're cultivating awareness, not a motionless body.

>> **'I felt bored, tired, frustrated, angry, annoyed, jealous, excited or empty.'** You're going to feel a variety of emotions in your mindfulness practise, just as you do in your everyday life. The difference is, instead of reacting to them automatically, you've got the valuable opportunity to watch them rise and fall. In the long run, these emotions will probably calm down a bit, but in the meantime you need simply to be aware of them – if you can, enjoy the show!

>> **'I had the experience of X (replace X with *any* negative experience),** which I didn't like.' People have both pleasant and unpleasant experiences in mindfulness meditation. The experience may be anything from deep sadness to feeling you're disappearing, or your arms may feel as if they're floating up. My theory is that your mind is releasing knots within your psyche out into your conscious mind, and freeing you from your own conditioning. This is part and parcel of the process – let the process unfold by itself if you feel you can. If you find the feeling coming up is a difficult one, try saying to yourself: 'This too will pass.'

If you're struggling a lot in your mindfulness practise, you're probably holding onto a desire for something. Maybe you desire to get rid of tension, a feeling of irritation, your mind wandering, or boredom. Maybe you're trying to *get* peace of mind, focus or relaxation. Make peace with your mindfulness practise. Let go of your desire to get anything out of the practise. Then, paradoxically, you'll find the practise far more enjoyable and peaceful.

WARNING

If you find yourself becoming very concerned or frightened in your mindfulness practise, and if the feelings are ongoing, you may need professional support for what's coming up for you. Get in touch with your doctor or suitable therapist.

WISE WORDS

LOVE IS A POWERFUL ATTITUDE

Once there was a little girl who was ill. She needed a blood transfusion, but had a rare blood type. The doctors searched for a blood match but to no avail. They then tested her younger, six-year-old, brother, and fortunately he was a match. The doctors and his mother explained to the boy that they needed his blood so that they could give it to his sister to help her get better. The boy looked concerned and said that he needed to think about it, which surprised them. After some time, he returned and agreed. The doctors laid the brother down on a bed next to his sister, and began transferring some blood. Before long, his sister began to get better. Then, suddenly, the boy called the doctor over and whispered in his ear, 'How long do I have left to live?' The boy thought that by giving blood, he'd die, which of course he wouldn't. That was why he took some time to decide before saying yes to giving his blood to his sister.

Chapter **5**

Humans Being Versus Humans Doing

Human beings love doing stuff. You go to work, have hobbies, socialise, and become an adept multi-tasker trying to fit everything into the day. But what about the *being* in human being?

Every day, in everything you do, your mind switches between *doing* mode and *being* mode. This doesn't mean that you switch between, say, typing an email and staring into space. Instead, it means *being* in the moment as you're *doing* a task. One mode of mind isn't better than the other. They're both helpful in different ways. However, using the wrong mode of mind for a particular situation can cause difficulties.

In this chapter, I explain how spending some of your time just *being* has huge and far-reaching advantages. I also tell you how to 'just be it.'

Delving into the Doing Mode of Mind

You know the feeling. You've got to get the kids ready, drop them off at school, pay the gas bill, pop that letter in the post, renew the car insurance, and make sure that you call your sister to see if she's feeling better. You're exhausted just thinking about everything! But you know you have to do it all. Your mind is in *doing* mode.

Doing mode is a highly developed quality in humans. You can think and conceptualise how you want things to be, and then work methodically in order to achieve them. That's part of the reason why people have been able to design computers and land on the moon – the products of doing mode.

Doing mode is certainly not a bad thing. If you want to get the shopping done, you need some doing mode! However, sometimes doing mode goes too far, and you start doing more and more without taking a break. That can certainly be draining.

Here are the hallmarks of the doing mode of mind:

> » **You're aware of how things *are*, and how they *should* be.** For example, if you need to renew your home insurance, you're aware that you currently haven't renewed the insurance, and that you need to at some point soon.

> » **You set a goal to fix things.** If you're in doing mode, you're setting goals for the way things should be. This problem-solving happens all the time without you being conscious of it. In the home insurance example, your goal may be to call several insurance companies or visit several websites to find the right deal for you.

> » **You try harder and harder to achieve your goal.** In doing mode, you feel driven. You know what you want and you try hard to get it. Doing mode is all about getting to the destination rather than considering anything else. So if an insurance company puts you on hold for too long, you begin to feel tense and frustrated. In this driven state of mind, you don't come up with creative solutions such as calling a different company or just trying at a quieter time.

> » **Most of your actions happen automatically.** You're not really aware when you're in doing mode. You're completing tasks on automatic pilot. Thoughts pop into your head, emotions emerge, and you act on them largely unconsciously. If the person you're speaking to on the telephone is rude, you may automatically react, making you both feel bad, rather than considering that the phone operator may have had a really long and bad day too.

> » **You're not in the present moment.** When engaged in doing mode, you're not connected with your senses, in the now. You're thinking about how things should be in the future, or replaying events from the past. You're lost in your head rather than focused in the moment. While you're placed on hold on the telephone, your mind may wander into anxious thoughts about tomorrow's meeting rather than you just taking the chance to have a break and look at the sky or gaze at the beautiful tree through the window.

REMEMBER

Doing mode isn't just the mode you're in when you're doing stuff. Even when you're sitting on the sofa, your mind can be spinning. You're in doing mode. Trying to run away from negative emotions or towards pleasant ones is also part of doing mode's speciality.

CRUISING ON AUTOPILOT

Aeroplanes have function called autopilot. When pilots push the button to trigger that function, they don't have to consciously control the aircraft – the plane flies by itself. People can also run on autopilot when they're in doing mode, although I haven't found the button for it yet! You may have had the experience when going to fetch something from another room. You walk down the stairs and into the room and . . . your mind's gone blank! You wandered off somewhere internally and forgot what you wanted. Or you're driving somewhere different and end up unconsciously driving to work. Oops! That's human autopilot in action.

Autopilot has some advantages, which is why it evolved in humans. Once something has become automatic, you don't need to consciously think about it again, and can give your attention to something else. Autopilot also saves some energy. Imagine if you had to think about every movement of your body when you were driving or walking – activities that involve hundreds of muscles; thinking in this way would be very tiring. In fact, you say someone has learnt something properly if he can do it automatically without thinking about it.

The problems of autopilot are that:

- **You can get trapped in autopilot.** You can spend your whole life in doing mode. With everything happening automatically, you have a lack of connection with the beauty of life. The blue sky, the green trees, the flight of a bird, the eyes of a child, become just ordinary or you don't even notice them. This kind of living leads to a sense of dissatisfaction.

- **You don't have a choice.** Autopilot is particularly dangerous in the field of thoughts and emotions. You may be thinking 'I'm useless,' 'I'm unlovable,' or 'I can't do that' automatically without even noticing it. Thoughts have a huge effect on emotions, especially if you believe the thoughts to be true. Automatic negative thoughts lead to unhelpful and difficult emotions. All you notice is that you're suddenly really low, or angry, or tired. However, if you're conscious of these negative thoughts, you have a choice as to whether you believe them or not.

WARNING

Doing mode is most unhelpful when applied to emotional difficulties. Trying to get rid of or suppress emotions may seem to work in the very short term, but before long the emotions rise up again. Being mode is a more helpful state of mind for understanding and finding out about emotions, particularly negative ones. See the later section 'Dealing with emotions using being mode.'

Embracing the Being Mode of Mind

Society values people achieving goals. You see people in the papers who have record amounts of money, or who've climbed the highest mountain. How many times has someone made the headlines for living in the moment?!

People are very familiar with and almost comforted by the doing mode of mind. To stop doing so much, whether physically or mentally, isn't easy. Doing feels attractive and exciting. However, people are beginning to realise that too much doing is a problem. In fact, a whole philosophy has arisen and lots of books have been written all about how you can slow down.

On the surface, the realm of *being* appears lifeless and boring. In actual fact, this couldn't be farther from the truth. Being mode is a nourishing and uplifting state of mind that's always available to you, in the midst of busy activity. You can be trading in the stock market or teaching young children maths – if you're conscious of your physical, emotional, and psychological state of mind – you're in being mode. In some ways, being mode isn't easy to cultivate, yet the rewards of accessing this inner resource far outweigh any difficulties in reaching it.

Here are some of the qualities of the being mode of mind:

>> **You connect with the present moment.** When you're in being mode, you're mindful of sight, sound, smell, taste or touch. Or you're consciously aware of your thoughts or emotions, without being too caught up by them. You're not intentionally getting lost in regrets about the past or concerns about the future.

>> **You accept and allow things to be as they are.** You're less goal-oriented. You have less of a burning desire for situations to change. You accept how things are before moving to change anything. Being mode doesn't mean resignation, it means active acceptance of the way things are at the moment. If you're lost but you have a map, the only way of getting anywhere is to know where you are to start with. Being mode is about acknowledging and accepting where you are.

>> **You're open to pleasant, unpleasant, and neutral emotions.** You're willing to open up to painful and unpleasant sensations or emotions without trying to run away from them. You understand that avoiding an emotion just locks you into the feeling more tightly.

The being mode of mind is what mindfulness endeavours to cultivate. Being mode is about allowing things to be as they are already. When you stop trying to change things, paradoxically they change by themselves. As Carl Jung said: 'We cannot change anything until we accept it.'

TIP

Don't accept an emotion just to try and make it go away. That's not acceptance. For example, say you're feeling a bit sad. If you accept it with a secret desire that the sadness will go away, you haven't fully accepted it yet. It's like offering to hug a friend but then not actually participating in the hugging. Instead, accept an emotion wholeheartedly if you can. After all, emotions are here to teach us something. Listen to your emotions and see what they have to say. This is a skill and certainly not easy at first, but with time and practise, you'll get better and better at accepting and making peace with your emotions.

THE HUNGRY TIGERS

WISE WORDS

The classic story of the hungry tigers points towards a different way of living.

One day a man was walking through a forest when a tiger spotted him and chased after him. The man ran out of the forest as fast as he could to escape the hungry beast. Eventually he stumbled and fell off the edge of a cliff. As he fell he managed to catch a vine, but continued to dangle precariously over the high drop. The tiger continued to watch him from above. Another pack of hungry tigers paced below the man. Then a mouse popped out of a crevice in the cliff. The mouse started gnawing the vine the man was clinging to. Suddenly, the man saw a beautiful plump strawberry glistening in the light. He plucked it and popped it into his mouth. How wonderful it tasted!

You can interpret this story in many ways. I like to think of the tiger above as worries about the past, and the high drop to the tigers below as concerns about the future. The suggestion is to come to your senses – enjoy the strawberry of the present moment, and engage in being mode! The story also offers hope: no matter how bad your past or future appears to be, you may be able to take some pleasure through connecting with your senses in the here and now.

Combining Being and Doing

Think of your mind as like the ocean. The waves rise and fall, but the still, deep waters are always there underneath.

You're tossed and turned in the waves when you're on the surface in doing mode. The waves aren't bad – they're just part of the ocean. Going farther down, the waves of doing rest on the still waters of being, as shown in Figure 5-1. Being is your sense of who you are. Being is characterised as a state of acceptance, a willingness to be with whatever is. Being is tranquil, still, and grounding.

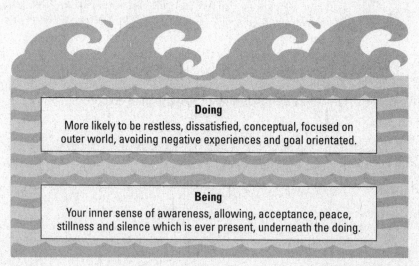

Doing
More likely to be restless, dissatisfied, conceptual, focused on outer world, avoiding negative experiences and goal orientated.

Being
Your inner sense of awareness, allowing, acceptance, peace, stillness and silence which is ever present, underneath the doing.

FIGURE 5-1:
The ocean of doing and being.

© John Wiley & Sons, Inc.

REMEMBER

Experience itself is neither doing nor being mode. You determine the mode by how you react or respond to the experience. Doing is getting actively involved in the experience in order to change it in some way. Being is simply seeing it as it is. That lack of fixing can result in a sense of calmness even when things are tricky.

Switching from doing to being doesn't require years of mindfulness training. It can happen in a moment. Imagine walking to work and worrying about all the things that you need to get done, and planning how you'll tackle the next project with the manager away on holiday. Suddenly you notice the fiery red leaves on a tree. You're amazed at the beauty of it. That simple connection with the sense of sight is an example of being mode. The mode of mind changes by shifting the focus of attention to the present moment. You're no longer on automatic pilot with all its planning, judging, criticising, and praising. You're in the present moment.

Even something as seemingly mundane as feeling your feet in contact with the ground as you walk is a move towards being mode, too. You can also notice the beauty of a tree, the sounds of birds chirping or the gentle sun on the back of your neck. Changing modes may not seem easy at first, especially when you're preoccupied by thoughts, but it gets easier through practise. You don't have to rush through life.

TIP

The key to a mindful way of living is to integrate both doing and being modes of mind into your life. Become aware of which mode you're operating in and make an appropriate choice about which is most helpful for the situation. You need to know where you are on the map before you can move on. Doing mode is important. You need to plan what you're going to do today, what food to buy, how to give feedback to a colleague, and how best to respond when your children start arguing. These activities make you human. However, as a human *being*, you need to integrate a being mode of mind into your doing in order to be fully awake to your life.

Overcoming Obsessive Doing: Distinguishing Wants from Needs

One of the most common addictions people have is work. What started as a 9 a.m. to 5 p.m. job can easily become a 5 a.m. to 9 p.m. job. Naturally, you need to work and earn enough cash to pay the bills. However, before you know it, you're trying to earn a bit more than you actually need. And then your neighbour gets that new car, and you're tempted to do the same. So you do, but it's a touch out of your budget. You go for that promotion, but you need to put in lots more hours – it's a slippery slope to more and more doing. If working long hours is what you want, you're fine, but if it's too much for you, or the long hours are having a negative impact on your relationships, consider looking into a different way of living.

You're excessively doing when your balance is tipped towards your wants rather than your needs. You need to keep a balance between what you want out of life and what you actually need. I define *wants* as desires that aren't really essential to your life, but that you seem to chase after, like an even bigger house or wanting absolutely everyone to like you. *Needs* are your basic necessities such as food, shelter, clothing, and a sense of security.

Here are some suggestions for reducing your wants and so helping you to have more time to access being mode:

>> Make a list of all the things you need to do today. Then prioritise. Ensure that you put mindfulness on the list too. That goes at the top!

>> Put some things on your to-do list that aren't urgent but are fun, like reading you favourite novel or taking the kids to the cinema. Let's throw an ice-cream in here too! Non-urgent activities give you a chance to have a breather from energy-draining doing mode.

>> Think about people you know who rarely rush from place to place. Ask them how they get everything done, or just spend more time with them. Hang out with those with a mindful disposition, and hopefully their mindfulness will rub off onto you.

>> Simplify your life. Remember who and what's most important in your life, and let go of the rest. As American writer and naturalist Henry David Thoreau said: 'Life is frittered away by detail. Simplify, simplify.'

>> Switch television channels when adverts come on. Adverts are designed to ignite dissatisfaction in you, making you want more, more, more. Or if you're feeling really mindful, just copy me and get rid of the television altogether. Why watch television when you can meditate or mindfully hang out with friends!

>> Invoke the being mode of mind whenever you're doing things. Connecting with your breath or the senses is a helpful way of accomplishing this.

Being in the Zone: The Psychology of Flow

Have you ever noticed that when you're eating your favourite food, you forget all your worries and problems? The experience is so lovely that the sense of who you are, what you do, where you come from, and whatever the plan is for tomorrow all vanish for a moment. In fact, most pleasures that you engage in result in you let-ting go of the sense of 'you' with all your problems and issues.

Imagine skiing downhill at high speed. You sense the wind whooshing past you, feel the cool mountain breeze, and enjoy the deep blue colour of the sky. You're *in the zone*, in the moment, at one with all around you. When you're in the zone, you let go of doing mode and come into being mode – the present moment.

This 'in the zone' state of mind is called *flow* by psychologist Mihaly Csíkszentmi-hályi. But what's flow got to do with the being mode of mind? Surely being in the zone is always about doing? Not quite. Practising mindfulness helps to generate flow experiences directly. Everything you do, you can do in the moment, giving you a deeper sense of aliveness.

Here's what you experience when you're in a state of flow:

>> You feel at one with the world.

>> You let go of your sense of being an individual and any worries and problems.

>> You're completely focused.

>> You feel very satisfied with what you're doing.

>> You're happy, although you don't really notice it at the time because you're so engrossed in whatever you're doing.

Understanding the factors of mindful flow

Csíkszentmihályi found some key factors that accompany an experience of flow. I've adapted them here so you can generate what I call a mindful flow experience. As long as you do a task mindfully, it's potentially going to be a flow experience.

Here are some of key factors of mindful flow and how you can generate them using mindfulness:

>> **Attention.** Flow experiences need attention. Mindfulness is all about attention, and mindfulness increases your level of attention with practise. Through regular mindfulness practise, your brain becomes better at paying attention to whatever you choose to focus on, making a flow experience far more likely. When driving, you simply pay attention to your surroundings rather than letting your mind wander off.

>> **Immediate feedback.** Flow needs immediate feedback as to how you're doing. When you're practising mindfulness, you're getting immediate feedback because you know at any time if you're paying attention or if your mind has wandered off for the last few minutes. So, if driving, you notice when your mind has drifted into dreaming about what's for dinner tonight, and you bring your attention gently back to the here and now.

>> **Sufficiently challenging.** Mindfulness is an active process of repeatedly rebalancing to come back to the present moment while the mind – doing what minds do – wants to pull you away into other thoughts. To drive in a mindful way from work to home would be a suitable challenge for anyone, potentially creating a flow experience.

>> **Sense of control.** When you're mindful of your thoughts and feelings that are arising, you've created a choice. You don't have to react to your thoughts or do what they tell you to do. This generates a sense of control as you become aware of the choices you have. If, while you're driving, someone cuts in front

of you, you've got the choice to either react and feel annoyed, or practise letting it go. Even if you do react, you can notice how you react and what effect the reaction has on your thoughts and feelings. Eventually, mindfulness goes beyond trying to control – you discover the flow experience is accessed through letting go rather than controlling your attention.

>> **Intrinsically rewarding.** As you carry out a task, you're doing it for the sake of itself. If you're driving your car to get home as fast as possible to have your cup of tea, you're not going to be in a flow experience. If you drive to simply enjoy each moment of the journey, that's different. You can feel the warmth of the sunshine on your arms, appreciate the colour of the sky while sitting in traffic, and marvel at the miracle of the human body's ability to do such a complex task effortlessly. You're in a flow experience.

WARNING

Normally, mindfulness would make you a safer driver rather than a more dangerous one. However, begin by being mindful of safer tasks like washing dishes or going for a walk before you attempt mindfulness of driving, just so you get used to being mindful. Don't use mindfulness of driving if you find the experience distracting.

Discovering your flow experiences

Everyone's had flow experiences. By knowing when you've been in flow, you can encourage more opportunities to experience it in the future. The following are some typical activities that people often find themselves flowing in. You may even find something here to try yourself:

>> **Reading or writing.** When you're fully engaged in a good book full of fascinating insights or a challenging storyline, you're in flow. You forget about everything else and time flies by. When writing in flow, words simply pop into your head and onto your page with effortless ease. You stop criticising what you're creating, and enjoy seeing the report or book pouring out of you. I've discovered how to do this myself by writing whatever words arise into my awareness first, and avoiding all self-judgement. Then I go back and edit the writing later on. In this way, the writing seems to flow naturally. This is an example of mindful writing.

>> **Art or hobbies (such as drawing, painting, dancing, singing, or playing music).** Most artistic endeavours involve flow. You're directly connected with your senses, and people often describe themselves as being 'at one with the music.' If you're forced to do a particular hobby, it may or may not be a flow experience, because the intrinsic motivation isn't there. Picture a friend being dragged onto the dance floor before he's had a drink and you know what I mean.

- » **Exercise (walking, running, cycling, swimming, and so on).** Some people love exercise so much that they get addicted to it. The rush of adrenaline, the full focus in the present moment, and the feeling of exhilaration make for a flow experience.

- » **Work.** Perhaps surprisingly, you can be in flow at work. Research has found that people are happier at work than they are in their leisure time. Work encourages you to do something with a focused attention, and often involves interaction with others. You need to give something of yourself. This can set the stage for flow. In contrast, watching television at home can drain your energy, especially if you're watching unchallenging programmes.

- » **Anything done mindfully.** Remember, anything that you do with a mindful awareness is going to generate a flow state of mind, from making love to making a cup of tea. Just let go of your judgement, be fully present as best you can, and see whether you can enjoy the experience.

Encouraging a Being Mode of Mind

Generally speaking, most people spend too much time in doing mode and not enough in being mode. Doing mode results in chasing after goals that may not be what you're really interested in. Being mode offers a rest – a chance to let go of the usual, habitual patterns of the mind and drop into the awareness that's always there.

REMEMBER

You can be in being mode even though you're doing something. Being mode doesn't necessarily mean that you're doing nothing. You can be busy working hard in the garden, and yet if your attention is right in the moment, and you're connecting directly with the senses, you can be in being mode.

Here are ten ways of switching from doing mode to being mode:

- » **When walking from place to place, take the opportunity to feel your feet on the floor, see the range of different colours in front of you, and listen to the variety of different sounds.** (Move to Chapter 6 to discover the art of mindful walking.)

- » **When moving from one activity to another, take a moment to rest.** Feel one complete in-breath and out-breath.

- » **Establish a regular mindfulness routine using formal mindfulness meditation practises.** (For more on this, head to Chapter 6.)

>> **Use the three-minute mini mindfulness meditation several times a day (see Chapter 7).** Whenever you catch yourself becoming excessively tense or emotional, use the mini meditation to begin moving towards being mode and opening up to the challenging experience, rather than reacting to try to avoid or get rid of the experience.

>> **Avoid multi-tasking whenever you can.** Doing one thing at a time with your full and undivided attention can engage being mode. Doing too many things at the same time encourages your mind to spin.

>> **Find time to do a hobby or sport.** These activities tend to involve connecting with the senses, which immediately brings you into being mode. Painting, listening to music, or playing an instrument, dancing, singing, walking in the park, and many more activities all offer a chance to be with the senses.

>> **When taking a bath or shower, use the time to feel the warmth of the water and the contact of the water with your skin.** Allow all your senses to be involved in the experience; enjoy the sound of the water and breathe in the scent of your favourite soap or body wash.

>> **When you're eating, pause before your meal to take a few conscious breaths.** Then eat the meal with your full attention. Check out Chapter 6 for ways to munch mindfully.

>> **Treat yourself to a half day or full day of mindfulness once in a while.** Wake up slowly, feel your breath frequently, and connect with your senses and with other significant people around you as much as you can. Chapter 8 sets out some suggestions for having a mindful day.

Dealing with emotions using being mode

Using doing mode in the area of thoughts and emotions is like using the wrong remote control to change the channel on your television. No matter how hard you push the buttons, the channel isn't going to change – and pushing the buttons harder just makes you more tired and breaks the remote control. You're using the wrong tool for the job.

Say you're feeling sad today. Doing mode may feel the emotion and use the problem-solving, goal-oriented mind to try to fight it, asking, 'Why am I sad? How can I escape from it? What shall I do now? Why does this always happen to me? Let me try watching television. Oh, I feel worse. What if this feeling never goes away? What if I feel depressed again?'

Doing mode sets thoughts spinning in your head, which just makes you feel worse. Your focus is on getting rid of the feeling instead of feeling the emotion. The more you fight the emotion, the stronger it seems to get. So, what's the solution?

Next time you have an uncomfortable feeling like sadness, anger, frustration or jealousy, try this exercise to get into being mode:

1. **Set your intention.** Let your intention be to feel the emotion and its effects as best you can with a gentle curiosity, kindness and acceptance. You're not doing so as a clever way to get rid of it. You're just giving yourself space to learn from the emotion rather than running away.

   All emotions, no matter how strong, have a beginning and an end.

2. **Feel the emotion.** Feel the emotion with care, kindness, and acceptance, as best you can. Open up to it. Notice where the emotion manifests itself in your body. Breathe into that part of your body and stay with it. Allow the emotion to be as it is. You don't need to fight or run away. Be with the experience.

3. **Step back from the emotion.** Notice that you can be aware of the emotion without being the emotion itself – create a space between yourself and the feeling. This is an important aspect of mindfulness. As you observe the feeling, you're separate from it in the sense that you're free from it. You're watching it. It's like sitting on a riverbank as the water rushes by rather than being in the river itself. As you watch the water (emotion) pass by, you're not in the river itself. Every now and then, you may feel like you've been sucked into the river and washed downstream. As soon as you feel this, simply step back out of the river again. Figure 5-2 illustrates this idea.

4. **Breathe.** Now simply feel your breath. Be with each in-breath and each out-breath. Notice how each breath is unique, different, and vital for your health and wellbeing. Then continue with whatever you need to do in a mindful way.

Finding time to just be

Are you a busy bee? Do you have too much to do to have time to be? One of the attractive things about mindfulness is that you don't have a fixed amount of time that you're 'supposed' to practise for. Your daily practise can be a mindfulness exercise for one minute or one hour – it's up to you. The other great thing about mindfulness is that you can simply be mindful of your normal everyday routine and in that way build up your awareness and *being* mode. That takes no time at all; in fact, it can save time because you're more focused on your activities.

These mindful practises require almost no time at all:

>> **When waiting in a queue, rather than killing time, engage your awareness.** Time is too precious to be killed. Notice the colours and sounds around you. Or challenge yourself to see whether you can maintain the awareness of your feet on the floor for ten full breaths. Even engaging in a friendly chat with someone can help you practise mindful listening.

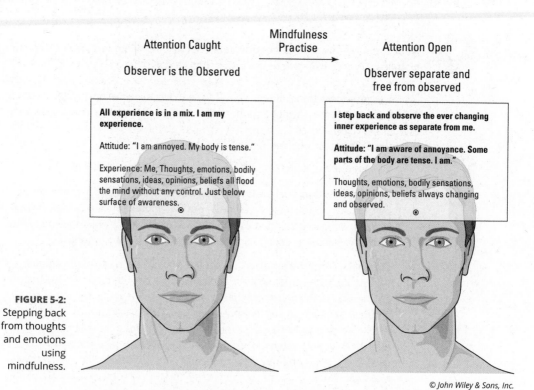

Attention Caught

Mindfulness Practise

Attention Open

Observer is the Observed

Observer separate and free from observed

All experience is in a mix. I am my experience.

Attitude: "I am annoyed. My body is tense."

Experience: Me, Thoughts, emotions, bodily sensations, ideas, opinions, beliefs all flood the mind without any control. Just below surface of awareness. ◉

I step back and observe the ever changing inner experience as separate from me.

Attitude: "I am aware of annoyance. Some parts of the body are tense. I am."

Thoughts, emotions, bodily sensations, ideas, opinions, beliefs always changing and observed. ◉

FIGURE 5-2:
Stepping back from thoughts and emotions using mindfulness.

© John Wiley & Sons, Inc.

>> **When you stop at a red traffic light, you have a choice.** You can let yourself get frustrated and impatient, or you can do traffic light meditation! Close your eyes and nourish yourself with three mindful breaths – very refreshing! If you get into this practise, you'll be hoping for red lights instead of green lights.

>> **The next time the phone rings, let it ring three times.** Use that time to breathe and smile. Telesales companies know that you can 'hear the smile' on the phone and ask employees to smile when they're on a call. You're in a more patient and happy state of mind when you speak.

>> **Change your routine.** If you normally drive to work, try walking or cycling for part of it. Speak to different friends or colleagues. Take up a new hobby. When you change your habits, you engage different pathways in the brain. You instinctively wake up to the moment and just be.

Living in the moment

You're always in the present moment. You've never been in any other moment. Don't believe me? Every time your mind worries about the past, when does it do it? Only in the present moment. Every plan you've ever made is only made in the present too. Right now, as you're thinking about what you're reading and comparing it with your past experience, you're doing so in this moment, now. Your plans for tomorrow can only be thought about now. Now is all you're ever in. So what's all the fuss about? The question is how you can connect with the here and now.

Here are some tips for living in the present moment:

>> **Value the present moment.** Spend time considering that the present moment is the *only* moment that you have. You then discover the value of focusing on the here and now. And once you experience how enjoyable present-moment living can be, you've created a powerful shift into a more mindful and happy lifestyle.

>> **Focus on whatever you're doing.** Be present in the little moments that fill your day, because the little moments aren't little; they're life. When you type, feel the contact between your fingers and the keyboard. When getting dressed, try giving it your full attention rather than allowing your mind to wander. When setting the table for dinner, feel the weight of the plates and utensils as you carry them. Appreciate how the table looks once you have set it. Enjoy doing tasks to the best of your ability. Living in the present is trickier than it sounds, but each time you try, you get a little better at it. Slowly but surely, you start really living in the moment.

>> **Reduce activities that draw you out of the moment.** I found that watching too much television sent my mind spinning, so I got rid of it. For you, you may need to reduce the time you spend on social media or surfing websites. Or it may be as simple as not lying in bed in the morning for too long, allowing youself to worry unnecessarily about the day. Nothing's wrong with any of these activities, but they don't encourage moment-by-moment living. They capture your attention and lead to a passive state of mind. Watching too many hours of Netflix while slumped on the sofa drains your energy much faster than an activity done with a gentle awareness.

>> **Establish a daily mindfulness practise.** Doing so strengthens your ability to stay in the present rather than being drawn into the past or pulled into the future. The strength of your daily habit extends into your everyday life, without you even trying. You hear the sound of that bird in the tree, or find yourself listening intently to your colleague in an effortless way. Now mindfulness becomes fun.

>> **Look deeply.** Consider and reflect on all the people and things that come together in each moment. For example, you're reading this book. The book's paper came from trees which needed sunshine and rain, soil and nutrients. The book was edited, marketed, printed, transported, distributed, and sold by

people. It also required the invention of the printing press, language, and more. You were taught English by someone to enable you to understand the words. This awareness of all that's come together and been provided for you to enjoy naturally creates gratitude and present-moment awareness. This is called *looking deeply*. You're connecting in the moment, and also seeing the bigger picture of how things have come together in an interconnected way. Looking deeply isn't thinking about your experience, but seeing your experience in a different way. You can try it in any situation – it transforms your perspective, and perspective transforms experience.

PLAY THIS

If you want to let go of your baggage from the past and future, try this mindful exercise. I discovered it from a mindfulness teacher and monk called Ajahn Brahm. This present–moment meditation is also available as an MP3 (Track 6), so you can plug in your headphones and enjoy being guided. To let go of the weight of the past and future:

1. **Find a nice comfortable position to sit or lie in.** Be kind to yourself, and ensure you're in a relaxed posture, loosening any tight clothing, removing any glasses you're wearing and slipping off your shoes if you wish.

2. **Take your time to take a few deep, smooth breaths.** Let each in-breath represent nourishment and energy. Let each out-breath signify letting go.

3. **Gently close your eyes. Imagine you're holding two heavy shopping bags. Imagine how heavy they feel.** Feel the strain on your fingers and how much effort it takes to hold both bags. Their weight is pulling you down. The strain makes you feel tired and tense.

4. **Let the bag in one hand represent your past.** Imagine the bag is labelled 'past.' The bag contains all your regrets and mistakes. All your successes and failures. Past relationships. The choices you've made and the sorrows you've felt. You may even be able to visualise all your past experiences contained within this heavy bag. Holding this bag all day is tiring.

5. **Imagine that you decide it's time to let go of the 'past' bag.** You want to put the bag down and have a rest. So imagine slowly lowering the bag to the ground. Eventually the bag makes contact with the ground, and as it does so, immediately you begin to feel a release. Eventually your whole bag, representing all your past, is down on the ground. You smile as you let go completely. Imagine your hand opening and imagine yourself feeling so much better. You're liberated from carrying your past around with you.

6. **In your other hand, you're holding a heavy bag signifying your future.** Imagine the word 'future' written on the bag. The bag contains all your hopes, dreams, and plans. And also all your anxieties and worries. All your concerns

and fears about what may or may not happen. Holding this hefty burden is no joke. The bag slows you down. But now you know how to put this bag, which is full of your future, down.

7. **Imagine that you slowly lower the 'future' bag until the bottom of the bag starts to make contact with the ground.** You begin to feel a relief. As you continue to lower the bag, all the weight is transferred to the earth. You feel an immense burden lifted. Your hand is now free, and you completely let go of your worries about the future.

8. **Imagine yourself standing with a bag representing your past on the floor on one side, and a bag representing your future on the floor on the other side.** Because you're standing between the past and future, where are you? You're in the best place to be: the present moment. Give yourself the go-ahead to feel free. The bags are perfectly safe on the ground. Rest in the joy of being in the present moment. Rejoice in the childlike innocence of the here and now – timelessness.

9. **Spend as much time as you want to in this experience of the present moment. And any time you feel you're carrying too much weight from the past or future, practise this mindful exercise and put the weights down again.**

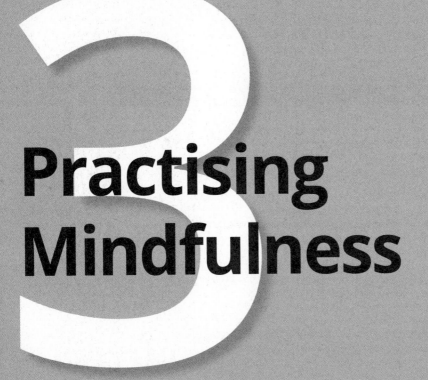

3
Practising Mindfulness

Explore the delights of practising mindfulness at any time of the day.

Find out how to design a mindfulness routine that is right for you.

Discover how to avoid the common pitfalls in the mindfulness game.

Chapter **6**

Getting Into Formal Mindfulness Meditation Practise

There are many ways to practise mindfulness in your everyday life. But if you want to take things further, you may want to explore mindfulness meditation.

Mindfulness meditation is like diving to the bottom of the ocean, where the water is more still. The waves (thoughts) are at the surface, but you're watching them from a deeper, more restful depth. To submerge to that peaceful depth takes time and patience. Extended meditations in the formal mindfulness meditation practises in this chapter offer the diving equipment for you to safely reach those tranquil places.

Formal practise is mindfulness meditation you specifically make time for in your day – it doesn't mean you need to put on a suit or a posh dress though! You decide when and for how long you're going to meditate, and you do it. A formal mindfulness routine lies at the heart of a mindful way of living. This chapter explores some formal mindfulness practises for you to do while lying down, sitting or walking.

Preparing Your Body and Mind for Mindfulness Meditation

Here are some useful pointers on preparing yourself to practise mindful meditation:

» You can practise the meditation any time and anywhere that suits you. For more help on deciding when and where you'll practise, see Chapter 9.

» Avoid meditating immediately after a big meal or when you're feeling very hungry; your stomach may then become the object of your attention rather than anything else.

» Try and find conditions conducive for meditation: ideally, somewhere that is not too noisy, with the right temperature for you and soft or natural lighting. Wear clothing that's loose and comfortable. None of these conditions are essential – it's possible to meditate anytime and anywhere – but if you're a beginner, these environmental factors help.

» You can be in any posture that feels comfortable for you for mindfulness meditation. If you're interested in advice on specific sitting postures, see further on in this chapter.

» Experiment by gently smiling when you meditate. This is a simple and powerful secret to help you enjoy meditation. Think of smiling as the most important posture in meditation. A cute little grin on your face sends a signal to your mind to be friendly towards yourself. You let go of being too serious or trying too hard; meditation can then become a joyful non-activity.

Savouring Mindful Eating Meditation

Starting with mindful eating meditation demonstrates the simplicity of meditation. Mindfulness meditation isn't about sitting cross-legged for hours on end; it's about the awareness you bring to each present moment. Mindfulness is about living with an open and curious awareness. Anything done with mindful awareness is meditation, including eating, driving, walking, talking and much more.

PLAY THIS

Try the following exercise, which is available as an audio track (Track 7):

1. **Place a small piece of fruit in your hand.** Imagine you dropped in from outer space and have never seen or tasted this fruit before. Spend a few minutes looking at the colour and texture. Explore the creases and folds of its skin, how

it catches the light as you rotate it, and how much varying detail it contains. Observe the skill in your fingers to be able to delicately hold and rotate the fruit precisely and at will.

2. **Bring the fruit towards your nose.** Feel the sensations in your arm as you bring the fruit towards your nose. As you breathe, notice whether the fruit has a scent, and the quality of it. Notice how you feel if the fruit doesn't have a scent. Spend a few minutes doing this.

3. **Hold the fruit to your ear.** Squeeze the fruit gently between your thumb and finger and listen to the sound it produces, if any. Perhaps it makes a quiet sound or no sound at all. When you've done this, bring your arm back down.

4. **Feel the texture of the fruit.** Close your eyes to tune in to the sense of touch more deeply. Feel the shape of the object and its weight. Gently squeeze the fruit and observe whether you can get a sense of its juice.

5. **Bring the fruit towards your mouth.** Are you salivating? If so, your body has already begun the first stage of digestion. Touch the fruit gently onto your upper and lower lips to see what sensations you can detect. Place the fruit inside your mouth, on your tongue. Do you have a sense of relief now, or frustration? Feel the weight of the fruit on your tongue. Move the fruit around your mouth, noticing how skilled your tongue is at doing this. Place the fruit between two teeth and slowly bring your teeth together. Observe the phenomenon of tasting and eating. Spot the range of experiences unfolding, including a change in taste and the fluxing consistency of the fruit as it slowly breaks up and dissolves. Be aware of yourself chewing and how you automatically start to swallow. Stay with the experience until you've finished eating.

6. **Notice the aftertaste in your mouth when you've finished eating the fruit.**

Now, reflect on these questions:

>> How do you feel having done that exercise?

>> What effect will this process have on your experience of eating?

>> What did you notice and find out?

REMEMBER

There's no correct experience in this mindful eating meditation. Different people have different experiences. You probably found it wasn't your normal experience of eating. The first thing to discover about all mindful meditations is that *whatever your experience is, it is your experience and it is correct and valid.*

By connecting with the senses, you move from automatic pilot mode to a mindful mode. (Refer to Chapter 5 for more about mental modes.) In other words, rather than eating while doing something else and not even noticing the taste, you deliberately turn your attention to the whole process of eating.

You may have found the taste of the fruit to be more vivid and intense than usual. Perhaps you noticed things about this fruit that you hadn't noticed before. Mindfulness reveals new things and transforms the experience itself, making for a deeper experience. If this is true of eating something ordinary like a piece of fruit, consider what effect mindfulness may have on the rest of your experiences in life!

You may have noticed that you were thinking during the exercise, and perhaps you felt you couldn't do the mindful eating properly because of thinking. Don't worry: you're pretty much *always* thinking, and it's not going to stop any time soon. What you can do is begin to become aware that it's happening and see what effect that has.

Calming with Mindful Breathing Meditation

If you're keen to try a short, simple, ten-minute sitting mindfulness meditation, this one's for you. This meditation focuses your attention on the breath and enables you to gently guide yourself back to your breathing when your attention wanders away.

PLAY THIS

This meditation is available as an audio track (Track 8) and shows you how to practise ten minutes of mindful breathing:

1. **Find a comfortable posture.** You can be sitting up in a chair, cross-legged on the floor or even lying down (see the later section 'Finding a posture that's right for you'). Close your eyes if you want to. And hold a charming little smile on your face.

REMEMBER

This is an opportunity to be with whatever your experience is from moment to moment. This is a time for you. You don't need to achieve anything. You don't need to try too hard. You simply need to be with things as they are, as best you can, from moment to moment. Relax any obvious physical tensions if you can.

2. **Become aware of the sensations of breathing.** Feel your breath going in and out of your nostrils, or passing through the back of your throat, or feel your chest or belly rising and falling. As soon as you've found a place where you can feel your breath comfortably, endeavour to keep your attention there.

Before long, your mind will take you away into thoughts, ideas, dreams, fantasies and plans. That's perfectly normal and absolutely fine. Just as soon as you notice that it's happened, gently smile again and you'll find your attention naturally returning to your breath. Try not to criticise yourself each time your mind wanders away. Instead, celebrate that you're back in the here and now. Understand that it's all part of the mindfulness process. If you find yourself criticising yourself or getting frustrated, say to yourself, 'It's okay . . . it's okay . . . minds naturally wander . . . gently come back to the breath.'

3. **Continue to stay with the meditation, without trying to control the depth or speed of your breathing.** If the breath changes, that's fine. If the breath stays the same, that's fine too. Everything's fine!

4. **After ten minutes, gently open your eyes.**

REMEMBER

All the timings I suggest in this book are for guidance only. You can be flexible and reduce or increase the time you meditate depending on your circumstances. I suggest you decide, before each sitting, for how long you're going to practise meditating and then stick to your decision. You can use an alarm with a gentle ring, or perhaps a countdown timer on your phone to indicate when you've finished. This avoids having to keep opening your eyes to check whether you need to bring the mindful meditation to a close.

If that was one of the first times you've practised meditation, you're starting a journey. The meditation may have felt fine or awful. That doesn't matter. What matters is your willingness to accept whatever arises and keep practising. Starting meditation is a bit like going to the gym for the first time in months: the experience can be unpleasant to begin with! Keep practising and try not to judge it as a good or bad meditation – there's no such thing. And remember, there's nothing to be frightened about in meditation either: if you feel too uncomfortable, you can simply open your eyes and stop the meditation. It's much better to do whatever feels right to you than trying to exactly follow my instructions. You know yourself better than anyone else.

A CURE FOR BREATHING BOREDOM

A meditation student went up to her teacher and said that she was bored of feeling the breath. Could a different technique make breathing more interesting? The teacher replied, 'Yes. Close your mouth and breathe with your nose. Then take your left arm and with the thumb block your left nostril. With your index finger block the other nostril. You can no longer breathe. In less than a minute, you'll enjoy your breathing more than anything else in the whole world. Try it for just 30 seconds and you'll find it hard to think about anything else but breathing.'

Remember how important your breathing is, and try not to take it for granted. Breathing is special.

Engaging in Mindful Movement

Moving and stretching in a slow and mindful way is a wonderful preparation for more extended meditation exercises. Movement can also be a deep formal meditation in itself, if you approach it with full awareness.

When practising mindful movement, tune in to the sensations of your breath as you move and hold different postures. Become aware of thoughts and emotions that arise, notice them, and shift your awareness back to the body. Be mindful when a stretch is slightly out of your comfort zone and begins to feel uncomfortable. Explore what being at this edge of your comfort zone feels like. Notice whether you habitually drive yourself through the pain, or whether you always avoid the discomfort completely. Be curious about your relationship with movement and stretching, and bring a playful attitude to your experience.

Practising mindful movement has many benefits. You can do the following:

TIP

>> **Explore limits and discomfort.** When you stretch, you eventually reach a limit beyond which the discomfort becomes too intense (the *edge*). Mindfulness offers the opportunity to explore your mind's reactions as you approach your edge. Do you try to push beyond it, often causing injury, or do you stay too far away, avoiding the slightest discomfort? By approaching the edge with a mindful awareness, you open up to uncomfortable physical sensations rather than avoiding them.

   You can transfer this skill of mindful awareness to your experience of difficult thoughts and emotions, encouraging you to stay with them and acknowledge them, and see what effect mindfulness has on them.

>> **Tune in to the sensations in your body and tune out of the usual wandering mind.** By focusing in on the range of feelings and sensations in your body, you bring yourself into the present moment. Mindful movement shows you a way of coming into the here and now. Most of the other formal meditation practises involve being still; you may find movement an easier door into mindful practise.

>> **Discover how to be mindful while your body is in motion.** You can transfer this discovery into your daily life and become more mindful of all the movement you do, such as walking, cooking, cleaning, and getting dressed. You're training your mind to be mindful in your day-to-day activities.

>> **Practise being kind to your body.** Mindful movement and stretching is an opportunity to relate to your physical sensations with a spirit of friendliness. Allow physical sensations to soften by feeling them with a sense of warmth and affection rather than resistance or avoidance.

BREATHING INTO DIFFERENT PARTS OF YOUR BODY

In mindfulness practise, I often mention 'breathing into' your toes or fingers or your discomfort. What does that mean? Your lungs don't extend into your toes! Here's how you breathe into a particular part of the body:

1. Feel the sensations in the particular part of the body you're working on.

2. As you breathe in, imagine your breath going from your nose up or down into that part of your body or experience.

3. When you breathe out, sense your breath going out of that part of the body and back out of your nose. Allow the sensations in that part of the body to gently soften as you do this.

If this technique doesn't work for you, try feeling the part of the body you're working on at the same time as feeling your breathing. Or try gently smiling as you feel that difficult sensation. Over time, this idea of breathing into your experience may naturally begin to make some sense. If it doesn't, don't worry. Trying different mindfulness tools allows you to find which ones work for you.

>> **Gain an understanding about life through movement practise.** When trying to balance in a yoga posture, notice how your body isn't stiff or still but continuously moving and correcting to maintain your balance. Sometimes you lose your balance and have to start again. In the same way, living a life of balance requires continuous correction, and sometimes you get it wrong. You just need to start again.

TIP

Consider other lessons about life you can take from doing a sequence of mindful yoga or any other mindful movement. Think about how you cope with the more challenging poses, or how you may compare yourself with others, or how you compete with yourself.

Trying Out the Body Scan Meditation

The body scan is a wonderful mindfulness practise to start your journey into contemplative practises. You normally do the body scan lying down, so you get a sense of letting go straight away.

Practising the body scan

Set aside at least half an hour for the body scan. Find a time when and a place where you won't be disturbed, and somewhere you feel comfortable and secure. Turn off any phones you have.

This is a time totally set aside for you, and for you to be with yourself. A time for renewal, rest, and healing. A time to nourish your health and wellbeing. Remember that mindfulness is about being with things as they are, moment to moment, as they unfold in the present. So, let go of ideas about self-improvement and personal development. Let go of your tendency for wanting things to be different from how they are, and allow them to be exactly as they are. Give yourself the space to be as you are. You don't even need to try to relax. Relaxation may happen or it may not. Relaxation isn't the aim of the body scan. If anything, the aim is to be aware of your experience, whatever it may be. Do whatever feels right for you.

REMEMBER

The body scan practise is very safe. However, if the body scan brings up feelings that you can't cope with, stop and get advice from a mindfulness teacher or professional therapist. However, if you can, open up to the feelings and sensations and move in close; by giving these feelings the chance to speak to you, you may find that they dissipate in their own time.

PLAY THIS

Follow these steps, which are available as an audio track (Track 9):

1. **Loosen any tight clothing, especially around your waist or neck.** You may like to remove your shoes.

2. **Lie down on your bed or a mat with your arms by your sides, palms facing up, and legs gently apart.** If you feel uncomfortable, place a pillow under your knees or just raise your knees. Experiment with your position; you may even prefer to sit up. You can place a blanket over yourself, because your body temperature can drop when you're still for an extended time. Hold a slight, gentle smile on your face for the duration of this practise. This helps to remind you to be kind to yourself and not to take any experience too seriously.

3. **Begin by feeling the weight of your body on the mat, bed, or chair.** Notice the points of contact between that and your body. Each time you breathe out, allow yourself to sink a little deeper into the mat, bed, or chair.

4. **Become aware of the sensations of your breath.** You may feel the breath going in and out of your nostrils, or passing through the back of your throat, or feel the chest or belly rising and falling. Be aware of your breath wherever it feels most predominant and comfortable for you. Continue for a few minutes.

5. **When you're ready, move your awareness down the left leg, past the knee and ankle and right down into the big toe of your left foot.** Notice the sensations in your big toe with a sense of curiosity. Is your big toe warm or

cold? Can you feel the contact of your socks, or the movement of air? Now expand your awareness to your little toe, and then all the toes in between. What do they feel like? If you can't feel any sensation, that's okay. Just be aware of lack of sensation.

6. **As you breathe, imagine the breath going down your body and into your toes. As you breathe out, imagine the breath going back up your body and out of your nose.** Use this strategy of breathing into and out of each part to which you're paying attention (see the nearby sidebar 'Breathing into different parts of your body').

7. **Expand your awareness to the sole of your foot.** Focus on the ball and heel of the foot. The weight of the heel. The sides and upper part of the foot. The ankle. Breathe into the whole of the left foot. Then, when you're ready, let go of the left foot.

8. **Repeat this process of gentle, kind, curious accepting awareness with the lower part of the left leg, the knee, and the upper part of the left leg.** Notice how your left leg may now feel different to your right leg.

9. **Gently shift your awareness around and down the right leg, to the toes in your right foot.** Move your awareness up the right leg in the same way as before. Then let it go.

10. **Become aware of your pelvis, hips, buttocks, and all the delicate organs around here.** Breathe into them and imagine you're filling them with nourishing oxygen.

11. **Move up to the lower torso, the lower abdomen, and lower back.** Notice the movement of the lower abdomen as you breathe in and out. Notice any emotions you feel here. See whether you can explore and accept your feelings as they are.

12. **Bring your attention to your chest and upper back.** Feel your rib cage rising and falling as you breathe in and out. Be mindful of your heart beating, if you can. Be grateful that all these vital organs are currently functioning to keep you alive and conscious. Be mindful of any emotions arising from your heart area. Allow space for your emotions to express themselves.

13. **Go to both arms together, beginning with the fingertips and moving up to the shoulders.** Breathe into and out of each body part before you move to the next one, if that feels helpful.

14. **Focus on your neck. Then move your mindful attention to your jaw, noticing whether it's clenched. Feel your lips, inside your mouth, your cheeks, your nose, your eyelids and eyes, your temples, your forehead (checking whether it's frowning), your eyes, the back of your head, and finally the top of your head.** Take your time to be with each part of your head in a mindful way, feeling and opening up to the physical sensations with curiosity and warmth.

15. **Imagine a space in the top of your head and soles of your feet. Imagine your breath sweeping up and down your body as you breathe in and out. Feel the breath sweeping up and down your body, and get a sense of each cell in your body being nourished with energy and oxygen.** Continue this for a few minutes.

16. **Now let go of all effort to practise mindfulness. Get a sense of your whole body. Feel yourself as complete, just as you are. At peace, just as you are.** Remember this sense of being is always available to you when you need it. Rest in this stillness.

17. **Acknowledge the time you've taken to nourish your body and mind. Come out of this meditation gently, being aware of the transition into whatever you need to do next.** Endeavour to bring this mindful awareness to whatever activity you engage in next.

Appreciating the benefits of the body scan meditation

The body scan meditation has many benefits:

» **Getting in touch with your body.** You spend most of your time in your head, constantly thinking, thinking, thinking. By practising the body scan, you're connecting with your own body and disconnecting from your mind with all its ideas, opinions, beliefs, judgements, dreams and desires. Thinking is a wonderful and precious aspect of being human, but by connecting with the sensations in the body, you tune in to the intelligence and wisdom of the body. Hearing what the body has to say is fascinating if you listen carefully and give your body the space to express itself. The body scan helps you acknowledge that understanding and insight comes not only from the thinking brain but from the whole body, a supremely intelligent system from which you can discover so much.

» **Letting go of doing mode and coming into being mode.** As you lie down to do the body scan, you can completely let go physically. Your mind can follow on from this and also begin to let go of thinking on automatic pilot. Through the body scan, you begin to move from the auto-pilot doing mode of mind into the being mode of mind, which is about allowing things to be just as they are (see Chapter 5 for more).

» **Training your attention.** The body scan alternates between a wide and a narrow focus of attention – from focusing on your little toe all the way through to the entire body. The body scan trains your mind to be able to move from detailed attention to a wider and more spacious awareness from one moment to the next. In other words, you're more able to zoom in and out of an experience – a skill you can use outside of meditation.

>> **Releasing emotions stored in the body.** Stressful events experienced from childhood, such as divorce or extreme discipline, cause great fear and can get locked and stored in the body as physical tension, an absence of sensation, or as a dysfunctional part of the body that causes, for example, problems with digestion. The body scan helps to release that stored-up emotion and tension. Some clients have had years of physical ailments relieved through the regular practise of the body scan meditation.

>> **Using the body as an emotional gauge.** Practising the body scan and becoming increasingly aware of your body enables you to become more sensitive to how your body reacts in different situations throughout the day. If you become stressed or nervous about something, you may be able to notice this earlier through the body, and so be able to make an informed choice as to what to do next. Without that awareness, you don't have a choice and face the possibility of unnecessarily spiralling down into unhelpful emotions and a tense body. For example, if you notice your forehead tightening up or your shoulders tensing in a meeting, you can do something about it rather than letting the tension unconsciously build and build.

DIAPHRAGMATIC BREATHING

Diaphragmatic or *belly breathing*, rather than just chest breathing, is the type of breathing that takes place when you're relaxed and calm. You can see it in babies and young children when they breathe. Their bellies come out as they breathe in, and go back in when they breathe out. This belly breathing is caused by a deep, relaxed breath in which the diaphragm goes up and down, pushing the stomach in and out. When you practise diaphragmatic breathing, you nourish your body with greater levels of oxygen, and the breathing is easier for the body. Many people find it therapeutic, and yoga emphasises it too. Try taking a few belly breaths before you start your meditation to help lead yourself into a more focused state of mind.

Here's how to do diaphragmatic breathing (see the accompanying figure):

1. Loosen any tight clothing, especially around your waist.

2. Get into a comfortable position, sitting or lying down.

3. Place one hand on your chest and the other on your belly.

4. As you breathe in and out, allow the hand on your belly to gently rise up and down while keeping the hand on your chest relatively still.

(continued)

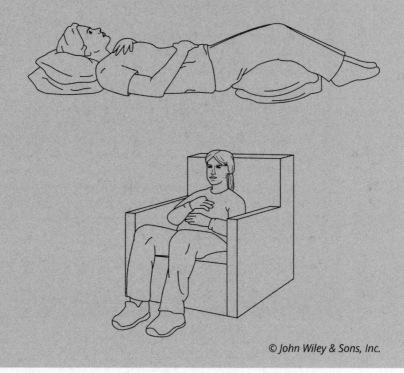

Diaphragmatic breathing may take some practise at first, but in time it becomes easy and natural. Practise as often as you want, and it soon becomes a healthy habit.

© John Wiley & Sons, Inc.

Overcoming body scan obstacles

The body scan seems easy on the surface. All you need to do is lie down, turn on the audio MP3, and guide your awareness through your body. In reality you're doing a lot more than that. If you've spent your life ignoring your body, trying a different approach takes both courage and determination. Problems may arise. Perhaps . . .

>> You felt more pain in your body than you normally do.

>> You wanted to stop the body scan.

>> You couldn't concentrate.

>> You fell asleep.

>> You became more anxious, depressed, or frustrated than when you started.

>> You couldn't do the body scan.

>> You didn't like the body scan.

>> You couldn't stop crying.

>> You couldn't see the point of the body scan.

All these are common experiences. Of course, experiences of pleasure and peace occur too! Remember the following sentence when you begin to struggle with the body scan and other long meditations:

You may not always like it – you just need to keep at it.

TIP

You may be struggling with your mindfulness meditation because you're seeking a particular outcome. Maybe you want your mind to shut up, or the pain to go away, or you want to get rid of your restlessness. Try letting go of these desires. The fewer desires you have, the more you're likely to enjoy the mindfulness practises. Make peace with whatever you're experiencing in the moment by becoming aware of it with friendliness. Look at the experience like you look at a little kitten, or a baby, or a really good friend: with affection, as best you can.

Enjoying Sitting Meditation

Sitting meditation is simply being mindful in a sitting position. In this section I share some common sitting postures and guide you through seated practise. Once you establish yourself in the practise, you can adapt it in any way that suits you.

Try sitting meditation after a couple of weeks' practising the body scan every day (explained in the previous section). The body scan helps you begin to get accustomed to paying attention to your breath and your body in an accepting and kindly way. You also begin to understand how easily the mind wanders off, and how to tenderly bring the attention back. The sitting meditation continues to develop your attention, bringing a wider range of present-moment experiences to be mindful of. Although your mind still strays into thoughts, you begin to shift your *relationship* to thoughts, which is a small but fundamental shift.

Finding a posture that's right for you

When it comes to postures in mindfulness practise, I offer all sorts of suggestions in this section. But the key principle is the following:

Find a posture that you feel comfortable with.

If you spend too much energy and experience unnecessary discomfort in a particular posture, you'll either be put off from the mindfulness practises or you'll associate mindfulness with painful experiences. There's no need for this. Mindfulness is about being kind to yourself, so be nice and comfortable when you're finding the right sitting posture for yourself.

When sitting for meditation, you may like to imagine yourself as a mountain: stable, grounded, balanced, dignified, and beautiful. Your outer posture is more likely to be translated in your inner world, bringing clarity and wakefulness.

Sit on a chair or on the floor, in any posture as long as your posture doesn't cause discomfort over time.

Sitting on a chair

Traditionally in the East for hundreds of years, most people sat on the floor, cross-legged. And that's why people like the Buddha are shown seated cross-legged on the floor when they are meditating. But if you, like most people in western society, are used to sitting on chairs every day, then sit on a chair for your meditation too! There's no need to force yourself to sit on the floor when you find it painful.

I don't believe in 'no pain, no gain,' especially in mindfulness. Instead, I say 'no pleasure, no leisure.' By this I mean if you make mindfulness enjoyable for yourself, you're much more likely to stick with it. Difficulties will arise in mindfulness practise, so anything you can do to make the experience a little easier is a good idea. That's being kind to yourself – what I like to call *kindfulness*.

Choose your favourite chair, and feel free to lean against the back on the chair if you wish. I urge you be comfortable and at ease, which is more likely to encourage a positive experience and therefore increase your chances of meditating regularly as part of your routine, if that's what you wish.

Don't worry if you find yourself feeling sleepy or falling asleep in your meditation. Falling asleep in meditation is usually a sign that you need the extra sleep! Call it beditation! And getting enough sleep is extremely good for your health and happiness. If you meditate regularly, you'll probably catch up on your sleep over time, and then you'll be falling awake instead of falling asleep! So gift yourself a nice, comfortable posture for your mindfulness meditation and see what happens.

There's only one important posture in mindfulness. And that's a little smile on your face!

REMEMBER

Sitting on the floor

You can also do seated meditation sitting in the more traditional posture on the floor if you wish. Some people find sitting on the floor more grounding and stable. And some people sit cross-legged on the floor to make them look cool when with their hippy friends – feel free to do whatever floats your boat.

On the floor, you can do the *kneeling posture*, shown in Figure 6-1, in which you support your buttocks using a meditation stool or a cushion. If you use a meditation stool, ensure that you have a cushion for it too, or you may find it uncomfortable.

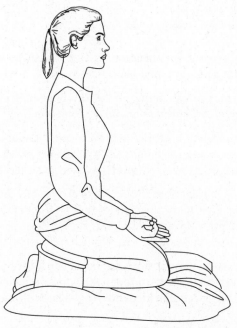

FIGURE 6-1:
Kneeling position with a meditation stool.

© John Wiley & Sons, Inc.

TIP

It's important to find a stool or cushion at the right height for yourself. Too high, and your back will feel strained and uncomfortable. Too low, and you're more likely to slump and feel sleepy.

Here are the instructions for the kneeling posture:

1. Begin by shaking your legs and rotating your ankles to prepare yourself for the posture.

2. Kneel on a carpet or mat on the floor.

3. **Raise your buttocks up and place the kneeling stool between your lower legs and your buttocks.**

4. **Gently sit back down on the kneeling stool.** Place a cushion on top of the kneeling stool if you haven't already done so, to make the posture more comfortable for yourself.

5. **Shift your body around slightly to ensure you're in a posture that feels balanced and stable.** You don't need to be overly rigid in your posture.

The other position is the *Burmese posture*. This simply involves sitting on a cushion and placing both lower legs on the floor, one folded in front of the other (shown in Figure 6-2).

The Burmese posture instructions are as follows:

1. **Shake your legs, rotate your ankles and have a stretch, however feels right for you.** This helps to prepare your body to sit.

2. **Place a mat or soft blanket on the ground. On top of that, place a firm cushion, or several soft cushions on top of each other.**

3. **Sit down by placing your buttocks on the cushion. Allow your knees to touch the ground.** If your knees don't touch the ground, either use more cushions or try one of the other postures suggested in this section.

4. **Allow the heel of your left foot to be close to or to gently touch the inside thigh of your right leg. Allow the right leg to be in front of the left leg, with the heel pointing towards your lower left leg.** If your legs aren't that supple, adjust as necessary, always ensuring you're comfortable.

5. **Invite your back to be quite straight but relaxed too. Gently rock back and forth to find the point where your head is balanced on your neck and shoulders. Tuck your chin in slightly, so the back of your neck isn't straining.**

6. **Place your hand on your knees, facing down or facing up with thumb and first finger gently touching. Alternatively, place a small cushion in your lap and place your hands on the cushion in any way that feels right for you.** I find that the cushion helps to prevent my shoulders being dragged forwards and down.

7. **Meditate to your heart's content.**

TIP

You'll find it more comfortable to sit on a firm meditation cushion, often called a *zafu*. Ordinary cushions on their own are too soft. The zafu helps to raise your hips above your knees, making the sitting position more stable. Alternatively, use lots of small cushions or fold a large cushion to give yourself better support. Find a position you're happy with.

FIGURE 6-2:
The Burmese
position.

© John Wiley & Sons, Inc.

Practising sitting meditation

The mindful sitting practise I describe here comprises several stages. To begin with, I recommend that you just do the first stage – mindfulness of breath – daily. Then, after about a week, you can expand the meditation to include mindfulness of breath and body, and so on.

If you find mindfulness of breath challenging, you can begin with any of the other tracks. For example, some people enjoy starting with mindfulness of sounds or simply feeling the sensation of their feet on the follor rather than the breath, and that's fine.

This book includes MP3 audio tracks that you can download for each stage of this sitting meditation. You can listen to them separately, or back to back for the full guided sitting meditation.

TIP

If you find the sitting posture too uncomfortable, you can do this mindfulness exercise lying down, or in any other posture that feels right for you. Go with what you prefer rather than forcing yourself to do what I suggest. This mindfulness exercise is available as an audio track (Tracks 10 to 14):

Practising mindfulness of breath (Track 10)

PLAY THIS

1. **Find a comfortable upright sitting posture on the floor or in a chair.**

2. **Remember that the intention of this practise to be aware of whatever you're focusing on, in a non-judgemental, kind, accepting and curious way.** This is a time set aside entirely for you, a time to be aware and awake to your experience as best you can, from moment to moment, non-judgementally. Hold a soft, gentle smile on your face.

3. **Become aware of the feeling of your breath.** Allow your attention to rest wherever the sensations of your breath are most predominant. This may be in or around the nostrils, as the cool air enters in and the warmer air leaves the nose. Or perhaps you notice it most in your chest as the rib cage rises and falls. Or maybe you feel it most easily and comfortably in the area of your belly, the lower abdomen. You may feel your belly move gently outwards as you breathe in, and back in as you let go breathe out. As soon as you've found a place where you can feel the breath, simply rest your attention there for each in-breath and each out-breath. You don't need to change the pace or depth of your breathing, and you don't even need to think about it – you simply need to feel each breath.

4. **As you rest your attention on the breath, before long your mind will wander off. That's absolutely natural and nothing to worry about. As soon as you notice it's gone off, realise that you're already back! The fact that you've become aware that your mind has been wandering is a moment of wakefulness. Now, simply label your thought quietly in your own mind. You can label it 'thinking, thinking' or if you want to be more specific: 'worrying, worrying' or 'planning, planning.' This helps to frame the thought. Then gently, kindly, without criticism or judgement, guide your attention back to wherever you were feeling the breath.** Your mind may wander off a thousand times, or for long periods of time. Each time, softly, lightly and smoothly direct the attention back to the breath, if you can.

5. **Continue this for about ten minutes, or longer if you want to.**

At this point, you can stop or carry on to the next stage, which is mindfulness of both breath and body:

Practising mindfulness of breath and body (Track 11)

PLAY THIS

6. **Expand your awareness from a focused attention on the breath, to a more wide and spacious awareness of the body as a whole.** Become aware of the whole body sitting in a stable, balanced and grounded presence, like a mountain. The feeling of breathing is part of the body, so get a sense of the whole body breathing.

7. **When the mind wanders off into thoughts, ideas, dreams, or worries, gently label it and then guide the attention back to a sense of the body as a whole, breathing as in Step 4.**

8. **Remember that the whole body breathes all the time, through the skin. Get a sense of this whole-body breathing.**

9. **Continue this open, wide, curious, kind, and accepting awareness for about ten minutes – or longer if you feel like it. If certain parts of your body become uncomfortable, choose to breathe into that discomfort, and note the effect of that, or slowly and mindfully shift your bodily position to relieve the discomfort. Whatever you choose, doing it mindfully is the important bit.**

At this point, you can stop or carry on to mindfulness of sounds.

Practising mindfulness of sounds (Track 12)

PLAY THIS

10. **Let go of mindfulness of breath and body and become aware of sounds.** Begin by noticing the sounds of your body, the sounds in the room you're in, the sounds in the building, and finally the furthest sounds outside. Let the sounds permeate into you rather than straining to grasp them. Listen without effort: let it happen by itself. Listen without labelling the sound, as best you can. For example, if you hear the sound of a plane passing, or a door closing, or a bird singing, listen to the actual sound itself – its tone, pitch, and volume – rather than thinking, 'Oh, that's a plane.'

11. **As soon as you notice your thoughts taking over, label the thought and tenderly escort the attention back to listening.**

12. **Continue listening for ten minutes or so.**

At this point, you can stop or carry on to mindfulness of thoughts and feelings.

Practising mindfulness of thoughts and feelings (Track 13)

PLAY THIS

13. **When you're ready, turn your attention from the external experience of sound to your inner thoughts.** Thoughts can be in the form of sounds you can hear or in the form of images you can see. Watch or listen to thoughts in the same way you were mindful of sounds: without judgement or criticism, and with acceptance and openness.

14. **Watch thoughts arise and pass away like clouds in the sky.** Neither force thoughts to arise nor push them away. As best you can, create a distance, a space, between yourself and your thoughts. Notice what effect this has, if any. If the thoughts suddenly disappear, see whether you can be okay with that too.

15. **Imagine that you're sitting on the bank of a river, as another way of watching thoughts. As you sit there, leaves float on the surface and continuously drift by. Place each thought that you have onto each leaf that passes you.** Continue to sit and observe your thoughts passing by.

16. **As soon as you notice your attention get stuck in a train of thought, calmly take a step back from your thoughts and watch them once again from a distance, as best you can.** (Every so often, your attention may get stuck in a train of thought; your mind just works that way.) If you criticise yourself for your mind wandering, observe that as just a thought too.

17. **Now try turning towards emotions. Notice whatever emotions arise, and whether they're positive or negative. As far as you can, open up to the emotion and feel it.** Notice where that emotion manifests itself in your body. Is it new or familiar? Is it just one emotion or several layers? Do you feel like running away from the emotion, or staying with it? Breathe into the feeling as you continue to watch it. Observe your emotion in a curious, friendly way, like a young child looking at a new toy.

18. **Continue to practise for ten minutes or so.** These subtle activities take time to develop. Just do your best and accept however you feel they've gone, whether you were successful at focusing or not.

At this point, you can stop or carry on to *choiceless awareness*, which is simply an open awareness of whatever arises in your consciousness: sounds, thoughts, the sensations in your body, feelings, or the breath. Here's how:

Practising choiceless awareness (Track 14)

PLAY THIS

19. **Just be aware of whatever arises, in an expansive, receptive, and welcoming way.** Put the welcome mat out for your experience. Notice whatever predominates most in your awareness and let it go again.

20. **If you find your mind wandering (and it's particularly easy to get swept up and away into thoughts when practising this), come back to mindfulness of breath to ground yourself, before trying again.** Become curious about what's happening for you, rather than trying to change anything.

21. **Practise for about ten minutes, then begin to bring the sitting meditation to a close.** Gently congratulate yourself for having taken the time to nourish your health and wellbeing in this practise, for having taken time out of doing mode to explore the inner landscape of being mode, and allow this sense of awareness to permeate whatever activities you engage in today.

Overcoming sitting meditation obstacles

One of the most common problems with sitting meditation is posture. After sitting for some time, the back, knees, or other parts of the body start to ache. When this happens, you have two choices:

» **Observe both the discomfort as well as your mind's reaction to it, while continuing to sit still.** I recommend this if the discomfort doesn't hurt too much. Mindfulness is about welcoming experiences, even if they feel unpleasant at first. What does the discomfort feel like exactly? What's its precise location? What do you think about it? Because all experience is in a state of flux and change, you may find that even your feeling of physical discomfort changes.

REMEMBER

» By you discovering how to stay with these sensations, your meditation skills flow into your everyday life. You can manage other difficult emotions and challenging problems in the same welcoming, curious, and accepting way, rather than fighting them. Your body and mind are one, so by sitting still, your mind has a chance to stabilise and focus too.

» **Mindfully move the position of your body.** If your bodily discomfort is overwhelming, you can, of course, move your body. That's a lovely act of kindness to yourself. Try not to react quickly to the discomfort. Instead, shift your position slowly and mindfully. In this way, you enfold your shift of position into the practise. You're responding instead of reacting, which is what mindfulness is about. Responding involves a deliberate choice by you: you feel the sensation and make a conscious decision about what to do next. Reacting is automatic, lacks control, and bypasses an intentional decision by you. By you becoming more skilful in responding to your own experience in meditation, your ability spills out into everyday life: when someone frustrates you, you can respond while remaining in control of yourself rather than reacting in an out-of-control way.

Besides arising from the posture, frustration can arise from the practise itself. You're so used to judging all your experiences that you judge your meditation too. But mindfulness means non-judgemental awareness. *Bad meditation doesn't exist – there's no such thing.* Sometimes you can concentrate and focus your mind, and other times it's totally wild. Meditation is like that. Trust in the process, even if it feels as if you're not improving. Mindfulness works at a level both above and below the conscious mind, so on the surface it may seem as though you're not getting anywhere. Don't worry: each meditation is a step forwards, because you've actually practised.

Stepping Out with Walking Meditations

Walking meditation is meditation in which the process of walking is used as a focus. The ability to walk is a privilege, and walking is a miraculous process that you can feel grateful for.

Imagine being able to walk to work in a mindful, calm, and relaxed way, arriving at your destination refreshed and energised. You can walk in a stress-free way with walking meditation. My students often say that walking meditation is one of their favourite practises. The walking gives them time out from an over-occupied mind. Meditative walking is also a good way of preparing for the other, more physically static, meditations.

Examining your walking habits

You probably rarely just walk. You may walk and talk, walk and think, walk and plan, or walk and worry. Walking is so easy that you do other things at the same time. You probably walk on automatic pilot most of the time. However, you can get into negative habit patterns and end up spending all your time planning when you walk, and rarely just enjoying the walking itself.

When you walk, you're normally trying to get somewhere. That makes sense, I know. In walking meditation, you're not trying to get anywhere. You can let go of the destination and enjoy the journey, which is what all meditations are about.

Practising formal walking meditation

In this section I describe a formal walking meditation, which means you make special time and space to practise the exercise. You can equally introduce an awareness of your walking in an informal way, when going about your daily activities. You don't have to slow down the pace at which you walk for that.

To practise formal walking meditation, sometimes called mindful walking, try the following steps, available as an audio track (Track 15):

PLAY THIS

1. **Decide for how long you're going to practise.** I suggest ten minutes the first time, but whatever you feel comfortable with. Also choose where to practise. The first time you try it, practise walking *very* slowly, so a quiet room at home may be best.

2. **Stand upright with stability.** Gently lean to the left and right, forwards and backwards, to find a central, balanced standing posture. Let your knees unlock slightly, and soften any unnecessary tension in your face. Allow your arms to

hang naturally by your sides. Ensure that your body's grounded, like a tree – firmly rooted to the ground with dignity and poise.

3. **Become aware of your breath.** Come into contact with the flow of each inhalation and exhalation. Enjoy breathing. Maintain a beautiful little grin on your face for the duration of this practise, if you can.

4. **Now slowly lean onto your left foot and notice how your sensations change. Then slowly shift your weight onto your right foot. Again perceive how the sensations fluctuate from moment to moment.**

5. **When you're ready, gradually shift most of your weight onto your left foot, so almost no weight is on the right foot. Slowly take your right heel off the ground. Pause for a moment here. Notice the sense of anticipation about something as basic as taking a step. Now lift your right foot off the ground and place it heel first in front of you. Become aware of the weight of your body shifting from the left to the right foot. Continue gradually to place the rest of the right foot flat and firmly on the ground. Notice the weight continue to shift from left to right.**

6. **Continue to walk in this very slow, mindful way for as long as you want.** When you finish, take some time to reflect on your experience.

Trying alternative walking meditations

Here are a couple of other ways of practising walking meditation that you can use while moving at your own pace.

Walking body scan

In this walking meditation, you gradually move your awareness up your body as you walk, from your feet all the way to the top of your head.

1. **Begin by walking as you normally do.**

2. **Now focus on the sensations in your feet.** Notice how the weight shifts from one foot to the other.

3. **Continue to move your mindful attention up your body.** Feel your lower legs as you walk, then your upper legs, noticing their movement.

4. **Now observe the movement and sensations in the area of the hips and pelvis.**

5. **Continue to scan your awareness to the lower and then upper torso, then your arms, as they naturally swing to help you keep balance.**

6. **Observe the sensation in your shoulders, your neck, your face, and then the whole of your head.**

7. **Now get a sense of the body as a whole as you continue to stroll, together with the physical sensation of the breath.** Continue this for as long as you wish.

Walking with happiness

This practise is recommended by world-famous mindfulness teacher Thich Nhat Hanh. This mindfulness exercise is about generating positive feelings as you walk. Try the following as an experiment. Have fun with it:

1. **Find a place to walk by yourself or with a friend.** Try to find a beautiful place to walk if possible.

2. **Remember that the purpose of walking meditation is to be in the present moment, letting go of your anxieties and worries.** Just enjoy the present moment.

3. **Walk as if you're the happiest person on earth.** Smile – you're alive! Acknowledge that you're very fortunate if you're able to walk.

4. **As you walk in this way, imagine you're printing peace and joy with every step you take.** Walk as if you're kissing the earth with each step you take. Know that you're taking care of the earth by walking in this way.

5. **Notice how many steps you take when you breathe in, and how many you take when you breathe out.** If you take three steps with each in-breath, in your mind say 'in – in – in' as you breathe in. And if you take four steps as you breathe out, say 'out – out – out – out.' Doing so helps you to become aware of your breathing. You don't need to control your breathing or walking; let it be slow and natural.

6. **Every now and then, when you see a beautiful tree, flower, lake, children playing, or anything else you like, stop and look at it.** Continue to follow your breathing as you do this.

7. **Imagine a flower blooming under each step you take.** Allow each step to refresh your body and mind. Realise that life can only be lived in the present moment. Enjoy your walking.

Overcoming walking meditation obstacles

Walking meditation doesn't create as many issues as the other meditations. However, here are a couple that often crop up, with ideas to solve them:

» **You can't balance when walking very slowly.** Walking straight at a very slow pace is surprisingly tricky. If you think that you may fall over, use a wall to support yourself. Additionally, gaze at a spot in front of you and keep your eyes fixed there as you walk forwards. As you practise, your balance improves.

» **Your mind keeps wandering off.** Walking meditation is like all other mindfulness practises. The mind becomes distracted. Gently guide your attention back to the feeling of the feet on the floor, or of the breath. No self-criticism or blaming is required.

Generating Compassion: Metta Meditations

Metta is a Buddhist term meaning loving kindness or friendliness. Metta meditation is designed to generate a sense of compassion both for yourself and towards others. All mindfulness meditations make use of an affectionate awareness, but metta meditations are specifically designed to deepen this skill and direct it in specific ways.

Many religious traditions and ancient cultures emphasise the need to love and care for yourself and those around you. When you're feeling particularly harsh and self-critical, metta meditation can act as an antidote and generate feelings of friendliness and affection. The reason metta meditation works is due to an important aspect of human beings: you can't feel both hatred and friendliness at the same time; by nourishing one, you displace the other. Metta meditation is a gentle way of healing your inner mind and heart from all its pain and suffering.

MEETING THE OLYMPIC MEDITATORS

Metta meditation is a skill you can develop in the same way as you can become skilful at tennis or driving: brain scans of experienced meditators have proved it. Renowned brain scientist Professor Richard Davidson and his team of neuroscientists at the University of Wisconsin–Madison in the USA have shown that short-term meditators can become more compassionate through metta-type meditations. Long-term meditators – so-called 'Olympic meditators' – who've spent over 10,000 hours meditating (not all at the same time!), have among the highest levels of wellbeing and compassion ever recorded in brain scans! In brain scan experiments, these expert meditators stepped out of uncomfortable and noisy scientific experiments after hours of testing with a smile on their faces – a reaction not seen before by scientists. The scientists proved that a sense of compassion is the most positive of positive emotions and is extremely powerful and healing for both body and mind.

TIP

If you're new to meditation, try some of the other meditations in this book first. When you've had some experience of those meditations, you're ready to try the metta meditation. Take your time with it: work through the practise slowly and regularly, and you're sure to reap the benefits.

Practising loving kindness meditation

Here's a guided metta meditation. Work through it slowly, taking it step by step. If you don't have the time or the patience to do all the stages, do as many as you feel comfortable with. Be gentle with yourself, right from the beginning. This meditation is available as an audio track (Track 16):

PLAY THIS

1. **You can practise loving kindness in a seated or lying down position. You can even practise it while walking.** What's most important isn't the position you adopt, but the intention of kindness and friendliness you bring to the process. Make yourself warm and at ease. Gently close your eyes or keep them half open, looking comfortably downwards.

2. **Begin by feeling your breath.** Notice the breath sensation wherever it feels most predominant for you. This awareness helps create a connection between your body and mind. Continue to feel your breath for a few minutes.

3. **When you're ready, see whether certain phrases arise from your heart for what you most deeply desire for yourself in a long-lasting way, and ultimately for all beings.** Phrases like:

   May I be well. May I be happy. May I be healthy. May I be free from suffering.

4. **Softly repeat the phrases again and again.** Allow them to sink into your heart. Allow the words to generate a feeling of kindness towards yourself. If that doesn't happen, don't worry about it: your intention is more important than the feeling. Just continue to repeat the phrases lightly. Let the phrases resonate.

5. **Now bring to mind someone you care about: a good friend or person who inspires you.** Picture the person in your mind's eye and inwardly say the same phrases to her. Don't worry if you can't create the image clearly. The intention works by itself. Use phrases like:

   May you be well. May you be happy. May you be healthy. May you be free from suffering.

   Send loving kindness to the person using these words.

6. **When you're ready, choose a neutral person: someone you see daily but don't have any particular positive or negative feelings towards.** Perhaps someone you walk past every morning or buy coffee from. Again send a sense of loving kindness using your phrases:

May you be well. May you be happy. May you be healthy. May you be free from suffering.

7. **Now choose a person you don't get on with too well.** Perhaps someone you've been having difficulties with recently. Say the same phrases again, from the mind and heart. This may be more challenging.

8. **Now bring all four people to mind: yourself, your friend, your neutral person, and your difficult person.** Visualise them or feel their presence. Try to send an equal amount of loving kindness to them all by saying:

   May we be well. May we be happy. May we be healthy. May we be free from suffering.

9. **Finally, expand your sense of loving kindness outwards, towards all living beings.** Plants, animals of the land, air, and sea. The whole universe. Send this sense of friendliness, care, loving kindness, and compassion in all directions from your heart:

   May all be well. May all be happy. May all be healthy. May all be free from suffering.

TIP

As a beginner, feel free to just do one of the stages to begin with. And if you find it difficult to start with sending loving kindness to yourself, start with imagining sending loving kindness to a friend. Then over time, you can include yourself.

If the metta phrases I suggest don't work for you, then here are other suggestions. Choose two or three and use them as your metta phrases. Or you can be creative and come up with your own, too:

>> *May I be at peace with myself and all other beings.*

>> *May I accept myself just as I am.*

>> *May I find forgiveness for the inevitable hurt peopole bring to one another.*

>> *May I live in peace and harmony with all beings.*

>> *May I love myself completely just as I am now no matter what happens.*

>> *May I be free from the suffering of fear and anger.*

>> *May I love myself unconditionally.*

Metta meditation can be a profoundly healing practise. Be patient with yourself and practise it slowly and lovingly. Let the phrases come from your heart and see what happens.

TIP

Once you become experienced at this meditation, you can even practise it while walking. However, remember to keep your eyes open, or you may mindfully bump into something!

Overcoming metta meditation obstacles

You may experience a few specific problems with metta meditation. Some common issues, with suggestions for overcoming them, include:

» **You can't think of a specific person.** If you can't think of a suitable friend, or neutral person, or someone you're having difficulties with, don't worry. You can miss that step for now, or just choose anyone. The intention of loving kindness is more important than the specific person you choose.

» **You say the phrases but don't feel anything.** This is perfectly normal, especially when you start. Imagine the phrases coming out of your chest or heart, rather than your head, if you can. Again, the feeling isn't as important as your attitude of friendliness in the practise. The feelings may come in the future, or may not – you don't need to worry about that.

» **Your mind keeps wandering off.** This is simply the nature of mind, and happens in all meditations. As always, as soon as you notice, kindly and gently bring your attention back to the practise. Each time you bring it back, you're strengthening your mind to pay attention.

» **You have great trouble with the difficult person.** You can skip this stage to begin with. Once you get more experienced in loving kindness meditation, you can then have another go in a few months. If you have a strong aversion to bringing a sense of kindness to the difficult person, try remembering that she's a human being, just like you. She too has her challenges in life, which may be why she behaves in the way she does. And she, too, ultimately wants to be happy and peaceful, although it may not seem that way on the outside. If these thoughts don't help either, try focusing on someone less difficult to begin with. Be patient with yourself: this isn't an easy process.

» **You feel very emotional.** Feeling emotional is a very common reaction. You may not be used to generating feelings in this way, and it can unlock deep-seated emotions. If you can, try to continue with the practise. If your emotions become overwhelming, try just the first phase, sending metta towards yourself, for the whole meditation. Doing just one phase for a whole meditation is perfectly fine. Alternatively, stop the practise and come back to it later, when it feels more appropriate.

Chapter **7**

Using Mindfulness for Yourself and Others

You probably appreciate the need to look after others. But are you aware of the need to look after yourself as well? You need to eat a balanced diet and exercise regularly for your health and wellbeing. You need to have the right amount of work and rest in your life. And you need to challenge yourself intellectually, to keep your mind healthy. You need to socialise and also save some time just for yourself. Achieving all this perfectly is impossible, but how can you strive to take care of yourself in a light-hearted way, without becoming overly uptight and stressed?

Mindfulness can help you look after both yourself and others. Being aware of your thoughts, emotions and body, as well as the things and people around you, is the starting point. This awareness enables you to become sensitive to your own needs and those of others around you, therefore encouraging you to meet everyone's needs as far as possible.

A caring, accepting awareness is the key to healthy living. Mindfulness is a wonderful way to develop greater awareness. This chapter details suggestions for looking after yourself and others through mindfulness.

Using a Mini Mindful Exercise

You don't need to practise mindfulness meditation for hours and hours to reap its benefits. Short and frequent meditations are an effective way of developing mindfulness in your everyday life.

Introducing the breathing space

When you've had a busy day, you probably enjoy stopping for a nice hot cup of tea or coffee, or another favourite beverage. The drink offers more than just liquid for the body. The break gives you a chance to relax and unwind a bit. The three-minute mini meditation, called the *breathing space* (illustrated in Figure 7-1 and 7-2), is a bit like a tea break, but beyond relaxation, the breathing space enables you to check what's going on in your body, mind, and heart – not getting rid of feelings or thoughts, but looking at them from a clearer perspective.

REMEMBER

Mindfulness is an awareness and acceptance exercise – not a relaxation exercise. Relaxation may come as a welcome side benefit. Let your intention be to become aware of your thoughts and emotions and allow them space to just be as they are, with curiosity and kindness, as best you can.

WISE WORDS

TREE, ROPE OR WALL? DESCRIBING AN ELEPHANT

Six blind people were asked to determine what an elephant looks like. Each of them was guided to the elephant and felt a different part. One felt a leg and said that the elephant was like a pillar. One felt the trunk and said that the elephant was like the branches of a tree. One felt the tail and said that the elephant was like a rope. Another felt the ear and said that the elephant felt like a fan. The one who felt the belly thought the elephant felt like a wall. And the one who felt the tusk said that the elephant was like a solid pipe. Then they all started arguing, insisting that they were right about the nature of the elephant. A wise person happened to be passing (they always do in these stories) and said that they were all right to a certain extent. If they felt other parts of the elephant they would get a different perspective.

The moral of the story? Mindfulness enables you to see both your outer and inner experience fully, shifting your perspective and helping you to resolve inner and outer conflicts. You begin to understand how other people can be restricted by their views because that's all they know – they're just feeling one part of the elephant. This insight can result in greater compassion and understanding.

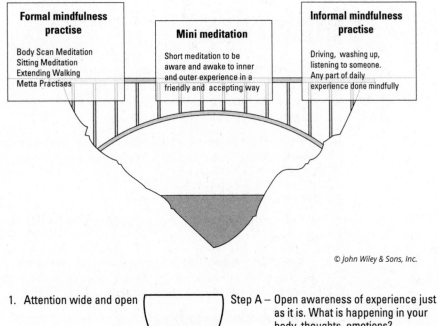

FIGURE 7-1:
How the breathing space acts as a bridge between formal and informal mindfulness practise.

Formal mindfulness practise

Body Scan Meditation
Sitting Meditation
Extending Walking
Metta Practises

Mini meditation

Short meditation to be aware and awake to inner and outer experience in a friendly and accepting way

Informal mindfulness practise

Driving, washing up, listening to someone. Any part of daily experience done mindfully

© John Wiley & Sons, Inc.

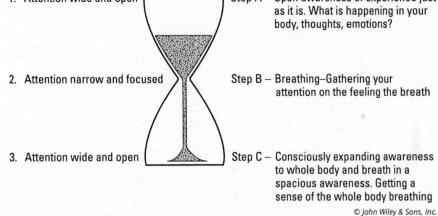

1. Attention wide and open

Step A – Open awareness of experience just as it is. What is happening in your body, thoughts, emotions?

2. Attention narrow and focused

Step B – Breathing–Gathering your attention on the feeling the breath

FIGURE 7-2:
The three-minute breathing space meditation progresses like an hourglass.

3. Attention wide and open

Step C – Consciously expanding awareness to whole body and breath in a spacious awareness. Getting a sense of the whole body breathing

© John Wiley & Sons, Inc.

Practising the breathing space

You can practise the breathing space at almost any time and anywhere. The meditation is made up of three distinct stages, which I call A, B, and C to help you to remember what to practise at each stage. The exercise doesn't have to last exactly three minutes: you can make it longer or shorter depending on where you are and how much time you have. If you only have time to feel three breaths, that's okay;

doing so can still have a profound effect. Follow these steps, which are available as an audio track (Track 17):

PLAY THIS

1. **Sit comfortably with a sense of dignity, but don't strain your back and neck.** You can sit upright or stand; even lying down on your back or curling up is acceptable. Sitting upright is helpful, because it sends a positive message to the brain – you're doing something different.

2. **Practise step A below for about a minute or so, then move on to B for a minute, ending with C also for a minute – or however long you can manage:**

Step A: Awareness:

Reflect on the following questions, pausing for a few seconds between each one:

   i. **What bodily sensations am I aware of at the moment?** Feel your posture, become aware of any aches or pains, or any pleasant sensations. Just accept them as they are, as far as you can.

   ii. **What emotions am I aware of at the moment?** Notice the feelings in your heart or belly area or wherever you can feel emotion.

   iii. **What thoughts am I aware of, passing through my mind at the moment?** Become aware of your thoughts, and the space between yourself and your thoughts. If you can, simply observe your thoughts rather than becoming caught up in them.

Step B: Breathing:

Focus your attention in your belly area – the lower abdomen. As best you can, feel the whole of your in-breath and the whole of each out-breath. You don't need to change the rate of your breathing – just become mindful of it in a warm, curious and friendly way. Notice how each breath is slightly different. If your mind wanders away, gently and kindly guide your attention back to your breath. Appreciate how precious each breath is.

Step C: Consciously expanding:

Consciously expand your awareness from your belly to your whole body. Get a sense of your entire body breathing (which it is, through the skin). As our awareness heightens within your body, notice its effect. Accept yourself as perfect and complete just as you are, just in this moment, as much as you can.

TIP

Experiment with having a very gentle smile on your face as you do the breathing space, no matter how you feel. Notice whether doing so has a positive effect on your state of mind. If it does, use this approach every time. You don't even need to say 'cheese'!

TIP

Imagine the breathing space as an hourglass. The attention is wide and open to start with and then narrows and focuses on the breath in the second stage, before expanding again with more awareness and spaciousness.

The breathing space meditation encapsulates the core of mindfulness in a succinct and portable way. The full effects of the breathing space are as follows:

>> **You move into a restful 'being' mode of mind.** Your mind can be in one of two very different states of mind: *doing* mode or *being* mode. Doing mode is energetic and all about carrying out actions and changing things. Being mode is a soothing state of mind where you acknowledge things as they are. (For lots more on being and doing mode, refer to Chapter 5.)

>> **Your self-awareness increases.** You become more aware of how your body feels, the thoughts going through your mind, and the emotion or need of the moment. You may notice that your shoulders are hunched or your jaw is clenched. You may have thoughts whizzing through your head that you hadn't even realised were there. Or perhaps you're feeling sad, or are thirsty or tired. If you listen to these messages, you can take appropriate action. Without self-awareness, you can't tackle them.

>> **Your self-compassion increases.** You allow yourself the space to be kinder to yourself, rather than self-critical or overly demanding. If you've had a tough day, the breathing space offers you time to let go of your concerns, forgive your mistakes and come back into the present moment. And with greater self-compassion, you're better able to be compassionate and understanding of others too.

>> **You create more opportunities to make choices.** You make choices all the time. At the moment, you've chosen to read this book and this page. Later on you may choose to go for a walk, call a friend, or cook dinner. If your partner snaps at you, your reaction is a choice to a certain extent too. By practising the breathing space, you stand back from your experiences and see the bigger picture of the situation you're in. When a difficulty arises, you can make a decision from your whole wealth of knowledge and experience, rather than just having a fleeting reaction. The breathing space can help you make wiser decisions.

>> **You switch off automatic pilot.** Have you ever eaten a whole meal and realised that you didn't actually taste it? You were most likely on automatic pilot. You're so used to eating, you can do it while thinking about other things. The breathing space helps to connect you with your senses so that you're alive to the moment.

Try this thought experiment. Without looking, remember whether your wrist watch has roman numerals or normal numbers on it. If you're not sure, or get it wrong, it's a small indication of how you're operating on automatic pilot.

You've looked at your watch hundreds of times, but not really looked carefully. (I explain more about automatic pilot in Chapter 5.)

>> **You become an observer of your experience rather than feeling trapped by it.** In your normal everyday experience, no distance exists between you and your thoughts or emotions. They just arise and you act on them almost without noticing. One of the key outcomes of the breathing space is the creation of a space between you and your inner world. Your thoughts and emotions can be in complete turmoil, but you simply observe and are free from them, like watching a film at the cinema. This seemingly small shift in viewpoint has huge implications, which I explore in Chapter 5.

>> **You see things from a different perspective.** Have you ever taken a comment too personally? I certainly have. Someone is critical about a piece of work I've done, and I immediately react or at least feel a surge of emotion in the pit of my stomach. But you have other ways of reacting. Was the other person stressed out? Are you making a big deal about nothing? The pause offered by the breathing space can help you see things in another way.

>> **You walk the bridge between formal and informal practise.** Formal practise is where you carve out a chunk of time in the day to practise meditation. Informal practise is being mindful of your normal everyday activities. The breathing space is a very useful way of bridging the gap between these two important aspects of mindfulness. The breathing space is both a formal practise because you're making some time to carry it out, and informal because you integrate it into your day-to-day activities.

>> **You create a space for new ideas to arise.** By stopping your normal everyday activities to practise the breathing space, you create room in your mind for other things to pop in. If your mind is cluttered, you can't think clearly. The breathing space may be just what the doctor ordered to allow an intelligent insight or creative idea to pop into your mind.

Using the breathing space between activities

Aim to practise the breathing space three times a day. Here are some suggested times for practising the breathing space:

>> **Before or after meal times.** Some people pray with their family before eating a meal to be together with gratitude and give thanks for the food. Doing a breathing space before or after a meal gives you a set time to practise and reminds you to appreciate your meal too. If you can't manage three minutes, just feel three breaths before diving in.

>> **Between activities.** Resting between your daily activities, even for just a few moments, is very nourishing. Feeling your breath and renewing yourself is very pleasant. Research has found that just three mindful breaths can change your body's physiology, lowering blood pressure and reducing muscle tension.

>> **On waking up or before going to bed.** A short meditation before you jump out of bed can be a wholesome experience. You can stay lying in bed and enjoy your breathing. Or you can sit up and do the breathing space. Meditating in this way helps to put you in a good frame of mind and sets you up for meeting life afresh. Practising the breathing space before going to bed can calm your mind and encourage a deeper and more restful sleep.

>> **When a difficult thought or emotion arises.** The breathing space meditation is particularly helpful when you're experiencing challenging thoughts or emotions. By becoming aware of the nature of your thoughts, and listening to them with a sense of kindness and curiosity, you change your relationship to them. A mindful relationship to thoughts and emotions results in a totally different experience.

Using Mindfulness to Look After Yourself

Have you ever heard the safety announcements on a plane? In the event of an emergency, cabin crew advise you to put your own oxygen mask on first, before you help put one on anyone else, even your own child. The reason is obvious. If you can't breathe yourself, how can you possibly help anyone else? Looking after yourself isn't just necessary in emergencies. In normal everyday life, you need to look after your own needs. If you don't, not only do you suffer, but so do all the people who interact or depend on you. Taking care of yourself isn't selfish: it's the best way to be of optimal service to others. Eating, sleeping, exercising, and meditating regularly are all ways of looking after yourself and hence others.

Exercising mindfully

You can practise mindfulness and do physical exercise at the same time. In fact, Jon Kabat-Zinn, one of the key founders of mindfulness in the West, trained the USA men's Olympic rowing team in 1984. A couple of the men won gold – not bad for a bunch of meditators! And in the more recent Olympics, several athletes claimed that mindfulness helped them to reach peak performance and achieve their gold medals.

TIP

Regular exercise is beneficial for both body and mind, as confirmed by thousands of research studies. If you already exercise on a regular basis, you know the advantages. If not, and your doctor is happy with you exercising, you can begin by simply walking. Walking is an aerobic exercise and a great way to practise mindfulness. (See Chapter 6 for a walking meditation.) Then, if you want to, you can build up to whatever type of more strenuous exercise you fancy. Approach each new exercise with a mindful attitude: be curious of what will happen, stay with uncomfortable sensations for a while, explore the edge between comfort and discomfort, and look around you.

TIP

Whatever exercise you choose, allow yourself to enjoy the experience. Find simple physical activities that make you smile rather than frown, and you're much more likely to stick with the discipline.

And if you find the word 'exercise' a turn off, called it 'physical activity' or simply 'moving your body' every day. Use words that are appealing to you.

To start you off, here are a few typical physical exercises and ideas for how to suffuse them with mindfulness.

Mindful running

Leave your music and phone at home. Try running outside rather than at the gym – your senses have more to connect with outside. Begin by taking ten mindful breaths as you walk along. Become aware of your body as a whole. Build up from normal walking to walking fast to running. Notice how quickly your breathing rate changes, and focus on your breathing whenever your mind wanders away from the present moment. Feel your heart beating and the rhythm of your feet bouncing on the ground. Notice whether you're tensing up any parts of your body unnecessarily. Enjoy the wind against your face and the warmth of your body. Observe what sort of thoughts pop up when you're running, without being judgemental of them. If running begins to be painful, explore whether you need to keep going or slow down. If you're a regular runner, you may want to stay on the edge a little bit longer; if you're new to it, slow down and build up more gradually. At the end of your run, notice how you feel. Try doing a mini meditation (described in the first section of this chapter) and notice its effect. Keep observing the effects of your run over the next few hours.

Mindful swimming

I usually only get a chance to go swimming when on holiday. But when I do, I really enjoy practising mindful swimming. The experience can be very meditative.

Begin with some mindful breathing as you approach the pool. Notice the effect of the water on your body as you enter. What sort of thoughts arise? As you begin to swim, feel the contact between your arms and legs and the water. What does the water feel like? Be grateful that you can swim and have access to the water. Allow yourself to get into the rhythm of swimming. Become aware of your heartbeat, breath rate, and the muscles in your body. At times, you may even feel at one with the water – enjoy that experience. When you've finished, observe how your body and mind feel.

Mindful cycling

Begin with some mindful breathing as you sit on your bike. Feel the weight of your body, the contact between your hands and the handlebars, and your foot on the pedal. As you begin cycling, listen to the sound of the wind. Notice how your leg muscles work together rapidly as you move. Switch between focusing on a specific part of your body like the hands or face to a wide and spacious awareness of your body as a whole. Let go of wherever you're heading and come back to the here and now. As you get off your bike, perceive the sensations in your body. Scan through your body and detect how you feel after that exercise.

Preparing for sleep with mindfulness

Sleep, essential to your wellbeing, is one of the first things to improve when people do a course in mindfulness. People sleep better, and their sleep is deeper. Studies found similar results from people who suffered from insomnia who did an eight-week course in MBSR (mindfulness-based stress reduction).

Sleep is about completely letting go of the world. Falling asleep isn't something you *do* – it's about *non-doing*. In that sense sleep is similar to mindfulness. If you're *trying* to sleep, you're putting in a certain effort, which is the opposite of letting go.

Here are some tips for preparing to sleep using mindfulness:

>> **Stick to a regular time to go to bed and to wake up.** Waking up very early one day and very late the next confuses your body clock and may cause difficulties in sleeping.

>> **Avoid over-stimulating yourself by watching television or being on the computer before bed.** The light from the screen tricks your brain into believing it's still daytime, and then it takes longer for you to fall asleep.

>> **Try doing some formal mindfulness practise like a sitting meditation or the body scan (refer to Chapter 6) before going to bed.**

>> **Try doing some yoga or gentle stretching before going to bed.** I've noticed cats naturally stretch before curling up on the sofa for a snooze. This may help

you to relax and your muscles unwind. Try purring while you're stretching, too – maybe that's the secret to their relaxed way of life!

>> **Do some mindful walking indoors before bed.** Take five or ten minutes to walk a few steps and feel all the sensations in your body as you do so. The slower, the better.

>> **When you lie in bed, feel your in-breath and out-breath.** Rather than trying to sleep, just be with your breathing. Count your out-breaths from one to ten. Each time you breathe out, say the number to yourself. Every time your mind wanders off, begin again at one.

>> **If you're lying in bed worrying, perhaps even about getting to sleep, accept your worries.** Challenging or fighting thoughts just makes them more powerful. Note them, and gently come back to the feeling of the breath.

REMEMBER

If you seem to be sleeping less than usual, try not to worry about it too much. In fact, worrying about how little sleep you're getting becomes a vicious circle. Many people sleep far less than eight hours a day, and most people have bad nights once in a while. Not being able to sleep doesn't mean something is wrong with you. A regular mindfulness practise will probably help you in the long run.

Looking at a mindful work–life balance

Work–life balance means balancing work and career ambitions on the one side, and home, family, leisure and spiritual pursuits on the other. Working too much can have a negative impact on other important areas. By keeping things in balance, you're able to get your work done quicker and your relationship quality tends to improve.

With the advent of mobile technology, or a demanding career, work may be taking over your free time. And sometimes you may struggle to see how you can re-dress this imbalance. The mindful reflection below may help.

TIP

Try this little reflection to help reflect on and improve your work–life balance:

1. Sit in a comfortable upright posture, with a sense of dignity and stability.

2. Become aware of your body as a whole, with all its various changing sensations.

3. Guide your attention to the ebb and flow of your breath. Allow your mind to settle on the feeling of the breath.

4. Observe the balance of the breath. Notice how your in-breath naturally stops when it needs to, as does the out-breath. You don't need to do anything – it just happens. Enjoy the flow of the breath.

5. When you're ready, reflect on this question for a few minutes:

    What can I do to find a wiser and healthier balance in my life?

6. Go back to the sensations of the breathing. See what ideas arise. No need to force any ideas. Just reflect on the question gently, and see what happens. You may get a new thought, image or perhaps a feeling.

7. When you're ready, bring the meditation to a close and jot down any ideas that may have arisen.

Refer to *Work/Life Balance For Dummies* by Katherine Lockett and Jeni Mumford (Wiley) or *Mindfulness at Work For Dummies* by Shamash Alidina and Juliet Adams (Wiley) for more on this topic.

Using Mindfulness in Relationships

Humans are social animals. People's brains are wired that way. Research into positive psychology, the new science of wellbeing, shows that healthy relationships affect wellbeing more than anything else does. Having high quality relationships is the biggest predictor of a happy, healthly life. Some researchers even found that being in high-quality relationships increases your life expectancy more than stopping smoking reduces your life span. That doesn't mean you should keep smoking and hang out with your pals, but it shows just how important having warm relationships is for human beings.

Psychologists have found that wellbeing isn't so much about the quantity of relationships but the quality. The good news is you can directly develop and enhance the quality of your relationships through mindfulness.

Starting with your relationship with yourself

Trees need to withstand powerful storms, and the only way they can do that is by having deep roots for stability. With shallow roots, the tree can't really stand upright. The deeper and stronger the roots, the bigger and more plentiful are the branches that the tree can produce. In the same way, you need to nourish your relationship with yourself to effectively branch out to relate to others in a meaningful and fulfilling way.

Here are some tips to help you begin building a better relationship with yourself by using a mindful attitude:

>> **Set the intention.** Begin with a clear intention to begin to love and care for yourself. You're not being selfish by looking after yourself; you're watering your own roots, so you can help others when the time is right. You're opening the door to a brighter future that you truly deserve as a human being.

>> **Understand that no one's perfect.** You may have high expectations of yourself. Try to let them go, just a tiny bit. Try to accept at least one aspect of yourself that you don't like, if you can. The smallest of steps make a huge difference. Just as a snowball starts small and gradually grows as you roll it through the snow, so a little bit of kindness and acceptance of the way things are can start off a positive chain reaction to improve things for you.

>> **Step back from self-criticism.** As you practise mindfulness, you become more aware of your thoughts. You may be surprised to hear a harsh, self-critical inner voice berating you. Take a step back from that voice if you can, and know that *you're not your thoughts*. When you begin to see this, the thoughts lose their sting and power. (The sitting meditation in Chapter 6 explores this.)

>> **Be kind to yourself.** Take note of your positive qualities, no matter how small and insignificant they seem, and acknowledge them. Maybe you're polite, or a particular part of your body is attractive. Or perhaps you're generous or a good listener. Whatever your positive qualities are, notice them rather than looking for the negative aspects of yourself or what you can't do. Being kind to yourself isn't easy, but through mindfulness and by taking a step-by-step approach, it's definitely possible.

>> **Forgive yourself.** Remember that you're not perfect. You make mistakes, and so do I. Making mistakes makes us human. By understanding that you can't be perfect in what you do, and can't get everything right, you're more able to forgive yourself and move on. Ultimately, you can learn only through making mistakes: if you did everything correctly, you'd have little to discover about yourself. Give yourself permission to forgive yourself.

>> **Be grateful.** Develop an attitude of gratitude. Try being grateful for all that you do have, and all that you can do. Can you see, hear, smell, taste, and touch? Can you think, feel, walk, and run? Do you have access to food, shelter, and clothing? Use mindfulness to become more aware of what you have. Every evening before going to bed, write down three things that you're grateful for, even if they're really small and insignificant. Writing gratitude statements each evening has been proven to be beneficial for many people. Try this for a month, and continue if you find the exercise helps you in any way.

>> **Practise metta/loving kindness meditation.** This is probably the most effective and powerful way of developing a deeper, kinder, and more fulfilling relationship with yourself. Refer to Chapter 6 for the stages of the metta practise.

Practising any one of the above activities regularly, even for just a minute or two per day, will help to raise your own wellbeing and help increase the quality of your relationships with others too. The secret is in regular practise rather than the length of the practise.

Dealing with arguments in romantic relationships: A mindful way to greater peace

Arguments are often the cause of many difficult interactions with others, especially in romantic relationships. Romantic relationships can be both deeply satisfying and deeply painful. And they're most difficult when disagreements arise. Sometimes (or often) those disagreements turn into arguments. Here's a typical scenario:

A: Why do you keep leaving your clothes lying on the floor in the bedroom? It looks so messy!

B: Why are you so picky! Relax, will you. It's not a big deal. You're always nagging about everything.

A: Me, nagging! Who's been doing all the cooking today? And all I ask is for you to pick up a few clothes, and that's too much effort. You're so childish.

B: Childish! Listen to yourself shouting about some clothes . . .

And so on. Your higher brain function becomes unavailable when you get into an argumentative state of mind. The frustration and emotional reactivity build with each sentence that each person says.

So, how on earth can mindfulness help when these small things start to escalate into a full-blown argument and a negative atmosphere? Mindfulness creates a mental and emotional inner space – some space between the moment when you feel your irritation rising and your decision to speak. In that space, you have time to make a choice about what to say.

If your partner accuses you of leaving clothes on the floor, you notice yourself getting defensive. But in that extra space you have, you can also think about your partner: he's had a long day, is tired and has a bit of a short fuse. From that understanding, you're able to say a few kind words or offer a little hug or massage. The situation begins to defuse itself.

That all-important few seconds between your emotional experience and your choice of words is created through mindfulness practise. As you become adept in mindfulness, you become less automatically reactive. You're conscious of what's happening within you and can make these better decisions.

Here's how to deal with potential arguments:

1. **Notice the emotion rising up in your body when your partner says something that hurts you.**

2. **Become aware of where you feel the emotion in your body and take a few breaths. Be as kind and friendly to yourself as you can.** Say to yourself, 'This emotion is difficult for me to feel right now . . . Let me gently breathe with it.' Make space for your emotions internally, and remember, you don't have to act from the feeling; you just need to notice the feeling.

3. **Choose the words you respond with wisely from your more mindful state of mind.** Perhaps begin with agreeing with part of your partner's statement. Soften your tone of voice. Let your partner know how you feel, if you can. And avoid making accusations – doing so will just feed the argument.

4. **As you begin to calm down, try to be more and more mindful.** Keep feeling your breathing. Or be conscious of your bodily sensations or other emotions. Gently smile if you can. This approach will make you less reactive and more likely to shift the conversation into more positive territory.

These steps are not easy for most people. You may like to share this practise with your partner so you can both have a go when tempers rise. And try applying this four step process in small arguments to begin with, and see how that goes. Small steps lead to big changes.

Engaging in deep listening

You can practise deep listening in order to relieve the suffering in us, and in the other person. That kind of listening is described as compassionate listening. You listen only for the purpose of relieving suffering in the other person.

Thich Nhat Hanh

Deep or mindful listening occurs when you listen with more than your ears. Deep listening involves listening with your mind and heart – your whole being. You're giving completely when you engage in deep listening. You let go of all your thoughts, ideas, opinions, and beliefs and just listen.

REMEMBER

Deep listening is healing. By healing, I mean that the person being listened to can feel a great sense of release and let go of frustrations, anxieties, or sadness. Through deep listening, true communication occurs: people want to be listened to more than anything else.

Deep listening comes from an inner calm. If your mind is wild, it's very difficult for you to listen properly. If your mind is in turmoil, go away to listen to your breathing or even to your own thoughts. By doing so, you give your thoughts space to arise out of the unconscious, and you thereby release them.

Here's how to listen to someone deeply and mindfully:

>> Stop doing anything else. Set your intention to listen deeply.

>> Look the person in the eye when he speaks and gently smile, if appropriate.

>> Put aside all your own concerns and worries.

>> Listen to what the person is saying and how he's saying it.

>> Listen with your whole being – your mind and heart, not just your head.

>> Cultivate empathy by putting yourself in their shoes - what would it be like for you to be feeling what they are feeling?

>> Observe posture and tone of voice as part of the listening process.

>> Notice the automatic thoughts popping into your head as you listen. Do your best to let them go and come back to listening.

>> Ask questions if necessary, but keep them genuine and open rather than trying to change the subject. Let your questions gently deepen the conversation.

>> Let go of judgement as far as you can. Judging is thinking rather than deep listening.

>> Let go of trying to solve the problem or giving the person the answer.

When you give the other person the space and time to speak without judging, he begins to listen to himself. What he's saying becomes very clear to him. Then, quite often, the solution arises naturally. He knows himself far better than you do. By jumping straight into solutions, you only reduce the opportunity that person has to communicate with you. So, when listening, simply listen.

REMEMBER

Accord to Zen Master Thich Nhat Hanh, the purpose of deep listening is to reduce suffering in others. This is achieved by using deep listening to let go of wrong perceptions. Your partner is seeing things from one perspective and you are seeing things from another perspective. Through deep listening, you can become aware of both your own wrong perceptions and the wrong perceptions of your partner. Even if you hear what you think is a wrong perception from your partner, keep listening deeply and compassionately and don't interrupt them. Once they've finished, kindly share what they shared, to be clear what they were saying. By understanding where they are coming from, you are in a better place to find a resolution.

MY JOURNEY INTO MINDFULNESS

Before I discovered the art of mindfulness, I thought the purpose of my life was to find happiness through getting a top degree, earning lots of money and finding the perfect relationship. I worked very hard to get the top marks at school, and when I went to university, I continued the search for happiness. I was excessively driven without a sense of deep purpose. I searched for ways of reducing the stress and eventually found mindfulness. I was very reluctant and sceptical at first: I spent a year deciding whether to learn it though a course. The meditation being offered seemed too mystical and spiritual for my scientific mind at the time.

In the end, after discovering some of the research into the benefits of mindfulness, I gave it a go and haven't looked back since! I discovered that happiness doesn't come as some future reward but is accessible in the simple pleasures of living in the moment. As I practise, it changes my relationship with myself. I don't feel the driving need to be successful in the way society prescribes. I have more time for myself. I'm a bit kinder towards myself. I'm on a journey and certainly haven't 'got there' (I don't think that I or anyone can be perfect in that sense).

More recently, I've discovered not to take mindfulness too seriously. Mindfulness isn't a religion or philosophy, but a creative way of living that each person uses in his own way. By having a light-hearted approach, I'm more relaxed about my own thoughts, words, and actions, and I allow life to unfold in a more natural way. If I remember to be mindful, that's great, but if I forget or have a lapse, that's human and not a problem at all. Above all, mindfulness allows the presence and inner space to cultivate a life that's rich, full and meaningful – that's the path I'm slowly treading. And if you're inspired by this mindful approach, we're walking along the same path together.

Being aware of expectations

Think about the last time someone annoyed you. What were your expectations of that person? What did you want him to say or do? If you have excessively high expectations in your relationships, you're going to find yourself frustrated.

Expectations are ideals created in your mind. The expectations are like rules. I expect you to behave; or to be quiet; or to make dinner every evening; or to be funny, not angry or assertive. The list is endless.

I've learnt to have low rather than high expectations with friends and family. I don't expect any huge presents on birthdays or any favours to be returned. I don't expect people to always turn up to meetings on time or to return phone calls. This way, I've discovered I'm less disappointed. And then I'm pleasantly surprised when a friend does call me, does a favour for me or is kind to me! If I had very high expectations, I'd be setting myself up for disappointment. With reduced expectations, you set the stage for greater gratitude and positivity in your relationships when others do reach out.

REMEMBER

If a person doesn't meet your expectations, you may react with anger, sadness, frustration, or jealousy. These emotions are natural to a certain extent, but if you experience them too frequently or too intensely, too much negative emotion harms your health and wellbeing. And just because you have high expectations or react emotionally when your expectations aren't met doesn't mean the other person is going to change, especially if you treat that person with emotional outbursts. However, if you're grateful and positive when others are kind and respectful to you, they are more likely to repeat that positive behaviour.

TIP

The next time you're about to feel annoyed, angry, or sad about an expectation of yours not being met, try the following mindfulness exercise. The practise helps you to move from an emotional or verbal reaction, to a mindful and balanced response. This is how:

1. **Don't speak yet.** A negative reaction just fuels the fire.

2. **Notice the sensations in your body.** Do you feel the pain of the unfulfilled expectation in your stomach, shoulders, or somewhere else? Does it have a shape or colour?

3. **Become aware of your breathing without changing it.** Is it deep or shallow? Is it slow or rapid? If you can't feel it, just count the out-breaths from one to ten. Or just to three if that's all you have time for.

4. **Imagine or feel the breath going into that part of the body.** Feel it with a sense of kindness and curiosity. Breathe into it and see what happens.

ARGUING WITH MONKS

Researchers wanted to see the effect of an argument and confrontation on an experienced meditator. They chose a monk who had extensive meditative practise behind him. The researchers found the most confrontational university professor to argue with the monk. They measured the men's blood pressure and heart rates during the conversation. The professor's heart beat started off very high, but the monk's stayed calm. As the conversation went on, the professor became calmer and calmer (but still didn't want to stop talking!). In this way, if you remain peaceful and calm, having established a mindfulness routine, you can spread a sense of wellbeing quite naturally as you talk to others. Your relationships flourish in this way.

5. **Take a step back.** Become aware of the space between you, the observer, and your thoughts and feelings, which are the observed. See how you're separate and therefore free of them. You're going you're your observer self, taking a step back, having a bird's-eye view of the whole situation from a bigger perspective.

6. **If necessary, go back to that person and speak from this wiser and more composed state of mind.** Don't speak unless you're settled and calm. Most of the time, speaking in anger may get what you want in the short term, but in the long term you leave people feeling upset. Play this by ear.

Looking into the mirror of relationships

Relationship is a mirror in which you can see yourself.

J Krishnamurti

All relationships, whether with a partner or work colleague, are a mirror that help you to see your own desires, judgements, expectations, and attachments. Relationships give an insight into your own inner world. What a great learning opportunity! You can think of relationships as an extension of your mindfulness practise. You can observe what's happening, both in yourself and the other person, with a sense of friendly openness, with kindness and curiosity. Try to let go of what you want out of the relationship, just as you do in meditation. Let the relationship simply be as it is, and allow it to unfold moment by moment.

Here are some questions to ask yourself as you observe the mirror of relationships:

>> **Behaviour.** How do you behave in different relationships? What sort of language do you use? What's your tone of voice like? Do you always use the same words or sentences? What happens if you speak less, or more? Notice your body language.

>> **Emotions.** How do you feel in different relationships? Do certain people or topics create fear or anger or sadness? Get in touch with your emotions when you're with other people, and see what the effect is. Try not to judge the emotions as good or bad, right or wrong: just see what they do.

>> **Thoughts.** What sort of thoughts arise in different relationships? What happens if you observe the thoughts as just thoughts and not facts? How are your thoughts affected by how you feel? How do your thoughts affect the relationship?

Being mindful in a relationship is more difficult than it sounds. You can easily find yourself caught up in the moment and your attention is trapped. Through regular mindfulness practise, your awareness gradually increases and becomes easier. Although mindfulness in relationships is challenging, it's very rewarding too.

Working with your emotions

'You make me angry.' 'You're annoying me.' 'You're stressing me out.'

If you find yourself thinking or saying sentences like these, you're not really taking responsibility for your own emotions. You're blaming someone else for the way you feel. This may seem perfectly natural. However, in truth, no one can affect the way you feel. *The way you feel is determined by what you think about the situation.* For example, say I accidentally spill a cup of tea on your work. If you think that I did it on purpose, you may think, 'You damaged my paperwork deliberately, you idiot,' and then feel angry and upset. You blame me for your anger. If you see it as an accident and think that I may be tired, you think, 'It was just an accident – I hope he's okay,' and react with sympathy. The emotion is caused by your thought, not by the person or the situation itself.

Rather than blame the other person for your anger, actually feel the emotion. Notice when it manifests in your body if you can. Observe the effect of breathing into it. Watch it with a sense of care. This transforms your relationship to the anger from hate to curiosity, and thereby transforms the anger from a problem to a learning opportunity.

An easy way to remember and manage your emotions is to use the acronyn ABC:

>> **A:** Activating event

>> **B:** Belief

>> **C:** Consequence

For example:

>> **Activating event:** A colleague doesn't turn up to a meeting.

>> **Belief:** You believe they must always be there on time.

>> **Consequence:** You feel annoyed.

Now go back and change your belief. Think differently, such as: 'People aren't always on time – that's a fact of life. Some people are just always late. Other times, they get held up in traffic or on a slow train.' Now you'll notice that you'll feel less annoyed.

So, be mindful of your beliefs whenever you feel a strong emotional reaction to someone else, and see whether changing the belief, or simply smiling at the belief, helps.

Seeing everyone as your teacher

Relationships are built on the history between you and the other person, whoever that may be. Whenever you meet another human being, your brain automatically pulls out the memory file on the person, and you relate to him with your previous knowledge of him. This is all very well when you're meeting an old and dearly loved friend, for example, but what about when you need to deal with someone you've had difficulties with in the past? Perhaps you may have had an argument or just don't seem to connect.

REMEMBER

When dealing with difficult people, it's worth remembering you have two ways of meeting another human being. The first way is to see your ideas, memories, thoughts, opinions, and beliefs about that person. That can be pretty boring and limiting, as you're not open to learning anything new. The other way is to actually see that person as he is, without the judgements and ideas and stories. This is meeting anew, meeting afresh, as if for the first time. Mindfulness is about meeting *all* experience afresh. When you connect with your senses, you're no longer in the realm of ideas, opinions, and beliefs. You're in the field of the present moment.

Meeting another human being in that way you can't help but feel a warmth towards him as well as a sense of wonder.

Here are some ways of dealing with difficult relationships:

» **Take five mindful breaths or carry out a mini meditation (check out Chapter 8) before meeting the other person.** This may help prevent the feeling of anger or frustration becoming overpowering. Simple, yet awesome!

» **Observe the difference between your own negative image about the person and the person himself.** As best you can, let go of the image and meet the person as he is by connecting with your senses when you meet him.

» **Understand the following, which Buddha is quoted as saying: 'Remembering a wrong is like carrying a burden on the mind.'** Try to forgive whatever has happened in your relationship. See whether that helps. Buddha usually knows what he's talking about!

» **See the relationship as a game.** Mindfulness is not to be taken too seriously, and nor are relationships. Often relationships become stagnant because you're both taking things too seriously. Allow yourself to lighten up. See the funny side. Crack a joke. Or smile, at least.

» **Consider what's the worst that may happen.** That question usually helps to put things back in perspective. You may be overestimating how bad the other person is, or the worst that he can realistically do to you.

» **Become curious about the kind of thoughts that arise in your head when you meet the difficult person.** Are the thoughts part of a familiar pattern? Can you see them as merely thoughts rather than facts? Where did you get these ideas from? This is an example of mindfulness of thoughts: becoming curious about your thinking patterns and noticing what's happening. You're not trying to fix or change; that happens by itself if you observe the current thought patterns clearly.

REMEMBER

Relationships are both rewarding and difficult. Don't be too hard on yourself if things don't work out. You have your own character, and sometimes you just don't connect with another person. Let go of the negatives from the past, as best you can, and follow your instincts. Allow things to unfold in their own natural way as best you can. And if it doesn't work out, it doesn't work out. You have another 7 billion people to try your mindful relationship skills on!

LAKE MEDITATION: DISCOVERING ACCEPTANCE

PLAY THIS

You can try this meditation, which is available as an audio track (Track 18):

This meditation is normally done lying down, but you can do it in any posture that's comfortable for you. Close your eyes softly. Feel your breathing for a few minutes. Now, when you're ready, imagine a beautiful lake. The lake is perfectly still and calm. The surface of the lake is so still it looks like a polished mirror. Majestic mountains are in the background, and the sky is predominantly blue, with a few small, white, fluffy clouds. The sky and mountains are reflected in the lake. Around the sides of this wonderful lake are old, mighty trees, with branches leaning out over the lake. A few birds fly across the lake in the distance. When the wind blows, small ripples and larger waves whip up on the surface, reflecting a dance of glints across the water. You're aware that, as the seasons change, the lake embraces the rain and fallen leaves, and in the winter may freeze on the surface. Deep under the surface, little changes or moves, and the water continues to teem with life. The lake openly accepts whatever is offered to it.

Now, when you're ready, allow yourself to merge and become one with the lake. As you lie or sit, you allow yourself to be the lake itself, if that makes sense to you. You're both the deep, still lake underneath and the ripples on the surface. Just allow yourself to absorb the slightest sense of what this may mean for you. In your compassion, kindness, and gentleness, you're supporting this body of water. As the weather changes, the water becomes muddied and gathers twigs and leaves. Can you softly allow all this to happen and continue to just be the lake? Appreciate how the changing conditions of the lake give it character, charm, and richness. Allow yourself to feel your own tranquillity and serenity underneath the turbulent surface. Is that possible to some extent? Are you able to allow the continual change that persistently unfolds around and in the lake to be part of the natural process of nature, and even embrace the beauty of it in yourself?

If you find it helpful, use this image of the lake to enrich your meditation practise from time to time. Even bringing it to mind as you go about your daily activities helps you to perceive life from a place of acceptance and peacefulness. Evoke the memory of how the lake can be both still, deep, and unmoving underneath, and disturbed at the surface. Recognise the continually fluxing thoughts and feelings of the mind and heart, and identify with the awareness that's both always there and just behind them. See your story, your world, your ideas, thoughts, dreams, opinions, and beliefs as part of that vast awareness, but not all of it. Enjoy the vision of the lake as it effortlessly reflects the sun and sky, birds and bees, plants and animals during the day, and the exquisite pale moon and twinkling stars at night, in the dark, cool sky – ever present, always changing, and yet always the same.

Chapter **8**

Using Mindfulness in Your Daily Life

Mindfulness is portable: you can be mindful anywhere and everywhere, not only on the meditation cushion or yoga mat. You can engage in a mindful state of mind while giving a presentation, feeding the cat, or hugging a friend. By cultivating a mindful awareness, you deepen your day-to-day experiences and break free from habitual mental and emotional patterns. You notice that beautiful flower on the side of the road, you become aware and release your tense shoulders when thinking about work, and you give space for your creative solutions to life's challenges. All the small changes you make add up. Your stress levels go down, your depression or anxiety becomes a bit more manageable, and you begin to be more focused. You need to put in some effort to achieve this, but a totally different effort to the kind you're probably used to; you're then bound to change in a positive way. This chapter offers some of the infinite ways of engaging this ancient art and modern science of mindfulness in your daily life.

Using Mindfulness at Work

Work. A four-letter word with lots of negative connotations. Many people dislike work because of the high levels of stress they need to tolerate. A high level of stress isn't a pleasant or healthy experience, so welcome any way of managing that stress with open arms.

WARNING

In many countries, managing the level of stress that employees face, and taking active steps to reduce stress, is a legal obligation. If you think that you're suffering from work-related stress, you need to consider talking to your manager or other appropriate person about the situation. Poor management standards are linked to unacceptably high levels of stress, and changes need to be made to ensure that stress is kept at reasonable levels, according to the Health and Safety Executive in the UK.

So how can mindfulness help with work?

>> Most importantly, mindfulness gives you the space to relate to your stress in a more healthy way.

>> Mindfulness has been found to lower levels of stress, anxiety, and depression.

>> Mindfulness leads to a greater ability to focus, even when under pressure, which then results in higher productivity and efficiency and more creativity.

>> Mindfulness improves the quality of relationships, including those at work.

REMEMBER

Mindfulness isn't simply a tool or technique to lower stress levels. Mindfulness is a way of being. Stress reduction is the tip of the iceberg. One business organisation I trained aptly said: 'Mindfulness goes to the heart of what good business is about – deepening relationships, communicating responsibly, and making mindful decisions based on the present facts, not the limits of the past.' When employees understand that giving mindful attention to their work actually improves the power of their brain to focus, their work becomes more meaningful and inspiring.

Beginning the day mindfully

Watching the 100-metre race in the Olympics, you see the athletes jump up and down for a few minutes before the start, but when they prepare themselves in the blocks, they become totally still. They focus their whole being completely, listening for the gunfire to signify the start. They begin in stillness. Be inspired by the athletes: begin your day with an inner stillness, so you can perform at your very best.

TIP

Start the day with a mindfulness exercise. You can do a full formal meditation such as a body scan or a sitting meditation (both these meditations are in Chapter 6), or perhaps some yoga or stretching in a slow and mindful way. Alternatively, simply sit up and feel the gentle ebb and flow of your own breath, or listen to the sounds of the birds as they wake up and chirp in the morning. Other alternatives include waking up early and eating your breakfast mindfully (see the mindful eating exercise in Chapter 6), or perhaps tuning in to your sense of smell, sight, and touch fully as you have your morning bath or shower; see what effect that has. That's better than just worrying about your day.

Dropping in with mini meditations

When you arrive at work, you can easily be swept away by it all and forget to be mindful of what you're doing. The telephone rings, you get email after email, and you're called into endless meetings. Whatever your work involves, your attention is sure to be sucked up.

This habitual loss of attention and going from activity to activity without really thinking about what you're doing is called *automatic pilot mode*. You simply need to change to mindful awareness mode. The most effective way of doing this is by one- to three-minute mini meditations, by feeling the sensation of your own breath as it enters and leaves your body. (Head to Chapter 5 for more about changing from automatic pilot.)

REMEMBER

The breathing space meditation (a type of mini meditation) consists of three stages. In the first stage you become aware of your thoughts, emotions, and bodily sensations. In the second stage you become aware of your own breathing. And in the third and final stage you expand your awareness to the breath and the body as a whole. For lots more on how to do the breathing space meditation, check out Chapter 7.

TIP

When you're at work, give a mini meditation a go:

>> **When?** You can do a mini meditation at set times or between activities. So when you've finished a certain task or job, you take time to practise a mini meditation before heading to the next task. In this way you increase the likelihood of being calm and centred, rather than flustered, by the time you get to the end of the day or working week. If you don't like the rigidity of planning your mini meditations ahead of time, just practise them whenever the thought crosses your mind and you feel you need to go into mindfulness mode.

Additionally, you can use the meditation to cope with a difficult situation, such as your boss irritating you. One way of coping with the wash of emotion that arises in such situations is to do a three-minute coping (breathing space) meditation (described in full in Chapter 7).

» **How?** Use any posture you like, but sit up if you wish to energise yourself through the practise. The simplest form of mini meditation is to feel your breathing. If you find your mind wanders a lot when feeling your breath, you can say to yourself 'in' as you breathe in, and 'out' as you breathe out. Alternatively, count each out-breath to yourself, going from one to ten. As always, when your mind drifts off, simply guide the attention gently and kindly back, even congratulating yourself for noticing that your mind had wandered off the breath. Remember to accept and embrace mind wandering as part of the mindfulness process.

» **Where?** You can do a mini meditation anywhere you feel comfortable. Usually, meditating is easier with your eyes closed, but that's not so easy at work! You can keep your eyes open and softly gaze at something while you focus your attention inwards. One of my clients goes to a special room at work for prayer and uses the space to meditate at lunchtime. If you work outside, try going for a slow walk for a few minutes, feeling your breathing and noticing the sensations of your feet as they gently make contact with the earth. Or if the weather is nice, perhaps you can lie down in the sunshine while lying on some grass as you practise some mindfulness.

TIP

You may dearly want to try out the mini meditation at work, but you simply keep forgetting. Well, why not make an appointment with yourself? Perhaps set a reminder to pop up on your computer, or a screen saver with a subtle reminder for yourself. One of my corporate clients popped a card on her desk with a picture of a beautiful flower. Each time she saw the picture, she took three conscious breaths. This helped to calm her and had a transformative effect on the day. Or, try a sticky note or a gentle alarm on your mobile phone – be creative in thinking of ways to remind yourself to be mindful.

Going from reacting to responding

A *reaction* is your almost automatic thought, reply, and behaviour following some sort of stimulus, such as your boss criticising you. A *response* to a situation is a more considered, balanced choice, often creative in reply to the criticism, and leads to solving your problems rather than compounding them.

You don't have to react when someone interrupts you in a meeting, takes away your project, or sends a rude email. Instead, having a balanced, considered response is most helpful for both you and your relationship with colleagues.

For example, say you hand in a piece of work to your manager, and she doesn't even say thank you. Later on you ask what she thinks of your work, and she says it's okay, but you can tell she doesn't seem impressed. You spent lots of time and effort to do a superb report, and you feel hurt and annoyed. You *react* by either automatically thinking negative thoughts about your manager and avoiding eye contact with her for the rest of the week, or you lash out with an outburst of accusations and feel extremely tense and frustrated for hours afterwards. Here's how you can turn this into a mindful response.

TIP

Begin to feel the sensations of your breath. Notice whether you're breathing in a shallow or rapid way because of your frustration, but try not to judge yourself. Say to yourself, 'in . . . out' as you breathe in and out. Expand your awareness to a sense of your body as a whole. Become mindful of the processes taking place inside you. Feel the burning anger rising from the pit of your stomach up through your chest and throat, or your racing heart and dry mouth when you're nervous. Honour the feeling instead of criticising or blocking the emotion. Notice what happens if you don't react as you normally do or feel like doing. Imagine your breath soothing the feeling. Bring kindness and curiosity to your emotions. This isn't an easy time for you – acknowledging that is an act of self-compassion.

You may discover that the very act of being aware of your reaction changes the flavour of the sensation altogether. Your relationship to the reaction changes an outburst, for example, to a more considered response. Your tone of voice may subtly change from aggressive and demanding to being slightly calmer and more inquisitive. The point is not to try and change anything, but just to sit back and watch what's going on for a few moments.

TIP

To help you to bring a sense of curiosity when you're about to react to a situation at work, try asking yourself the following questions slowly, one at a time, and giving yourself time for reflection:

>> What feeling am I experiencing at the moment, here at work? How familiar is this feeling? Where do I feel the feeling in my body?

>> What thoughts are passing through my mind at the moment? How judgemental are my thoughts? How understanding are my thoughts? How are my thoughts affecting my actions at work?

>> How does my body feel at the moment? How tired do I feel at work? What effect has the recent level of work had on my body? How much discomfort can I feel at the moment in my body, and where is the source of it?

>> Can I acknowledge my experiences here at work, just as they are? Am I able to respect my own rights as well as responsibilities in the actions I choose? What would be a wise way of responding right now, instead of my usual reaction? If I do react, can I acknowledge that I'm not perfect and make my next decision a more mindful response?

Perhaps you'll go back to your manager and calmly explain why you feel frustrated. You may become angry too, if you feel this is necessary, but without feeling out of control. Perhaps you'll choose not to say anything today, but wait for things to settle before discussing the next step. The idea is for you to be more creative in your *response* to this frustration rather than *reacting* in your usual way, if your usual way is unhelpful and leads to further problems.

The benefits of a considered, balanced response as opposed to an automatic reaction include:

>> Lower blood pressure. (High blood pressure is a cause of heart disease.)

>> Lower levels of stress hormones in your blood stream, leading to a healthier immune system.

>> Improved relationships, because you're less likely to break down communication between colleagues if you're in a calmer state of mind.

>> A greater feeling of being in control, because you're able to choose how you respond to others rather than automatically reacting involuntarily.

REMEMBER

You don't sweep your frustration or anger under the carpet. Mindfulness isn't about blocking emotions. You do the opposite: you allow yourself to mindfully feel and sooth the emotions with as much friendliness and kindness as you can muster. Even forcing a smile can help. Mindfulness is the only way I know of effectively overcoming destructive emotions. Expressing out-of-control anger leads to more anger: you just get better at it. Supressing anger leads to outbursts at some other time. Mindfulness is the path to easing your frustration through being genuninely curious and respectful of your own emotional experiences.

Solving problems creatively

Your ideas need room. You need space for new perceptions and novel ways of meeting challenges, in the same way that plants need space to grow, or they begin to wither. For your ideas, the space can be in the form of a walk outside, a three-minute mini meditation, or a cup of tea. Working harder is often not the best solution: working smarter is.

If your job involves dealing with issues and problems, whether that involves people or not, you can train yourself to see the problems differently. By seeing the problems as challenges, you're already changing how you meet this issue. A *challenge* is something you rise to – something energising and fulfilling. A *problem* is something that has to be dealt with – something draining, an irritation. Studies have found people who learn to see problems as positive challenges have a more enjoyable experience of navigating a solution.

TIP

To meet your challenges in a creative way, find some space and time for yourself. Write down *exactly* what the challenge is; when you're sure what your challenge is, you find it much easier to solve. Try to see the challenge from a different person's perspective. Talk to other people and ask how they'd deal with the issue. Become mindful of your immediate reactive way of dealing with this challenge, and question the validity of it.

Practising mindful working

Mindful working is simply being mindful of whatever you do when you work. Here are some examples of ways of being mindful at work:

>> **Start the day with a clear intention.** What do you need to get done today? What attitude do you wish to bring to your day? Perhaps kindness or focus, for example. How will you ensure you're best able to achieve what you intend to do? What barriers could prevent you achieving your intention and how can you best remove or manage them? For example, if your intention is to be focused and you're likely to get distracted in the office, can you work from home or in another part of the office?

>> **Be mindful of your everyday activities.** For example, when typing, notice the sense of touch between your fingers and the keyboard. Notice how quickly your mind converts a thought into an action on keys. Are you striking the keys too hard? Are your shoulders tense; is your face screwing up unnecessarily? How's your posture? Are you taking breaks regularly to walk and stretch?

>> **Before writing or checking an email, take a breath.** Is this really important to do right now? Reflect for a few moments on the key message you need to get across, and remember it's a human being receiving this message – not just a computer. After sending the message, take time to feel your breath and, if you can, enjoy it. Notice how easy it is to be swept away for hours by the screen.

>> **When the telephone rings, let the sound of the ring be a reminder for you to be mindful.** Let the telephone ring a few times before answering. Use this time to notice your breath and posture. When you pick it up, speak and listen with mindfulness. Notice both the tone of your own voice and the other person's. If you want to, experiment by gently smiling as you speak and listen, and become aware of the effect that has.

>> **When you get a text message or other ping sound from your smart-phone, just pause for a moment.** Do you need to check your phone right now or are you in the middle of something? If it's not an ideal time to check, is now a good time to switch off your phone so that you can focus and finish the

work you're doing? These small moments of choice can make a difference to your whole day.

>> **No matter what your work involves, do it with awareness.** Awareness helps your actions become clear and efficient. Connect your senses with whatever you're doing. Whenever you notice your mind drifting out of the present moment, just gently bring it back.

>> **Make use of the mini meditations to keep you aware and awake at work.** The meditations are like lampposts, lighting wherever you go and making things clear.

USING MINDFUL LEADERSHIP

If you're a leader in an organisation, responsibility goes with the job. Good leaders need to make effective decisions, manage emotions successfully, and keep their attention on the big picture. In their book *Resonant Leadership* (Harvard Business School Press), Richard Boyatzis and Annie McKee highlight the need for mindfulness in order for leadership to be most effective. They found that the ability to manage your own emotions and the emotions of others, called emotional intelligence, is vitally important for an effective leader, and to achieve this, you need to find a way to renew yourself.

Renewal is a way of optimising your state of mind so you're able to work most effectively. The stress generated through leadership puts your body and mind on high alert and weakens your capacity for focus and creativity. Renewal is a necessary antidote for leadership stress, and one key way science has found to achieve this is through mindfulness.

Neuroscience has shown that optimistic, hopeful people are naturally in an *approach* mode of mind. They *approach* difficulties as challenges and see things in a positive light. Other people have more *avoidant* modes of mind, characterised by *avoiding* difficult situations and denying problems rather than facing up to them. Mindfulness practised for just eight weeks has been shown to move people from unhelpful, *avoidant* modes to more helpful, creative, emotionally intelligent, *approach* modes of mind, leading to a greater sense of meaning and purpose, healthy relationships, and an ability to work and lead effectively.

For example, one of my clients, a CEO of a medium-sized corporation, felt isolated and highly stressed. Through practising tailor-made mindfulness techniques, he began to renew himself, see the business more holistically, take greater time to make critical decisions, and communicate more effectively with his team about the way forwards. He now practises mindfulness on a daily basis for 10 minutes, as well as using other strategies during the day, to create renewal.

Trying single-tasking: Discovering the multi-tasking myth

Everyone does it nowadays: texting as we walk, or checking emails as we speak on the phone. People multi-task to be efficient, but most of the time it actually makes you *less* efficient. And from a mindfulness perspective, your attention becomes hazy rather than centred.

Many studies by top universities show that multi-tasking leads to inefficiency and unnecessary stress. Some reasons to avoid multi-tasking and to mindfully focus on just one task at a time instead are that doing so will help you to:

>> **Live in the moment:** In one hilarious study, researchers asked people who walked across a park whether they noticed a clown on a unicycle. People who were glued to their phones didn't notice it! Others did.

>> **Be efficient:** By switching between two tasks, you take longer. It's quicker to finish one task and then the other. Switching attention takes up time and energy and reduces your capacity to focus. Some experts found a 40 per cent reduction in productivity due to multi-tasking.

>> **Improve relationships:** A study at the University of Essex found that just by having a phone nearby while having a person-to-person conversation had a negative impact. Give your partner your full attention as much as possible. Most people don't realise how much of a positive effect simply giving your partner your mindful awareness has.

>> **De-stress:** A study by the University of California found that when office workers were constantly checking email as they were working, their heart rates were elevated compared with those of people focusing on just one task.

>> **Get creative:** By multi-tasking, you over-challenge your memory resources. There's no space for creativity. A study in Chicago found that multi-taskers struggled to find creative solutions to problems they were given.

Finishing by letting go

You may find letting go of your work at the end of the day very difficult. Perhaps you come home and all you can think about is work. You may spend the evening talking angrily about colleagues and bosses, or actually doing more work to try to catch up with what you should've finished during the day. This impacts on the quality and quantity of your sleep, lowering your energy levels for the next day. This unfortunate negative cycle can spin out of control.

REDUCING TEACHER STRESS

Teaching in schools in considered one of the most stressful jobs in the world. When I was a full-time schoolteacher, almost all my time was taken up in planning lessons and marking books. I worked until the early hours of the morning and turned up the next day in a daze. The books were marked, but I was of no real use to the children; I easily lost patience with them, and made mountains out of molehills. I was 'sweating the small stuff.'

By meditating for 20 minutes or so when I reached home, I was able to let go of all the worries and anxieties of the workplace and allow my evening to be that little bit more enjoyable. I prioritised my time and ensured that I found more time to exercise and socialise. The mindfulness gently drew me out of the undue stress, as well as helping me to organise my work and life more effectively.

REMEMBER

You need to draw a line between work and home, especially if your stress levels feel unmanageable. Meditating as soon as you get home, or on your way home (see the following section), provides an empowering way of achieving this. You're saying 'enough.' You're taking a stand against the tidal wave of demands on your limited time and energy. You're doing something uplifting for your health and wellbeing, and ultimately for all those around you too. And you're letting go.

To let go at the end of the day most powerfully, choose a mindful practise that you feel works best for you. You may choose one of the formal mindfulness meditation practises in Chapter 6. Or take up a sport or hobby in which you're absorbed by gentle, focused attention – an activity that enables the energy of your body and mind to settle, and the mindfulness to indirectly calm you.

Using Mindfulness on the Move

I always find it amusing to see people from abroad on the Underground transport system in London, looking at the trains with awe and taking plenty of photos. Other commuters look up, almost in disgust, before burying their heads back in a book or newspaper or checking their phones. When people are on holiday they live in the moment, and the present moment is always exciting. The new environment is a change from their routine. Travelling is another opportunity to bring mindfulness to the moment.

Walking mindfully

Take a moment to consider this question: what do you find miraculous? Perhaps you find the vastness of space amazing; perhaps you find your favourite book or band a wonder. What about walking? Walking is a miracle too. Scientists have managed to design computers powerful enough to make the Internet work and for man to land on the moon, but no robot in the world can walk anywhere nearly as smoothly as a human being. If you're able to walk, you're lucky indeed. To contemplate the miracle called walking is the beginning of walking meditation.

Normally, in the formal walking meditation (as described in Chapter 6), you aren't trying to get anywhere. You simply walk back and forth slowly, being mindful of each step you take, with gratitude. However, when walking to work or wherever you're going, you have a goal. You're trying to get somewhere. This creates a challenge, because your mind becomes drawn into thinking about when you're going to arrive, what you're going to do when you get there, and whether you're on time. In other words, you're not in the moment. The focus on the goal puts you out of the present moment.

TIP

Practise letting the destination go. Be in the moment as you walk. Feel the breeze and enjoy your steps if you can. If you can't enjoy the walk, just feel the sensations in your feet – that's mindfulness. Focus more on the process and less on the outcome. Keep bringing your mind back into the moment, again and again, and, hey presto, you're being mindful as you walk.

Driving mindfully

If everyone did mindful driving, the world would be a safer and happier place. Don't worry: it doesn't involve closing your eyes or going into a trance! Try this mindful driving exercise, and feel free to be creative and adapt it as you like. Remember, don't read this book while you're driving: that would be dangerous.

1. **Set your intention by deciding to drive mindfully.** Commit to driving with care and attention. Set your attitude to be patient and kind to others on the road. Leave in plenty of time to get to where you're going, so you can let go of overly focusing on your destination.

2. **Sit in the driver's seat and practise a minute or so of mindful breathing.** Feel your natural breath as it is, and come into the present moment.

3. **Start your car.** Get a sense of the weight and size of the car – a machine with tremendous power, whatever its size, and with the potential to do much damage if you drive irresponsibly, or to be tremendously helpful if you drive with mindful awareness and intelligence. Begin making your way to your destination.

4. **Be alert.** Don't switch on the music or news. Instead, let your awareness be wide and perceptive. Be aware of what other vehicles and people are doing all around you. Let your awareness be gentle, rather than forcing and straining it.

5. **See how smoothly you can drive.** Brake gradually and accelerate without excessive revving. This type of driving is less stressful and more fuel efficient.

6. **Every now and then, briefly check in with your body.** Notice any tension and let it go if you can, or become aware and accept it if you can't. You don't need to struggle or fight with the tension.

7. **Show a healthy courtesy to your fellow drivers.** Driving is all about trusting and co-operating with others. Use any opportunities you can to be kind to your fellow drivers.

8. **Stay within the speed limit.** If you can, drive more slowly than you normally do. You'll soon grow to enjoy that pace, and may be safer.

9. **Take advantage of red traffic lights and traffic jams.** If the lights are about to change to red, stop rather than speed through. Smile when you meet traffic. Getting annoyed will not get you to your destination any faster. This is a great opportunity to do traffic meditation! This is a time to breathe. Look out of the window and notice the sky, the trees, and other people. Let this be a time of rest for you, rather than a time to become anxious and frustrated. Remember that stress isn't caused by the situation but by the attitude you bring to the circumstance. Bring a mindful attitude, just as an experiment, and see what happens. You may discover a different way of living altogether.

Travelling mindfully on public transport

If you travel on a bus, train, or plane, you're not in active control of the transport itself, and so can sit back and be mindful. Most people plug themselves into headphones or read, but mindfulness is another option. Why not exercise your mind while travelling? If commuting is part of your daily routine, you can listen to a guided mindfulness exercise or just practise by yourself. If you think you'll go deeply into meditation, ensure that you don't miss your stop by setting the alarm on your watch or phone.

The disadvantage of practising mindfulness in this way is the distractions. You may find yourself being distracted by sudden braking or the person who keeps snoring right next to you. I suggest that you practise your core mindfulness meditation in a relatively quiet and relaxed environment, such as your bedroom, and use an mindfulness exercise while travelling as a secondary meditation. Ultimately there are no distractions in mindfulness: whatever you experience can be the object of your mindful attention.

Here are some specific mindfulness experiments to try out while on the move:

1. **See whether you can be mindful of your breath from one station to the next, just for fun.** Whether you manage or not isn't the issue: this is just an experiment to see what happens. Do you become more mindful or less? What happens if you put more or less effort into trying to be mindful?

2. **Hear the various announcements and other distractions as sounds to be mindful of.** Let the distractions be part of your mindful experience. Listen to the pitch, tone, and volume of the sound, rather than thinking about the sound. Listen as you'd listen to a piece of music.

3. **See whether you can tolerate and even welcome unpleasant events.** For example, if two people are talking loudly to each other, or someone is listening to noisy music, notice your reaction. What particular thought is stirring up emotion in you? Where can you feel the emotion? What happens when you imagine your breath going into and out of that part of your body?

4. **Allow your mindful awareness to spill into your walk to wherever you're going.** As you walk, feel your feet making contact with the ground. Notice how the rate of your breathing changes as you walk. Allow your body to get into the rhythm of the walk, and enjoy the contact of the surrounding air with your skin as you move.

Using Mindfulness in the Home

Not only is doing mindfulness meditation and exercise at home convenient, but it also helps you to enjoy your everyday activities as well. Then, rather than seeing chores as a burden, you may begin to see them as opportunities to enjoy the present moment as it is.

Waking up mindfully

When you wake up, breathe three mindful breaths. Feel the whole of each in-breath and the whole of each out-breath. Try adding a smile to the equation if you like. Think of three things you're grateful for – a loved one, your home, your body, your next meal – anything. Then slowly get up. Enjoy a good stretch. Cats are masters of stretching – imagine you're a cat and feel your muscles elongate having been confined to the warmth of your bed all night. If you want to, do some mindful yoga or tai chi.

Then, if you can, do some formal mindful meditation. You can do five minutes of mindful breathing, a 20-minute sitting meditation, or a body scan meditation – choose what feels right for you.

Doing everyday tasks with awareness

The word 'chore' makes routine housework unpleasant before you've even started. Give your chores a different name to help spice them up, such as dirt-bursting, vacuum-dancing, mopping 'n' bopping, or home sparkling!

The great thing about everyday jobs, including eating, is that they're slow, repetitive physical tasks, which makes them ideal for mindfulness. You're more easily able to be mindful of the task as you do it. Here are a couple of examples to get you started.

Washing dishes

Recently, one of my clients who works from home found mindful dishwashing a transformative experience. She realised that she used to wash dishes to have a break from work, but when washing up she was still thinking about the work. By connecting with the process of dishwashing, she felt calmer and relaxed, renewed and ready to do a bit more creative work.

Have a go:

1. **Be aware of the situation.** Take a moment to look at the dishes. How dirty are they? Notice the stains. See how the dishes are placed. What colour are they? Now move into your body. How does your physical body feel at the moment? Become aware of any emotions you feel – are you annoyed or irritated? Consider what sort of thoughts are running through your mind; perhaps, 'When I finish this, then I can relax,' or 'This is stupid.'

2. **Begin cleaning, slowly to begin with.** Feel the warmth of the water. Notice the bubbles forming and the rainbow reflections in the light. Put slightly less effort into the scrubbing than you may normally, and let the washing-up liquid do the work of cleaning. When the dish looks completely clean, wash the bubbles off and see how clean the plate looks. Allow yourself to see how you've transformed a grimy, mucky plate into a spotless, sparkling one. Now let it go. Place the dish on the side to dry. Be childlike in your sense of wonder as you wash.

3. **Try to wash each dish as if for the first time.** Keep letting go of the idea of finishing the job or of the other things you could be doing.

4. **When you've finished, look at what you've done.** Look at the dishes and how they've been transformed through your mindful awareness and gentle activity. Congratulate yourself on having taken the time to wash the dishes in a mindful way, thereby training your mind at the same time.

All meditation is like mindfully washing dishes. In mindfulness you're gently cleaning your mind. Each time your attention wanders into other thoughts and ideas, you become aware of the fact and gently step back. Each step you take back from your unruly thoughts is a cleansing process.

Vacuuming

Using the vacuum cleaner, another common activity in many people's lives, is usually done while your mind is thinking about other things – which isn't actually experiencing the process of vacuuming. Try these steps to experience mindfulness while vacuuming:

1. **Begin by noticing the area you want to clean.** What does it look like and how dirty is the floor? Notice any objects that may obstruct your vacuuming. Become mindful of your own physical body, your emotions, and thoughts running through your mind.

2. **Tidy up the area so you can use the vacuum cleaner in one go, without stopping, if you can.** This ensures you have time to get into the rhythm of the activity without stopping and starting, helping you to focus.

3. **Switch the vacuum cleaner on.** Notice the quality of the sound and feel the vibrations in your arm. Begin moving the vacuum cleaner, getting into a calm rhythm if possible, and continue to focus your mindful attention on your senses. Stay in the moment if you can, and when your mind takes your attention away, acknowledge that and come back into the here and now.

4. **When you've finished, switch off and observe how you feel.** How was the process different to how you normally vacuum the floor? Look at what you've done and be proud of your achievement.

Eating mindfully

Regular, daily mindfulness practise is a key aspect of mindful eating. This acts as a foundation from which you can build a mindful-eating lifestyle. The discipline of mindfulness makes you aware of your emotions and thoughts. You begin to notice the kinds of situations, thoughts, and emotions that lead you to eating particular foods.

Here's how to eat a meal mindfully:

1. **Remove distractions.** Turn off the television, radio, and all other electronics. Put aside any newspapers, magazines, and books. All you need is you and your meal.

2. **Carry out three minutes of mindful breathing.** Sit with your back upright but not stiff, and feel the sensations of your breathing. Alternatively, try the three-minute breathing space detailed in Chapter 7.

3. **Become aware of your food.** Notice the range of colours on the plate. Inhale the smell. Remember how fortunate you are to have a meal today and be grateful for what you have.

4. **Observe your body.** Are you salivating? Do you feel hungry? Are you aware of any other emotions? What thoughts are going through your head right now? Can you see them as just thoughts rather than facts?

5. **Now slowly place a morsel of food into your mouth.** Be mindful of the taste, smell, and texture of the food as you chew. Put your cutlery down as you chew. Don't eat the next mouthful until you've fully chewed this one. At what point do you swallow? Have you chewed the food fully?

6. **When you're ready, take the next mouthful in the same way.** As you continue to eat mindfully, be aware of your stomach and the feeling of being full. As soon as you feel you've had enough to eat, stop. Because you've been eating slowly, you may find that you feel full up sooner than usual.

7. **If you feel full but still have the desire to eat more, try doing another three minutes of mindful breathing.** Remember that the thought 'I need to eat' is just a thought. You don't have to obey the thought and eat if that's not the best thing for you.

Try eating in this way once a day for a week or two, and become mindful of the effect it has.

Second hunger: Overcoming problem eating

When you eat, you need to:

» Eat the right amount of food, neither too much nor too little, to maintain a healthy weight.

» Eat the right types of food for you to meet your daily nutritional needs.

However, you may not eat just to meet those needs. In reality you may eat to:

>> Avoid feeling bored.

>> Cope with a sense of anger.

>> Fill a feeling of emptiness within you.

>> Satisfy a desire for some taste in particular (such as sweet or fatty food).

>> Help you cope with high levels of stress.

This 'comfort' eating, or emotional eating as it's sometimes called, tends to operate on an unconscious level, driving your cravings for food.

Emotional eating is like a second hunger, to satisfy the need for psychological wellbeing. Your emotions are eating rather than your stomach. You're using the food to calm your mind. This can lead to an unhealthy eating cycle. You experience a negative emotion, so you eat food to cope with the emotion, which leads to a temporary feeling of satisfaction but, before long, the negative emotion returns.

Mindful eating offers a way of becoming more aware of the inner thoughts and emotions driving your tendency to eat. Through a mindful awareness you begin naturally to untangle this web and begin to discover how to eat in a healthy and conscious way, making the right choices for you.

Additionally, you may like to try these strategies:

>> **Hunger reality check**. Before eating, notice whether your hunger is physical or emotional. If you've eaten recently and your tummy isn't rumbling, perhaps you can wait a little longer and see whether the sensation passes.

>> **Keep a food diary**. Simply writing down everything you eat for a few weeks is often an eye-opener. You may begin to see patterns emerging.

>> **Manage boredom**. Rather than using boredom as a reason to eat, try doing an activity such as mindful walking, or call a friend and be really aware of your conversation.

>> **Avoid extreme dieting**. By depriving yourself of certain foods, you may end up fuelling your desire for that food. Instead, treat yourself occasionally and eat the food mindfully. Actually tasting the treat makes it even tastier!

Living Mindfully in the Digital Age

I've got a smartphone, but it's not very smart. My phone sends me text messages just when I'm writing a chapter for a new book. It rings when I'm driving. Its addictive nature beckons me to check social media when I'm supposed to be drifting off to sleep.

The digital age has brought huge benefits: from saving lives in emergencies, to sharing information with the world, the advantages are countless. But without mindfulness, living in the digital age can drive you crazy! If you don't turn your phone or computer off from time to time, your attention can be completely hijacked by websites, incoming messages, social media, games and more. Gadgets are so compelling.

If you think that the digital age is getting too much, check out the suggestions in this section to get yourself back in control.

Assessing your level of addiction to technology

Nowadays, people seem to use their phones a lot. A recent survey of over 4,000 users found that . . .

>> Average smartphone users checks their phones 47 times a day.

>> 85 per cent of smartphone users will check their phone when speaking with friends and family.

>> 80 per cent of smartphone users check their phone within an hour of waking up or going to sleep.

>> Almost half of all smartphone users have tried to limit their usage in the past.

When you find you're spending more time on your phone than interacting with real people, it may be time to reassess your phone usage. Smartphone addiction is often fueled by Internet overuse, as it's often the games, apps and online worlds that are most compelling.

Here's a quiz I've developed to get an idea of just how addicted you are to your phone:

1. **You're doing some work and a phone rings in another room. Do you:**

    a. Take no notice: it must be someone else's; your phone is normally off.

    b. Ignore it and check it later.

c. Walk casually to pick it up.

d. Run to pick up the phone, sometimes tripping over or stubbing your toe in the process, and getting annoyed by anyone in the way.

2. **You're planning a holiday, but the hotel has no Wi-Fi and no phone signal. Will you go?**

   a. Yes, why not?

   b. Oh, I'd love the chance to get a break from my devices. Heaven!

   c. Probably wouldn't go there.

   d. No way! How can I have a vacation without my phone and/or laptop – that doesn't make sense. I need a good phone signal and superfast Internet 24/7.

3. **Where's your phone right now?**

   a. My what? Oh, phone . . . Err, no idea. I'm not sure if I have a phone actually.

   b. Somewhere around here.

   c. In this room.

   d. It's right here – my beautiful, precious phone.

4. **What do you use your phone for?**

   a. Phone calls, of course. What else is it for?

   b. Calls and texts from time to time. Mainly emergencies.

   c. Call and texts. And picking up emails sometimes too. A few pictures.

   d. Everything. It's my life! Facebook, Twitter, WhatsApp, Instagram, Snapchat, email, texting, photos, video, playing games, fitness, Skype. Oh yes, and ocassionally phone calls too.

5. **Do you keep your phone nearby as you sleep?**

   a. No way!

   b. Sometimes. Or just for my alarm clock. Don't really check last thing at night or first thing in the morning.

   c. Quite often. Send the odd text and maybe have a peek at my messages first thing in the morning too.

   d. Every night. I sleep with my phone. It's the last thing I look at before falling asleep and the first thing I see when I wake up. It's a compulsion.

Add up your score: letter a is 1 point, b is 2 points, c is 3 points, and d is four points.

5–10 points: you're not really addicted to your phone at all – you're probably too busy meditating.

11–15 points: you like your phone, but not that much. You're still in control and can live comfortably without it.

16–18 points: you're pretty dependent on your phone for many things. You might like to take a little break from your phone from time to time.

19–20 points: you love your phone. What if you lose your phone? Or it gets stolen? Make sure you have some moments in the day where you take a break from your device and do some mindful walking or stretching, or sit and meditate away from your phone. If you feel that your phone usage is out of control, try some of the tips in the section below to help, or consider getting professional help if you feel overwhelmed.

Using mindfulness to get back in control

If you've discovered that you're using digital devices to the point that they're having a negative impact on your work or social life, it's time to get back in control.

You can manage overuse of digital devices in many ways. It's not as hard as you may think. In fact, once you start using some of these strategies, you may find that you don't even want to look at your mobile devices.

Here are some techniques that you can try:

» **Engage in other activities.** You can participate in a new hobby regularly, such as knitting, gardening or playing an instrument. By paying mindful attention to your hobby and keeping your phones and computers out of the way, you'll develop greater mindfulness. And you can also get on with a few household chores – you'll feel good once they're done. Again, keep your devices switched off and try focusing on the chore – it can be soothing and enjoyable to polish the dining table or clear your desk with full attention and a little smile.

» **Make good use of flight mode, or switch your phone off.** When I have an important task to do, I try to remember to keep my phone off or simply in flight mode. That way, I can't be disturbed. The iPhone even has a new mode called 'do not disturb.' This prevents calls and alerts from coming through. So, from 9pm to 8am I set my phone to 'do not disturb' to automatically prevent any more calls or messages coming in.

>> **Set boundaries.** Just before you go to bed, it's important not to look at screens too much. Television, laptops and phones emit a light which signals to your body that it's still daytime. Then you may have trouble falling asleep and may wake up tired. Also, you may not want to be disturbed at other specific times in the day. For example, when walking through the park keep your phone off and enjoy nature and the people around you. And obviously, when you're with friends or family or eating a meal, switch your phone off or leave it out of the way. If distancing yourself from your phone sounds like a challenge, just try it once and see how that goes. Eventually, it can feel freeing to leave your gadgets behind.

>> **Switch off notifications.** Does your computer beep each time an email comes through? Does your phone make a noise each time someone chats to you on social media or sends you a message? If so, you can end up with perpetual distraction. Every time you're doing one task, you're distracted by another. The more you keep switching your attention, the less your mindful awareness develops. Turn off as many notifications as you can. This way, you can focus on doing whatever you need to do with awareness.

>> **Be kind to yourself when you slip up.** Ever had that feeling of frustration when you've spent the last hour or so just surfing the Internet rather than finishing your work? I have. But when you do eventually catch yourself doing this, don't beat yourself up too much. It's okay. Everyone has their downtime and gets distracted. Say to yourself, 'It's okay. Let me take a break from my computer and phone and have a little mindful walk. I'll then come back with a smile and get on with my tasks. Everyone gets too caught up with the barrage of technology nowadays.'

REMEMBER

If you feel you need more help to reduce your Internet usage, consider an evidence-based therapy like Cognitive Behavioural Therapy or Acceptance and Commitment Therapy to ease your compulsive behaviour and change your perception about internet usage. Professional help can offer alternative ways of dealing with the underlying emotions and thoughts that may be fueling your smartphone use.

Using technology to enhance mindful awareness

If you're looking for a way to enhance your mindfulness, you may want to avoid technology altogether – and that's understandable. Use of technology can distract your mind. But for you, using digital devices may be part of your everyday life. Switching them off for an extended period may seem impossible to achieve. In such a case, I encourage you to make good use of mindfulness apps, websites and more.

You can download and use apps for mobile devices like phones and tablets. Simply search for 'mindfulness' or 'meditation' in the app stores and you'll find lots of resources – take your pick. New apps come out every week! Popular ones at the moment are Insight Timer, Calm or Headspace. But there are many more.

If you use social media a lot, following people or organisations that offer mindful images, tweets and resources may help you. If you want to follow my work, just search for my name, Shamash Alidina, on your social media channel of choice. I usually share mindfulness tips and quotes. And feel free to say "Hi" too!

You can also use software to help you focus mindfully on your work. My favourite free software that helps me to focus and be productive on my computer is called Self Control. It's available free for Apple Mac computers, and there are equivalent software products for Windows PCs.

For example, I do my best creative work in the mornings. So today, I wanted to focus for a few hours on writing this article. I switched on the Self Control program until noon. I blocked all my social media websites and my email, which can easily suck me in. With those areas blocked, I can mindfully focus on my writing. Then I can deal with emails, social media and meetings in the afternoon.

It's ironic that as a mindfulness specialist, I need a self-control app to prevent me from using social media sites and email! It just goes to show how addictive they can be for us all and how we can use technology tools to help manage our usage.

Chapter 9

Establishing Your Own Mindfulness Routine

Learning a new language takes time, effort and patience. You need to dedicate yourself and at the same time not expect rapid progress. You try to practise regularly, preferably daily. You can learn the language by using phone apps, books, television programmes, videos, websites, or in person through a teacher – whatever way best suits your lifestyle and learning methods. Learning mindfulness has some similarities. You can begin in many different ways, as long as you practise regularly and with a certain commitment and the right attitude and intention. (Refer to Chapters 4 and 5 for more about nurturing your attitudes and intention.) If you find committing yourself to a mindfulness practise difficult, you're not alone; you can try a different approach, adjust your practise method, explore possible barriers and look for support as you discover the language of mindfulness.

Remember that when you learn a language, you can measure your progress – by, say, the number of new words you know. You can't measure progress in mindfulness so easily. Mindfulness is about being exactly where you are right now and exploring the landscape, enjoying the scenery and being as you are, whatever that means for you. No matter how long you've been practising mindfulness, the present moment is always the same and yet always fresh, new and full of possibilities.

In this chapter I introduce the eight-week mindfulness-based stress reduction course and explore how to choose which element of mindfulness is best for you to practise. I also give you some ideas you can use if you want to take your mindfulness meditation even deeper.

Trying an Evidence-Based Mindfulness Course

Perhaps one of the most well-proven mindfulness courses is an eight-week programme called *mindfulness-based stress reduction* (MBSR), originally developed at a clinic at the University of Massachusetts medical school by Jon Kabat-Zinn. The course has been researched many times with thousands of people and has proved to be effective at managing stress, so the recommended practises are certainly worth a go. If, after the eight weeks, you've felt no change has happened and sense that mindfulness isn't for you, you can drop the practise. If you found the programme helpful, you can go on to develop your own practise, having experienced the range of meditative exercises.

TIP

If you want to try this course, begin the programme by making a personal commitment to suspend your judgement and follow the recommended practises for eight weeks. After that, decide whether mindfulness is something for you. You can ask others in your life to help support you over the next eight weeks, or at least to give you some space to engage in mindfulness meditations daily for the next couple of months. Keep a journal on hand during the eight weeks to record your progress and any thoughts or emotions that arise.

Week One: Understanding automatic pilot

You operate on an automatic pilot far more than you may think you do. You may have experienced driving a car for a significant time before realising you were lost in thoughts, worries, or daydreams. This may be okay for a little while, but if your whole life is run automatically, you miss the show. Your mind thinks the same old thoughts, you may react unnecessarily when things don't go your way, and your stress is compounded without you being fully aware of this process. Mindful awareness, as opposed to automatic pilot, allows for the possibility of responding to situations by offering you choice – a freedom from the mechanical, reactive, habitual patterns of your mind. (Refer to Chapter 5 for more about overcoming living on automatic pilot.)

MAKING THE MIND–BODY CONNECTION

The root meaning of the phrase *to heal* is literally 'to make whole.' Mindfulness meditation leads to a sense of being whole and complete, a sense of seeing the perfection of yourself, just the way you are, no matter what may be wrong with you.

One of the key ways modern medicine broke down the wholeness of being human was by splitting up the body and the mind as two distinct, separate entities. Your attitudes, opinions and beliefs weren't thought to affect your physical health. Ample evidence now shows strong links between your inner attitudes and your physical health and wellbeing. In this context, healing means to make whole the connection between mind and body and to see the mind and body as two parts of the same entity. Through practising mindfulness you see how your mind influences everything from the rate of your breathing to the way you treat your colleagues at work, and how an emotional rollercoaster ride on a Monday may be influencing your flu-like symptoms on Wednesday. This doesn't mean that 'you're causing' yourself to become ill by thinking certain thoughts, but simply that the way your body functions is linked to the level of stress you experience.

This is the practise for Week One:

>> Begin the week by engaging in the 'eating a piece of fruit' meditation described in Chapter 6. Record in your journal what effect the exercise has on you. Reflect on the effect of operating on automatic pilot in your daily life. What are you missing out on? What effect is unawareness having on your thoughts, emotions and body, as well as your relationship with yourself, others and the world?

>> Practise the body scan meditation (explained in Chapter 6) daily, using the MP3 provided with this book. Play the MP3 and follow the guidance as best you can. Each day, note whether you practised and how you found the meditation. Don't worry if you don't enjoy it; persevere with it. Experiment with doing the body scan at different times of the day to see what works best for you.

>> Choose a routine daily activity to practise mindfully. This can be brushing your teeth, showering, getting dressed, walking or driving to work, speaking with your partner, cooking, cleaning or anything you can think of. Bring a sense of curiosity to your experience. What matters is not what you choose, but your commitment to being aware of what you're doing, as you're doing it.

Week Two: Dealing with barriers

Daily meditation practise can be pretty challenging. Meditation provides the space for a whole range of trapped thoughts and emotions to rise to the surface, often the ones you want to avoid most. The tendency of the mind is to judge experiences as good or bad. The idea of mindfulness is to be aware of these judgements and let them go. The most important thing is to keep practising, no matter what your experience is. And try not to beat yourself up when you don't manage to do the practises. Instead, just gently understand that, as a human being, you're not flawless. Pick yourself up and when you're ready, try again.

REMEMBER

The aim of the body scan or any other meditation isn't relaxation, so don't worry if you don't feel relaxed. The aim is simply to be aware of whatever your experience is, as far as you can. The experience may be unpleasant, and you may feel more tense by the end of the session, but that's still as good a meditation as any other; your mind may just be doing an emotional 'detox' – who knows? Just be patient and try not to judge the experience.

This is the practise for Week Two:

» Continue to practise the body scan daily using the MP3. You may now know the best time for you to practise meditation, and be able to stick with it. Make a short record in your journal, even just a sentence, of how the experience of the body scan is for you, on a daily basis.

» Choose another daily routine activity to do with mindfulness, in addition to the one you selected in Week One. Try pausing for a breath or two before starting the activity, and then connect with your senses, noticing the thoughts and emotions playing in your mind.

» Practise being mindful of your breath for ten minutes a day, by simply sitting comfortably straight and feeling the sensation of your breath. If your mind naturally wanders off, congratulate yourself for noticing and guide your attention kindly back to the breath sensation. Avoid paying attention to self-criticism; if criticism does arise in your awareness, note the negative thought as just another thought and turn your attention back to the breath. See Chapter 6 for how to practise mindfulness of breath in more detail.

» Start a pleasant events diary and use it to write down your thoughts, feelings and bodily sensations when you experience something pleasant, in as much detail as you can. In this way, you become more aware of how you automatically react to pleasant experiences. See Chapter 13 for details on how to do this.

Week Three: Being mindful in movement

One of the beauties of mindfulness is that you don't have to be sitting still to be mindfully aware. This week is an opportunity to explore mindfulness in movement. This is also an opportunity to reflect on the power of focusing on the breath. The breath can act like an anchor: a place always available, right under your nose, to draw you into the present moment. Being aware of your breath while focusing on something challenging can enable you to see the difficulty from a different angle, softening the tension a little.

Try this practise for Week Three:

» On days one, three and five, practise about 30 minutes of mindful walking or stretching. Many people enjoy developing mindfulness through yoga or tai chi and find the approach very powerful. (You can refer to *Yoga For Dummies* by Georg Feuerstein and Larry Payne (Wiley) or *Tai Chi For Dummies* by Therese Iknoian (Wiley) for ways to do this.)

» On days two, four and six, practise the body scan using the MP3.

» Begin practising the mini meditation called the three-minute breathing space three times a day (explained in Chapter 7). You may be more likely to remember to do the breathing space if you decide at the beginning of the week exactly when you want to practise.

» Complete an unpleasant events diary in your journal (see Chapter 13 for details) on a daily basis. This means writing down one thing each day that was unpleasant for you, and the sensations in your body, the thoughts going through your mind at the time, and how you felt emotionally.

Week Four: Staying present

This week, focus on the present moment. Reflect on the quality of this moment now. How does it compare with thinking about the past or the future? What effect does focusing on the here and now have on your thoughts and emotions?

You react to experience in one of three ways:

» Attachment to pleasant experiences

» Aversion to unpleasant experiences

» Indifference to everyday experiences

Holding onto pleasant experiences leads to fear of what happens when you lose them. For example, chasing a good feeling could make you feel anxious as soon as that happy feeling subsides. And aversion from an unpleasant experience leads to stress each time you have a bad time. So if you avoid the feeling of anxiety by not socialising, your anxiety will probably be even higher next time you do need to socialise. Going into automatic pilot when facing a neutral event means you miss out on the mystery and wonder of being alive.

This week, focus on your aversion to unpleasant experiences. You, like everyone on the planet, have to face difficulties from time to time. The question is *how* you meet the challenge: do you run away from, suppress, or fight the feelings? Is there another way? However you meet difficulties, by becoming more mindful of the process, your reactions begin very slowly to untangle themselves. You begin to consider the possibility of responding in a way that reduces rather than com-pounds your stress.

Here's your practise for Week Four:

>> On days one, three and five, practise 15 minutes of mindful movement – stretching or walking – followed by 15 minutes of mindful breathing.

>> On days two, four and six, practise the 30-minute guided sitting meditation explained in Chapter 6, using the MP3 provided.

>> Practise the three-minute breathing space meditation three times a day at times predetermined by you.

>> Additionally, practise the three-minute breathing space when something unpleasant happens. Write in your journal what effect the meditation has on your experiences.

>> Become aware of times of stress. How do you react to the stress? Do you create a block, resist or suppress the stress, or shut down? Become aware of what's happening in your body. When you react in a certain way to the stress, what's going on for you? What effect does staying present with a difficulty have on your response? Allow yourself to be deeply curious about your relationship to stress.

Week Five: Embracing acceptance

This week, try allowing things to be as they are, rather than immediately wanting to change them. For example, if someone irritates you, rather than reacting immediately, just stay with the feeling of irritation. Feel it in your body and notice your automatic thoughts. If you feel a headache coming on, observe what happens if you let the pain be just as it is, and watch it rise and fall. What effect does allow-ing, accepting and acknowledging have on unpleasant and pleasant sensations?

If you want to become more relaxed, the first step is to allow things to be as they are, however they are. If you feel frustrated, the feeling is already there, so rather than getting frustrated about that too, try to begin accepting the frustration. Notice the thoughts, feelings and bodily sensations that go along with the frustration. You can try saying to yourself, 'It's okay; whatever it is, it's okay. It's already here. Let me feel it.'

REMEMBER

Acceptance isn't resignation: you're facing up to the difficulty rather than running away. Mindfulness involves accepting awareness and using it as a way to change, not resigning yourself to a situation in which change will never happen.

Try this practise for Week Five:

» Practise the guided sitting meditation using the MP3, noticing how you react to thoughts, emotions and bodily sensations. Record any observations in your journal.

» Do the three-minute breathing space meditation three times a day. Try to connect it with everyday activities at times such as meal times, after waking up and just before going to sleep.

» Practise the three-minute breathing space when you're going through a difficulty. Use the practise to explore your thoughts and feelings rather than trying to get rid of them, if you can.

» Explore the difference in responding in a controlled way to more challenging situations, whether they occur during meditation or not, rather than reacting uncontrollably to your experience. Become more aware of your reactions and the thoughts and emotions that drive them.

Week Six: Realising that thoughts are just thoughts

Usually, when you think of something, like 'He hates me' or 'I can't do this,' you accept it as a fact, a reality. You may believe that almost any thought that pops into your awareness is an absolute truth. If your mind habitually pops up negative or unhelpful thoughts, seeing the thoughts and images as facts has stressful consequences. However, you can free yourself of this burden. Switch things around and try seeing thoughts as automatic, conditioned reactions rather than as facts. Question the validity of thoughts and images. Step back from the thoughts, if you can and don't take them to be you, or reality. Just watch them come and go and observe the effect of this.

REMEMBER

Thoughts are just thoughts, which may or may not be true. Thoughts are mental events: words or images popping up in your mind. You don't have to be *in* your thoughts; you can be the observer of your thoughts. This gives you a sense of inner space and distance from your thoughts and chance to see them for what they are – just thoughts.

When you're feeling challenged, read Chapter 13 and see whether you can identify what types of thoughts are taking place.

Practise for Week Six:

>> Now you can begin to mix and match as you wish. Combine the sitting meditation, the body scan and mindful movement for 30–45 minutes a day. You can split the time into two or three parts, and spread them out through the day. Some days you may choose not to use the MP3.

>> Practise the three-minute breathing space three times a day, and additionally practise when a difficulty or challenge arises for you. Notice any recurring patterns, notice the effect of mindful breathing on your body, and let the mindfulness spread into whatever you're facing next.

>> If you can make time, practise a day of silent mindfulness meditation. See the section 'Setting aside a day for mindfulness' later in this chapter for how you can plan and do this mindfulness day.

Week Seven: Taking care of yourself

The activities you choose to do, from moment to moment and from day to day, strongly influence how you feel. By becoming aware of the activities that uplift you and the activities that deplete you, you may be able to adjust the choices you make to best take care of yourself.

Here's your practise for Week Seven:

>> Choose any formal mindfulness meditations you like – such as the body scan, sitting meditation, or a combination of the meditations – and practise them daily, with or without the MP3.

>> Continue to practise the three-minute breathing space three times a day and when a difficulty arises. Try making a wise choice after or during a difficulty.

>> Design a stress warning system in your journal by writing down all the warning signs you have when under excessive stress, like feeling hot or behaving impatiently, and then write down an action plan you can follow

to reduce the stress, such as a mini meditation, going for a walk, or talking to a friend. Refer to your action plan when you next feel overly stressed and notice what effect it has.

Week Eight: Reflection and change

Sometimes, when faced with a problem, no matter how hard you try, no matter how much effort you put into solving the problem, you're still stuck with the difficulty. Nothing seems to work. If you keep trying, you may become more and more tired, and perhaps move farther from a solution rather than nearer. In such circumstances, stop trying to solve the issue, and accept the circumstance for now. In this act of kindness to yourself, a solution may or may not arise. However, you're likely to feel less angry, frustrated, stressed, or depressed. The feeling of helplessness arises when you keep trying and no benefit seems to manifest itself. Acceptance is a change in itself.

WISE WORDS

You may already know the serenity prayer, which seeks:

The serenity to accept the things I cannot change;

The courage to change the things I can; and

The wisdom to know the difference.

In this last week of the course, reflect on how the experience has been for you. What have you found most helpful? What aspects would you like to integrate into your daily practise? Write your thoughts in your journal.

And finally, your practise for Week Eight:

➤ Decide which formal mindfulness practise you want to do for the next week, and carry out your decision as best you can.

➤ At the end of Week Eight, reflect on how the eight weeks of the course went for you, recording your thoughts in your journal. Consider some of these questions to help with your journal entries. How did your level of stress change over the course of the eight weeks? How did you meet difficulties in your life while engaging in this course? How can you adapt the mindfulness practises to integrate them into your life?

➤ Congratulate yourself for reaching this point, no matter how much or how little mindfulness you actually managed to do. The practise of mindfulness on a daily basis isn't an easy one to do: any mindfulness you managed is better than none at all.

STICKING TO YOUR DECISIONS

Research has found that the longer you practise mindfulness for each day, the greater the benefit. Experiments have also shown that even short bouts of mindfulness – even a few minutes or a few mindful breaths – have positive effects on your wellbeing.

How long you decide to practise mindfulness for each day depends on your motivation for meditating in the first place. Deciding how long to meditate for depends on:

- Your intentions
- Your past experience with meditation or prayer
- How committed you are to reaping the long-term benefits of meditation
- Your level of discipline

The important thing is: *once you've decided how long you're going to meditate, stick to your decision*. This is *very* important for training your mind. If you practise for as long as you feel like and then get up, you're acting on a feeling. You stop being mindful if your mind says so. However, if you've decided to meditate for ten minutes and after five minutes feel like getting up, you still stay put. This makes you experience feelings of restlessness or boredom, frustration or agitation. What's the benefit of this? Well, you're taking a stand. *You* are saying to *your mind*, 'Thank you for your idea, but I'm in charge here. I've decided to sit still for ten minutes and feel the sensations of my breathing to help me to focus and stay calm.' The mind eventually calms down. You're no longer a slave to what your mind throws at you. This is the *freedom* of mindfulness: you're free to choose what you do and how you act, rather than your mind choosing. You are not your thoughts.

Choosing What to Practise for Quick Stress Reduction

How do you decide what you're going to eat for dinner tonight? Your decision probably depends on how hungry you or your family are, who's cooking, the food in the fridge, the day of the week, the meal you ate yesterday, and so on. Many factors come into account. How do you decide which mindfulness meditation to practise today when establishing your own mindfulness routine? I give you some options in this section.

Many people come to mindfulness for stress reduction. Stress has an impact on everyone. If you're alive, you're going to experience stress. The question is, how do you handle the stress?

Trying to get rid of your stress by brute force can just increase it. Imagine you're trying to pull open a door that has a sign saying push. No matter how hard you pull, the door won't open! If you pull hard enough, the door handle may fall off, which won't help. Stress can come from doing, doing, and more doing. You can't use the same frantic approach for stress reduction. Stress reduction requires you to stop constantly doing – or to start non-doing. This is what mindfulness offers.

Try practising the following tips daily over a period of a few weeks, and see what happens:

» For quick stress reduction, try the three-minute breathing space meditation (covered in Chapter 7 and on the MP3). This mindfulness exercise cleverly includes a little bit of all the different types of mindfulness meditation in one neat, bite-size package. How cool is that? You don't have to use the MP3 once you've got the hang of it, and you don't even have to close your eyes. If you're at work, you can softly gaze at the bottom of the computer screen, or pop to the lavatory and practise there – why not?! It's quiet (hopefully!), you can lock the door, lower the lid and sit down. Your boss might even wonder why you look so serene every time you step out of the toilet!

» Try ten minutes of mindful breathing, using the MP3 track or practising on your own. Ideally, do this meditation in the morning to set yourself up for the day, but if you don't like that, do it any time of the day that suits you, or whenever you feel stressed.

» Walking meditation is a wonderful practise to integrate into your day. You're then combining some gentle exercise with mindfulness – a powerful combination for stress reduction. Head to Chapter 6 for the walking meditation.

» Spend ten minutes or more stretching your body in a mindful way. Use any stretching movements you prefer. The stimulation of the body as you stretch draws your attention out of your mind and into the physical sensations. If you have time during the day, you can also engage in the odd gentle stretch now and then. Remember, the most important thing is to be aware of the feelings in the body and mind as you stretch, in a kind and gentle way. Keep breathing mindfully as you move – let go of any tendency to hold your breath if you can.

» Spend some time seeing a stressful situation from the other person's perspective or just a different perspective, to help you relieve stress.

» Before you go to sleep, think of three things you're grateful for. Doing so relieves stress and has a beneficial long-term effect. See Chapter 4 for more on gratitude.

Also, write down all the events in your day that caused you stress. What was going through your mind? What fixed ideas did you have? Do you notice any patterns? Watch out for these patterns the next time you're in a stressful situation, and notice what effect being aware of the repeating pattern has.

USING MINDFULNESS FOR SELF-DISCOVERY

Many people use mindfulness as a way to *self-discovery*. This is about deepening your own understanding of who you are and your relationship with yourself, others and the wider environment. In meditation, your conceptual mind with its thoughts and ideas stops being the only reference point for you.

You discover the concept of being separate from everything else as you grow up. Babies don't identify with their own bodies. The baby looks in wonder at its own foot just as it may look at a bunch of keys. There's no sense of me and not me. Humans have a deep-seated need to feel part of a bigger whole, whether socially or spiritually. Albert Einstein is attributed with the following striking observation:

> A human being is a part of the whole, called by us 'Universe,' a part limited in time and space. He experiences himself, his thoughts and feelings as something separated from the rest – a kind of optical delusion of his consciousness. This delusion is a kind of prison for us, restricting us to our personal desires and to affection for a few persons nearest to us. Our task must be to free ourselves from this prison by widening our circle of compassion to embrace all living creatures and the whole of nature in its beauty.

This is the 'task' of mindfulness. You're seeing this 'optical delusion' as Einstein puts it, as the self-limiting thoughts and beliefs about who you are and your place in the world. Through mindfulness comes insight, and you begin to see this prison of separation and, in doing so, are released, even if only momentarily. But each moment of freedom is nourishing and uplifting, and energises and motivates you to keep walking on the journey towards healing, wholeness, health and self-discovery. Remember, you don't need to travel far for this: the present moment is right here, right now.

Going Even Deeper

So you've established a mindfulness routine. You feel you're ready for the next step. If you feel called to do so and can set aside the time and resources, you can progress in your practise by meditating for more extended periods of time. This section offers ways for you to step beyond your routine and find further support in your journey.

Discovering the value of silence

We live in a busy, noisy world. Just today I've spoken to friends and family members. I've exchanged messages with others. I've watched some YouTube videos and even created one!

Among all this noise and busyness, there's little silence. And when you do find yourself in a quiet place, like on a beach or in a forest or meadow, you may be tempted to call a friend or capture the experience with photos. Constantly communicating can become an impulsive habit rather than a choice.

I'd like to invite you to explore something different if you haven't already: being silent. Explore the value of being silent rather than talking or communicating with others for a period of time. This includes not watching television or surfing the net, or even reading. Just get away from the world of language. This can be for a few hours, a full day, or perhaps longer if you attend a retreat.

Most people think being silent is impossible for them. But why not give it a try? You've got nothing to lose and may discover a whole new way of being that you can revisit from time to time.

It's a bit like believing the earth is flat. If you hold that belief, you won't explore. But if you've got the guts to go to the edge to see what happens, you discover a whole new landscape. In the same way, if you believe that being silent won't teach you anything new, you won't try. But if you're willing to give it a go, who knows what beautiful new inner landscapes you may be able to explore?

The benefits of refraining from speaking for some time include:

>> A chance for the chatty mind to calm down, so that you can see clearly and observe with greater depth and clarity

>> An opportunity to reflect upon your life and consider what's going well and which direction you want to take in the future

>> Time to process and let go of any pent-up emotions that you may have knowingly or unknowingly supressed

>> Greater levels of creativity

>> A extended period of time to de-stress, heal and find some inner peace

You don't need to force yourself to be silent. Have a go when you feel ready to do so.

Setting aside a day for mindfulness

In this day and age, people work very hard. You're working hard for your employers or your own business, or perhaps you're at home, looking after your parents or children. Even looking after yourself requires time, energy and effort. Mindfulness meditation offers some respite, a chance to stop doing, to stop fulfilling your endless needs and desires to help others or yourself, and to simply *be*. Have you ever treated yourself to a whole day of non-doing? This doesn't mean watching television all day, or just sleeping all day; even when you sleep, your mind can be in overdrive, going from one dream to another. By non-doing, I mean using the time to let go of excessively thinking about the past or worrying about the future – to softly reside in the here and now.

TIP

A day of mindfulness is a beautiful gift you can give yourself. The idea is to spend a whole day in mindful awareness, ideally being silent. Here are some instructions on practising this exercise:

1. **The evening before, place a reminder next to your bed and around the house that you're going to spend the day mindfully.** Be clear in your mind that you're going to keep the phone, computer, television and other electronics switched off. Drift off into sleep by feeling your breathing as you lie in bed.

2. **When you wake up on your day of mindfulness, begin the day with some mindful breathing as you lie in bed.** Feel each in-breath and each out-breath mindfully. If you like, smile gently. Spend some time reflecting on what you're grateful for: your home, your relationships, your income, your family, your body, your senses, or whatever you feel you have that perhaps others don't.

3. **Slowly and mindfully step out of bed.** If you have a pleasant view from your window, spend some time looking outside. Enjoy looking at the trees, or grass, or the people walking purposefully to fulfil their needs. Look, if you can, without encouraging judgements and reactions. Your mind is bound to wander off into other thoughts and worries – just gently bring your attention back as soon as you realise.

4. **Practise some formal mindfulness meditation.** You can do the body scan meditation, for example.

5. **Have a bath or shower.** Do this at a leisurely pace. Take your time, even if you feel like rushing for no apparent reason. Feel the sensations of the water on your body – in many places throughout the world people have to walk for hours to collect water, so be grateful for the easy access you have to water.

6. **Take your time making your breakfast.** Connect with your senses and keep bringing your attention into the here and now. Pause for a few moments before you start eating your breakfast. Ensure that you've tasted and fully chewed each mouthful before you start the next one. This is mindful eating.

7. **You may choose to spend the mid-morning going for some walking meditation or doing some mindful yoga or perhaps a little gardening.** Whatever you choose to do, do it with a gentle, kindly awareness. Avoid spending more than a few minutes reading a book or a magazine. The idea is to connect with your senses rather than encourage the mind to think too much.

8. **Spend some time preparing and eating lunch.** Again, allow the process to unfold in a leisurely way. You don't need to rush. If feelings of boredom, restlessness, or frustration arise, see whether you can offer them the space to come to pass – to surface and diminish again. Eat your meal with gratitude and attention; chew each morsel unhurriedly.

9. **Engage in gentle physical activity after lunch, or perhaps have a siesta.** Why not? Connect your senses with another hobby of your choice. Every now and then, practise the breathing space meditation for a few minutes to help bring you into the present moment. You may even choose to do another extended meditative practise, such as a sitting meditation or some mindful yoga or tai chi. Don't be surprised if you begin to find the whole process challenging or emotional. You may not be used to giving yourself so much room to simply be present, and this can allow unprocessed thoughts and emotions to release themselves into your consciousness. Be as kind and patient with yourself as you're able to be.

10. **Continue to allow the day to unfold in this way, eating, resting, walking and practising meditation.** If you can't help cleaning out a cupboard or organising your paperwork, really take your time with the actions, doing things one step at a time.

11. **Having prepared and eaten your evening meal, which is ideally the lightest of the meals you've had during the day, you can rest and relax before going to bed.** Lie in bed and ride on the waves of your own breathing, allowing yourself to doze naturally into a slumber.

Joining a group

Meditation is often spent sitting down with your eyes closed, in silence. Not much banter goes on; nobody's cracking open the beers. So, why on earth would you need to bother joining a mindfulness meditation group? Here are some reasons:

>> **By attending a regular group, you commit to practising frequently.** Without such a commitment, you may lose momentum and end up not meditating, even though you really want to and find it valuable.

>> **Your meditation is deeper when practising in a group.** Many of my clients say this when they attend a class. You're less likely to fidget unnecessarily when sitting with others; if the body remains relatively still, the mind also calms down. You're also more likely to make a little more effort in your sitting posture, sitting straighter and with dignity. People who are spiritually inclined believe that by meditating together, you create a certain positive energy in the room that generates a favourable atmosphere, intensifying the quality of the meditation.

>> **You often end up making friends with people who enjoy meditation.** This can create a 'positive feedback' system within your social circle, because the more time you spend with other fellow meditators, the more you think about mindfulness and remember to practise and the more you're likely to hear about the latest and greatest book, teacher, or retreat. You begin to support each other in other areas of life too, which is always nice.

How do you go about choosing a group? You may be able to find a mindfulness meditation group in your area by searching on the Internet. You don't have to join a mindfulness group, however. You can join any type of meditation group and, through trial and error, find one you feel comfortable with. Most Buddhist organisations practise some form of mindfulness meditation. And increasingly, yoga centers offer mindfulness groups or classes.

TIP

If you can't find a group for you, consider setting up one yourself. I know one couple who started a weekly group that grew naturally by itself, just by word of mouth, until they had about 15 regular members. In each session, you just need a period of silence for meditation – perhaps 30 minutes or so – and then a period to explore and share how the practise and week have gone. You may want to read a paragraph of text from a book on mindfulness. After that, I suggest some time simply to socialise over a cup of tea and a few delicious biscuits. In the summer, I organise mindful walks and picnics in parks or by the river – perhaps these are the kind of events you too can set up.

Finding an appropriate retreat

When you've been practising mindfulness for at least a few months, you may be ready to attend a mindfulness retreat. This is a magnificent opportunity for you to develop your mindful practise and discover more about yourself. Retreats can be any length from one day to several years! I strongly recommend you begin with the one-day retreat, then gradually extend to a weekend, then a week, and if you're very serious in your practise, you can go for even longer.

Retreats cost between £20 and £200 for a day, or £150 and £2,000 for a week, which includes all food and accommodation. Buddhist retreats usually invite an additional donation for the teachers and organisers, who sometimes work voluntarily.

Here are some of the questions to ask before booking yourself on a mindfulness retreat:

- >> **Is the retreat in silence?** Silence offers a powerful way of intensifying your meditative discipline, as explained earlier. If you feel that going on a silent retreat is a little too much, especially to begin with, you can try and find a mindfulness holiday, combining meditation with free time to relax and socialise too. Then try a silent retreat at a future date, when you feel ready.

- >> **Is the teacher experienced?** In most retreats, the person leading is normally quite experienced, but this is worth checking, especially if you're attending for an extended period.

- >> **What's a typical schedule for the day?** Find out the time at which you're expected to wake up, so you know what you're letting yourself in for. And check how much time is spent in the day meditating too. Waking up at 4 a.m. and meditating in two-hour stretches throughout the day may be too much for you, and may put you off meditation altogether. You can find many retreats with far gentler schedules if you look around.

WARNING

- >> **Is it a cult?** If the organisation says things like 'Our way is the best/only way' or 'If you stop following us, you'll derail/die/suffer/never be happy,' then say thank you and walk away. Many wise organisations run meditation retreats but, as with everything, a few suspect ones do too. If the organisation says 'You're free to walk away at any time' or 'Our way is one way of practising meditation, but there are many other ways that you're welcome to investigate if you wish' or 'Ultimately, only you can discover what is the best way for you to meditate, through your own observation and experience,' you're probably with a good organisation. Good luck with the search.

The best way to find a retreat is to get a recommendation. If you don't know who to ask, try searching online. Some are Buddhist, or some other religion, and others are purely secular. Most retreats welcome people of all faiths, or no faith. Even if the retreats aren't in your area, they may lead you to find a suitable retreat within easy reach. Some are silent retreats. Others combine mindfulness with a holiday, so you can do some mindfulness together with a group and have some time to relax and unwind in your own way too, exploring your surroundings – these can be great fun. I taught such a retreat recently in Morocco, near the Atlas mountains – a real joy. I look forward to offering more retreats in the future.

Chapter **10**

Dealing with Setbacks and Transcending Distractions

When you first learnt to walk you must have fallen over hundreds, if not thousands, of times before you could balance on two legs. But you didn't give up. You probably giggled, got up, and tried again. Learning mindfulness is a similar process. When you first try to be mindful, you're going to fall over (well, not literally I hope, unless you're trying the lesser-known hopping-on-one-leg meditation). But setbacks are part of the process of mindfulness. The question is how you deal with them. If you see setbacks as learning opportunities rather than failures, you're bound to succeed. Each time a problem occurs, you simply need to get up and try again, with a smile if possible. In the end, you may realise that mindfulness isn't about achieving a certain state of mind, but about meeting each experience in a warm, accepting way. This chapter shows you how.

REMEMBER

Everyone accesses mindfulness in their own sweet way. For you, the mindfulness meditations in this book may just not feel right. In such a case, you can cultivate mindfulness through gardening, cooking, running, cleaning or some other way. If meditating doesn't appeal, consider which daily activity you could do, or already do, in a mindful way, by fully focusing your attention in that moment. Walking your dog in a local park, for example, can be your daily mindfulness practise if done consciously and with an open mind. Discover your unique daily mindful moment.

Getting the Most Out of Meditation

Mindfulness meditation means setting aside time to intentionally pay attention to a certain aspect of your experience with a kindly acceptance from moment to moment, as best you can. So, for example, you can pay attention to your breathing as it enters and leaves your body, accepting the rate of the breathing just as it is. Mindfulness meditation can also go on to consciously be aware and open to all your experiences from moment-to-moment – your breath, body, sounds, the thought about your shopping list, the feeling of boredom and so on.

REMEMBER

Ultimately, *you have nothing to get out of meditation.* I know that sounds pretty crazy, but it's an important point. Meditation isn't a way of *getting* something, because you already have everything you need to be whole and complete. Rather, meditation is about letting go. All the benefits of meditation (which I cover in Chapter 2) are best seen as side effects. Meditation is about being with whatever your experience is, whether pleasant or unpleasant, and seeing what unfolds. Meditating is a bit like doing your favourite hobby. If you like painting, you paint. If you paint for the love of painting rather than looking for an outcome, you paint in an effortless and joyful way. Meditation is like painting: if you spend your time looking for the benefits, you kind of spoil the fun.

Making time

If you're interested in developing the art of meditation, try engaging in some form of meditation every day, called *formal practise.* Whether you choose to meditate for five minutes or one hour is up to you, but making a daily connection with meditation has a profound effect.

Too busy to meditate daily? I know the feeling. Life is full of so many things to do that finding time to practise meditation can be hard. But you find time to brush your teeth, get dressed, and sleep. You find the time for chores, because you have to. You don't feel right if you fail to do these things. Meditation is like that too. Once you get into the rhythm of daily meditation, you don't feel right if you haven't had your daily fix of it. That's when you find the time to meditate.

SHARPENING YOUR TOOLS

Once upon a time there was a woodcutter. He had lots of trees to cut down and was working frantically, puffing and sweating away to complete his work on time. A wise person happened to be passing through (they always do in these stories) and asked, 'Why are you working so hard trying to cut that tree down? Wouldn't it be easier and faster if you took the time to sharpen your axe?' The woodcutter looked up at the wise person and said, 'Can't you see how many trees I need to cut down today? I don't have time to sharpen the axe!'

Our own lives can be a bit like that. If you find the time to meditate, to sharpen the axe of your mind, you can save much time and energy in your life. Yet a common reaction to meditation is, 'I'm too busy!' If you ever have that thought, think about the woodcutter and the time he'd have saved by sharpening his tools.

REMEMBER

The great thing about mindfulness is that you can practise it at any time. Right now, you can become aware of the fact that you're reading. You can feel the position of your body as you're reading this sentence. That's mindfulness. When you put this book down and walk somewhere, you can feel the sensations of your feet on the floor, or the tension in your shoulder, or the smile on your face. When you're aware of what you're doing, that's mindfulness. These small moments of mindfulness add up to make a positive difference to your day.

Too busy to be mindful? Well, I've got good news for you. Practising mindfulness actually saves time. Research has found that meditators work more efficiently than others. Or, you may say that meditation makes time.

Rising above boredom and restlessness

Boredom and restlessness are like opposite poles of an energy scale. Boredom is associated with a lack of enthusiasm and connection, whereas restlessness implies energy that's pumping through the body, itching to burst out. Mindfulness is designed to observe both of these states and find a balance between the two.

Boredom

Meditation can sound like the ultimate boring activity. Sit there and do nothing. What could be more boring? Even watching paint dry may sound like a more exciting prospect. Society seems geared up to help you avoid boredom. Television adverts are short and snappy to grab your attention, and mobile phones help to distract you at any moment that a hint of boredom arises. These continual forms of distraction make you bored more quickly and more easily. Meditation is a courageous step against the tide.

Boredom generally implies a lack of connection, or that you're thinking about the past or future instead of the present. If you're finding attending to your breathing boring, imagine if your head was plunged into water: you'd suddenly become very interested in breathing! Each breath is unique and different. Noticing feelings of boredom and moving your focus back to your breathing is all part of the process of mindfulness, and quite natural.

Excessive feelings of boredom may indicate that you're forcing yourself into the mindfulness practise. Try easing off your effort and bringing self-kindness to your practise. Feel your breath with a sense of friendliness and warmth. Watch your bodily sensations in the way you watch a puppy or cute little baby. And try practising the loving kindness meditation (kindly head to Chapter 6 for more on this).

TIP

The following techniques can help you work with the feelings of boredom during meditation:

>> **Acknowledge the feeling of boredom.** Boredom is the feeling that has arisen, so accept it in this moment.

>> **Notice the thoughts running through your mind.** Perhaps, 'Ohhhh, I can't be bothered!' or 'What's the point of doing this?'.

>> **Get interested in boredom.** Allow yourself to become curious. Where did the boredom come from? Where's it going? Can you feel boredom in certain parts of your body? Notice the desire to sleep or do something else other than continuing to practise.

>> **Connect your attention to the sensations of breathing and see what happens to boredom.**

>> **Take a step back from the emotion of boredom.** If you're aware of the boredom, you're not the boredom itself. Observe the boredom from this stance of a decentred, detached awareness, as if the boredom is separate from you.

Observing boredom can be very interesting. When boredom arises, you see the thoughts and feelings that run through you every time you get bored. These feelings can rule your life without you noticing. As you become aware of them, the feelings begin to loosen and let go. Your mental programmes are shadows, and through the light of mindfulness the programmes lose their apparent reality and disappear, without you doing anything much.

Restlessness

Restlessness is similar to boredom, but is associated with excessive levels of energy, and is a common mental state. You run around all day doing a million and one things and then when you sit down to meditate, your mind's still racing.

TIP

Try these three ways of coping with restlessness:

>> **Begin your meditation practise with some mindful movements.** You may choose to do some mindful walking or perhaps mindful yoga (both talked about in Chapter 6). This helps to slowly calm your mind so that you're able to practise some sitting or lying down meditations.

>> **Observe your restlessness without reacting to it.** Feel the restlessness in your body. What's your mind telling you to do? Continue to sit, despite what the mind says. This is a powerful meditation, a routine that gently trains the mind to do what you tell it to do rather than the other way around. You're beginning to take control, rather than your mind being in control. Just because your mind is restless you don't have to run around like a headless chicken doing what it tells you to. The mind can say things like, 'Oh, I can't stand this. I need to get up and do something.' You can watch this show going on in the mind, breathe into it, and guide your attention back to the inhalation and exhalation. You can even answer back in your head, saying words like, 'Thank you mind for your activity. But let's continue to practise mindfulness for a little bit longer. Then we can move around after that.'

>> **Ask your mind what it wants to do.** An alternative approach to the last tip would be to ask your mind, 'I see you're feeling very restless today. What would you like to do?' Perhaps your mind may think it wants to go for a run or have a snack or something else. If the suggestion sounds fair, go ahead and do it! And importantly, notice what happens. Does your mind settle down after that and more willing to be a bit more mindful? This is what I call a 'kindful' approach and can be a very soothing way to work with your mind. In essence, you're making friends with your mind rather than battling your mind. Ultimately you can decide what approach works best for you.

Staying awake during mindful meditation

Due to the stresses of life or constant busyness and digital stimulation, you may not be getting enough sleep. Or your sleep may not be of a high quality. In either case, you may find yourself falling asleep rather than 'falling awake' in your mindfulness practise. That's okay. You probably need sleep more than mindfulness anyway. So allow yourself the time to sleep restfully. No need to fight with yourself. Then, once you've caught up on your sleep, mindfulness can start to help you feel more awake in a refreshed and rejuvenated way.

Ultimately, sleep and mindfulness are opposites, as shown in Figure 10-1. When you fall asleep you're at a low level of consciousness – lower than during normal everyday life. Mindfulness is designed to heighten your state of awareness, so that it's greater than it is during your normal daily existence.

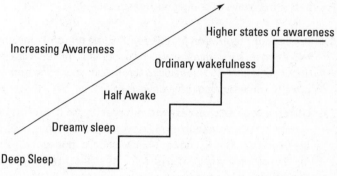

FIGURE 10-1: The different levels of consciousness.

Sometimes your mind makes you feel sleepy in order to avoid the mindfulness practise. Sleepiness during mindfulness meditation is very common and you're certainly not alone if you experience it. Don't beat yourself up about it. Sometimes, becoming sleepy is a clever trick your mind plays to prevent you from facing up to difficult thoughts or emotions (see the later section 'Getting over difficult emotions'). If you start to feel sleepy, begin to recognise the feeling.

TIP

Try these suggestions to cope with or avoid sleepiness:

>> **Ensure that you get enough sleep.** If you don't get enough sleep, you're likely to fall asleep in your next meditation.

>> **Take a few deep, slow breaths.** Repeat a few times until you feel more awake.

>> **Don't eat a big meal before meditating.** If you feel hungry before a meditation, eat a small snack beforehand rather than a three-course meal.

>> **Stand up and do some mindful stretching, yoga, tai chi or walking.** Then go back to your sitting or lying-down meditation.

>> **Experiment with meditating at different times of day.** Some people feel wide awake in the mornings, others in the afternoon or evening. Find the right time for you.

>> **Open your eyes and let some light in.** In some meditation traditions, all meditations are done with eyes half or fully open for the duration of the

practise. Experiment to see what works for you. When doing this, continue to focus on your breath, body, sounds, sights, thoughts, or emotions – whatever you've decided to make the focus of your mindful awareness.

>> **Become mindful of the state of mind called sleepiness.** This is difficult, but worth a try. Before you feel too sleepy, notice and get curious about how your body, mind, and emotions feel. This can sometimes dissipate the sleepiness and enable you to cope with it next time it happens.

Ironically, one of the first benefits of meditation that many of my students report is better sleep. Through practising mindfulness meditation, people seem to be able to allow difficult thoughts to be released from the brain, enabling the state of sleep to arise more naturally when necessary.

REMEMBER

If you do find yourself falling asleep despite your best efforts, don't worry about it too much. I find many of my students overly criticising themselves for falling asleep. If you fall asleep, you fall asleep: you probably needed it. Enjoy the snooze; night-night!

Finding a focus

When you sit for meditation, how do you decide what to focus on?

TIP

Think of your breathing as your anchor. A ship drops its anchor whenever it needs to stop. By being mindful of a few breaths, you're dropping your anchor. These breaths bring your body and mind together. Breathing can be conscious or unconscious, and focusing on breathing seems to have a wonderful way of creating a state of relaxed awareness. Your breathing also changes with your thoughts and emotions, so by developing a greater awareness of it you can regulate erratic feelings on a daily basis. The simple sensations of your breath as it enters and leaves your body can be like drinking an ice-cool, refreshing drink on a hot, stuffy day. So, don't forget to breathe.

THERE'S A TIME AND A PLACE!

I had a meditation student who, when we meditated together, kept bowing his head and then jolting it up. At the end of the meditation, I asked him if he was feeling sleepy. He said, 'Not at all. When I learnt meditation, my teacher kept doing that, so I thought that was part of the meditation practise and copied him!' His teacher was, of course, falling asleep when teaching this student, and the student innocently imitated him.

After you feel you've established your attention on breathing, you can go on to focus on bodily sensations, thoughts, feelings, or the different parts of the body, as I describe in Chapter 6.

Re-charging enthusiasm

When you've established yourself in a mindfulness meditation practise, getting into a routine is easy. The habit of practising mindfulness regularly is certainly helpful, but not if you do so in a mechanical way. If you get the feeling that you're doing the same thing every day and keep falling asleep, or you just sit there with no real purpose, then it's time to re-charge your enthusiasm.

TIP

Here are some ideas for firing up your enthusiasm:

>> **Do a different mindfulness practise.** Look through this book or refer to the resources in Part 3 for ideas.

>> **Join a mindfulness group or go on a retreat.** One or other is almost certain to shift something in you. See Chapter 9 for tips on this.

>> **Try doing your practise in a different position.** If you normally sit, try lying down or walking. You can even dance, skip or do the can-can and be mindful at the same time.

>> **Change the time when you practise meditation.** Usually morning is best, but if you're just too sleepy then, try after work or before lunch, for example.

>> **Treat yourself to a day of mindfulness.** Spend the whole day – right from the moment you open your eyes in the morning to the time you go to bed at night – doing nothing in particular, apart from being mindful. Let the day unfold naturally, rather than controlling it too much. Give yourself permission to enjoy the day.

>> **Get in touch with a mindfulness meditation teacher or try attending a course or workshop.** See whether there's a good teacher in your area, through a Google search. Some readers of this book have attended my live online mindfulness teacher training or coach training; by learning ways of helping others to meditate, they discovered more about their own mindfulness practise too. Get in touch with my team to find out more by emailing info@shamashalidina.com or visiting shamashalidina.com

REMEMBER

Practise is important, whether you feel enthusiasm or not. Keep going, and see what benefits you gain from your practise in the long term.

Dealing with Common Distractions

Distractions – whether internal or external – are a part of mindfulness experience in the same way as these words are part of this book. They go hand in hand. If you find yourself frustrated, criticising the distraction, and getting annoyed, feel it, let it be part of the mindfulness practise, and gently guide your attention back to the breathing or the focus of your meditation.

Getting frustrated can be a mind pattern, and watching and noticing the frustration rather than reacting to it may gradually change the pattern. Being distracted during meditation is a very common experience, a part of the learning process. Expect some frustration, and then see how to cope with it rather than trying to run away from it.

TIP

Reduce external distractions to a minimum. A few precautions to take are:

>> Switch off or unplug all your phones.

>> Turn off all televisions, computers, and pretty much anything electronic.

>> Ask anyone else in your home to give you some quiet time if possible.

The very effort you make to reduce distractions can have a beneficial effect on your practise. If you still get distracted, remember that everyday events always get in the way of the practise; listen to the sounds and let them become part of the practise rather than blocking them out.

You can manage internal distractions in the following ways:

>> **Just do it.** If you need to deal with something particularly urgent or important, do it before you start meditating. Your mind can then be at rest during the meditation.

>> **Take a step back from thoughts.** Watch the stream of thoughts that arise in your mind like clouds that pass across the sky. See the thoughts as separate from you, and note what effect that separation has.

>> **Welcome your thoughts for a while.** This is a great approach. Just allow all the thoughts to enter your consciousness. Welcome them. You'll probably find that the more you welcome your distractions, the fewer distractions pop into your head. It's a fun experiment!

>> **Be patient.** Remember that it's natural for the mind to think. Label each thought with a word such as 'thinking' or 'planning,' and then gently invite the attention back to your breathing.

Handling unusual experiences

Meditation isn't about getting a certain experience, but about experiencing whatever is happening right now. Blissful experiences come and go. Painful experiences come and go. You just need to keep watching without holding onto either. The practise itself does the rest. Meditation is far, far simpler than people think.

DON'T THINK ABOUT GIRLS; DON'T THINK ABOUT GIRLS

One of my favourite mindfulness teachers at the moment is a monk called Ajahn Brahm. Here's a story he often tells to teach the importance of not fighting the distractions in your mind.

When Ajahn Brahm was a young monk, he came across a beautiful, peaceful monastery in Thailand. It was so quiet there. The traffic noise came from one car a week, driving along the nearest road. And there were no sounds of planes flying overhead. It was perfect for meditation.

So Brahm settled into a routine of daily meditation in a nearby cave. The temperature and atmosphere in there couldn't be better. His meditation went well for a few weeks, but then he faced a problem. His mind started thinking about his past girlfriends. Were they still single? Maybe they'd like to meet up again? 'Stop thinking about that!' he ordered his mind. But that didn't work. No matter how hard he tried, his mind kept thinking about girls. And for a monk vowing for a life of chastity, these weren't very 'monkish' thoughts. He wanted to meditate, not think about other stuff. Brahm felt helpless.

Then one day, after asking a statue of Buddha for inspiration, Brahm had an idea: he'd do a deal with his mind! Every day at 3 p.m. he would let his mind think whatever thoughts it wanted to. The rest of the time, his mind had to focus on Brahm's breathing. So he tried that the next day. Unfortunately, that didn't work. All day, from 4 in the morning to the afternoon, Brahm battled with his mind and couldn't focus on his breathing at all. Finally came the afternoon. Brahm lay down and as he had promised and let his mind think whatever it wanted. He prepared for an hour of 'unmonkish' thoughts. But instead, something amazing happened. For that full hour, he was mindful of every single breath! Wow!

Ajahn Brahm discovered something very important that day about his mind. Never fight with your mind. Make friends with it. By consciously allowing your mind to wander if it wants to, you'll be rewarded with a calmer, gentler, and more mindful mind.

TIP

In meditation you may sometimes experience floating (just imaginary; I'm not talking about levitating yet!), flashing lights, flying pigs, or pretty much anything the mind can imagine You can also sometimes experience your body moving, stretching or shaking for example. Whatever unusual experiences arise, remember that these are just experiences and come back to the focus of the meditation. These experiences do happen, so you're not alone. In mindfulness you don't need to judge or analyse these experiences: simply let them go, as far as you can, and then come back to the senses. If you find yourself really struggling or feeling unwell, gently come out of the meditation and try again later; take things slowly, step by step. And if they happen so often that you find them overwhelming, get in touch with a very experienced mindfulness teacher for some support.

Learning to relax

The word 'relax' originally comes from the Latin word meaning to loosen or open again. Relax is such a common word. 'Just relax,' people say. If only it were so simple. How do you relax during meditation? Essentially by learning to accept the tension you're currently experiencing, rather than fighting with it.

TIP

Consider this scenario. You feel tense. Your shoulders are hunched up, and you can't let go. What do you do? Try the following steps if tension arises during your meditation:

1. **Become aware of the tension.** Get a sense of its location in your body. Recall that the aim of mindfulness is not to relax but to be curious and explore your experience.

2. **Notice whether the tension has an associated colour, shape, size or texture.** Allow yourself to be curious about it rather than trying to get rid of the tension.

3. **Feel right into the centre of the tension and breathe into it.** Feel the tense part of the body as you simultaneously feel your natural breathing. Just be with the tension as it is. Say words like 'softening' in your mind to see what effect that has.

4. **Notice whether you have any feeling or desire to get rid of the tension.** As best you can, let go of that too and see whether you can accept the sense of tension a little bit more than you do already.

5. **Send kindness and curiosity to that part of your body.** You can do this by gently smiling towards the sensation, or by placing your warm hand on the tension and caring for that part of your body or wishing that part of your body well. And try asking that tense part of your body, 'What brings you here? Is there anything you wish to communicate to me?' Find out what the cause of the tension is rather than trying to eliminate the feeling.

Fighting to let go of tension just leads to more stress and tension. That's because trying implies effort, and if the tension doesn't disappear you can end up more frustrated and angry. A warm, gentle acceptance of the feeling is far more useful.

Meditation can lead to very deep relaxation. However, relaxation is not the aim of meditation: meditation is ultimately an aimless activity.

Developing patience

Whenever I'm at a party and I'm asked what I do, I explain that I'm a trainer of mindfulness meditation. One of the comments I often get back is along the lines of, 'Oh, you must be patient. I don't have the patience for teaching anything, let alone meditation.' I don't think patience is something that you have or don't have: you can develop it. You can train your brain to become more patient. And it's a muscle worth building.

Mindfulness is patience training – especially the meditations. To commit to connect with the breath or the senses requires patience. If you feel impatient in your meditation practise but continue to sit there, you're beginning to train the patience muscle. Observe the feeling of discomfort. See whether your impatience stays the same or changes. Just as your muscles hurt when you're training in the gym, sitting through impatience is painful, but gradually the feelings of impatience and discomfort diminish. Keep pumping that iron!

You may be impatient for results if you're a beginner to mindfulness. You've heard of all the benefits of mindfulness and so you want some. That's fair enough. However, because meditation requires patience, when you begin to practise regularly you'll see that the more impatient you are, the fewer 'results' you get.

If you can't cope with being still and feeling your breath for ten minutes, try five minutes. If that's too much, try two minutes. If that's too much, try ten seconds. *Begin with however long you can manage*, and build it up, step by step. The most important thing is to keep at it, practise as regularly as you can, and gradually increase the time you practise for. Eventually, you'll become a super-patient person. Think of those huge bodybuilders who started off skinny but by taking small steps achieved Olympic weightlifting standards. Believe that you can develop patience, and take the next step.

Learning from Negative Experiences

Think back to the first time you met a dog. If your first encounter with a dog was pleasant, you're likely to think that dogs are wonderful. If, as a child, the first thing a dog did was bite you or bark excessively, you probably think dogs are aggressive. Your early experiences have a big impact on your attitudes and ways of coping later in life. By learning to see that a negative experience is just a momentary thing rather than something that lasts forever, you can begin to move forwards.

Mindfulness is similar. If you happen to get lucky and have a few positive experiences to start with, you'll stick with it. But if you don't, please don't give up. You've only just begun the journey, and you have a lot more to discover. Stay with it and work through any negative experiences you encounter.

Dealing with physical discomfort

In the beginning, sitting meditation will probably be uncomfortable. Learning to cope with that discomfort is an important hurdle to jump in your meditation adventure. When the muscles in your body get used to sitting meditation, the discomfort will probably diminish. For most people, sitting on a chair is the most comfortable and beneficial way to start.

TIP

To reduce physical discomfort when meditating, you can try several things:

>> **Sitting on a chair:**

- Try raising the back two legs of the chair using books or wooden blocks, and see whether that helps.

- You may be sitting at an angle. Gently lean forwards and backwards and to the left and right to find the middle point.

- Lean against the back of the chair.

- Ensure that you're not straining too much in the way you sit.

>> **Sitting on a cushion on the floor:**

- Experiment with using cushions of different sizes.

- Slowly and mindfully stand up, stretch with awareness, and sit back down.

REMEMBER

You can always lie down for mindfulness practises. You don't have to sit up if it's too uncomfortable for you. There's no rules here. Do what feels right for you.

Getting over difficult emotions

Many of my clients come to mindfulness with difficult emotions. They suffer from low mood, anxiety, or are stressed at work. They're trying to cope with anger, lack of confidence, or are burnt out. Often they feel as if they've been fighting their emotions all their lives and are now just too tired to keep fighting. Mindfulness is the final resort – the answer to coping with their difficulties. What mindfulness asks of people (to stop running away from themselves and to transcend difficulties as they arise in awareness, moment by moment) is both very simple and very challenging. As soon as you get a glimmer of the effect mindfulness has, your trust in the process grows and a new way of living emerges.

TIP

The next time you face difficult emotions, whether you're meditating or not, try the following exercise:

1. Feel the emotion present in the here and now.

2. Label the emotion in your mind, and repeat it (perhaps 'fear, fear').

3. Notice the desire to get rid of the emotion, and as far as you can, gently be with it.

4. Be mindful of where you feel the emotion in your body (most emotions create a physical sensation in the body).

5. Observe the thoughts running through the mind.

6. Breathe into the emotion, allowing your breathing to help you observe what you're feeling with warmth and friendliness. Say in your mind, 'It's okay. Let me gently be with this feeling. It will pass.'

7. Become aware of the effect of this exercise on your relationship to the emotion for a few moments. Are you a little more accepting of it?

TIP

Try to get a sense of the gentleness of this exercise. Look at the emotion as you would a flower: examine the petals, smell its fragrance, and be tender with it. Think of the emotion as wanting to talk to you, and listen to it. This is the opposite of the normal way people meet emotion, by bottling it up and running away.

If this all sounds too overwhelming, take it step by step. Make the tiniest step you can manage towards the feeling. Don't worry about how small the step is: it's the intention to move towards the difficult emotion rather than run away that counts. A very small step makes a massive difference, because it begins to change the pattern. This is the positive snowball effect of mindfulness.

When you first move towards difficult emotions, they may grow bigger and feel more intense, because you're giving them your attention. This is absolutely normal. Try not to get frightened and run away from these emotions. Give yourself some time, and you'll find that your emotions flux and change and aren't as fixed as you've always believed.

Every time you try to avoid, suppress or push away your feelings, it's like you're putting fuel in a fire, as the emotions are given more strength. The idea with mindfulness is to accept, allow and make space in your mind and heart for the emotions to be there. Knowing everyone experiences such emotions, you then focus your attention on whatever you need to do in your life rather than trying to fix your feelings.

Accepting your progress

Mindfulness meditation is a long-term process: the more time and skillful effort you put in, the more you get out of it. Mindfulness isn't just a set of techniques that you do to see what you get immediately: it's a way of living. Be as patient as you can. Keep practising, little and often, and see what happens. Most of the time your mind may wander all over the place and you may feel you're not achieving anything. This isn't true: just sitting down and making a commitment to practise daily for a certain time has a tremendous effect; you just can't see its effect in the short term.

Think of mindfulness as planting a seed. You plant the seed in the most nourishing soil you can find, you water it daily, and you allow it to grow in a sunny spot. What happens if you poke around in the soil to see how it's doing? You disturb the progress of course. Germinating a seed takes time. But there's no other way. You just need to regularly water your seed and wait.

Be patient about your progress. You can't see a plant growing if you watch it, even though it's actually growing all the time. Every time you practise meditation you're growing more mindful, although it may seem very difficult to see from day to day. Trust in the process and enjoy watering your seed of mindfulness.

Going beyond unhelpful thoughts

'I can't do meditation' or 'It's not for me' are some comments I heard when I was last at a health and wellbeing conference. These attitudes are unhelpful, because they make you feel as if you can't meditate, no matter what. I believe everyone can learn meditation. 'I can't do meditation' actually means 'I don't like what happens when I look at my mind.'

Some common thoughts with useful antidotes to remember are:

>> **'I can't stop my thoughts.'** Mindfulness meditation isn't about stopping your thoughts. It's about becoming aware of them from a detached perspective.

>> **'I can't sit still.'** How long can you sit still for? A minute? Ten seconds? Take small steps and gradually build up your practise. Alternatively, try the moving meditations detailed in Chapter 6.

>> **'I don't have the patience.'** Meditation is perfect for you! Patience is something you can build up, step by step, too. Start with short meditations and increase them to increase your patience.

>> **'It's not for me.'** How do you know that if you haven't tried meditating? Even if you've tried it once or twice, is that enough? Commit to practising for several weeks or a few months before deciding whether mindfulness meditation is suitable for you.

>> **'This isn't helping me.'** This is a common thought in meditation. If you think this, just make a mental note and gently guide your attention back to your breathing. Mindfulness is a long term process and way of living, not a quick fix.

>> **'This is a waste of time.'** How do you know that for sure? Thousands of scientific studies and millions of practitioners are unlikely to be totally wrong. Mindfulness is beneficial if you stick to it.

Thoughts of failure have an effect only if you approach meditation with the wrong attitude. With the right attitude, there's no failure, only feedback. By feedback, I mean that if you think your meditation didn't work for some reason, you now know what doesn't work and can adjust your approach next time. Think of when you were a child learning to talk. Imagine how difficult that must have been! You'd never spoken in your life and yet you learnt how to talk at only a few years old. As a young child you didn't know what failure meant, so you kept trying. Most of the time what came out was 'ga-ga' and 'goo-goo,' but that was okay. Step by step, before you knew it, you were speaking fluently. It was you that achieved that, and it's you that can also learn to be mindful, small step by small step.

REMEMBER

There's no such thing as a good or bad meditation. You sit down to practise meditation – or you don't. It doesn't matter how many thoughts you have or how bad you feel in the meditation. What matters is trying to meditate and making a little effort to cultivate the right attitude.

Finding a Personal Path

The journey of mindfulness is a personal one, although it affects every person you meet, because you interact with them in a mindful way. Many people have walked the path before, but each journey is unique and special. In the end you learn from your own experience and do what feels right for you. If meditation doesn't feel appropriate, you probably won't do it. However, if some quiet, calm voice or feeling underneath all the chatter seems to resonate with the idea of mindfulness, you begin taking steps. You decide in each moment the next course of action that can best deal with setbacks and distractions. These choices shape your personal mindfulness journey.

Approaching difficulties with kindness

When you face a difficulty in life, how do you meet it? How you relate to your difficulty plays a big role in the outcome. Your difficulties offer you a chance to put mindfulness into practise and see these difficulties in a different way. How do you meet problems? You can turn towards them or away from them. Mindfulness is about turning towards them with a sense of kindness rather than avoidance.

Difficulties are like ugly, scary shadows. If you don't look at them properly, they continue to frighten you and make you think they're very real. However, if you look towards them, even though the difficulties scare you, you begin to understand what they are. The more light you shine on them, the more they seem to lose their power. The light is mindfulness or a kindly awareness.

People can be very unkind to themselves through self-criticism, often learnt at a young age. The learnt behavioural pattern of self-criticism can become like an automatic reaction any time you face difficulties or you make mistakes. The question is, how do you change this harsh, critical inner voice that keeps attacking you? The mindful approach is to listen to it. To give it space to say what it wants to say, and to listen, but in a gentle, friendly way, as you may listen to a young child or a piece of beautiful music. This ends up breaking down the repetitive, aggressive tone, and ends up calming and soothing the self-criticism a little. Just a tiny shift in your attitude towards these thoughts makes all the difference in dealing with difficulties. You're going on a powerful journey of running away and avoidance to moving towards with courage and kindness.

TIP

If a strong memory or worry of a past or present difficulty comes up in your practise of meditation, try taking the following steps:

1. **Become aware of the fact that something challenging has come up for you that keeps drawing your attention.**

2. Observe what effect this difficulty has on your physical body and emotions at the moment.

3. Listen to the difficulty as you would listen to a friend's problems, with a warm sense of empathy rather than criticism.

4. Say to yourself words like, 'It's alright. Whatever the difficulty is, it's okay. Let me feel it for this moment.'

5. Accept the difficulty just as it is for the time being.

6. Step back from the experience into your observer self. Be a witness of your thoughts and emotions rather than being entangled in them. Create that space between you and your inner experience, like watching clouds floating through the sky.

7. Breathe into it and stay with the sensations, even if they seem to grow larger at first. With practise, stay with the feeling of the difficulty for longer.

8. When you're ready, gently go back to the focus of the meditation.

REMEMBER

Everyone experiences difficulties of varying degrees from time to time. Mindfulness is here to help you to be with the difficulty if you can't change the circumstances that are causing it.

Understanding why you're bothering

In the middle of your mindfulness meditation practise, you may start thinking, 'Why am I bothering to do this?' and 'I'm wasting my time.' This is quite a normal thought. Simply notice the thought, gently say to yourself something like 'It's just another thought,' and turn your attention back to the breath or other focus of meditation. When you practise for a while and begin to see the benefits of meditation, your trust in the process grows and your doubts diminish.

If you feel as if you've forgotten why you're practising mindfulness in the first place and are lacking motivation, refer to Chapter 3.

Realising that setbacks are inevitable

When I first learnt to meditate, I tried too hard. I thought I had to *get* something. I sat up extremely straight in a stiff way, rather than comfortably. Each time my mind wandered away from the breath, I hauled it back instead of kindly guiding it back to the breathing. I waited for an experience. I kept trying to clear my mind completely. Sometimes it felt wonderfully blissful, and I thought I'd got it! But then it went away. So, there I was again, trying to *get* it. I felt I was going through setback after setback.

MEDITATION MAESTRO

Meditation is similar to training to be a musician. You may love playing music, but you need to put in the practise every day. Some days are great, and wonderful sounds emerge from your instrument – you feel at one with the harmony of the piece. Other days are tough. You don't want to practise, you can't see the point, you feel like giving up. But the musician still perseveres. Deep down you know the magic of music and trust that your practising will pay off. You play music because you love music.

Meditation is the same. You have good and bad days, but if you know deep down that it's important for you, you keep putting in the time. That depth of motivation and vision is the secret to making the most of meditation.

In fact, I was going through a learning process, beginning to understand what mindfulness was all about. You can only have a setback if you're trying to get something or go somewhere. If you have no goal, you can't really have a setback. Ultimately, mindfulness is about letting go of the destination and focusing on the journey.

Imagine you're sitting at home and you decide you're going to go home. What do you need to do? You guessed it: nothing! You're already there. The journey of mindfulness is like that. You feel as if you're getting closer to true meditation, but really *each moment you practise* is true meditation, no matter what your experience.

Setting realistic expectations

If you think that mindfulness is going to make you feel calm and relaxed and free of all problems straight away, you're going to have a hard time. When you first learn to drive, you don't expect to be an expert after one lesson. Even after you pass the test, it takes years to become a good driver. Mindfulness, like any other learning experience, takes time too. Have realistic expectations about mindfulness.

Here are ten realistic expectations to reflect on:

>> 'My mind will wander around. This is what happens in mindfulness, even if it's for a few breaths.'

>> 'There's no such thing as a good or bad meditation. It's like when a small child does a scribble for drawing. It just is what it is.'

>> 'Mindfulness isn't about getting certain experiences. It's about being with whatever arises, moment to moment, with acceptance.'

>> 'I'll sometimes feel calm and sometimes feel agitated and tense in mindful practise.'

>> 'Mindfulness and meditation is a long-term practise. I'll gradually learn to let go of my expectations as I practise.'

>> 'It may be difficult to motivate myself to practise every day, especially at the beginning. Some days I may forget to practise. That doesn't mean I should immediately give up.'

>> 'Sometimes I may feel worse after a mindfulness exercise than before. This is part of the learning process that I need to understand.'

>> 'I can never know how I've benefited from mindfulness. I can only practise every day and see what happens.'

>> 'Even after years of mindfulness practise, I may sometimes feel I haven't progressed. This isn't a fact but an idea. Mindfulness works subtly and below conscious awareness, and so I can't know what's happening there.'

>> 'Mindfulness isn't about what I pay attention to. It's about *how* I pay attention. It's about my attitude. Can I bring a bit more acceptance, kindness or curiosity to this moment now? That's the question.'

4 Reaping the Rewards of Mindfulness

Discover the wonderful ways in which mindfulness can help you, from boosting your wellbeing to dealing with anxiety.

Try some of the techniques used in mindfulness therapy to manage depression.

Find out how to teach mindfulness to children and pick up some useful tips on mindful parenting.

Chapter **11**

Discovering Greater Happiness

'd just started my career. I had a job with a proper salary going straight into my bank account – much more money than any pocket money or student loan I'd received. The feeling was exhilarating: I'd made it! All those years at school, all those exams at university, slogging away, and now I'd made it. Now what? Spend it of course, I thought. So I went out and spent it. A new car, clothes, the latest gadgets and gizmos – and yet the pleasure was short lived. Before long, that sense of emptiness I'd unconsciously been running from returned. Something was missing. Chasing after stuff wasn't the way to happiness, even though the whole of society seemed to advertise that it was. My search for real and lasting happiness began.

This chapter explores the relationship between the science of happiness and the art of mindfulness. By applying the findings of what makes a happy life along with the contemplative exercises of mindfulness, you can explore ways to be more content and peaceful in your life.

Discovering the Way to Happiness

Before we dive into exploring ways to a happier life, let's take a moment to understand what happiness is.

Most people think of happiness as simply feeling good. Is that true? If feeling good is your definition of happiness, you can never be fully happy. Why? Because the feeling of happiness is just one of many emotions you experience as a human being, like sadness, disgust, anger, fear and surprise. You can't just have one feeling all the time – it's impossible. So defining happiness as just feeling good is simply unhealthy.

Another approach is to define happiness as living a rich, full and meaningful life. This way of defining happiness was suggested by the Ancient Greek philosophers who called it *eudaimonia*, which means human flourishing. Cultivating a rich, meaningful life is also the aim of a well researched mindfulness-based therapy called Acceptance and Commitment Therapy (which is covered in Chapter 13).

I've found this approach to be a powerful way to wellbeing. Rather than focus on my day-to-day happiness levels, I focus on cultivating a meaningful life pursuing actions based on my core values.

A happy life, in this way of thinking, doesn't mean I won't experience pain or hardship along the way. On the contrary, by stepping out of my comfort zone and doing what really matters, I do and will experience painful thoughts and emotions. But I can use the mindfulness skills of stepping back from my thoughts and kindly accepting my emotions as I pursue my dreams. In this way, my day-to-day moods and negative thoughts can come and go as they wish, and they don't need to impact the actions I take. I mainly focus my efforts and attention on what I can choose: the daily actions I take to create a purposeful life.

Happiness requires effort and skill

You may think that if your needs of food, shelter, clothing and loving relationships are met, you'll naturally be happy. Unfortunately, this isn't true. You could have all these things and many more luxuries and yet feel miserable. Why? Because as human beings, happiness is not our natural state. Otherwise, most people with enough money and friends would be happy. Of course, we know that's not true. Depression is the number one disability in the world according to the World Health Organisation.

Humans have evolved primarily to *survive*, not to be happy. So although we may feel good when we eat some delicious food or have a nice time with friends, the feeling soon passes and our mind wants the next thing.

This quote sums up happiness well:

> Happiness is like a butterfly, the more you chase it, the more it will evade you, but if you notice the other things around you, it will gently come and sit on your shoulder. – Henry David Thoreau

Mindfulness doesn't make the feeling of happiness into a goal. Instead, mindfulness teaches you to accept and learn from the rich range of emotions you experience as a human being. As a member of the human family, you're going to feel hurt, sad, angry, shame, guilt and sorrow, as well as happiness.

Denying, suppressing or fighting your negative thoughts and emotions has one effect – they come back stronger. Your life then revolves around trying to get rid of difficult emotions rather that directly focusing on creating a meaningful life.

Being kind, curious and accepting of your difficult thoughts has another effect – they ease, so you can turn your attention on getting on with life doing what matters most to you.

Cultivating happiness in your life has scientifically proven benefits:

>> **Happiness improves your relationships.** You have more friends and get on better with them.

>> **Happiness boosts your intelligence.** No matter how smart you are, you use those brain cells well.

>> **Happiness makes you more optimistic.** You see the bright side in most situations. And your optimism makes you feel happier too.

>> **Happiness makes you live longer and more healthily.** You have lower blood pressure and fight off diseases more effectively.

>> **Happiness supercharges your creativity.** You're capable of coming up with new and innovative ideas for home and work.

REMEMBER

Thinking of happiness as a feeling will encourage you to chase the emotion in an unhealthy way. Instead, focus on finding out what's most important in your life and your values and take action to move towards them. Use your mindfulness and acceptance skills to manage the difficult emotions and let happiness come and go as a side-effect.

Exploring your ideas about happiness

Everyone has their own ideas about happiness means to them. You may have ideas about happiness that you're not even aware of.

TIP

An interesting way of finding out your ideas about happiness is a technique called sentence completion. Complete the following sentences quickly with five or six different answers, without thinking too much:

> The things that truly make me happy are . . .
>
> To be 5 per cent more mindful in my life, I need to . . .
>
> To be 5 per cent happier in my life I need to . . .

Keep your answers handy. Practise this exercise daily for a few weeks to see what kind of answers you get. You may need to act on them, or you may not. Just by becoming aware of your responses, you naturally begin to move towards becoming happier.

Challenging assumptions about happiness

The most common assumption about happiness we've explored is that *pleasure equals happiness*. By maximising the number of positive feelings and minimising the number of negative ones, a happy life is created. It turns out that this is a very small part of the picture. Research shows that pleasure alone doesn't lead to any greater sense of life satisfaction. So, although nothing's wrong with staying in luxurious hotels and enjoying your favourite food, these activities just result in a fleeting feel–good effect.

That money equals happiness is another popular belief. The relationship between happiness and money is really interesting, because society gears itself towards acquiring more money and therefore hoping for more happiness. One experiment compared the happiness of big lottery winners with the happiness of people who had been in a serious accident and become paralysed. That's a serious test: what a comparison! The results showed that after two years, the people who won the lottery went back to the happiness level they'd been at before. The same happened with the paralysed accident victims. Isn't that amazing? Whether you become paralysed or win the lottery, you end up with the same level of happiness in the long term.

This effect is due in part to a process called the *hedonic adaptation* – the tendency for humans to go back to their previous level of happiness despite a positive or negative event or life change. This happens because you quickly get used to your new experiences. For example, think about how you feel when you purchase a sparkly new pair of shoes or the latest smartphone. You feel so excited at first,but soon get used to the purchase. And before long, you see a better product and start longing for that. Annoying but true!

If you live in the U.S., you'll find this study interesting. Research on almost half a million Americans found their happiness levels went up as their income went up to $75,000. But beyond that, more money had no effect on their happiness. That figure probably is the sweet spot where basic needs are met.

TIP

Imagine that you're able to sell your happiness. Once you've sold it, you'll never be happy again – your happiness will be gone. Will you sell your happiness, and for how much? Maybe £1,000? Most people say no. How about £50,000? That gets people thinking, but usually the answer is no. How about a million pounds in cash – crisp £50 notes – in exchange for your happiness? Think about that for a moment. A million pounds. Will you sell it? A million pounds can buy you a lot of stuff, but you'll get no happiness in return. How about a billion pounds?

I find the question of selling happiness an interesting one because it really gets you to reflect on how much you value happiness. But you sell your happiness very easily in the short term. You sell your happiness when you can't find a parking space, if your partner irritates you, or a demanding manager is rude to you. It's easy to forget how much your happiness is worth. Perhaps it's priceless?

WISE WORDS

In the wonderful book called *Happiness,* Buddhist monk Matthieu Ricard states that wellbeing is a deep sense of serenity that *underlies and permeates all emotion states,* including joy and sorrow. This sense of being, or *wellbeing,* is cultivated through 'mind training' (mindfulness and meditation). Mind training involves becoming aware of destructive emotions like jealousy and anger. Rather than acting on them, which just reinforces the self-perpetuating process, watch them arise in your awareness, without judgement. As you watch the negative feelings rise up in you and refrain from acting, or reacting, these feelings naturally subside in their own time. This doesn't mean you spend all day trying to force a grin on your face (although apparently that actually helps), but you see different emotional states as opportunities to find out about them and create an emotional balance between them. You're not pushing them away or grabbing hold of them – just calmly observing them, from moment to moment.

A HAPPINESS RECIPE

I found a sense of happiness through the following 'recipe:'

- A **regular practise** of mindfulness, both in meditation and in everyday life

- An attitude of **gratitude** for what I have

- **Valuing social relationships** and reaching out to spend time with others

- **Letting go** of anything outside my control and accepting life as it is in the present moment

- Having **meaningful goals** in my life that are in line with my core values, and enjoying the journey towards achieving them rather than getting fixated on results

- Practising **stepping back from my ruminative thinking**

- Learning to **accept and make peace with difficult thoughts and emotions** rather than fighting, suppressing or denying them

- Taking **small steps** to cultivate positive habits every day

- Having a light-hearted approach – **laughing** uncontrollably from time to time

- Working with a **sense of service** for the community

I'm far from perfect, and some days tend to go better than others of course. But that doesn't matter to me so much. I no longer think of happiness as just a feeling, and I'm not checking all the time if I'm happy or not. Instead, happiness is about cultivating a deep, rich and meaningful life in line with my values. The practise of mindfulness is always available to me and helps me to access my inner resources for healing, wellness and peace. Consider what your happiness recipe is, and write it down. Which ingredients do you need to be truly happier?

Applying Mindfulness with Positive Psychology

Positive psychology is the scientific study of strengths that enable individuals and communities to thrive. The field is based on the belief that people want to lead meaningful lives, cultivate what is best from within themselves and to enhance their experience of work, love and play.

Mindfulness is one of the powerful tools in the positive psychology toolkit, because evidence demonstrates a link between mindfulness practise and levels of deeper wellbeing.

Psychology traditionally studied people's problems. Psychologists were interested in reducing human misery. This is certainly not a bad thing and has resulted in a number of mental illnesses now being treatable. Through evidence-based talking therapies and sometimes drugs, psychology has helped people to reduce their suffering. The problem is that in their rush to help suffering people, psychologists forgot about how to help human beings have flourishing lives. So psychologists can try to help move people from unhappy to neutral, but they haven't considered how to go from neutral to flourishing. If you drive a car, you know that you can't get very far in neutral! Positive psychologists focus on helping people thrive.

Understanding the three ways to happiness

Happiness is not something ready made. It comes from your own actions.

Dalai Lama

Positive psychology describes three different ways to happiness. You can try use all three interchangeably and consider what approaches are likely to work best for you in the long-term.

Pleasure

Maximising the amount of pleasure you experience leads to some feelings of happiness. Eating your favourite chocolate, going out to watch a film, or going shopping are all examples of seeking pleasure. Being grateful for the experiences you're having or have had can help to enhance the happy experience and make it more long lasting. Pleasant experiences make you feel happy temporarily, but if you keep repeating them they become unpleasant. For example, eating one bar of chocolate is delicious, but not 100 bars of chocolate!

Engagement or flow

With flow, you give 100 per cent of your attention to and are at one with whatever you're doing, whether pleasurable or not. Flow usually requires some effort on your part. The activity involved is just challenging enough to hold your relaxed attention. Refer to Chapter 5 for a complete description of flow.

REMEMBER

You can develop a state of flow in anything you do, if you give it your full attention. This is where mindfulness comes in: developing a relaxed, calm, focused awareness from moment to moment. Even washing the dishes or walking the dog is an opportunity to live in this state of flow, a condition of happiness. Give full attention to whatever you're doing, whenever you remember.

Meaning

Living a meaningful life involves knowing your values and using them in the service of something larger than yourself. We live in an individualistic society, and the word 'service' isn't often thought to be attractive. However, helping others is often found to be the core ingredient for a happy, fulfilling life.

Don't worry: you don't necessarily have to change your job or lifestyle to lead a meaningful life. If you're a lawyer who wants to make as much money as possible, that severely limits your overall sense of happiness. The same work can offer more meaning, with the right motivation. Justice, equality, the inner desire to help others – all give you a much greater sense of meaning and purpose in such a career.

Other ways of creating greater meaning include volunteer work or joining a religious or spiritual group. Simply performing acts of kindness wherever you can gives life greater meaning. You don't have to make a massive world-changing difference: cracking jokes with friends, making tea for everyone at the office or organising a group holiday all count, if they are important values to you.

TIP

Take a few moments to reflect on what your core values are. Values are the direction you wish your life to go. For example, some of my core values are courageous compassion, creativity, fun and truth. Then consider an area in your life where you wish to achieve a goal, like, for example, going on a date. Then take some time to consider which value you'd like to apply to your goal. So let's say it's creativity and fun. So you could ask someone if they'd like to go on a date to somewhere fun. In that way, you'll be motivated to achieve your goal and more likely to have a nice time, because it truly likes up with fun, something you value. Chose a domain of your life and have a go. This is a mindful and reflective way to take action to move towards a more fulfilling life.

Using your personal strengths mindfully

Positive psychologists carefully analysed a range of strengths and virtues, and found 24 of them to be universally significant across cultures. By discovering and using your strengths in your work and home life you achieve a greater sense of wellbeing because you're doing something you're good at and that you love doing.

Table 11-1 shows the 24 key signature strengths under six key categories. Scan through the list and reflect on what you think are your five main strengths or virtues.

TABLE 11-1 **The 24 Signature Strengths**

Wisdom	Courage	Love	Justice	Temperance	Transcendence
Creativity	Bravery	Intimacy	Responsibility	Forgiveness	Appreciation
Judgement	Perseverance	Kindness	Fairness	Self-control	Gratitude
Curiosity	Integrity	Sociability	Leadership	Humility	Optimism
Love of learning	Enthusiasm			Caution	Humour
Perspective					Spirituality

The great thing about discovering your signature strengths is finding a strength you never knew you had. I found out that one of my strengths was kindness. I never thought of that as a strength, but it is. And it makes me happy to offer kindness to others. You too can dust off your undiscovered strengths and apply them to your life.

Link your strengths with your mindfulness practise by becoming more aware of when you do and don't use your strengths. Also, notice what effect mindfulness meditation has on your signature strengths – for example, you may find that you become better at leadership as your confidence grows, or that your general level of curiosity increases.

For example, say one of your undiscovered strengths is a love of learning, but your job is boring and seems to involve repeating the same thing every day. How can you use your love of learning? Well, you do an evening course, start a master's degree or make time to read more. Or you can integrate your strength into your work in a mindful way. Become aware of each of the tasks you do and think about what makes that task boring. Look at co-workers and discover what attitudes others have that make them feel differently about the job. Discover something new about the work every day, or research ways of moving on to a more suitable career. By doing so, you use your strength and feel a bit better every day.

To increase your day-to-day feelings of happiness, try this:

>> Discover your signature strengths. You can discover your own strengths for free at www.authentichappiness.org.

>> Use your signature strengths in your daily life wherever you can and with a mindful awareness.

>> Enjoy focusing more on the process and less on the outcome.

LOOKING ON THE FUNNY SIDE OF LIFE

One of my top five signature strengths turns out to be humour. Now, let me make it clear, that doesn't mean I'm going to be the next big hit on the comedy circuit. It means I particularly love laughing and making others laugh. I never thought of it as a strength until I discovered that I rated highly for it in the signature strengths test I did online. Now I know that, I value time to be with friends and colleagues who like to see the funny side of life. I also use it to see life in a light-hearted way when things aren't going my way, and let myself clown around regularly. I apply this value when I need to achieve a goal in my life too, and I try and make the process fun for myself and others. In this way, I'm more motivated and certainly more likely to enjoy whatever I'm doing. I still haven't worked out how to make doing my accounts funny, so if you have any ideas, let me know!

Mindfulness is an important practise, but if you take it too seriously you miss out on an important attitude. By discovering your own signature strengths, you can spend more time developing them in a mindful way. When I'm coaching clients in mindful living, I sometimes recommend identifying strengths as an beneficial approach.

Writing a gratitude journal

The human brain is designed to remember things that go wrong rather than right. This is a survival mechanism and ensures that you don't make the same mistake again and again, which may be life-threatening if you live out in the jungle and need to remember to avoid the tigers. If you don't live in the jungle, focusing on the negative is a problem. The antidote for the human brain's tendency to look for what's going wrong is to consciously focus on what's going well – in a nutshell, gratitude. And research has found gratitude to be very effective.

A gratitude journal is a powerful and simple way of boosting your happiness. The journal is simply a daily record of things in your life that you're grateful for. Research has found that if, at the end of each day, people reflect on what made them grateful, their levels of gratitude increase and people feel significantly happier. It works!

TIP

Here's how to write an effective gratitude journal:

1. **Get a book or diary in which you can make a daily record.** As long as it has sufficient space for you to write three sentences every day, that's fine. Make sure you leave it by your bedside to help remind you to practise. That's important.

2. **Every evening, before you go to bed, write down three things that you're grateful for.** Try to vary what you're grateful for. Writing that you're grateful for your cat, apartment, and car every single day isn't as effective as varying it, unless you really mean it and feel it. You don't have to choose huge things: anything small, even if you feel only slightly grateful about it, will do. Examples include having a partner (or not having a partner!), enjoying a conversation at work, a relaxing drive home, a roof over your head. You're training your gratitude muscle. The more you practise, the better you get at focusing on what's going well in your life. Include why you're grateful for that thing to deepen the experience.

3. **Notice what effect your gratitude diary has on the quality and quantity of your sleep and how you generally feel throughout the day.** By checking in on how you're feeling and what effect the exercise is having, you're able to fine-tune it to work for you. Noticing the benefits of gratitude also helps to motivate your practise.

4. **Continue to practise regularly if you find it beneficial.** After a while, gratitude will become a pleasant habit.

If you don't like doing your gratitude journal in the evening, try the morning, like me. Reflect on what you were grateful for on the previous day, or in life in general.

Through practising mindfulness meditation, you may naturally find that you're grateful for the simpler things in life and feel happier as a result. Writing a gratitude journal complements your daily mindfulness practise very well (refer to Chapter 9 for a daily routine). Both gratitude and mindfulness are proven to boost your happiness, so you're sure to feel more emotionally resilient over time. You can even write the journal together with a loved one, to deepen your relationship.

If you don't like writing a journal, simply think about what's going well in your life as you drift off to sleep, or even on your morning commute.

TIP

The *gratitude visit* is a very popular experiment among positive psychologists, because it's so powerful. Think of someone who made a big difference to your life who you haven't properly thanked. Write a letter to express your gratitude to that person. Really take your time to reflect on all the ways you value this lovely person. If you can, arrange to visit the person and read the testimonial to him. Even three months later, people who express their gratitude in this way feel happier and less depressed. Add mindfulness to this exercise by simply being aware of your thoughts and feelings that arise as you do the exercise. See what happens. I did this recently for my friend on her birthday and she loved it, and she did the same for me on my birthday!

Savouring the moment

Savouring the moment means becoming aware of the pleasure in the present time by deliberately focusing attention on it. The process of savouring includes mindfulness but includes some practises that are different too. Here are some ways of developing this skill:

>> **Mindfulness.** Being aware of what you're doing in the moment is the only way of ultimately savouring the moment. If your mind and heart are in two different places, you miss the joy of the moment – the breeze that passes through the trees or the flower on the side of the pavement. Most of the exercises in this book help you to grow your inner muscle of mindfulness. In savouring, the idea is to be mindful of the pleasant aspects of the experience in particular.

>> **Sharing with others.** Expressing your pleasure to those around you turns out to be a powerful way of savouring the moment. If you notice a sunset or beautiful sky, share your pleasure with others. Letting someone know about the pleasure it gave you helps to raise the positive feeling for both of you. However, don't forget to look carefully at the beautiful thing first – sometimes it's easy to get carried away talking and miss the beauty of the moment itself.

PAINTING JOY

Last year, I decided to paint the walls my living room. Now, you may see this as a boring task with no particular opportunity apart from getting the room painted, or you may see it as a fantastic chance to be absolutely 100 per cent mindful of the task. I decided to try the mindful approach.

I felt the bristles on the brush as I dipped the brush into the thick paint, connected with the sensations in my arm as I moved the brush over to the edge of the wall, and enjoyed watching the colour magically release itself from the brush and onto the surface. As I got into a calm, rhythmic movement, I gradually lost my usual sense of self and was at one with the painting. By the time I finished, I felt energised and uplifted. I'd been fortunate enough to enter the state of flow, or mindful awareness.

Think about a task that you find boring or repetitive, try to give the task your full mindful awareness and see what happens.

>> **Seeking new experiences.** Vary your pleasurable experiences rather than repeating the same ones over and over again – it's a happier experience. I love pushing my boundaries and trying out new things because I feel like I'm pushing myself outside my comfort zone, and the experience naturally makes me more mindful and helps me learn something new.

And if you like ice cream, eat it once in a while and with full mindful awareness rather than feeling guilty about it. That's practising savouring!

Helping others mindfully

Of the three ways of achieving satisfaction in life (pleasure, engagement, and meaning), engagement and meaning are by far the most effective, and of the two, *meaning has been found to have the most positive effect.*

To achieve deeper meaning, you work towards something that's greater than yourself. This involves doing something for others – or, in other words, helping others. A meaningful life is about meeting a need in the world through your unique strengths and virtues. By serving a greater need, you create a win–win situation: the people you help feel better, and you feel better for helping them.

Compassion motivates us to relieve others of suffering. Research shows that compassion has deep evolutionary benefits. Your heart rate slows down, and you release the social bonding hormone called oxytocin and experience feelings of pleasure. Research on even short courses in cultivating compassion has found that people report long-term feelings of happiness.

Going back to the Dalai Lama, he states:

> *'If you want others to be happy, practise compassion. If you want to be happy, practise compassion.'*

I often attend talks by the Dalai Lama or volunteer for his public events. The Dalai Lama almost radiates warmth and compassion in the way he speaks to and interacts with others. Recently, I watched him speaking with a bishop on stage in Italy. As the Dalai Lama spoke to the bishop, he held his hand as if the two were good friends. The Dalai Lama stated that he'd love to attend one of the bishop's religious ceremonies. And he shared the importance for us all to respect each other's religion to create greater harmony in the world. These are all acts of compassion.

Here are the Dalai Lama's suggestions to develop greater compassion and therefore happiness in your life:

» **Understand what true compassion is.** Compassion isn't desire or attachment. When you're genuinely compassionate for your partner, you wish for him to be happy. The ultimate form of compassion for your partner means that even if he behaves negatively or leaves you, you're happy for him if he's happy. That's not easy! Just start by imagining yourself in his shoes when he goes through a tough time, and wish for his difficulties to end soon.

» **Realise that, like you, everyone wants to be happy and not suffer.** Once you begin to see how we're all the same underneath our thin layer of skin, you feel greater compassion for others. Compassion grows when you see how everyone's essentially the same, with the same desires and the same essential needs.

» **Let go of anger and hatred.** You can do this by investigating your feelings of anger and hatred for others. Do they serve you? Do they make you feel happier? Even when you think that your anger gives you the energy to act on injustices, look more closely: anger shuts down your rational brain and can make your actions destructive and unkind. Investigate and observe mindfully for yourself. Notice the difference between acting as if you're angry and actually being angry. The former is less destructive.

» **See compassion as strong, not weak.** Compassion and patience are mistakenly thought of as weak. Actually they offer great strength. People who react quickly with anger are not in control of themselves. Whereas someone who listens, is patient and compassionate is tremendously resilience and strong. Think of people like Gandhi, Mother Teresa and Martin Luther King Jr. They are considered incredibly compassionate, wise and courageous, not weak at all.

» **Be grateful for your enemies.** If you want to learn tolerance and patience – qualities of compassion – you can't learn from your friends. You need a challenge. So when someone annoying comes into your life, be thankful for the opportunity to cultivate compassion! Understand that this person has a deep desire for happiness, just like you do. He may be looking for happiness in the wrong way. Wish that he finds a better path to happiness and therefore doesn't suffer so much. If he suffers more, he may just cause more pain for others.

» **Treat whoever you meet as an old friend, or as a brother or sister.** That makes you feel happier straight away!

» **See beyond people's outer appearances.** They may look different, dress differently, or act differently. But remember that underneath we're all the same. We're all part of the same human community.

TESTING SELFISH AND SELFLESS HAPPINESS

In positive psychology classes, teachers sometimes give students the task of doing something for their own happiness followed by doing something to make someone else happy.

Students who do something for their own pleasure – like watching a film, eating out in a restaurant, or surfing on the Internet – find the happiness to be short-lived and lacking in depth.

The students then do something that will make someone else happy, such as giving their partner a massage or complimenting a friend. Students always find that making others happy is far more enriching and fulfilling than just making themselves happy, with the sense of happiness lasting for much longer.

Why not try making someone happy today?

By cultivating compassion, you make a positive contribution to the world. When you feel a little happier, you make the world a happier and more peaceful place to live. The planet is our home, and the best way to protect it is through compassion – positive relations with others. Ultimately, it's vital for the survival of our species.

TIP

A great way to develop your capacity for compassion is to practise the loving kindness mindfulness meditations in Chapter 6.

REMEMBER

Doing things just for your own happiness doesn't really work. Imagine cooking a meal for the whole family and then just eating it yourself and watching the rest of the family go hungry. Where's the fun in that? The food may taste good, but without sharing you miss something really important. Happiness is the same. If you practise mindfulness just for your own happiness and for no one else, the mindfulness has a limited effect. Expand your vision and allow your mindfulness to expand to benefit all, and you'll find it far more fulfilling. Each time before you practise, recall the positive effect mindfulness has on both yourself and those around you, ultimately making the world a better place to live in. (Refer to Chapter 6 for an exercise in metta meditation, which encourages kind feelings for yourself and others.)

Generating Positive Emotions with Mindfulness

Mindfulness is about offering a warm, kind, friendly, accepting awareness to your moment-by-moment experience, whatever that may be. For this reason, any practise of mindfulness, in the long term, develops your ability to generate positive feeling towards your inner (thoughts, emotions) and outer (world) experience. To develop this further, try the exercises in this section.

REMEMBER

Mindfulness practise is like training in the gym. You may feel uncomfortable at first, but through regular practise you get better at being mindful in each moment. Because it's such a gradual process, you may not notice any change at first, but just trust in the process and give it a decent try. Keep going to the brain gym!

Breathing and smiling

A smile makes you master of yourself. When you smile, you realise the wonder of the smile.

Thich Nhat Hanh

Research has found a connection between the muscles you use to smile and your mood. You smile when you feel good – but interestingly, simply smiling makes you feel good. It works both ways.

You can test this out for yourself. Try smiling right now and simultaneously think a negative thought. Can you? I find that smiling certainly has an effect over negative mood.

Smiling's contagious: have you noticed how infectious a smile is? If you see someone smiling, you can't help but do the same. It also reduces stress: by deliberately becoming aware of your breathing and smiling, you act against the body's automatic defence mechanism and allow a more restful and calm state to occur.

Thich Nhat Hanh, a world-famous Zen teacher, has dedicated his life to the practise of mindfulness. One of his recommended practises is breathing and smiling. He offers the following meditation. Try reciting these lines as you breathe in and out:

Breathing in, I calm body and mind.

Breathing out, I smile.

Dwelling in the present moment

I know this is the only moment.

PLAY THIS

Have a go at this mindful smiling exercise, which is available as an audio track (Track 19):

1. Sit in a really nice warm and cosy place, where you feel safe and comfortable.

2. Take a few moments to stretch your arms. As you do so, gently smile.

3. Come back to a relaxed seated posture, or any other posture that feels right for you.

4. Gently close your eyes. Hold that gentle smile on your face, even if you don't actually feel happy or smiley at the moment.

5. Enjoy the feeling of each in- and out-breath. Imagine your breath has the quality of happiness within it. With each in-breath, you're breathing in smile energy.

6. As you breathe in, say to yourself: 'Breathing in, I calm my body and mind.'

7. As you breathe out, say to yourself: 'Breathing out, I smile.'

8. While you continue this exercise, simply say to yourself 'breathing' on each in-breath and 'smiling' on each out-breath.

9. Persevere for a few minutes to see what happens. The process may feel fake, contrived, or uncomfortable. Or it may feel great!

10. Stop this exercise after around five to ten minutes. Notice how you feel having completed this process.

REMEMBER

Smile, especially when you don't feel like it or it feels unnatural. Even if you don't feel great, smiling has a small effect. You're planting the seeds of happiness. With time, the seeds are sure to grow.

Mindful laughter

Everyone enjoys a good laugh. A good belly laugh has physical, mental, and social benefits.

Physically, laughter relaxes your whole body, decreases your stress hormones, releases endorphins (your body's natural feel-good hormone), and improves heart and blood vessel function. Mentally, you'll feel less anxious and be more resilient to life's stressors. And socially, laughter brings people closer to you, and through it you can defuse conflict more easily and enhance teamwork.

I've combined mindfulness practise with laughter yoga (developed by Dr Madan Kataria) to enhance the process. In this way, you don't have to find a reason to laugh: you can laugh any time!

Here are a few of the key principles:

>> **You don't need a reason to laugh.** You don't need to have jokes, comedy routines, or anything like that. You can if you'd like, but it's not necessary – simply having a playful attitude and creating sounds of laughter is sufficient.

>> **Fake it until you make it.** The idea is to do fake laughs. If they turn into real laughs, great. If not, that's fine too! With practise, you'll get better at it. It'll feel very strange at first, but just persevere and you'll find yourself laughing for real at the silliness of the whole thing!

>> **Be conscious and enjoy the experience, however it goes.** Most people aren't used to laughing much. And many people don't laugh at all. So it'll take time at the beginning. With experience, you'll be laughing more easily. It's just a matter of getting used to it. Because the neurons in your brain that fire together, wire together, with practise you'll be able to enjoy and laugh more easily at life's ups and downs.

TIP

Have a go at this mindful laughter exercise. You can do this exercise with a friend or even with a group of friends or family members:

1. **Begin by doing a mindfulness exercise together with a smile on your face.** Any mindfulness meditation from this book is fine. The breathing and smiling exercise above is a good one.

2. **Now look someone in the eye and, as you clap, say, 'Ho, ho, ha, ha, ha.'** Make the sounds of laughter. Be as playful with this as you can. Be non-judgemental and let go of your inhibitions if you can. Be like a child for just the next few minutes.

3. **Try the handshake laugh. As you and your friend shake hands, look each other in the eye and do some fake laughs.** You may find yourself finding it funny. But if not, no worries. You're just warming up.

4. **Take a few moments to just calmly breathe and stretch between these laughter exercises.**

5. **Now sit in a circle or facing each other and laugh.** Any kind of fake silly laugh will suffice. Have eyes open or closed. Listening to the laughter of others can kick off your own laughter. Laughter is contagious. Let the joy bubble up inside you. And remember: there's no need to think you're doing it incorrectly if your laugh isn't a real one at the moment. You're just starting the journey of mindful laughter. Get serious about laughter by seriously laughing!

6. **Finish with another mindfulness exercise in this book.** It can be simply mindfulness of breath or some relaxing mindful walking. Or lie down and try doing the body scan meditation.

TIP

If you really don't enjoy this approach to laughter, try to watch more comedies or spend time with people who make you laugh. See the funny side of things, and avoid taking things too seriously, by asking, 'Is there a more light-hearted way of seeing this situation?'

MINDFULNESS INCREASES HAPPINESS: THE PROOF

Jon Kabat-Zinn of the University of Massachusetts Medical School, and Richard Davidson, Professor of Psychology and Psychiatry of University of Wisconsin-Madison, and their colleagues have proved that mindfulness increases happiness.

The researchers randomly split a group of employees at a biotech company into two groups. The first group did an eight-week course in mindfulness-based stress reduction (MBSR), and the others did nothing. The electrical activity of their brains was studied before and after the training.

After eight weeks, the people who did the mindfulness training had greater activation in a part of the brain called the left prefrontal cortex. This part of the brain is associated with positive emotions, wellbeing and acceptance of experience. Left prefrontal cortex activated people normally describe themselves as interested, excited, strong, active, alert and enthusiastic. In comparison, right prefrontal cortex activated people describe themselves as afraid, nervous, scared, upset and distressed.

The experiment showed that just eight weeks of mindfulness meditation training in a busy workplace environment can have positive effect on happiness. Other studies with more experienced meditators suggest that these changes in the brain become a permanent feature – explaining the mild grin on the faces of experienced meditation practitioners.

Releasing Your Creativity

What is creativity? Where does creativity come from? How can you become happier and more creative? Good questions! The act of creativity is a deep mystery. If creativity is a mechanical process in which you do such and such, it ceases to have its intrinsic uniqueness.

For example, I'm being creative by writing this book. I simply type the words that come into my mind. I don't know where the thoughts are coming from: they seem to arise into awareness and vanish again in the same mysterious way. Creativity is a beautifully magic process that seems to be a natural part of the Universe. By using ways to calm your mind, you find the creative process naturally unfolds itself, which increases your happiness.

Exploring creativity

Play is an important aspect of creativity. If you're willing to play and have fun, creativity is sure to follow on. When you play, you engage the more creative right side of the brain. You let go of the usual rules. If you stick to the normal rules, you can't come up with something new. The new is born from transforming the way you see things.

Let's say, for example, that you're trying to think of something different to do with the family this weekend. Here's one way to get the creative juices flowing:

1. **Write down what you want to achieve.** For example, I'm looking for an exciting weekend getaway with the whole family, to cheer us all up and so that we can have fun together.

2. **Let go of the problem.** Allow the mind to slow down and connect with the breath for five minutes or more.

3. **Write down several things you've done at weekends for fun.** For example, staying over at your sister's place, going to the nearest beach, staying over at your friend's house, going to local museums, playing different sports.

4. **Change your perspective. Imagine you're very rich or you don't have a family, or you live in a forest. What would you do then?** For example, if you were very wealthy, you might fly to a bigger city for the weekend; if you didn't have children, you might book a romantic weekend getaway; if you lived in the forest, you might start building a tree house.

5. **Now see what ideas can be used from that.** For example, you can travel by train or budget airline to a relatively cheap hotel in a city you haven't been to before, you can ask your neighbours whether you can stay at their country home for the weekend, or you can find a hotel that caters for children while you spend some quality time with your partner.

To be highly creative, you need to calm the mind completely. Many research papers show that a calm and relaxed mind is far more creative than an anxious and stressed one. This stage of creativity is called incubation: you allow your mind to incubate your challenge and see what creative solutions arise.

When you're calm, your thoughts aren't firing off too often, so you have space for creative ideas to rise to the surface. Creativity is a bit like looking for treasure at the bottom of a lake. If the water is choppy and murky, you can never see the treasure below. But if the lake is clear and calm, you can easily see it. Mindfulness gives space for the mind to become calm, and at the same time raises your level of awareness. You're not forcing calmness, you're just creating the right conditions for it to happen.

I often get new ideas when practising informal mindfulness. I can be going for a stroll through my local park, looking at the trees, or enjoying the blueness of the sky when a new idea pops into my head. I usually carry around a small notebook in which to jot ideas down. I don't do this when I'm doing formal mindfulness meditation, however, because that would be a distraction. I don't *try* to get ideas or force them to come up.

REMEMBER

Keep your mind engaged in the moment, and ideas naturally arise. Recall, if you're trying to remember where you left your keys, no matter how hard you try, you can't remember where they are. Then you forget about it, and whoosh – the location shoots into your head. This almost effortless approach is part of the way creativity works.

Look at Figure 11-1.

FIGURE 11-1:
Optical illusion.

If you haven't seen this illusion before, you probably see a series of random dots. Now try feeling your breath, becoming aware of the feelings and sensations in your body for a few moments, and then look again in a more relaxed way. As best you can, let go of any frustrations or desires to 'get it.' Spend a few minutes doing this. Look at the image just as it is. Has it changed? Can you see it from a different perspective? Be patient and see what unfolds. I'm going to tell you now, are you ready . . . it's a Dalmatian. If you still can't see the dog, what can you do? You can ask someone else, come back to it later, or try looking from different angles – in other words, you look for creative alternative ideas. Can you see how getting frustrated may be a natural reaction but isn't helpful?

This shows how the same thing (that picture) can be seen in two different ways. One seems random, and the other a fairly clear image of a dog. We create our reality. If you let go and look deeply, other realities can unfold. The interesting thing is, once you've 'seen' it, you can't forget it! Sometimes you may do this with problems too: seeing the same problem instead of new and innovative approaches to a solution. Try letting go of the obvious answer: walk away, meditate, do something else, and come back to the challenge later on with a refreshed and therefore more creative and happier mind.

MOMENTS OF GENIUS

Arguably one of the greatest scientific creative thoughts in the last hundred years didn't occur in a lecture theatre or seminar with top scientists. It arose in the relaxed, curious, open and questioning mind of a teenager. Einstein's greatest moment of genius occurred to him when he was 16 years old, strolling along and dreaming about what it would feel like to ride on a beam of light – which led to his famous theory of relativity. I call that state of mind 'mindfulness of thought': Einstein allowed the mind to wander but was aware of thoughts and ideas arising.

Inventors need to be aware to spot everyday problems that need a new invention. James Dyson was vacuuming in his home when he realised the top-of-the-range vacuum cleaner was losing suction and getting clogged up. He became aware of this (mindfulness) and then went on to design over 5,000 different prototypes before coming up with his famous bagless vacuum cleaner.

Another inventor, George de Mestral, embodied the mindful attitude of curiosity. He was walking his dog on a beautiful summer's day in Switzerland and returned home to find burrs – plant seed sacs – stuck to his dog and his own trousers. With his burning curiosity, he examined the burrs under a microscope to discover that they were covered in tiny hooks which clung onto the loops in his trousers. In that moment, he had the idea to invent Velcro, made of hooks on one side and loops on the other. Genius!

Creating conditions for originality

You can do this mindfulness exercise to kick–start your creativity. Mindfulness helps you to consider your challenge, allows time for incubation, and makes the space for new ideas to arise. As an example, I'm going to use this exercise to think of new ways to better serve mindfulness teachers who I've already trained and who currently get a monthly coaching call from me.

Here's how:

1. **Consider the challenge and state it clearly in a sentence in your mind.** For example, 'I'm looking for a simple, powerful way to better serve my existing mindfulness teachers so they become happier and more effective mindfulness teachers.'

2. **Sit or lie down in a comfortable posture, with a smile.** Have a gentle smile on your face to remind yourself to have fun and be playful – the foundations of creativity.

3. **Be mindful of whatever you like.** For example, right now I'm in a park, and so am enjoying being mindful of the sounds of the birds. You can choose what you prefer – your breathing, your body sensations, your thoughts – whatever is predominant for you now. Practise for a least a few minutes.

4. **After your mindfulness time is up, see which ideas pop into your head.** As I did this exercise, an idea arose in my mind: to offer an advanced mindfulness teacher training programme online for those who've done my basic course. That would help them improve the quality of their teaching. I could also offer to train them to teach compassion-type meditations rather than just mindfulness-based approaches. Did any ideas come up for you?

5. **If no ideas come to mind, do the exercise again.** Remember to see whether you can enjoy the mindfulness exercise rather than making it a struggle.

6. **If you still have no ideas or feel agitated, try going for a mindful stroll or have a mindful cup of tea or coffee.** You may just need to give your brain a rest!

Through this exercise you begin to allow your inner creative space to fill with fresh, new ideas. You clear out the old limiting ideas to make space for the brand new ones. Feel free to interrupt the mindfulness practise at any time to write your ideas down, because this isn't a formal meditation practise but a creativity exercise, so allow yourself to have fun with it and experiment. Enjoy!

Chapter **12**

Reducing Stress, Anger and Fatigue

D ifficulties are part and parcel of life – you can't stop them, unfortunately. What you *can* stop is the way you meet and relate to challenges. Perhaps you habitually go into denial, or maybe you throw yourself in head first and end up overly tired. If you can face the difficulty in the right way, you can take the heat out of the problem and even use the energy generated by the issue to manage your emotions and activities.

Mindfulness offers you the opportunity to become more intimate with your own habitual patterns of operation. If you haven't really noticed how you currently meet challenges, you're bound to have a hard time assessing whether your approach is useful. Whether the way you react is helpful or not depends on what effect your reaction has. If you have no clear idea of the effects, you're not bene-fiting from experience – you're just replaying a record again and again. As this chapter shows, by becoming even slightly more mindful, your awareness grows and something can shift – and the smallest shift can make the biggest difference. As astronaut Neil Armstrong said (sort of): one small step for you; one giant leap for your wellbeing!

Using Mindfulness to Reduce Stress

If you feel you're suffering from too much stress, the temptation is to immediately find ways to reduce it. But mindfulness takes a radically different approach. Mindfulness is saying rather than diving in to immediately reduce your stress, try exploring your relationship to the stress. Become curious about the stress and all your thoughts, feelings and sensations around the experience.

Having said that, research shows that mindfulness does reduce stress, in the short and long term, even well after people have completed training in mindfulness. This is because many people choose to continue to practise some form of mindfulness as part of their daily routine years later, because they found it so helpful. In this section I explore the various ways stress creeps up on you, and how mindfulness can help you meet stress in a different way.

Understanding your stress

Stress is a natural and everyday occurrence. Whenever you have a challenge to meet, doing so triggers the physiological reaction of stress. Stress isn't an illness, but a state of body and mind. However, if your stress level is very high, or goes on for too long, then you can suffer from both physical and mental ill health.

REMEMBER

Stress isn't always a bad thing: when you or someone near you faces a physical danger, stress is helpful. For example, if you see a child running out in the street, the stress response provides you with the energy and focus you need to run and stop her. However, if you're lying in bed, worrying about your tax bill, stress isn't helpful: the result is that you don't sleep. If this stress goes on for too long, your health is likely to suffer.

Stress researcher Richard Lazarus found that stress begins with you *interpreting* the situation as dangerous or difficult and rapidly deciding what resources you have to cope with the challenge. If you interpret an event as dangerous or difficult and you feel you don't have the resources to cope, you experience a stress reaction. This is why one person loves going on a rollercoaster, whereas for another the experience is a living nightmare.

When you interpret a situation as challenging, your body's primitive nervous system is hard-wired to automatically begin a chain of reactions in your body. This includes stress hormones being released into the bloodstream, your pupils enlarging, perception of pain diminishing, attention becoming focused, blood moving from the skin and digestive organs into the muscles, breath and heart rate rising, blood pressure increasing, and more sugars being released into your system, providing you with an immediate source of energy.

In this state of body and mind, called the *fight–flight–freeze response*, you see almost everything as a potential threat. You're in an attack mode and see things from a survival, short-term point of view, instead of seeing the long-term impact of your words and actions. You fight the situation, run away or simple freeze, unable to take action.

Imagine that your boss tells you how poor your last presentation was, and that you're not working hard enough. If you *interpret* this as a personal attack, your blood pressure rises, your pupils dilate, you sweat and feel anxious. Your body behaves as if you're about to be attacked by a life-threatening bear, and you're ready to fight, flee, or freeze. However, if you interpret the situation as 'the boss is in a bad mood' or 'she says the same to everyone – it's no big deal,' you're less likely to trigger so great a stress reaction. The interpretation is far more important than the 'reality' of the situation, from a stress point of view.

Research shows that everyone has an optimum level of stress. Think of stress levels like the pressure of a pencil on a piece of paper. If you push too hard (high levels of stress), you tear the paper or snap the pencil. If you press too lightly (too little stress), nothing you draw can be seen, which is dissatisfying. The optimum balance is between the two. Then a beautiful drawing can emerge. Too little stress leads to a lack of motivation, and too much leads to over-stimulation and ill health. Mindfulness can help you cope with higher levels of pressure before your stress reaction becomes too highly activated.

Here I break down the forms of stress into the following categories and offer some mindful ways to ease them:

>> **Physical stress:** This is when your body is under too much pressure. You may be sitting in one position for long periods, or lifting very heavy weights or exercising your body excessively. Reduce this by simply trying to take more time off and by practising the body scan (Chapter 6) to learn to be kinder to your body.

>> **Mental stress:** This arises if you have too much work to do in too short a space of time. Time pressure can cause stress. Thinking too much and worrying are sources of mental stress. Reduce this stress by practising mini meditations regularly (Chapters 7 and 8) and perhaps mindful walking (Chapter 6).

>> **Emotional stress:** This is often due to relationship issues. Perhaps you've had a communication breakdown with someone or feel very depressed, anxious, or lonely. Practising compassion meditations (Chapter 6) or forgiveness meditation (Chapter 4) can really help here.

>> **Spiritual stress:** Your life lacks a sense of meaning or purpose. You may feel disconnected from other people or nature. The compassion meditations (Chapter 6) and meditating in nature can help. Reading mindfulness books, spending more time with friends or getting some life coaching may help too.

Noticing the early signs of stress

How do you know when you're *beginning* to get too stressed about something? What are your early warning signs? Does your eye start twitching, or do you begin to get a headache? Perhaps you lose patience easily, or begin worrying. By becoming more aware of your early reactions to stress, you can begin to take appropriate action before the stress spirals out of control.

When the pressure gets too much for me, my shoulders tense up and I find it harder to smile, I'm less likely to chat to friends, and generally begin to take life far too seriously! I remember being like this the last time I had a really tough deadline to meet and had far too much work to get done in the allocated time.

Regular mindfulness meditation and doing your daily activities with a mindful awareness makes you more aware of your own thoughts, feelings, bodily sensations and behaviour. You're more likely to be aware when stress levels begin to rise, and you can then take appropriate action.

Take a few moments to reflect on the last time you were stressed. Did you notice what was happening to your body? Which parts became tense? Was it your tummy or jaw? How did your behaviour change? Did you call up your drinking buddies or some other particular friend? What sorts of emotions did you feel? Anxiety or sadness? What thoughts were going through your mind? Negative thoughts about yourself or others? Look out for these changes when facing your next challenge. Then you can begin to practise using mindfulness to relate to your stress in a curious, kind and accepting way.

Assessing your stress

You may find that a stress diary is a useful way of assessing your level of stress from day to day. Stress diaries make you more mindful of the areas in your life that cause you stress in the short term, as well as your own reaction to the stress. This knowledge makes you more aware of the onset of stress and your response to it, allowing you to make more helpful choices to lower your stress levels if they're too high, or at least to view your stress in a more useful way.

TIP

Designate a notebook as your stress diary, and try the following. Write down:

>> How stressed you feel on a scale of one to ten, with ten being extremely stressed

>> What caused the stress

>> The thoughts going through your mind, your emotions, and bodily sensations like headache or tense shoulders

>> How you're responding to the stress – in other words, your actions

Often, running away from what causes you stress isn't a good idea, unless you're in a dangerous situation. Avoiding the feeling of stress is called experiential avoidance. By avoiding situations that cause you stress, the next time you're faced with the challenge, you'll probably find it even more stressful. If you can, turn towards your difficulties mindfully, in small and manageable steps. You'll then be taking steps towards what's important to you rather than being controlled by your stress.

Moving from reacting to responding to stress

When experiencing stress, I call the things that you do automatically, without even thinking about it, stress *reactions*. If you're lucky, some of your reactions may be helpful and therefore dissipate the stress. More often than not though, automatic reactions to stress are unhealthy and lead to further stress. A *response* is more mindful, includes some time for reflection, is aware rather than automatic, and tends to be more helpful.

Your reactions to stress are partly based on what you assimilated in childhood, are partly genetic, and partly based on your own experiences with stress. If whoever brought you up reacted in a certain way to stress, you have a greater chance of behaving in a similar way. Your own experience of ways of dealing with stress also comes into the equation. Perhaps you've always drunk several cups of coffee when you're feeling stressed, and find the caffeine helps you to get your work done. Although you may feel that this is effective, caffeine is a stimulant, and the more you drink the *more* stressed you'll probably become. Changing these small habits can make a surprisingly big difference.

Reacting automatically implies a lack of choice. Through practising mindfulness, you begin to have a greater choice of ways to respond, and can thereby achieve a more satisfactory outcome.

TIP

Make a list of the unhelpful and helpful ways in which you deal with stress:

>> Unhelpful reactions may include drinking too much alcohol or caffeine, negative thinking, zoning out, working even harder, avoiding the situation or eating too much or too little food.

>> Helpful responses may include going for a walk, exercising, meeting up with friends, meditating, moving towards your challenge or listening to music.

As you make your list, don't been too hard on yourself. Instead, laugh or at least smile at your shortcomings. Hey, no one's perfect!

Become more aware of the choices you make following a stressful event, and begin choosing small helpful strategies such as going for a walk. Make use of mindfulness skills to help you make wiser choices. Remember to give yourself a nice big pat on the back when you make a positive choice, even if you'd normally think of it as too small or insignificant an event to reward yourself for. Every little helps!

Here's the two-step mindfulness process for responding rather than reacting when you feel your stress levels rising:

1. **Notice your current reactions.** What are your body, mind, and emotions doing? Are they showing the signs of stress? Acknowledge the fact that you're experiencing stress and that's perfectly natural. Observe how you're reacting to the stress. Your *body* may be tense in certain places. Perhaps you're having indigestion or have had a cold for weeks. Your *behaviour* may be different to usual. You may be snapping with anger for the smallest thing. You may not be making time to meet up with friends. Your *emotions* may be fluctuating. You may feel tired or out of control. Your *thoughts* may be predominantly negative. You may have trouble concentrating. At this stage, you just need to become aware of what's happening, without judging the situation as bad or wrong – just be mindful, without the judgement if you can. By becoming conscious of what's happening within you, *the experience is already transforming*. This is because you're *observing* the stress, rather than *being* the stress. As the *observer* of an experience, you're no longer tangled up in the emotions themselves. You can't be what you observe.

2. **Choose a mindful response.** Now, from an awareness of the level of stress you're experiencing and how you're currently coping with that stress, you can make a wise, mindful choice as to the best way to cope. You know yourself better than anyone else does – you need to decide how best to cope with the stress. As you become aware of your own inner reactions, you make space for creative action to arise, rather than the habitual, well-worn paths you've chosen many times before.

   Here are some suggestions for a mindful response to your stress:

   - **Take as many mindful breaths as you have time for.** Even one nice big deep breath has positive physiological benefits, and everyone can do that.

   - **Do a three-minute mini meditation (refer to Chapter 7) or practise a formal mindfulness meditation for a more extended period.**

   - **Go for a walk, perhaps in the park, or do some yoga, tai chi. or stretching exercises.**

- **Avoid excessive alcohol, caffeine, drugs, and sugary or fatty foods.** And if you do indulge by mistake, see whether you can forgive rather than berate yourself. You're human after all.

- **Talk to someone or socialise.** Even sending a little text message is better than nothing.

- **Watch a hilarious comedy. Or just laugh for no reason.** See Chapter 11 on mindful laughter.

- **Observe the stress rise up in your body and mind and then fall away.** Consider yourself as the witness of stress – whole, complete, and free just as you are. Pretend that the stress is separate from you, which it is in some ways. You can be like the sky (awareness) observing the clouds (stress) as they come and go. The sky is unaffected by clouds, and so you can observe and be unaffected by the stress.

- **Do some mindful exercise such as running, swimming, or cycling.** You can practise vigorously or gently. Experiment to see what you find most helpful.

- **See stress positively.** Think about how stress energises you, releases oxytocin (a hormone that encourages connection with others) and gets you moving. A recent major study found that if you can shift your mindset about stress, the stress goes from being destructive to healthy. Seeing stress in a positive way was even shown to increase people's life expectancy by many years!

Breathing with your stress

Your breath is a particularly helpful ally in coping with stress. Many relaxation programmes are well aware of the power of the breath in regulating stress, and recommend deep breathing to manage it.

Usually, in mindfulness, you simply need to be aware of your breath and don't have to change your breathing rate. However, here are some different techniques you can use to help relieve stress:

» **Diaphragmatic or belly breathing.** You can do this lying down, sitting up with your back straight, or in whatever position suits you. Take a natural breath and allow your belly to fill up with air. Allow the breath to release as you normally do. Repeat for as long as you feel necessary. Feel each breath coming in and going out of your body. (See Chapter 6 for more about diaphragmatic or belly breathing.)

WASHING AWAY STRESS WITH RAIN

Mindfulness groups sometimes take an approach with the acronym RAIN for a mindful way of dealing with emotions. Just as rain falls equally on everyone and provides for your body, so can RAIN help to transform your inner world. Follow these four steps next time you find yourself getting too stressed, anxious, angry or any other overwhelming experience for you.

- **R**ecognise that a strong emotion is present.

  Often, you can easily be swept up by the emotion itself, and immediately begin acting on it. Emotions can be such an integrated part of who you are that you don't give the feeling due credit. Begin with recognition of the emotion. Say to yourself, 'Ah, I'm feeling stressed at the moment,' for example.

- **A**ccept that the emotion is there.

  With strong emotions, sometimes the natural reaction is to pretend that the feeling isn't really present. In this step, you accept that at this precise moment, you're experiencing anger. You can even say to yourself, 'I accept I'm experiencing a strong feeling at the moment.' You aren't being passive and giving in to the feeling. If you don't accept what's here now, you can't hope to manage the emotion in any way.

- **I**nvestigate thoughts, feelings, and bodily sensations.

  In this third step, you're not trying to analyse, but instead to observe what's going on in your mind, heart, and body. It's time to be curious! What thoughts are running through your head? What feelings are you mindful of? What areas of your body feel tense, or burning, or warm, or relaxed? How does your body feel as a whole? Do you have a burning, throbbing, unpleasant sensation, or is the physical expression of the emotion quite pleasant? Where is the core of the emotion located exactly, and what effect does a sustained mindful awareness have on the physical aspect of your experience? Simply observe the sensations.

- **N**on-identification with the passing emotion.

  Emotion has the word motion in it. Emotions are always moving, fluxing, and changing. No emotion stays completely fixed forever. This final step is to try to distance yourself and create a space between yourself and your emotion. By you offering a space, the emotion is more likely to do what emotions do quite naturally, which is to keep moving. Remember that you're not your anger. Emotions come and go, but you don't come and go: you're always here. Another way of seeing this is like clouds in the sky. The clouds come and go; some are black, some are white and fluffy. No matter what happens to the clouds, the sky itself remains unaffected. In the same way, emotions come and go, but your awareness, like the sky, is free.

>> **Counting your breaths.** Adopt a comfortable posture and close your eyes if you want to. Feel your breath coming in and out. Each time you breathe out, count. Begin with one, and work your way up to ten. When you reach ten, start again from one. If at any point you lose count, begin again at one. You may find it difficult to get past the number two or three before your mind goes off into worries or dreams – no problem. All that matters is that as soon as you notice that your mind's drifted off, you start again at one, *without criticising yourself if you can.*

>> **Breathing and smiling.** Sometimes your joy is the source of your smile. And sometimes your smile is the source of your joy. So if you feel stressed, lift up the corners of your mouth as you feel your breathing. For more on breathing and smiling, see Chapter 11.

>> **Deep mindful breathing.** Take a deep breath and allow your belly to fill up with air. Hold your breath for a few seconds and then slowly release the breath. Repeat for as long as you feel comfortable. As you breathe out, allow yourself to let go of all tension and stress as best you can. If you can't, you don't need to worry – just try again later.

>> **Mindful breathing with other activities.** Mindful breathing while engaging in day-to-day activities provides a calming and nourishing antidote to stress. If you're doing a simple or repetitive activity, become aware of your breathing as you do it. For example, as you walk, feel your breath and notice how your breathing rate changes. If you're waiting for your computer to start up, or you're in a queue, or hanging up the clothes on the washing line, simply allow some of your awareness to go to the feeling of your breath.

As you practise, you may become great friends with your own breath. You look forward to being with the breath and noticing its calming, rhythmic flow.

Using your mind to manage stress

Stressors don't cause stress on their own. First, you need to interpret the stress as a problem that may have a negative impact on you. Then the stress reaction occurs. This simple but fundamental process can be seen in Figure 12-1 below. Remembering that you're the observer of your stress rather than the stress itself helps you to become free, and stress becomes less of a problem.

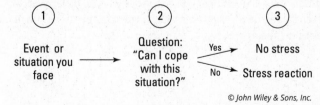

FIGURE 12-1: Stress, interpretation and the observer.

© John Wiley & Sons, Inc.

Use the following tips to lower your level of stress by becoming aware of how you interpret challenges:

>> **Write down the thoughts that are causing you stress.** For example, if you've just suffered a relationship breakdown, just keep writing whatever comes into your head. Nobody else but you needs to see what you write, so be totally honest. The process of writing helps to slow your mind down, and enables you to tackle the stressful thoughts one at a time. Having written them, remember that thoughts are just thoughts – not necessarily facts. Your stress is caused not so much by the thoughts, but *because you believe them to be true*. Seeing thoughts as just sounds and images that pop in and out of consciousness reduces their impact significantly.

>> **See the big picture.** What effect does seeing things from a different angle have on the situation? How would you feel if you were in someone else's shoes? This may be the person who seems to be causing the stress, or someone else – you choose! Or, imagine you're zooming up into the sky, away from your life. See your own town, your region, your country. Keep imagining that you're zooming out of the planet to the solar system and beyond! Is your stress still such a big issue?

>> **Consider what's the worst that could happen.** Sometimes you may imagine the situation to be worse than it actually is. By considering the worst, you may realise things aren't that bad.

>> **Break down the problem.** If you have a big problem and can't face up to the issues, try splitting the problem into small steps. Then take things one step at a time. For example, if you've lost your job and are short of cash, the first step to getting a new job may be to rewrite your CV (résumé). You can even break that down to phoning a friend to help you write one, or getting a book from your local library on writing CVs.

>> **See problems in a different way.** If you see difficulties in life as challenges, your mind may automatically begin to start searching for helpful solutions. If all you see are problems, you're more likely to feel drained and stressed by their weight on your shoulders. See challenges as opportunities to discover new things about yourself and your resilience, rather than problems to be avoided or coped with. Think of this challenge as something that's come into your life to teach you a wiser, kinder way of living.

>> **Discuss the cause of the stress with someone.** The process of talking about your issue is likely to help you to see aspects you never even thought of. And even if you don't, the very act of talking about the issues you're facing helps to dissipate their potency.

>> **Let go of perfectionism.** Perfectionism is a common reason for high levels of stress. Understand that being perfect is impossible to achieve. Adjust your standards by lowering them a little. You can try aiming for 80 per cent perfection and see whether that helps. Notice how the imperfection of a tree with its wonky branches and lack of symmetry is also its beauty. In the same way, see the beauty of your imperfections. This is the ancient Japanese philosophy of *wabi-sabi*.

>> **Appreciate what's going well.** Think of all the things that are going well for you at the moment and write them down. They don't need to be big things – anything you're even slightly grateful for will suffice. Doing so encourages you to feel less stress. You're still breathing? You have a roof over your head? You have a friend? Anything is fine.

LIFE IS THE WAY YOU SEE

How often you experience high levels of stress is at least partly, if not completely, dependent on the way you see things. This old Muslim mystical (Sufi) story illustrates the point beautifully.

A young traveller from another country entered a new territory. She saw an old man sitting under a tree and asked the man, 'What are the people like in this country?' The old man looked up and asked, 'How do you find the people in your own country?' The young woman enthusiastically replied, 'Oh, they are kind, hospitable and generous.' 'Well,' replied the old man with a gentle smile, 'you'll find the people of this country to be kind and friendly too.'

A little later on in the afternoon, another traveller was passing through into the country. He too spotted the old man under the tree, and asked, 'Hey, what are the people like in your country?' The old man asked, 'What are they like in your own country?' 'Terrible,' he sighed. 'They're always fighting, often inhospitable and sly.' The old man answered, 'I'm afraid you'll find the people of this country to be the same as in yours.'

The secret to transforming the level of stress you experience is to change the way you see life. Practising any of the mindfulness exercises in this book regularly will help you to make this change.

Cooling Down Your Anger

Anger can be healthy if the emotion is controlled and used sparingly. For example, if you're being treated unfairly, you may need to *act* angrily to ensure that you're treated justly and with respect. However, being out of control when you're angry can cause tremendous harm both to yourself and to your relationships with others. Cooling down anger isn't an easy process and requires a clear decision, effort, and support from others. Mindfulness can help, as this section shows.

Understanding anger

Anger is a normal human emotion. If you're mistreated, feeling angry is perfectly natural. The problem is knowing what to do with the emotion that arises if you hurt yourself or others with the anger.

Anger arises when you feel something *should* happen but it *doesn't*, for example if you receive poor customer support for something you've bought, or you see how much crime has gone up in your city and feel angry because the government *should* be taking more action.

I don't really have outbursts of anger. The last time I had to *act* in an angry way was during a visit to India a few years ago. A shoe polisher insisted that she wanted to polish my shoes, so we agreed a price and she polished them. Then she tried to charge me ten times more. I refused. She then wouldn't give my shoes back. So I decided to act as if I was angry to get my shoes back! It worked. I had to raise my voice, and I attracted a little crowd. I then gave the shoe polisher the agreed price, which she promptly threw back at me. I was disappointed with her but felt sorry for her too. She was poor, and perhaps I should have given her more money. But this is a simple example of how acting angry can help you get your shoes back!

REMEMBER

Acting angry and *being* angry are different. When you act angry, you don't experience a lack of control or a loss of reason. You can switch straight back to smiling when you need to.

Different situations make different people angry. Like all emotions, anger depends on the *interpretation* of the situation, rather than the situation itself. If someone at a checkout gives you the wrong amount of change and you see this as a mistake, you probably forgive her straight away and think nothing of the oversight. However, if you think that she did this to you on purpose, you're more likely to become annoyed, frustrated or angry. So, it's *your interpretation* that causes the anger, not the situation itself.

ANGER IN THE AISLES

A manager at a supermarket overheard an employee who was helping a customer pack her bags with groceries. The customer said, 'Do you know when you'll get some?' The bagger replied, 'No, I don't know. We may not have any all week, or maybe even longer.' The customer said, 'Oh. Okay, thanks. Bye,' and walked off.

The manager glared at the bagger and chased after the customer saying, 'We'll have some in tomorrow. Don't worry, I'll guarantee we'll get it for you.' He then turned back to the bagger and was furious. 'Don't ever, ever say that we don't have something. And if we don't have it, say we'll have it in by tomorrow. That's the policy. You're useless! What did she want anyway?' 'She wanted rain,' replied the bagger.

When you're stressed out, you're more likely to see things the wrong way.

Anger arises from a thought or series of thoughts. Anger doesn't just come up on its own. You may not be aware of the thought causing the anger you feel, but a thought must have arisen for the emotion to surface. For example, if you think 'That cashier is out to rip me off', you feel anger surging through your body almost instantly afterwards.

REMEMBER

You experience certain physical sensations when angry, such as tensing your shoulders, tightening your stomach, a headache, clenching your hands or jaw, poor concentration, feeling sweaty, increasing your breathing rate, restlessness, and a fast heart rate. Mindfulness of anger includes watching for these signs in your body.

Coping when the fire rises up

You arrive home and your partner hasn't cooked any food. You were working late, and you begin to feel anger rising up in you. What do you do? You know that logically you're far better off talking calmly about the issue and resolving the conflict rather than spoiling the evening with an argument. Here's how:

1. **Become aware of the physical sensation of anger in your body.** Notice the sensations in your stomach, chest, and face. Become aware of your rapid heart and breathing rate. Observe whether your fists or jaw are clenched. Witness the tension in the rest of your body.

2. **Breathe.** Breathe into the physical sensations of your body. Close your eyes if you want to. You may find counting out ten breaths helpful. Imagine the breath entering your nose into your belly, and as you breathe out, imagine the breath going out of your fingers and toes, if you find this useful.

3. **Continue to stay with the sensations as best you can.** Bring a sense of kindness and gentleness to your feelings of anger. Look at the discomfort in the way you would look at scenery – taking your time and being with the landscape of your inner self. Try to see the anger as an opportunity to understand about the feeling, how the burning rises up in your being, and how the breath may or may not have a cooling effect on the flame within you.

4. **Notice your thoughts.** Thoughts like 'It's not fair' or 'I'm not having this' feed the fire of anger. Notice what effect you have by letting go of these thoughts, for your own health and wellbeing more than anything else. If you can't let go of the thoughts, which is common, just continue to watch the way thoughts and feelings feed into each other, creating and recreating the experience of anger as well as other feelings like guilt, frustration, and sadness. If you have lots of energy pumping through your body, try walking around the room and feeling the contact between your feet and the ground. Alternatively, instead of walking, you can try slow, mindful stretching, feeling the body as you extend your various muscle groups.

5. **Step back.** Take a step back from your internal experiences. Notice that you're the observer of your thoughts and emotions and not the thoughts and emotions themselves. Just as images are projected onto a screen, but the screen itself is unaffected, so thoughts, emotions, and sensations arise in awareness, but you, as awareness, are untouched.

6. **Communicate wisely.** As soon as the main force of your anger has dissipated, you may need to communicate your feelings with the other person. Begin with 'I' statements instead of 'you' accusations. If you blame the other person for your feelings, you're more likely to make her act defensively. If you say 'I felt angry when you didn't cook dinner' rather than 'You made me angry when you didn't cook dinner,' you're taking responsibility for your feelings. As you continue to communicate, stay aware and awake to your own feelings, and let go of any aggression if you can – less aggression and more honesty are more likely to lead to a harmonious and productive conversation and result.

Coping with anger is a challenging task, and nobody can follow these steps perfectly. The idea is to keep these steps in mind and follow them with small levels of frustration rather than outright anger. When you do, you become more adept at cooling the flames of anger.

Here are some other ways of managing your feelings of anger:

>> **Be mindful of the thought patterns that feed your anger.** These include:

- **Over-generalising** by using sentences like 'You *always* ignore me' or 'You *never* respect me.' When you notice this, say 'Ah, over-generalising mind!'

- **Mind-reading** by thinking you *know* what the other person is thinking, and often predicting the thoughts as negative, such as 'I know you think I nag you too much.' When you spot this, you can think 'My mind is mind-reading. Thanks!'

- **Blaming** others for your own anger with thoughts like 'You always make me angry' or 'It's all their fault.' Instead, take responsibility for your anger.

» **Take mindful physical exercise.** By exercising regularly, you build up a greater resilience to stress, and this may dissipate some of your anger. By exercising mindfully (see Chapter 7), paying attention to all the physical sensations as you perform an exercise, you simultaneously build up your mindfulness muscles too, leading to greater levels of awareness and less reactive, automatic-pilot behaviour.

» **Connect with your senses.** Listen to the sounds around you or listen mindfully to some music. Smell some of your favourite calming scents. Eat a snack as slowly as you can, chewing and tasting with as much awareness you can muster. Have a shower or bath and connect with the sensations on your skin. Look out of your window and enjoy the sky, clouds, trees, or rain.

» **Question your reaction.** Ask yourself questions like: 'Is this worth it?' 'Is this important in the big picture?' 'How else can I respond in this situation?' 'What is a more helpful thing to do now?'

Figure 12-2 shows how you can use mindfulness to dissipate the anger cycle.

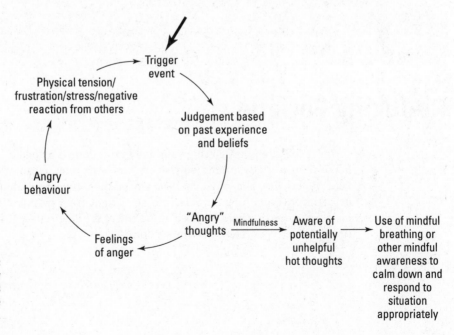

FIGURE 12-2: Seeing how mindfulness dissipates the anger cycle.

DEALING WITH THE ROOTS OF ANGER

If you have a short fuse, you may wonder why you get angry so easily. For many people, the reason is a difficult upbringing. If those who cared for you were often angry, being angry is the only way in which you understood how to react to situations. If your parents or carer treated you badly, you're bound to have feelings of anger trapped inside. Highly stressful and traumatic events can also lead to anger.

If you easily react with anger, you may be using the anger to cover up other, deeper feelings. The anger acts as a protection, to prevent you from becoming aware of more subtle feelings of fear, shame, guilt or embarrassment.

By becoming mindful of the feelings behind your anger, you can begin to unlock the emotional chains that may be controlling you. One way of doing this is by feeling the emotion as you notice it arising, and being aware when it manifests itself in your body. By feeling this with openness and kindness rather than criticising yourself, you begin the healing process within yourself.

Coping with your anger as the emotion arises is a bit like fire-fighting. Dealing with the cause of the anger when you're not in the midst of the emotion is like fitting a smoke alarm and acting before things become out of hand.

Powerful ways of dealing with the roots of anger include mindfulness meditation and forgiveness meditation. Loving kindness meditation, or metta meditation, can also be very effective (covered in Chapter 6).

For an entire book's worth of tips and strategies on coping with anger, see *Anger Management For Dummies* by Gillian Bloxham and W Doyle Gentry (Wiley).

Reducing Fatigue

If you're full of energy, getting your daily tasks done is a doddle – you may come home from work brimming with energy, able to cook, clean, go out with your friends, socialise, and generally have a good time. If you're lacking in the energy department, everything becomes a drag – right from getting out of bed in the morning, to getting back into bed at the end of the day. You can find some helpful tips to reduce your fatigue in this section.

Assessing your energy levels

Begin by assessing your energy levels in a typical week or month. You can do this by simply making a note in your diary or journal. You'll find several benefits of doing this:

>> You discover how your energy levels change from one day to the next.

>> You see at what times of the day you have the most energy available to tackle your more challenging tasks.

>> You may begin to see patterns: certain foods or certain physical activities may be boosting or draining your energy levels.

Practise some mindfulness meditation on a daily basis, just to see what effect the exercise has on your energy levels. Mindfulness isn't a short-term fix but a long-term way of meeting life in a healthy way; any improvements in energy may take some time but be long lasting, so persevere with your practise.

Discovering energy drainers

Some activities are similar to energy leeches – they suck energy out of your system. By discovering and mindfully reflecting on what takes energy out of you, you can begin to reschedule your lifestyle, or reduce your intake of energy drainers. Energy drainers include:

>> **Too much stress.** If you allow yourself to become overly stressed out and don't take steps to manage the stress, you stand to burn lots of your energy. This is because the stress reaction, or fight or flight response, pushes all your energy reserves out of your digestive and immune system and into your muscles. If you keep engaging the stress reaction again and again, your energy reserves gradually become more and more depleted. Use the mindfulness tips earlier in this chapter to help combat stress.

>> **Too much thinking.** If you take your thoughts too seriously, you give your mind undue attention. This tends to feed the mind and encourages you to think more and more. The brain uses a massive 20 per cent of all your energy – if you give thoughts too much attention, they spiral out of control, zapping your energy. Take a step back from thoughts, and don't let thoughts become your master.

>> **Too much sugar.** Although sugar may seem to uplift your energy in the short term, your energy levels soon plummet. Reduce your intake of refined sugar and watch out for low-fat foods that contain high levels of sugar to make them taste good. Read *Mindful Eating For Dummies* by Laura Dawn (Wiley) to learn how to be more mindful with food.

>> **Skipping breakfast.** Lots of research shows the benefits of eating a healthy breakfast. In fact, people who don't eat breakfast not only lack energy but are also more likely to put on weight due to overeating later on in the day.

If you're feeling tired, sometimes you need to rest and sometimes you need to ignore your thoughts and do an energizing activity like mindful brisk walking. Just because your mind says, 'Why am I so low on energy? I'm tired. I want to sleep again,' doesn't mean you need to listen to it. Remember, you get to decide what's best for you, not just your mind. That's freedom.

Finding what uplifts you

You can take control of your energy levels by taking active, healthy steps to raise your liveliness. Keep in mind that you want the kind of energy that's revitalises you rather than the kind that makes you overly excited! Too much of a 'high' eventually results in you crashing out as you burn your energy rapidly. That's okay from time to time when you want to have fun, but not all the time.

Do the following with a mindful, gentle awareness:

>> **Engage in mindful physical activity.** Rather than draining your energy, regular bodily movement actually gives you a boost. This may be due to the release into your brain of a chemical called serotonin that helps you feel better and less frustrated or stressed. Health organisations recommend 30 minutes of vigorous physical activity on a daily basis, which can include a brisk walk to the shops and back. Anything that gets your heart beating, your breathing rate up, and makes you a bit sweaty and out of breath is classified as a vigorous exercise. Read Chapter 7 for more about mindful physical exercise.

>> **Enjoy mindful, regular meals.** Eating smaller portions on a regular basis rather than having a few big meals is healthier and helps to maintain your energy levels. Wholegrain rye bread, porridge, pasta, beans, lentils and noodles all contain energy that is released slowly into your body, helping to sustain you throughout the day. Eat mindfully too, by looking at your food, tasting as you eat, eating one mouthful at a time and not doing anything else when eating.

>> **Drink plenty of water.** Aim to drink six to eight glasses of water a day, and more if you're exercising. Become more aware of your feeling of thirst, or better still, drink before the feeling arises in case you're already dehydrated. As you drink, remember how lucky you are to have water available to you, and feel the water in your mouth and how it has a cooling effect as it goes down into your stomach.

>> **Find your joy.** Make time for activities that you enjoy. You may simply be working too hard. If you can't change that, see what small things you can do to make your work more fun. Spend time with friends and family that are 'mindful' – whatever that means for you. Try smiling more and do mindful laughter exercises (see Chapter 11). Tell someone a joke. Move towards laughter, playfulness or creativity. Act in a silly or childlike way from time to time. Try and see the funny side of life if you can.

>> **Meditate.** Both informal mindfulness and a formal meditation on a daily basis help to increase your energy levels. This is because mindful awareness helps ultimately to step out of your habitual, energy-draining thinking patterns, even if just for a moment. As you continue to practise on a daily basis, your tendency to ruminate diminishes, and therefore your energy levels increase to a healthy level. You find little pockets of peace, calm and rejuvenation.

TIP

Does your mind wander off for long periods of time every time you practise a mindfulness exercise? Do you end up feeling even more tired? If so, stop doing the meditation. Open your eyes for a few moments and reflect on what were the initial thoughts that hooked you into your trains of thought. Then have another go, being mindful of not getting hooked into those particular thoughts. Do this a few times if necessary. Through this process, you'll be able to spot the thoughts that hook you in early on, and you may feel more energized as your mind is ruminating less.

Using meditations to rise and sparkle

Here's an energising meditation, which is available as an audio track (Track 20), that you can practise whenever you want to focus on increasing your energy levels:

PLAY THIS

1. **Sit or lie down in a suitable posture for yourself in this moment.** You may choose to sit up straight in a chair, or lie down on your bed.

2. **Adjust your intention of this meditation to simply be with whatever arises without trying to push things away or grab hold of experiences.** Let your attitude be one of curiosity and kindness.

3. **Feel the gentle rhythmic sensations of your own breathing.** Feel the sensations of the breath from moment to moment, non-judgementally. Just allow the breathing to happen by itself. As you breathe in, imagine you're breathing in nourishing, fresh, energising oxygen into your body. Get a sense of this nutritious oxygen permeating your whole body, feeding each cell generously. As you breathe out, imagine any toxins being released out of your system. Breathe out anything that's troubling you, and let go of unhelpful thoughts, emotions, ideas, or sensations.

4. **With each breath you take, feel more energised and uplifted.** Essentially you're a container of energy, interchanging with the energy all around. Get a sense of this as you continue to breathe. Feel the exchange of energy with your surroundings – both a give and take process; a cycle.

5. **Now come back to a sense of awareness of the breath: breathing itself.** Enjoy the in-breaths and out-breaths with a spirit of acceptance, caring, and empathy.

6. **As you come towards the end of this meditation, notice your transition into a normal, wakeful state.** Continue to be mindful of this exchange of energy taking place with your surroundings as you go about your daily activities.

The following are a couple additional helpful meditations to provide an energy boost:

PLAY THIS

>> **Body scan.** You can do this practise no matter how tired you feel. You simply need to listen to the *Mindfulness For Dummies* Track 9 while lying down on the floor, a mat, or a bed. Even if you're unable to concentrate for much of the time, something will shift. You may drop a stressful idea, you may drift into a restful sleep, or you may feel immediately energised by the end of the practise. (See Chapter 6 for a full description of the body scan.)

PLAY THIS

>> **Three-minute breathing space.** This meditation (Track 17) is ideal if you don't have much time available. If you can find the time and discipline to practise this exercise several times a day, you'll begin to become aware of the kinds of thoughts and emotions running through your system, sapping your vital energy. (Refer to Chapter 7 for a description of the breathing space.)

Chapter **13**

Using Mindfulness to Combat Anxiety, Depression and Addiction

"You are not your illness."

D epression, anxiety and addiction present serious challenges in our society. According to the World Health Organization, depression is the planet's leading cause of disability, affecting over 300 million people worldwide. About one in six people suffer from clinical depression at some point in their lives. About one in twenty people experience *generalised anxiety* at some point in their lives – feeling anxious all day.

Medical evidence suggests that mindfulness is very powerful in helping people with recurrent depression, and studies with anxiety and addiction have been promising too. If you suffer from any of these conditions, following the mindfulness advice in this chapter can really help you.

In fact, most researchers agree that the most well proven approach for people with a range of mental health challenges is called Cognitive Behavioural Therapy (CBT). And the latest form of these therapies make use of mindfulness and acceptance. The most popular are Acceptance and Commitment Therapy (ACT) and Mindfulness-Based Cogntive Therapy (MBCT). You will learn more about them in this chapter.

WARNING

If you think that you suffer from a medical condition, please ensure that you visit your doctor before following any advice here. If you currently suffer from depression as diagnosed by a health professional, wait until the worst of the illness is over and you're in a stronger position to digest and practise the mindfulness exercises in this chapter. Often mindfulness can work well together with other therapy or (in some cases) medication – again check with your doctor before you begin, so he can best advise and support you.

Exploring Acceptance and Commitment Therapy

There are lots of evidenced-based approaches to different mental health challenges. But a new approach has gained popularity that seems to work for a range of conditions as it has been designed by looking at the way all human minds seem to work. It's an approach called *Acceptance and Commitment Therapy*, or ACT (pronounced as one word, not A-C-T).

Here's a great way to summarise ACT:

> **Client**: I want to change BUT I'm too anxious.
>
> **ACT Therapist**: You want to change AND you have feelings of anxiety showing up.

The client believes that he or she needs to fix themselves by getting rid of the feeling of anxiety before they can take action. ACT has shown this approach isn't necessary or helpful.

ACT is radically different from other forms of therapy because the goal of ACT is not symptom reduction. Sounds crazy but it's true! In other words, it's not about reducing your feelings of depression, anxiety or difficult thoughts, memories, urges or sensations.

So what's it about then? The aim of ACT is to help you live a rich and meaningful life by learning to accept your difficult thoughts and feelings that will show up along the way. Having said this, almost every study on ACT has found that through being open, mindful, accepting and commiting to a more meaningful life, symptoms do reduce.

ACT is also different from the other mindfulness-based therapies in that it's not based on a fixed program of sessions. Instead, it can be shared creatively with clients in whatever ways seems appropriate. It can be taught one to one, in groups, in schools, the workplace or any other community. The approach itself is flexible.

QUICKSAND IN ACTION

Imagine a man is going for a walk and falls into some quicksand. He starts to shout and struggle. He tries to swim out of the sand but only gets deeper. He tries to use his feet to force himself out of the sand but sinks deeper still. No matter what he tries to do, he just can't seem to get out of the quicksand. In fact, the harder he tries, the faster he seems to sink. He starts to give up all hope.

A passerby hears the commotion and says, 'Hey, stop trying to struggle to get out!'

'What are you talking about! I have to struggle; otherwise, I'll sink deep into the sand!' replied the man.

'It's your struggles that are causing you to sink. Try this: stop struggling for a moment. Rather than trying to push yourself out, spread your whole body over the sand. Try to stay fully in contact with the sand.'

The man thinks this is crazy advice! By coming into even more more contact with the sand, surely he'll sink deeper and faster. But he realizes he's tried everything else, and nothing has worked. So he decides to give it a go. He tentatively spreads himself out on the sand and stops struggling for a bit. Wow, he stops sinking as much! When he finds the courage to spread himself open on the sand, he stops sinking altogether. He can then think more clearly, find his energy and ask for a rope so he can be pulled out gently and safely. Now he can get on with his life.

This metaphor is often used in ACT. It shows that when you struggle and fight with your difficult thoughts and emotions (the quicksand), you sink deeper into them and feel as if you have to struggle even more. It's understandable because painful experiences are very uncomfortable, but fighting or running just makes things worse. The answer is counterintuitive: instead of struggling, avoiding or running away from your pain, stop and open up to your difficult internal experiences. Accept them, be with them, feel them and then move on mindfully. That's the route to freedom – not fighting your inner experience.

ACT is powerful because it's not just a tool to help you when you happen to be suffering from depression or anxiety, for example. It's a way to build everyone's mental and emotional resilience by increasing what is called *psychological flexibility*. Psychological flexibility is the ability to stay present and do what's most important for you in the long term, bringing along any tricky thoughts, emotions, memories or sensations that may come along for ride.

ACT, through increasing people's psychological flexibility, has been proven to help with a range of clinical conditions, including depression, obsessive compulsive disorder (OCD), workplace stress, chronic pain, the stress of terminal cancer, anxiety, post-traumatic stress disorder (PTSD), anorexia, heroin abuse, marijuana abuse and schizophrenia.

REMEMBER

In ACT, a meaningful life is achieved by helping you find out what your core values are and what your heart's calling is. You are then encouraged to take action to live your values everyday and use mindfulness skills to make room for any difficult thoughts and feelings that will arise along the journey.

All human minds suffer – it's natural

ACT has another radical idea compared to other therapies. ACT assumes that a normal, natural, healthy human being, with enough food, shelter, clothing and loving relationships will still experience much suffering.

REMEMBER

A natural, normal and healthy human mind is highly susceptible to mental suffering, which explains why mental health conditions are so common. In fact, here's an astonishing statistic: Twice as many people suffer from mental health difficulties than by diabetes, heart disease, strokes, cancer and lung disease combined.

This suffering emanates from the way you deal with the pain that arises in your mind. By learning the six flexibility skills of ACT (discussed in the next section), you can increase your psychological flexibility. With greater flexibility, you will still experience painful experiences, but your suffering will decrease.

Six core skills of ACT

To be psychologically flexible, which leads to a healthy and meaningful life according to over 1,000 scientific studies, you need to cultivate the following six skills (depicted in Figure 13-1):

>> **Cognitive defusion:** The skill to be able to see thoughts as just thoughts and notice when you get hooked by thoughts, especially unhelpful thoughts, that could prevent you living in line with your values. When faced with unhelpful

thoughts, you practise seeing the thoughts as just words and pictures, and you then create a separation between you and your thoughts. One way to do this is to think, 'My mind is having the thought. . . .'

>> **Acceptance:** Instead of avoiding difficult thoughts and feelings, you develop the skill of being open to all your inner experiences and don't struggle with them so much. Make space for the difficult inner experiences in your mind. Remember, you don't have to like them – you're just allowing them to be there because avoiding them just leads to more suffering.

>> **Contact with the present moment:** You develop the skill of being present to your moment to moment awareness, and you have the flexibility to move your attention wherever you choose. A simple way to come into the moment is to push your feet into the ground and feel both of your feet.

>> **Values:** You develop skills to live your life according to the principles and beliefs that you possess.

>> **Committed action:** You work to do the things that bring meaning and value to your life.

>> **Observer self:** You have the skill to step back from identifying yourself with whatever you r thoughts tell you who you are in your self-story.

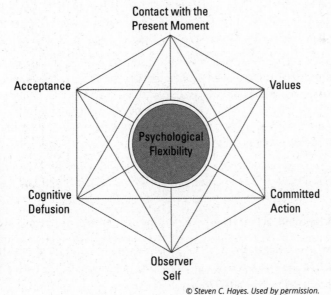

FIGURE 13-1:
In ACT this diagram is often called the *Hexaflex*, these are the 6 skills for developing psychological flexibility.

© *Steven C. Hayes. Used by permission.*

Doing ACT exercises

Here are a few ACT exercises for you to try:

» **Action speaks louder than thoughts.** Say in your mind, 'I can't lift my right hand. I can't do it.' And at the same time, lift up your right hand. Do this at least five times. This short exercise shows you that just because you have a thought doesn't mean it's true!

» **Thank your mind.** Let's say you have the thought, 'I'm so behind in my work. I'll never finish it.' Then simply say, 'Thank you mind!' Wait for the next thought to pop up in your mind. Again say, 'Thanks for sharing mind. Anything else you wish to say?' Doing this will help to improve your relationship with your mind and also create a separation between you and your mind so that you become less fused with your thoughts.

» **Sing your thoughts out aloud.** If you have a sticky, unhelpful thought, sing it to the tune of a song, like 'Happy Birthday.' For example, 'I will never finish my work. I will never finish my work. I will never finish my worrrkkkkkkkk. I'll never finish my work.' This approach helps you to see that the thoughts you're having are simply words or images in your mind – not absolute truths. And it can be quite funny too!

» **Explore 'yes.'** Look around wherever you are reading this. As you see different things, say 'no' either out aloud, or in your mind. Get a sense of judgement and dislike of the different objects you look at. You could even shift your posture into one of avoidance or defense – tensing your muscles and closing in your chest. As you do this, notice how you feel.

Now, do the same exercise but internally say 'yes' to what you see. Get a sense of the objects being fine just the way they are, a sense of being open to them as they are. Put yourself in a more open body posture too, with your chest more open, shoulders back and arms unfolded. How was that experience? How was it different to when you said 'no'?

You may begin to get a sense of the difference between an attitude of avoidance and acceptance. See if you can notice this with specific thoughts, emotions, urges and sensations.

» **Try mindful feet** Here's one of many mindful exercise used in ACT that has proven to be powerful as it doesn't just teach you the skill of being present. You also develop the skill of having a flexible attention. Set a timer for 2 minutes and feel the sensations in your left foot. Notice what you noticed. Then set a timer again for 2 minutes and feel your right foot. Again notice how that was and how it was different to the left foot. Then, finally, set a timer for 2 minutes and feel both feet at the same time.

>> **Imagine you're sitting at a bus stop.** You just need to sit at the bus stop, and one bus after another keeps stopping and moving on. Each time a bus arrives, place whatever thought is in your head onto the side of the bus, and let the bus drive off. This exercise trains you to separate the thought from your mind and not to get fused or 'hooked' to your thoughts. You also step into a sense of being the observer self rather than identifying yourself with your thoughts.

>> **Use your magic wand.** Imagine I have a magic wand and I waved it and all the things you feel you need to achieve are done for you. You feel completely confident and happy. You don't need to impress anyone again or prove anything to anyone. You can do whatever you want in your life from now on. In this scenario . . .

What would you do with your life?

How would you spend your time?

How would you act differently?

How would you talk to yourself and others differently?

What would change?

This exercise can give you some clues about your values and what's important for you. By answering these questions, you can begin setting small, achievable goals that correlate with your values.

There are literally hundreds of exercises you can do in ACT. To find out more, check out *Acceptance and Commitment Therapy For Dummies* by Freddy Jackson Brown and Duncan Gillard or *Get Out of Your Mind and Into Your Life* by Steven C. Hayes.

Dealing Mindfully with Depression

Of all mental health conditions, recurring depression has most clearly been shown to respond to mindfulness. If the body of evidence continues to grow, mindfulness may go on to become the standard treatment for managing depression all over the world. This section explains what depression is and why mindfulness seems to be so effective for those who have suffered from several bouts of depression.

Understanding depression

Depression is different to sadness.

Sadness is a natural and healthy emotion that everyone experiences from time to time. If something doesn't go the way you expect, you may feel sad. The low mood may linger for a time and affect your thoughts, words and actions, but not to a huge extent.

Depression is very different. When you're depressed, you just can't seem to feel better, no matter what you try.

Unfortunately, some people still believe that depression isn't a real illness. Depression *is* a real illness with very *real symptoms*.

According to the NHS, if you have an ongoing low mood for most of the day every day for two weeks, you're experiencing depression and you need to visit your doctor. The symptoms of depression can include:

>> A low, depressed mood

>> Feelings of guilt or low self-worth

>> Disturbed sleep

>> A loss of interest or pleasure

>> Poor concentration

>> Changes to your appetite

>> Low energy

Understanding why depression recurs

Depression has a good chance of being a recurring condition, and to understand why, you need to understand the two key factors that cause mild feelings of sadness to turn into depression:

>> **Constant negative thinking (rumination).** This is the constant, repetitive use of self-critical, negative thinking to try to change an emotional state. You have an idea of how things are (you're feeling sad) and how you want things to be (feeling happy, relaxed or peaceful). You keep thinking about your goal and how far you are from your desired state. The more you think about this gap, the more negative your situation seems and the further you move away from your desired emotion. Unfortunately, thinking in this way – trying to fix the problem of an emotion – only worsens the problem and leads to a sense of failure as depression sets in. Rumination doesn't work, the reason being that

emotions are part of being human. To try to fix or change emotions by simply thinking about what you want doesn't work. Rumination is a hallmark of the *doing mode* of mind, explained in Chapter 5.

» **Intensely avoiding negative thoughts, emotions and sensations (experiential avoidance).** This is the desire to avoid unpleasant sensations. But the process of experiential avoidance feeds the emotional flame rather than reducing or diminishing the emotion. Running away from your emotions makes them stronger.

When you first suffer from depression, you experience negative thoughts, a negative mood and sluggishness. When this occurs, you create a connection between these thoughts, feelings and bodily sensations. Even when you feel better, the underlying connections are still there, lying dormant. Then, when by chance you feel a little sad, as everyone does, you begin to think, 'Here we go again. Why is this happening to me? I've failed,' and so on. The negative thoughts recur. This triggers the negative moods and low levels of energy in the body, which creates more negative thinking. The more you try to avoid your negative thoughts, emotions and sensations, the more powerful they become. This is called the downward mood spiral, as shown in Figure 13-2.

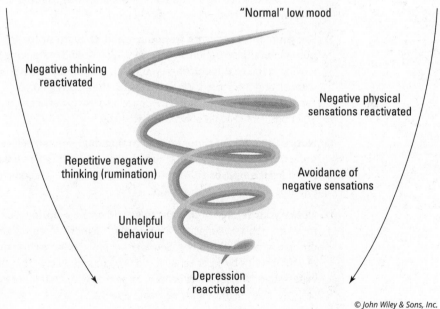

"Normal" low mood

Negative thinking reactivated

Negative physical sensations reactivated

Repetitive negative thinking (rumination)

Avoidance of negative sensations

Unhelpful behaviour

Depression reactivated

FIGURE 13-2: Downward mood spiral.

© *John Wiley & Sons, Inc.*

Using mindfulness to change your relationship to low mood

One of the key ways in which depressive relapse occurs and is sustained is through actively trying to avoid a negative mood. Mindfulness invites you to take a different attitude towards your emotion. Depression is unpleasant, but you see what happens if you approach the sensation with kindness, curiosity, compassion and acceptance. This method is likely to be radically different to your usual way of meeting a challenging emotion.

When you experience a low mood, try one of these exercises as an experiment and see what happens:

» **Identify where in your body you feel the emotion.** Is your stomach or chest tight, for example? What happens if you approach that bodily sensation, whatever the sensation is, with kindness and curiosity? Can you go right into the centre of the bodily sensation and imagine the breath going into and out of the sensation? What effect does that have? If you feel too uncomfortable doing that, how close can you get to the unpleasant feeling in your body? Try playing with the edge of where you're able to maintain your attention in your body, neither pushing too hard nor retreating away. Try saying to yourself: 'It's okay, whatever I feel, it's okay, let me feel it.'

» **See yourself as separate from the mood, thought or feeling.** You're the observer of the sensation, not the sensation itself. Try stepping back and looking at the sensation. When you watch a film, you have a space between yourself and the screen. When you watch the clouds going by, a space separates you from the clouds. A space also exists between you and your emotions. Notice what effect this has, if any.

» **Notice the kinds of thoughts you're thinking.** Are they self-critical, negative thoughts, predicting the worst, jumping to conclusions? Are the thoughts repeating themselves again and again? Bring a sense of curiosity to the patterns of thought in your mind.

» **Notice your tendency to want to get rid of the emotion.** See if you can move from this avoidance strategy towards a more accepting strategy, and observe what effect this has. See whether you can increase your acceptance of your feelings by 1 per cent – just a tiny amount. Accept that this is your experience now, but won't be forever, so that you can temporarily let go of the struggle, even slightly, and see what happens.

UNDERSTANDING AVOIDANCE AND APPROACH MODES

The more you try to avoid an emotion, the greater the emotion grasps hold of you and strengthens. However, by approaching the emotion, you begin to open up the possibility of releasing yourself from its hold. By approaching the sensations with a sense of kindliness, compassion and gentleness, you create the possibility of allowing and accepting your present-moment experience as it is. You let go of the possibility of a downward mood spiral created by an avoidance mode of mind.

Professor Richard Davidson, top neuroscience professor at the University of Wisconsin-Madison and friend of the Dalai Lama, has shown that the avoidance mode of mind is associated with activation of the right prefrontal cortex part of the brain (commonly seen in those in depression), and the approach mode of mind is associated with greater activation in the left prefrontal cortex part of the brain (commonly seen in more positive people). He's also shown that mindfulness helps to move people's brain activation from right to left, in other words from avoidance mode to approach mode. This creates a healthier, more open, detached stance towards emotions, thereby allowing them to operate in a more natural way. In a nutshell, mindfulness can train your brain to become healthier!

>> **Try doing a three-minute breathing space as described in Chapter 7.** What effect does this have? Following the breathing space, make a wise choice as to what is the most helpful thing for you to do at the present moment to look after yourself.

>> **Recognise that recurring ruminative thinking and having a low mood are a part of your experience and *not part of your core being*.** An emotion arises in your consciousness and at some point diminishes again. Adopting a de-centred, detached perspective means you recognise that your low mood *isn't* a central aspect of your self – of who you are.

Discovering Mindfulness-Based Cognitive Therapy (MBCT)

Mindfulness-based cognitive therapy (MBCT) is an eight-week group programme based on the mindfulness-based stress reduction (MBSR) course described in Chapter 9. The MBSR course has been found to be very helpful for people with a range of physical and psychological problems. MBCT was specifically adapted for those who've suffered repeated episodes of depression. Research so far has proven that MBCT is 50 per cent more effective than the usual treatment for those suffering from three or more episodes of depression.

MBCT is a branch of a more general form of therapy called cognitive behavioural therapy (CBT), which holds that thoughts, feelings and actions are intimately connected. The way you think affects the way you feel and the activities you engage in. Conversely, the way you feel or the activities you undertake affect the way you think, as shown in Figure 13-3.

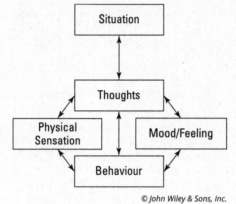

FIGURE 13-3: The relationship between thoughts, feelings and activities.

Traditional CBT encourages you to challenge unrealistic negative thoughts about yourself, others or the world. (Discover more in *Cognitive Behavioural Therapy For Dummies* by Rhena Branch and Rob Willson (Wiley).) Mindfulness-based cognitive therapy takes a slightly different approach. Rather than deliberately considering alternative thoughts, you move towards your unpleasant thoughts, emotions and physical sensations in a more de-centred, kind, curious and compassionate way – in other words, mindfully. The emphasis isn't on changing the experience but on being with the experience in a different way. You develop the ability to do this through mindfulness meditation.

If you want to do the MBCT course on your own using this book, you can follow the eight-week MBSR course described in Chapter 9, and in addition do the activities in this chapter. This isn't the same as doing a course with a group and a professional teacher, but gives you an idea of what to expect and certainly may help you.

THE SCIENTIFIC BASIS OF MINDFULNESS

A recent survey in the USA found that more than 40 per cent of mental health professionals do some form of mindfulness therapy to encourage healing in both the body and mind. In group clinical settings, mindfulness is applied mainly through two programmes:

- **Mindfulness-based stress reduction (MBSR):** An eight-week training in mindfulness meditation for reducing stress in those with a wide range of medical conditions.

- **Mindfulness-based cognitive therapy (MBCT):** Based on the eight-week MBSR course, with added elements of cognitive behavioural therapy, developed to address the problem of relapse in clinical depression, and now being tested and used for a wide variety of ailments.

Dr Jon Kabat-Zinn and colleagues developed MBSR in a hospital setting at the University of Massachusetts Medical School in 1979.

The scientific evidence proving the medical benefits of mindfulness is impressive. Here's a small sample of the research on mindfulness so far:

- More than 200 patients with chronic pain were referred for mindfulness treatment, and large overall improvements in physical and psychological wellbeing following MBSR were observed for the majority.

- A study on the use of MBSR for patients with anxiety disorders showed significant reductions in anxiety and depression scores for more than 90 per cent of the patients.

- In an experiment, some patients with psoriasis were given a guided mindfulness meditation to listen to while in a light box. Those patients healed four times faster than the patients without the mindfulness audio in the light box. This shows that mindfulness itself seems to accelerate the healing effect.

- Several trials have shown that MBCT is effective in preventing relapse in depression, showing that in patients with three or more previous episodes of depression, MBCT reduced the recurrence rate by 55 per cent.

Chapter 9 explores MBSR.

Pleasant and Unpleasant Experiences

In everyday life, you experience a whole range of different experiences. They can all be grouped into pleasant, unpleasant and neutral experiences. Pleasant experiences are the ones you enjoy, like listening to the birds singing or watching your favourite television programme. Unpleasant experiences may include having to sit in a traffic jam or dealing with a difficult customer at work. Neutral experiences are the ones you just don't even notice, like the different object in the room you're in at the moment, or the taste of the tea or coffee you're drinking. Mindfulness encourages you to become curious about all aspects of these experiences.

You can probe your experiences through the following exercise, which is normally done over two weeks:

TIP

Take a sheet of paper, or use your journal, and create four columns. Label them 'experience,' 'thoughts,' 'feelings,' 'bodily sensations.' Under each column heading, write down one experience each day that you found to be pleasant. Write down the thoughts that were going through your head, the feelings you experienced at the time, and how your body felt under the appropriate columns. Continue this each day for a whole week.

The following week, repeat the exercises, but this time for an unpleasant experience each day. Remember, you don't need to have very pleasant or unpleasant experiences – even a small, seemingly insignificant experience will suffice.

The purpose of this exercise is to do the following:

>> Help you to see that experiences aren't one big blob. You can break down experiences into thoughts, feelings and bodily sensations. This makes difficult experiences more manageable rather than overwhelming.

>> Notice your automatic, habitual patterns, which operate without you even knowing about them normally. You learn how you habitually grasp onto pleasant experiences with a desire for them to continue, and how you push away unpleasant experiences, called experiential avoidance, which can end up perpetuating them.

>> Learn to become more curious about experiences instead of just judging experiences as good or bad, or ones you like or dislike.

>> Encourage you to understand and acknowledge your unpleasant experiences rather than just avoid them.

Interpreting thoughts and feelings

You can do this visualisation exercise sitting or lying in a comfortable position:

1. Imagine you're walking on one side of a familiar road. On the other side of the road you see a friend. You call out his name and wave, but he doesn't respond. Your friend just keeps on walking into the distance.

2. Write down your answers to the following questions:

- What did you feel in this exercise?
- What thoughts did you have?
- What physical sensations did you experience in your body?

If you think, 'Oh, he's ignored me. I don't have any friends,' you're more likely to feel down, and perhaps your body may slump. If you think, 'He couldn't hear me. Oh well, I'll catch up with him later,' you're unlikely to feel affected by the situation. The main purpose of the exercise is to show that your *interpretation* of a situation generates a particular feeling, rather than the situation itself.

Almost all people have a different response to this exercise, because they have a different *interpretation* of the imagined event. If you're already in a low mood, you're more likely to interpret the situation negatively. Remember: *thoughts are interpretations of reality, influenced by your current mood.* Don't consider your thoughts to be facts, especially if you're in a low mood. *Thoughts are just thoughts, not facts.*

Combating automatic thoughts

Mindfulness encourages you to recognise and deal with negative automatic thoughts that can prolong depression or cause it to worsen.

Consider the following statements (adapted from Kendall and Hollon's 'Automatic Thoughts Questionnaire,' Cognitive Therapy and Research, 1980):

- » I feel as if I'm up against the world.
- » I'm no good.
- » I'll never succeed.
- » No one understands me.
- » I've let people down.
- » I don't think that I can go on.

» I wish I were a better person.

» I'm so weak.

» My life's not going the way I want it to.

» I'm so disappointed in myself.

» Nothing feels good anymore.

» I can't stand this anymore.

» I can't get started.

» Something's really wrong with me.

» I wish I were somewhere else.

» I can't get things together.

» I hate myself.

» I'm worthless.

» I wish I could just disappear.

» I'm a loser.

» My life is a mess.

» I'm a failure.

» I'll never make it.

» I feel so helpless.

» My future is bleak.

» It's just not worth it.

» I can't finish anything.

How much would you believe these thoughts right now if any one of them popped into your head? How much would you believe them if any one of them popped into your head when you were in your lowest mood? *These thoughts are attributes of the illness called depression, and aren't to do with your true self.*

By considering depression in a detached way, you become more detached from the illness. You see depression as a human condition rather than something that affects you personally and almost no one else. You see depression as a condition that's treatable through taking appropriate steps.

Alternative viewpoints

Alternative viewpoints are the different ways in which you can interpret a particular situation or experience.

TIP

This exercise from MBCT shows how feelings affect thoughts, and thoughts affect feelings. The exercise is similar to the 'Interpreting thoughts and feelings' exercise earlier in the chapter, but focuses more on how you interpret situations depending on how you're already feeling.

Consider the following scenario: You've just been *criticised* by your boss for your work, and you feel low. You walk past one of your colleagues and are about to say something to him, and he says he's really busy and can't stop. Write down your thoughts and feelings.

Now consider a different scenario: Your boss has just *praised* you for doing an excellent job. You walk past one of your colleagues and are about to say something to him, and he says he's really busy and can't stop. Write down your thoughts and feelings.

You probably found very different thoughts and feelings in the two different circumstances. By understanding that your thoughts and feelings are influenced by your interpretation of a situation, you're less likely to react negatively. Mindfulness allows you to become more aware of your thoughts and feelings from moment to moment, and offers you the choice to respond to a situation in a different way, knowing that your thoughts are just thoughts, or interpretations, rather than facts.

De-centring from difficult thoughts

Practise the three-minute breathing space meditation (explained in Chapter 7) and then ask yourself some or all the following questions. Doing so helps you to de-centre or step back from your more difficult thoughts and helps you to become more aware of your own patterns of mind. Here are the questions:

>> Am I confusing a thought with a fact?

>> Am I thinking in black and white terms?

>> Am I jumping to conclusions?

>> Am I focusing on the negative and ignoring the positive?

>> Am I being perfectionist?

>> Am I guessing what other people are thinking?

>> Am I predicting the worst?

>> Am I judging myself or others overly harshly?

>> What are the advantages and disadvantages of thinking in this way?

>> Am I taking things too personally?

Listing your activities

TIP

Make a list of all the typical activities you do in a day, such as preparing food, getting dressed, travelling to work, interacting with others, hobbies, sports, evening classes and so on. Then label each activity as nourishing or depleting. Nourishing activities make you feel uplifted and enthusiastic, giving you energy and joy. Depleting activities drain your energy, making you feel low in vitality and dull in attention. Consider what you can do to increase the number of nourishing activities and decrease the number of depleting activities in your daily routine.

Now list activities that give you a sense of mastery or pleasure. Activities that offer a sense of mastery are those that are quite challenging for you, such as tidying up a cupboard, making a phone call you've been avoiding, or forcing yourself to get out of the house to meet a friend or relative. Activities that offer pleasure may include having a hot bath, watching a film or going for a gentle stroll.

When you feel stressed or low in mood, choose a 'mastery' or 'pleasure' activity. Prior to making your choice, carry out the three-minute breathing space meditation to help bring mindfulness to the experience.

Making wise choices

When experiencing a low mood, a depressing thought, a painful sensation or a stressful situation, practise the three-minute breathing space and choose what to do next, which may include these options:

>> **Mindful action.** Go back to doing what you were doing before, but in this wider, more spacious, being mode of mind (Chapter 5 explains a being mode of mind). Do each action mindfully, perhaps breaking the activity into small, bite-size chunks. The shift may be very small and subtle in your mind, but following the breathing space, you'll probably feel different.

>> **Being mindful of your body.** Emotions manifest in your physical body, perhaps in the form of tightness in your jaw or shoulders. Mindfulness of body invites you to go to the tension and feel the sensations with an open, friendly, warm awareness, as best you can. You can breathe into the sensation, or say 'opening, acknowledging, embracing' as you feel the

uncomfortable area. You're not trying to get rid of the sensations, but discovering how to be okay with them when the sensations are difficult or unpleasant.

>> **Being mindful of your thoughts.** If thoughts are still predominant following the breathing space, focus your mindful awareness onto what you're thinking. Try to step back, seeing thoughts as mental events rather than facts. Try writing down the thoughts, which helps to slow them down and offers you the chance to have a clear look at them. Reflect on the questions listed in the section 'De-centring from difficult thoughts.' Bring a sense of curiosity and gentleness to the process if you can. In this way, you're trying to create a different relationship to your thoughts, other than accepting them as 100 per cent reality no matter what pops up in your head.

>> **A pleasant activity.** Do something pleasant like reading a novel or listening to your favourite music. While engaging in this activity, primarily engage your attention on the activity itself. Check in to notice how you're feeling emotionally and how your body feels, and be mindful of your thoughts from time to time. Try not to do the activity to force any change in mood, but instead do your best to acknowledge whatever you're experiencing.

>> **A mastery activity.** Choose to do something that gives you a sense of mastery, no matter how small, such as washing the car, going for a swim or baking a cake. Again, give the activity itself your full attention. Notice whether you're trying to push your feelings out, going back to habitual doing mode (Chapter 5), and instead allow yourself to accept your feelings and sensations as best you can, which is being mode (Chapter 5). Bring a genuine sense of curiosity to your experience as you go about your activity.

Using a depression warning system

Writing out a depression warning system is a good way of nipping depression in the bud rather than letting it spiral downwards. Write down the following:

1. **The warning signs** you need to look out for when depression may be arising in you, such as negative thinking, oversleeping or avoiding meeting friends. You may want to ask someone close to you to help you do this.

2. **An action plan** of the kind of things you can do that are helpful, such as meditation, yoga, walking or watching a comedy, and make a note of the kind of things that would be unhelpful, too, that you need to try to avoid if you can (perhaps changing eating habits, negative self-talk or working late).

Calming Anxiety: Let It Be

Anxiety is a natural human emotion characterised by feelings of tension, worried thoughts, and physical changes like increased blood pressure. You feel anxious when you think that you're being threatened. Fear is part of your survival mechanism – without feeling any fear at all, you're likely to take big risks with no concern about dangerous consequences. Without fear, walking right on the edge of a cliff would feel no different to walking in the park – not a safe position to be in!

REMEMBER

Anxiety and panic can be due to a combination of factors, including your genes, the life experiences you've had, the current situation you're in, and whether you're under the influence of drugs, including caffeine.

This section looks at how mindfulness can help with managing your anxiety and fear, whether the feelings appear from time to time or whether you have a clinical condition such as generalised anxiety disorder (GAD), where you feel anxious all the time.

Feel the fear . . . and make friends with it

Eliminating fearful thoughts isn't easy. The thoughts are sticky, and the more you try and push them out, the stronger the worries and anxieties seem to cling on. In this way, you can easily get into a negative cycle in which the harder you try to block out the negatives, the stronger they come back.

Mindfulness encourages you to face up to all your experiences, including the unpleasant ones. In this way, rather than avoiding anxious thoughts and feelings, which just makes them stronger and causes them to control your life, you begin to slowly but surely open up to them, in a kind and gentle way, preventing them building up out of proportion.

Perhaps this analogy may help. Imagine a room filling up with water. You're outside the room trying to keep the door closed. As more and more water builds up inside the room, you need to push harder and harder to keep the door shut. Eventually you're knocked over, the door flings open and the water comes pouring out. Alternatively, you can try opening the door very slowly at first, instead of pushing the door shut. As you keep opening the door, you give the water a chance to leave the room in a trickle rather than a deluge. Then you can stop struggling to keep the door shut. The water represents your inner anxious thoughts and feelings, and the opening of the door is turning towards the difficult thoughts and feelings with a sense of kindliness, gentleness and care, as best you can.

Using mindfulness to cope with anxiety

If you worry a lot, the reason for this is probably to block yourself from more emotionally distressing topics. For example, you may be worrying whether your son will pass his exams, but actually your worry-type thoughts are blocking out the actual feeling of fear. Although the worry is unpleasant and creates anxiety, the thoughts keep you from feeling deeper emotions. However, until you open up to those deeper emotions, the worry continues.

Worry is an example of experiential avoidance, described earlier in the chapter. Mindfulness trains you to become more open and accepting of your more challenging emotions, with acknowledgement, curiosity and kindness. Mindfulness also allows you to see how you're not your emotions, and that your feelings are transient, and so it helps you to reduce anxiety. Mindfulness encourages you to let go of worries by focusing your attention on the present moment.

Here's a mindful exercise for anxiety:

1. **Get comfortable and sit with a sense of dignity and poise on a chair or sofa.** Ask yourself: 'What am I experiencing now, in the present moment?' Reflect on the thoughts flowing through your mind, emotions arising in your being, and physical sensations in your body. As best you can, open up to the experiences in the here and now for a few minutes.

2. **Place your hand on your belly and feel your belly rising and falling with your breath.** Sustain your attention in this area. If anxious thoughts grasp your attention, acknowledge them but come back to the present moment and, without self-criticism if possible, focus back on the in- and out- breath. Continue for a few minutes.

3. **When you're ready, expand your awareness to get a sense of your whole body breathing, with wide and spacious attention as opposed to the focused attention on the breath alone.** If you like, imagine the contours of your body breathing in and out, which the body does, through the skin. Continue for as long as you want to.

4. **Note your transition from this mindfulness exercise back to your everyday life.** Continue to suffuse your everyday activities with this gentle, welcoming awareness, just to see what effect mindful attention has, if any. If you find the practise supportive, come back to this meditation to find some solace whenever you experience intrusive thoughts or worries.

WELCOMING THE NOISY NEIGHBOURS

Your anxious thoughts are like the music from a noisy neighbour. Mindfulness isn't so much about trying to force the neighbour to stop, which may or may not work, but about listening to the noise in a different way. When you're listening to your favourite piece of music, you let the sounds come into you, you open yourself fully to the rhythm. In the same way, you need to open up and listen to your thoughts and feel the underlying emotions without trying to fix or change them – just acknowledging them as they are.

Training your mind like this isn't an easy process and takes practise. The 'music' (your anxious thoughts) may or may not change – all you can control is your attitude towards them. Let the attitude be one of curiosity and kindness as far as you can.

REMEMBER

Mindfulness isn't about trying to get rid of your anxiety, or any other difficult experience. Mindfulness offers the possibility of developing a healthy stance towards your unpleasant experience. The unpleasant experience is here, whether you want it or not. You can try distracting yourself in the short term, but this is tiring and tends not to work in the long term. The invitation of mindfulness is a radical one: to take a courageous, challenging step towards the difficulty, whatever the difficulty is, and see what unfolds. This act of acknowledgement changes your relationship with the anxiety and therefore gives freedom for that emotion to move on, when you're ready.

Being with anxious feelings

If you want to change anxiety, you need to begin with the right relationship with the anxiety, so you can be with the emotion. Within this safe relationship, you can allow the anxiety to be there, neither suppressing nor reacting to it. Imagine sitting as calmly as you can while a child is having a tantrum. No tantrum lasts forever, and no tantrum stays at exactly the same level. By maintaining a mindful, calm, gentle awareness, eventually and very gradually the anxiety may begin to settle. And even if it doesn't go away, by sitting calmly next to it, your experience isn't quite such a struggle.

TIP

You don't need to face anxiety head-on straight away. You can take these steps over a period of days, weeks or months:

1. **Observe how you normally react when anxiety arises; or if you're always anxious, notice your current attitude towards the emotion.**

2. **Consider the possibility of taking a more mindful attitude towards the anxiety.**

3. **Feel the anxiety for about a minute with as much kindness and warmth as you can, breathing into it.**

4. **Notice the colour, shape and texture of the feeling. What part of your body does it manifest in?** Does the intensity of the sensation increase or decrease with your mindful awareness? Explore the area somewhere between retreating away from and diving into the anxiety, and allow yourself to be fascinated by what happens on this edge with your kindly, compassionate awareness.

5. **Watch the feeling as you may look at a beautiful tree or flower, with a sense of warmth and curiosity. Breathe into the various sensations and see the sensations as your teacher.** Welcome the emotion as you may welcome a guest, with open arms.

This isn't a competition to go from Steps 1 to 5 but is a process, a journey you take at your own pace. Step 1 is just as important, significant and deep as Step 5. Remember that these steps are a guide: move into the anxiety, or whatever the emotion is, as you see fit. *Trust in your own innate wisdom to guide your inner journey.*

Overcoming Addiction

An addiction is a seemingly uncontrollable need to abuse a substance like drink or drugs or to carry out an activity like gambling. Addictions interfere with your life at home, work or school, where they cause problems.

If you're suffering from addiction, remember that you're not alone. In the USA, for example, 23 million are addicted to alcohol or other drugs. And over two-thirds of people who suffer from addiction abuse alcohol.

The good news is, help is available. If you've tried and failed at overcoming your addiction, don't give up. There's hope, with all the support out there. Mindfulness is one of many ways to overcome addiction.

WARNING

Not sure whether you're suffering from addiction? It can be hard to admit if you're addicted to something. But recognising and accepting your addiction is the first step in change. Ask yourself the following questions:

>> Do you use more of the substance or participate in the activity more now than in the past?

>> Do you experience urges or withdrawal symptoms when you don't have the substance or activity?

>> Do you ever lie to others about your use of the substance or your behaviour?

If the answer is yes, consider consulting a health professional for a more accurate evaluation and appropriate advice. A health professional can refer you to all sorts of support – many organisations can help in treating addiction. Cognitive behavioural therapy (CBT) and motivational enhancement therapy (MET) have been found to be very effective treatments.

WARNING

Mindfulness itself is an ancient practise, going back at least 2,500 years. But, clinically speaking, mindfulness is a new approach for overcoming addiction, and the evidence for the approach is at the very early stages of being gathered, although it's positive so far.

Understanding a mindful approach to addiction

Once you're addicted, your actions are the opposite of mindful: they're automatic. This example describes a process that happens almost unconsciously each time you smoke a cigarette:

1. You're sitting at work on your desk and you feel a bit lethargic and tired.

2. You feel the urge to smoke a cigarette. It's actually a physical sensation in your body, but usually you don't know where the sensation is in your body.

3. You immediately think: 'I need to smoke.' (You don't often consciously register this thought – it just happens in your brain.)

4. You very quickly find yourself standing up and walking out of the building with the packet of cigarettes and a lighter in your hands (usually without awareness – a conscious choice is rarely made).

5. The act of taking a cigarette out, lighting it and drawing in the smoke happens quickly and automatically (you may be lost in other thoughts).

6. The urge is satisfied for now and the lethargy gone. You're rewarded with a feeling of pleasure (dopamine is released in your brain). The cycle repeats again in a few hours.

Mindfulness offers you a way to identify the thoughts and emotions that are driving your addiction, and gives you a *choice* rather than just the automatic compulsion and action of depending on the addictive behaviour.

You discover that just because you have an urge to do something doesn't mean you have to do it. You can just experience the urge until it passes.

ADDICTION AND THE BRAIN

Most scientists now consider addiction a long-term disease. This is because addiction changes the structure and function of the brain. Just as a piece of clay changes when you squeeze it, so the brain's internal structure changes with addiction.

Changes happen in the brain due to the experience of pleasure and consequent action. When you experience anything pleasurable, the brain releases dopamine. A delicious meal, receiving money or taking a drug all result in a dopamine release. The greater the intensity, speed and reliability of dopamine release, the greater the chance of addiction.

Drugs cause a massive surge of dopamine in your brain. This begins to make changes in the way the memory, motivation and survival system areas of your brain work. This is how just wanting the substance turns into a compulsion. Addiction is much more than just a desire.

The huge surge of dopamine creates the experience of pleasure and overwhelms your brain. Your brain isn't designed to deal with so much dopamine. The ability to experience pleasure diminishes as your pleasure system gets overloaded and, to some extent, damaged. You need more of the substance or activity to get the same experience of pleasure.

At this point, compulsion takes over. Your memory reminds you of the past pleasure you experienced, and you are compelled to recreate that experience by taking more of the substance or further engaging in the behaviour.

This is why addiction is so powerful and how everyday willpower doesn't seem to help.

Discovering urge surfing: The mindful key to unlocking addiction

One brilliant way of managing the urges that arise in addiction is called *urge surfing*. It's a different way of meeting the reactive behaviour of addiction. Acting on strong cravings, when in an automatic pilot mode, doesn't help you in the long term. By urge surfing, you don't have to act on the urge or craving that you experience.

PLAY THIS

Listen to the urge surfing meditation (Track 21). The steps when you have an urge are:

1. **Find a comfortable posture.** You can sit, lie down, or even walk slowly – whatever you prefer. See whether you can relax your body a little and let go of any areas of tension. Begin by taking a deep breath and slowly breathing out.

2. **Notice that you have an urge to smoke, drink, gamble or whatever else it is for you.**

3. **Be mindful of your body.** Turn your attention to your physical bodily sensations. Where do you feel this urge in your body? Is it in one particular place or is it all over your body? What's does the urge actually feel like?

4. **Be mindful of your thoughts.** Notice and acknowledge the thoughts that are arising for you right now. Is it a familiar pattern of thoughts? Are they negative or judgemental thoughts? See whether you can step back from those thoughts, as if you're an observer of the experience, rather than getting too caught up in the thoughts, if you can. Watch the thoughts like bubbles floating away.

5. **Be mindful of your feelings.** Notice the feeling of the urge. The feeling may be very uncomfortable. That doesn't make it bad or good – it's just the nature of the feeling. Notice your judgement of 'I like this experience' or 'I don't like this experience.' Remember that the feeling isn't dangerous or threatening in itself.

6. **Allow the experience to be as it is.** See whether you can be with the experience without a need to get rid of it or to react to it by engaging in the behaviour that's not helpful for you. Just practise being with the experience, the urge, the craving, the compulsion, in the present moment.

7. **Notice how the urge is changing.** Perhaps the urge is increasing or decreasing for you. Maybe it's staying just the same.

8. **If the urge is increasing, imagine a wave in the ocean approaching a beach.** The waves rises higher and higher. But once it reaches its peak, it begins to come down again. Imagine your urge is like the wave. It'll continue to grow in intensity but will then naturally go down again. It won't keep growing forever. See whether you can just be present with the urge as it rises and falls. Ride the wave. You may even like to imagine yourself surfing the wave, the urge. Make use of your breathing. Keep 'surfing that urge.' Perhaps see your breath like a surf board that supports you as you surf the wave of your urge.

9. **Notice how you've managed to surf this urge for all this time.** This tool is always available for you, no matter how strong your urge or however intense your emotion or whatever thoughts arise for you.

TIP

Try reflecting on what you really want when you're in the midst of your craving. Usually it's not the substance or behaviour you're craving. Maybe you're feeling lonely or stressed? Or maybe you want freedom from circumstances or emotions at this time?

Think of your urge like a tantrum that a child has. If you give the child a sweet, they'll quieten down. But they've learnt to be rewarded for screaming. So before long they'll have another tantrum. So what's the solution? Just to be nice to them, but don't to give them any sweets. Eventually the tantrum will stop. The next time they start screaming, if, again, you just hold them or hug them but don't give them any sweets, the tantrum will end sooner. Eventually they'll stop having tantrums altogether. Being kind to the child without giving them sweets is like being mindful of your urge without satisfying your urge.

REMEMBER

Each time you ride out your urge, your craving gets weaker. Each time you satisfy that urge with a smoke or a drink, for example, you strengthen your craving. Every small effort you make counts.

TIP

If you want to boost your willpower, try one of the following ideas suggested by Kelly McGonigal, author of a fabulous book called The Willpower Instinct, Avery Publishing Group, 2013:

>> Get enough sleep. Aim for around eight hours if possible.

>> Mediate daily.

>> Exercise. Even a few minutes of walking is a great idea. You don't have to be too intensive. Make it mindful walking to make it even more powerful.

>> Slow down your breathing to four to six full breaths a minute – that can boost your willpower when you need it.

SMOKER'S HELL?

In one fascinating experiment, researcher Sarah Bown from the University of Washington asked a group of smokers to come into a lab. Half were taught the urge-surfing approach and the other half weren't.

Then the whole group sat around a large table and the smokers were asked to take over 20 minutes to light a single cigarette. Each process was slowed down, guided and made mindful: taking the new packet out of the pocket, taking the cellophane off, smelling the new packet, looking at the packet, choosing a cigarette, taking it out of the packet, smelling the cigarette, putting it in the mouth, taking out the lighter, looking at the lighter, lighting the lighter, lighting the cigarette and experiencing smoking the cigarette. That's torture for a smoker!

After the experiment, even though the group weren't asked to reduce the number of cigarettes they smoked, the part of the group that had been taught urge surfing had cut back by 37 per cent. The other group smoked as much as before.

Managing relapse: Discovering the surprising secret for success

As someone once told me: 'I've been a smoker for 20 years. I've given up hundreds of times.'

Most people who want to give up an addiction are able to stop for a short period, but in a moment of difficulty or mindlessness they begin using the object of their addiction again. This is to be expected. Everyone's human and will mistakenly go back to the drug, drink or whatever.

How do you treat yourself when you have a relapse? Most people think that if they're hard on themselves when they accidently relapse, they'll get better. In fact, amazingly, the opposite has been found to be true in research.

Studies have found one of secrets of those that manage to give up long term: self-compassion. For example, people addicted to alcohol were less likely to have a major relapse if they were more forgiving of themselves when they had a drink.

The more kind and forgiving you can be with yourself when you relapse, the more likely it is that the relapse be a one-off. But if you beat yourself up, thinking, 'Oh, I'm such an idiot. I can't even give up drinking. I'll never do it,' the worse you feel. And the worse you feel, the more you feel the need to find some false comfort in your addiction.

This is a powerful approach if you're dealing with an addiction. When you do manage to give up, let's say a drug, for a few days, congratulate yourself each day. And when you end up relapsing on a bad day, tell yourself that you've made a one-off mistake and can go back to being drug-free again. Remind yourself that you've had four days of no drugs and one day having taken the drug. That's four out of five – pretty good!

See whether you can manage a few more days without the substance – see whether you can sit with that urge a bit longer. See whether you can take the time to meditate, perhaps simply feeling your breathing, for a couple more minutes today. Be extra nice to yourself.

Chapter **14**

Getting Physical: Healing the Body

Mindfulness for people with serious medical problems was initially adopted in the USA, and now the approach is rapidly being adopted all over the world. Doctors who'd exhausted all traditional medical routes referred patients to a stress-reduction clinic that used mindfulness to help people cope with pain, anxiety and stress.

As the patients engaged in mindfulness, they began to discover a different way of relating to their challenging experiences. They began to feel better, despite their medical problems. The symptoms didn't necessarily disappear, and the aim of mindfulness wasn't to make them go away. The patients found a different way of coping with the illness: from a state of wholeness and wisdom, rather than fear and disharmony.

This chapter explores why mindfulness may be beneficial for those suffering from a chronic health condition, and offers a variety of different ways of beginning that journey. You certainly don't have to be ill to benefit from mindfulness, but thousands suffering from serious medical conditions have found relief through mindfulness.

Contemplating Wholeness: Healing from Within

The word 'heal' is related to the Old English word for whole ('hal'). The word 'health' originally meant wholeness.

Get a sense of what being whole means for you, and as you read this chapter, continue to reflect. Mindfulness is about going to that capacity you have to be aware, whole and free, no matter how broken you feel your body to be. This is a totally different way of seeing what healing truly means, but seems to lead to a peace of mind conducive to feeling better.

Physical disease, or dis-ease, isn't just a problem with the body, but a problem for the mind too. As I explore in this section, your mind and body are inseparable – a whole. When you suffer from a disease, you need to look after both your body and mind to best manage your difficulties. You also need to consider how a sense of being whole can come about whatever happens to your body. Everyone's physical body perishes in the end – how can you live so that this process is dignified rather than full of stress, anxiety and the feeling of being broken?

REMEMBER

When you practise mindfulness, you practise an act of love. You're befriending yourself, slowly but surely. You're engaging in an activity for yourself, to look after and nurture your own health and wellbeing.

In mindfulness meditation you may at some point connect with your own deep, innate sense of wholeness. You begin to touch a depth of relaxation, of peace, of calm, that you may not have been aware of beforehand. This encounter with your own wholeness is profoundly healing in the sense of feeling at peace with yourself and with an inner conviction that things are going to be okay, however they work out. Your ill heath, your body, your thoughts, the emotions that arise and pass away, aren't everything. They're a part of the whole. The thought, 'It's all my fault; I'm completely useless,' is just a thought, not a fact. When you begin to touch this inner wholeness, your illness becomes less threatening. You become more optimistic in both the present moment and the future. From your more detached, free and light-hearted stance, your perception of your predicament shifts, and you allow more space for your body to heal as best it can, while taking all the medical treatment as appropriate.

TIP

Mindfulness helps you to see things from a bigger perspective. If, due to your disease, you feel low and down, out of control, and that you just can't dig yourself out of the hole that you're in, you probably feel depressed, isolated, lonely and afraid. However, consider the same situation from a bigger perspective: remember that you're suffering in the same way as many others. You can become aware of both the suffering you feel and those aspects of you that are healthy and well. Although you may have a bad back, what about the parts of your body that are functionally well? Mindfulness shifts the fixed patterns of the mind and enables you to see from eyes of wholeness. Then perhaps you can forgive yourself for feeling down – you're human after all.

Seeing the Connection between Mind and Body

Imagine you're scared of spiders. As you walk downstairs before dawn, you can see a shape on the floor in the gloom. 'It's a spider!,' you think. Your heart starts pounding and you begin to sweat. You're not sure whether you should even move, in case you disturb the spider. Your thoughts go wild. Then you look again and notice that the shape doesn't look quite right. You switch on the light to discover it's only a mark on the carpet! You feel relieved.

When you saw the mark as a spider, a whole series of changes took place in your body. You experienced the changes because of what you thought and interpreted the mark to be – in other words, because of your mind. When you realised it was just a stain on the carpet, a set of calming reactions took place. The object remained exactly the same. The way you changed your bodily reaction was by bringing curiosity to your experience and then switching on the light. Through awareness and curiosity, you begin to interpret things differently, to see them as they actually are rather than what you *think* they are.

By becoming more skilful in the way you use your mind, you can create the conditions to help rather than hinder the healing process. If you're experiencing high levels of chronic stress that you find overwhelming, it'll reduce the effectiveness of your immune system – the power of your body to self-heal. So any creative ways of relating to the stress in a different way is likely to have some positive effect.

Here's a very short exercise you can try that clearly demonstrates the link between your mind and body:

1. **Make yourself comfortable sitting or lying down and close your eyes if you want to.**

2. **Imagine you are hungry and are about to eat your favourite food.** You can smell the food and see it on your plate. Take a few minutes to imagine what the food looks and smells like. You take a piece of the food and begin eating. Imagine the taste of the delicious food in your mouth.

3. **Notice any changes happening in your body.** Are you salivating? Do you feel the desire to have this food now? Do you feel certain emotions manifesting themselves in your body? Are some parts of your body becoming tense or relaxed?

This short exercise (or form of torture, with all this talk about food!) again shows how your mind can directly have an effect on your body. All you did in this exercise was use your mind to create images in your head. And yet all sorts of physical changes took place in your body. You may now even go off to cook this food you've been imagining. In the same way, using your mind in the right way can go on to create positive, healing effects in your body.

APPRECIATING THE POWER OF PLACEBOS

A *placebo* pill is a non-active substance, usually made of sugar, which has no actual medicine in it. Whenever scientists want to test a new drug, they compare the drug with a placebo. Amazingly, many studies show that patients feel better after taking a placebo rather than the real medicine. How? The answer lies in your belief system. If you believe that a pill is going to help you, the positive belief seems to accelerate the healing process.

Here are some interesting facts about placebos:

- **Placebos seem to release natural painkillers from your body into the bloodstream, if you *believe* that the pill is a painkiller.** This can have the equivalent effect of that of a moderate dose of morphine!

- **Expensive placebos work better than cheap ones.** I love this fact! In one experiment, researchers gave patients a placebo, telling half the patients that the pill cost $2.50, and telling the other half it cost 10 cents. The group that thought they had the more expensive pills experienced less pain when given a mild electric shock in their hands. Ouch!

- **Placebo surgery is where the patients think they've had surgery, but no actual surgery has taken place.** For ethical reasons placebo surgery is rarely carried out. In a study done in 2013, published in the New England Journal of Medicine, 146 patients with a particular form of knee damage were randomly assigned to have either actual surgery or placebo surgery. After 12 months, at no point did the actual surgery group report less pain or better function than the placebo surgery group.

The placebo effect is powerful and proves how the mind can actually affect the healing process.

Accepting Your Limits

You have a certain amount of time and energy on this planet. If you didn't have any limits on time, you'd live forever. If you didn't have any limits on your energy, you'd never need to sleep. So, how can you best use the time and energy you do have? If you try to do more and more, you eventually break down. You're better off becoming aware of your limits and acknowledging them, but continuing to push those boundaries every now and then, in a healthy and mindful way.

At one point in my career, I believed that I could do anything and everything. I took on more and more jobs and responsibilities. I was doing more but achieving less. By the end of the day I was exhausted, my energy levels were very low and I was just about finding time to meditate, just to keep going. One day I woke up and thought 'enough is enough' – why sacrifice my health and wellbeing for the sake of yet another promotion and a bit of extra cash? I began to reduce the responsibilities that I could reduce, and looked for more efficient and creative ways of doing the things I had to do. In this way, I enjoy challenging myself, and testing my limits, but I don't overdo it.

WARNING

Don't confuse accepting or acknowledging your limits with feeling defeated. If you suffer from a long-term health condition for example, you don't have to give up and curl up in the corner for the rest of your life. Accepting your limits means accepting that your body isn't well and you need to start taking small steps to begin improving your condition, as your doctor advises. You may need support from a group, or from your own friends or family. You also need to remember that you won't magically transform, and that therefore you need to work at accepting your limits slowly but surely.

Accepting limits reminds me of what bees do. When a bee is stuck in a room, it continues to fly into the closed window, thinking that it can go through. If the bee could see that the window is a limit, and it's not possible to get out that way, it wouldn't keep knocking into the window until it died. If you find yourself hitting limits again and again, and getting frustrated, be imaginative and try a different approach – don't keep flying into the window just because the view looks great on the other side. Try a radically different approach.

Rising above Your Illness

To rise above your illness means to separate yourself from your illness rather than to identify yourself with the disease. In this way, you may become less overwhelmed by your condition.

Dana Jennings, who suffered from cancer, wrote in a *New York Times* blog:

> *Being able to laugh in the face of cancer lets you continue to own yourself, as hard as that might be, rather than ceding ownership to the disease. A good laugh reminds you that you are not your cancer.*

You are not your illness. Laughter may be one way of reminding yourself of that fact, and mindfulness is another. Some days are better than others. Some days may be dark, and you may need just to hang on until things lighten up a bit. Remembering that 'I am not my illness' may help.

Recently, when I was practising a mindful meditation, my body felt lighter and lighter, in a pleasant way. I felt completely calm and at ease. Everything was okay with the world. At that point in time, I didn't identify with my body and yet I felt completely at ease and fine with the experience. In fact, I felt as if I was truly myself. Experiences such as this remind me that my body isn't as solid and real as I normally think. I like to think: 'I am not my body but I am aware of my body. I am the awareness – aware of thoughts, feelings, my body and the world around me.' In this sense of wholeness, you experience a freedom from the chains of thinking 'I'm ill' or 'I'm incomplete,' to achieve the freedom of being, of resting, in the sense of 'I'm alone.' In this context, I mean alone as in 'al-one' or 'all one,' the original meaning of the word alone. This is the opposite of feeling lonely and isolated. It's a feeling of being connected to yourself and the world around you.

Don't use mindfulness to try to chase certain pleasant experiences. Whatever you experience in mindfulness practise is okay – mindfulness isn't good or bad. The sense of wholeness is your true nature, right here and right now, not just in some exotic mindful experience. Experiences come and go, but awareness is always here, whether you want to be aware or not. Identify with that presence and you're immediately reminded of your own sense of wholeness.

Using Mindfulness to Accept Pain

Acute pain is a sharp pain lasting for a short time, sometimes defined as less than 12 weeks. Medicine is quite good at treating acute pain. *Chronic pain* is pain that lasts for over 12 weeks, and doctors have a much harder time treating such a condition. Many consider chronic pain as one of the most underestimated health-care problems in the world today, having a massive effect on both the patient and being a major burden on the health-care system.

DEALING WITH A HEADACHE

As I write, my head is aching. So, what do I do? Mindfulness is about awareness, so I become aware of the sensation in my head. I notice that my shoulders are tensing up due to the pain, so I breathe into them, and the tension seems to melt a little. I also take frequent breaks and drink lots of water. I remember that I'm not my headache. The headache arises and at some point is going to pass away. The actual experience of pain only exists in this moment. I don't need to 'tolerate' the pain, because even if I stop tolerating it, the pain is still there. Tolerating is a state of extra unnecessary tension. I can also become aware of the shape, size, colour and texture of the pain sensation in my head. I breathe into the pain, and some resistance eases around the pain. I know that the pain only exists from one moment to the next. I notice and let go of the desire for the headache to go away.

This may give you some idea of the spirit with which to practise mindfulness when coping with a painful sensation. The idea is to turn your attention towards the difficulty and become really curious about it – but not to try and get rid of it. I suppose it's a bit like trying to soothe a crying baby: getting angry usually doesn't help. By giving the baby your attention, although it's uncomfortable when she's crying, you're able to meet her needs.

The World Health Organization found that between a half and two-thirds of people with chronic pain struggle to exercise, enjoy normal sleep, perform household chores, attend social activities, drive a car, walk or have sexual relations.

It has repeatedly been found that those who complete an eight-week mindfulness programme find their level of pain reduced. This is surprising, because mindfulness asks you to go into the place that hurts and allow the sensation to be there, rather than to fight with the pain itself. The following sections explain how this may work.

Knowing the difference between pain and suffering

Pain is inevitable. Suffering is optional. Pain is a sensation that you're bound to experience from time to time. In fact, pain is often a very useful sensation – without pain, you'd go around damaging yourself without realising it. If you've ever been anaesthetised in your mouth by your dentist, you know how easy it is to bite the inside of your cheek, even making it bleed, without realising.

Suffering is different. Suffering is something you create yourself, often unknowingly. Say you suffer from arthritis. Each morning, when you wake up, for a split second you just experience the raw sensation – the pain of having arthritis. Then, within a second or so, your mind begins to interpret the experience: 'That stupid disease. Why me? I bet I got it because of the unhealthy food I used to eat. It's not fair. I'm so annoyed! It's all my fault. What will happen in the future?' Unhelpful judgements, interpretations and predictions all lead to suffering.

A useful formula to remind you of the difference between pain and suffering is:

Pain x Resistance = Suffering

In other words, the more you resist or fight or deny or avoid your pain, the greater the suffering you experience. I'm not saying it's going to be easy to reduce your urge to resist pain – resistance is the automatic response to pain. But through the tools and approaches in this book, you can learn to reduce that reaction and therefore begin to find relief from your suffering.

REMEMBER

Pain can be emotional: feelings of sadness, loneliness, grief, anxiety or anger. Suffering is the way you meet those emotions. If you're curious about them and almost welcome them rather than trying to push them away, fight or block them, you're unlikely to create much suffering. However, if you avoid the emotions through addictions like drugs or excessive alcohol use, to avoid these feelings, you're likely to increase your own suffering.

All the avoidant strategies can't make the pain go away, they just numb it for the time being. This can be helpful in the short term to help you to cope, but by avoiding the painful sensations or emotions, you sustain and feed them. Suffering is something you can begin to manage and control by looking more carefully at the thoughts and feelings you're experiencing – the very act of turning towards painful experiences begins to change the level of suffering you have.

WISE WORDS

Here's a quote from Nisargadatta, a famous Indian spiritual teacher. He experienced the pain of throat cancer in the latter years of his life:

Pain is physical, suffering is mental. Beyond the mind there is no suffering. Pain is essential for the survival of the body, but none compels you to suffer. Suffering is due entirely to clinging or resisting; it is a sign of our unwillingness to move on, to flow with life. As a sane life is free of pain, so is a saintly life free from suffering. A saint does not want things to be different from what they are; he knows that, considering all factors, they are unavoidable. He is friendly with the inevitable and, therefore, does not suffer. Pain he may know, but it does not shatter him. If he can, he does the needful to restore the lost balance, or he lets things take their course.

BEING INSPIRED BY OTHERS

Here are some of the kinds of things my clients with chronic pain conditions say about the effect of mindfulness, which may help you to cope with your pain, and offer you some ways to apply mindfulness.

'I suffer from a chronic pain condition – if I move around for an hour or so on one day, my body is in agony the next day. Mindfulness is pretty much the only thing that has helped relieve the pain I've suffered in the last six years. I can't really move my body, and most therapies require some sort of movement. With the body scan, or mindfulness of breathing, I can lie down on the floor and do the meditation without actually moving. That's a wonderful thing. By the end, I feel really tired, but also as if I've released lots of tension I've been holding for weeks or even months.'

'I have severe lower back pain. The pain goes shooting down my leg every time I move. I thought the pain was there 24 hours a day, seven days a week. Having done the mindfulness training, the biggest thing I've realised is that there are moments in the day when I have no pain. That's really important for me.'

Working with pain

It's helpful to be clear about what your aim is when practising mindfulness. Your aim is not to reduce your feeling of pain. Instead, the idea is to make space for the experience of pain to be there, acknowledge that you are not your pain but the observer of your pain, and to flexibly begin moving your attention and taking action to creating a rich and meaningful life, in line with what's most important for you.

Here are a few things to remember about pain when applying mindfulness to the condition:

>> **Pain can only exist in the present moment.** You only need to cope with this moment now. By worrying about the rest of the day, week, month or year, you begin to create suffering for yourself.

>> **Tension increases pain.** By becoming aware of the sensation of pain and imagining the breath going into and out of the area of pain, the tension naturally begins to release, thereby reducing the pain. However, if the tension

stays, that's okay too – your intention is all you can control here. Become aware of the actual sensation of the pain itself. Notice where the pain is located in the body. Does it have an associated shape, size, texture or colour?

» **Trying hard to reduce pain doesn't really work.** (This is just like how trying hard to relax can create more tension.) By discovering how slowly but surely to acknowledge and accept your pain, your experience may change for the better.

Here's a mindfulness exercise you can try to help you through your pain:

1. **Adopt any position that you feel comfortable in for a few minutes.**

2. **Feel the sensation of your own breathing.** Be aware of your breath with a lightness, a kindness and a sense of gratitude as far as you can.

3. **Notice how the pain grabs your attention time and again.** Try not to criticise yourself for this. Understand that this is a difficult practise and guide your awareness gently back to the feeling of the in-breath and out-breath around the nose, chest, belly or wherever else you find it most easy to focus on. Continue for a few minutes.

4. **Now bring your attention to the sensation of the pain itself.** This may feel frightening, or you may be very reluctant to try moving your attention to the pain. However, if you've never done this before, why not give it a go? Imagine your breath going into and out of the centre of the pain, or however close you can comfortably move to the pain.

5. **You may find saying the following words to yourself helpful, as you breathe in and out.** You may want to make a nice, slow recording of it – perhaps with music in the background if you like – and play the recording back to yourself:

   Breathing in, I am aware I am breathing in,

   Breathing out, I am aware I am breathing out.

   Breathing in, I am aware of pain,

   Breathing out, I am aware of pain.

   Breathing in, I am aware of pain,

Breathing out, I know I am not my pain.

Breathing in, I begin to accept the pain

Breathing out, I make space for the pain to be there.

Breathing in, I am aware of tension,

Breathing out, I know I am not my tension.

Breathing in, I am aware of anger,

Breathing out, I know I am not my anger.

Breathing in, I am aware of sadness,

Breathing out, I know I am not my sadness.

Breathing in, I am aware of anxiety,

Breathing out, I know I am not my anxiety.

Breathing in, I take things moment by moment,

Breathing out, this is the only moment.

Breathing in, I know I am awareness,

Breathing out, I know I am free.

You can change the wording to whatever you feel comfortable with. Feel free to experiment. Practise at least once a day and note the effect.

THE BUTTERFLY OF THE MIND

The Diving Bell and the Butterfly is the title of a book by Jean-Dominique Bauby that was later made into a film. Bauby, editor of the French *Elle* magazine, wrote the whole book after becoming paralysed, communicating by blinking his left eye when his companions spoke the correct letter of the alphabet. He explores the value of the simple things in life, and the experience of feeling trapped in his body, like being in a diving bell, while his mind flits around like a butterfly. The book is a reminder of what you have rather than what you don't have – of how precious life is, despite the pain and suffering. As one critic said: 'Read this book and fall back in love with life.'

Using Mindfulness during Ill Health

In the mindfulness–based stress reduction clinic, a popular saying is: 'If you can breathe, there's more right with you than wrong with you.' You don't even have to be able to sit up or to move to benefit from mindfulness. Mindfulness is mind training, and so no matter what the condition of your body, you can still train your mind.

Mindfulness is used to support those with cancer, heart disease, diabetes and a whole range of other chronic conditions. How does it support you when you have such a physical disease? Here are some ways:

>> Mindfulness offers you a way to support yourself and build some inner resilience so you aren't overwhelmed by the looming decisions you may need to make and difficulties you may meet. Making choices about your treatment is an extra stressor when you're unwell. With mindfulness, you can access a greater clarity of thought.

>> Mindfulness offers a way of connecting with something other than just your physical body, making you feel more grounded. The illness may have a physical impact and cause changes to your appearance. Your whole sense of personal identity and self-worth can be questioned when you look different as you gaze at yourself in the mirror.

>> Ultimately, mindfulness is about realising that you're more than just your body, mind and heart. You're more than your fleeting thoughts and fluxing emotions. You're more than your illness. Through the practise of mindfulness and a natural self-enquiry that arises, you begin to discover a different dimension of yourself, a dimension in which illness no longer overwhelms you.

>> Mindful awareness can help you to spot unhelpful and untrue thoughts, thereby defusing their potency. If you're ill, stress increases not only for you but also for your family and friends, when you all need greater support and calm. Some people even believe that they've brought the disease upon themselves due to stress. This belief leads to further distress.

>> The space offered in mindfulness may help you to uncover a direct experience of an understanding through which life and death begin to make sense on some level. Serious illness puts you face to face with the prospect of death. Facing death may force you to reflect on your priorities, on what is most important in your life.

Illness isn't all negative. Surprisingly, research has shown there are positive effects of terminal illness. Some patients report increased spirituality, a deeper appreciation and a generally more positive perception of partners and significant others. Some people report greater compassion and willingness to express emotions. Higher levels of spirituality indicate that the patient senses that the illness is part of a bigger picture, and is more likely to be at peace amidst such challenging life circumstances. The phenomenon of this re-prioritisation and personal development seems to occur when people overcome their trauma, and is called post-traumatic growth.

REMEMBER

You can develop mindfulness in two main ways, even when you're feeling ill: either by practising mindfulness exercises and meditations, or by living in a mindful way whenever it comes to mind in the moment. So when you're lying in bed waiting for the doctor, you can try and enjoy some deep, mindful breaths. When you're waiting for your test results, you can slowly walk up and down and feel the sensations in your feet – that's mindful walking. When you spot yourself saying negative, harsh words to yourself, you can try soothing yourself with some words of self-kindness, or remember that you're not alone with this condition – many others are in a similar or worse situation all over the world. You don't need to beat yourself up just because you can't find the time or motivation to meditate. Any short mindful exercise counts.

Aiding the healing process

When you sit down to meditate, any aches, pains and physical discomfort that you may have managed to ignore during the course of the day become more apparent. The practise of mindfulness is about allowing and managing these uncomfortable feelings rather than totally distracting yourself from them; you use them in a positive way.

Mindfulness can make you feel empowered. Even if you can't move a muscle in your body, you're able to do something within your mind that may do you some good. In this way, you're able to be proactive at a time in your life when you feel most powerless. Mindfulness can feel like a lifebuoy when you're struggling to stay afloat. What a relief!

I can't guarantee that mindfulness will help you heal – but there's a chance it can, so it's worth a shot, especially if the practise makes you feel a bit better.

All the mindfulness exercises in this book can help you at a time of illness – choose whatever appeals to you. The following are a selection of some practises you can do to help reduce stress and aid the healing process:

>> **Mindfulness of breath.** Practise focusing your attention on your breathing. If you find focusing on the breath too difficult due to any pain you feel, try counting your breaths or saying 'in' and 'out' to yourself as you breathe in and out. Even managing just one mindful breath is a great start. Allow yourself to become aware of the natural, life-giving energy of your breathing as it finds its

instinctive rhythm. As you breathe, you may become aware of a physical tightness in the body that restricts the breathing process. Allow and accept this, and breathe into the tension. If the tension melts, fine; if the tension doesn't, that's also fine.

» **Mindfulness of body.** Being mindful of your body is a particularly important stage if you're unwell. Bring as much kindness as you can to your experience. If you aren't too overwhelmed by the sensation of pain, allow and accept it as far as you can. Feel the sensation of pain in a neutral way, staying with the feeling and doing nothing else. In addition to kindness, bring some curiosity to your experience, as best you can. The more nurturing and gentle you can be in your relationship with your body, the better. Try some yoga, stretching or tai chi if they help to soothe the pain.

» **Mindfulness of thoughts and emotions.** In mindfulness, you can welcome your thoughts and emotions rather than resisting them. You may want to use your breath to anchor yourself in the present moment every now and then when you find yourself swept away by thoughts, as happens very often. Notice the nature of your thoughts. Are they catastrophic? Are they always about the illness? Do they focus on the future all the time? What about your emotions? Allow yourself to move into your emotions rather than resist them. Notice in what part of the body they manifest themselves and use your breath to soothe them. Trust in your own capacity to heal, to make whole.

» **Mindfulness of being.** Become aware of your own sense of identity – be aware of the sense of 'I am.' Experiment with letting go of your identification with your body, your mind, your emotions, your health and illness, your desires and fears. Keep coming back to the sense of being, the sense of 'I am.' Rest in this state of 'beingness.' If you find yourself getting lost in thoughts, imagine that your thoughts are simply dancing on top of your awareness. Remember that your thoughts and feelings are like waves in an ocean of being that is you. Expect thoughts to arrive rather than resisting or fighting them. Just as clouds aren't distractions for the sky, so thoughts aren't distractions for your mindfulness practise. Just be.

Chapter **15**

Sharing Mindfulness with Children

O nce you've begun to develop your own mindfulness practise, you can consider how to share mindfulness with your children too. Mindfulness can help children to become calmer, more focused and emotionally intelligent. Mindfulness is a very natural process that children can practise from a young age. In this chapter you can find lots of fun exercises to train your child or teenager in mindfulness, as well as some mindful parenting tips to help keep your family smiling in the challenging but rewarding art of bringing up children.

Children and Mindfulness: A Natural Combination

Young children are naturally in the moment. Babies are like mini Zen masters! Since they haven't learnt language, they see things as they are. A set of keys, a light bulb, or the eyes of another human being are awe-inspiring for them. All actions they take are spontaneous. One moment they can be crying, and the next moment they completely let go of the past and laugh. They eat when they're hungry, sleep when they're tired, and walk when they want to walk. Their minds are full of curiosity – they can't help but explore. They're naturally full of love, which you can see beaming out of their eyes. Babies are often happy just to 'be.' They can look around and shake their legs and arms, and that's enough. They love to play and don't take things too seriously. Babies don't see themselves as separate individuals; they simply do what they do and go with the flow. Many of these qualities are the essence of mindfulness.

What they can't so easily do is manage their emotions. They act on what they think or feel, without much reflection. They can be at the mercy of anger, bursting into tears if their wishes are not met. Children don't enjoy feeling overwhelmed and often will ask to be led in a mindfulness exercises once they've tasted the benefits of feeling more present and centred. Mindfulness gives them a choice about how to respond to life's challenges, big and small, and offers them a possibility of acting more wisely.

As their minds are so pliable, these skills can set them up for a lifetime of greater mindfulness and wellbeing. And with wiser, kinder children, we create a wiser and kinder world too.

As babies grow up and begin to develop individuality, they begin to lose the sense of joy in just 'being' and can end up going from one thing to another, looking for a source of entertainment but lacking the attention to stay with it. When your child is age 5 upwards, you can begin to teach him some very simple mindfulness exercises to help give him some relief from his overactive mind, helping him to find out how to calm himself down.

As children approach their teenage years, they battle with a huge influx of hormones and struggle with the demands that the world makes upon them. They become more serious as individuality takes a firm hold, and begin to suppress emotions. Some simple mindfulness exercises, like mindful breathing for a few minutes, can offer your child a method to focus the mind inwards and not spiral out of control each time something doesn't go his way.

HAVING A MINDFUL PREGNANCY AND CHILDBIRTH

Pregnancy and childbirth are usually both exciting and scary times. But one thing's for sure: being pregnant is an emotional rollercoaster.

Pregnancy can be a joyous experience but is often painful too. Medication isn't normally recommended during pregnancy, which makes the pain more challenging to cope with. Because mindfulness has been found to help with chronic pain, mindfulness is being researched for pregnancy as an approach to pain management. One of the most common areas of concern for women is the feeling of losing control and not being able to cope. Mindfulness helps women to decouple the physical sensation of pain from their negative thoughts and emotions. With this approach, women experience less anxiety, and that may have a positive knock-on effect of reducing the feeling of physical pain.

The value of mindfulness extends to the birth, too. Research has found that some women are able to manage labour without the pain relief that's offered. Further questions have revealed that such women have more positive empowering experiences from labour rather than resisting labour. They tend to use expressions like 'going with the flow,' 'being present' and 'pain is your friend not your enemy.' These are attitudes that these women seem to naturally possess. But the research shows that all women can learn these attitudes and skills.

Mindfulness offers a middle path during childbirth: it gives women permission to be mindful and aware of the experience of labour, but not to feel self-judgemental if they need pain relief. Another helpful aspect of mindfulness around pregnancy is in managing depression. Over one in ten suffer depression around the time of pregnancy and childbirth and afterwards. With mindfulness being used to prevent the reoccurrence of depression during pregnancy, this can be a great time to learn about mindfulness to manage the challenging feelings.

Here are three little tips if you're pregnant right now:

- **Slow down.** Pregnancy is a great time to take things easy. Try not to overschedule. Enjoy naps in the afternoon, and take naps more often. Once your child is born, you'll be busy. Do just one thing at a time. Enjoy relaxing while you can.

- **Get enough sleep.** If you're struggling to sleep, which is common in pregnancy, try doing some soothing body scan meditations. Mindful body-awareness exercises can be relaxing while lying down. Bring a self-compassionate attitude to the mindfulness practises – in other words, bring a feeling of affection towards yourself and your baby as you meditate.

- **Adapt your routine.** If you're used to doing a long mindfulness practise in the mornings, but are now struggling to achieve this, adapt. You'll need to adapt again when your baby's born, so doing this is good practise. Thirty minutes of mindful yoga may need to turn into a five-minute stretch and then some ten-minute body scan meditations through the day when you can fit them in.

It's worth noting that men go through as much post-natal depression as women, and so it's a great idea to offer training in mindfulness to fathers as well as mothers to be.

Teaching Mindfulness to Children

Before you attempt to teach your children the art of mindfulness, consider how they learn. By adopting the right attitude to this important and challenging endeavour, you're more likely to avoid unnecessary frustration. Follow these tips when teaching mindfulness:

>> **Be light-hearted.** Children don't like taking things too seriously, so bringing an element of play and fun is important. At the same time, be clear in your mind what the purpose of each mindfulness exercise is, and explain it to your children. (See the next section for ideas for exercises.)

>> **Keep the sessions short.** Children's attention spans just aren't as long as those of adults. You need to adjust the length of the session as appropriate for the child.

>> **Reduce talk and increase action.** Avoid talking about how much mindfulness helps you and how wonderful it is. You're better off practising more mindfulness and letting your child learn from what you do rather than what you say.

>> **Remember that some days will be better than others.** Some days you may feel as if nothing works – then suddenly, your child may sit quietly without distraction, for no apparent reason. So their engagement will depend on their mood at the time, and whether they've slept enough, eaten, had some exercise, and other such factors.

>> **Avoid using force.** If your child doesn't want to do a mindful exercise, you can't force him. This just creates a negative idea about mindfulness. Mindfulness isn't like learning the piano, or maths. Mindfulness requires a desire to practise with a sense of curiosity, and using force can't generate the right attitude. Instead, be creative and try something completely different. (See the later exercises in this chapter for ideas.)

Setting an example

Children learn far more from who you *are* what you *do* than from what you *say*. Children naturally copy others, especially people they respect. If a child sees you meditating, he's likely to be curious about what you're doing and why you're doing it. In this way you draw your child towards mindfulness, rather than forcing mindfulness upon him.

If you practise very little mindfulness, but think that your child would benefit from the practise, you may have a hard time convincing him of the benefits. He may have seen you react to your stress in unhelpful ways, getting unnecessarily angry and becoming frustrated over small things. Your child may pick up on these reactions and unconsciously begin copying them instead.

If you practise mindfulness on a regular basis and genuinely put in the time, effort and energy to develop it in your life, your child is going to pick up on this too. He'll notice how you try to calm down when you become upset; how you practise mini mindfulness exercises when things become overwhelming for you; how you're firm when you need to be firm, and light-hearted at other times. If your child sees you making genuine efforts to cultivate mindfulness, he's likely to pick up on this. Even if he doesn't show calm and controlled behaviour at the moment, the memory of his positive perceptions of mindfulness will stay with him, and is likely to flower as he gets older.

Taking baby steps

Don't expect your child to start with a 30-minute, mindful-breathing exercise the first time you teach him. You may not even be able to do the eating meditation with a raisin or any other food. (See Chapter 6 for the eating meditation.) If your child feels bored, he's likely to give up immediately and do something more interesting instead. You'd probably have a hard time trying to convince him to explore the boredom or to get interested in the cause of boredom!

If you have high expectations about your child practising mindfulness, you may be disappointed. Keep your expectations reasonably low and be happy with any small progress. Ultimately, mindfulness is about being in the present moment, so any time at all is very valuable and better than nothing.

Playing Mindfulness Games and Exercises

Children love games. Games help to focus your child's mind and at the same time have an element of fun. Then, in this more focused state of mind, you can do a short guided imagery for a minute or so – and with young children, that's enough. I know a couple of schools that do this, and the children really look forward to doing the mindful exercises – they enjoy both the fun and the release of any anxieties and stresses in their systems.

Use your intuition to decide which games to use, but be brave too and try some that you initially doubt. You never know what will happen until you try! Some can be adapted for older children – just use more appropriate props, more adult language and extend the length of the mindful exercises slightly.

You can do these games with one child or more.

Connecting with the whole universe

Here's a nice, visual exercise that gives the sense of connecting full with the world around them. A great positive way to introduce your child to a fun, mindful exercise. This can be a calming exercise that helps them to get their energy out and feel centred.

1. Ask your child to stand with feet hip-width apart and close his eyes.

2. Tell him to stretch up to the sky as if he could touch the clouds and breathe in as deeply as he can.

3. Then tell him to breathe out and try and touch his toes

4. On the next inbreath, tell him to imagine he is scooping up the whole universe in his arms – the earth, the clouds, the sky, the planets, the sun and all the stars. He can lift the whole universe above his head as he breathes in deeply!

5. As he breathes out, tell him to wiggle his fingers and sprinkle the whole universe over himself and you and anyone else around with a nice big smile. He can make a magical sound as he breathes out and sprinkles.

6. He can repeat this cycle three times, each time feeling as if he is lifting more and more of the universe and sprinkling it out further and further. Encourage him to imagine he is becoming one with the universe.

7. Then repeat this cycle one more time, but more calmly and slowly.

8. Finish with him hugging himself, feeling his breathing and imagining he and the universe and connected and peaceful and one. Give him some time to notice the natural sensation of his breathing.

Teddy bear

This exercise helps to encourage belly breathing, and also to focus the attention on the breathing:

1. Ask your child to lie down on the floor, a mat or a bed.

2. Place a teddy bear or any other favourite toy on your child's belly and ask her to become aware of the toy as it rises and falls.

3. Encourage your child to be curious about how often the teddy bear goes up and down. Can she make it go up and down a little more slowly? How does that make her feel inside?

Paper windmill spinning

This game is a way of focusing your child's attention on his breathing. The visual cue of a colourful paper windmill is far more interesting to your child than just feeling his breath alone.

Here are the steps:

1. Give your child a colourful paper windmill (pinwheel). Let her play with it for a while, and then tell her you're going to practise being curious together.

2. Ask her to blow as softly as he can and to observe what happens. Ask her to see how slowly he can make the paper windmill turn. How does this make her feel?

3. Ask her to blow as hard as possible, and see how fast the paper windmill turns. What happens to all the colours? How does this make her feel?

4. Ask her to experiment with a long or short breath, and notice how long the paper windmill turns for.

5. Ask her to breathe normally, and to watch what happens to the paper windmill. Again, ask him how he feels.

6. Finally, ask her to put the paper windmill down and feel his breath without it. Ask her whether he can feel calm and relaxed even without the paper windmill, just by feeling his own breath.

It's okay, whatever the weather

When your child is in a grumpy mood, it's nice to be able to offer a mindful exercise to help him acknowledge the feeling and also create a sense of separation between him and his feeling – an important mindfulness skill.

1. Ask your child to find a comfortable, relaxed sitting or lying-down posture with his eyes closed, if that feels okay for him.

2. Ask him to share his 'internal weather' – this means, if he could describe how he was feeling, what weather would it be. If he's in a grumpy mood, it may be rainly, cloudy, thundering or as if there's a tornado in his mind.

3. Ask him to describe the weather in as much detail as possible. This gives him permission to accept how he's feeling as sense some separation.

4. Then ask him to zoom out and away from the weather so that he can see the crazy weather, but it's not so close to him, if he can. Or if he can't do that, ask him to look around to the other side and see if the weather is different.

5. Invite him to take three, slow, deep mindful breaths. As he breathes out, he's breathing away the difficult weather in a gentle way – not pushing it away but just making space for himself.

Be a friend with the world

This is a powerful exercise to practise with your children. It is a children's version of the loving kindness mediation described in Chapter 6. If your children really like the exercise, they may be happy to do the meditation every day before going to sleep. They may find that they sleep more deeply and feel calmer and refreshed the next day. Pause after giving each instruction, to give your child plenty of time to experience the exercise.

For the meditation:

1. Ask your child to find a comfortable, relaxed sitting or lying-down posture with his eyes closed, if that feels okay for him. Let her use her favourite pillow, cushion or blanket.

2. Ask her to remember something that makes her feel happy. She may recall a game she played with a friend, a favourite hobby or much-loved cuddly toy. Adjust according to the age of your child.

3. Ask her to place both his hands over her chest and imagine the feeling of warmth, peace and happiness grow from there to all over his body and even the room around him. She can imagine it as a warm, golden light filling her heart.

4. Tell her to imagine this golden light spreading to everyone in her family, then to all of her friends, all of the children in her class, her school and her town, even those she doesn't get on with very well. Then to all people on the planet, living in all the different countries. The golden light enteres everyone's heart and makes them smile, no matter how grumpy they are. Then to all animals and plants on earth, including those that live high up in the air and down in the deepest oceans. Mention different trees and animals she is fond of.

Some children may find difficulty in wishing happiness to people they don't like or to animals such as spiders. Explain that this friendly energy includes every living thing, and just as they want to be happy, so do others want to be happy too.

TIP

Experiement with different words. You can use friend energy, loving light, peace or joyfulness for example. Or better still, ask your child which word they find most soothing.

Bubble meditation

I've tried this mindful visualisation with children from age 10 upwards, and they all seem to like it. You can also try the exercise for younger children too – just simplify the language a little.

The steps are as follows:

1. Ask your child to sit or lie down in a comfortable position. Allow him to use pillows and blankets to make himself cosy. You don't need to ask him to sit up straight for this meditation. He can close his eyes if he's okay with that.

2. Say to him: 'Imagine you have a small, shiny bubble in your hand, that can't be burst. Imagine dropping that bubble on the floor in front of you, and watching it gently expand until it's so big you can step inside it. In fact, the bubble is the size of a large, spacious room. Then, step inside the bubble. Now, imagine you can instantly decorate the inside of this bubble in any way you like. You can cover it with blankets of your favourite colour or paint the walls and ceiling just as you like. You can have games machines, expensive televisions, and your favourite music playing in the background – whatever you want. Your favourite food is available whenever you need it. Consider all the sights, sounds, smells, tastes being just how you like them to be inside your bubble. You feel really relaxed, comfortable and safe inside this bubble of yours.' Allow him time to really enjoy his own personal bubble that he's created for himself. Children often like imagining what to put inside his bubble, and so you can extend this for more than five minutes.

3. Now allow some time to practise mindfulness. Say to him: 'Notice how your body feels right now. Which parts feel relaxed? Become aware of your own gentle in and out breath. Enjoy the feeling of your breathing. Feel how soothing the experience is. Breathe in any feeling of happiness and breathe out any stress.'

4. Say to your child: 'Now you've created and enjoyed your own personal bubble, you're ready to keep this personal bubble of yours for later on. You step out of your bubble and see the bubble shrinking so you can hold the bubble in your hand once again. Now imagine the bubble becomes so small it can move inside your hand and up your arm. Allow the bubble to go into the centre of your chest, where your heart is. You can keep your bubble here for safety, and any time you feel you need to go back into your bubble, you can.'

5. Bring the meditation to a close by asking your child to gently open his eyes, and then discuss how the practise went.

Mindful drawing

This exercise trains your child to be mindful of shape, colour, and light and shade. This is particularly helpful for children who resist traditional mindfulness meditation with their eyes closed, because drawing doesn't feel like meditation at all, and yet they're training their attention for detail with a sense of curiosity.

This exercise goes like this:

1. Ask your child to draw an object in the room. She can look at the object as she draws.

2. When she's finished, you can both compare the picture with the actual object. Which bits are close to the reality and which bits aren't quite right? Emphasise that this isn't a competition, more of an experiment to see what happens.

3. If the child wants to, you can repeat the exercise and see how much better the second drawing is through paying attention.

Mindful body scan

Children are far more likely to give their attention to the world around them rather than to their own bodies. This exercise helps to bring their attention back to their physical body, training their attention to focus on one part at a time; they also discover how to move their attention from one part of the body to another. Children can then use this capacity to hold and move their attention in their daily lives.

TIP

Here are the steps for the mindful body scan:

1. Ask your child to lie down in a quiet and relaxing place. He can close his eyes if he wants to.

2. Ask him to name each part of his body, beginning with his toes and moving up to his head. After naming each part, ask him to tell you how that part of the body feels. After naming the part of the body, the child can move it; this changes the feeling and brings a bit of fun to the exercise too.

3. When you get to the top of his head, gently ring a bell and ask him to put his hand up when he can no longer hear the bell. The bell is a way of expanding the attention from a sharp, focused one to a wider, more expansive and open awareness. By asking him to identify when the sound turns into silence, he is drawn naturally into the peaceful silence, and can feel more calm and refreshed.

You can also make this body scan more visual by telling them to imagine a peaceful light beams into each part of their body, making them more aware and accepting of the feelings in that part of their body.

Supporting Teens with Mindfulness

It's not easy being a teenager. If you cast your mind back to those days, you may recall mood swings, frustration with parents, annoying teachers, scary exams and the constant battle to fit in with your peers.

Teenagers often judge themselves harshly, with questions like: 'Why do I look fat? Why do I have a massive spot on my nose just when I managed to get a hot date? Why aren't I pretty? Why doesn't she fancy me?' With all these thoughts hijacking the brain, it's no wonder life is tough for teens. If you're honest with yourself, you still have judgmental and self-critical thoughts in your mind to this day. They may be a little different, but are still there.

The adolescent brain experiences more intense emotions than a child or adult's brain does. This has evolved in nature, because *emotions* are designed to create *motion*. In *Brainstorm: The Power and Purpose of the Teenage Brain* by Daniel Siegel (Published by Tarcher, 2014), the teenage brain has evolved to motivate the teenager to prepare to move away from home. So teenagers' mood swings are not their fault – it's the way their brains work.

TIP

Take a few moment to reflect on what your challenges were as a teenager. How may mindfulness have helped you? How would you have liked to be introduced to mindfulness?

Poor mental health of young people is a large and growing concern. This is not due to just more awareness about mental health – sadly, even suicides by young people are on the increase, being the leading cause of death in 15-19 years olds worldwide. I think that, as a society, we need to do something about these alarming statistics.

Introducing mindfulness to teens

Mindfulness can be a great help to teenagers. With the cocktail of emotions that teens face, mindfulness can be used to help teens anchor themselves in the present by connecting with their senses, and thereby feel a little more in control.

When introducing adolescents to mindfulness, don't use it as a way make them behave better. If that's your attitude, it's likely to backfire. Instead, offer mindfulness for the sake of it.

REMEMBER

The aim of mindfulness is not to feel better but to get better at feeling.

Teenagers need you to treat them like adults. They're human beings, don't forget! The more respect you can show them, the better they'll be able to listen to you.

Offer short mindfulness exercises to teens. Around 10 minutes is a good length of time. A longer session of 15–20 minutes is acceptable for more relaxing exercises like the body scan, which can be done lying down.

With time, many of the mindfulness meditations offered in this book can work for teens.

These tips may help you:

>> **Use appropriate language.** I think 'mindfulness' is quite a good word. The word 'meditation' has all sorts of connotations that may put teenagers off. Some people call it 'relaxation,' but as I mention in Chapter 1, mindfulness is not relaxation – that's just a side effect that sometimes occurs. Teens may be interested if you explain the difference between mindfulness and relaxation.

>> **Use examples and role models that they can relate to.** Think about the group of teenagers (or the individual teenager) you're speaking to, and what kind of things they're interested in. Tell them about famous personalities who are into mindfulness. Examples of meditators include Oprah Winfrey, Arianna Huffington, Bill Ford (executive chairman of Ford), Hugh Jackman (aka 'Wolverine'), Russell Brand, the Dalai Lama and many more.

>> **Respect them, like they're adults.** In my experience, the more you can show respect to teenagers as if they're adults, the better they'll respond. With the inner practise of mindfulness, you certainly can't force it upon anyone. By being mindful yourself, you set the stage and provide an example for them to follow you.

TIP

Here's a simple little exercise for teens to try:

1. Mindful Three: Three things with three senses.

Notice what you can see around you. Which three different objects can you see? Notice their colour and shape.

2. Now listen. Which three different sounds can you hear? Notice the pitch and volume.

3. Now feel the physical sensations in your body. Which three different sensations can you feel? What do the sensations actually feel like?

That's a quick, easy way to get into mindfulness using three senses.

Helping teens with exam stress

Being a teenager without the stress of writing exams is difficult enough. But the added pressure of relentless testing can tip teenagers into anxiety or depression. If you want to help your teenager manage the stress of exams, mindfulness can help.

You can introduce teens to mindfulness in several ways:

>> Show them this or another appropriate book on mindfulness. Perhaps suggest a couple of specific chapters for them to look at.

>> Give them a guided mindfulness audio from this book to try – aim for one that's between three and ten minutes long to begin with. Or invite them to practise mindfulness with you in a comfortable environment.

>> Help them to find a time of day that's right for them – mornings, afternoons or early evenings are all good.

>> Share the short mini mindfulness meditation, and let them use that several times a day, especially at times when they're feeling higher-than-normal levels of stress.

You can give these 'mindful' tips to your teenager in the run-up to exam day:

>> **Sleeping is like plugging your phone in at night.** That's the best way your phone will work best if it's fully charged. The same goes for you. Make it a priority to go to bed on time. It's tempting to revise more and more, but the less sleep you have, the harder you make it for your brain to recall facts.

>> **Start the morning with a short mindfulness practise.** You can do a short body scan or listen to the short mindfulness guided audio tracks that come with this book.

>> **Avoid last-minute revision.** In my experience of doing last-minute revision, all I remembered was the stuff I revised at the last minute, and everything else somehow got lost! If you do revise at the last minute, observe to see whether it works for you or not.

>> **Do a mini mindful exercise just before you start your exam.** Take three conscious deep breaths before you open the exam paper. Or if you feel pressured to open the exam paper when everyone else does, do so, but then do your three deep, mindful breaths. Then take your time over the first question. Exams are like building a house. You need to take your time to build nice solid foundations early on. The first question is your foundation upon which to build.

>> **If you're struggling to answer the questions, don't panic.** Now's the time to stop writing for a few moments and gather yourself. Feel your body on the chair and your feet on the floor to bring you into the present moment. Try putting your pen down and opening and closing your hands a few times, noticing how that feels. Then make a fresh start with the next question, reading the question carefully. Don't give up!

>> **Treat your exam like you're a patient.** When you go to see the doctor, do you want the doctor to rush or to listen carefully to your questions and answer them accurately? Of course you want the doctor to listen and take their time. Rushing exams will lower your grade, not increase it. Take your time and read each question at half the speed at which you normally read. See whether that helps you to answer the question more accurately.

Discovering 7/11 breathing

This is a nice, easy exercise for teenagers to use to deal with the anxiety of exams. Actually, younger children and adults can equally benefit from it. This breathing technique switches on your relaxation response, and if you notice the sensation of your breathing, the exercise can be a mindfulness experience too.

TIP

You can do this exercise anywhere: on a bus, on a train, sitting at home, lying down or even while gently walking. Here's how:

1. As you breathe in, count to seven in your head. Count at a rate that feels comfortable for your breath. Don't count too slowly, otherwise it'll be too difficult to do.

2. As you breathe out, count to 11.

3. Repeat Steps 2 and 3.

4. Whenever you mind wanders off, just forgive yourself, smile and start again. That's cool!

5. Stop after five to ten minutes, or sooner if you feel too relaxed or light headed!

As you do the 7/11 breathing exercise, consider these tips:

>> You need to breathe in a bit faster than you breathe out. The in-breath is slightly harder, and the out-breath a little softer.

>> This takes a bit of practise, like anything else. You'll get better at it after you've done it a few times. Eventually it may get so enjoyable it's slightly addictive, which is good!

TAKING MINDFULNESS INTO SCHOOLS

Worldwide, there is a rapidly growing movement to bring mindfulness into schools.

If you're a parent or guardian and would like to see mindfulness offered in your child's school, try organising a conversation with the head teacher, or ask whether any other teachers are interested in mindfulness. Meeting with and suggesting your idea to teachers who are passionate about mindfulness may help to give the idea momentum. Sharing information and good quality books and articles about mindfulness in schools is like watering the seed of an idea. With a bit of luck, eventually the idea will sprout. Either a teacher will convince the management it's a good idea, or the management itself will begin to take steps to organise an action plan within the school.

If you're a teacher and would like to learn to teach mindfulness and offer it to other teachers or students, see whether you can find a teacher training programme either online or in your local area. (You obviously need to have experience in practising mindfulness and experiencing the challenges and benefits of the practise before you can learn to share the approach with others.)

>> Combine this exercise with visualising yourself in a peaceful place if you like. That's what I call mindful visualisation, if you allow yourself to stay conscious within the experience.

>> If the numbers 7/11 don't work for them, let them find numbers that do. Maybe 3/4 or 5/5.

Mindful Parenting

I think that parenting is probably the most difficult, stressful, important and fulfilling responsibility in the world. A good parent needs not only to nurture the child with food, shelter and clothing, but to develop the child's mind too. Your behaviour as a parent often reflects what your own parents were like, even if you want to change and improve upon certain areas. However, parents often end up repeating the cycle in subtle ways, passing on unhelpful behaviours. Fortunately, mindful parenting can help to break the cycle.

Being present for your children

How can mindfulness help with parenting? Mindful parents are aware of and awake to their actions and the actions of their children. This is very important in bringing up a child. Children crave attention. For children, attention is like love. If they don't receive sufficient attention, they misbehave until they get that attention – even being told off is preferable to being ignored. Attention is a fundamental need for a child. How can you give that attention if you're not attentive yourself? Mindfulness offers ways to hone your attention skills to help bring up a child in a more harmonious and peaceful way.

Here are the benefits of parenting in the present moment:

>> **You can meet your child's needs.** By living in the present moment, you're more able to meet your child's needs as necessary. You notice if your child needs to eat or sleep or just play. You notice if actually all that he needs is a hug. Each moment is different and fresh, and what worked yesterday may not work today. Your child is one day older and different – living moment by moment helps you to see this.

>> **You can meet your own needs.** By being aware and awake to the present sensations in your own body, and noticing the way you react to situations, you're also better able to look after yourself. Parenting is very tiring, and when you're over-tired you can end up making decisions that just create more difficulties rather than solutions. Awareness of your own reactions helps you to sense when this is happening and to take whatever appropriate action is necessary.

>> **You cultivate gratefulness.** Living in the present moment helps you to be grateful for what you have rather than ungrateful for what you don't. You may notice how much work you have to do, or how frustrated you are by your children's behaviour, but thinking about what isn't going according to plan is draining. Living in the present enables you to see what's going well and what you do have. You may have healthy children and a nice home; you may be having a spell of good weather; or you may have a supportive partner or friend.

>> **You see things afresh.** One of the other key aspects of mindfully living in the present is adopting an attitude of 'beginner's mind.' (For more on seeing things afresh, jump to Chapter 4.) This involves seeing things freshly, as if for the first time. If you have a baby, you're able to see how he's always living in beginner's mind. Babies look around the room or area with wonder. By living with this same attitude, you're more able to meet the ever-changing challenge of parenting in the present moment.

>> **You free yourself from worries.** Living and parenting moment by moment means you can let go of regrets about the past and worries about the future. Neither of them exist in the present moment. Do you have any problems at all, right now, if you don't think about them? All worries, concerns, fears and anxieties arise from leaving the here and now, the present moment. All you need to do is take things one day at a time – or, better still, one second at a

time. You may be worrying about how your children will be tomorrow, or next week, month or year. All you can possibly do is your best, right here and now, and let go of what has happened or may happen.

Trying out tips for mindful parenting

Here are a few tips for practising mindful parenting:

>> **Be present for your child.** The greatest present you can give your child is your presence. Live in the moment and as if everything in front of you is your teacher. Your child will observe and copy this on some level.

>> **Find the balance between love and discipline.** If you're too lenient your children become spoilt, but if you're too harsh your children become overly cold and closed. Set clear boundaries, but ensure that you praise good behaviour and attitudes, and don't just criticise their errors.

>> **Trust your intuition.** Your sense of the best thing to do is more intelligent than logical thinking – your intuition has access to all your unconscious learning that has operated in humanity for thousands of years. Use a combination of your head and heart in your decisions.

>> **Look for a balance in situations.** You can't get your own way all the time, and neither can your child. But perhaps a place in between satisfies you both to a certain extent and feels right.

>> **Imagine things from your child's perspective.** What's it like to be dominated by adults most of the time? How does your child feel if adults' seemingly silly desires are all they can think about? If you were your child, how would you want your parents to act towards you?

>> **Take some time to meditate every day, even if for a short period of time.** Don't force your child to do the same, but answer his questions about meditation honestly and simply, and play mindful games with him when you can.

>> **Practise mindful listening.** Listen to your child as if you're listening to a piece of music or the sounds of nature. Listen with a gentle attentiveness and respond as necessary. Listening to your child can be like a mindfulness meditation.

>> **Observe your own behaviour as much as you observe your child's behaviour.** See how you like to do what you like doing, just as your child likes to do what *he* likes doing.

>> **Look after yourself.** Ensure that you eat properly, sleep enough (I know this can be difficult), and take exercise. You may need to be really creative to fit some of these things into your daily schedule.

>> **Be light-hearted.** You don't need to take things too seriously. If you made a mistake in your parenting, don't beat yourself up about the fault – instead see whether you can laugh or at least smile about it. You're human after all, and so is your child.

MULLA NASRUDDIN STORIES

Children love stories of Nasruddin, known throughout the Middle East. The stories seem to suggest that Nasruddin was foolish, but they all contain gems of hidden wisdom within. Here are a few examples:

- Nasruddin was on his hands and knees one dark evening, under the light of a street lamp. A neighbour came out to ask what the problem was. Nasruddin said he had dropped his keys and so was looking for them. The neighbour helped him search but couldn't find the keys. In the end the neighbour asked: 'Where exactly did you drop them?' Nasruddin said, 'Over there,' pointing to his front door. The neighbour retorted: 'Then why are you looking under the lamp?'! Nasruddin replied: 'Because there's light here.'

- One day Nasruddin went into his favourite coffee shop and said: 'The moon is more useful than the sun.' An old man asked: 'Why?' Nasruddin replied: 'We need the light more during the night than during the day.'

- A friend asked Nasruddin: 'How old are you?' 'Fifty,' he replied. 'But you said the same thing two years ago!' 'Yes,' replied Nasruddin, 'I always stand by what I've said.'

- 'When I was in the desert,' said Nasruddin to his friend, 'I caused an entire tribe of horrible and bloodthirsty people to run.' 'How did you do it?' 'Easy. I just ran, and they ran after me.'

- Nasruddin, who wasn't used to public speaking, arose in confusion and said nervously: 'M-m-my f-f-friends, when I c-c-c-came here tonight only God and I knew what I was about to say to you. Now, only God knows!'

- Nasruddin was sitting chatting with a neighbour, when his son came up the road holding a chicken. 'Where did you get that chicken?' Nasruddin asked. 'I stole it,' said his son. Nasruddin turned to his neighbour and said proudly: 'There's my boy. He may steal, but he won't lie.'

You can find more stories, in full, at www.nasruddin.org.

5

The Part of Tens

Find ten tips for practising daily mindfulness.

Explore ten different ways to practise mindfulness that can really help you.

Discover ten common ideas about mindfulness that just aren't true.

Investigate ten different resources including books, films and websites.

Chapter **16**

Ten Top Tips for Mindful Living

Mindfulness is simple in essence – it's about cultivating present-moment awareness more than anything else – but the difficulty is in practising mindfulness consistently. This chapter gives you a series of short, easy ways of integrating the principles of mindfulness into your everyday life. Don't underestimate their value – they may take relatively little time and seem overly simplistic, but many of these tips have been proven to be effective. Try them out for yourself and hold back your judgement until you've given the tools a try for at least a few weeks.

Spending Some Quiet Time Every Day

Having some quiet time every day is the most important tip I can give you. I can't emphasise enough the importance of connecting with some form of mindfulness practise on a daily basis, preferably for ten minutes or more. By deliberately practising mindfulness every day, you strengthen your mind's ability to be more aware and awake.

If you want to be more mindful, you need daily training, just as when if you want to become fitter, you need to exercise your body on a daily basis. If you only exercised once a week, you wouldn't benefit as much. Your mind goes back to its original state even more quickly than the body does.

To practise mindfulness on a daily basis can involve sitting still and feeling the sensation of your breathing, or doing some yoga, or simply sitting in your garden and looking at the trees and birds with a warm drink before starting work.

Here are some ways to ensure that you remember to be mindful every day:

» Use the principle of *habit stacking*. Practise at the same time and in the same place every day, following from an existing habit in your routine. This way, mindfulness becomes part of your routine like brushing your teeth, and you're much more likely to remember.

» Don't push yourself too much. If ten minutes seems too long, just do whatever you can manage. You can gradually build up the time for which you practise.

» Put reminders on your mirror, refrigerator, computer or phone. When you see the reminder, do a little meditation.

Connect with People

In the first instant that you meet someone, within a split second, you judge her. You may think that she's too fat or too thin, you don't like her hairstyle, she reminds you of someone you don't like. Your mind instantly tries to categorise, which is why first impressions are so important in interviews. The moment you make an initial judgement of a person, you begin to look for evidence to support your theory. If she doesn't look you in the eye properly, or fails to say thanks, you take these moments as evidence about her, and your opinion becomes more fixed. Then you create an image in your mind. You think that you know this other person, when all you know are your own judgements of her.

When you meet someone, connect with your senses rather than your ideas. Look the person in the eye in a natural way. Listen to what she has to say, rather than thinking about what you're about to say. Be curious and ask questions rather than imposing your own perceptions so much. See things from the other person's point of view – what would you be like in that person's situation? How would you feel, and what would you want? By being less juedgemental of others, you'll also become less juedgemental of yourself, and vice versa.

REMEMBER

Mindfulness is about paying attention with a sense of warmth and kindness, as well as a sense of curiosity and openness. Bring these attitudes to the relationship and see what happens.

Enjoy the Beauty of Nature

The clearest way into the Universe is through a forest wilderness.

JOHN MUIR

Nature has a way of drawing a mindful awareness from you, rather than you forcing yourself to be mindful. Walking among old trees with their branches overhanging the path you're treading, smelling the scent of freshly cut grass, or listening to the birds sing and the twigs crunching under your feet, you can't help but be aware in the moment. Gardening is also a wonderful way of connecting with nature and experiencing 'flow' (explained in Chapter 5); absorb yourself in tasks such as weeding and planting and enjoy the fruits of your labours as you see tiny shoots grow into beautiful plants and flowers.

TIP

If you have a garden or live near a park or a bit of greenery, realise how fortunate you are. Take time to reconnect with mother nature – make time for doing so. Nature is a miraculous living being, and you're part of that life. As a child you may have loved to play in natural surroundings, jumping in puddles and sliding in mud. With your acute senses, perhaps you were quite happy to explore and observe all day long if permitted. Try reconnecting with a childlike innocence and visit a natural environment, whatever that means to you.

In a famous study in a care home, half the elderly folk were given a plant to look after themselves, and the other half were given a plant but told that the nurses would look after it. Those who had responsibility to water and nurture the plants lived significantly longer than the others. The study concluded that responsibility gave the elderly a sense of control, leading to longer life. The study also suggests that not only looking at nature in a passive way, but also growing plants and ensuring that they thrive as best you can, is a healthy and life-enhancing activity to engage in on a regular basis.

Change Your Daily Routine

Humans are creatures of habit. If you think about the things you've done today, they're probably the same things you've done many times before. One way of being more mindful is to change your routine. Yes, you have to get up, get dressed, go to work and so on, but you don't have to do all that in exactly the same way. And what about the way you spend your free time (if you're lucky enough to have free time!)? Do you always do the same hobbies, watch the same kind of movies, read the same type of books, meet the same sort of people, think the same sort of thoughts? The answer is probably yes.

Try changing your routine to boost your mindful awareness. When you're in your routine lifestyle, your mind goes into a sleep state. You're less likely to notice the good things happening around you. You're unable to think creatively.

By making just small changes in your routine, your brain wakes up. You gently nudge yourself out of your comfort zone. And in that more awakened state, you're immediately more mindful.

For example, today I had a cup of tea before my mindfulness practise, which I don't normally have. It's a small change, but it helped me stay present in my practise and has had a positive knock-on effect on my day!

TIP

Choose one of these options to help shift out of your automatic-pilot living.

>> Meet up with a friend you haven't seen for ages.

>> Drive to work without switching on the radio.

>> Pick up a random book next time you're in a bookshop or library and read a chapter.

>> Try signing up to an evening class to learn a new skill such as painting, photography or pottery – ideally something that may push you out of your comfort zone a little.

>> Switch around your daily morning routine – maybe have breakfast before having a shower, or vice versa.

>> Do a random act of kindness today. Make tea for a coworker. Pick up some litter from the ground. Or even just take extra care of some plants or your pet today.

See the Wonder of the Present Moment

Yesterday is history, tomorrow a mystery, today is a gift, that's why it's called the present.

This moment is the *only moment* you have, and you have it right now. Memories of the past come up in the present moment. Ideas of the future are shaped by past experience and projected into an imagined tomorrow. In reality, this present moment is all that's available.

If you're currently going through a difficult time, you probably don't think that the present moment is wonderful at all. That's okay. You can remember that you don't have to worry too much about the future and only need to cope with whatever you're facing here and now. In this sense, being in the present moment is helpful – you don't need to worry about the future.

TIP

To really appreciate the present moment, feel your senses. Connect with your sense of sight. Notice the range of different colours in front of you. Reflect on the fact that this experience of colour is partly due to a large amount of biochemical reactions rapidly turning into electrical impulses going into your brain, leading to this incredible experience called colour. What would it be like to see colour for the first time? How would you describe the experience to someone who'd never seen colour before? Try looking without naming objects or people – just connect with the bare awareness of light itself. Be grateful you have eyes that are able to see in the first place. Look with the effortless gaze of a child.

Another way to really connect with the present is to focus on your breathing. Think these words while breathing in and out, if you find them helpful:

>> Breathing in: 'I am in the present moment.'

>> Breathing out: 'This is a wonderful moment.'

If you don't like feeling your breathing, you could try feeling your feet on the floor, listening to the sounds around you or simply gazing at the sky curiously for a few moments. Experiment! Find what you find most enjoyable or engaging.

Listen to Unpleasant Emotions

How do you see the wonder of the present moment if you feel down, upset or annoyed? In these situations, don't try to impose a different emotion on what you're experiencing. Be in the present moment and open up the emotion as best you can. Give yourself time to feel it rather than immediately running from it. Remember that all emotions have a beginning and an end – try to see the feeling as a temporary visitor. Additionally, see yourself as separate from the emotion. The emotion rises and falls, but you maintain a sense of stability and greater emotional balance.

Imagine that someone turns up at your front door and rings the doorbell. You decide to ignore the sound. The bell rings again and again. You get frustrated and try all sorts of ways of distracting yourself from the sound of the doorbell, but you can't. And all that work distracting yourself means you can't get on with your day. By simply opening the door and allowing the person ringing the bell to come in, you can stop all your avoidance strategies and do what matters. You're facing your fears. You're looking towards the unpleasant emotions rather than running away (which is an understandable response).

Moving towards the emotion, without forcing it to go away, often has the effect of dissipating the emotion. The emotion comes in, has a cup of tea or whatever, and off it goes. The emotion just wanted some mindful awareness. The idea is to offer just that – becoming aware of the emotions you spend so much time running away from with a kind, curious, open, non-judgemental awareness, as best you can. Explore and discover what effect this has on negative emotions in the long run, not to get rid of them, but to learn from them.

WARNING

If you practise mindfulness to try to get rid of an emotion, that's not mindfulness. That's avoidance, which is the opposite of what we're trying to cultivate. Avoidance is like putting fuel in the fire of your emotions: They'll just get stronger. The idea is to *allow* the emotion space to be in your awareness, acknowledge and learn from it, and then to continue on with whatever matters to you. You are above your emotions as you're aware of them. You don't need to let the emotion rule your life.

Chapters 12 and 13 are all about how mindfulness can help you deal with unpleasant emotions.

Remember That Thoughts Are Just Thoughts

If you had the thought, 'I'm a flying, pink chimpanzee,' you obviously wouldn't believe it. That's a crazy idea. Then why do you believe thoughts like 'I'm useless' or 'I'll never get better' or 'I can't go on?' They're thoughts too, that have just popped into your head. Don't believe everything you think. Your mind often makes assumptions and inferences that simply aren't true. 'I'm feeling low at the moment' may be true, but 'I'll always be depressed' is not. 'I find it annoying when she doesn't do her chores' may be true, but 'She never helps me' is unlikely to be true.

Thoughts are just words, images and sounds that pop up in your mind. But most of the time, you get hooked to your thoughts and believe them to be true. But you don't have to.

As you discover how to observe the nature of your mind in mindfulness, you realise from experience that thoughts are always arising in your mind, no matter how much mindful practise you do. Even people who've been practising mindfulness for years have plenty of thoughts. The thoughts aren't going to stop. You simply need to change your relationship to thoughts. Seeing thoughts as just thoughts rather than facts makes a world of difference. If the thought 'I'm pathetic' comes up and you believe whatever arises in your mind, you're bound to feel low and uneasy. However, if exactly the same thought comes up and you're mindful of it, you see it as just a thought and not a fact. This takes much of the sting out of the thought, and you're free to dismiss it and carry on with whatever you're doing, relatively untouched. This is freedom. Freedom, or peace of mind, isn't about *stopping* your thoughts, but seeing thoughts as just thoughts and not giving them too much attention, and not believing them as reality. I believe that reality is contained in the here and now, beyond ideas and concepts. This implies that you're not your mind – you're the observer, the silent witness, always complete, whole and free.

REMEMBER If you practise meditation regularly, you begin naturally to take a step back from your thinking. Normally, if you have a thought, you act on it, especially if you aren't fully conscious of the thought. In meditation, you observe the thought without acting on it. You see your thoughts as a pattern, as energy moving through your mind.

Be Grateful Every Day

Gratitude is the best attitude! Gratitude is when you discover how to want what you have and not want what you don't have. Usually, people want what they don't have and don't want what they do have. This is bound to lead to a sense of dissatisfaction. You can practise gratitude right now. Think about this book in your hand at the moment. Millions of people in the world don't have a single book. Think about the fact that you can read – another skill inaccessible to millions.

Gratitude requires mindfulness. Let's say you're cooking. To be grateful of how fortunate you are to have food available to you requires you to be mindful, and that brings you into the present moment.

When I'm feeling a bit down, which is sometimes a sign that I'm focusing on things that aren't going well, I find myself practising gratitude. Just reflecting for a moment and trying to think of five things I'm grateful for helps to put things into perspective. It may or may not make me feel better, but at least I'm considering things from a more realistic perspective.

Here are some ways to nurture feelings of gratitude:

>> **Sleep with gratitude.** Before going to sleep, spend a minute or two thinking about five things you're grateful for. They can be very simple things, and you don't have to feel hugely grateful for them. Just go through each one and see what effect that has on your sleep. To enhance the experience, consider why you're grateful for them too.

>> **Say thank you.** This is a simple act but very powerful. Saying thank you is both an act of gratitude and kindness – you're making clear to the other person that you've recognised her generosity.

>> **Carry out an action to say thanks.** Send a thank-you card or a small gift, or do something like making coffee or helping someone with her work. As the old saying goes, actions speak louder than words.

>> **Try being grateful for things you wouldn't normally be.** For example, when things are difficult, you can be grateful for the challenge the difficulty offers. Be grateful for access to running water or for your ability to hear. Or try being grateful for being alive in the first place – perhaps this is the greatest miracle.

Here's an extract from a wonderful poem by an unknown author, on thanks and gratitude:

Be thankful that you don't already have everything you desire. If you did, what would there be to look forward to?

Be thankful when you don't know something, for it gives you the opportunity to learn.

Be thankful for the difficult times. During those times you grow.

Be thankful for your limitations, because they give you opportunities for improvement.

Be thankful for your mistakes. They will teach you valuable lessons.

Be thankful when you're tired and weary, because it means you've made a difference.

It's easy to be thankful for the good things.

A life of rich fulfilment comes to those who are also thankful for the setbacks.

Find a way to be thankful for your troubles, and they can become your blessings.

328 PART 5 **The Part of Tens**

Use Technology Mindfully

Just as plants and animals evolve to better survive and thrive in their environment, technology has also evolved over time. And part of technology's evolution is to become both faster and more addictive. With the advent of smartphones, you can use technology from the very moment you wake up until you drift off to sleep. And even if you wake up in the middle of the night, you can find yourself checking social media or surfing the web before you know it.

Video games are another form of technology that's highly addictive. Some people spend so long playing games, it affects their work and home lives and has even lead to marriage breakups.

I'm not dismissing the huge benefits of technology, but you need to manage your use of digital devices. Here are some tips:

>> **Have a digital detox day or half day once a week.** Give your brain a break.

>> **Charge your phone in your kitchen at night.** This is a clever way of keeping your phone away from the side of your bed each night. This way you can start your mornings mindfully and tech-free.

>> **Be courteous.** Switch off your phone at mealtimes or when out with friends and family. Challenge yourself and see whether you can resist the temptation to check your phone at the table, even if your friend does.

>> **Go for a walk without your phone.** If you're not used to this, you'll probably find the experience strange at first and then tremendously refreshing. I love doing this regularly.

>> **Make a note of how many times you check your phone in a day.** That's an experience of mindfulness in itself. Average users check their phones over 100 times a day! Switch off your phone for chunks of the day and find something more enjoyable to do with your time.

>> **Surf the urge to use technology.** When you feel the desire to use technology but don't really have to, notice the feeling in your body. See whether you can ride that urge, just feeling it and relaxing into it. Each time you do that, your addiction will lessen until eventually the urge will disappear completely.

Breathe and Smile!

You'll find that life is still worthwhile, if you just smile.

CHARLES CHAPLIN

The muscles in your face link with your feeling of happiness. When you're happy, you smile – you know that of course. But did you know that smiling can make you feel better? Try the process right now, no matter how you feel. Simply hold a subtle, gentle smile as you read these sentences. Continue for a few minutes and note what effect the smiling has. Combine this with feeling your own breathing.

TIP

You can apply this technique of feeling your breathing and smiling gently in a systematic way every day for ten minutes, or while you're going about your daily activities. Think of it as yoga for your mouth! In this way you can be mindful doing whatever you're doing, whether washing the dishes, writing a report or waiting in a queue. Each moment is an opportunity to come back to the here and now, the present moment. You don't need anything extra – your breath and smile are both highly portable!

You may feel reluctant to smile right now, because you don't think that the smile is genuine. You'll smile when you're happy, not now. All I can say is, try it out. Yes, you're bound to feel unnatural at the beginning but that soon goes. Just give it a try, even though it feels strange, and see what happens after a time. As someone said to me once: 'Fake it till you make it!'

REMEMBER

Mindfulness is not about forcing your yourself to feel better – it's more about bringing a sense of curiosity to your feelings and thoughts and gaining information from them, whatever you're experiencing. Being aware of thoughts or feelings and accepting them as they are is far more important than trying to *change* your thoughts or feelings.

Chapter **17**

Ten Ways Mindfulness Can Really Help You

Mindfulness provides a plethora of benefits that I hope you'll experience for yourself. As soon as you start being mindful on a regular basis you'll find mindfulness quite addictive! In this chapter I give you a snapshot of the benefits of mindfulness, many of which are backed up by scientific research.

Training the Brain

Until fairly recently, scientists thought that the connections and structure of the adult brain were fixed, because changing the brain's connections would be far too complex.

Now we know the truth: your brain *can* change! Scientists looked at violinists' brains and found that the part of the brain responsible for finger dexterity was much bigger for violinists compared with non-violinists. They also studied London taxi drivers, who need to know all the complex road networks and 10,000 different streets in London ('the knowledge'). When scientists compared the cabbies' brains with 'normal' brains, they found that the part responsible for location was significantly *bigger*. The longer the drivers worked, the more significant the change.

The evidence proves that through training and simple everyday experience, the physical brain actually changes. Repetitive experience changes the brain more than anything else does. The discovery that the brain changes in response to experience is now called *neuroplasticity*, and it gives everyone tremendous hope – you can *change your brain* through training at any age!

With the help of the Dalai Lama, top neuroscientist Professor Richard Davidson scanned the brains of meditating monks who'd engaged in a prolonged meditation for a minimum of 10,000 hours (not all in one go!). The meditation the monks did was a compassion meditation, similar to the metta meditation described in Chapter 6. The monks' brains totally changed through the practise of this meditation. The front left part of the brain (left prefrontal cortex if you're really curious) associated with positivity was activated – in fact, it went off the scale! No scientist had ever seen so much positive effect in a human being before. The scientists found that the monks' entire brains had been rewired to be more positive. This proves that mindfulness and compassion aren't fixed, but are skills that you can train in.

Okay, monks' brains become more positive because they spend most of their time meditating. But what about you and me? We don't have time to meditate for that long. Can short lengths of time meditating mindfully help? Does the brain improve after, say, 30 minutes a day for two weeks?

The incredible answer is yes. Scientists have also looked at short-term mindfulness meditation. People were randomly assigned to two groups. One group trained in cognitive behavioural therapy to show group members how to see challenges in their lives with greater positivity. The other group was trained in metta (mindful loving kindness) meditation. Some of those in the metta group had greater activation in the brain region signifying positivity and also reported greater love for themselves compared with those in the cognitive behavioural therapy group. Helpful changes did indeed happen within a fortnight of practise.

So mindfulness meditation does change the brain, and the more you practise, the greater the positive change within your brain. One more reason to download the MP3 Audio tracks that accompany this book and start meditating!

Improving Relationships

Several studies show that people's relationships tend to improve when they begin to practise mindfulness. Several reasons indicate why this may be the case.

Mindfulness can switch off stress. When you feel threatened by a nasty remark or overly challenged at work or home, your body and mind engage in a stress response. You become less understanding and more reactive and judgemental. Obviously, this can have a detrimental effect on personal relationships. You may snap easily when your partner asks what's wrong, or respond emotionally when you come home to realise that dinner hasn't been cooked. Mindfulness makes you more conscious of your day-to-day life, making you less likely to react unhelpfully. You have more mental space and time to make better choices in the way that you respond to situations.

REMEMBER

Mindfulness develops your capacity to accept your experience from moment to moment. This accepting stance translates itself into improved relationships with others. In knowing how to be more accepting of another person's faults (nobody's perfect!), you're more likely to develop greater understanding and increase the possibility of noticing people's positive qualities.

Being judgemental isn't the greatest relationship booster in the world. However, research shows that mindful meditators are less judgemental and more focused in the moment, even when they're not meditating. This may explain why your relationships improve once you start meditating – you're connecting with what other people say rather than wasting your energy judging them.

Mindfulness leads to higher levels of empathy and compassion for both yourself and others. A more caring attitude naturally leads you to give greater levels of attention and helps you to see from other people's perspective. Ultimately, a feeling of love is at the heart of any meaningful relationship, and, as love grows in mindfulness, the quality of relationships naturally deepens.

Boosting Creativity

Your creativity depends entirely on your state of mind. You can't expect to have exciting and perceptive ideas if your mind is overworked and jam-packed with opinions and points of view. Creativity requires letting go of the old to make way for the new. Mindfulness meditation is about being aware of your thoughts without judging them; this lack of judgement allows new and unique ways of thinking to arise. In most creativity exercises, the emphasis is always to stop judging ideas and just let them flow – in a mindfulness practise called choiceless awareness, described in Chapter 6, you do exactly the same thing.

Research published in the journal *Consciousness and Cognition* in 2012 was the first study to show that people who rate themselves as being more mindful are better able to solve insight problems – problems that require a shift of perception and novel thinking to find solutions.

REMEMBER

Mindfulness, over the long term, leads to a calmer state of mind. When the conscious mind settles down, you begin to access the immense creative capacity and knowledge of the subconscious mind. You normally only access this creativity when sleeping, so doing so is almost totally out of your control. With mindfulness, the creative ideas that arise are more practical. Most of my good ideas have arisen while mindfully meditating. By giving my mind the opportunity and space just to be, I tap into my creativity, accessing idea after idea.

Reducing Depression

Some types of depression are thought to be caused by repetitive negative thinking patterns (rumination) and avoiding uncomfortable thoughts and feelings rather than facing up to them (experiential avoidance). Mindfulness, as part of mindfulness-based cognitive therapy explained in Chapter 13, helps combat depression in several ways. Mindfulness:

>> **Develops your capacity to stay with, experience and face difficult experiences and emotions instead of avoiding them.** Avoiding difficult emotions has been found to be the key way in which relapsing into depression occurs. You can gradually develop an attitude of acceptance, kindness and curiosity towards experience through regularly practising mindfulness, enabling a healthier approach towards emotions.

>> **Shifts you towards a 'being mode' of mind.** This being mode (described in full in Chapter 5) enables you to witness your depression as something that rises and falls within you, rather than as a core part of who you are. You can step back from your internal experience in a beneficial way and see things from a bigger perspective. This shift in perspective helps to prevent you from seeing the depression as something that'll never end, changing the idea 'I'm depressed' to 'The feeling of depression is here at the moment, but not forever. All feelings have a beginning and an end.'

>> **Helps you to understand the patterns of the mind.** Being mindful helps you to see how your mind easily goes into an unaware 'automatic pilot' mode, which leads to negative thinking cycles, leading to further depression. Becoming aware of these habits of mind is the first step to beginning to see them from a different perspective and thereby reducing their potency.

>> **Develops healthier habits of mind.** Depression is deepened through rumination. Mindfulness disables this negative thinking cycle by encouraging you to connect your attention to the present moment. This focus reduces the inner resources devoted to rumination. As mindfulness develops into a habit, when mild feelings of sadness arise, your likely response is to focus on the sensations in your body rather than spiralling into major depression.

Turn to Chapter 13 for much more on combating depression with mindfulness.

Reducing Chronic Pain

Incredible as it sounds, mindfulness can actually reduce chronic pain. Participation in Dr Jon Kabat-Zinn's mindfulness-based stress reduction (MBSR) programme has shown, in several research studies, the benefits of mindfulness for those suffering from chronic pain.

In one study, 90 patients suffering chronic pain were trained in mindfulness meditation for ten weeks. Experts observed a significant reduction in pain, negative body image, negative moods, anxiety and depression. The patients also engaged in more activity, including everyday activity such as preparing food and driving, which they'd struggled with before. The use of pain-reduction drugs decreased and feelings of self-esteem increased. These patients did much better than a group that underwent normal pain-management programmes.

The most exciting aspect was the result of a follow-up four years later. The majority of the chronic pain patients reported that most of their improvements had lasted or even improved further. This was probably due to the fact that, incredibly, over 90 per cent of the participants continued to practise some form of mindfulness meditation. This is a major achievement, considering they'd trained four years previously.

All these positive benefits may be partly due to the way mindfulness can train you to accept difficult bodily sensations instead of trying to resist them or pretending the discomfort isn't there. Paradoxically, acceptance seems to reduce the pain. You discover how to feel the pain and experience it as a moment-to-moment feeling rather than avoiding it and tensing up your muscles. You can help the muscles around the painful region relax, thereby reducing the pain itself.

Giving Deeper Meaning to Life

Before I started practising mindfulness, I found life rather hollow and empty. I had friends and family, a comfortable place to live and a good career, but something was definitely missing. Life was a bit of a grind and lacked zest and vitality. I still remember the first mindfulness class I attended. The teacher calmly talked about the nature of awareness and how, through regular practise, you can become more aware. This need for awareness resonated with me – the whole thing made sense. However, I lacked discipline to begin with, and discovered that a lack of a regular mindfulness meditation routine didn't really work. With further practise, many wonderful teachers and good fortune, I was able to deepen my mindfulness practise. The practise itself became a driving force for a more meaningful and authentic life.

REMEMBER

In a popular, mindful therapeutic approach called Acceptance and Commitment Therapy (ACT), the goal is to help clients live a rich and meaningful life. This is achieved by helping them to find out what their core values are and encouraging them to take action. They are taught mindfulness skills to help them accept and navigate any unhelpful thoughts and feelings. This leads to greater psychological flexibility and a life with greater vitality. See Chapter 13 for more on ACT.

Managing Stress and Anxiety

Stress and anxiety are slightly different. Stress is your response to a challenging situation, and anxiety is one effect of that stress. Anxiety is more fear-based and a reaction to the stress itself. Mindfulness can help with both.

Stress is part and parcel of life. Challenges in life cause you stress. Some stresses can feel great: a new relationship, completing a fun yet tricky job or playing sports. They cause no harm. But the problem is when the stress feels overwhelming and unrelenting. Many health issues are caused by this chronic, unsustainable level of stress.

When it comes to mananging stress in a mindful way, this Serenity Prayer (or Serenity Reflection) is key:

> *Grant me the serenity to accept the things I can't change, the courage to change the things I can change and the wisdom to know the difference.*

The idea is to change what you can change and accept what you can't.

So take action if you can. Quit that job if your boss is consistently unreasonable. Walk to work rather than taking the train if your commute is horrible. Change any stressors that feel like unhealthy levels of stress.

For those things that you can't change, change your relationship to those challenges. If you can't quit your job, can you become more curious about why your boss reacts the way he or she does? If you have a deadline that you must meet, notice your negative thought:

'I can't do it'

Change it to this:

'I notice I'm having the thought I can't do it'

This small change can shift your perspective and ease your stress.

When you feel your stress levels getting excessively high, just do a short mini-meditation, as described in Chapter 7, can give you a bit of mental space to decide what's the best way to respond to the challenge.

WISE WORDS

Dr. Richard Lazarus, world-famous stress researcher and psychologist, defined stress as 'a particular relationship between the person and the environment that is *appraised* by the person as taxing or exceeding his or her resources and endangering his or her wellbeing.' I like his insight. The definition explains how an event may be stressful for you, but not for someone else – the level of stress experienced depends on whether you see the situation (the stressor) as something you can cope with.

Here's an example of how mindfulness can help in many different levels. Say your boss has a tendency to lose his cool easily and shouts at you often, even though you're doing your best. How would mindfulness help? Read through the three ways listed below.

Firstly, by being more mindful, you'll notice the fact that you're stressed. You may feel your jaw tightening or your shoulders hunching before you even get to work. Then when your boss shouts at you, you're more aware of the choices you have. You know what effect saying nothing, reacting with insults, or storming out would have. The very fact of being aware of your reactions changes them. You naturally begin to move from *reacting* to negative events to *responding* with greater wisdom. You begin to think more creatively, which may include behaving more assertively.

Secondly, through regular practise of mindfulness meditation, you give your body and mind a rest. Instead of spending your time doing and achieving this and that, you provide a space for yourself to simply be. This 'being' mode is tremendously nourishing and uplifts your inner resources for responding calmly rather than stressing out.

Thirdly, you begin to see things from a different perspective. Although your car won't start this morning, at least it gives you a chance for a cup of tea while you wait for a mechanic. Even though there's a big queue at the bank, at least you have enough money to live on, unlike many unfortunate people. You may even use the opportunity to practise mindfulness as you wait in the queue.

What about anxiety? How can mindfulness help with that? Feeling anxious is a perfectly natural human emotion when you're facing with a tough challenge. However, responding to feeling anxious in a unmindful way compounds the feeling, making it into a issue.

Everyone experiences feelings of anxiety in their lives, perhaps before an interview or an exam. However, if you suffer from a generalised anxiety disorder, the feeling becomes a part of your day-to-day existence. Anxiety can significantly disrupt activities you found easy to do in the past.

TIP

When a situation makes you feel anxious, your temptation will be to avoid the situation. I don't recommend that. Your mind is trying to reduce your anxiety, but the strategy of avoidance will backfire. The more you try to avoid anxiety, the more you are allowing the emotion to rule your life, and the stronger the anxiety will get. A much healthier strategy is to move towards your challenge – approach rather than avoid. Use mindfulness exercises to become curious and accept your feelings of anxiety, knowing that it'll pass in its own time.

Anxiety and worry are based on thinking about the future. You may be concerned about what will happen later, next month or next year. Your mind drifts into predicting negative future outcomes and thereby generates challenging emotions. Mindfulness counteracts this by encouraging you to live in the here and now, from moment to moment and non-judgementally. You begin to free yourself from your dangerously drifting mind and allow yourself to emerge in the sensory world of the present.

REMEMBER

Mindfulness enables you to step back from the contents of your mind and emotions. You discover how to identify less with the thoughts going through your mind and to realise that they're just thoughts, rather than facts. This enables your thoughts to lose their power, which therefore reduces the anxiety. You don't have to think 'I am anxious.' Instead you can think 'I'm the observer of this anxiety, and as the observer, I'm untouched by it.'

Surprisingly, research has found that *trying* to stop worrying increases the worry. Through being more mindful, you change your *relationship* to thoughts, being more compassionate and accepting of them rather than trying to eliminate them. This mindful approach seems to be far more effective than trying to prevent worrying thoughts completely. Read Chapter 13 for more about using mindfulness to combat anxiety.

Dealing with Addiction

Do you have any addictions? Maybe to coffee or cigarettes? Or maybe you're addicted to shopping, gambling, the Internet? Or are you addicted to reading *For Dummies* books? Joking aside, addiction to substances like alcohol or drugs or to activities like gambling obviously has serious negative consequences for you and your loved ones. The good news is that initial findings on mindfulness are showing promising results.

For example, one study published in 2017 in the *International Journal of Neuropsychopharmacology* invited 68 heavy drinkers to participate in an experiment. The group was randomly split into two groups: a relaxation group and a mindfulness group (although they were not told they were doing mindfulness or relaxation). Both groups were given an 11-minute audio recording to listen to. The relaxation group were given a guided relaxation audio, encouraging them to calm their mind and ease the tension in their muscles. The mindfulness group were given a guided audio encouraging them to notice the physical sensations in their body, the emotions they were experiencing and thoughts they had – all the mindfulness approaches shared in this book. The word 'mindfulness' wasn't even used in the audio to avoid bias.

The groups were also give small flash cards, reminding them of the technique they had learnt and to use the strategy whenever they felt the urge to drink.

One week later, the mindfulness group were drinking 35-percent less alcohol on average. The relaxation group showed no significant change at all. Amazingly, they were not even practising that much as they used the audio on average 3 to 4 times per week for 5 to 10 minutes. This study shows again how a big change can come through small, consistent efforts.

The reason mindfulness works so well is probably because you learn to root out your craving. In some studies, for example, researchers offer a four-step process for managing craving:

>> R – Recognise you're experiencing a craving and allow yourself to gently be with the experience.

>> A – Accept the moment as it is – no need to distract or avoid your feeling.

> » I – Investigate your experience. Ask yourself: 'What's going on in my body right now?'

> » N – Note your experience – perhaps you feel a sense of pressure, tightness, an ache, tension or heat. Realise that these are just bodily sensations which will pass. Ride the wave of this experience until it passes.

For more on mindfulness for addiction, see Chapter 13.

Regulating Eating Habits

Are you aware of what you eat? Do you taste each mouthful and chew it thoroughly before swallowing? Do you give your attention to what you're eating, or do you distract yourself with television, newspapers or books? Do you use food as a way of coping with unpleasant emotions?

If you feel empty inside, you may eat to help try to fill that space. Or every time you're worried, you may grab a bar of chocolate. Perhaps stress drives you to open the fridge door or makes you limit your food to feel more in control. Mindfulness offers a different way of regulating and coping with your difficult and uncomfortable emotions rather than by eating or avoiding eating.

REMEMBER

Mindful eating is about becoming more aware of the process of preparing and eating food, being less judgemental and more accepting of your current eating habits. Mindful eating also includes being aware of the messages your body sends to you, and using that awareness to determine how much or little to eat. Through this increased awareness, you can choose what to eat and what not to eat from a wiser state of mind. You're able to savour the taste of the food and enjoy the process of eating. With awareness, you're more likely to be in touch with physical hunger and able to notice when you've eaten sufficiently. So mindful eating can even help you maintain a healthy weight!

Increasing Your Happiness

Everybody wants to be happy. All your actions can be explained as your personal desire for greater happiness. The question is, what's the best way to increase happiness? It turns out that simply trying to think positively doesn't work – you need to engage in something regularly that uplifts your sense of wellbeing in a more authentic way.

Positive psychologists – scientists who study happiness – think that mindfulness is the answer. Mindfulness seems to train the brain to naturally become more positive and increases resilience. Resilience is the capacity to cope with stress and catastrophe in a healthy way. It ensures that you bounce back to your happy self sooner rather than later following difficulties. It also strengthens your capacity to cope with difficulties in the future. Regular mindfulness exercises change the very structure of your brain, helping to increase your resilience in difficult times.

Through practising mindfulness on a regular basis, you also begin to discover that happiness is an inside job. You can have all the money and power in the world, but if your thoughts are very negative and you believe your thoughts to be true, you're not going to be happy. Conversely, you can have very few possessions, but if your mind is naturally open, receptive and positive, having practised mindfulness daily, you're bound to experience a deeper sense of wellbeing.

REMEMBER

Happiness is not just about feeling good. I like to think of happiness as living a rich and purposeful life, pursuing what makes life worth living – what the ancient Greeks called *eudaimonia*, or flourishing. This approach can lead to painful experiences in the short term, and that's ok – that's life! Mindfulness can be used to step back and accept your unhelpful thoughts and emotions as you move toward a more fulfilling life.

TIP

Here's a simple mindful exercise to help you to happiness. Every day, look at a stranger and think in your mind: 'May you be well, may you be happy.' This makes you notice someone different and creates a positive wish in your mind. It'll probably make you smile too!

Chapter **18**

Ten Mindfulness Myths to Expose

When I told a friend of mine that I teach mindfulness, he said, 'I don't think that's for me – my mind's full enough already, buddy!' Mindfulness isn't about filling up the mind, of course. Mindfulness isn't just meditation either. If you want to ensure that you've got the right idea about mindfulness, check out this chapter and do some 'mind emptying' – take this opportunity to root out any wrong ideas you may have about the ancient and modern science and art of mindfulness.

Mindfulness Is All about the Mind

You may have heard this quip: 'What is mind? Doesn't matter. What is matter? Never mind!'

As a human being you have the capacity to think. In fact, you can't help but think. Thinking seems to happen whether you like it or not. Thinking is almost like breathing, and probably happens more frequently. Some experts estimate humans think up to 60,000 thoughts a day! Mindfulness isn't all about the mind; it takes a step back from thinking rather than stops thinking.

Mindfulness can more appropriately be called heartfulness. In ancient Eastern languages like Sanskrit or Pali, the words for mind and heart are the same, so perhaps the word 'mindfulness' is a little misleading. What does heartfulness mean? If you have an open, warm heart you may be: kind, gentle, caring, accepting, understanding, patient, trusting, joyful, honest, grateful, light-hearted, loving and humble. Perhaps you're not all of those things, but I share those words to express the spirit of mindfulness with you. The idea is to bring one or more heart qualities to your mindful awareness. Naturally, you can't bring *all* of them in at the same time, but you can get a sense of the kind of attitude to bring to your awareness.

REMEMBER

Mindfulness isn't a cold, harsh awareness. A thief needs to be attentive when planning to steal something, but that isn't mindfulness. Mindfulness has a sense of kindness as well as curiosity about it.

If, when you're being mindful, you sense you're being critical, struggling a lot and being unkind to yourself, or you think that your attention doesn't have a warmth about it, don't beat yourself up. You'll end up frustrated. Simply be aware of whatever you're being mindful of, and in its own time some kindness will naturally grow. You don't need to force things too much – the less you force things, the better.

TIP

Some people think that mindfulness means you need to think about whatever you're focusing on. This isn't quite right. If you're being mindful of your breathing, this means you're feeling the sensation of the breathing in your body – you're not trying to think about the breathing.

Mindfulness Isn't for Restless People

Are you a busy, active and perhaps restless person? Always on the go? If so, mindfulness may sound as if it's too passive for you. But actually, mindfulness is great way to uproot restlessness and replace it with an inner joy.

Many of the mindfulness exercises and meditations are about slowing down. But that's not the aim. The purpose is to cultivate a greater level of awareness and warm-heartedness towards yourself and what's happening around you. It's possible to achieve this whether you're sitting still or moving your body.

Restlessness isn't a fixed part of your personality that'll never change. Mindfulness rewires your brain. If you practise mindfulness regularly, beginning with just a few minutes a day, you learn to be with the feeling of restlessness without reacting to it. You discover that the feeling of restlessness arises and eventually passes away. But there's more to discover. You may find that your life was being *driven* by the feeling of restlessness. It doesn't have to be. With time and effort, the feeling of restlessness is replaced with a greater sense of inner peace and satisfaction.

As always, I don't promise it'll be an easy or quick fix, but the journey can begin with just a five-minute daily mindfulness of breath meditation. So do have a go if you'd like to overcome restlessness.

TIP

If you find it difficult to sit still for even a few minutes, try mindful movement. Be aware of your bodily sensations as you stretch up, try to touch your toes or as you go for a run in your local park.

Mindfulness Is Positive Thinking

You can interpret all situations in a positive or negative way, but it's helpful to regard situations optimistically rather than always expecting the worst. Through your regular practise of mindfulness you become more aware of your own thought patterns, both negative and positive. When negative thoughts arise, mindfulness helps you to recognise your own habitual reactions. You may try seeing the situation differently, whether positively or more realistically, and see what effect that has. Mindfulness doesn't tie you into any positive thinking rules – you just bring a sense of curiosity to the experience.

WARNING

I don't recommend fighting with negative thoughts. Battling with your own mind creates a struggle, and you can end up increasing the level of negativity in yourself. The more you fight a thought, the stronger the thought becomes.

Ultimately, mindfulness takes a step back from all thoughts, both negative and positive. Thoughts are thoughts, not necessarily facts. You can't control thoughts completely – all you can do is watch, take a step back, and stop reacting to your thoughts. The more you can do that, the more you feel in control and the less you feel helpless and stressed. Chapter 5 has more about detaching yourself from thoughts.

Mindfulness Is Only for Buddhists

Buddhists don't have the exclusive rights to mindfulness. Mindfulness, or a mindful awareness, is a universal human attribute and skill, a fundamental quality of being alive, just like eyes, ears and a stomach are part of a human body. To be mindful is to be aware, and awareness is not and cannot be attributed to any one religion.

However, mindfulness *was* investigated and developed by Buddha and followers of Buddha. Therefore, if you want, you can read and study more about mindfulness in Buddhist texts, no matter what your religious beliefs. You can also find out about mindfulness in several other religions and philosophies such as Hinduism, Taoism, Advaita, Sufism and many more. However, you find out far more by just being mindful yourself and exploring and learning through your own experience.

WISE WORDS

As one modern sage, Nisargadatta, said: 'The greatest Guru is your inner self.' Even the Buddha often said: 'Don't simply believe what I am saying – find out for yourself in your own experience.'

Mindfulness isn't a religion or belief system. If anything, mindfulness points towards an approach to living. The mission of the Center for Mindfulness in Massachusetts is simply 'an awakened and compassionate world.' If you really want a goal for your mindfulness practise, I think that to become more awakened and compassionate is a good one.

If you're religious and look deeply into your own faith, you're likely to find some way or system to strengthen the capacity to let go of conceptual thinking and train your quality of attention. So, you don't need to change your religion to find mindfulness a meaningful discipline. To be mindful is to develop the innate human capacity to be aware – you can be of any faith or no faith at all and be mindful.

Mindfulness Is Only for Tough Times

Mindfulness is used to alleviate depression, chronic pain, anxiety, addiction relapse, stress, and high blood pressure, and even to manage the stress and treatment of cancer. Initial results in these areas are very encouraging, and the application of mindfulness is sure to develop along with all the other treatments.

However, mindfulness isn't only for the hard times. Consider this: you can't just start saving money in a recession. You need to save money in the good times too, so when things are really difficult you have some cash to help you out. In fact, saving money is much easier and more effective when times are good. In the same way, you can benefit by developing your mindfulness discipline when things are going relatively well. When the going gets tough, you can naturally bring your mindfulness skills to the challenge, and dip into your inner resources to help you cope.

When I first began practising mindfulness, partly for managing stress, I never understood the far-reaching effect of the practise. For example, I used to struggle if I had to speak to more than a small group of people; now I'm lucky enough to feel able to deliver lectures to hundreds of people. I still have feelings of anxiety show up, and on a good day, I make space and accept that experience rather than avoid it. My focus is on accepting what I feel and moving on rather than trying to fix emotions, which is impossible. This is the power of mindfulness. Although your mindfulness practise may be used to deal with a problem to start with, if you persevere, mindfulness goes on to nurture all sorts of different areas of your life.

As you begin to understand and practise mindfulness, you notice benefits. At this stage, some people stop practising. Life seems to be going well, you've resolved the issues, and you kind of forget about the mindfulness and meditation . . . until the next disaster strikes! And then you reach out for help again. Coming and going to and from mindfulness meditation is part of the natural process, but in the end you come to realise that without a daily discipline, your life is a bit of a roller-coaster. The meditation makes the ride that little bit smoother.

Mindfulness Is a Set of Techniques

A technique is usually a quick method of achieving a certain outcome, like counting to ten to help calm yourself down when you feel angry. You may have a certain technique for hitting a golf ball, or a technique for reducing conflict in a conversation. Techniques are great for achieving certain results, but they have their limitations too. If you get too stuck on one technique, you can't branch out to new ways of doing things. Sometimes you may get defensive about your particular technique and become actively unwilling to try something different – in this way, techniques can stifle development.

Mindfulness isn't a technique, because fundamentally mindfulness isn't goal-orientated. This is quite a difficult concept to grasp, because you're probably used to doing things to achieve something. Why would you bother doing something to achieve, ultimately, nothing? Mindfulness has benefits, but if you practise to achieve a particular outcome, you limit its potency. A good scientist does an experiment without forcing a certain outcome – all the scientist wants to do is find the truth of the situation by observing the outcome. If the scientist is looking for a particular outcome, perhaps if the experiment is sponsored by a drug company, you're wary of the results because they may be biased. In the same way, if you look for a certain outcome with mindfulness, you're being biased and not really trying the mindfulness wholeheartedly.

Mindful awareness is about being aware of your inner and outer experience, *whatever that experience is.*

Paradoxically, mindfulness underlies and enhances the quality of all other techniques. Without awareness you can't use a technique. The less aware you are, the less likely it is that whatever technique you're using will work. For example, if you use a technique to reduce stress by letting go of negative thinking, but you're not really aware of your thoughts, how do you hope to succeed?

This book does contain lots of tips and techniques to encourage mindfulness, but ultimately mindfulness itself isn't a technique.

Mindfulness is about letting go of doing. It is about simply being as you are. Being yourself, whatever you think of yourself. Being yourself isn't a technique. You can't *do* non-doing. Non-doing means letting go of all techniques with their desired outcomes and just *being*.

Mindfulness Isn't for Me

Some people may not be keen on mindfulness, perhaps due to misconceptions and stereotypical views about the practise. Mindfulness doesn't even have to be connected with the typical picture of a meditator: someone sitting cross-legged, perhaps burning incense, aimlessly navel-gazing for some future spiritual high. But mindfulness is for anyone interested in becoming more aware, more awake, more alive, more connected. Although mindfulness meditation is an extremely helpful way of developing greater mindfulness, you can also simply pay a bit more attention every time you go for a walk, have a chat with your colleagues or play sport. You may spend a few minutes feeling your breathing as you rest on the sofa before switching on the television. These are simple ways of waking up to your life and letting go of automatic pilot. I don't know anyone who can't do with a greater dose of awareness.

You may think that you can't do mindfulness because you're too impatient, too stressy or too anxious. But mindfulness develops your capacity to be patient, kind, attentive, calm and happy, so you may be the perfect person to try mindfulness! To say you're not patient enough to do mindfulness is like saying you're too unfit to exercise. If you don't exercise at all, you'll never be fit. However, take things easy to begin with – try a short, five-minute mindfulness exercise every day and build from there. Or try some mindful walking for a few minutes. Go to Chapter 6 for ways to practise walking meditations.

Some people think that mindfulness is something weird to do with religion, or some cultish idea. Mindfulness is feeling your own breathing, or listening to the sounds around you, or really tasting the food in front of you. Mindfulness is another word for kindly awareness – nothing mysterious in that sense. You can make mindfulness whatever you want – there are no rules in this game. Some people practise mindfulness for spiritual or religious reasons, just as some people burn incense for religious reasons – that doesn't mean incense is for religious people only!

Mindfulness Meditation Is Relaxation

Relaxation exercises are often designed to loosen the muscles in your body, and the aim of relaxation is to become less tense. So relaxation has a clear goal, and you have various methods for achieving it.

Mindfulness is different. If anything, the goal of mindfulness is greater awareness of your thoughts, feelings, sensations, urges and memories. Or a greater awareness of your surroundings. In mindfulness, you're encouraged to move towards difficult thoughts and emotions with mindful attitudes rather than avoid them. That's very different to relaxation, isn't it. Through this approach, you learn to see that thoughts and emotions are experiences arising and falling into your awareness, and you may step into being like a passive observer of your experience rather than an active 'doer.' You are moving from fighting, suppressing or fixing your private experiences to accepting, observing and allowing them to be as they are.

Relaxation is often, but certainly not always, a very welcome side effect of meditation. However, when you first practise mindfulness, you may feel more tense by the end, and that's perfectly fine! When I first began practising mindfulness, I was trying to do it well and my attention was overly intense. My body became tense trying to focus, as I tried in vain to force thoughts out. This led to more tension but was part of the learning process.

REMEMBER

Mindfulness can sometimes release deep-seated trapped emotions that your sub-conscious mind has hidden away and works hard at keeping out. The process can create more tension temporarily as you face your demons. However, the sooner you release the emotion, the better. As the emotion rises into your conscious mind, the feeling can dissolve, sometimes relaxing a part of the body that has been tense for years. (Chapter 10 has more about dealing with mindfulness bringing up painful emotions.)

Mindfulness Can Be Used Instead of Therapy or Medicine

Mindfulness certainly can't be used *instead of* therapy or medicine. If you suffer from a clinical condition, you need to follow your doctor's recommendations. However, *in addition to* medical advice, you can normally develop a mindfulness practise to support your healing process. Mindfulness helps to manage your stress levels, and can reduce your blood pressure and boost your body's immune function.

Recent evidence suggests medication for mental health conditions such as depression and anxiety are sometimes overprescribed, but you will need to seek medical advice and do your own research to decide what's the best option for you.

Medical professionals can sometimes refer patients to a mindfulness-based stress reduction (MBSR) course, a mindfulness-based cognitive therapy (MBCT) course or Acceptance and Commitment Therapy (ACT), empowering patients to take a more proactive part in looking after their own health and wellbeing though the application of mindfulness. This way of developing inner resources and enhancing resilience to stress has been found to be profoundly wholesome. Chapter 9 goes into more detail about MBSR, and Chapter 13 explains more about ACT.

REMEMBER

There are many changes in your lifestyle that can significantly support your mental health, including physical activity, socialising regularly, spending time with a caring listener, eating a healthy diet, going to bed on time, spending some time volunteering and reducing or cutting out alcohol and junk food. By doing a little bit of mindfulness every day, even literally just a few minutes, you will be a better position mentally to make wiser choices for your health and wellbeing. See Chapter 3 for tips on how to create positive habits in your life.

Mindfulness Is Complicated and Boring

How you view mindfulness depends on the rules you create in your head about the process. Here's some rules that are unhelpful but often come up: Mindfulness should be relaxing and enlightening; my mind should be blank; I should feel comfortable; I shouldn't feel emotional; if I don't do it every day I've failed; if it feels difficult I must be doing it incorrectly.

You need to be aware of the kind of rules you've created in your head about mindfulness. Any 'must,' 'should' or 'ought' is the sign of a rigid rule laid down in your mind. Life has the tendency to flow wherever it wants to go, therefore you find, time and again, your inner rules being broken and frustration and boredom arising.

Mindfulness is simple but not easy. The simple bit is that mindfulness is about being aware and paying attention. The not-so-easy bit is having the discipline to practise regularly and the ability to trust in the process, no matter how wild your mind appears to be.

Mindfulness has a sense of simple flow about it: doing less rather than more; thinking less rather than more; going with the flow of life rather than spending life wrestling with complications created by the mind.

I'll give you an example of the simplicity yet difficulty of mindfulness. Right now, if you're aware of the weight of this book in your hand, you're being mindful. If you walk out of the room you're in and feel your feet on the ground, you're being mindful. So mindfulness is simple. However, the difficult bit is overcoming your current habitual thought patterns, which have been strengthening for however long you've been on this planet, and are naturally very powerful. When you put this book down and walk off, notice how long it takes before you're lost in an ocean of thoughts, feelings, stories, frustrations and desires.

If you find mindfulness boring, you have a few choices:

>> Reduce the length of time for which you are practising mindfulness.

>> Become curious about boredom.

>> Let the feeling of boredom go, and re-focus on the present moment again and again.

>> Accept the boredom as part and parcel of life and keep being mindful – the boredom will soon pass.

Ultimately, no matter how much trouble you have being mindful, and no matter how confused or bored you may be occasionally, you have a deep and powerful aspect of yourself that nothing can ever touch. Awareness is a mysterious aspect of being human that remains beyond the understanding of science. Awareness is always there, at the root of your being – ever shining, ever knowing. Even when you're lost in thought or caught up in the darkest, most frightening emotion or situation, you're aware, at some level, of what's going on, both inside and outside yourself. See that part of you, your observer self, as always free, whole and complete.

Chapter **19**

Ten Paths to Further Study

So you've begun the exciting journey into mindfulness and want to find out more. Well, you're in luck. Mindfulness is a hot topic, and you can find all sorts of different resources to support your mindfulness practise. Browse through this chapter to see whether anything catches your eye.

Websites

You can find out just about everything you need to know about mindfulness on the Internet. The problem is there are so many different websites, it's hard to know where to start. Here are a few to help you to begin mindfully exploring.

ShamashAlidina.com

If you like my approach in this book, you may enjoy spending a few minutes browsing my website and subscribing to my electronic newsletter and blog. My organisation offers training and online teacher training in mindfulness. I also write a blog post every week or two and share it to be my electronic newsletter subscribers. My mindfulness courses are offered online or I can come and run a workshop or retreat near you if you or someone in your area invites me.

Visit www.shamashalidina.com for training or for free resources, including the following:

>> **Online free 7-day online course in mindfulness**

>> **Free e-mail newsletter and 'weekly wisdom' e-mails when you subscribe**

>> **Online eight-week mindfulness or kindfulness courses**

>> **Certified Mindfulness teacher training online programs (our most popular offering)**

>> **One-to-one coaching, usually over online video calls**

If you're on social media, you can follow me, get in touch and feel free to ask questions – I'll do my best to respond! See facebook.com/shamashalidina or twitter.com/shamashalidina or instagram.com/shamashalidina or www.linkedin.com/in/shamashalidina.

And feel free to get in touch via email to find out what resources would be most suitable to you on info@shamashalidina.com.

Greater Good Science Centre

The mission of The Greater Good Science Centre is to 'study the psychology, sociology, and neuroscience of well-being, and teach skills that foster a thriving, resilient and compassionate society.' It sounds very grand, but the centre's website is fantastic and the web pages are enjoyable to read.

Visit the centre at greatergood.berkeley.edu and browse through the core themes, which are: gratitude, altruism, compassion, empathy, forgiveness, happiness and, last but not least, mindfulness. The articles are well written and well researched. I'd also recommend their online courses.

Mindful.org

Mindful.org celebrates being mindful in all aspects of daily living. It's an ideal resource if you're interested in various forms of mindfulness practise. The website offers a range of stories, practical news, insights and tips.

Visit www.mindful.org and read sections on:

» Education

» Mind and Body

» Parenting and Family

» Relationships

» Workplace

Books, Magazines and Films

I recommend that you continue to nourish your mindfulness practise with a range of different writers to help deepen your understanding of yourself. Here are some resources that I have enjoyed and still do.

Book: Wherever you go, there you are

This book by Jon Kabat-Zinn (published by Piatkus) is simple and easy to read, covering a wide range of topics on mindfulness. Kabat-Zinn developed the mindfulness-based stress reduction course detailed in Chapter 9, so he definitely knows a thing or two about mindfulness!

The chapters in this book are nice and short, so it's ideal to pick up and read for a few minutes before or after doing a mindfulness meditation. The book is perfect for beginners and contains something for more experienced practitioners too.

Book: Peace Is Every Step

Thich Nhat Hanh (pronounced Tik N'yat Hawn) is a Vietnamese Zen Buddhist monk, poet, scholar and peace activist. Nhat Hanh has written many books, and I particularly enjoyed reading this one (published by Rider).

The author begins the book with this passage:

> Every day, when we wake up, we have 24 brand new hours to live. What a precious gift! We have the capacity to live in a way that these 24 hours will bring peace, joy and happiness to ourselves and others.

EVERYTHING IS CONNECTED

Part of the purpose of mindfulness, according to Thich Nhat Hanh, is to see how you're interconnected with everything else and not a separate entity that exists in isolation. This *interbeing* leads to a sense of peace and wellbeing and reduces feelings like anger and frustration. You come to see that if you're angry towards another person, you're in a way being angry towards yourself. If you're hammering a nail into a piece of wood and accidentally hit your left hand with the hammer in your right hand, your left and right hand don't start fighting each other! On the contrary, your right hand cares about and soothes the pain in the left hand, because the two hands are one. In the same way, if you begin to see how you're interconnected with everything else, you experience greater compassion (one of the most positive emotions you can have) and respect for things and people around you.

Thich Nhat Hanh is probably one of the world's most famous teachers of mindfulness. Because of his lifelong commitment and efforts for peace in Vietnam, he was nominated for the Nobel Peace Prize in 1967 by Martin Luther King, Jr.

You can find many gems in this book to help transform your daily life and achieve conscious awareness of, and gratitude for, what you do. The simplicity and poetry of Thich Nhat Hanh's words make them a joy to read. The book is in short sections that you can read in a few minutes and then reflect on, – ideal before or after meditating to set you up for the day.

Book: Mindfulness: An Eight-Week Plan for Finding Peace in a Frantic World

This is one of the most popular books on mindfulness. Co-authored by Professor Mark Williams, former head at Oxford University's Mindfulness Centre, and Danny Penman, a journalist, this book details an eight-week mindfulness course for people suffering from the challenges of everyday stress. The book includes short mindfulness exercises, 10–15 minutes long, so it's ideal if you lead a busy life and don't have time for the longer mindfulness meditations.

Do take a look and see whether it appeals to you.

Magazine: Mindful

This is the only quality monthly magazine that I know dedicated to celebrating the 'mindfulness movement.' Packed with well-written articles, the magazine contains ideas for applying mindfulness at home and work, as well as the latest research findings on mindfulness, fascinating interviews, recommended mobile apps and more.

Currently, both digital and print versions are available, so you can access *Mindful* wherever you are in the world.

Film: Inside Out

Inside out is Disney Pixar's award winning film that came out in 2015. This is a fabulous film to introduce children (and adults) to the different emotions you experience, the voices in your head and the danger of not accepting our more difficult emotions. The content was researched by leading mindful specialists, so you can rest assured that you'll be learning something valuable in this fun movie for the whole family.

The film teaches the different core emotions all humans experience, the problem with fixating on one emotion, the danger of avoiding unpleasant emotions, the fact that you can be the observer of your thoughts rather than getting hooked by your thoughts and the power of acceptance and kindness.

Film: Room to Breathe

This documentary film is about the transformation of a struggling school in San Francisco as the students are introduced to the practise of mindfulness meditation. Stressed-out teachers face the option of either continuing the battle to gain the focus of frustrated students or trying to share the ancient practise of mindfulness to help develop the students' ability to be present. Find out how a young mindfulness teacher from Berkeley, facing the students' lack of discipline, lack of respect for authority and little interest in learning anything works through the challenge.

The film is particular interesting for anyone who works with children or has any interest in the power of mindfulness.

Retreats

You can deepen your experience of mindfulness by attending a retreat. Retreats offer you an extended period away from your usual environment and responsibilities – often in silence. In this setting, your mind has more time to settle, and through the practises of mindfulness meditation you gain insights and grow in wisdom as you meditate.

This sort of opportunity is rare, so if you get such a chance I encourage you to have a go. If you're never spent a day not talking, why not try it out and see what happens? You may find it fascinating how your mind reacts to the experience. For many people, the experience is restful, energising and a bit like a mental detox.

Some of these programs offer full silent retreats; others have a mixture of silence and time to chat too!

Mindfulness-based retreat centres worldwide

The following retreat centres offer mindfulness-based silent retreats:

>> Insight Meditation Society, Barre, Massachusetts, USA

>> Spirit Rock, Woodacre, California, USA

>> Insight Meditation Community of Washington, Cabin John, Maryland, USA

>> Southern Dharma, Hot Springs, North Carolina, USA

>> Boundless Way Zen, Worcester, Massachusetts, USA

>> San Francisco Zen Center, San Francisco, California, USA

>> Zen Center of San Diego, San Diego, California, USA

>> Zen Community of Oregon, Clatskanie, Oregon, USA

>> Karme Choling, Barnet, Vermont, USA

>> Shambhala Mountain Center, Red Feather Lakes, Colorado, USA

>> Gaia House, Devon, UK

>> Amravati, Hertfordshire, UK

>> Shapham Trust, Devon, UK

>> Jhana Grove Retreat Centre, Australia

>> Vipassana Meditation Centers (worldwide)

This is not an exhaustive list, but it gives you some ideas of places to look. Most of these centres are in the USA, but when you look on their websites you may find links to recommended centres near your country or even near where you live.

Vipassana Meditation Centers are located worldwide and are based on the SN Goenka tradition. In my experience, people tend to either love these centres or find them a bit too intensive. I personally would not recommend them for beginners. Check the website or speak to someone who's been there to see whether it's right for you.

Jiddu Krishnamurti is considered one of the great philosophers, speakers and writers of the last hundred years, and I've read many of his books and often stayed at his centre in the UK for a personal retreat. He was against the idea of gurus and organised religion, so he's not considered as an authority as such. You can find his retreat centres and study centres around the world. The centres are designed to explore his teachings and are very open and relaxed, rarely with any set timetable. His ideas emphasise the importance of being present, seeing the limits of thought, taking responsibility for what's happening in the world and connecting with the beauty of nature. His popular quotes include 'You are the world and the world is you' and 'Truth is a pathless land.' Find the list of international centres at https://kfoundation.org/worldwide.

If you're looking for a centre completely not associated with religion, get in touch with a secular mindfulness teacher like me. Many secular mindfulness teachers now offer retreats. The easiest way to find a such a teacher may be to search on the Internet for one in your area and then check the credentials and experience of the teacher on the associated website.

Check the timetables and schedule for any retreat. If you're a beginner and think you may feel intimidated with a whole week or more, try to start with just a day or weekend retreat. And don't feel you have to attend every meditation session: take some breaks if you need to, and go at a gentle pace rather than pushing yourself too much. It is a re*treat* after all, not a re*torture*!

I also offer tailor-made retreats upon request or group retreats for the public from time to time. Get in touch if you're interested!

Plum Village and related centers

Plum Village is a Buddhist retreat centre founded by world-famous Buddhist monk, Thich Nhat Hanh, in southern France. I've attended several retreats there and enjoy the light-hearted atmosphere mixed with the incisive and fascinating talks every morning. The retreat was partly in silence, especially at meal times. Everyone seems to enjoy the silence. But there's also plenty of time to talk, socialize and volunteer. The summer retreats are family friendly, so you can bring the kids along too! There are specific groups and fun activites for children, so they won't get bored and will have a chance to experience some mindfulness too.

Other retreat centres now follow the same approach:

» **Blue Cliff Monastery:** In 80 acres of beautiful woodland, about one and half hours north of New York City, USA, this is home to monks and nuns, who welcome you to come and practise mindfulness with them.

» **Deer Park Monastery:** On 400 acres in the glorious mountains of southern California, USA, Deer Park is a place of serenity, home to 17 monks and 19 nuns. Visit and practise mindfulness there.

» **Magnolia Grove Monastery:** In Batesville, Mississippi, USA, more than 30 monks and nuns in residence, welcome visitors who wish to practise meditation and mindfulness with every breath and every step.

» **Nhap Luu Monastery**: A two-hour drive from Melbourne, Australia, the sisters at Stream Entering Nhap Luu Monastery welcome visits and overnight stays at certain times of the year, including regular days of mindfulness.

Check the respective websites to find out the best time to arrive and leave.

If you attend a summer retreat, here's a typical schedule:

5:30 a.m.	Rise
6:00 a.m.	Sitting and walking meditations
7:30 a.m.	Breakfast
9:00 a.m.	Lecture by one of the monastics
12:30 p.m.	Lunch
2:00 p.m.	Rest
3:00 p.m.	Class/study time
6:00 p.m.	Dinner
8:00 p.m.	Exercise
9:30 p.m.	Silence begins
10:30 p.m.	Lights out

If that sounds appealing and you like the teachings of Thich Nhat Hanh, look out for his summer retreat and book yourself in! Visit www.plumvillage.org or the websites of the other retreat centres for more details.

Index

childbirth, mindful, 302–303

children

  about, 301

  being present for your, 315–317

  mindful body scan and, 310

  mindful parenting, 315–318

  mindfulness and, 301–303

  mindfulness games and exercises, 305–310

  teaching mindfulness to, 304–305

  teens and mindfulness, 311–315

choiceless awareness, practising, 122

choices

  breathing space for increasing, 135

  making wise, 276–277

choosing groups, 189–190

chronic pain

  defined, 292

  reducing, 335

clarifying intentions, 51–53

cognitive behavioural therapy (CBT), 270, 282

Cognitive Behavioural Therapy For Dummies (Branch and Willson), 270

cognitive defusion, as a core skill of ACT, 262–263

combating automatic thoughts, 273–274

'comfort' eating, 169

commitment

  about, 45–46

  resistance to practice, 58–59

committed action, as a core skill of ACT, 263

communication, anger and, 252

compassion, 228–229

connecting

  with people, 322–323

  with your senses, 29, 232

Consciousness and Cognition (journal), 334

contact with the present moment, as a core skill of ACT, 263

coping

  with anger, 251–253

  with anxiety, 279–280

  with pain, 295–297

cost of retreats, 190

counting breaths, 247

courage, as category for strengths, 223

'cracked pot' adage, 23

creating

  attentive minds, 30–32

  conditions for originality, 237

  positive emotions with mindfulness, 220–233

  time, 194–195

  wise choices, 276–277

creativity

  about, 161

  boosting, 333–334

  releasing, 234–237

  as a strength, 223

cues, 48, 50

cult, 191

curiosity

  cultivating, 70–72

  as a strength, 223

cycling, mindful, 139

D

daily life

  about, 153

  changing your routine, 323–324

  intentions, 51–57

  mindfulness at work, 154–162

  mindfulness in the digital age, 170–174

  mindfulness in the home, 165–169

  mindfulness while traveling, 162–165

  preparing for mindfulness, 57–59

Dalai Lama (spiritual leader)

  about, 15

  on brains, 332

  on compassion, 227–229

Davidson, Richard (professor), 127, 269, 332

de Mestral, George (inventor), 236

de-centring, from difficult thoughts, 275–276

decision-making

  improving, 28

  sticking to, 184

deep listening, engaging in, 144–146

deep mindful breathing, 247

Deer Park Monastery, 360

depression

L

lake meditation, 152
laughter, mindful, 231–233
laughter yoga, 232
Lazarus, Richard (researcher), 240, 337
leadership
  mindful, 160
  as a strength, 223
learning
  from failure, 80–81
  from negative experiences, 205–208
  to relax, 203–204
letting go
  about, 72–73, 348
  of doing mode, 112
  through forgiveness, 76–78
  in workplace, 161–162
limits, acknowledging your, 291
listening
  deep, 144–146
  to unpleasant emotions, 325–326
  to your thoughts, 27–28
listing activities, 276
living in the moment, 96–99, 161
location, for daily mindfulness practice, 47–48
long-term vision, 17
looking deeply, 97–98
love
  as an attitude, 81
  as category for strengths, 223
love of learning, as a strength, 223
loving kindness meditation
  exercise, 308–309
  practising, 128–129, 143
low mood. *See* depression

M

magazines, as resources, 355–357
Magnolia Grove Monastery, 360
managing
  addiction, 339–340
  with anger, 251–253

with anxiety, 279–280
barriers, 178
boredom, 169
emotions using being mode, 94–95
feelings, 33
internal distractions, 201
with pain, 295–297
pain with mindfulness, 292–297
physical discomfort, 05
relapse to addiction, 286
sleepiness, 198–199
stress with your mind, 247–249
unusual experiences, 202–203
Man's Search for Meaning (Frankl), 35
mastery activity, 277
MBCT (mindfulness-based cognitive therapy), 269–271
MBSR (mindfulness-based stress reduction), 176, 233, 269, 271, 335
McGonigal, Kelly (author)
  The Willpower Instinct, 285
McKee, Annie (author)
  Resonant Leadership, 160
meal times, using breathing space before/after, 136
meaning
  achieving deeper, 227
  to life, 336
  as a way to happiness, 222, 227
measuring
  addiction level to technology, 170–172
  energy levels, 255
  stress, 242–243
medicine, using mindfulness with, 350
meditation
  bubble, 309
  energising, 257–258
  for fatigue, 257–258
  forgiveness, 77–78
  formal, 11, 136
  getting the most out of, 194–200
  informal, 11, 136
  lake, 152
  loving kindness, 128–129, 143, 308–309
  metta, 127–130, 143

mindful breathing, 106–107, 185, 299–300
mindful eating, 104–106, 167–168, 256, 340
mindfulness, 11, 104, 194, 295–297, 349
mini, 155–156
reducing tension during, 203–204
sitting, 115–123
walking, 124–127, 163, 185
meditation, body scan
about, 23–24
aim of, 178
benefits of, 112–113
children and, 310
for energy boost, 258
obstacles to, 114–115
practising, 110–112
walking, 125–126
meditation, breathing space
about, 132–133
for entering being mode, 135
practising, 133–136
for quick stress reduction, 185
stages of, 155
for turning off automatic pilot, 135–136
using between activities, 137
mental stress, 241
MET (motivational enhancement therapy), 282
metta meditations
about, 127–128
obstacles to, 130
practising, 143
practising loving kindness meditation, 128–129
mind
calming the, 26–32
managing stress with you, 247–249
mind-body connection
about, 177
seeing the, 289–290
Mindful (magazine), 356–357
mindful awareness
about, 348
enhancing, 173–174
mindful breathing meditation
about, 106–107
for ill health, 299–300

with other activities, 247
for quick stress reduction, 185
mindful childbirth, 302–303
mindful cycling, 139
mindful drawing exercise, 310
mindful driving, 163–164
mindful eating
about, 167–168, 340
for fatigue, 256
meditation, 104–106
mindful exercise, 137–139
mindful feet, 264
mindful flow, 91–92
mindful helping, 227–229
mindful laughter, 231–233
mindful leadership, 160
mindful living, 321–330
mindful meditation, staying awake during, 197–199
mindful movement, 108–109, 179
mindful parenting, 315–318
mindful physical exercise
for anger, 253
for fatigue, 256
mindful pregnancy, 302–303
mindful running, 138
mindful smiling, 230–231
mindful swimming, 138–139
'mindful visualisation' exercise, 53–54
mindful waking up, 165–166
mindful walking, 163
mindful working, 159–160
mindful work-life balance, 140–141
mindful yoga, 109
mindfulness. See also specific topics
applying with positive psychology, 220–229
apps for, 174
attitudes of, 63
being mode and, 334
benefits of, 11–17, 21–39, 331–341
boredom of, 350–351
changing relationship to low mood with, 268–269
children and, 301–303
compared with relaxation, 14
coping with anxiety with, 279–280

About the Author

Shamash Alidina has been teaching mindfulness since 1998. He was invited to experiment with a short mindfulness exercise whilst studying in a 'practical philosophy' evening class, and caught the mindfulness bug! He was amazed at the power of mindfulness to transform his state of mind, both during the mindful meditation itself and through exercises in day-to-day life. He decided to dedicate his life to learn and teach mindfulness to others. He taught mindfulness to groups of adults, and then additionally taught in a children's school in London called St. James for eight years, which integrated mindfulness and meditation into the curriculum. He's been working in the field of mindfulness on a full-time basis since 2010.

Shamash formally trained for three years at Bangor University's Centre for Mindfulness in Wales. He also holds a masters degree in Chemical Engineering and a masters degree in Education.

He runs his own successful training organisation, *ShamashAlidina.com*, to introduce mindfulness to the general public, give talks, workshops, coaching, as well as offer fully online mindfulness teacher training. He has taught mindfulness all over the world, including the USA, Australia, New Zealand, the Middle East and Europe. Shamash is also cofounder of the world's first Museum of Happiness in London.

Shamash has been interviewed by many national newspapers and magazines and has appeared on radio and television. He has featured in mindfulness campaigns and blogs weekly on his main passions: mindfulness, compassion, wisdom, happiness, positive psychology and acceptance, and commitment therapy. He currently lives in London.

Dedication

This book is dedicated to my two favourite teachers: Ajahn Brahm and Steven Hayes. Ajahn Brahm for teaching me the importance of kindness and playfulness when practising and teaching mindfulness. And Dr. Steven Hayes for his dedication to use science to help me discover what seem to be the core ways the human mind creates suffering and how to cultivate greater psychological flexibility for a healthier, happier life and world.

Authors' Acknowledgments

I would like to thank Tim Gallan for his encouragement whilst editing this third edition of the book. And thanks to the very patient Tracy Boggier for overseeing this edition of the book and making it happen.

I would like to thank Iona Everson over the production of the second edition of the book. And I would like to thank Jennifer Prytherch and Nicole Hermitage who originally commissioning me to write the first edition of this book. And I would also like to wholeheartedly extend my thanks to the whole production team at Wiley. This book is certainly a team effort!

I'd like to thank all my family members. In particular, thanks to my brother, Aneesh, who first suggested the idea of *Mindfulness For Dummies,* and my parents Manju and Fateh, who support me throughout my life. Much gratitude to the support of family members Nirupa, Amy, Shona, Ashok, Parul, Nikhil and Amisha. I'd like to especially acknowledge my late uncle Vijay, who passed away relatively recently and who was a proud supporter of my work.

Big thanks to my wonderful friends for their support (together with why I think they're great!): Vicky (full of compassion), Kush (wise and peaceful), Yvonne (caring and insightful), John (warm and funny) Harpal (kind and funny), Trevor (kindfully 'joining the dots' for all), Michal (visionary outlook and kindness), Patrycja (compassionate being), Maneesh (caring and big thinker), BKC (fun and reflective), Mimi (courageously kind) and Gioia (passionately kind). Plus my lovely friends from the Museum of Happiness of course! I don't have a chance to see some of you often, but rest assured, I often think of you. And apologies to any of you I've forgotten — it just means mindfulness has not improved my memory!

Huge gratitude to Teresa, my friend and chief happiness officer, who you'd chat to if you contact us. She has been one of the longest standing supporters of my work. And much thanks to Diana too, our chief technology officer, who's also been a longtime supporter. We're a great team.

I would like to thank Steven Hickman, director of the UCSD Center for Mindfulness, for his support of my work, and for writing a beautiful foreword to this book.

Finally I'd like to thank the teachers who continue to inspire me with mindfulness, wisdom and compassion through their talks and writing: The Dalai Lama, Matthieu Ricard, Ajahn Brahm, Jon Kabat-Zinn, Mark Williams, Paul Gilbert, Kristin Neff, Steven Hayes, Russ Harris, Ramana Maharshi and Nisargadatta. Thank you for inspiring others to look deep within and for sharing the beauty of this mysterious gift we have — life itself.

Publisher's Acknowledgments

Acquisitions Editor: Tracy Boggier
Project Editor: Tim Gallan
Technical Reviewer: Anthony Santero

Production Editor: Magesh Elangovan
Cover Image: © Philippe LEJEANVRE/ Getty Images

Leverage the power

Dummies is the global leader in the reference category and one of the most trusted and highly regarded brands in the world. No longer just focused on books, customers now have access to the dummies content they need in the format they want. Together we'll craft a solution that engages your customers, stands out from the competition, and helps you meet your goals.

Advertising & Sponsorships

Connect with an engaged audience on a powerful multimedia site, and position your message alongside expert how-to content. Dummies.com is a one-stop shop for free, online information and know-how curated by a team of experts.

- Targeted ads
- Video
- Email Marketing

- Microsites
- Sweepstakes sponsorship

20 MILLION PAGE VIEWS **EVERY SINGLE MONTH**

15 MILLION UNIQUE VISITORS PER MONTH

43% OF ALL VISITORS ACCESS THE SITE **VIA THEIR MOBILE DEVICES**

700,000 NEWSLETTER SUBSCRIPTIONS **TO THE INBOXES OF** *300,000* UNIQUE INDIVIDUALS EVERY WEEK

# of dummies

Custom Publishing

Reach a global audience in any language by creating a solution that will differentiate you from competitors, amplify your message, and encourage customers to make a buying decision.

- Apps
- Books
- eBooks
- Video
- Audio
- Webinars

Brand Licensing & Content

Leverage the strength of the world's most popular reference brand to reach new audiences and channels of distribution.

For more information, visit **dummies.com/biz**

PERSONAL ENRICHMENT

 **Staying Sharp** dummies
9781119187790
USA $26.00
CAN $31.99
UK £19.99

 **Facebook** dummies
Carolyn Abram
9781119179030
USA $21.99
CAN $25.99
UK £16.99

 **Guitar** dummies
Mark Phillips
Jon Chappell
9781119293354
USA $24.99
CAN $29.99
UK £17.99

 **Investing** dummies
Eric Tyson, MBA
9781119293347
USA $22.99
CAN $27.99
UK £16.99

 **Beekeeping** dummies
Howland Blackiston
9781119310068
USA $22.99
CAN $27.99
UK £16.99

 **Digital Photography** dummies
Julie Adair King
9781119235606
USA $24.99
CAN $29.99
UK £17.99

 **Meditation** dummies
Stephan Bodian
9781119251163
USA $24.99
CAN $29.99
UK £17.99

 **Pregnancy** ALL-IN-ONE dummies
6 Books
9781119235491
USA $26.99
CAN $31.99
UK £19.99

 **Samsung Galaxy S7** dummies
Bill Hughes
9781119279952
USA $24.99
CAN $29.99
UK £17.99

 **iPhone** dummies
Edward C. Baig
Bob "Dr. Mac" LeVitus
9781119283133
USA $24.99
CAN $29.99
UK £17.99

 **Crocheting** dummies
Karen Manthey
Susan Brittain
9781119287117
USA $24.99
CAN $29.99
UK £16.99

 **Nutrition** dummies
Carol Ann Rinzler
9781119130246
USA $22.99
CAN $27.99
UK £16.99

PROFESSIONAL DEVELOPMENT

 **Windows 10** dummies
Andy Rathbone
9781119311041
USA $24.99
CAN $29.99
UK £17.99

 AutoCAD dummies
Bill Fane
9781119255796
USA $39.99
CAN $47.99
UK £27.99

 Excel 2016 dummies
Greg Harvey, PhD
9781119293439
USA $26.99
CAN $31.99
UK £19.99

 **QuickBooks 2017** dummies
Stephen L. Nelson, MBA, CPA, MS in Taxation
9781119281467
USA $26.99
CAN $31.99
UK £19.99

 **macOS Sierra** dummies
Bob "Dr. Mac" LeVitus
9781119280651
USA $29.99
CAN $35.99
UK £21.99

 **LinkedIn** dummies
Joel Elad, MBAs
9781119251132
USA $24.99
CAN $29.99
UK £17.99

 **Windows 10** ALL-IN-ONE dummies
10 Books
Woody Leonhard
9781119310563
USA $34.00
CAN $41.99
UK £24.99

 **SharePoint 2016** dummies
Rosemarie Withee
Ken Withee
9781119181705
USA $29.99
CAN $35.99
UK £21.99

 **Fundamental Analysis** dummies
Matt Krantz
9781119263593
USA $26.99
CAN $31.99
UK £19.99

 Networking dummies
Doug Lowe
9781119257769
USA $29.99
CAN $35.99
UK £21.99

 **Office 2016** dummies
Wallace Wang
9781119293477
USA $26.99
CAN $31.99
UK £19.99

 Office 365 dummies
Rosemarie Withee
Ken Withee
Jennifer Reed
9781119265313
USA $24.99
CAN $29.99
UK £17.99

 Salesforce.com dummies
Liz Kao
Jon Paz
9781119239314
USA $29.99
CAN $35.99
UK £21.99

 **Coding** dummies
Nikhil Abraham
9781119293323
USA $29.99
CAN $35.99
UK £21.99

dummies.com

dummies ®
A Wiley Brand